FAST TRACK TO A 5

Preparing for the AP* Physics B Examination

To Accompany
College Physics
8th Edition
by Raymond A. Serway, Chris Vuille, and Jerry S. Faughn

and

College Physics
9th Edition
by Raymond A. Serway and Chris Vuille

Edward Pascuzzi
Stony Brook University, Stony Brook, New York

G. Patrick Zober
Yough Senior High School, Herminie, Pennsylvania

Patricia Zober
Ringgold High School, Monongahela, Pennsylvania

BROOKS/COLE
CENGAGE Learning™

Australia • Brazil • Japan • Korea • Mexico • Singapore • Spain • United Kingdom • United States

*AP and Advanced Placement Program are registered trademarks of the College Entrance Examination Board, which was not involved in the production of, and does not endorse, this product.

ISBN-13: 978-0-8400-6878-1
ISBN-10: 0-8400-6878-6

Brooks/Cole
20 Channel Center Street
Boston, MA 02210
USA

Cengage Learning is a leading provider of customized learning solutions with office locations around the globe, including Singapore, the United Kingdom, Australia, Mexico, Brazil, and Japan. Locate your local office at: **www.cengage.com/global**

Cengage Learning products are represented in Canada by Nelson Education, Ltd.

To learn more about Brooks/Cole, visit
www.cengage.com/brookscole

Purchase any of our products at your local college store or at our preferred online store
www.cengagebrain.com

Printed in the United States of America
1 2 3 4 5 6 7 15 14 13 12 11

CONTENTS

ABOUT THE AUTHORS

EDWARD PASCUZZI has taught Honors and AP Physics over the past fifteen years in New York State. The driving force behind the creation of the AP course at his school, Ed has earned a number of awards for his teaching and 90 percent of his students who have taken the AP Physics B Exam have scored 3 or better. Holding degrees in both Physics and Astrophysics, Ed has also served as Lead Teacher for QuarkNet, an NSF sponsored program aimed at helping physics teachers introduce particle physics into their curriculum. With QuarkNet, Ed taught particle physics workshops at both Fermilab and Brookhaven National Laboratory. He is also an avid astronomer and photographer who has co-authored an introductory astronomy book and has contributed as a staff photojournalist for *Airways* magazine. In his spare time, Ed enjoys spending time with his family and friends and is also an active glassblower.

DR. G. PATRICK ZOBER, PhD Physics, has spent most of his professional career of forty years teaching AP B and AP C Physics in Pennsylvania. He is a former AP Physics Exam grader for the ETS and a current AP Physics Consultant for the College Board. G. Patrick also spends part of his summers conducting AP Physics Workshops for a number of colleges and universities and the State of West Virginia. Besides teaching high school, he has taught Intermediate Mechanics, Engineering Physics, and Modern Physics at several colleges and universities. He has served as a Physics Consultant to the Pennsylvania Department of Education and several higher education publishers. G. Patrick is retired, writes fiction, and enjoys classical music, travel, and digital photography.

PATRICIA J. ZOBER, MS Physics, has forty years plus of experience in teaching AP B and AP C Physics at Ringgold High School in western Pennsylvania. An AP Physics Consultant with the College Board and a former AP Physics Exam grader for the College Board, she also presents AP Physics workshops. Besides her teaching duties, Patricia is science department chairperson and serves as district-wide science curriculum coordinator. She also has taught Intermediate Mechanics and Engineering Physics at local colleges and universities. Patricia is a member of the Selection Committee for the Pennsylvania Governor's School in Science, and has served as In-Service Presenter for the Pennsylvania Standards in Science Education. She also serves as consultant to several academic publishing firms. In her spare time, Patricia reads, travels, and is involved with TEAMS and Science Olympiad.

PREFACE

As a science, physics deals with the *how* of natural phenomena, but being a science of Physics, it is necessarily concerned also with *how much*. This means that you will encounter numerical problems consistently throughout the first course in Physics. Too often, students are intimidated by such problems; many people believe that solving these kinds of problems requires some special intuition that they lack. Our aim is to help you realize that you can solve such problems using strictly logical methods that require no extraordinary gifts. To accomplish this goal, this guide presents a brief summary of the topics covered in an AP Physics B course, paying special attention to the meanings of the equations of physics. These equations are simply shorthand expressions for relationships between physical concepts. Sample problems, worked out in detail, illustrate these equations using a procedure based upon logical approach and careful analysis. In this manner, we hope to help you learn how to set up and tackle the problems and questions of AP Physics B.

To solve a problem involving any concept, you must first have a clear understanding of the meaning of that concept. Thus, the topic summaries, definitions, and defining equations that you will find in this guide play particularly important roles. We have focused the presentation of concepts on problem solving, testing your mastery of the concepts with both multiple-choice questions and free-response problems. We hope that this guide will help you view the numerical problems you encounter as applications to the Laws and Principles of Physics, and that you will find it a helpful aid in problem-solving.

Edward Pascuzzi
G. Patrick Zober
Patricia J. Zober

Acknowledgments

We are deeply indebted to John Haley and Margaret Lannamann of O'Donnell and Associates for all their guidance, and in particular to John for his input, patience, organizational skills, and occasional nudges. A special thanks goes to Alison Zetterquist of Cengage Learning for her advice and assistance. The authors wish to thank Karen Hutchison and Joseph Stieve for their timely reviews of the many chapters of the manuscript. We extend a special acknowledgment to Joseph A. Sholtis, Jr. and John R. Bell for their invaluable and extensive input and assistance. Finally, we express special gratitude to Theo and Strong Vincent for all the timely reminders about mealtime and when it was time to turn off the computers for the night.

G. Patrick and Patricia Zober

I would like to personally thank my family and friends for their support and encouragement during the production of the manuscript for this book, and more importantly, I greatly appreciate the kindness and assistance of Mr. John Haley and Ms. Margaret Lannamann, both of whom provided countless suggestions and support during the creation of this work. Additionally, my thanks are also extended to reviewers Karen Hutchison and Joseph Stieve, as well as to all those involved in the editing and final production of this work, without whose diligence this effort would not have been possible.

Edward Pascuzzi

Part I

Strategies for the AP Test

PREPARING FOR THE AP* PHYSICS B EXAMINATION

Advanced Placement can be exhilarating. Whether you are taking an AP course at your school or you are working on AP independently, the stage is set for a great intellectual experience.

Sometime after New Year's Day, however, when the examination begins to loom on a very real horizon, Advanced Placement can seem downright intimidating. In fact, offered the opportunity to take the examination for a lark, even adults long out of high school refuse. If you dread taking the test, you are in good company.

The best way to deal with an AP examination is to master it, not let it master you. If you can think of these examinations as a way to show off how much physics you know, you have a leg up. Attitude *does* help. If you are not one of those students, there is still a lot you can do to sideline your anxiety. This book is designed to put you on a fast track. Focused review and practice time will help you master the examination so that you can walk in with confidence and score a 5.

WHAT'S IN THIS BOOK

This book is keyed to *College Physics*, 8th edition and 9th, by Serway and Vuille, but because it follows the College Board Topic Outline, it is compatible with all AP B Physics textbooks. It is divided into three sections. Part I, strategies for the AP Test, offers suggestions for getting yourself ready, from signing up to take the test and sharpening your pencils to organizing a free-response essay. At the end of Part I, you will find a Diagnostic Test. This test has all the elements of the AP Physics B Examination, but the 70 multiple-choice questions are organized according to the College Board Topic Outline. When you go through the answers at the end of the Diagnostic Test, you will see how the examination is weighted for each content area.

Part II, A Review of AP Physics B, is made up of 17 chapters, again following the College Board Topic Outline. These chapters are not a substitute for your textbook and class work; they simply review the AP Physics B course. At the end of each chapter, you will find 15 multiple-choice questions and 2 free-response problems based on the material of that chapter. Again, you will find page references at the end of each answer directing you to the discussion on that particular point in *College Physics*.

Part III, Practice Tests, has two complete AP Physics B level examinations. At the end of each test, you will find the answers,

---

* AP and Advanced Placement Program are registered trademarks of the College Entrance Examination Board, which was not involved in the production of, and does not endorse, this product.

explanations, and references to *College Physics* for the multiple-choice and free-response problems.

At the end of the book you will find AP Tables of Information. These tables include information you may need when you take the tests in this book. The tables will also appear in your test booklet when you take the exam.

SETTING UP A REVIEW SCHEDULE

If you have been doing your homework steadily and keeping up with the course work, you are in good shape. Organize your notes, homework, and handouts from class by topic. Reference these materials as well as your textbook and this study guide when you have difficulty in a specific section. Even if you've done all that—or if it's too late to do all that—there are still some more ways to get it all together.

To begin, read Part I of this book. You will be much more comfortable going into the test if you understand how the test questions and problems are designed and how best to approach them. Then take the Diagnostic Test to see where you are right now.

Take out a calendar and set up a schedule for yourself. If you begin studying early, you can chip away at the review chapters in Part II. You'll be surprised—and pleased—by how much material you can cover in a half an hour a day of study for a month or so before the test. Look carefully at the sections of the Diagnostic Test; if you missed a number of questions in one particular area, allow more time for the chapters that cover that area of the course. The practice tests in Part III will give you more experience with different kinds of multiple-choice questions and the wide range of free-response problems.

If time is short, skip reading the review chapters (although you might read through the chapter subheadings) and work on the multiple-choice and free-response problems at the end of each review. That will give you a good idea of your understanding of that particular topic. Then take the tests in Part III.

If time is *really* short, go straight from Part I to Part III. Taking practice tests over and over again is the fastest, most practical way to prepare. You cannot study physics by reading it like a novel. You must actively do problems to gain understanding and excel in your performance. Athletes don't perform well just by reading books about their sport or by watching others. They must get up and practice. So, you too, just like athletes, must practice, practice, and practice if you want to do your best!

BEFORE THE EXAMINATION

By February, long before the exam, you need to make sure that you are registered to take the test. Many schools take care of the paperwork and handle the fees for their AP students, but check with your teacher or the AP coordinator to make sure that you are on the list (especially if you have a documented disability and need test accommodations). If you are studying AP independently, call AP Services at the College Board for the name of the local AP coordinator, who will help you through the registration process.

The evening before the exam is not a great time for partying, nor is it a great time for cramming. If you like, look over class notes or drift through your textbook, concentrating on the broad outlines, not the small details, of the course. You might also want to skim through this book and read the AP tips.

The evening before the exam *is* a great time to get your things together for the next day. Sharpen a fistful of no. 2 pencils with good erasers; bring a scientific calculator with fresh batteries. You may bring a programmable calculator; the memory will not be erased or cleared by the test administrator. It must not have a typewriter-style keyboard. Bring a watch but turn off the alarm if it has one; get a piece of fruit or a power bar and a bottle of water for the break. Make sure that you have your social security number and whatever photo identification and admission ticket are required. Then relax. Get a good night's sleep.

On the day of the examination, it is wise not to skip breakfast; studies show that students who eat a hot breakfast before testing get higher grades than students who do not. Be careful not to drink a lot of liquids, necessitating a trip to the bathroom during the test. Breakfast will give you the energy you need to power you through the test, and more. You will spend some time waiting while everyone is seated in the correct room for the correct test, and that's before the test has even begun. With a short break between Section I and Section II, the AP Physics B exam lasts for more than three hours, so be prepared for a long morning. You do not want to be distracted by a growling stomach or hunger pangs.

Be sure to wear comfortable clothes, taking along a sweater in case the heating or air conditioning is erratic. Be sure, too, to wear clothes you like—everyone performs better when they think they look better— and by all means wear your lucky socks.

You have been on the fast track. Now go get a 5!

TAKING THE AP* PHYSICS B EXAMINATION

The AP Physics examination consists of two sections: Section I has 70 multiple-choice questions, and Section II has 6 or 7 free-response problems. You will have 90 minutes for the multiple-choice portion. You will not be allowed to use a calculator for the multiple-choice questions. The questions are collected, and you will be given a short break. Then you then have 90 minutes for the free-response problem section.

AP Physics B Exam – Distribution of Questions and Problems

	Weighting	Possible Topics	Time Allowed
Section I	50%	Multiple-choice questions	90 minutes
Section II	50%	Free-response problems	90 minutes

STRATEGIES FOR THE MULTIPLE-CHOICE SECTION

Here are some rules of thumb to help you work your way through the multiple-choice questions.

- **Multiple-Choice scoring** Each correct answer is worth one (1) point, and by a recent change to AP scoring, you will no longer lose points for incorrect answers. Therefore it is well worth your time to answer every question, even if you have to guess. There are five possible answers to each question. If you are unable to narrow down the choices at all, you have a 20% chance of guessing correctly. If you can eliminate even one response, it will always improve your chances of guessing correctly. Your best strategy is to work your way through the entire multiple-choice section, answering all questions to which you know the answers. If you skip a question, be careful to skip that line on the answer sheet as well. Then go back and work on the questions you have skipped, being sure to fill in all answers.
- **Read the question carefully** Pressured for time, many students make the mistake of reading the questions too quickly or merely skimming them. By reading a question carefully, you may already have some idea about the correct answer. You can then look for it in the responses.
- **Eliminate answers you know are incorrect** You can write on the multiple-choice questions in the test book. As you read through the responses, draw a line through any answer you know is wrong.
- **Read all the possible answers and then choose the one you believe is correct** AP examinations are written to test your precise knowledge of a subject. Some of the responses may be partially correct, but there is only one response that is completely true.

- **Mark and skip tough questions** If you are hung up on a question, mark it in the margin of the question book. Make sure to skip that question on your answer sheet, too. But save time to come back to it later, since you want to answer all questions.
- **Calculational questions** In either calculational or approximation type multiple-choice questions, you may be asked to find the solution to a problem that requires minimal mathematics. These computations are done without the use of a calculator. These types of questions usually end with the word *nearly*.
- **The acceleration due to gravity** In the multiple-choice part of the test, it is advisable to use 10 m/s² as the acceleration to approximate an answer.

TYPES OF MULTIPLE-CHOICE QUESTIONS

There are various types of multiple-choice questions. Here are some suggestions for approaching each type.

CLASSIC/BEST RESPONSE QUESTIONS

These questions are the most common type of multiple-choice question. They simply require you to read the question and select the most correct answer. For example:

1. Sources of electromagnetic radiation whose waves have the same phase relationship at all times are described as
   (A) continuous
   (B) coherent
   (C) dispersed
   (D) interfered
   (E) monochromatic

ANSWER: B. By definition, coherent sources of electromagnetic radiation are those whose emitted waves have the same phase relationship at all times. Other sources are described as incoherent.

LIST AND GROUP QUESTIONS

In this type of question, there is a list of possible answers, and you must select the answer that contains the correct group of responses. For example:

1. Which of the following quantities are vectors?
   I. instantaneous velocity
   II. distance traveled
   III. average acceleration
   (A) II only
   (B) I and II
   (C) II and III
   (D) I and III
   (E) I, II, and III

ANSWER: D. A vector quantity expresses both magnitude and direction. Both instantaneous velocity and average acceleration are vectors. Distance traveled is a scalar because direction is not specified. Cross out all items that contain response II. You have narrowed down the possible responses to (D).

Noncalculational Computations

These questions require computations without the use of a calculator. Simple mathematics and the choice of the correct physics equation will be involved. For example:

1. The work done by friction on a 15-kg body pulling it horizontally in a straight line for 15 m when the coefficient of friction between the contact surfaces is given by $\mu_k = 0.4$ is most nearly what value?
   (A) 60 J
   (B) 90 J
   (C) –60 J
   (D) –590 J
   (E) –890 J

Answer: E. The work done by friction is negative because friction is a degrading forces, thus eliminating responses (A) and (B) because they are both positive. The force of friction is given by $f = -\mu_k N = -\mu_k mg = (0.4)$ (15 kg)(10 m/s²) = –60 N. The work done by friction is $W = fx = (-60 \text{ N}) (15 \text{ m}) = -900$ J. This answer is most nearly choice (E).

STRATEGIES FOR THE FREE-RESPONSE PROBLEM SECTION

Section II of the AP Physics B exam comes with a table of equations and constants. This table, which appears after the practice tests in this guide, includes numerical values of some physical constants and conversion factors and states some conventions used in the exams.

- Check the radian/degree mode on your calculator. Set it in the degree mode.
- Scan all the questions in the section you are working in and mark those that you know you can answer correctly. Do these problems first.
- You will be provided with an answer booklet as well as an insert that contains the same questions as the answer booklet, but without the spaces. You can remove the insert for reference. All your work and answers for each problem must be shown in the answer booklet. No credit will be given for work shown on the insert, but you may write on it.
- Show all your work. Partial credit will be awarded for problems if the correct work is shown but the answer is not present or is incorrect. In problems involving calculations, box or circle your final answer.
- Points are awarded in the scoring of a problem. The awarding of the points is done by the problem rubric. Points are never taken away.
- Cross out incorrect answers and work with an "X" rather than spending time erasing.
- Be clear and organized in your work. If a grader cannot clearly understand your work, you may not receive full credit. Neatness goes a long way.
- Free-response problems will have sets of parts: (a), (b), (c), and so on. Attempt to solve each part. Even if your answer to part (a) is

incorrect, you still may be awarded points for the remaining parts of the question if the work is correct to that point.

■ Some free-response problems may not have numbers associated with them.

■ Units are important in your answers. Place units in each and every step and in the final answer.

■ You do not need to work the problems in order.

■ You should be able to recognize that equations of the form $y = mx + b$ are linear with a slope m and a vertical intercept b. An equation of the form $x = at^2 + bt + c$ is parabolic. An equation of the form $PV = k$ is hyperbolic. You should be able to distinguish between these curves.

■ In graphing P versus V, P is plotted along the vertical axis and V along the horizontal axis. When graphing $s = f(t)$, s is plotted along the vertical axis and t along the horizontal axis.

■ An answer by itself is not enough. The reader (grader) must see how the solution evolves. A good rule of thumb to follow is to write or derive a working equation, substituting using units, and the final answer with correct units. Circle or box the answer.

SAMPLE PROBLEMS AND SCORING

SAMPLE PROBLEM 1

(15 points) A wood block of mass M is held at rest at the top of an inclined plane of length x and height h that makes an angle θ with the horizontal. The block is released from rest and undergoes uniform acceleration down the plane. The coefficient of friction between the contact surfaces is μ.

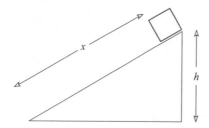

(a) The block slides a short distance down the plane; show and label all the forces acting on the block.

(b) In terms of the coefficient of friction μ, the mass M of the block, the acceleration due to gravity g, and the angle θ of inclination of the inclined plane, what is the frictional force f acting on the block?

(c) Using energy considerations and in terms of the length of the plane x, μ, g, and θ, what is the velocity of the block at the instant it reaches the bottom of the plane?

(d) In terms of g, μ, and θ, what is the acceleration of the block down the plane?

(e) In terms of M, x, μ, g, and θ, what impulse is generated on the block?

Sample Problem 1 Rubric
15 points total
   (a) 3 points

1 point is awarded for each correctly drawn and labeled vector.	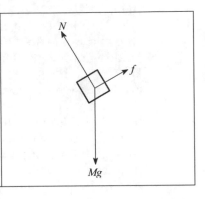

(b) 2 points

	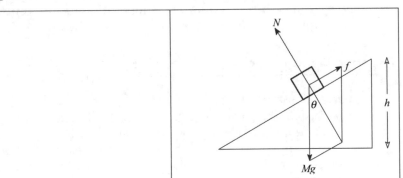 Friction is defined as $f = \mu N$. The normal is related to the weight vector as
1 point is awarded for recognizing that the normal force is related to the weight by the cosine function.	$$\cos\theta = \frac{N}{mg}$$
1 point is awarded for the statement of friction in terms of μ, M, g, and θ.	$$f = \mu Mg \cos\theta$$

(c) 4 points

1 point is awarded for writing an expression of the law of mechanical energy, including the work done by a nonconservative force.	$$-W_f = \Delta K + \Delta U$$ $$-fx = K - K_0 + U - U_0$$
1 point is awarded for showing that the work done by the nonconservative force is negative (–).	The initial kinetic energy is zero and the final potential energy is zero, giving $$-fx = K - 0 + 0 - U_0$$ $$K = U_0 - fx$$ Substituting yields $$\frac{1}{2}Mv^2 = Mgh - \left(\mu Mg\cos\theta\right)x$$ Next, h must be eliminated: 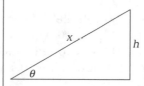
1 point is awarded for expressing h in terms of x and θ.	$$h = x\sin\theta$$ Substituting and dividing out mass M gives $$\frac{1}{2}v^2 = gx\sin\theta - \mu gx\cos\theta$$ $$v^2 = 2gx\,(\sin\theta = \mu\cos\theta)$$
1 point is awarded for the expression of v in terms of x, g, μ, and q.	$$v = \sqrt{2gx\,(\sin\theta - \mu\cos\theta)}$$

(d) 2 points

1 **point** is awarded for recognizing the equation to be used.	$v^2 = v_0^2 + 2ax$
1 **point** is awarded for the correct expression.	$2gx(\sin\theta - \mu\cos\theta) = 0 + 2ax$ $a = (\sin\theta - \mu\cos\theta)g$

(e) 3 points

2 **points** are awarded for a statement of the impulse–momentum theorem.	$J = \Delta p$ $J = M(v - v_0)$ $J = Mv$
1 **point** is awarded for the correct expression.	$J = M\sqrt{2gx(\sin\theta - \mu\cos\theta)}$
1 **additional point** is awarded if no extraneous forces are drawn in part (a).	

SAMPLE PROBLEM 2

(15 points) A 3.00-g bullet leaves the muzzle of a horizontally mounted rifle with a speed v_0 of 300.0 m/s. The bullet strikes and passes completely through a 0.400-kg wooden block suspended from a long cord. The impulse gives the block a speed V of 1.50 m/s as it exits the block. Ignore air resistance.

(a) Determine the speed of the bullet as it exits the block.
(b) Find the elevation of the center of mass of the block just after the bullet exits.
(c) What is the work done on the block by the bullet?
(d) Calculate the quantity of thermal energy produced as the bullet passes through the block.

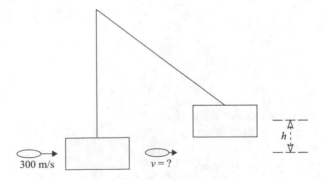

SAMPLE PROBLEM 2 RUBRIC
15 points total
(a) 3 points

	The total initial momentum equals the total final momentum.
1 point is awarded for the law of conservation of linear momentum.	$\Sigma p_0 = \Sigma p$ $Mv_0 = MV + mv$ $v = \dfrac{mv_0 - MV}{m}$
1 point is awarded for the correct substitution with the correct units.	$v = \dfrac{(0.003\ \text{kg})(300.0\ \text{m/s}) - (0.40\ \text{kg})(1.50\ \text{m/s})}{0.003\ \text{kg}}$
1 point is awarded for the correct answer with the correct proper units.	The velocity v of the bullet as it exits the block is $v = 100\ \text{m/s}$

(b) 5 points

2 points are awarded for recognizing that energy is conserved.	The kinetic energy of the block just after the bullet leaves equals the gravitational energy the block gains. $\dfrac{1}{2}MV^2 = Mgh$ 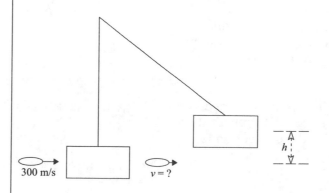 The mass M on both side divides out, giving $V^2 = 2gh$

1 point is awarded for the correct substitution with the correct units.	$h = \sqrt{\dfrac{V^2}{2\,g}} = \sqrt{\dfrac{(1.50 \text{ m/s})^2}{2(9.8 \text{ m/s})}}$
2 points are awarded for the correct answer with the correct proper units.	The block is elevated by $h = 0.34$ m

(c) 4 points

2 points are awarded for recognizing that the work done is the gain in potential energy.	Work done equals the change in gravitational energy.
1 point is awarded for the correct working equation.	$W = \Delta U = Mgh$ $W = (0.40 \text{ kg})(9.8 \text{ m/s}^2)(0.34 \text{ m})$
1 point is awarded for the correct answer with the correct proper units.	$W = 1.3\,J$

(d) 3 points

	Total energy before = total energy after $K_0 = K + U + Q$ $Q = K_0 - K - U$ $Q = \dfrac{1}{2}mv_0^2 - \dfrac{1}{2}mv^2 - Mgh$
1 point is awarded for expressing the thermal energy in terms of the kinetic energies and the gain in gravitational potential energy.	
1 point is awarded for the correct substitution with the correct units.	$Q = \dfrac{1}{2}(0.003 \text{ kg})(300.0 \text{ m/s})^2 - \dfrac{1}{2}(0.003 \text{ kg})(100 \text{ m/s})^2$ $- (0.40 \text{ kg})(9.8 \text{ m/s})^2(0.11 \text{ m})$ The thermal energy developed in the block is $Q = 119.6\,J$.
1 point is awarded for the correct answer with the correct proper units.	$Q = 120\,J$

A DIAGNOSTIC TEST

This diagnostic test will give you some indication of how you might score on the AP Physics B exam. Of course, the exam changes every year, so it is never possible to predict a student's score with certainty. This test will also pinpoint strengths and weaknesses on the key content areas covered by the exam.

AP Physics B
Section I: Multiple-Choice Questions
Time: 90 minutes
70 Questions

DIRECTIONS: Each of the following questions or incomplete statements is accompanied by five suggested answers or completions. Select the correct response to each question.

Hand calculators are not allowed on this part of the test.

The Table of Information is allowed, but not the AP Physics B Equations.

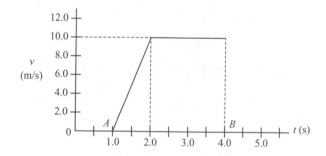

1. The motion of an automobile is shown as a function of time in the graph. The distance traveled from point A to point B is approximately
   (A) 12 m.
   (B) 15 m.
   (C) 20 m.
   (D) 22 m.
   (E) 25 m.

2. A particle travels along a curved path between two points P and Q as shown. The displacement of the particle does not depend on
   (A) the location of P.
   (B) the location of Q.
   (C) the distance traveled from P to Q.
   (D) the shortest distance between P and Q.
   (E) the direction of Q from P.

3. At time $t = 0$, an object is observed at $x = 0$; and its position along the x axis follows this expression; $x = -3t + t^3$, where the units for distance and time are meters and seconds, respectively. What is the object's displacement Δx between $t = 1.0$ s and $t = 3.0$ s?
   (A) –20 m
   (B) –2 m
   (C) +2 m
   (D) +16 m
   (E) +20 m

4. A football kicked from rest has an initial horizontal velocity component V_x and an initial vertical velocity component V_y. At the moment the ball is at the highest point of its trajectory, which of the following correctly state the acceleration and the vertical and horizontal velocity components of the ball?

	VERTICAL VELOCITY	HORIZONTAL VELOCITY	ACCELE- RATION
(A)	V_y	V_x	0
(B)	V_y	0	0
(C)	0	V_x	0
(D)	0	0	g
(E)	0	V_x	g

5. A rock is shot vertically upward from the surface of Earth with speed v_i and lands at the same location from which it was shot while spending T seconds in the air. Neglecting air resistance, which of the following expressions best describes the maximum height that the rock reaches?
   (A) $\dfrac{v_i^2}{2g}$

   (B) $v_i T$

   (C) $\dfrac{1}{2}g\left(\dfrac{T}{2}\right)^2$

   (D) $\dfrac{1}{2}gT^2$

   (E) $\dfrac{v_i^2}{2gT}$

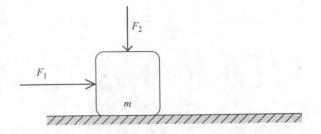

6. A block is pushed across a horizontal surface by the forces F_1 and F_2 shown. If the block moves with an acceleration of 2.0 m/s², $F_1 = 15.$ N, $F_2 = 10.$ N, and $m = 2.5$ kg, which of the following is an approximation of the coefficient of kinetic friction between the block and the surface?
   (A) 0.15
   (B) 0.29
   (C) 0.35
   (D) 0.40
   (E) 0.61

7. A book with zero acceleration is resting on the surface of a stationary table. Consider the following four forces that arise in this situation;
   (1) The force of the Earth pulling on the book
   (2) The force of the table pushing on the book
   (3) The force of the book pushing on the table
   (4) The force of the book pulling on the Earth

   Which pair of forces, excluding "action–reaction" pairs, must be equal in magnitude and opposite in direction?
   (A) 1 and 2
   (B) 1 and 3
   (C) 1 and 4
   (D) 2 and 3
   (E) 2 and 4

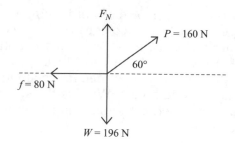

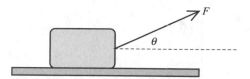

Questions 8 and 9 refer to the diagram shown in which a force P pulls on a crate of mass m along a rough surface. Other forces acting on the crate are also shown in the diagram; W represents the crate's weight, F_N represents the normal force on the crate, and f is the frictional force.

8. Which statement best describes the motion of the crate?
   (A) The crate must be at rest.
   (B) The crate must be moving with constant velocity.
   (C) The crate must be moving with constant acceleration.
   (D) The crate may be either at rest or moving with constant velocity.
   (E) The crate may be either at rest or moving with constant acceleration.

9. What is the magnitude of F_N, the normal force, on the crate?
   (A) 57 N
   (B) 80 N
   (C) 160 N
   (D) 196 N
   (E) 230 N

10. A 10-kilogram block is set moving with an initial speed of 6 m/s on a rough horizontal surface. If the force of friction is 20 N, approximately how far does the block slide before it stops?
    (A) 1.5 m
    (B) 3 m
    (C) 6 m
    (D) 9 m
    (E) 18 m

11. As shown, a block of mass m is pulled along a rough horizontal floor to the right by an applied force F.

    The normal force exerted on the block by the floor is
    (A) mg
    (B) $F \sin \theta$
    (C) $mg - F \cos \theta$
    (D) $mg + F \cos \theta$
    (E) $mg - F \sin \theta$

12. The amount of energy needed to power a 0.10-kilowatt lightbulb for 1 minute would be just sufficient to lift a 1.0 kilogram object through a vertical distance of
    (A) 12 m.
    (B) 75 m.
    (C) 100 m.
    (D) 120 m.
    (E) 610 m.

13. A 5.00-kilogram block of ice is sliding across a frozen pond at 2.00 m/s. A 7.60-newton force is applied in the direction of motion. The ice block slides 15.0 meters, and then the force is removed. The work done by the applied force is
    (A) −735 J.
    (B) −114 J.
    (C) +20 J.
    (D) +114 J.
    (E) +735 J.

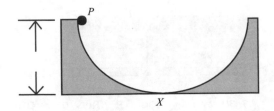

14. As shown, a rounded block that does not rotate is placed at point P at the top end of a rough circular track and is released from rest. The block slides along the arc past the bottom of the track (point X). Which is true of the height to which the block rises on the other side of the track?

(A) It is equal to $\dfrac{\pi h}{2}$.

(B) It is equal to $\dfrac{h}{4}$.

(C) It is equal to $\dfrac{h}{2}$.

(D) It is equal to h.

(E) It is between zero and h, the exact height depending on how much energy is transferred to friction.

15. A rock is dropped from a high tower and falls freely under the influence of gravity toward Earth's surface. Which one of the following statements is true concerning the rock as it falls?

(A) It will gain an equal amount of momentum during each second.

(B) It will gain an equal amount of kinetic energy during each second.

(C) It will gain an equal amount of speed for each meter through which it falls.

(D) It will gain an equal amount of momentum for each meter through which it falls.

(E) The amount of momentum it gains will be proportional to the amount of potential energy that it loses.

16. A 1.0-kilogram ball has a velocity of 12 m/s downward just before it strikes the ground and bounces up with a velocity of 12 m/s upward. What is the change in momentum of the ball?

(A) zero

(B) 12 kg · m/s, downward

(C) 12 kg · m/s, upward

(D) 24 kg · m/s, upward

(E) 24 kg · m/s, downward

17. A railroad car of mass m is moving at a speed v when it collides with a second railroad car of mass M, which is initially at rest. The two cars lock together instantaneously and then move along the track as one object. What is the speed of the combined cars immediately after the collision?

(A) $\dfrac{(v)}{2}$

(B) $\dfrac{mv}{M}$

(C) $\dfrac{Mv}{m}$

(D) $\dfrac{(m+M)v}{m}$

(E) $\dfrac{mv}{(m+M)}$

18. Planet Earth exerts the necessary centripetal force on an orbiting satellite to keep it moving in a circle at constant speed. Which statement best explains why the speed of the satellite does not change even though there is a net force exerted on it?

(A) The satellite is in equilibrium.

(B) The acceleration of the satellite is zero.

(C) The centripetal force has magnitude mv^2/r.

(D) The centripetal force is canceled by the reaction force.

(E) The centripetal force is always perpendicular to the velocity.

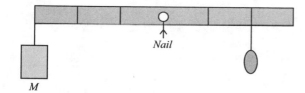

M

19. A uniform wooden board of length L and mass $8M$ is attached loosely to a wall by a nail at its center as shown. A block of mass M hangs from a massless string attached to the left end of the board a distance $L/2$ away from the nail. Another block of unknown mass is also hung on a massless string from the board, but at the right end, a distance of $L/3$ away from the nail. The system remains in equilibrium. Which of the following best represents the mass hanging on the right?

(A) $\dfrac{M}{2}$

(B) $\dfrac{M}{3}$

(C) M

(D) $2M$

(E) $\dfrac{3M}{2}$

20. A car enters a horizontal, curved roadbed of radius 50 m. The coefficient of static friction between the tires and the roadbed is 0.20. What is the maximum speed with which the car can safely negotiate the unbanked curve before slipping?

(A) 5 m/s
(B) 10 m/s
(C) 20 m/s
(D) 40 m/s
(E) 100 m/s

21. What is the kinetic energy of a satellite of mass m that orbits Earth, of mass M, in a circular orbit of radius R?

(A) zero

(B) $\dfrac{1}{2}\left(\dfrac{GMm}{R}\right)$

(C) $\dfrac{1}{4}\left(\dfrac{GMm}{R}\right)$

(D) $\dfrac{1}{2}\left(\dfrac{GMm}{R^2}\right)$

(E) $\dfrac{GMm}{R^2}$

22. In simple harmonic motion, which of the following best describes when the magnitude of the acceleration of the oscillating object is a minimum?

(A) When the displacement is a maximum.
(B) When the speed is zero.
(C) When the displacement is zero.
(D) When the restoring force is a maximum.
(E) When the speed is a between maximum and minimum.

23. Mars has a mass 1/10 that of Earth and a diameter half that of Earth. The magnitude of the acceleration of a falling body near the surface of Mars is most nearly

(A) 0.25 m/s².
(B) 0.5 m/s².
(C) 2.0 m/s².
(D) 4.0 m/s².
(E) 25.0 m/s².

24. Which of the following is a correct expression for the maximum speed of a mass m oscillating on a spring of spring constant k, whose amplitude of motion is A?

(A) $\sqrt{\dfrac{Ak}{m}}$

(B) $\sqrt{A^2 mk}$

(C) $\sqrt{\dfrac{A^2 m}{k}}$

(D) $\sqrt{\dfrac{A^2 k}{m}}$

(E) Akm

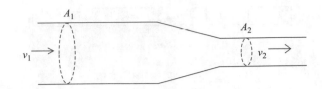

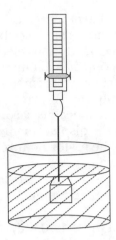

25. As shown in the figure, an object of mass 0.4 kilogram that is suspended from a stationary scale is submerged in a liquid contained in a beaker. If the reading on the scale is 3.0 newtons, then the buoyant force that the liquid exerts on the object is most nearly
(A) 0.25 N.
(B) 0.33 N.
(C) 0.75 N.
(D) 1.0 N.
(E) 1.3 N.

26. A submarine is operating at a depth of 100.0 m below the surface of the ocean. If the air inside the submarine is maintained at a pressure of 1.0 atmosphere, what is the magnitude of the force that acts on the rectangular hatch 2.0 m × 1.0 m on the deck of the submarine (the density of the sea water is 1025 kg/m³)?
(A) 980 N
(B) 2.0×10^3 N
(C) 5.0×10^4 N
(D) 9.8×10^5 N
(E) 2.0×10^6 N

27. An incompressible liquid flows along the pipe as shown, in which A_1 is the area of the pipe segment shown, v_1 is the fluid speed at A_1. The fluid then passes into a different pipe segment, which has area A_2, yielding the fluid speed v_2. The ratio of the speeds v_2 to v_1 is

(A) $\dfrac{A_1}{A_2}$.

(B) $\dfrac{A_2}{A_1}$.

(C) $\sqrt{\dfrac{A_1}{A_2}}$.

(D) $\sqrt{\dfrac{A_2}{A_1}}$.

(E) $\dfrac{v_1}{v_2}$.

28. A copper rod and a steel rod are to have lengths L_c and L_s such that the difference between their individual lengths is the same at all ambient temperatures. If the coefficients of linear expansion of copper and steel are α_c and α_s, respectively, which of the following best relates their lengths and expansion coefficients?

(A) $\dfrac{L_C}{L_S} = \dfrac{\alpha_C}{\alpha_S}$

(B) $L_C - L_S = \alpha_C - \alpha_S$

(C) $\dfrac{L_C}{L_S} = \dfrac{\alpha_S}{\alpha_C}$

(D) $\dfrac{L_C}{L_S} = \sqrt{\left(\dfrac{\alpha_C}{\alpha_S}\right)}$

(E) $\dfrac{L_C}{L_S} = \sqrt{\left(\dfrac{\alpha_S}{\alpha_C}\right)}$

29. Water enters a pipe of diameter 0.03 m with a velocity of 3.0 m/s. The water encounters a constriction where its velocity is 12.0 m/s. What is the diameter of the constricted portion of the pipe?
(A) 3.3×10^{-3} m
(B) 7.5×10^{-3} m
(C) 1.0×10^{-2} m
(D) 1.5×10^{-2} m
(E) 1.1×10^{-1} m

30. A 2.00-kilogram metal object requires 5.02×10^3 joule of heat to raise its temperature from 20.0°C to 40.0°C. Which of the following is most likely the specific heat capacity of the metal?
(A) 63 J/(kg · °C)
(B) 126 J/(kg · °C)
(C) 251 J/(kg · °C)
(D) 502 J/(kg · °C)
(E) 1000 J/(kg · °C)

31. An ideal gas at 0°C is contained within a rigid vessel. The temperature of the gas is increased by 1°C. What is P_f / P_I, the ratio of the final to initial pressure?
(A) 274/273
(B) 273/274
(C) 1/2
(D) 1/10
(E) 1/273

For Questions 32 and 33, refer to the PV plots.

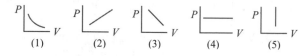

32. Which of the graphs best represents an isobaric process?
(A) Graph (1)
(B) Graph (2)
(C) Graph (3)
(D) Graph (4)
(E) Graph (5)

33. Which of the graphs best represents a thermal process in which $\Delta U = 0$?
(A) Graph (1)
(B) Graph (2)
(C) Graph (3)
(D) Graph (4)
(E) Graph (5)

34. A match is placed in an oxygen-filled cylinder that has a movable piston. The piston is moved downward so quickly that no heat escapes as the match suddenly ignites. What kind of change is demonstrated in this process?
(A) an isobaric compression
(B) an adiabatic compression
(C) an isothermal compression
(D) an isochoric compression
(E) a change of heat capacity

35. A Carnot, or ideal, heat engine operates between 27°C and 177°C. The engine's efficiency is approximately
(A) 22%.
(B) 33%.
(C) 56%.
(D) 76%.
(E) 100%.

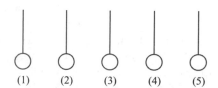

36. Five Styrofoam balls [(1) through (5) as shown] are suspended from insulating threads. Several experiments are performed on the balls and the following observations are made:
I. Ball (1) attracts (2) and repels (3).
II. Ball (4) attracts (2) and has no effect on (5).
III. A negatively charged rod attracts both (1) and (5).

What are the charges, if any, on each ball?

	Ball (1)	Ball (2)	Ball (3)	Ball (4)	Ball (5)
(A)	+	−	+	0	+
(B)	+	−	+	+	0
(C)	+	−	+	0	0
(D)	−	+	−	0	0
(E)	+	0	−	+	0

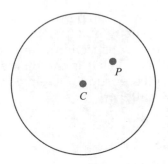

37. A −4.0-μC charge is located 0.30 m to the left of a +6.0-μC charge. What is the magnitude and direction of the electrostatic force on the positive charge?
    (A) 2.4 N, to the left
    (B) 2.4 N, to the right
    (C) 4.8 N, to the right
    (D) 4.8 N, to the left
    (E) 7.2 N, to the left

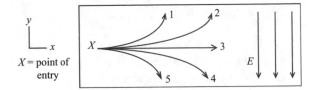

38. Two particles of the same mass carry charges +3Q and −2Q, respectively. They are shot into a region that contains a uniform electric field E as shown. The particles have the same initial velocities in the positive x direction. The lines, numbered 1 through 5, indicate possible paths for the particles. What will be the resulting paths for these particles?
    (A) Path 1 for +3Q and path 4 for −2Q
    (B) Path 5 for +3Q and path 2 for −2Q
    (C) Path 4 for +3Q and path 3 for −2Q
    (D) Path 2 for +3Q and path 5 for −2Q
    (E) Path 3 for +3Q and path 2 for −2Q

39. Which one of the following statements is true concerning the strength of the electric field between two oppositely charged parallel plates?
    (A) It is zero midway between the plates.
    (B) It is a maximum midway between the plates.
    (C) It is a maximum near the positively charged plate.
    (D) It is a maximum near the negatively charged plate.
    (E) It is constant between the plates except near the edges.

40. The hollow metal conducting sphere shown is given a net positive charge. Point C is the center of the sphere, and point P is any other point within the sphere. Which of the following is true of the electric field at these two points?
    (A) It is zero at C, but at P it is not zero and is directed outward.
    (B) It is zero at C, but at P it is not zero and is directed inward.
    (C) It is zero at P, but at C it is not zero.
    (D) It is zero at both points.
    (E) It is not zero at either point.

41. Which of the following is true concerning capacitors?
    (A) Capacitors can be used to store charge or energy or to trigger a timed electrical event.
    (B) When a capacitor is connected to a battery, the charge on one conductor of the capacitor increases with time indefinitely as long as the capacitor is connected to the battery.
    (C) Capacitors are not electrically polarized.
    (D) When a parallel plate capacitor is charged, one conductor has a positive charge and the other has a negative charge of twice that amount.
    (E) When a parallel-plate capacitor is charged, the two conductors have charge of the same sign (both positive or both negative).

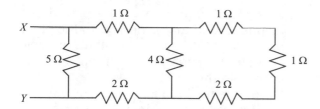

42. The equivalent resistance between points X and Y in the circuit segment shown in the diagram is closest to
    (A) 2.5 ohms.
    (B) 3.0 ohms.
    (C) 4.0 ohms.
    (D) 4.5 ohms.
    (E) 6.0 ohms.

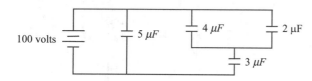

43. The equivalent capacitance of the circuit grouping shown is most nearly
    (A) $10/7$ μF.
    (B) $3/2$ μF.
    (C) $7/3$ μF.
    (D) 7 μF.
    (E) 14 μF.

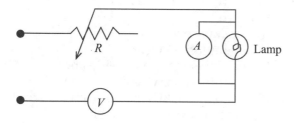

44. The circuit shown in the diagram was wired for the purpose of measuring the resistance of the lamp. Inspection shows that
    (A) voltmeter V and the variable resistor R should be interchanged.
    (B) the circuit is correct as is.
    (C) the ammeter A should be in parallel with R, not with the lamp.
    (D) the meters V and A are incorrectly placed and should be interchanged.
    (E) the lamp and V should be interchanged.

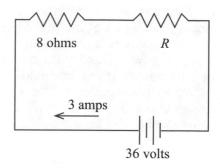

45. What is the value of the resistance R in the circuit shown?
    (A) 2 ohms
    (B) 4 ohms
    (C) 10 ohms
    (D) 12 ohms
    (E) 20 ohms

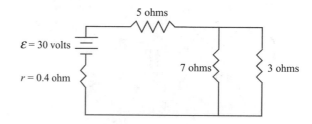

46. A circuit containing the three resistors shown (5 ohms, 7 ohms, and 3 ohms) is connected to an emf $\mathcal{E}$ of voltage 30 volts with an internal resistance of 0.4 ohm. Which of the following is the current in the 5-ohm resistor?
    (A) 2 amps
    (B) 4 amps
    (C) 8 amps
    (D) 13 amps
    (E) 225 amps

47. An electron is moving with a speed of 3.5×10^5 m/s when it encounters a magnetic field of 0.60 T. The magnetic field makes an angle of 60.0° with respect to the electron's velocity. What is the magnitude of the magnetic force on the electron?
    (A) 2.9×10^{-14} N
    (B) 3.4×10^{-14} N
    (C) 1.7×10^{-13} N
    (D) 3.2×10^{-13} N
    (E) 4.9×10^{-13} N

48. Two electrons are located in a region of space where the magnetic field is zero. Electron *A* is at rest, and electron *B* is moving westward with a constant velocity. A nonzero magnetic field directed eastward is then applied to the region. In what direction, if any, will each electron be moving after the field is applied?

	ELECTRON *A*	ELECTRON *B*
(A)	at rest	westward
(B)	northward	eastward
(C)	at rest	eastward
(D)	southward	downward, toward Earth
(E)	upward, away from Earth	westward

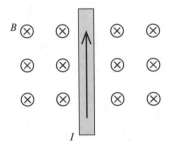

49. A wire in the plane of the page carries an electric current *I* directed upward as shown. If the wire is located in a uniform magnetic field *B* directed into the page, the force on the wire resulting from the magnetic field is
(A) directed into the page.
(B) directed out of the page.
(C) directed to the right.
(D) directed to the left.
(E) zero.

50. A 0.50 T magnetic field is directed perpendicular to the plane of a circular loop of radius 0.25 m. What is the magnitude of the magnetic flux through the loop?
(A) 0.049 Wb
(B) 0.098 Wb
(C) 0.20 Wb
(D) 0.39 Wb
(E) zero

51. A conducting loop of wire is placed in a magnetic field that is normal to the plane of the loop. Which one of the following actions will not result in an induced current in the loop?
(A) Rotate the loop about an axis that is parallel to the field and passes through the center of the loop.
(B) Increase the strength of the magnetic field.
(C) Decrease the area of the loop.
(D) Decrease the strength of the magnetic field.
(E) Rotate the loop about an axis that is perpendicular to the field and passes through the center of the loop.

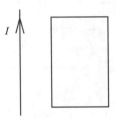

52. A long straight wire (shown) is in the plane of a rectangular conducting loop. The straight wire carries an increasing electric current in the direction shown. The current in the rectangle is
(A) zero.
(B) clockwise.
(C) counterclockwise.
(D) clockwise in the left side and counterclockwise in the right side.
(E) counterclockwise in the left side and clockwise in the right side.

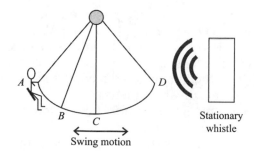

Stationary whistle

Swing motion

53. As shown, various positions of a child in motion on a swing are shown from the side. Letters *A* and *D* represent the child's highest position on the swing, whereas letter *C* represents her lowest position on the swing. Somewhere in front of the child a stationary whistle is blowing. At which position(s) will the child hear the highest sound frequency from the whistle?
(A) at both *A* and *D*
(B) at *B* when moving toward *A*
(C) at *B* when moving toward *C*
(D) at *C* when moving toward *B*
(E) at *C* when moving toward *D*

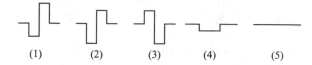

(1)   (2)   (3)   (4)   (5)

54. Which combination of pulses shown above would interfere to produce the situation shown in image (4)?
(A) If (2) were superimposed onto (3).
(B) If (1) were superimposed onto (3).
(C) If (1) were superimposed onto (2).
(D) If (3) were superimposed onto (5).
(E) None of the pulses can be combined to form wave pattern (4).

55. The greatest number of beats per second will be heard from which pair of tuning fork frequencies?
(A) 300 Hz and 302 Hz
(B) 543 Hz and 537 Hz
(C) 786 Hz and 781 Hz
(D) 45 Hz and 48 Hz
(E) 1236 Hz and 1240 Hz

56. Which of the following best represents the frequency of a standing wave on a string of length *L* fixed at both ends with one antinode?
(A) $\dfrac{5v}{2L}$

(B) $\dfrac{2v}{L}$

(C) $\dfrac{v}{2L}$

(D) $\dfrac{v}{L}$

(E) $\dfrac{3v}{2L}$

57. In a Young's double-slit experiment, green light is incident on the two slits. The inference pattern is observed on a screen. Which one of the following changes would cause the fringes to be more closely spaced?
(A) Reduce the slit separation distance.
(B) Use red light instead of green light.
(C) Use blue light instead of green light.
(D) Move the screen farther away from the slits.
(E) Move the light source farther away from the slits.

58. A beam of white light is incident upon a glass prism in air. When the light enters the prism at an oblique angle and emerges as a band of colors, which of the following is primarily responsible for this?
(A) Some of the color components of the white light are absorbed by the glass, and only the remaining components are observed.
(B) Only some of the color components are refracted by the glass, and these are the ones that are observed.
(C) White light in the prism is subjected to diffraction causing the light to spread into its component colors.
(D) The index of refraction of the glass depends on the light's different wavelengths, so the color components are refracted at different angles.
(E) White light is separated into its color components by total internal reflection within the prism.

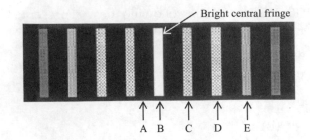

Bright central fringe

A B C D E

59. The interference pattern shown was obtained in a double-slit experiment using light of wavelength 600 nm. Five fringes of the pattern are labeled A through E as shown. Which fringe is 300 nm closer to one slit than to the other?
(A) A
(B) B
(C) C
(D) D
(E) E

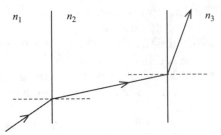

n_1 n_2 n_3

(Note: diagram drawn to scale)

60. The figure shows the path of a portion of a ray of light as it passes through three different materials, originating from region 1 (of index of refraction n_1), passing through region 2 (of index of refraction n_2), and finally passing into region 3 (of index of refraction n_3). What can be concluded concerning the refractive indices of these three materials?
(A) $n_1 > n_2 > n_3$
(B) $n_3 < n_1 < n_2$
(C) $n_1 < n_2 < n_3$
(D) $n_1 < n_3 < n_2$
(E) $n_2 < n_1 < n_3$

61. When an object is placed 15 cm from a lens, a virtual image is formed. Which one of the following conclusions is incorrect?
(A) The lens may be a convex or concave.
(B) If the image is reduced, the lens must be a diverging lens.
(C) If the image is upright, the lens must be a diverging lens.
(D) If the lens is a diverging lens, the image distance must be less than 15 cm.
(E) If the lens is a converging lens, the focal length must be greater than 15 cm.

62. A concave mirror has a radius of curvature of 30 cm. How close to the mirror should an object be placed so that the rays travel parallel to each other after reflection?
(A) 10 cm
(B) 15 cm
(C) 30 cm
(D) 45 cm
(E) 60 cm

63. Which one of the following statements concerning the image formed by a concave spherical mirror is correct?
(A) When the object distance is less than the focal length, the image is virtual.
(B) When the object distance is larger than the focal length, the image is virtual.
(C) When the object is at the center of curvature, the image is formed at infinity.
(D) When the object distance is less than the focal length, the image is inverted relative to the object.
(E) When the object distance is larger than the focal length, the image is upright relative to the object.

64. Which of the following correctly describes the de Broglie wavelength λ of an electron of mass m that is moving with a speed v, where $v \ll c$?
(A) $\lambda = \dfrac{h}{mv}$

(B) $\lambda = hf$
(C) $\lambda = pc$

(D) $\lambda = \dfrac{h}{v}$

(E) $\lambda = \dfrac{mv}{h}$

65. In the photoelectric effect, the maximum speed of the electrons emitted by a metal surface when it is illuminated by light depends on which of the following?
   I.   The intensity of the light
   II. The frequency of the light
   III. The nature of the photoelectric surface

   (A) I only
   (B) III only
   (C) I and II only
   (D) II and III only
   (E) I, II, and III

66. After Rutherford bombarded gold foil with alpha particles, he concluded that the volume of the atom was predominately empty space. Which observation led him to this conclusion?
   (A) The great majority of the incident alpha particles was not deflected.
   (B) Some of the alpha particles were deflected 180°.
   C) The paths of the deflected alpha particles were hyperbolic.
   (D) The gold nuclei absorbed the great majority of the incident alpha particles.
   (E) Predicting the final paths of the alpha particles was nearly impossible.

67. Which of the following was one of the Bohr postulates concerning the model of the atom?
   (A) Electrons can, under certain circumstances, exhibit wave-like properties.
   (B) Electrons can occupy only certain, quantized energy levels in the atom.
   (C) All light is composed of photons.
   (D) All atoms are mostly empty space.
   (E) Electrons and protons are uniformly spread throughout the atom, like a pudding.

68. An atom with one electron has an ionization energy of 24 eV. If an electron makes a transition from an excited energy state where $E = -6$ eV to the ground state and a photon is released, what is the approximate wavelength of the photon?
   (A) 18 nm
   (B) 33 nm
   (C) 69 nm
   (D) 120 nm
   (E) 180 nm

69. A nucleus with N neutrons and Z protons emits an alpha particle and then a positron. After this emission, which of the following best describes the nucleus' atomic and neutron numbers?
   (A) The nucleus still has Z protons and N neutrons.
   (B) The nucleus now has $Z - 3$ protons and $N - 1$ neutrons.
   (C) The nucleus now has $Z - 2$ protons and $N - 2$ neutrons.
   (D) The nucleus now has $Z - 1$ protons and $N - 3$ neutrons.
   (E) The nucleus now has $Z - 3$ protons and $N - 2$ neutrons.

70. During beta decay, what happens to the mass number and the atomic number of an element?
   (A) The mass number decreases by 4, and the atomic number decreases by 2.
   (B) The mass number does not change, and the atomic number decreases by 2.
   (C) Neither the mass number nor the atomic number change.
   (D) The mass number does not change, and the atomic number increases by 1.
   (E) The mass number increases by 2, and the atomic number increases by 1.

STOP
END OF SECTION 1
IF YOU FINISH BEFORE TIME IS CALLED, YOU MAY CHECK YOUR WORK ON THIS SECTION. DO NOT GO ON TO SECTION II UNTIL YOU ARE TOLD TO DO SO.

AP Physics B
Section II: Free-Response Problems
Time: 90 minutes

DIRECTIONS: Solve each of the following problems. Unless the directions indicate otherwise, respond to all parts of each question.

Hand calculators are permitted on this part of the test.

The Table of Information and the AP Physics B Equations are allowed.

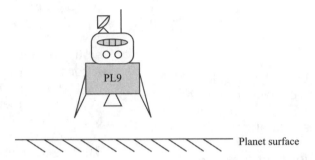

Planet surface

1. An interplanetary space probe called Planetary Lander 9 (PL9) has a mass of 2.0×10^4 kg and lands on a newly discovered planet far from Earth. Following is a table containing data from PL9's descent onto the planet, during which time its rockets provided a constant upward descent thrust of 1.3×10^5 N to slow the craft for a period of 40 seconds. PL9 has measured the radius of the planet it is landing on as 5.0×10^6 m.

t (s)	v (m/s)	Remarks
0.0	−20.0	Begin timing
10.0	−16.0	Altitude = H
20.0	−11.0	
30.0	−4.0	
40.0	0.0	$h = 0.0, v = 0.0$

(a) Plot the velocity versus time of the PL9 craft on the following axes.

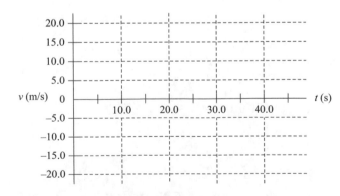

(b) Calculate the acceleration of the PL9 craft during its descent.
(c) Calculate the altitude of the PL9 craft when the timing began at $t = 0$ seconds.
(d) Calculate the value of H.
(e) Calculate the surface value of g for this planet (assume it is constant for the duration of the PL9's descent).
(f) Calculate the mass of the planet onto which the PL9 craft has landed.

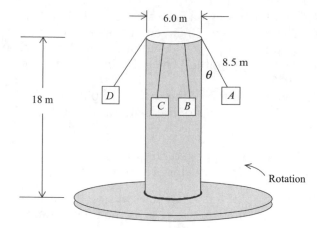

2. As shown, an amusement park ride moves in a uniform circular path with small baskets (labeled A, B, C, and D) suspended by cables of length 8.5 meters. Baskets A and B contain riders, however baskets C and D are empty. Note that the inner cylinder diameter is 6.0 meters and its height is 18 meters above level ground. Basket A extends to an angle of 36°.
   (a) Calculate the speed of the riders in basket A.
   (b) Calculate the period of the riders in basket A.
   (c) Calculate the acceleration of the riders in basket A.
   (d) The total mass of the riders in basket B is 3 times that of the mass of riders in basket A.
      (i) To what angle would the cable of basket B extend to? Justify your answer.
      (ii) What is the speed of basket B relative to basket A? Justify your answer.

   While at top speed, the cable holding basket C breaks just as it is in the position shown.

   (e) Calculate the time it takes basket C to reach the ground.
   (f) Calculate the horizontal distance traveled by basket C from the point of release to the point of impact with the ground.

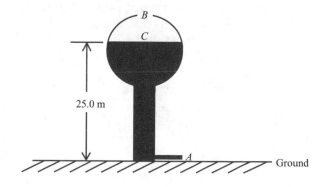

3. As shown, a town's water tower has a water level that is 25.0 meters above ground level (point *C*), the top of which (point *B*) is vented (open) to the atmosphere. When a valve in a pipe of diameter 16.0 cm is opened at *A*, water can flow outward (the height of the pipe above ground level at *A* is negligible). The valve in the pipe is initially closed. The density of the water is 1000 kg/m³.
    (a) Why is there a vent in the top of the tower? Explain briefly.
    (b) Calculate the absolute pressure of the water at point *A* just inside the pipe when the valve is closed.

    The valve at point *A* is now opened and the water is allowed to flow nonviscously; the speed of the water at point *C* during this time is negligible.

    (c) Determine the pressure of the water just *outside* the flow pipe at point *A*.
    (d) Calculate the speed of the water as it exits the pipe at point *A*.
    (e) Calculate the volume flow rate of the water as it exits the pipe at point *A*.
    (f) If 1.0 U.S. gallon of water contains approximately 3.875×10^{-3} cubic meters of water, how many gallons of water exit this pipe at point *A* every second?

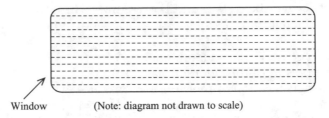

    Window   (Note: diagram not drawn to scale)

4. As shown, a typical automobile rear window contains approximately 20 thin copper wire strips of approximate radius 1.0×10^{-5} m which act to defrost or defog the window when moisture builds up on the interior. The resistivity of the copper is 1.72×10^{-8} Ω•m and the length of each wire is 1.211 meters.
    (a) Calculate the resistance of one strand of this wire.
    (b) If this group of wires is connected in parallel to a 12.0-volt power source of negligible internal resistance, determine the amount of power delivered to the window by this entire group of 20 wires.
    (c) The energy *Q* required to cause a temperature change ΔT of a liquid of mass *m* is given by $Q = mc\Delta T$, where *c* is the specific heat of the liquid. If 5.0 grams of water condenses on the window interior at a temperature of 25.0°C, how much time does it take this wire strand to heat this moisture to 100°C? The specific heat of water is 4186.0 J/kg °C.
    (d) Determine the amount of electric current required to heat the window.

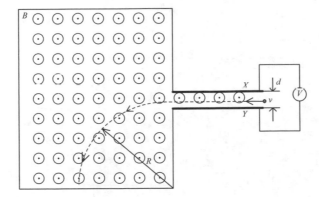

5. As shown, a particle of unknown mass m and charge q is injected from rest to a speed of $v = 4.2 \times 10^6$ m/s undeflected through a parallel plate capacitor represented by X and Y. The plates are separated by a distance of $d = 6.0 \times 10^{-2}$ m, and a constant potential difference V is maintained between them. A uniform magnetic field B of magnitude 2.0 T directed out of the page exists both between the plates and in a region to the left of them, as shown. After the particle passes into the region to the left of the plates where only the magnetic field exists, its trajectory is circular with a radius $R = 0.50$ m, part of which is shown by the dashed line.
   (a) What is the sign (+ or −) of the charge of the particle? Explain how you determined this.
   (b) On the diagram of the capacitor shown, clearly indicate the direction of the electric field between the plates. Explain how you determined this.

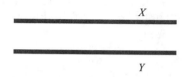

   (c) Determine the acceleration of the charge while it is passing through the region to the left of the capacitor.
   (d) Determine the magnitude of the potential difference V between the plates of the capacitor.
   (e) Determine the ratio of the charge to mass (q/m) of the particle.
   (f) It is discovered that, at one point immediately after the particle is injected into the capacitor, it curves upward and collides with plate X. Provide an explanation for this.

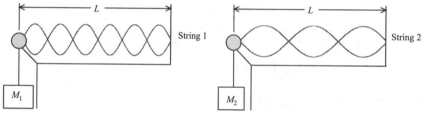

6. As shown, two identical strings, fixed at both ends, are held tightly at their left ends by masses M_1 and M_2, respectively, suspended over pulleys. At their right ends, a wave generator (not shown) operates such that string 1 has the shape shown and that waves on it move at 28.0 m/s. Similarly, a wave generator oscillates string 2 such that it has the shape shown and that waves on it travel at 19.8 m/s. Both strings have a mass of 25.0 grams and the value of L is 2.0 meters.
   (a) Determine the value of M_1 and M_2.
   (b) Determine the period of the waves on each string.
   (c) Suppose now the two waves and their mechanisms are connected to a large hollow wooden box to generate sound waves to make a musical instrument. Calculate the frequency of the beats resulting from the superposition of the two waves.
   (d) If typical human hearing is responsive to sound waves ranging in frequency from 55 Hz to 18,000 Hz, describe what a person would hear from this device.

7. A particular metal in a photovoltaic cell has a threshold frequency of 4.25×10^{14} Hz. A nearby variable wavelength light source shines monochromatic light onto the metal.
   (a) What is the kinetic energy of the photoelectrons from this metal when the incident light has a frequency of 4.25×10^{14} Hz? Explain your answer.
   (b) Calculate the work function of the metal in the photovoltaic cell.

   The source is adjusted so that light of wavelength 3.25×10^{-7} m is now incident upon the metal.

   (c) Calculate the average speed of the photoelectrons ejected from this metal.
   (d) Calculate the de Broglie wavelength of an ejected photoelectron.
   (e) On the axes below, construct a graph of the kinetic energy versus frequency for the situation described previously.

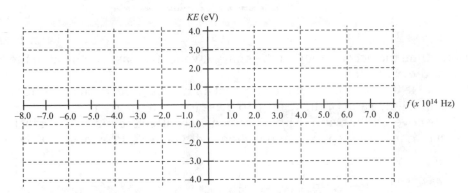

   (f) Calculate the slope of the graph created for part (e). What is the significance of the slope?
   (g) Briefly answer each of the following;
      (i) Describe what must be done to the light source in order for it to emit a greater number of photoelectrons from the metal.
      (ii) Describe what must be done to the light in order for it to emit more energetic photoelectrons.

SCORING THIS TEST

ANSWER KEY FOR MULTIPLE-CHOICE QUESTIONS

1. E	11. E	21. B	31. A	41. A	51. A	61. C
2. C	12. E	22. C	32. D	42. A	52. C	62. B
3. E	13. D	23. D	33. A	43. D	53. E	63. A
4. E	14. E	24. D	34. B	44. D	54. A	64. A
5. A	15. A	25. D	35. B	45. B	55. B	65. D
6. B	16. D	26. E	36. C	46. B	56. C	66. A
7. A	17. E	27. A	37. A	47. A	57. C	67. B
8. D	18. E	28. C	38. B	48. A	58. D	68. C
9. A	19. E	29. D	39. E	49. D	59. A	69. B
10. D	20. B	30. B	40. D	50. B	60. B	70. D

EXPLANATIONS FOR THE MULTIPLE-CHOICE ANSWERS

1. **E** The distance traveled during the time from A to B may either be calculated directly from the kinematics equation $d = v_i \Delta t + \frac{1}{2} a \Delta t^2$ or simply by finding the area under the curve. In doing the latter, the area under the curve from $t = 1$ s to $t = 2$ s is that of a triangle: $d_1 = \frac{1}{2}(base)(height) = \frac{1}{2}(1\,s)\left(10\frac{m}{s}\right) = 5$ m. Similarly, the distance traveled from $t = 2$ s to $t = 4$ s is $d_2 = (base)(height) = (2\,m)\,10\frac{m}{s} = 20$ m. Therefore, the entire distance traveled from A to B is $d_{tot} = d_1 + d_2 = 25$ m, which is choice (E) (*College Physics* 8th ed. pages 34–37/9th ed. pages 35–38).

2. **C** Displacement, unlike distance, is a vector quantity that does not depend on the precise path taken, but instead depends only on the final ending location relative to some starting fixed reference point. Thus, the displacement from P to Q is not the curved path, but a line drawn from P to Q in the northeasterly direction (*College Physics* 8th ed. pages 24–46/9th ed. pages 25–47).

3. **E** The location of the object at $t = 1$ second is found by $x(1) = -3(1) + (1)^3$ or $x(1) = -2$ meters. At $t = 3$ seconds, the position of the object is $x(3) = -3(3) + (3)^3$ or $x(3) = +18$ meters. Therefore, the displacement Δx of the object between 1 and 3 seconds is from -2 meters to $+18$ meters, which is $+20$ meters, choice (E) (*College Physics* 8th ed. pages 24–46/9th ed. pages 25–47).

4. **E** At the peak of its path, a projectile stops moving upward, and thus $V_y = 0$; however, recall that the horizontal velocity of all projectiles is constant, and thus the value of V_x at the peak is the same as that when the object was launched. Additionally, since the object is in freefall during the duration of its flight, its acceleration is always g, -10 m/s^2 (*College Physics* 8th ed. pages 62–65/9th ed. pages 63–68).

5. **A** Using the equation $v_f^2 = v_i^2 + 2gd$ in the vertical direction will provide the answer (where $v_f = 0$ at the top of the path and $g = -10$ m/s^2); $v_f^2 = v_i^2 + 2gd$ becomes $0 = v_i^2 + 2gd$. Solving for d gives $-v_i^2 = 2gd$ or $\frac{v_i^2}{2g} = d$. The negatives cancel; thus, choice (A) is the closest correct answer (*College Physics* 8th ed. pages 62–68/9th ed. pages 63–70).

6. **B** In the vertical direction, the block is in static equilibrium, so that $\Sigma F_y = 0$ gives $N = mg + F_2$ (1). In the horizontal direction, there is a net force, and thus an acceleration, so that $\Sigma F_x = ma_x$ gives $F_1 - f_k = ma$ (where $f_k = u_k N$), or $F_1 - u_k N = ma$ (2). Thus, substituting equation (1) into (2) where N appears gives the following: $F_1 - u_k (mg + F_2) = ma$ or, $u_k = (F_1 - ma)/(mg + F_2) = 0.29$ (using $g = 10$ and $m = 5/2$), which is choice (B) (*College Physics* 8th ed. pages 83–92, 94–108/9th ed. pages 86–89, 98–112).

7. **A** The action–reaction pairs are (1) and (4) (Earth pulls on book, book pulls on Earth) and (2) and (3) (table pushing on book, book pushing on table) and thus they are excluded according to the directions of the question. Therefore, choices (C) and (D) may be eliminated. As for choice (A), the force of Earth pulling on the book is w (1) and the force of the table pushing on the book is the normal force N (2), which are both equal but opposite, so it is the correct answer. Forces (1) and (3), choice (B), and forces (2) and (4), choice (E), are not opposing forces (*College Physics* 8th ed. pages 92–94/9th ed. pages 94–98).

8. **D**   Note that the frictional force $f = 80$ N acts to the left, which is balanced by the component of P toward the right horizontal axis, $P \cos 60°$, which is also equal to 80 N. Because of this, the object could be at rest or moving with constant velocity (static and dynamic equilibrium, respectively), but it is certainly not accelerating. Therefore, choice (D) most accurately describes this situation (*College Physics* 8th ed. pages 83–92, 94–108/9th ed. pages 86–89, 98–112).

9. **A**   In this case, it is necessary to apply $\Sigma F_y = 0$, which gives $F_N + 160 \cos 60° - w = 0$. Solving for F_N gives $F_N = w - 160 \cos 60°$ which becomes $F_N = 196$ N $- 138.6$ N $= 57.4$ N, choice (A) (*College Physics* 8th ed. pages 83–92, 94–108/9th ed. pages 86–89, 98–112).

10. **D**   Sketching the free body diagram will show that the only force acting horizontally is the kinetic friction force, $f_k = \mu_k N$. Therefore, applying $\Sigma F = ma$ in the x direction gives $\Sigma F = ma = \mu_k N = \mu_k(mg)$ which gives the acceleration as $a = \mu_k g$. Additionally, the distance d can be found by the kinematics equation $v_f^2 = v_i^2 + 2ad$. Substituting for a and solving for d will give $v_f^2 - v_i^2 = 2ad$ or $\dfrac{v_f^2 - v_i^2}{2a} = d$ and finally $\dfrac{v_f^2 - v_i^2}{2(\mu_k g)} = d$. Lastly, to solve this, it is necessary to find the coefficient of friction, μ_k using $f_k = \mu_k N$ as follows: $20 = \mu_k(mg) = \mu_k(10$ kg$)(10$ m/s$^2)$ or $\mu_k = 2/10$. Therefore, d can be calculated, with $v_f = 0$, $v_i = 6$ m/s and $g = 10$ m/s^2 (units omitted for clarity); $d = \dfrac{v_f^2 - v_i^2}{2(-\mu_k g)} = \dfrac{0-36}{2(-\frac{2}{10})(10)} =$ 9 meters, choice (D). Note that $a = \mu_k g$ must be negative as it opposes the motion of the object, which therefore cancels with the -36 in the numerator. Note this may also be solved using the work-energy theorem, $W = \Delta K$ (*College Physics* 8th ed. pages 83–92, 94–108/9th ed. pages 86–89, 98–112).

11. **E**   In the vertical direction, the block is in static equilibrium, so that $\Sigma F_y = 0$ gives $\Sigma F_y = 0$ or $N + F_y - w = 0$ so that $N = w - F_y$. Therefore, $N = w - F \sin \theta$ or $N = mg - F \sin \theta$, which is choice (E) (*College Physics* 8th ed. pages 83–92, 94–108/9th ed. pages 86–89, 98–112).

12. **E**   The given quantities are $\Delta t = 60$ s, $mg = 10$ N, $P = 0.1 \times 10^3$ W, and $d = ?$ Since d (or r) is the unknown, the only relations that connect r with power and energy are $P = \dfrac{W}{\Delta t}$ and $W = F \Delta r \cos \theta$ (here, $\cos \theta = -1$ since $\theta = 180°$). Thus, it is necessary to solve for W and then substitute it into the equation for work to solve for r. Therefore, $P \Delta t = F \Delta r$ solving for r gives $\dfrac{P \Delta t}{F} = \Delta r$. Omitting units for clarity and substituting gives $\dfrac{(0.1 \times 10^3)(60)}{10} = \Delta r = 600$ m, closest to choice (E) (*College Physics* 8th ed. pages 119–122,143–146/9th ed. pages 124–129, 147–152).

13. **D**   This is a straightforward application of the definition of work, $W = F \Delta r \cos \theta$ where $\cos \theta = 1$ since $\theta = 180°$, as the force $F = 7.6$ N and the displacement $r = 15$ m are in the same direction. Noting the calculation must be done longhand, this becomes $W = F \Delta r \cos \theta = (7.6$ N$)(15$ m$)(1)$ or $W = + 114$ J. Note that the quantity is positive as work done by the force to cause the displacement (F and Δr in the same direction) to add energy to the system (as opposed to friction which removes energy, and would thus be negative) (*College Physics* 8th ed. pages 119–149/9th ed. pages 124–154).

14. **E**   As an application of energy conservation, the block's total energy is mgh, which is then transformed into kinetic energy and transferred to friction during its downward slide. At the very bottom of the arc, where $h = 0$, the block's kinetic energy must be

less that *mgh* because of this "loss" of energy to friction, which similarly is the same reason the block cannot rise to *h* on the right side of the arc. Therefore, choice (E) is correct (*College Physics* 8th ed. pages 127–135/9th ed. pages 132–139).

15. **A** Since the rock accelerates uniformly, increasing its speed by 9.8 m/s each second, it would therefore follow that the rock's momentum would also increase uniformly by the same amount, each second, since the magnitude of momentum ($p = mv$) is directly proportional to the object's speed. Since kinetic energy depends on the square of the velocity, (B) cannot be correct, and since speed squared is proportional to distance fallen (by $v_f^2 = v_i^2 + 2ad$), (C) and (D) are also incorrect. Lastly, (E) is incorrect because momentum cannot be equated to a form of energy (*College Physics* 8th ed. pages 42–46, 119–149, 161–166/9th ed. pages 43–47, 124–153, 167–172).

16. **D** Since momentum is a vector, it is imperative that direction of the ball's velocity be incorporated into the change of momentum equation $\Delta p = \Delta mv$. Therefore, $\Delta mv = mv_f - mv_i$, which becomes $m (v_f - v_i) = 1.0$ kg [+12 m/s – (–12 m/s)] = + 24 kg · m/s (i.e., upward) (*College Physics* 8th ed. pages 161–166/9th ed. pages 167–172).

17. **E** Applying the conservation of momentum before and after the collision, then solving for v_f gives $p_{isys} = p_{fsys}$, which becomes $mv = (m + M)v_f$. Therefore, $v_f = \dfrac{mv}{(m + M)}$ (*College Physics* 8th ed. pages 161–166, 169–176/9th ed. pages 167–172, 175–182).

18. **E** The primary features of uniform circular motion include centripetal (center-seeking) force and acceleration; however, the velocity of the object is tangent to the circle's path, which therefore reinforces the circular motion. Since *v* is tangent to the path and *a* is radially directly, *v* and *a* must be perpendicular, which prevents the object from decelerating. Therefore, choice (E) is correct (*College Physics* 8th ed. pages 199–207/9th ed. pages 207–214).

19. **E** Since it is stated that the board is in equilibrium, apply $\sum \tau = 0$ to determine the unknown mass on the right, noting that the torque due to the left mass is counterclockwise (+) and that due to the right mass is clockwise (–). With the rotation axis chosen at the center, where the board is nailed, the torque that arises from the board is zero since its lever arm *r* is zero. Calling the right mass *m*, this becomes: $\sum \tau = \left(\dfrac{L}{2}\right) Mg + 0 + - \left(\dfrac{L}{3}\right) mg$ or $\left(\dfrac{L}{2}\right) Mg = \left(\dfrac{L}{3}\right) mg$. Since *L* and *g* are common to both sides, they cancel to give the final answer, $m = \left(\dfrac{3}{2}\right) M$, which is choice (E) (*College Physics* 8th ed. pages 228–232, 236–239/9th ed. pages 235–239, 244–247).

20. **B** Sketching a free-body diagram will help to show that $f_{smax} = \mu_s N = \sum F_c = \dfrac{mv^2}{R}$, which becomes $\mu_s N = \dfrac{mv^2}{R}$. Applying $\sum F = 0$ in the *y* direction gives $N = mg$ so the previous equation for centripetal force now becomes $\mu_s (mg) = \dfrac{mv^2}{R}$, and solving for speed *v* gives $v = \sqrt{\mu_s gR} = \sqrt{\left(\dfrac{2}{10}\right)(10)(50)} = 10$ m/s, which is choice (B) (*College Physics* 8th ed. pages 199–207/9th ed. pages 207–214).

21. **B** The kinetic energy of the satellite at any moment is given by $K = \frac{1}{2} mv^2$ and $\sum F = ma = \dfrac{mv^2}{R}$ is balanced by the gravitational pull $F = \dfrac{GMm}{R^2}$, which is therefore written

$$\frac{\cancel{m}v^2}{\cancel{R}} = \frac{GM\cancel{m}}{R^{\cancel{2}}}$$, which gives $v^2 = \frac{GM}{R}$. Substituting this into the K equation then gives $K = \frac{1}{2}mv^2 = \frac{1}{2}m\left[\frac{GM}{R}\right]$ or $K = \frac{1}{2}\left(\frac{GMm}{R}\right)$, which is choice (B) (*College Physics* 8th ed. pages 127–135, 199–207/9th ed. pages 132–139, 207–214).

22. **C** The magnitude of the acceleration of an object in SHM is $a = \dfrac{kx}{m}$, showing that a and x are directly related. Therefore, acceleration is a minimum at minimum displacement, which occurs when the oscillating mass is passing through equilibrium at $x = 0$, the time when it has the greatest speed v and the smallest restoring force $F = -kx$. This therefore eliminates choices (A), (B), (D), and (E) (*College Physics* 8th ed. pages 425–428, 431–436/9th ed. pages 437–441, 443–448).

23. **D** The question is asking for g for Mars (i.e., g_M). For a mass m near the surface of Mars, the gravitational force it experiences is equivalent to its weight, which can be written as $F_g = mg = \dfrac{GMm}{R^2}$, which becomes $\cancel{m}g = \dfrac{GM\cancel{m}}{R^2}$ where M is M_M (mass of Mars). Note that you must perform this calculation without a calculator, fractions are left as is for ease of calculation (note units are omitted for clarity). This becomes

$$g_m = \frac{GM_M}{R_M{}^2} \approx \frac{G\left(\frac{1}{10}\right)M_E}{\left(\frac{1}{2}R_E\right)^2} \approx \frac{\left(\frac{1}{10}\right)GM_E}{\left(\frac{1}{4}\right)R_E{}^2} \approx \left(\frac{4}{10}\right)g_E \approx 4\,\frac{m}{s^2}$$

which is choice (D) (*College Physics* 8th ed. pages 207–211/9th ed. pages 214–217).

24. **D** During the oscillation of the mass m, it has maximum elastic potential energy PE_s at the endpoints of its motion (where $x = A$). As it passes through equilibrium (where $x = 0$), this elastic potential energy is transferred into kinetic energy K, which is its maximum at equilibrium, and thus occurs where the speed v of the mass is the greatest. Therefore, by energy conservation $K = P'E_s$, which becomes $\dfrac{1}{2}mv^2 = \dfrac{1}{2}kx^2$ solving for v gives $v = \sqrt{\dfrac{A^2k}{m}}$, which is choice (D) (*College Physics* 8th ed. pages 127–135, 425–428, 431–436/9th ed. pages 132–139, 437–441, 443–448).

25. **D** If the liquid were not present, then the downward force acting on the scale would simply be the weight of the object, or $w = mg = (0.4\ kg)(9.8\ m/s^2)$ or about 4. newtons, with only two forces in the free-body diagram (T upward and w downward, both 4 N). With the addition of the liquid, supplying an upward buoyant force, there are now three forces in the free-body diagram: T upward, F_B upward, and W downward. Since $w = 4\ N$ and the scale is now reading 3 N, then $\Sigma F = 0$ applied to the vertical direction gives a remaining force of 1 N, which must be the buoyant force. Therefore, $F_B = 1.0$ N, which is choice (D) (*College Physics* 8th ed. pages 284–290/9th ed. pages 293–299).

26. **E** Since the submarine is submerged to 100 meters, it will first be necessary to find the gauge pressure ($P_g = \rho gh$) as the goal is to find the force F on the hatch, which will be done using $P = F/A$. Thus, $P_g = \rho gh = (1025\ kg/m^3)(10\ m/s^2)(100\ m) = (1.025 \times 10^3)$ $(1 \times 10^3) = 1.025 \times 10^6\ N/m^2 = P_g$. Then, since $PA = F$, we can substitute $(1.025 \times 10^6$

N/m²)(1.0 m × 2.0 m) = 2.05 × 10⁶ N = F, which is choice (E) (*College Physics* 8th ed. pages 276–284/9th ed. pages 279–281, 288–293).

27. **A** This problem also involves using the condition of fluid continuity, $A_1 v_1 = A_2 v_2$, where A (= πr^2) is the cross-sectional area of the pipe, and r is the pipe's radius. Here, though, as all that is being asked for is the ratio of the fluid speeds $\frac{v_2}{v_1}$. By the continuity equation, this becomes $A_1 = A_2 \frac{v_2}{v_1}$ or $\frac{A_1}{A_2} = \frac{v_2}{v_1}$, which is choice (A) (*College Physics* 8th ed. pages 290–293/9th ed. pages 299–302).

28. **C** According to the equation of linear thermal expansion, the change in length (ΔL) is proportional to the change in temperature (ΔT). Therefore, if we wish to have two different materials have the same change of length, they must satisfy the condition (C is for copper, and S is for steel): $(\Delta L)_C = (\Delta L)_S$ or $L_C \alpha_C \Delta T = L_S \alpha_S \Delta T$. Since each must have the same temperature change, these cancel from each side, thus giving $\frac{L_C}{L_S} = \frac{\alpha_S}{\alpha_C}$, which is choice (C) (*College Physics* 8th ed. pages 328–335/9th ed. pages 337–343).

29. **D** This problem involves using the condition of fluid continuity, $A_1 v_1 = A_2 v_2$, where A (= πr^2) is the cross-sectional area of the pipe, and r is half the pipe's diameter, or radius. Note the checklist should be $r_1 = 3/2 \times 10^{-2}$ m, $v_1 = 3$ m/s, $v_2 = 12$ m/s, and $r_2 = ?$ (Note fractions are used to make the hand calculation easier and quicker). Rearranging for r and then substituting values gives the following: $\pi r_1^2 v_1 = \pi r_2^2 v_2$

or $\sqrt{\frac{r_1^2 v_1}{v_2}} = r_2$. This becomes (omitting units for clarity) $r_2 = \sqrt{\frac{\left(\frac{3}{2} \times 10^{-2}\right)^2 (3)}{(12)}}$ or

$r_2 = \sqrt{\frac{\left(\frac{9}{4} \times 10^{-4}\right)(1)}{(4)}} = \sqrt{\frac{9}{16} \times 10^{-4}} = \frac{3}{4} \times 10^{-2}$ m. The diameter, therefore, is twice as large, or 1.5 × 10⁻² m, which is choice (D) (*College Physics* 8th ed. pages 290–293/9th ed. pages 299–302).

30. **B** The relationship between the change in temperature (ΔT) and the heat gained or lost (Q) by a mass (m) is $Q = mc\,T$. Therefore, all that is necessary is to solve for c and substitute the known variables: $\frac{Q}{m\Delta T} = c$ or $\frac{5.2 \times 10^8}{(2)(20°)} = c$ ~ 126. J/kg· °C, which is choice (B) (*College Physics* 8th ed. pages 355–357/9th ed. pages 365–366).

31. **A** To solve this problem, it is necessary to use the ideal gas law, $PV = nRT$ both before and after the temperature change. Since nR is a constant (i.e., the container is closed), the entire process can be written as $\frac{P_1 V_1}{T_1} = nR = \frac{P_2 V_2}{T_2}$. "Rigid vessel" means that the volume does not change after the temperature is raised; therefore, the gas law now gives $\frac{P_1 V_1}{T_1} = \frac{P_2 V_2}{T_2}$ or $\frac{P_1}{T_1} = \frac{P_2}{T_2}$, which is then written $\frac{T_2}{T_1} = \frac{P_2}{P_1}$. This simply means that the ratio of the pressures is simply the ratio of the temperatures (in Kelvin), which becomes $\frac{274}{273} = \frac{P_2}{P_1}$, or answer choice (A), noting that 0°C is 273 K (*College Physics* 8th ed. pages 335–340/9th ed. pages 343–347).

32. **D**   An isobaric process is a constant pressure process and, thus, on a *PV* plot would be represented by a straight horizontal line (since *P* is on the vertical axis). This is only shown by graph (4), answer choice (D) (*College Physics* 8th ed. pages 385–399/9th ed. pages 395–410).

33. **A**   In AP Physics, since thermal work *W* represents the work done *on* a system (not *by* the system), the first law of thermodynamics is written $\Delta U = Q + W$. A process, therefore, in which $Q = -W$ constitutes a zero change of internal energy ($\Delta U = 0$). The only type of process in which this occurs is an isothermal process, since ΔU is directly related to ΔT by the relation $\Delta U = \frac{3}{2} nR\Delta T$. Thus, the correct answer is (A), as graph (1) denotes an isotherm (*College Physics* 8th ed. pages 385–399/9th ed. pages 395–410).

34. **B**   As the problem states, the volume *V* of the cavity can therefore be changed, and as the piston is moved downward, *V* decreases rapidly. By the ideal gas law, $PV = nRT$, the pressure *P* must increase to keep the *PV* product constant. The resulting rapid increase of pressure causes a corresponding rapid increase of temperature, *T*, which occurs with no addition of heat *Q* from outside the cylinder. Therefore, since $Q = 0$, it must represent an adiabatic process, and since the volume is being reduced, it is an adiabatic compression, choice (B) (*College Physics* 8th ed. pages 385–399/9th ed. pages 395–410).

35. **B**   The efficiency of a Carnot cycle between T_H (high temperature) and T_C (low temperature) is $e = \dfrac{T_H - T_C}{T_H}$ where the temperatures must be in degrees Kelvin (which is °C + 273). Here, 27°C is 300 K and 177°C is 450 K. Therefore, the efficiency becomes $e = \dfrac{450 - 300}{450} = \dfrac{150}{450} = \dfrac{1}{3}$ or 33%, or choice (B) (*College Physics* 8th ed. pages 399–408/9th ed. pages 410–418).

36. **C**   This is a direct application of the law of electrostatics, which states like charges repel and unlike charges attract; however, it is important to keep in mind that a neutral object will attract either a positively or negatively charged object. Here, the first condition that (1) repels (3) implies that they must be like in charge, which immediately eliminates choice (E). Next, according to the statement that (4) has no effect on (5) implies that both are neutral, which means choices (A) and (B) can be eliminated. Lastly, the statement that a negative rod attracts both (1) and (5) implies that one of these two balls may be positively charged and one may be neutral, which eliminates choice (D). Therefore, (C) is the correct choice (*College Physics* 8th ed. pages 497–502/9th ed. pages 513–518).

37. **A**   This is a straightforward application of Coulomb's law, $F = \dfrac{kq_1 q_2}{r^2}$, used to calculate the electrostatic force between two charges q_1 and q_2 separated by a distance *r*. Since the two charges are opposite and thus experience an attractive force, the direction of the force on the positive charge must be toward the left, which permits the elimination of choices (B) and (C). Substituting values will allow *F* to be found; $F = \dfrac{(9 \times 10^9)(4 \times 10^{-6})(6 \times 10^{-6})}{(3 \times 10^{-1})^2} = \dfrac{(9 \times 10^9)(4 \times 10^{-6})(6 \times 10^{-6})}{9 \times 10^{-2}} = \dfrac{24 \times 10^{-8}}{1 \times 10^{-2}} = 2.4\text{N}$, which is choice (A) (*College Physics* 8th ed. pages 500–505/9th ed. pages 517–522).

38. B The nature of the electric force F on a charged particle q that is moving in a uniform electric field E is such that it is dictated by the magnitude and sign of the charge according to $F = qE$. Since electric field lines are drawn from regions of positive charge to negative charge, this shows that the top of the diagram is + (also signifying that the paths 1 and 2 must be negative charges, by the law of electrostatics) and the bottom is − (also signifying that the paths 4 and 5 must be positive charges). Additionally, since the force is proportional to the magnitude of the charge, the greater the charge, the greater the force, which means that $3Q$ must have a greater arc than charge $2Q$. Thus, charge $3Q$ must follow path 5 and charge $2Q$ must follow path 2. As path 3 is straight, it could only be taken by a neutral particle, and therefore the following choices; (C) and (E) can be eliminated. Therefore, the best answer is choice (B) (*College Physics* 8th ed. pages 505–512/9th ed. pages 522–528).

39. E The electric field E within a capacitor is designed to be uniform in strength due in part to both the dielectric immersed in the capacitor and the parallel plate charge distribution. Since the charge distribution is not uniform near the plate edges, the field E varies and decreases there, with field lines curving. Thus, the best choice is (E) (*College Physics* 8th ed. pages 546–549, 561–562/9th ed. pages 562–565, 578–579).

40. D A hollow conducting sphere holds all of its charge on the outside of the shell, as such charges are free to migrate according to the law of electrostatics. Since electric fields arise from charges and charge distributions, there can be no electric field in the interior of the sphere, as no charges are present there. Therefore choice (D) is the correct answer (*College Physics* 8th ed. pages 520–521/9th ed. pages 536–537).

41. A Capacitors are typically devices composed of sections (plates) of conductors, each with either a positive or negative charge depending upon how they are connected to a voltage source. As time passes, the capacitor charges until it reaches a fixed value, whereupon it holds energy according to $W = qV$ (where $q = CV$ is the charge on the capacitor plates). Upon releasing this charge, the capacitor can perform a function (such as flashing a bright light for a camera) as it releases a burst of energy from this stored charge. Therefore, choice (A) is the correct answer (*College Physics* 8th ed. pages 546–549, 555–562/9th ed. pages 562–565, 571–579).

42. A This is a straightforward application of adding n resistors connected in both series ($R_s = \sum_i R_i$) and in parallel $\dfrac{1}{R_p} = \sum_i \dfrac{1}{R_i}$. Working back from the right-most part of the connections toward XY shows the three right-most resistors are in series, as they share the same current. Their total resistance is 4 Ω, shown below on the left. Next, the two right-most 4 Ω resistors are in parallel, and thus $\dfrac{1}{R_{tot}} = \dfrac{1}{4} + \dfrac{1}{4}$ or $R_{tot} = \dfrac{4}{2}$ or 2 Ω, shown below, center. Third, the 1 Ω, 2 Ω, and 2 Ω resistors are in series, whose total resistance is 5 Ω, shown below on the right.

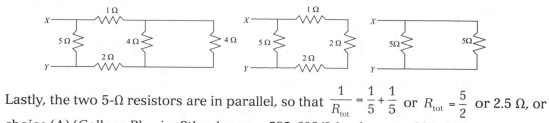

Lastly, the two 5-Ω resistors are in parallel, so that $\dfrac{1}{R_{tot}} = \dfrac{1}{5} + \dfrac{1}{5}$ or $R_{tot} = \dfrac{5}{2}$ or 2.5 Ω, or choice (A) (*College Physics* 8th ed. pages 595–603/9th ed. pages 617–625).

43. **D**   Capacitors in series add inversely ($\frac{1}{C_s} = \Sigma_i \frac{1}{C_i}$), whereas capacitors in parallel add directly ($C_p = \Sigma_i C_i$). Therefore, in this circuit, the $4\mu F$ and $2\mu F$ capacitors are in parallel, and their sum is $6\mu F$ (below, left). Next, this $6\mu F$ capacitor is in series with the $3\mu F$ capacitor, meaning their total capacitance is found by $\frac{1}{C_{tot}} = \frac{1}{3} + \frac{1}{6} = \frac{3}{6}$; therefore, C for that branch is $2\mu F$ (below, right).

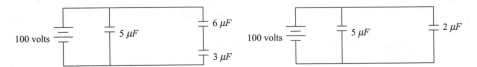

Lastly, the $5\mu F$ and $2\mu F$ capacitors are in parallel, and simply add to give C_{tot} for the entire circuit, which is $7\mu F$, answer choice (D) (*College Physics* 8th ed. pages 549–555/9th ed. pages 565–571).

44. **D**   This question tests the knowledge of meter placement within a circuit, as both the ammeter *A* and voltmeter *V* are incorrectly placed, eliminating choice (B). Voltmeters, since they are measuring voltages, must be placed like resistors in parallel, which share the same voltage. Similarly, ammeters are placed to measure current *I* and therefore must be in line (i.e., in series) with resistors, which share the same current. Thus, the correct answer is (D) (*College Physics* 8th ed. pages 574–575/9th ed. pages 595–596).

45. **B**   Since both the total current I_{tot} and the total voltage V_{tot} are given, one can simply use Ohm's law to solve for R_{tot}, which can then yield the value of R. $V_{tot} = I_{tot} R_{tot}$ or 36 volts = 3 amps (8 + R) ohms. This then becomes 12 = 8 + R so that R = 4 ohms, choice (B) (*College Physics* 8th ed. pages 594–598/9th ed. pages 616–620).

46. **B**   First, find the equivalent resistance for the 7 Ω and 3 Ω connected in parallel. This becomes $\frac{1}{R_{eq}} = \frac{1}{7} + \frac{1}{3}$ with a common denominator of 21. Thus, R_{eq} = 21/10 or 2.1 Ω. Therefore, the total resistance of the circuit becomes; R_{eq} = 5 Ω + 2.1 Ω + 0.4 Ω (since they are in series) or R_{eq} = 7.5 Ω. Then, by Ohm's law, $V_{tot} = I_{tot} R_{tot}$ or 30 volts = I_{tot} (7.5 ohms). Thus I_{tot} = 30/7.5 or 4 amps, which is choice (B) (*College Physics* 8th ed. pages 594–603/9th ed. pages 616–625).

47. **A**   By the scalar form of the magnetic force equation $F = qvB \sin\theta$ (where θ is 60°) this becomes $F = (1.6 \times 10^{-19} C)\left(3.5 \times 10^5 \frac{m}{s}\right) 0.60T \sin 60° = 5.6 \times 10^{-14} (0.60)(0.866) = 3.0 \times 10^{-14}$ N, which is closest to choice (A) (*College Physics* 8th ed. pages 630–633/9th ed. pages 652–655).

48. **A**   The magnetic force on a charged particle is described by the magnetic force equation $F = qvB \sin\theta$, which states that a velocity *v* must exist for a force to exist. In the case of electron A, since it is at rest, it will remain at rest, and thus experience no force, eliminating choices (B), (D), and (E). Similarly, electron B will also experience a zero force due to the fact that it is traveling 180° to the **B** field because sin 180° = 0 and will therefore continue moving westward. Therefore, the correct choice is (A) (*College Physics* 8th ed. pages 630–633/9th ed. pages 652–655).

49. **D** By the right-hand rule (with the hand flat and uncurled), the thumb in the direction of the current I, the fingers point into the page in the direction of the **B** field, and the palm points in the direction of the force left in this case. Therefore, choice (D) is correct (*College Physics* 8th ed. pages 630–636/9th ed. pages 652–658).

50. **B** The flux of any vector field is simply the product of that vector quantity and the area of the region through which it is passing. Therefore, magnetic flux (Φ_m) is the product of the magnetic field B, the area A of the loop through which it passes and the cosine of the angle between the vector field and the surface normal ($\phi_m = BA\cos\theta$). Therefore, this becomes $\phi_m = (0.50\text{ T})\pi(0.25\text{ m})^2\cos 0° \approx \left(\dfrac{1}{2}\right)3.14\left(\dfrac{1}{16}\right)(1) \approx \dfrac{1}{10}$ weber. Thus, the closest choice is (B) (*College Physics* 8th ed. pages 664–666/9th ed. pages 688–691).

51. **A** According to Lenz's law, in order for a current to be induced in this loop, it must experience a time rate of change of magnetic flux through its area, which could not occur if rotated about an axis that is parallel to the external magnetic field. The flux would change if the field strength were altered, if the area were altered, or if the loop were to rotate about an axis perpendicular to the magnetic field such that it presents a changing area to the field. Therefore, all choices but (A) are eliminated (*College Physics* 8th ed. pages 666–676/9th ed. pages 691–701).

52. **C** The B field due to the upward current is increasing into the page on the right side where the loop rests. Therefore, the magnetic flux through the loop due to this increasing current is also increasing. Therefore, by Lenz's law, the current that will be induced in the loop will be set up to oppose this change, which caused the increasing inward flux. As a result, the loop creates a current I such that an outward-facing magnetic field exists in the loop, which by the right-hand rule (thumb traces the current and fingers curl outward from the inside of the loop) will set up a counterclockwise current I in the loop. This eliminates all choices but (C) (*College Physics* 8th ed. pages 666–676/9th ed. pages 691–701).

53. **E** By the Doppler effect, which states that when a wave source and an observer are approaching each other, the observer's detected wave frequency (or pitch, in the case of sound) from the source will increase, and that if these two objects recede from each other the detected wave frequency (or pitch) will decrease. The best answer here is (E). When at location C, the child is traveling the fastest in her swing, and since the Doppler effect also depends on the speed of either the observer or source, she will hear the greatest increase of pitch at this location (*College Physics* 8th ed. pages 468–473/9th ed. pages 482–488).

54. **A** Here, the principle of wave superposition states that the sum of the individual amplitudes of interfering waves will produce a net effect, creating a momentary wave with a new amplitude whose value is equal to the sum of the individual amplitudes. Therefore, to produce the straight shape shown in (4), two regions which are lower than they are high must combine at the center to produce the rectangular trough shown in (4). This can only be created if wave (2) is superimposed onto wave (3), as shown here:

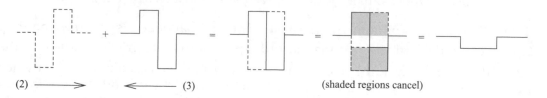

(2) ⟶   ⟵ (3)   (shaded regions cancel)

Therefore, the correct answer is (A) (*College Physics* 8th ed. pages 448–450/9th ed. pages 461–462).

55. **B** Beat frequency is most pronounced when the difference between individual beats $(f_2 - f_1)$ yields the largest value. Therefore, of the choices provided, the greatest beat frequency occurs between the pair of frequencies that span the most range; taking the differences of each to find the greatest one gives 2 Hz for (A), 6 Hz for (B), 5 Hz for (C), 3 Hz for (D), and 4 Hz for (E). Therefore, the greatest beat frequency occurs between 543 Hz and 537 Hz, choice (B) (*College Physics* 8th ed. pages 484–486/9th ed. pages 499–500).

56. **C** The expression for the fundamental frequencies on a standing wave of n antinodes is $f = \dfrac{nv}{2L}$ so that here, where $n = 1$, this becomes $f = \dfrac{nv}{2L} = \dfrac{(1)v}{2L} = \dfrac{v}{2L}$, which is answer choice (C) (*College Physics* 8th ed. pages 475–479/9th ed. pages 489–494).

57. **C** The distance x_m between bright fringes in the slit interference pattern is proportional to the wavelength λ of the light incident upon the double-slit apparatus according to the relation $x_m \approx \dfrac{m\lambda L}{d}$, where L is the distance from the double slit to the screen and d is the distance between slits. Therefore, if the desire is to have the fringes more closely spaced, assuming L and d remain unchanged, then the wavelength λ must be reduced by moving toward the blue end of the visible spectrum. Therefore, choice (C) best indicates this. Choice (A) suggests reducing d, all of which would increase x_m, choice (B) suggests increasing the wavelength λ, and choice (D) suggests increasing L (choice (E) has no relation to x_m) (*College Physics* 8th ed. pages 791–795/9th ed. pages 825–829).

58. **D** This question deals with light refracting according to color, as each color (or wavelength λ) of light has a different index of refraction n according to the relation $n_1\lambda_1 = n_2\lambda_2$. This effect, known as dispersion, creates the visible rainbow often seen when using either a prism or a lens that is uncorrected for chromatic aberration. The best answer, therefore, is choice (D) (*College Physics* 8th ed. pages 737–746/9th ed. pages 767–775).

59. **A** The path difference δ between a ray drawn from one slit in the Young's double-slit experiment to the screen where the interference pattern exists, and the line drawn from the other slit, is an integral number of half wavelengths, as given by $\delta = d\sin\theta = \left(m + \dfrac{1}{2}\right)\lambda$, the condition for destructive interference. The integer m represents the number of the dark fringe from the central bright fringe, were $m = 0$ is the first dark fringe, $m = 1$ is the second, $m = 2$ is the third, and so on. Therefore, moving outward from the bright central fringe, these values of the path difference δ become $\left(\dfrac{\lambda}{2}\right), \left(\dfrac{3\lambda}{2}\right), \left(\dfrac{5\lambda}{2}\right)$, and so on, or simply an odd number of half wavelengths. The first dark fringe, therefore, produces a path difference shown of $\left(\dfrac{\lambda}{2}\right)$, which means that fringe (A) is one-half wave closer to one slit than to the other, answer choice (A) (*College Physics* 8th ed. pages 791–795/9th ed. pages 825–829).

60. **B** The speed of light v in a transparent material depends inversely on the index of refraction n of the material according to the relation $n = \dfrac{c}{v}$. Therefore, the higher the n, the lower the speed and therefore the smallest angle of refraction would occur. Similarly, the lower the n, the higher the speed, and the larger the angle of refraction would be. Thus, in the diagram for this problem, the greatest speed occurs

in the medium with the largest angle of refraction, which is n_3, suggesting that n_3 is the lowest of the indices shown (since its refractive angle is the largest). Similarly, the next highest index of refraction would be n_1, and the highest index of refraction is n_2, best shown by answer choice (B) (*College Physics* 8th ed. pages 736–742/9th ed. pages 765–771).

61. **C** The orientation of the image viewed by either a convex (converging) or concave (diverging) lens depends primarily on the object location relative to the focal point f. For the diverging lens, all images seen through the lens are upright and therefore virtual; however, no information is given concerning the focal length or object distance so it cannot be determined for certain if the lens in question is a diverging one. Similarly, a converging lens could produce an upright, virtual image of the object as well, provided the object is placed inside the focal point f. Again, however, no statement is made concerning a focal point. Therefore, it cannot be stated with certainty that the lens is either concave or convex, which implies that choice (C) is the incorrect statement (*College Physics* 8th ed. pages 773–782/9th ed. pages 805–815).

62. **B** As the question states that the concave mirror has a radius of curvature R of 30 cm, it is therefore immediately known by the relation $R = 2f$ that the focal point $f = 15$ cm. Additionally, the object must be placed directly at the focal point for all reflected rays of light to exit the mirror parallel to each other, producing no image. Therefore, the best answer is choice (B), as illustrated in the diagram (*College Physics* 8th ed. pages 762–764/9th ed. pages 793–795).

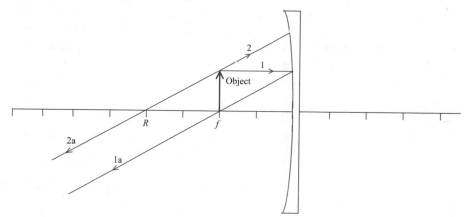

63. **A** As shown by all ray diagrams in Chapter 16, each answer choice may be evaluated: Choice (A) is correct, as objects placed inside f produce upright, virtual and larger images. Choice (B) is incorrect, as moving the object outside of f creates an inverted, real image. Choice (C) is incorrect also, as objects placed at R produce an exact image of themselves, but inverted, and real. An object placed at f produces rays that converge at infinity. Choice (D) is the opposite of choice (A) and is thus incorrect, and lastly, choice (E) is incorrect; objects placed outside of f produce images that are inverted and real (*College Physics* 8th ed. pages 762–764/9th ed. pages 793–795).

64. **A** The expression for the de Boglie wavelength is $\lambda = \dfrac{h}{p}$, which is $\lambda = \dfrac{h}{mv}$, best shown by choice (A) (*College Physics* 8th ed. pages 880–883/9th ed. pages 922–925).

65. **D** According to the relationship $K = hf - W_o$, which dictates the photoelectron energy when light of a certain frequency is incident upon a photoelectric surface, K is proportional to the frequency of the light f and to the work function W_0 (a characteristic of the photoelectric surface). K is independent of the light's intensity

as the energy necessary to release the electrons is quantized according to $E = hf$. Therefore, the answer that best describes this is choice (D) (*College Physics* 8th ed. pages 872–875/9th ed. pages 913–916).

66. **A** In Rutherford's gold foil experiment, several thousand incident alpha particles passed through the foil with little deflection for every one alpha particle that was deflected back at nearly 180°. Therefore, the likely conclusion to be made was that, as a result, there was simply very little volume to the atomic nucleus, presenting very little target to the incident alpha particles. Thus, the best answer is (A) (*College Physics* 8th ed. pages 891–892, 913/9th ed. pages 934–935, 957–959).

67. **B** The Bohr postulates are as follows: (1) electrons move in circular orbits with the Coulomb force providing the centripetal acceleration, (2) only quantized electron orbits are permitted, and no energy is lost due to orbital radiation, (3) radiation is only emitted or absorbed which causes electrons to "jump" up or down to a different orbital level, and (4) the circumference of the orbits are quantized in units of $n\hbar$. Therefore, the only correct answer is choice (B) as the other choices, some of which may be physically correct, do not state any of Bohr's postulates (*College Physics* 8th ed. pages 892–899/9th ed. pages 935–942).

68. **C** By Planck's work, the quantized energy of a photon is $E = hf = \dfrac{hc}{\lambda}$ where λ is the photon wavelength, the subject of the question. In this particular atom, it is stated that the electron makes a transition such that its original energy is –6 eV and its final energy is that of the ground state, which here must be –24 eV, as it is stated that 24 eV is the ionization energy of the atom. Therefore, the energy E emitted by the electron in this transition is simply the change of energy between these two levels, or 18 eV. To determine λ, simply substitute this energy value and the constants h and c and carefully solve by hand;

$$\lambda = \frac{hc}{E} = \frac{(4.14 \times 10^{-15} \text{eV} \cdot \text{s})(3.0 \times 10^{8} \text{m/s})}{18 \text{ eV}} \approx \frac{(4 \times 10^{-15} \text{ eV} \cdot \text{s})(3 \times 10^{8} \text{m/s})}{2 \times 10^{1} \text{ eV}}$$

$$\approx \frac{(12 \times 10^{-7} \text{ m eV})}{2 \times 10^{1} \text{ eV}} \approx 6 \times 10^{-8} \text{m}$$

which is 60×10^{-9}m or 60 nm, closest to answer choice (C) (*College Physics* 8th ed. pages 870–872/9th ed. pages 911–913).

69. **B** In nuclear physics, the nucleus of element X has protons P plus neutrons N, which add to give the mass number A. Similarly, the number of protons P is represented by Z, the atomic number, such that A and Z are represented in the format $^A_Z X = ^{P+N}_P X = ^{mass \#}_{atomic \#} X$. In this problem, this fictitious decay can therefore be notated

as $^A_Z X \rightarrow ^{A'}_{Z'} Y + ^4_2 \text{He} + ^0_{+1} e$, or, it may also be written $^{P+N}_P X \rightarrow ^{P'+N'}_{P'} Y + ^4_2 \text{He} + ^0_{+1} e$. Determining the final number for N' and Z' can be found by simply balancing the superscripts (nucleon number) and the subscripts (proton number) as follows:

Subscripts:
$P = P' + 2 + 1$; therefore, $P' = P - 3$, but since P is the same as Z, we can write $Z' = Z - 3$.

Superscripts:
$A = A' + 4 + 0$ or $A' = A - 4$. However, since $A' = P' + N'$ and $A = P + N$, this can be written $(P' + N') = (P + N) - 4$.

From the subscripts analysis, substituting $P = P' + 3$ for P now gives $(P' + N') = (P' + 3) + N - 4$, which becomes $P' + N' = P' + N - 1$ or $P' - P' + N' = N - 1$. Therefore, $N' = N - 1$. From both the superscript and subscript analysis, the new atomic number Z' is now

$Z-3$ and the new neutron number N' is now $N-1$, which is answer choice (B) (*College Physics* 8th ed. pages 913, 921–924/9th ed. pages 957–959, 965–971).

70. **D** In nuclear physics, the nucleus of element X has protons P plus neutrons N, which add to give the mass number A. Similarly, the number of protons P is represented by Z, the atomic number, such that A and Z are represented in the format $^A_ZX = ^{P+N}_P X = ^{\text{mass \#}}_{\text{atomic \#}}X$. Thus, when a beta particle $\left(^0_{-1}e\right)$, or electron, is emitted, the decay reaction can be written as $^A_ZX \rightarrow ^{A'}_{Z'}Y + ^0_{-1}e$, where $^{A'}_{Z'}Y$ represents the new configuration of the element.

Since charge and nucleon number are conserved in the decay reaction, the following can be written: $Z = Z' - 1$ and $A = A' + 0$. Thus, solving for Z' and A', the new atomic number Z' becomes $Z + 1$, and the new mass number A' becomes $A - 0$, or remains unchanged. Therefore, the best answer is choice (D). While this may seem counterintuitive, recall that in beta + decay that the additional proton is converted, via the weak force, to a neutron, a positron, and a neutrino, which does not occur in isolation as it requires an input of energy (*College Physics* 8th ed. pages 913, 921–924/9th ed. pages 957–959, 965–971).

ANSWERS TO FREE-RESPONSE PROBLEMS

1. (15 points)

(a) 2 points

Data points which are plotted are depicted as demarcated circled points. Additionally, a best-fit line is drawn as it is stated that the lander's thrust is constant during the descent, which implies constant acceleration. The "X" marks are slope points on the line

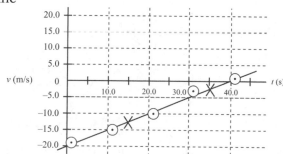

[1 point for all data points from the table plotted correctly to ±0.3 grid space]
[1 point for a best-fit straight line (i.e., approximately one to two points above or below the line)]

(*College Physics* 8th ed. pages 24–47/9th ed. pages 25–46)

(b) 2 points

The acceleration is the slope of the velocity–time graph. Taking two slope points shown in the plot, this becomes $a = slope = \dfrac{rise}{run} = \dfrac{-2.5-(-12.5)}{(35-15)} = 0.5$ m/s² $= a$.

[1 point for using the correct equation for slope and for not using data points for slope]
[1 point for substitution with units and the correctly calculated answer]

(*College Physics* 8th ed. pages 24–47/9th ed. pages 25–46)

(c) 2 points

The displacement of the craft is the area under the v versus t graph. Thereafter, the scalar value of the displacement can be used to find the craft's height. The area under the graph from 0 s to 40 s is simply the area of a triangle, $A = ½$ (*base*) (*height*). Therefore, $A = ½ (40 \text{ s})(-20 \text{ m/s}) = -400$ meters, or the height of the craft is 400 meters at $t = 0$

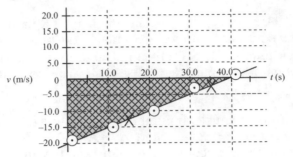

[1 point for determining the displacement by correct calculation of area under the plot]
[1 point for knowing the difference between displacement and height and providing the correct answer with the correct unit]

(*College Physics* 8th ed. pages 24–47/9th ed. pages 25–46).

(d) 3 points

The area under the v graph is the displacement of the craft, which is the sum of the area of the shaded rectangle and the shaded triangle from 0 s to 10 s.

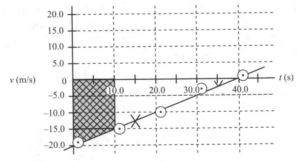

This is $(10.0 \text{ s})\left(-15.0\dfrac{\text{m}}{\text{s}}\right) + \dfrac{1}{2}(10.0 \text{ s})\left(-5.0\dfrac{\text{m}}{\text{s}}\right) = -150 \text{ m} + -25 \text{ m} = -175 \text{ m}$

[1 point for using the correct method to determine the displacement via area under the plot from 0 s to 10 s.]
[1 point for substitution with units and the correctly calculated answer]

ALTERNATE SOLUTION USING KINEMATICS

The displacement of the craft for the first 10 seconds is first found using the kinematics equation $v_f^2 = v_i^2 + 2ad$, as $v_i = -20$ m/s and $v_f = -15$ m/s (keeping in mind that the acceleration of the craft is ½ m/s²). $v_f^2 = v_i^2 + 2ad$ or $(-15 \text{ m/s})^2 = (-20 \text{ m/s})^2 + 2\left(\dfrac{1}{2}\text{m/s}^2\right)d$. Solving gives $d = -175$ m. Thereafter, the absolute value of this displacement must be subtracted from the 400-meter height found in part (c), which will then give the height H above the planet's surface. Therefore, this becomes $H = 400 \text{ m} + (-175 \text{ m})$ or $H = 225$ m.

[1 point for realizing the previous value must be subtracted from 400 m and presenting an answer with the correct units]

(*College Physics* 8th ed. pages 42–46/9th ed. pages 43–47)

(e) 3 points

A free body diagram and the application of $\sum F = ma$ is necessary to solve for the planet's acceleration due to gravity, g, where T is the upward thrust and w is the craft's weight. The diagram follows:

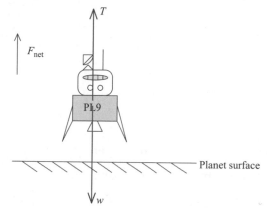

Therefore, $\sum F = ma$ gives $T - mg = ma$. Solving for g yields $\dfrac{T - ma}{m} = g$.

[1 point for correctly applying a correct statement of Newton's second law]
[1 point for correctly solving for the gravitational acceleration g]

Substituting (omitting units for clarity) gives the final solution:

$$g = \frac{T - ma}{m} = \frac{(1.3 \times 10^5) - \left[(2.0 \times 10^4)\left(\dfrac{1}{2}\right)\right]}{(2.0 \times 10^4)} = 6.0 \text{ m/s}^2$$

[1 point for substitution with units and the correctly calculated answer]

(*College Physics* 8th ed. pages 83–92, 94–101/9th ed. pages 86–95, 98–105)

(f) 3 points

The gravitational force F_g exerted by the planet on the PL9 craft is simply the weight mg of the craft. Therefore, the following may be used to solve for M, the planet's mass (note m is the mass of PL9):

$$F_g = \frac{GM\cancel{m}}{R^2} = \cancel{m}g \quad \text{Solving for } M \text{ gives } \quad M = \frac{gR^2}{G}$$

so that substituting values gives $\dfrac{(6.0)(5.0 \times 10^6)^2}{(6.67 \times 10^{-11})} = M = 2.3 \times 10^{24}$ kg

[1 point for correctly equating the gravitational force to the craft's weight mg]
[1 point for correctly solving for the planetary mass M]
[1 point for substitution with units and the correctly calculated answer]

(*College Physics* 8th ed. pages 207–211/9th ed. pages 214–217)

2. (15 points)
(a) 4 points

This is a situation of uniform circular motion in which $\sum F_C = \dfrac{mv^2}{R}$ with the free-body diagram of basket A (and tension components) as shown. In this case, the horizontal component T_x provides the centripetal force F_C, which, with $\sum F_y = 0$ in the vertical direction, can be used to determine the speed v.

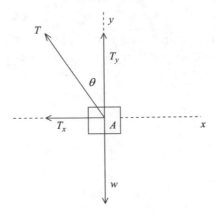

In the x direction this becomes $\sum F_c = T_x = T\sin\theta = \dfrac{mv^2}{R}$ and in the y direction, which is equilibrium, $T_y - mg = 0$ or $T\cos\theta = mg$.

[1 point for a correct application of Newton's second law to circular motion and for correctly deriving the x and y components of the tension force]

Since both m and T are unknown, the speed v must be determined by solving one equation in terms of the other variables and substituted. Therefore, $T\cos\theta = mg$ becomes $T = \dfrac{mg}{\cos\theta}$, which will be used to replace T in the first equation. Thus, $T\sin\theta = \dfrac{mv^2}{R}$ becomes $\left(\dfrac{mg}{\cos\theta}\right)\sin\theta = \dfrac{mv^2}{R}$. Notice that m cancels and $\dfrac{\sin\theta}{\cos\theta}$ is replaced by $\tan\theta$. Solving for v gives $v = \sqrt{(Rg\tan\theta)}$.

[1 point for correctly solving a system of equations with two unknowns to determine v]

Next, to calculate v, it is necessary to determine R, the radius of the circular path taken by basket A. Noting the right triangle formed by the cable,

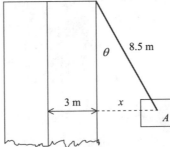

the value of R is 3 m + x, where $x = 8.5\sin 36° = 5$ m, or $R = 8$ m. Now, v can be calculated: $v = \sqrt{(8)(9.8)\tan 36°} = 7.5$ m/s.

[1 point for correctly determining the radius R of the circular path]
[1 point for correct substitution with units and the calculation of v]

(*College Physics* 8th ed. pages 196–206/9th ed. pages 203–214)

(b) 2 points

The period T can be calculated from the velocity equation for uniform circular motion, given by $V_{avg} = \dfrac{\Delta d}{\Delta t}$, which becomes $v = \dfrac{2\pi R}{T}$. Solving for T yields $T = \dfrac{2\pi R}{v}$ so that substituting values gives (omitting units for clarity) $T = \dfrac{2(3.14)(8)}{7.5}$ or $T = 6.7$ s.

[1 point for correctly deriving the period equation applied to circular motion]

[1 point for correct substitution with units and the calculation of T with its unit]

(College Physics 8th ed. pages 25–30, 198–206/9th ed. pages 22–33, 203–214)

(c) 2 points

The centripetal acceleration a_c can be calculated from $a_c = \dfrac{v^2}{R}$. Substituting values gives $a_c = \dfrac{(7.5)^2}{8} = 7.0 \text{ m/s}^2$, which is less than 1$g$ experienced by a stationary object near the surface of Earth.

[1 point for correctly deriving the period equation applied to circular motion]
[1 point for correct substitution with units and the calculation of a with its unit]

(College Physics 8th ed. pages 196–206 /9th ed. pages 203-214)

(d) 2 points
   (i) 1 point

Solving the speed equation ($v = \sqrt{(Rg\tan\theta)}$) for the angle θ shows also that the angle is independent of m, and thus all baskets will extend to the same angle: $\theta = \tan^{-1}\left(\dfrac{v^2}{Rg}\right)$, or 36°.

[1 point for correctly stating the independence of angle and mass using the speed equation]

   (ii) 1 point

As in the <u>solution</u> to (a), the speed v of the riders is independent of the mass m ($v = \sqrt{(Rg\tan\theta)}$) and thus both the more massive and less massive baskets will have the same speed.

[1 point for correctly stating the independence of speed and mass using the speed equation]

(College Physics 8th ed. pages 196–206/9th ed. pages 203–214)

(e) 3 points

In the y direction, apply the kinematics equation $d_y = v_{iy}\Delta t + \dfrac{1}{2}a_y\Delta t^2$, which gives $d_y = \dfrac{1}{2}a_y\Delta t^2$ as $v_{iy} = 0$ for horizontally projected objects. The height of basket, d_y, however, must carefully be determined, as it is not simply the height of the cylinder, 18 meters. Noting the right triangle,

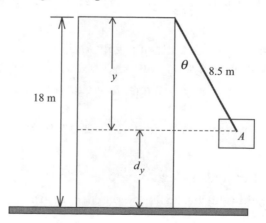

the value of d_y is 18 m − y, which is 18 m − 8.5 cos 36° = 18 m − 6.9 m. Therefore, d_y = 11.1 m, and the fall time is then calculated from the kinematics equation: $\sqrt{\dfrac{2d_y}{g}} = t$, which becomes $\sqrt{\dfrac{2(11.1)}{(9.8)}} = t = 1.5$ s.

[1 point for correctly using the kinematics equation in the y-direction, with $v_{iy} = 0$]
[1 point for correctly using geometry to determine the value of $d_y = 0$]
[1 point for correct substitution with units and the calculation of t with its unit]

(*College Physics* 8th ed. pages 62–68/9th ed. pages 63–71)

(f) 2 points

In the x direction, apply the kinematics equation $d_x = v_{ix}\Delta t + \dfrac{1}{2}a_x\Delta t^2$, which, since $a_x = 0$ for a projectile, becomes; $d_x = (7.5 \text{ m/s}) (1.5 \text{ s}) = 11.$ m

[1 point for correctly using the kinematics equation in the x direction, with a = 0]
[1 point for correct substitution with units and the calculation of d_x with its unit]

(*College Physics* 8th ed. pages 62–68/9th ed. pages 63–71)

3. (10 points)

(a) 1 point

The vent exists at the top of the tower in order to equalize the pressure between the inside of the tower and the outside.

[1 point for any correct statement concerning the equalization of pressure between the interior and exterior of the water tower]

(*College Physics* 8th ed. pages 283–284 /9th ed. pages 292–293)

(b) 2 points

The absolute, or total, pressure at point A arises from both the pressure due to the 25-m-high column of water plus the overlying pressure due to the atmosphere. Therefore, $P = P_o + pgh$ becomes $P = 1.01 \times 10^5 + (1000)(9.8)(25.0) = 3.5 \times 10^5$ pascal.

[1 point for any indication that absolute pressure is the sum of the overlying air pressure plus the gauge pressure]

[1 point for a correct calculation, with units, of the absolute pressure at point A]

(*College Physics* 8th ed. pages 276–284/9th ed. pages 279–282, 288–293)

(c) 1 point

The pressure just outside of the flow pipe at point A is simply the pressure of the air at sea level, which is 1 atm, or 1.01×10^5 pascal.

[1 point for any correct statement yielding the pressure outside is equal to 1 atm or the equivalent]

(*College Physics* 8th ed. pages 281–282/9th ed. pages 292–293)

(d) 3 points

Here, use Bernoulli's equation applied to the top of the liquid (point C) and at the bottom of the liquid where it exits the pipe (point A); $P_C + \rho g y_C + \dfrac{1}{2}\rho v_C^2 = P_A + \rho g y_A + \dfrac{1}{2}\rho v_A^2$.

Preparing to solve for v_A gives the following: $P_C - P_A + \rho g y_C - \rho g y_A + \dfrac{1}{2}\rho v_C^2 = +\dfrac{1}{2}\rho v_A^2$.

[1 point for a correct expression and application of Bernoulli's equation]

Note that at the very top of the liquid, v_c is nearly zero, and that both pressures P_C and P_A are equal at 1 atm. This therefore reduces to $\rho g y_C - \rho g y_A = \frac{1}{2}\rho v_A^2$, which can easily be solved for v_A as $\sqrt{2g(y_C - y_A)} = v_A$. Therefore, $v_A = \sqrt{2(9.8)(25)} = 22.1$ m/s

[1 point for consistent/correct substitutions of variables in Bernoulli's equation]
[1 point for a correct calculation, with units, of the speed of the liquid]

(*College Physics* 8th ed. pages 293–296/9th ed. pages 302–305)

(e) 2 points

To determine volume flow rate (Av), the area A of the pipe must be determined, which is simply $A = \pi r^2$ (note the pipe's diameter of 16 cm is given, so its radius is 8 cm, or 0.08 m). Therefore, volume flow rate = Av = (3.14) (0.08)² (22.1) = 0.44 m³/s

[1 point for determining and calculating the necessary area of the pipe]
[1 point for a correct calculation, with units, of the volume (not mass) flow rate]

(*College Physics* 8th ed. pages 290–293/9th ed. pages 299–302)

(f) 1 point

By factor label method, cubic meters cancel to give = 113.5 gallons/s.
$$\left(\frac{0.44\,\frac{m^3}{s}}{1}\right) \times \left(\frac{1\ \text{gallon}}{3.875\times 10^{-3} m^3}\right)$$

[1 point for a correct employment of factor label method/dimensional analysis with a correct calculation, with units, of the number of gallons per second]

(*College Physics* 8th ed. page 10/9th ed. pages 10–11)

4. (10 points)

(a) 2 points

The resistance of a single conducting wire of length L, resistivity ρ, and cross-sectional area A is given by $R = \frac{\rho L}{A}$. Note that the problem only provides the radius r of the wire, not the area, which is determined by πr^2.

[1 point for realizing and calculating the necessary area of the wire]

Therefore, substituting values gives (omitting units for clarity) $R = \frac{\rho L}{A} = \frac{\rho L}{\pi r^2} = \frac{(1.72\times 10^{-8})(1.211)}{(3.14)(1.0\times 10^{-5})^2} = 66$ ohms

[1 point for a correct calculation using the wire resistance formula, including units]

(*College Physics* 8th ed. pages 575–579/9th ed. pages 596–599)

(b) 3 points

This is essentially a parallel circuit with 20 resistors in parallel, whose total resistance R_{tot} can be calculated using $\frac{1}{R_p} = \sum_i \frac{1}{R_i}$ where $i = 20$.

[1 point for correctly realizing this is an arrangement of 20 resistors in parallel and for using the correct parallel equivalent resistance equation]

To determine the total power P_{tot}, it is necessary to use one of the three power equations, here $P_{tot} = \dfrac{V_{tot}^2}{R_{tot}}$ being the most useful as both the total voltage and total resistance are known or will be found. The total resistance becomes

$$\frac{1}{R_p} = \Sigma_i \frac{1}{R_i} = 20\left(\frac{1}{66.3\,\Omega}\right), \text{ or } R_{tot} = 3.32\ \Omega$$

[1 point for a correct calculation and usage of the parallel equivalent resistance equation, including units]

The total power is $P_{tot} = \dfrac{(12)^2}{3.32} = 43.4$ watts.

[1 point for a correct calculation and usage of the power equation, including units]

(*College Physics* 8th ed. pages 580–584, 598–603/9th ed. pages 601–604, 620–625)

(c) 3 points

The energy dissipated by the parallel wire strand serves to warm the moisture (which is simply water) to the vapor point of 100°C. This energy, which is, $P\Delta t$ is equivalent to the energy $Q = mc\Delta T$ required to warm the moisture, by energy conservation (an important assumption is that little to no energy is transferred to the air). Therefore, $P\Delta t = mc\Delta T$.

[1 point for a correct statement that energy is PΔt]
[1 point for a correct statement equating energy the energy transfer PΔt = mcΔT]

Solving for the time gives $t = \dfrac{mc\,T}{P} = \dfrac{(5.0 \times 10^{-3})(4186)(75)}{43.4} = 36.2$ s.

[1 point for a correct calculation of the time, including substitution with units]

(*College Physics* 8th ed. pages 580–584/9th ed. pages 601–604)

(d) 2 points

By using the total values for resistance, current, and voltage in Ohm's law, $V_{tot} = I_{tot}R_{tot}$, it is possible to solve for the current I_{tot}. Therefore, $\dfrac{V_{tot}}{R_{tot}} = I_{tot}$ becomes

$\dfrac{12}{3.3} = 3.6$ amps.

[1 point for the correct application of Ohm's law]
[1 point for a correct calculation of the electric current, including units]

(*College Physics* 8th ed. pages 575–579/9th ed. pages 596–599)

5. (15 points)

(a) 2 points

The hand rules can be used to determine if this charge fits the profile of a negative or positive particle. With the hand held flat at the point where the particle just exits the capacitor, the thumb points in the direction of the particle's velocity, the fingers point in the direction of the *B* field (out of the page) and the open palm points in the direction of the force, which should be toward the center of the circular path (i.e., centripetal). Using the right hand (for a positive particle) shows that this is incorrect, however, using the left hand (for a negative particle) shows that is correct. Thus, the particle is negative.

[1 point for correctly stating that the charge is negative]
[1 point for a correct explanation alluding to the use of the hand rules]

(*College Physics* 8th ed. pages 639–641/9th ed. pages 661–664)

(b) 2 points

It is clearly shown that the net force on the particle is zero as it passes linearly through the capacitor, and since the magnetic force F_B is downward as the particle enters the magnetic-field only region, this must indicate that the electrostatic force F_E on the particle is upward while in the capacitor. As it was determined that the charged particle is negative, the only way it could experience and upward electrostatic force in the capacitor is if the top plate (*X*) is correspondingly positive. Therefore, since electric field lines are drawn from positive to negative regions, the electric field lines *E* must point from *X* to *Y* in the capacitor, as shown

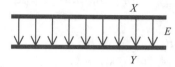

[1 point for correctly sketching straight downward facing arrows emanating from plate X and touching plate Y]
[1 point for a correct explanation of the nature of both the electric and magnetic forces in the capacitor]

(*College Physics* 8th ed. pages 510–511, 546–548/9th ed. pages 526–528, 562–565)

(c) 2 points

While the particle passes through the magnetic-field only region, it is subjected to the Lorentz force, which supplies the centripetal force F_c. Therefore, in this region, the particle's acceleration is centripetal acceleration, given by $a_c = \dfrac{v^2}{R}$.
A direct substitution yields $a_c = \dfrac{(4.2 \times 10^6 \, \text{m/s})^2}{0.5 \, \text{m}} = 3.5 \times 10^{13}$ m/s².
[1 point for correctly realizing the particle experiences a centripetal acceleration]
[1 point for a correct calculation and substitution with units]

(*College Physics* 8th ed. pages 198–206/9th ed. pages 203–214)

(d) 4 points

As previously described, the particle is in equilibrium between plates *X* and *Y*, as the upward electrostatic force F_E balances the downward magnetic force F_B. Using the condition for equilibrium, it is possible to then calculate *V* using the relation $V = Ed$ between the capacitor plates. Thus, $\sum F = 0$ gives $-F_B + F_E = 0$ or $F_B = F_E$ in between plates *X* and *Y*.

[1 point for correctly providing a statement of dynamic equilibrium, $\sum F = 0$]
[1 point for correctly stating that $F_B = F_E$]

As it is necessary to solve for *E* to find the potential difference *V*, substituting for these forces gives $qvB \sin 90° = qE$ or $E = vB$.

[1 point for correctly deriving the relationship E = vB]

Substituting this into $V = Ed$ and then solving gives $V = Ed = (vB)d =$ (
4.2×10^6 m/s$)(2T)(6.0 \times 10^{-2}$ m$) = 5.0 \times 10^5$ volts.

[1 point for a correct substitution into V = Ed with a calculation and substitution with units]

(*College Physics* 8th ed. pages 546–548, 628–631/9th ed. pages 562–565, 650–655)

(e) 4 points

In the magnetic-field only region, the magnetic force $qvB\sin 90°$ supplies the centripetal force $F_c = \dfrac{mv^2}{R}$ and so the following can be written in order to determine the ratio $\dfrac{q}{m}$: $\sum F_c = qvB\sin 90° = \dfrac{mv^2}{R}$.

[1 point for correctly providing a statement that the net force = $\dfrac{mv^2}{R}$]

[1 point for correctly stating that the magnetic force provides the centripetal force]

Therefore, $qB = \dfrac{mv}{R}$ or $\dfrac{q}{m} = \dfrac{v}{BR}$.

[1 point for correctly deriving the equation for q/m]

Substituting (omitting units for clarity) gives $\dfrac{q}{m} = \dfrac{4.2 \times 10^6 \text{ m/s}}{(2 \text{ T})(0.5 \text{ m})} = 4.2 \times 10^6 \text{ C/kg}$.

[1 point for a correct calculation and substitution with units]

(*College Physics* 8th ed. pages 628–631, 637–640/9th ed. pages 650–655, 661–664)

(f) 1 point

The only possible explanation for observing the particle collide with plate X is that the magnetic field is reversed by 180° such that it now points into the page. Therefore, both the magnetic and electric forces on the particle are upward

[1 point for a correct statement that the magnetic field direction has been reversed]

(*College Physics* 8th ed. pages 628–631, 637–640/9th ed. pages 650–655, 661–664)

6. (10 points)

(a) 3 points

The speed of a wave through a taut string is given by $v = \sqrt{\dfrac{Tension}{m/L}}$ where the tension is caused by the hanging masses and m/L is the linear density of the string (μ). Therefore, this equation must be solved for tension F, which equals $M_1 g$ and $M_2 g$ for each string, respectively.

[1 point for correctly stating/deriving the wave speed on a string]

This becomes $v^2 \mu = F = Mg$. Solving for M finally gives $\dfrac{v^2 \mu}{g} = M$.

[1 point for correctly solving the wave speed equation for M]

Substituting gives $\dfrac{(28 \text{ m/s})^2 \left(\dfrac{0.025 \text{ kg}}{2 \text{ m}} \right)}{9.8 \text{ m/s}^2} = M_1 = 1.0 \text{ kg}$

$$\frac{(19.8 \text{ m/s})^2 \left(\dfrac{0.025 \text{ kg}}{2 \text{ m}} \right)}{9.8 \text{ m/s}^2} = M_2 = 0.5 \text{ kg}$$

[1 point for correct substitution (with units) and calculation of each hanging mass M]

(*College Physics* 8th ed. pages 447–448/9th ed. pages 459–461)

(b) 4 points

The period T and frequency f are reciprocals of one another according to $T = \dfrac{1}{f}$. Therefore, if frequency can be determined, so can period. Since the waves formed on both strings are standing waves, it is necessary to use the harmonic frequency relationship between antinode number n and speed v of the wave, which is $f = \dfrac{nv}{2L}$ (note that this equation is easily derived from the given wave shapes and from $v = f \lambda$).

[1 point for correctly stating/deriving the harmonic frequency equation for string standing waves]

Note that for string 1, $n = 6$ (i.e., six antinodes) while $n = 3$ for string 2.

[1 point for correctly determining the antinode number for each standing wave]

Substituting values to find each wave frequency gives

$$f_1 = \frac{nv_1}{2L} = \frac{6(28 \text{ m/s})}{2(2 \text{ m})} = 42 \text{ Hz} \quad \text{and} \quad f_2 = \frac{nv_2}{2L} = \frac{3(19.8 \text{ m/s})}{2(2 \text{ m})} = 15 \text{ Hz}.$$

[1 point for correct substitution (with units) and calculation of each wave frequency]

The wave periods are now $T_1 = \dfrac{1}{f_1} = \dfrac{1}{42} = 2.4 \times 10^{-2}$ s and $T_2 = \dfrac{1}{f_2} = \dfrac{1}{15} = 6.7 \times 10^{-2}$ s.

[1 point for correct substitution (with units) and calculation of each wave period]

(*College Physics* 8th ed. pages 475–479/9th ed. pages 490–494)

(c) 2 points

The beat frequency f_b that occurs as a result of two interfering sound waves of different frequency is simply the difference Δf of the two frequencies. Therefore, for this situation, this becomes $\Delta f = f_{high} - f_{low} = 42 \text{ Hz} - 15 \text{ Hz} = 27 \text{ Hz}$.

[1 point for correctly stating the beat frequency equation]

[1 point for correct substitution (with units) and calculation of the beat frequency]

(*College Physics* 8th ed. pages 484–486/9th ed. pages 499–500)

(d) 1 point

As stated the lower frequency limit of human hearing is approximately 55 Hz, which therefore suggests that this device would be inaudible to humans.

[1 point for correctly stating that this frequency is inaudible to humans]

7. (15 points)

(a) 2 points

Note that the frequency given in the problem is the threshold frequency f_0 of the metal in question. Since the work function $W_0 = hf_0$, the relation $K_{max} = hf - \phi$

(sometimes written $K_{max} = hf - W_0$), gives the following: $K_{max} = hf - hf_0$ or $K_{max} = 0$. Therefore, light that is incident at the threshold frequency has only enough energy for the metal's electrons to become unbound and gives them no additional energy to serve as kinetic energy.

[1 point for stating that the kinetic energy of the photoelectrons is zero]
[1 point for providing a correct explanation]

(*College Physics* 8th ed. pages 870–875/9th ed. pages 911–916)

(b) 2 points

The work function ϕ (or W_0) is the product hf_0, which is therefore

$\phi = (4.14 \times 10^{-15} \text{ eV} \cdot \text{s})(4.25 \times 10^{14} \text{ Hz}) = 1.76 \text{ eV}$.

[1 point for stating the relation between work function and threshold frequency]
[1 point for a correct calculation and substitution with units]

(*College Physics* 8th ed. pages 870–875/9th ed. pages 911–916)

(c) 3 points

By the relation $K_{max} = \dfrac{hf}{\lambda} - \phi$, the kinetic energy must first be calculated, and from $K_{max} = \dfrac{1}{2}mv^2$ the average speed v can be determined (note that $hf = \dfrac{hc}{\lambda}$, where λ is the wavelength of the incident light): $K_{max} = \dfrac{hc}{\lambda} - \phi = \dfrac{(4.14 \times 10^{-15} \text{eV} \cdot \text{s})(3.0 \times 10^8 \text{ m/s})}{(3.25 \times 10^{-5} \text{ m})} - 1.76 \text{ eV} = 2.06 \text{ eV} = K_{max}$. To determine the speed, solve the kinetic energy equation for v: $K_{max} = \dfrac{1}{2}mv^2$ becomes $\sqrt{\dfrac{2K_{max}}{m}} = v$

so that $v = \sqrt{\dfrac{2K_{max}}{m}} = \sqrt{\dfrac{2(2.06 \text{ eV}) \times (1.60 \times 10^{-19} \text{J/eV})}{(9.11 \times 10^{-31} \text{kg})}} = 8.51 \times 10^5 \text{ m/s}$.

[1 point for a correct replacement of f with $\dfrac{c}{\lambda}$]

[1 point for a correct calculation, and substitution with units, of K_{max}]

[1 point for a correct calculation, and substitution with units, of v]

(*College Physics* 8th ed. pages 870–875/9th ed. pages 911–916)

(d) 2 points

The de Broglie wavelength is calculated by $\lambda = \dfrac{h}{p}$ where p is the momentum ($p = mv$) of the ejected photoelectron. This becomes $\lambda = \dfrac{h}{p} = \dfrac{h}{mv} = \dfrac{(6.63 \times 10^{-34} \text{J} \cdot \text{s})}{(9.11 \times 10^{-31} \text{kg})(8.51 \times 10^5 \text{ m/s})} = 8.55 \times 10^{-10} \text{ m}$ or $8.55 \text{ Å} = \lambda$.

[1 point for a correct calculation, and substitution with units, of p]
[1 point for a correct calculation, and substitution with units, of λ]

(*College Physics* 8th ed. pages 880–883/9th ed. pages 922–925)

(e) 2 points

The data points W and f are depicted as demarcated circled points and the "X" marks are slope points on the line whose coordinates are shown.

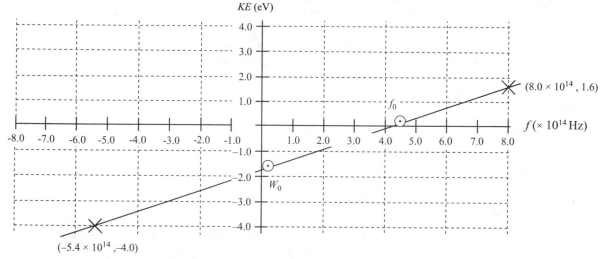

[1 point for all data points from the table plotted correctly to ±0.3 grid space]
[1 point for a correctly drawn line]

(f) 2 points

Taking the coordinates of the two slope points shown in the plot, this becomes

$$\text{slope} = \frac{rise}{run} = \frac{1.6\ \text{eV} - (-4.0\ \text{eV})}{(8.0 \times 10^{14}\ \text{Hz}) - (-5.4 \times 10^{14}\ \text{Hz})} = \frac{5.6\ \text{eV}}{(13.4 \times 10^{14}\ \text{Hz})} = 4.18 \times 10^{-15}\ \text{eV} \bullet \text{s}.$$

The significance of the slope of the K versus f plot is that it is Planck's constant, h.

[1 point for a correct calculation, and substitution with units, of the slope]
[1 point for a correct statement that the slope is Planck's constant, h]

(College Physics 8th ed. pages 870–875/9th ed. pages 911–916)

(g) 2 points

(i) 1 point

Once the source is emitting light at or above the threshold frequency, the number of emitted photoelectrons can be increased by increasing the intensity (i.e., brightness) of the light.

[1 point for a correct statement pertaining to increasing the light intensity]

(ii) 1 point

Again, once the source is emitting light at or above the threshold frequency, photoelectrons possessing more kinetic energy will be emitted from the atom only if the frequency of the incident light is increased. Doing so will increase the energy hf of the photons, which will in turn transfer more energy to the ejected electrons

[1 point for a correct statement pertaining to increasing the light frequency and/or energy, or decreasing its wavelength]

(College Physics 8th ed. pages 870–875/9th ed. pages 911–916)

Calculating Your Score

Section I: Multiple-Choice

_____ × 1.2857 = _____

Number Correct   Weighted Section I Score
(out of 70)   (If less than zero, enter
                 zero; do not round)

Section II: Free Response

Question 1 _____ × 1.0000 = _____
            (out of 15)   (Do not round)

Question 2 _____ × 1.0000 = _____
            (out of 15)   (Do not round)

Question 3 _____ × 1.0000 = _____
            (out of 15)   (Do not round)

Question 4 _____ × 1.0000 = _____
            (out of 15)   (Do not round)

Question 5 _____ × 1.0000 = _____
            (out of 15)   (Do not round)

Question 6 _____ × 1.0000 = _____
            (out of 15)   (Do not round)

Question 7 _____ × 1.0000 = _____
            (out of 15)   (Do not round)

Sum = _____

Weighted Section II Score
(Do not round)

Composite Score

_____ + _____ = _____
Weighted   Weighted   Composite Score
Section I Score   Section II Score   (Round to nearest
                              whole number)

AP Grade Conversion Chart

Composite Score Range	AP Grade
112–180	5
85–111	4
57–84	3
40–56	2
0–39	1

Part II

A Review of AP Physics B

1

KINEMATICS

Unless otherwise stated, the effects of air resistance in this chapter and the rest of the book is negligible.

WHAT IS KINEMATICS?

(College Physics 8th ed. pages 24–46/9th ed. pages 25–47)

Kinematics is the study of the movement of objects in a straight line in one dimension such as cars, trains, planes, and electrons in particle physics labs. Probably the most important and ever-present type of such motion known is *free fall*, the type of motion experienced by an object that is under the influence of only the pull of a planet's gravity. Kinematics can be separated into two main categories: problems that are solved algebraically using the five main kinematics equations (shown below) and problems that are solved by analyzing graphs (an introduction to calculus).

First, the concepts of displacement, velocity, and acceleration must be firmly understood. Velocity describes the distance covered by a moving object in a given time, noting its direction. For example, if a runner covers a displacement d of 800 m east on a track in a time interval Δt of 5 minutes, the runner's average velocity $\bar{v}$ is

$$\bar{v} = \frac{\Delta d}{\Delta t} = \frac{800 \text{ meters}}{300 \text{ seconds}} = \textbf{2.67 m/s east = average velocity}$$

In this example, we calculated the runner's average *velocity*, not the average *speed*; speed is a scalar quantity and has no direction, whereas velocity is a vector quantity and must have both size and a direction.

Similarly, if the runner changes velocity (called *acceleration*) in a certain time, that rate of change of velocity can also be calculated. Suppose the runner accelerates from 2.7 m/s east to a velocity of 5.0 m/s east in 4.0 s. Thus, we can calculate the acceleration as follows:

$$a = \frac{\Delta v}{\Delta t} = \frac{5.0 \text{ m/s} - 2.67 \text{ m/s}}{4.0 \text{ s}} = \textbf{0.6 m/s}^2 \textbf{ east = acceleration}$$

To perform calculations on Section 1 of the AP Physics exam successfully, the following five equations of motion for the subject of kinematics must be committed to memory.

$$\bar{v} = \frac{\Delta d}{\Delta t}$$

$$\bar{v} = \frac{v_i + v_f}{2}$$

$$a = \frac{\Delta v}{\Delta t}$$

$$v_f^2 = v_i^2 + 2ad$$

$$d = v_i \, \Delta t + \tfrac{1}{2} a \, \Delta t^2$$

TYPES OF MOTION

(*College Physics* 8th ed. pages 31–44/9th ed. pages 33–38)

Before embarking on further problems, we must understand that linear motion actually encompasses two types of motion:

1. Constant velocity is when an object does not change its velocity (that is, it does not speed up or slow down).
2. Constant acceleration is when an object changes its velocity uniformly (that is, it does speed up or slow down).

A simple thought experiment can help you discern between these two motions. Imagine that a car dripping oil on the road moves with both constant speed and constant acceleration. Because the car doesn't accelerate when moving with constant velocity, it therefore covers equal distances in equal times. Thus, the oil drops will appear equally spaced:

When the car instead stops at a traffic light and then accelerates uniformly, the dot spacing must now change. Because the car starts moving very slowly, the dots must first appear close together, but they then start to spread farther apart, showing that the car is speeding up. Thus, after the car starts from rest, the dots will be spaced in this manner:

A type of problem dealing with constant acceleration is an object moving under the influence of gravity, which *always* accelerates (either uniformly slowing down or uniformly speeding up). This motion is called *free fall*. Neglecting the influence of air resistance, near the surface of Earth the rate at which an object accelerates due to gravity is –9.8 m/s², meaning that for every 1 s of travel, the object's velocity will change by 9.8 m/s. For the sake of brevity and ease of problem solving in AP Physics, this value of *g* is often rounded to –10.0 m/s².

PERFORMING KINEMATICS CALCULATIONS

When performing calculations, it is extremely important to remember that all equations of kinematics must be used with their appropriate vector quantities. Most physics teachers abide by the convention that any vector pointing downward or to the left must be written with a negative sign (which must be included in the calculation) and any vector pointing upward or to the right is written with a positive sign. With the aid of the five kinematics equations stated above, this crucial standard can be easily solidified by the following example.

SAMPLE PROBLEM 1

A stone is released from a balloon while the balloon is descending at a constant speed of 10.0 m/s. Neglecting air resistance, the speed of the stone after 20.0 s is closest to what value?
(a) 2160 m/s
(b) 1760 m/s
(c) 210 m/s
(d) 176 m/s
(e) 107 m/s

SOLUTION TO PROBLEM 1

Making a checklist of the given quantities gives the following information:

$$v_i = -10.0 \text{ m/s} \quad a = -10.0 \text{ m/s}^2 \quad \Delta t = 20.0 \text{ s} \quad v_f = ?$$

Two valuable aspects of this problem that each student must discover are that the stone is initially moving downward (and thus has a *negative* initial velocity) and that it is in free fall and is subjected to the downward force due to gravity (thus, $a = g = -10 \text{ m/s}^2$). Therefore,

$$a = \frac{\Delta v}{\Delta t} = \frac{v_f - v_i}{\Delta t} \qquad \text{or} \qquad -10 \text{ m/s}^2 = \frac{v_f - (-10 \text{ m/s})}{20 \text{ s}}$$

and **$v_f = -210$ m/s.**

This answer suggests that the velocity is either downward or to the left; notice the problem asked only for the *speed* of the stone and not the *velocity*, thus making choice the correct answer.

SAMPLE PROBLEM 2

A stone dropped off a 175-meter-high building would land on the ground in approximately how many seconds?
(a) 3 s
(b) 4 s
(c) 6 s
(d) 18 s
(e) 36 s

SOLUTION TO PROBLEM 2

Here, the word *dropped* (or, often in physics problems, *released from rest*) is key and suggests the initial velocity is zero. Also, because the stone is falling downward, it is being displaced in the downward direction with a displacement d of −175 m, not simply 175 m. Failing to incorporate the negative sign will render the calculation incorrect. Thus, the checklist is as follows:

$$v_i = 0.0 \text{ m/s} \qquad a = g = -10 \text{ m/s}^2 \qquad d = -175 \text{ m} \qquad \Delta t = ?$$

Looking through the five kinematics equations, the one that will solve this problem is $d = v_i \, \Delta t + \frac{1}{2} a \Delta t^2$. Thus, substituting yields $-175 = \frac{1}{2} (-10) \Delta t^2$, or $\Delta t = \mathbf{6 \ s}$, which is choice (c).

GRAPHICAL ANALYSIS

(*College Physics* 8th ed. pages 34–37/9th ed. pages 35–38)

Recognizing graphs and performing graphical calculations with them is vital to achieving success in the subject of graphical analysis of kinematics. Nearly all graphs are constructed with time (*t*) as the dependent variable on the horizontal axis. On the vertical axis, however, any one of three possible variables can be plotted: distance (or displacement), speed (or velocity), or acceleration. First, recall constant velocity and constant acceleration motions.

GRAPHS FOR CONSTANT VELOCITY MOTION

Three types of graphs illustrate the motion of constant velocity:

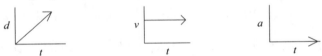

Notice that distance increases evenly with time (recall "equal distances in equal times"), velocity is unchanging (hence the straight horizontal line), and, as expected, acceleration is zero (because the velocity is constant).

GRAPHS FOR CONSTANT ACCELERATION MOTION

There are also three graphs for the motion of constant acceleration:

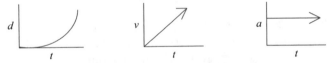

For these graphs, notice that distance covered by the object *becomes larger* during equal amounts of time, which is why the first (and only) plot is parabolic. Also, because the object is accelerating uniformly, it must gain velocity by the same amount every second and thus the middle plot is linear (hence the meaning of acceleration: velocity increasing or decreasing by the same amount for all equal time intervals). Finally, notice that the acceleration plot must be horizontal because the acceleration is constant.

SLOPE (RATE OF CHANGE)

A fundamental aspect of science is to discern the rate of change of a quantity (which in calculus is a *derivative*). In graphical analysis of kinematics, it is possible to find the rate of change of the displacement (which is *velocity*) and the rate of change of the velocity (which is *acceleration*). To determine these rates from graphs, simply find the *slope* of a particular line segment on a graph. When doing so, keep in mind the following:

1. The slope of a line is the change of the vertical divided by the change of the horizontal, or *rise over run*:

$$\text{slope} = \frac{\Delta \text{ vertical}}{\Delta \text{ horizontal}}$$

This identity is the same as $a = \Delta v / \Delta t$ and $\bar{v} = \Delta d / \Delta t$.

2. The slope of a vertical line is undefined (that is, infinity), or the maximum rate of change.

3. The slope of a horizontal line is zero, or no rate of change.

An easy way to remember these points for solving graphical problems is the following mnemonic:

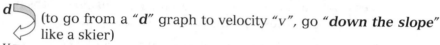 (to go from a "*d*" graph to velocity "*v*", go "**down the slope**" like a skier)

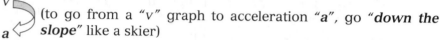 (to go from a "*v*" graph to acceleration "*a*", go "**down the slope**" like a skier)

SAMPLE PROBLEM 3

The following graph shows the displacement *d* versus time *t* for a car trip.

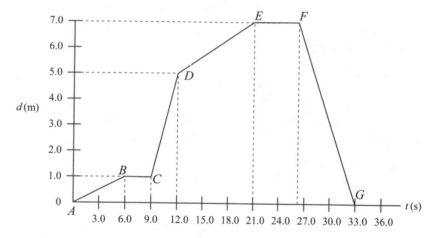

Displacement vs. Time for a Car Drive

(a) Describe the type of motion during each segment of the trip: *AB*, *BC*, *CD*, *DE*, *EF*, and *FG*.

(b) What distance did the car travel for the first 21.0 s of the trip?

(c) What is the car's average velocity from *C* to *D*?

SOLUTION TO PROBLEM 3

(a) *AB* = constant velocity; *BC* = stopped; *CD* = constant velocity; *DE* = constant velocity; *EF* = stopped; *FG* = constant velocity.

(b) For segment *AB*, the car traveled 1.0 m. For segment *BC*, the car was stopped and thus traveled 0.0 m. For segment *CD*, the car traveled from 1.0 m to 5.0 m, or a total of 4.0 m. For segment *DE*, the car traveled from 5.0 m to 7.0 m, or a total of 2.0 m. For segment *EF*, the car was stopped and thus traveled 0.0 m. For segment *FG*, the car traveled from 7.0 m back to 0.0 m (its reference or starting point) and thus traveled 7.0 m.

Thus, the total distance traveled is 1.0 m + 0.0 m + 4.0 m + 2.0 m + 0.0 m + 7.0 m = **14.0 m.**

(c) Again, we have to calculate the slope of the segment *CD*. The question is asking for *v* and we have a *d* graph, so according to the mnemonic above, we need to find the slope of segment *CD*. Thus,

$$\text{slope} = \frac{\Delta \text{ vertical}}{\Delta \text{ horizontal}} = \frac{5.0 \text{ m} - 1.0 \text{ m}}{12.0 \text{ s} - 9.0 \text{ s}} = \textbf{+1.3 m/s.}$$

AREA UNDER THE CURVE

Often seen as the "reverse" of finding the slope of a graphed function, the calculation of area under a curve also offers valuable kinematic information. In calculus, this calculation is known as *integration*. For the purposes of AP Physics, such calculations are kept elementary, using graphs that typically are linear. Follow these guidelines for calculating area under a curve:

1. The area under a horizontal line is the area of a square or rectangle: length × width.
2. The area under a diagonal line is the area of a triangle: $\frac{1}{2}$ (base × height).
3. It may be necessary to find both the area of a square and the area of a triangle; add them together to find the total area.
4. The area under an acceleration graph is the velocity of the object.
5. The area under a speed graph is the displacement traveled.

An easy way to remember this for solving graphical problems is the following mnemonic device:

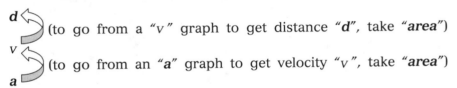

d (to go from a "*v*" graph to get distance "***d***", take "***area***")

v (to go from an "***a***" graph to get velocity "*v*", take "***area***")
a

SAMPLE PROBLEM 4
The following graph shows the velocity *v* versus time *t* for a running cheetah.

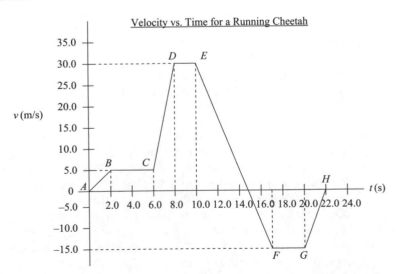

(a) Describe the cheetah's motion during segments *CD*, *DE*, and *EF*.

(b) Determine the cheetah's displacement during the first 15 s.
(c) Determine the cheetah's acceleration from E to F.
(d) What is the cheetah's instantaneous velocity at $t = 20$ s? Describe its significance.
(e) Is the cheetah's displacement for the entire 22-s trip positive or negative? Support your answer with appropriate calculations.

SOLUTION TO PROBLEM 4

(a) Recalling the graphs for the motion of constant velocity and of constant acceleration described earlier, we find that segment CD represents a changing velocity (that is, constant acceleration motion); segment DE shows an unchanging, constant velocity (that is, constant velocity motion); and segment EF also represents a uniformly changing velocity (because the slope is the same). Notice that the cheetah's velocity reaches zero at 15 s. Thereafter, the cheetah is moving in the opposite direction (indicated by the negative graph) toward its starting point. During segment EF, however, the cheetah still displays the same rate of change of velocity (that is, constant acceleration motion).

(b) Displacement from a velocity graph is determined by calculating the area under the curve during each interval. Notice that the units, just like the numbers, behave algebraically. First, find the displacement of each segment.

DISPLACEMENT FROM A to B:

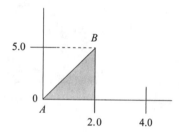

The shaded area of the triangle shown is $\frac{1}{2}$ (base × height) = $\frac{1}{2}$ (2 s × 5 m/s) = **+5.0 m**.

DISPLACEMENT from B to C:

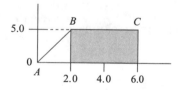

The shaded area of the rectangle shown is base × height = 4 s × 5 m/s = **+20.0 m**.

DISPLACEMENT from C to D:

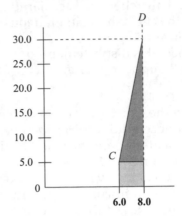

The shaded area of the rectangle shown plus the shaded area of the thin darker triangle shown is base × height = 2 s × 5 m/s = 10.0 m plus $\frac{1}{2}$ (base × height) = $\frac{1}{2}$ (2 s × 25 m/s) = 25 m, or **+35.0 m total.**

DISPLACEMENT from D to E:

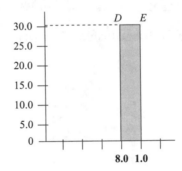

The shaded area of the rectangle shown is base × height = 2 s × 30 m/s = **+60.0 m.**

Therefore, the entire displacement for the first 15 s is the sum of the above values, or **+120 m.**

(c) Recalling that slope of the velocity graph gives acceleration, all that is required here is to determine the slope of segment EF:

$$\text{acceleration} = \text{slope} = \frac{\Delta \text{ vertical}}{\Delta \text{ horizontal}} = \frac{-15.0 \text{ m/s} - 30.0 \text{ m/s}}{17.0 \text{ s} - 10.0 \text{ s}}$$
$$= \mathbf{-6.4 \text{ m/s}^2}$$

(d) Time $t = 20$ s corresponds to point G, which, by reading the graph, gives $v = -15.0$ m/s. Therefore, the cheetah is traveling back toward its starting point, in a direction opposite to how it was traveling during the first 15 s of its trip.

(e) From answering part (b) first, we already know the cheetah is +120 m from its starting point. Therefore, it is necessary to find the displacements for segments 15 s to F, FG, and GH.

DISPLACEMENT from 15 s to *F*:

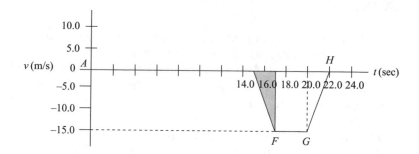

The shaded area of the triangle shown is $\frac{1}{2}$ base × height = ½ (2 s × [−15 m/s]) = **−15.0 m**.

DISPLACEMENT from *F* to *G*:

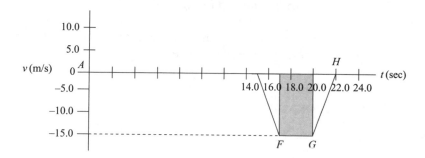

The shaded area of the rectangle shown is base × height = 3 s × (−15 m/s) = **−45.0 m**.

DISPLACEMENT from *G* to *H*:

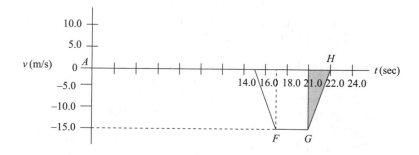

The shaded area of the triangle shown is $\frac{1}{2}$ (base × height) = $\frac{1}{2}$ (2 s × [−15 m/s]) = **−15.0 m**.

Therefore, the entire displacement for the 22-s trip is +120 m + (−15 m) + (−45 m) + (−15 m) = +45 m (that is, it is positive). The cheetah's final position is still to the right of its starting point and never passed this mark during its trip.

KINEMATICS: STUDENT OBJECTIVES FOR THE AP EXAM

▪ You must know the general relationships among position, velocity, and acceleration for the motion of a particle in a straight line.

▪ You must know how to identify, sketch, and mathematically interpret graphs of each of these variables (position, velocity, and acceleration) as functions of time for both constant velocity and constant acceleration motions.

▪ You must be able to use the equations noted above to solve one-dimensional constant acceleration motion problems.

MULTIPLE-CHOICE QUESTIONS

No calculators are permitted in this section.

1. The diagram shown represents the linear motion of a car. Which of the following statements is true?

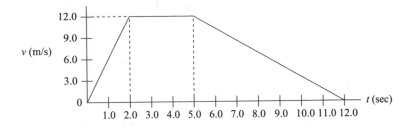

(A) The car accelerates, stops, and then reverses direction.
(B) The car accelerates at the greatest rate during the first 2.0 s of its motion.
(C) The car is in motion for only 9.0 s.
(D) The car accelerates at –12.0 m/s² for the last 4.0 s of its motion.
(E) The car returns to its starting point at $t = 9.0$ s.

2. A car starting from rest accelerates linearly at a constant rate of 2.50 m/s². What distance will the car cover in 12.0 s?
(A) 180.0 m
(B) 120.0 m
(C) 30.0 m
(D) 15.0 m
(E) 2.0 m

3. Ball *A* is dropped out of a window. At the same instant, ball *B* is thrown downward from the same window and ball *C* is thrown upward from the same window. Which statement concerning the balls is necessarily true?
   (A) At some instant after it is thrown, the acceleration of ball *C* is zero.
   (B) All three balls strike the ground at the same time.
   (C) All three balls have the same velocity at any instant.
   (D) All three balls have the same acceleration at any instant.
   (E) All three balls reach the ground with the same velocity.

4. A brick is dropped from a height of 4.9 m. The brick will impact the ground in approximately how many seconds?
   (A) 0.6 s
   (B) 1.0 s
   (C) 1.2 s
   (D) 1.4 s
   (E) 2.0 s

5. Of the following situations, which one is impossible?
   (A) a body having velocity east and acceleration east
   (B) a body having velocity east and acceleration west
   (C) a body having a zero velocity and nonzero acceleration
   (D) a body having constant acceleration and variable velocity
   (E) a body having constant velocity and variable acceleration

6. Which of the following is a scalar quantity?
   (A) speed
   (B) velocity
   (C) displacement
   (D) acceleration
   (E) acceleration due to gravity

7. A feather, initially at rest, is released in a vacuum 12.0 m above the surface of Earth. Which of the following statements is correct?
   (A) The maximum speed of the feather is 9.8 m/s.
   (B) The acceleration of the feather decreases until it moves with constant (terminal) velocity.
   (C) The acceleration of the feather remains constant during the fall.
   (D) The acceleration of the feather increases during the fall.
   (E) The acceleration of the feather is zero.

8. A ball is thrown vertically upward from the surface of Earth. Consider (1) the speed of the ball, (2) the velocity of the ball, and (3) the acceleration of the ball. Which of the following choices are zero when the ball has reached the maximum height? Choose all that apply.
   (A) (1)
   (B) (2) only
   (C) (1), (2), and (3)
   (D) (1) and (3)
   (E) (1) and (2)

9. A rock is dropped from a height h above the ground. It falls and hits the ground with a speed of 11.0 m/s. From what height should it be dropped so that its speed upon hitting the ground is 22.0 m/s? Neglect air resistance.
   (A) 1.4h
   (B) 2.0h
   (C) 3.0h
   (D) 4.0h
   (E) 0.71h

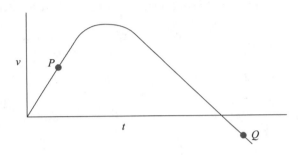

10. The diagram shown is a velocity–time plot for a linearly moving car. At point Q, what must be happening to the car?
    (A) It is moving with zero acceleration.
    (B) It is experiencing no displacement.
    (C) It is traveling underground.
    (D) It is reducing speed.
    (E) It is traveling in the reverse direction relative to that of point P.

11. A westward acceleration is suggested by which of the following situations?
    (A) The car travels westward at constant speed.
    (B) The car travels eastward and speeds up.
    (C) The car travels westward and slows down.
    (D) The car travels eastward and slows down.
    (E) The car starts from rest and moves toward the east.

12. How much time would it take a racing car to increase its speed from 10.0 m/s to 30.0 m/s if it accelerates uniformly over a distance of 80.0 m?
    (A) 2.0 s
    (B) 4.0 s
    (C) 5.0 s
    (D) 8.0 s
    (E) The answer cannot be calculated it because acceleration is unknown.

13. Starting from rest, a particle confined to move along a straight line is accelerated at a rate of 5.0 m/s². Which one of the following statements accurately describes the motion of this particle?
   (A) The particle travels 5.0 m during each second.
   (B) The particle travels 5.0 m only during the first second.
   (C) The speed of the particle increases by 5.0 m/s during each second.
   (D) The acceleration of the particle increases by 5.0 m/s² during each second.
   (E) The final speed of the particle will be directly proportional to the distance that the particle covers.

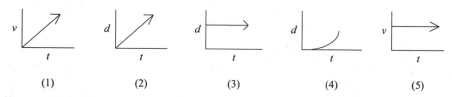

(1)   (2)   (3)   (4)   (5)

14. Above are five graphs that could represent the motion of an object moving in one dimension. Which of the following combinations of the numbered graphs best represents an object undergoing constant (nonzero) acceleration?
   (A) graphs (2) and (4)
   (B) graphs (1), (2), and (4)
   (C) graphs (1) and (4)
   (D) graphs (1), (4), and (5)
   (E) graph (4) only

15. A stone is dropped from a height of 49 m. Two seconds later, a similar stone is thrown downward from the same height. If the two stones hit the ground at the same time, what was the approximate initial velocity of the second stone?
   (A) –15 m/s
   (B) –25 m/s
   (C) –35 m/s
   (D) –45 m/s
   (E) –55 m/s

FREE-RESPONSE PROBLEMS

1. A football player returns a kickoff from the very end of a 100-yard-long (91.0-m-long) field and runs to the other end of the field with the ball, covering the entire length of the field. The first 18.0 m of his run are covered in 2.5 s while undergoing constant acceleration, starting from rest. Thereafter, he runs at constant speed, and during the final 9.0 m he slows for 1.5 s with a constant acceleration until stopping in the end zone for a touchdown.
   (a) Determine the distance covered by the player while moving at constant velocity.
   (b) Determine the player's constant acceleration during the first 18.0 m of the run.
   (c) Determine the player's speed at the end of the first 2.5 s of his run.
   (d) Determine the player's constant acceleration during the final 9.0 m of his run.

(e) Determine the total amount of time the player takes to run the full 100 yards (91.0 m).

(f) On the axes provided, accurately sketch the player's speed during his entire run.

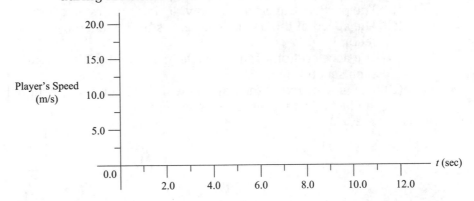

2. Two hikers are climbing a hillside when one throws a 9.0-kg backpack straight upward with a velocity of +20.0 m/s. The second hiker, who has run to an outcrop, manages to catch the backpack while it is descending and at a location that is 5.0 m above the point from which it was originally thrown.

(a) Determine the acceleration of the backpack during its movement through the air.

(b) Determine the velocity of the backpack the moment it was caught by the other hiker.

(c) Determine the amount of time the backpack was in the air.

(d) On the axes provided below, accurately sketch the backpack's velocity and acceleration during its time in the air until the moment before it is caught.

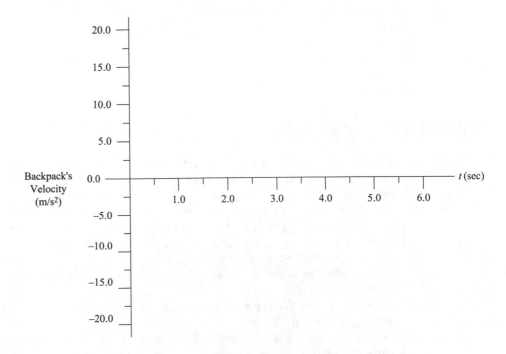

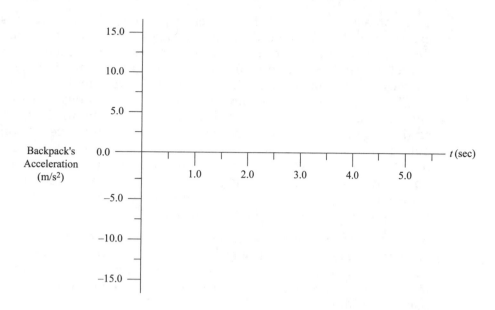

ANSWERS

MULTIPLE-CHOICE QUESTIONS

1. **B** The slope of the velocity graph gives the acceleration, and thus the car accelerates at 6 m/s² from 0 s to 2 s and at 12/7 m/s² from 5 s to 12 s, suggesting choice (B) is correct. Between 2 s and 5 s, the car moves with constant velocity, which serves to eliminate choices (A), (C), and (D). The velocity values are all above the t axis indicate that the car is continuing in the positive direction, and so choice (E) is incorrect. Thus, choice (B) is the only correct answer (*College Physics* 8th ed. pages 34–37/9th ed. pages 35–38).

2. **A** The checklist gives $v_i = 0$ ("starts from rest"), $a = 5/2$ m/s², and $\Delta t = 12.0$ s, respectively. Because the unknown is distance d, we can use $d = v_i \Delta t + \frac{1}{2} a \, \Delta t^2$. Substituting gives $d = +\frac{1}{2}\left(\frac{5}{2}\right)(12)^2 = \frac{5}{2}(72) = 5(36) =$ **180.0 m** (*College Physics* 8th ed. pages 31–44/9th ed. pages 33–45).

3. **D** Because all objects falling near the surface of Earth will accelerate at the same rate, choice (D) is the most obvious correct choice, which eliminates choice (A) because any object, even if it momentarily stops while in free fall, still experiences a downward gravitational acceleration. Because all the balls are not released the same way, none of them can have the same velocity at any instant, eliminating choices (B), (C), and (E). Thus, the best answer is choice (D) (*College Physics* 8th ed. pages 42–46/9th ed. pages 43–47).

4. **B** The checklist gives $v_i = 0$ ("dropped"), $a = -10$ m/s², $d = -4.9$ m, and $\Delta t = ?$, respectively. Solving for Δt gives $d = v_i \Delta t + \frac{1}{2} a \, \Delta t^2$, which becomes $-4.9 = \frac{1}{2}(-10) \Delta t^2$ or $-4.9 = (-5) \Delta t^2$. Therefore, $t =$ **1 second** (*College Physics* 8th ed. pages 31–44/9th ed. pages 33–45).

5. E Upon accelerating, an object's velocity and acceleration vectors are parallel, in the same direction. Similarly, upon decelerating, the object's velocity and acceleration vectors oppose each other. Therefore, choices (A) and (B) *are* possible and are thus incorrect choices. At the top of the tossed ball's path, its velocity is zero, but it still experiences a downward gravitational pull, indicating that choice (C) is possible (and is not correct for the question). Similarly, as that ball accelerates downward, it has a constant acceleration but has a variable (changing) velocity, and thus choice (D) is also a possible situation. When an object moves with unchanging velocity, however, it is impossible for it to have any acceleration, and thus choice (E) is impossible and answers the question correctly (*College Physics* 8th ed. pages 24–46/9th ed. pages 25–47).

6. A *Vectors* are quantities with both size and direction, but *scalars* are simply quantities with only size and no direction. All choices listed are vectors, except for speed, which has no direction and is thus a scalar. Therefore, choice (A) is correct (*College Physics* 8th ed. pages 24–46/9th ed. pages 25–47).

7. C Because it is stated that this problem occurs in a vacuum, it denotes true free fall in which all objects fall with same constant rate (that is, –9.8 m/s²). Thus, we see immediately that choice (C) is the correct choice and that choice (E) is incorrect. Similarly, choice (D) is impossible because the value of g is constant for a 12.0-m fall. As for the maximum speed, a quick calculation using $v_f^2 = v_i^2 + 2ad$ becomes $v_f^2 = 0 + 2(-10)(-12) = 120$, or $v_f \approx 11.0$ m/s, which shows that the impact speed of the feather is 11.0 m/s, thus eliminating choice (A). Therefore, choice (C) is correct (*College Physics* 8th ed. pages 42–46/9th ed. pages 43–47).

8. E In all parts of its path, the ball's acceleration will always be g or –9.8 m/s² near the surface of Earth. Therefore, the acceleration in (3) is never zero at the top of the path, and thus any choice with (3) in it—that is, choices (C) and (D)—can be eliminated. At the top of the path, however, the ball stops moving and thus has both zero speed and zero velocity, leading to (1) and (2) as being correct. Thus, the correct answer is choice (E) (*College Physics* 8th ed. pages 42–46/9th ed. pages 43–47).

9. D The checklist gives $v_i = 0$, $a = -10$ m/s², $v_f = ?$, and $d = ?$ Notice, however, that one final speed is exactly twice that of the other (22.0 m/s versus 11 m/s) and that the question asks for the height for the larger speed. The important relation that must be used for each speed is as follows: $v_f^2 = v_i^2 + 2ad$, which becomes $(-11)^2 = (0)^2 + 2(-10)h$ or $121 \approx 20h$, and thus $h = \mathbf{6}$ **m**; and $v_f^2 = v_i^2 + 2ad$, which becomes $(-22)^2 = (0)^2 + 2(-10)h$ or $484 \approx 20h$, and thus $h = \mathbf{24}$ **m**. Clearly, the second value of h is about *four times* that of the first. Simply observing the equation above will show the square dependency between v_f and the displacement d. Therefore, the best answer is choice (D) (*College Physics* 8th ed. pages 31–44/9th ed. pages 33–45).

10. E Noticing the negative velocity near Q suggests the car has briefly stopped (where the graph crosses the t axis) and is now moving in the opposite direction, giving choice (E) as the most likely correct answer. Because the slope of the v graph gives the acceleration, it also

implies that choices (A) and (B) are incorrect because an accelerating object is being displaced. Choice (D) cannot be correct because the plot is increasing in the negative direction, suggesting its speed is increasing even though it is moving in the opposite direction. Therefore, the only correct answer is choice (E) (*College Physics* 8th ed. pages 34–37/9th ed. pages 35–38).

11. **D** When an object has a westward acceleration, it suggests it is either moving westward and speeding up (velocity and acceleration both point west) or it is moving eastward and slowing down (velocity points to the east and acceleration to the west), yielding choice (D) as being correct. Choice (A) is incorrect as it states constant speed, choice (B) is a situation in which both velocity and acceleration point east, and choice (C), as with choice (E), suggests acceleration points to the east. Thus, choice (D) is the only correct answer (*College Physics* 8th ed. pages 34–37/9th ed. pages 35–38).

12. **B** The checklist gives $v_i = 10.0$ m/s, $v_f = 30.0$ m/s, $a = ?$, $t = ?$, and $d = 80.0$ m. Therefore, first find acceleration: $v_f^2 = v_i^2 + 2ad$ becomes $(30)^2 = (10)^2 + 2(a)80$ or $800 = 160a$, or $a = 5.0$ m/s^2. Then, find the time using $a = \dfrac{\Delta v}{\Delta t} = \dfrac{v_f - v_i}{\Delta t}$ or $5 = \dfrac{30 - 10}{\Delta t}$ or $t = 4$ s (*College Physics* 8th ed. pages 31–44/9th ed. pages 33–45).

13. **C** Because we only know that $a = 5.0$ m/s^2, all that can be determined is that the particle's speed changes by 5.0 m/s every second, immediately seen by choice (C). Similarly, choice (D) is eliminated. In addition, no time values are given and therefore no determination about distance covered can be calculated, eliminating choices (A) and (B).

Choice (E), however, is nearly correct, according to the relationship $v_f^2 = v_i^2 + 2ad$ or $v_f \propto \sqrt{2ad}$. The final speed would be proportional to the *square root* of distance, not distance, thus making choice (E) incorrect. Therefore, the correct answer is (C) (*College Physics* 8th ed. pages 31–44/9th ed. pages 33–45).

14. **C** Graph (1) depicts velocity increasing uniformly (constant acceleration), whereas graph 2 depicts displacment increasing uniformly (constant velocity). Graph (3) depicts an object stopped, graph (4) depicts displacement increasing quadratically (constant acceleration), and graph (5) depicts velocity unchanging (constant velocity). Therefore, the graphs that best show constant acceleration are graphs (1) and (4), or choice (C) (*College Physics* 8th ed. pages 34–37/9th ed. pages 35–38).

15. **D** The time for the first stone to fall is from $d = \dfrac{1}{2}gt^2$, so solving for t gives $t_{fall} = \sqrt{\dfrac{2d}{g}}$ or $t_{fall} = \sqrt{\dfrac{2(-49)}{(-10)}}$, which gives a fall time of a little more than 3 s. Because the second stone is thrown 2 s later, it will take a little more than 1 s to reach the ground. Therefore, $d = v_i \Delta t + \dfrac{1}{2}a \Delta t^2$ becomes $-49\,\text{m} = v_i (1\,\text{s}) + \dfrac{1}{2}(-10\text{m/s}^2)(1\,\text{s})^2$, or $v_i \sim$ **−45 m/s** (*College Physics* 8th ed. pages 31–44/9th ed. pages 33–45).

Free-Response Problems

1. (a) Because the problem says that the player first accelerates for 18.0 m, runs at constant speed, and then finally decelerates during the last 9.0 m, he has therefore accelerated for a distance of 18.0 m + 9.0 m, or 27.0 m. Therefore, the distance he covers moving at constant speed must be 91.0 m – 27.0 m, or **64.0 m**.

    (b) The checklist gives a_1 = ?, v_i = 0 m/s, d = 18.0 m, and Δt = 2.5 s, and we can use the kinematics equation $d = v_i\,\Delta t + \frac{1}{2}a\Delta t^2$. Thus, 18.0 m $= 0 + \frac{1}{2}(a)(2.5)^2$, or 36.0 m $= (a)(6.25)$, or a_1 = **5.8 m/s²**.

    (c) The checklist gives a_1 = 5.8 m/s², v_i = 0 m/s, d = 18.0 m, Δt = 2.5 s, and v_f = ? Using the following equation and substituting the values listed above will give $a = \dfrac{\Delta v}{\Delta t} = \dfrac{v_f - v_i}{\Delta t}$, which becomes 5.8 m/s² $= \dfrac{v_f - 0}{2.5\ \text{s}}$, or v_f = **14.0 m/s**.

    (d) The checklist gives a_2 = ?, v_i = 14.0 m/s, v_f = 0, d = 9.0 m, and Δt = 1.5 s. Using the following equation and substituting the values listed above will give $a = \dfrac{\Delta v}{\Delta t} = \dfrac{v_f - v_i}{\Delta t}$, which becomes $a = \dfrac{0 - 14.0\ \text{m/s}}{1.5\ \text{s}}$, or a_2 = **–9.3 m/s²**.

    (e) The variable checklist gives a = 0, $v_i = v_f$ = 14.4 m/s, d = 64.0 m, and Δt = ? The problem states the first 18.0 m are run in 2.5 s and the last 9.0 m are run in 1.5 s, so the remainder of the time is spent running the other 64.0 m. Therefore, 2.5 s + 1.5 s = 4.0 s for the regions of acceleration. The time covered in the region of constant velocity is from $d = v_i\,\Delta t + \dfrac{1}{2}a\Delta t^2$ or 64 m = 14.4 m/s(Δt), or Δt = 4.4 s. Therefore, the entire time spent running the length of the field is 4 + 4.4 = **8.4 s**.

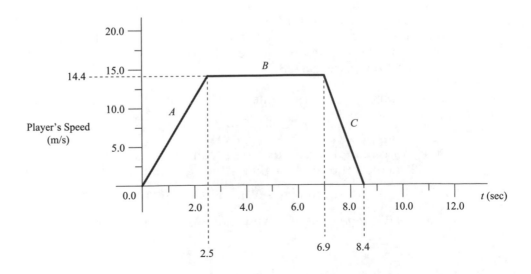

(f) For the first 18 m (or 2.5 s), the player accelerates uniformly from rest and reaches a speed of 14.4 m/s as shown by segment *A* in the graph (which must be a diagonal line). From 2.5 s to 6.94 s, the player is moving with constant velocity, a horizontal line at v = 14.4 m/s (segment *B* in the graph). Finally, the deceleration during the last 1.5 s occurs from 6.94 s to 8.44 s, when the player reaches a speed of 0 m/s from a speed of 14.4 m/s (segment *C* in the graph, also a diagonal straight line to denote acceleration).

(*College Physics* 8th ed. pages 31–44/9th ed. pages 33–45)

2. (a) Because the stone is in free fall near the surface of Earth, it accelerates at a rate of **–9.8 m/s²** (or **9.8 m/s² downward, toward the center of Earth**).

(b) The checklist gives a = –9.8 m/s², v_i = +20.0 m/s, d = +5.0 m, and v_f = ? Here, we can use the kinematics equation $v_f^2 = v_i^2 + 2ad$, or $v_f^2 = (20.0 \text{ m/s})^2 + 2(-9.8 \text{ m/s}^2)(5.0 \text{ m})$, or v_f = **–17.4 m/s.**

(c) The checklist gives a = –9.8 m/s², v_i = +20.0 m/s, d = +5.0 m, v_f = –17.4 m/s, and Δt = ? Here, use the following kinematics equation to determine the time of flight, substituting all variables as necessary from the above checklist; $a = \dfrac{\Delta v}{\Delta t} = \dfrac{v_f - v_i}{\Delta t}$, or –9.8 m/s² = $\dfrac{-17.4 \text{ m/s} - (+20.0 \text{ m/s})}{\Delta t}$, giving Δt = **3.8 s.**

(d) To determine the values of the velocity along the path of the backpack, it is necessary first to find the time to the top, where the velocity is zero. So, $a = \dfrac{\Delta v}{\Delta t} = \dfrac{v_f - v_i}{\Delta t}$, or –9.8 m/s² = $\dfrac{0 - (+20.0 \text{ m/s})}{\Delta t}$, or Δt_{top} = **2.04 s.** Therefore, a diagonal line must go from t = 0 s to t = 2.04 s, where it must cross the time axis (where v = 0,

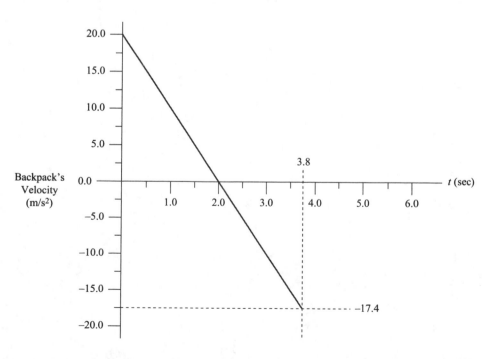

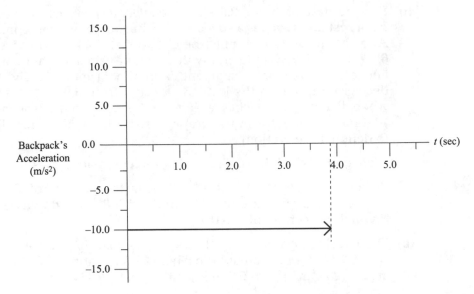

which is the peak of the path). The bag is in the air for a total of 3.8 s, which signifies that it is moving for another 3.8 s – 2.04 s after its peak, which is 1.76 s. Therefore, the rest of the plot must extend for another 1.76 s. In addition, because the backpack is now descending, the plot must be below the time axis because it is now a negative velocity down to –17.4 m/s. The final plot is shown above.

(*College Physics* 8th ed. pages 34–44 /9th ed. pages 35–47)

2

PROJECTILE MOTION

Projectiles involve anything that is shot (or *projected*) either horizontally or at any angle ("oblique" projectiles). A projectile may be a stone shot off a cliff, a kicked football, a thrown basketball, or a bullet exiting from a gun. Projectile motion is simply kinematics in two directions (horizontal and vertical), with one crucial aspect: both of these directions *must* be treated separately when problem solving. All the rules of kinematics from Chapter 1 must be applied carefully to both the horizontal and vertical motions of a projectile.

HORIZONTAL PROJECTILES

(*College Physics* 8th ed. pages 54–70/9th ed. pages 9th ed. pages 56–71)

A horizontal projectile is simply an object that is initially shot *horiontally*, or parallel to the ground, with an initial horizontal velocity (n_{ix}) and no initial vertical velocity ($n_{iy} = 0$). The moment the projectile is freed from the device that provided its original impulse, the force due to Earth's gravity accelerates the object downward. Thus, this projectile simultaneously moves vertically (*y* direction) and horizontally (*x* direction) with a path (*trajectory*) as shown:

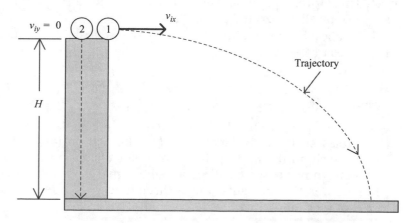

Often, it is thought that a gravitational force acts horizontally to carry the projectile, but that is a key misconception. Imagine a marble horizontally launched while another marble is simultaneously dropped from the same height. Although the second marble moves only vertically due to the gravitational force acting on it, the first marble moves both downward and horizontally. That the two marbles strike the ground at the same time proves that these two motions are independent and that no horizontal force affects the flight of the first marble (after it was launched). In addition to solidifying the independence of the horizontal and vertical motions of the projectile, it also proves that the time to cross is equal to the time it takes to fall from the same height.

On closer examination, we can sketch both the vertical and horizontal velocities of the marble as well as the downward gravitational acceleration g:

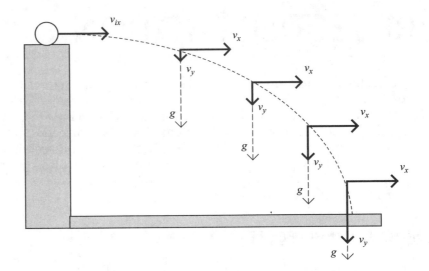

The nature of the two motions of any projectile are evident from this diagram. In the horizontal x direction, the projectile's motion is constant velocity because no horizontal force exists to alter the velocity, and in the vertical y direction, the projectile experiences constant acceleration due to the force of gravity. Notice that although the downward velocity vector increases in magnitude, the downward acceleration (g) remains constant. For ease of calculation, on Earth, that rounded value is -10.0 m/s^2. Therefore, you can *always* write $a_x = 0$ and $a_y = -10.0$ m/s^2 as well as $v_{iy} = 0$ for all horizontal projectiles.

The following problem-solving tips will help you set up and solve projectiles problems quickly.

AP Tip

Get into the habit of distinguishing horizontal and vertical variables such as displacement (d), acceleration (a), and velocity (v) by writing the appropriate x or y subscripts on them as soon as you know in which direction the equation must be applied. Remember that because these directions are independent, you *cannot* mix subscripts.

AP Tip

When making a checklist of knowns and unknowns for a *horizontal* projectiles problem, you can *immediately* write

$$v_{iy} = 0 \text{ m/s}$$
$$a_x = 0 \text{ m/s}^2$$
$$a_y = -10.0 \text{ m/s}^2$$

SAMPLE PROBLEM 1

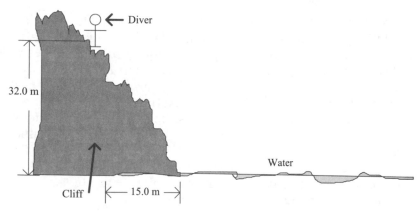

Cliff divers in Acapulco, Mexico, dive from a 32.0-m-high cliff. The rocks at the cliff base extend outward (horizontally) 15.0 m before clear water begins as shown.
(a) Determine the amount of time it takes the diver to reach the water.
(b) Determine the minimum horizontal velocity of the diver such that he clears the 15.0 m of rock at the base of the cliff and lands in the water.

SOLUTION TO PROBLEM 1

(a) Variable Checklist: $a_x = 0$, $a_y = -10.0 \text{ m/s}^2$, $v_{iy} = 0$, $d_y = -32.0$ m, $d_{x\,min} = 15.0$ m, $\Delta t = ?$

Recalling that the diver's fall time is the same as if he simply jumped straight downward, the following equation applied in the y-direction will give

$$d_y = v_{iy}\Delta t + \tfrac{1}{2}a_y \Delta t^2$$

Substituting, this equation becomes

$$d_y = \tfrac{1}{2}g\Delta t^2 = \tfrac{1}{2}(-10.0 \text{ m/s}^2)\Delta t^2 = -32.0\text{m}$$

or

$$-32.0 \text{ m} = (-5.0 \text{ m/s}^2)\,\Delta t^2$$

Thus, $t = 2.6$ s.

(B) Variable Checklist: $a_x = 0$, $a_y = -10.0 \text{ m/s}^2$, $v_{iy} = 0$, $d_y = -32.0$ m, $d_{x\,min} = 15.0$ m, $\Delta t = 2.6$ s, $v_{ix} = ?$

For the diver to just clear the 15.0-m span of the rocks, he must travel horizontally a minimum of 15.0 m. Thus, using the following equation in the horizontal x direction will give

$$d_x = v_{ix}\Delta t + \tfrac{1}{2}a_x\Delta t^2$$

Substituting values (and the time of 2.6 s), this equation becomes 15.0 m = v_{ix} (2.6 s), or v_{ix} = **5.9 m/s**.

OBLIQUE PROJECTILES

(*College Physics* 8th ed. pages 54–70/9th ed. pages 56–71)

An oblique projectile is an object that is projected at a certain angle relative to the horizontal, such as a kicked football, a batted baseball, or a hit golf ball. Even though an oblique projectile also travels in two directions (x and y), during the first part of its trajectory the object slows as it ascends (as a result of the downward pull of gravity, g), indicated by the decreasing magnitude in n_y. At the peak (A), it momentarily stops (where $n_y = 0$) and then descends, speeding up as it does (indicated by the increasing magnitude of n_y). During the entire time the object is airborne, it is always pulled downward by the planet's gravity (i.e., gravity does not "shut off" particularly at the peak). As shown, an oblique projectile's two motions must also be treated separately to solve problems correctly.

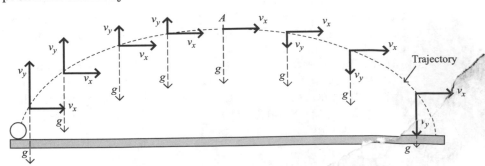

A second vital difference between horizontal projectiles and oblique projectiles is that the oblique projectile's initial velocity has *components* acting in both the horizontal and vertical directions. Thus, as shown here, the initial velocity v_y must be resolved into the components v_{ix} and v_{iy}:

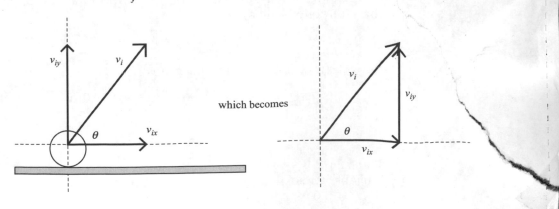

which becomes

Therefore, using the right triangle relationships for sine and cosine gives $v_{ix} = v_i \cos\theta$ and $v_{iy} = v_i \sin\theta$, and by the Pythagorean theorem, $v_i^2 = v_{ix}^2 + v_{iy}^2$.

HOW FAR DOES IT GO?

(*College Physics* 8th ed. page 54–70/**9th ed. pages 54–70**)

Sometimes, it may be necessary to calculate the entire horizontal distance traveled by the projectile (called the *range*) when no information about time of flight is given simply by using the range equation. In addition, it is helpful to use this relationship to note how range depends on initial launch angle. Although range can easily be derived using the kinematics equations in the horizontal direction (and eliminating the time variable), it is

$$\text{range } R = \frac{v_i^2(\sin 2\theta)}{g}$$

This equation shows that for a launch angle of 45°, 2(45°) is 90°, so sin 90° gives 1.0, which indicates that the greatest projectile range occurs when the object is shot at 45°. Launch angles both below and above the value of 45° give ranges that are lower than that at 45°. Notice also the square dependence of R on v_i.

WHAT IS THE TIME OF FLIGHT?

(*College Physics* 8th ed. pages 54–70/**9th ed. pages 54–70**)

Some oblique projectiles problems require us to determine the entire time of flight for a symmetrical path (i.e., a path that starts and stops at the same height relative to the ground or another fixed reference point). Because the parabolic path is symmetrical, finding the time of flight is simply twice the time it takes the projectile to reach its maximum height. Considering that v_i and the launch angle q are nearly always given, the time to the top may easily be found using the following equation in the vertical y direction:

$$a_y = \frac{\Delta v_y}{\Delta t}$$

where $a = g$, which then becomes

$$g = \frac{v_{fy} - v_{iy}}{\Delta t}$$

A useful tip for solving these kinds of equations is to choose the launch point as the initial location (*i*) and then choose the peak of the trajectory as the final location (*f*), which is where $v_y = 0$.

SAMPLE PROBLEM 2

A golfer hits a golf ball upward at 50.0 m/s at an angle of 30° relative to the ground. Shortly thereafter, the ball lands on the same level ground some distance from where it was hit.

  (a) Determine the time of flight of the ball.

(b) Determine the maximum height of the ball.

(c) Determine the range of the ball.

Solution to Problem 2

(a) Variable Checklist: $a_x = 0$, $a_y = -10.0$ m/s^2, $v_{ix} = 50.0 \cos 30° = 43.0$ m/s, $v_{iy} = 50.0 \sin 30° = 25.0$ m/s

Using the acceleration equation, we can immediately find the time to the top. Then, by symmetry, we can double it to find the entire flight time (notice the appropriate use of positive and negative):

$$g = \frac{v_{fy} - v_{iy}}{\Delta t}$$

which becomes

$$-10.0 \text{ m/s}^2 = \frac{0 - (+25.0 \text{ m/s})}{\Delta t}$$

So,

$$t = \frac{-25.0 \text{ m/s}}{-10.0 \text{ m/s}^2} = 2.5 \text{ s}$$

Therefore, the time of flight is approximately **5.0 s**.

(b) Variable Checklist: $a_x = 0$, $a_y = -10.0$ m/s^2, $v_{ix} = 50.0 \cos 30° = 43.0$ m/s, $v_{iy} = 50.0 \sin 30° = 25.0$ m/s, $\Delta t_{total} = 5.0$ s, $d_{y\,max} = ?$

Using the equation for displacement in the y direction, we can solve for d_y:

$$d_y = v_{iy}\Delta t + \tfrac{1}{2}a_y\Delta t^2$$

Notice that no variable drops out (in contrast to horizontally projected objects) and that we cannot use the full time of flight because the highest point occurs after only half the flight time has passed. Substituting, we have

$$d_y = (25.0 \text{ m/s})(2.5 \text{ s}) + \tfrac{1}{2}(-10.0 \text{ m/s}^2)(2.5 \text{ s})^2$$

Therefore, the maximum height is d_y = **31 m**.

(c) Variable Checklist: $a_x = 0$, $a_y = -10.0$ m/s^2, $v_{ix} = 50.0 \cos 30° = 43.0$ m/s, $v_{iy} = 50.0 \sin 30° = 25.0$ m/s, $\Delta t_{total} = 5.0$ s, $d_{y\,max} = 31$ m, $d_x = ?$

Here, it is possible to use either the range equation or the kinematics equation for d_x. Using the range equation gives

$$R = \frac{v_i^2(\sin 2\theta)}{g}$$

$$R = \frac{(50)^2 \left[\sin (60)\right]}{10.0 \text{ m/s}^2} = 217 \text{ m}$$

Using the kinematics equation gives

$$d_x = v_{ix}\Delta t + \tfrac{1}{2}a_x\Delta t^2$$

$$d_x = 43.0 \text{ m/s}(5.0 \text{ s}) + \tfrac{1}{2}(0)(5.0 \text{ s})^2 = 215 \text{ m}$$

Thus, the range of the golf ball is approximately **216 m**.

SAMPLE PROBLEM 3

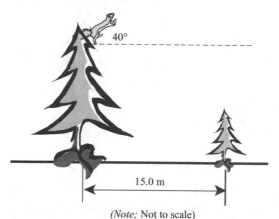

15.0 m

(Note; Not to scale)

A flying squirrel launches itself from the top of a stationary tree as shown. The squirrel leaves the tree with a velocity of 6.0 m/s at 40° relative to the level ground below and approaches a shorter tree located 15.0 m from the point of projection.

    (a) Determine the time it takes the squirrel to reach the plane of the second tree, 15.0 m away.

    (b) Determine the vertical displacement of the squirrel when it lands in the second tree.

    (c) Determine the final speed of the squirrel the moment it lands in the second tree.

SOLUTION TO PROBLEM 3

    (a) Variable Checklist: $a_x = 0$, $a_y = -10.0$ m/s^2, $v_{ix} = 6 \cos 40° = 4.59$ m/s, $v_{iy} = 6 \sin 40° = 3.86$ m/s, $d_x = 15.0$ m, $\Delta t_{cross} = ?$

Because there is no horizontal acceleration, the following equation may be used with $a_x = 0$:

$$d_x = v_{ix}\Delta t + \tfrac{1}{2}a_x\Delta t^2$$

which becomes 15.0 m = (4.59 m/s) $\Delta t + 0$, or $\Delta t_{cross} = $ **3.3 s.**

    (b) Here, calculate d_y, the moment the squirrel reaches the location of the tree, 15.0 m away. Variable Checklist: $a_x = 0$, $a_y = -10.0$ m/s^2, $v_{ix} = 6 \cos 40° = 4.59$ m/s, $v_{iy} = 6 \sin 40° = 3.86$ m/s, $d_x = 15.0$ m, $\Delta t_{cross} = 3.3$ s, $d_y = ?$
Now use the displacement equation in the vertical y direction:

$$d_y = v_{iy}\Delta t + \tfrac{1}{2}a_y\Delta t^2$$

which becomes $d_y = (3.86$ m/s$)(3.3$ s$) + \tfrac{1}{2}(-10.0$ m/s$^2)(3.3$ s$)^2$ or $d_y = $ **−42.0 m.** In other words, the squirrel is about 42 m below its launch point.

    (c) Variable Checklist: $a_x = 0$, $a_y = -10.0$ m/s^2, $v_{ix} = 6 \cos 40° = 4.59$ m/s, $v_{iy} = 6 \sin 40° = 3.86$ m/s, $d_x = 15.0$ m, $\Delta t_{cross} = 3.3$ s, $d_y = -42.0$ m, $v_f = ?$

To calculate v_f, it is necessary to determine the vector components v_{fx} and v_{fy}. Because v_x is already known (and is a constant, 4.59 m/s), once we find v_{fy}, the Pythagorean theorem will provide v_f. So,

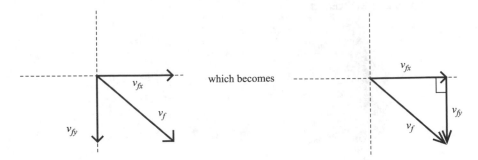

$$v_{fy}^2 = v_{iy}^2 + 2a_y d_y$$

which becomes $v_{f_y}^2 = (3.86 \text{ m/s})^2 + 2(-10.0 \text{ m/s}^2)(-42.0 \text{ m})$, or $v_{fy} = -29.0$ m/s (negative because it is downward). Therefore, using the Pythagorean theorem, v_f becomes $v_f^2 = v_{fx}^2 + v_{fy}^2$, which becomes $v_f^2 = (4.59 \text{ m/s})^2 + (-27.9 \text{ m/s})^2$, or $v_f =$ **29.6 m/s.**

PROJECTILE MOTION: STUDENT OBJECTIVES FOR THE AP EXAM

- You should understand the general motion of a particle in two dimensions.
- You should understand the motion of a projectile in a gravitational field so that you can write down expressions for the horizontal and vertical components of position and velocity, and sketch or identify said components.
- You should be able to use the equations of motions learned in Chapter 1 to analyze the motion of an oblique projectile.
- You should know how to resolve an initial velocity vector into its components.
- You should understand that you must treat x and y motions *independently* when solving projectiles problems.
- You should be able to calculate both the range and flight time of an oblique projectile.
- You should know this section's Problem-Solving Tips and how to apply them.

MULTIPLE-CHOICE QUESTIONS

1. A ball is projected horizontally off the roof of a building with a speed of 14.0 m/s. If the height of the roof is 80.0 m and air resistance is negligible, what is the approximate time the ball is airborne?
   (A) 16.0 s
   (B) 3.0 s
   (C) 9.0 s
   (D) 81.0 s
   (E) 4.0 s

2. An object moving horizontally with speed V falls off the edge of a vertical cliff and lands a distance D from the base of the cliff. If it instead lands a distance 2D from the base of the cliff, how fast was it moving? Assume air resistance is negligible.
   (A) V
   (B) $\sqrt{2}\, V$
   (C) 2V
   (D) 4V
   (E) It cannot be determined unless the height of the cliff is known.

3. A physics student standing on the edge of a cliff throws a stone vertically downward with an initial speed of 10.0 m/s. The instant before the stone hits the ground below, it is traveling at a speed of 30.0 m/s. If the physics student were to throw the stone *horizontally* outward from the cliff instead, with the same initial speed of 10.0 m/s, approximately how fast would the stone be traveling just before it hits the ground? Assume air resistance is negligible.
   (A) 10.0 m/s
   (B) 20.0 m/s
   (C) 30.0 m/s
   (D) 40.0 m/s
   (E) It cannot be determined unless the height of the cliff is known.

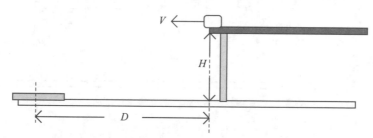

4. A block of mass M is moving horizontally with constant speed V on a frictionless tabletop as shown. A short pan, whose center is a distance D from the table edge, is placed on the level floor. Which of the following equations best represents an expression for the height H that the table must be so that the mass lands directly at the center of the pan? Assume air resistance is negligible.

   (A) $H = \dfrac{2D^2}{gV}$

   (B) $H = \tfrac{1}{2}g\left(\dfrac{D}{V}\right)^2$

   (C) $H = \dfrac{gD^2}{V^2}$

   (D) $H = \sqrt{gV}\left(\dfrac{D^2}{V^3}\right)$

   (E) $H = \sqrt{2gV}$

5. A bullet is shot vertically upward from a pistol while on the flatbed back of a pickup truck that is moving in a straight line on a level, horizontal roadway at a speed of 20.0 m/s. If air resistance is negligible, what is the bullet's landing point?
   (A) It lands in front of the truck, ahead of where it was launched.
   (B) It lands behind the truck, behind where it was launched.
   (C) It lands in the flatbed of the truck, close to the point from which it was launched.
   (D) Its landing point is dependent on the bullet's mass.
   (E) Its landing point is dependent on the value of *g*.

6. A projectile is fired from a gun and has initial horizontal and vertical components of velocity equal to 30.0 m/s and 40.0 m/s, respectively. Assuming air resistance is negligible, approximately how long does it take the projectile to reach the highest point in its trajectory?
   (A) 1.0 s
   (B) 2.0 s
   (C) 4.0 s
   (D) 8.0 s
   (E) 16.0 s

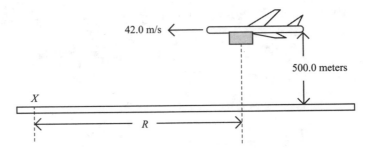

7. An airplane in level flight at an altitude of 500.0 m is moving horizontally with a speed of 42.0 m/s as shown. At what approximate distance *R* should it release a 900.0-kg package such that it hits the target *X*?
   (A) 150.0 m
   (B) 295.0 m
   (C) 424.0 m
   (D) 2.55×10^3 m
   (E) 1.50×10^4 m

8. A projectile is fired with an initial speed of 30.0 m/s at an angle of 60° above the horizontal. What is the magnitude of the horizontal component of the projectile's displacement at the end of 2.0 s?
   (A) 30.0 m
   (B) 50.0 m
   (C) 15.0 m
   (D) 26.0 m
   (E) 60.0 m

9. A spring-loaded gun is aimed horizontally and is used to launch identical balls with different initial speeds. The gun is at a fixed position above the floor. If the second projectile is fired with two times the speed as that of the first projectile, how would the horizontal range be affected?
   (A) The range for both projectiles would be the same.
   (B) The range of the second projectile would be half as much as that of the first projectile.
   (C) The range of the second projectile would be about 1.4 times larger than that of the first projectile.
   (D) The range of the second projectile would be smaller than that of the first by a factor of 1.4.
   (E) The range of the second projectile would be twice as large as that of the first projectile.

10. A football is kicked with a speed of 22.0 m/s at an angle of 60° relative to the positive x direction. At that instant, an observer rides past the football in a car that moves horizontally on a level roadway with a constant speed of 11.0 m/s in the positive x direction. According to the observer in the car, what will happen to the ball? Assume air resistance is negligible.
    (A) It will follow a path that is straight up and down in the y direction.
    (B) It will follow a path that is straight across in the positive x direction.
    (C) It will follow a hyperbolic path.
    (D) It will follow a parabolic path.
    (E) It will follow a straight line that is angled (less than 90°) with respect to the x direction.

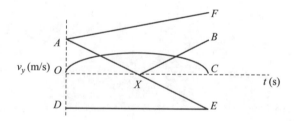

11. Which of the lettered segments on the graph best represents a graph of the vertical velocity (v_y) versus time (t) for a projectile shot at an angle of 45° above the horizontal?
    (A) OC
    (B) DE
    (C) AXB
    (D) AXE
    (E) AF

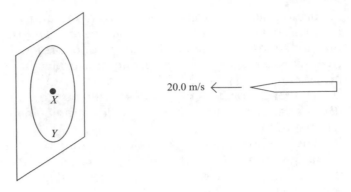

12. A dart is thrown horizontally at 20.0 m/s toward target X as shown. If the dart hits point Y (directly below X) 0.1 s later, what is the approximate vertical distance of XY?
    (A) 2.0 m
    (B) 1.0 m
    (C) 0.5 m
    (D) 0.1 m
    (E) 5.0×10^{-2} m

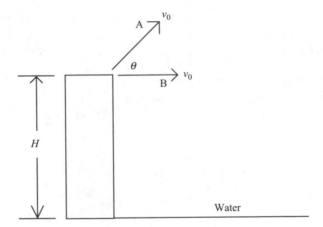

13. As depicted, person A throws a stone of mass M with initial velocity v_0 at an angle θ (relative to the horizontal) from a bridge that is a height H above water level. At the same instant, person B throws a stone of mass $2M$ with the same initial velocity but in the horizontal direction. Which of the following statements is correct concerning the speeds of each stone (v_A and v_B thrown by persons A and B, respectively) and the times (t_A and t_B) at which the stones impact the water, assuming air resistance is negligible?
    (A) $v_A < v_B$ and $t_A > t_B$
    (B) $v_A > v_B$ and $t_A < t_B$
    (C) $v_A < v_B$ and $t_A = t_B$
    (D) $v_A = v_B$ and $t_A > t_B$
    (E) $v_A = v_B$ and $t_A = t_B$

14. Two steel balls, one of mass 1.0 kg and the other of mass 2.0 kg, simultaneously roll off the edge of the same horizontal table, each leaving with the same velocity. Which of the following statements is correct?
   (A) Both balls will hit the floor at approximately the same horizontal distance from the base of the table.
   (B) The less massive ball will travel twice the horizontal distance the base of the table than does the more massive ball.
   (C) The more massive ball travels twice the horizontal distance from the base of the table as does the less massive ball.
   (D) The less massive ball travels $\sqrt{2}$ times farther from the base of the table than does the more massive ball.
   (E) The more massive balls travels $\sqrt{2}$ times farther from the base of the table than does the less massive ball.

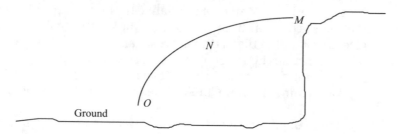

15. A stone is thrown horizontally with a speed v off a hillside cliff. The stone follows the path *MNO* as shown. Which vector best represents the direction of the acceleration of the stone at point *N*?

(A)

(B)

(C)

(D)

(E)

FREE-RESPONSE PROBLEMS

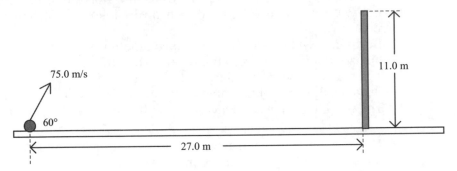

1. A ball of mass 0.3 kg, initially at rest, is projected from ground level toward a wall that is 27.0 m away. The ball's velocity the moment it is projected is 75.0 m/s at 60° relative to the horizontal as shown, and the wall is 11.0 m high. During its flight, the ball impacts nothing else and is not subjected to air resistance.
   (a) Determine the magnitude of the vertical and horizontal components of the ball's velocity.
   (b) Determine the time it takes the ball to reach the plane of the wall.
   (c) The ball passes over the wall. Determine the ball's distance above the wall the moment the ball passes over the wall.
   (d) On the graph shown below, make an appropriate sketch of the horizontal velocity component of the ball during its flight until it reaches the plane of the wall.

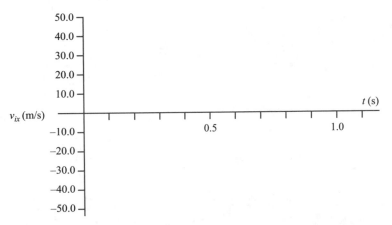

   (e) Has the ball passed over the wall before, after, or at the highest part of its trajectory? Defend your answer with appropriate calculations.

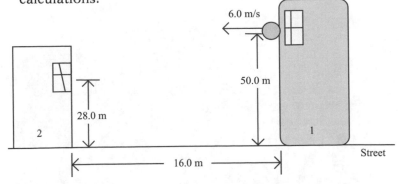

2. A person in apartment building 1 throws a ball horizontally at a speed of 6.0 m/s out a window toward nearby apartment building 2, which is 16.0 m away, as shown. The location in the window from which the ball leaves is 50.0 m above the street, and the center of the second window in building 2 is 28.0 m above the street as shown. The entire height of the window in building 2 is 1.5 m.
   (a) Determine the amount of time it takes the ball to reach apartment building 2.
   (b) Using appropriate calculations to defend your answer, determine whether or not the ball goes into the window in building 2. If it does not, how far above or below the window center does it pass?
   (c) Determine the final speed of the ball the moment it reaches the closest plane of the wall of building 2.
   (d) Explain why your answer to part (c) is larger than the initial speed (6.0 m/s) of the ball.

ANSWERS

MULTIPLE-CHOICE QUESTIONS

1. **E** The time of flight can be found by analyzing the vertical motion using the kinematics equation $d_y = v_{iy} \, \Delta t + \frac{1}{2} a_y \Delta t^2$. Because $v_{iy} = 0$, this equation becomes $d_y = \frac{1}{2} a_y \Delta t^2$, and solving for t gives $t_{fall} = \sqrt{2d_y/g}$. Substituting values gives $t_{fall} = \sqrt{2(80)/10} = \sqrt{160/10} = \sqrt{16}$, or $= \mathbf{4 \ s}$ (*College Physics* 8th ed. pages 62–68/9th ed. pages 63–71).

2. **C** Recalling that the x motion is constant velocity, the kinematics equation $v_x = D/\Delta t$ can give us the answer. Solving for D gives $D = v_x \Delta t$, showing that if D were doubled, it could only mean that v must have also doubled to have caused an increase in the displacement. Therefore, choice (C) is the only correct statement (*College Physics* 8th ed. pages 62–68/9th ed. pages 63–71).

3. **C** Here, we must use information about the first stone to solve for the fall time:

$$g = \frac{v_{fy} - v_{iy}}{t}$$

$$-10.0 \ \text{m/s}^2 = \frac{-30.0 \ \text{m/s} - (-10.0 \ \text{m/s})}{\Delta t}$$

or $\Delta t = 2.0$ s. Next, calculate the cliff height (i.e., the displacement of the stone) using $v_f^2 = v_i^2 + 2gd$, which gives $(-30.0 \ \text{m/s})^2 = (-10.0 \ \text{m/s})^2 + 2(-10 \ \text{m/s}^2)d$, or $d = -40.0$ m. For the second stone ($v_{iy} = 0$), find v_{fy} using $v_{fy}^2 = v_{iy}^2 + 2gd$, which becomes $v_{fy}^2 = (0)^2 + 2(-10 \ \text{m/s}^2)(-40.0 \ \text{m})$, or $v_{fy} = -28.0 \ \text{m/s}$. Because $v_f = \sqrt{v_{fy}^2 + v_{fx}^2}$ is the Pythagorean theorem for the right triangle vector equation as the stone impacts the ground and because v_{fx} is 10.0 m/s, the answer becomes

$$v_f = \sqrt{v_{fy}^2 + v_{fx}^2}$$

$$v_f = \sqrt{(-28.3 \text{ m/s})^2 + (10.0 \text{ m/s})^2}$$

or v_f = **30.0 m/s** (*College Physics* 8th ed. pages 62–68/9th ed. pages 63–71).

4. **B** From the equations for constant acceleration in the vertical direction, use $d_y = v_{iy} \Delta t + \frac{1}{2} a_y \Delta t^2$, with $v_{iy} = 0$ and $d_y = H$, which becomes $H = \frac{1}{2} g \Delta t^2$. In addition, because the horizontal velocity V is given, the time to fall vertically must be found by realizing that it also equals the time to travel horizontally the distance D. Using the constant speed relation in the horizontal direction gives $D = V t_{fall}$, or $t_{fall} = D/V$. Thus, combining gives an expression for the height H as requested: $H = \frac{1}{2} g t^2 = H = \frac{1}{2} g (D/V)^2$, which is choice (B) (*College Physics* 8th ed. pages 62–68/9th ed. pages 63–71).

5. **C** The moment the bullet is launched, it already possesses the same horizontal velocity of the truck because it was on the vehicle prior to launch. In addition, because all projectiles travel with constant velocity in the x direction, the bullet will therefore always travel horizontally at 20.0 m/s and will remain over its launch point (as long as the truck's velocity does not change). Therefore, the person who fired the bullet will always be directly under it as it travels, and the bullet should land back at its starting point (*College Physics* 8th ed. pages 62–65/9th ed. pages 63–68).

6. **C** Recall that the vertical velocity at the top of the path ($v_{y\ top}$) is equal to zero (object stops momentarily). In addition, the horizontal velocity component given in this problem is immaterial because it has no bearing on the projectile's vertical motion. The time of flight for any projectile to its highest point can be calculated from

$$g = \frac{v_{y\ top} - v_{oy}}{t_{top}}$$

which becomes

$$-10.0 = \frac{0 - 40.0}{t_{top}}$$

or t_{top} = **4 s** (*College Physics* 8th ed. pages 62–68/9th ed. pages 63–71).

7. **C** First, find the fall time of the projectile using the equation for constant acceleration in the vertical direction, $d_y = v_{iy} \Delta t + \frac{1}{2} a_y \Delta t^2$, with $v_{iy} = 0$ and $d_y = H$, which becomes $H = \frac{1}{2} g \Delta t^2$, or $t_{fall} = \sqrt{2H/g}$. Substituting yields $t_{fall} = \sqrt{2(500)/10}$, or $t_{fall} = 10$ s. Horizontally, the projectile moves a distance R in this 10 s, and the relation that allows us to find R is given by $R = v t_{fall}$, which is from $v = D/t_{fall}$. Therefore,

$R = 42(10)$, or **R = 420 m** (*College Physics* 8th ed. pages 62–68/9th ed. pages 63–71).

8. **A** Because the horizontal motion of a projectile is constant velocity (i.e., no acceleration), the kinematics equation for displacement can be used to calculate the horizontal distance d_x: $d_x = v_{ix}\Delta t$, where the horizontal velocity component v_{ix} must be calculated from the right triangle relationship of $\cos 60° = v_{ix}/v_i$. Therefore, $v_{ix} = v_i \cos\theta$, or $v_{ix} = 30 \cos 60°$. Substituting yields $d_x = [30 \cos(60°)](2s)$, or **d_x = 30 m** (*College Physics* 8th ed. pages 57–60/9th ed. pages 58–62).

9. **E** In the horizontal (x) direction, we have $v_x = (D/\Delta t)$, which becomes $D = v_x\Delta t$ to show the linear relationship between D and v_x. Thus, if v_x were to double, it could only mean that D must also double (because the time to fall depends on the vertical height of the cliff, not on the horizontal distance). Therefore, choice (E) is the only correct statement. In addition, choices (A) through (D) cannot be correct because there exists a linear relation between the horizontal velocity of a projectile and the horizontal distance it covers (*College Physics* 8th ed. pages 67, 54–70/9th ed. pages 69, 56–71).

10. **A** Here, notice that the observer's horizontal speed of 11.0 m/s is exactly the same as the horizontal velocity component of the kicked ball, found by the right triangle relationship $v_{ix} = v_i \cos 60° = 22.0(0.5) = 11.0$ m/s. Therefore, because the ball and the observer are both moving horizontally at the same speed, the observer will see the ball directly in front of him. For the first half of the ball's trip, however, it ascends, which the observer sees as he follows the ball horizontally. At the top of the path, the ball will reverse direction and descend, but the observer will still be in line with the ball because both move off horizontally with the same speed, until the ball impacts the ground (*College Physics* 8th ed. pages 62–65/9th ed. pages 63–68).

11. **D** As a projectile ascends, its vertical *velocity* component decreases in magnitude due to the downward gravitational force exerted on it. As a result, its vertical velocity is zero at the peak of the trajectory (indicated by segment AX on the graph). Because the question asks about *velocity* (and not speed), *direction* of the projectile's vertical velocity on its downward descent is vital, which, although increasing in magnitude, is a *negative* value because it is pointing downward (negative direction). Therefore, segment AXB, and therefore choice (C), is eliminated, leaving the segment XE as the correct downward velocity. Thus, (D) is the correct choice (*College Physics* 8th ed. pages 62–65/9th ed. pages 63–68).

12. **E** Again, use the kinematics equation in the vertical direction, $d_y = v_{iy}\Delta t + \frac{1}{2}a_y\Delta t^2$, with $v_{iy} = 0$ and $d_y = H$, which becomes $H = \frac{1}{2}g\Delta t^2$. Substituting yields $H = \frac{1}{2}(-10)(\frac{1}{10}) = \frac{1}{2}(-10)(\frac{1}{100}) = \frac{1}{2}(\frac{-10}{100}) = \frac{1}{2}(\frac{1}{10})$, or **H = 1/20 m**, which is equivalent to 0.05 m (division without a calculator is a must), or choice (E) (*College Physics* 8th ed. pages 62–68/9th ed. pages 63–71).

13. **D** For the fall time, the most crucial piece of the problem is that stone A will travel in a large parabolic arc before reaching the horizontal line marking its launch point, all in time t_1. Thereafter, the time to fall height H will be called t_2. Clearly, because stone B covers only time t_2, the time for stone A must be greater by the sum $t_1 + t_2$. Therefore, t_A will be greater than t_B. Mathematically, we can solve by using

$$g = \frac{v_{y\ top} - v_{oy}}{t_{top}}$$

Therefore, the time for the full trip along the arc for stone A is, by symmetry, twice the time to the top (t_{top}). Keeping in mind that $v_{y\,top} = 0$, we have $t_{total} = 2t_{top} = 2v_{oy}/g$, which we will call t_1 as described above. In addition, both stones must fall through height H, whose fall time can be found by $H = \frac{1}{2}gt^2$, or $t_{fall} = \sqrt{2H/g}$, which we will call t_2 as described above. Therefore, the travel time for stone A, $t_1 + t_2$, becomes $2v_{oy}/g + \sqrt{2H/g}$. The travel time for stone B, however, is only t_2, which is just $\sqrt{2H/g}$. Therefore, t_B must be greater than t_A. So, either choice (A) or (D) may be correct at this point.

For the impact speed, we can use the right triangle composed of the horizontal and vertical velocity components to find the final velocity by $v_f = \sqrt{v_{fy}^2 + v_{fx}^2}$, where v_{fy} can be calculated by $v_{fy}^2 = v_{oy}^2 + 2gH$.

The difference between the two stones, however, is that stone A has a smaller horizontal component than stone B simply because of the nonzero launch angle. Stone A's v_{fx} will be smaller by a factor of $\sin \theta$; all stone B's horizontal velocity, however, is equal to its launch velocity. The final vertical velocities of the stones (v_{fy}) differ also, but in the opposite sense. Stone A's final vertical velocity component is larger than that of stone B due to the extra term v_{oy} in the equation at the end of the previous paragraph. Stone B, because it was launched horizontally, has no v_{oy} component and therefore has a smaller v_{fy} velocity component. As a result, both stones impact with the same speed. Therefore, choice (D) is the only correct answer (*College Physics* 8th ed. pages 62–68/9th ed. pages 63–71).

14. **A** Recall that the horizontal velocity of a projectile remains constant during its motion and that the motions discussed in kinematics are independent of the projectile's mass. The vertical motion, however, is not constant velocity and is affected by the acceleration due to gravity, and both balls will experience this effect equally, independent of mass. (Their velocities will change equally, however, bear in mind that the *force* on each does depend on the individual masses.) Without air resistance, each ball will therefore travel in the same manner both vertically and horizontally (*College Physics* 8th ed. pages 42–44/9th ed. pages 43–45).

15. **A** Because projectile motion is a case of free fall (motion under the action of only gravitation), the only possible direction for the

acceleration of any projected object must be toward the center of Earth, or toward the ground, below the projectile. Notice that, under the action of only gravity, there is no horizontal acceleration (or component of such an acceleration), which therefore eliminates all other choices (*College Physics* 8th ed. pages 42–44, 62–65/9th ed. pages 63–68).

FREE-RESPONSE PROBLEMS

1. (a) This question involves basic trigonometry of the right triangle as shown here:

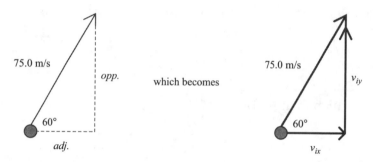

Thus, $\sin 60° = v_{iy}/75.0$ and $\cos 60° = v_{ix}/75.0$ so that v_{iy} = **65.0 m/s** and v_{ix} = **38.0 m/s** (*College Physics* 8th ed. pages 57–60/9th ed. pages 58–62).

(b) To calculate the time the ball is airborne until it reaches the wall, it is necessary to calculate the time it travels horizontally for the entire 27.0 m distance to the wall. Therefore, we can use the displacement equation in the x direction: $d_x = v_{ix} \Delta t + \frac{1}{2}a_x \Delta t^2$, and because $a_x = 0$ for all projectiles, it is just $d_x = v_{ix} \Delta t$ Therefore, substituting yields 27.0 m = (38.0 m/s)(Δt), or Δt = **0.7 s** (*College Physics* 8th ed. pages 62–68/9th ed. pages 63–71).

(c) Here, it is necessary to calculate the vertical distance d_y of the ball the moment it has traveled horizontally for 27.0 m, or simply for 0.7 s. Using the same equation (but in the y direction), $d_y = v_{iy} \Delta t + \frac{1}{2}a_y \Delta t^2$, and because no term is zero, we have $d_y = (65.0$ m/s$)(0.7$ s$) + \frac{1}{2}(-10.0$ m/s$^2)(0.7$ s$)^2 = 43$ m above the ground. Thus, the height of the ball above the wall is 43 m – 11.0 m, or **32.0 m** (*College Physics* 8th ed. pages 62–68/9th ed. pages 63–71).

(d) Because all horizontal motion of projectiles is constant velocity motion, this plot of v_{ix} is a horizontal straight line. In addition, when the ball reaches the plane of the wall, it has traveled for only 0.7 s and thus the line must end at $t = 0.7$ s on the plot. From part (a), the value for v_{ix} is 38.0 m/s. The plot is as shown (*College Physics* 8th ed. pages 57–60, 62–68/9th ed. pages 63–71).

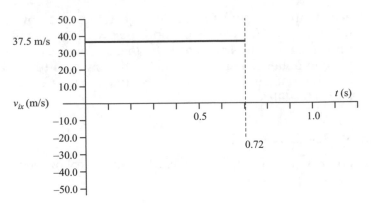

(e) Find the time to the maximum height, where $v_y = 0$, using $a = \Delta v / \Delta t$, or

$$g = \frac{v_{fy} - v_{iy}}{\Delta t_{top}}$$

which then becomes

$$-10.0 \text{ m/s}^2 = \frac{0 - 65 \text{ m/s}}{\Delta t_{top}}$$

Solving for the time to the top gives 6.5 s, which suggests that the ball passes over the wall well before it ever reaches its highest point. Remember that the time calculated in part (b) was only 0.7 s (*College Physics* 8th ed. pages 62–68/9th ed. pages 63–71).

2. (a) To determine the time the ball is airborne until it reaches the wall of apartment building 2, it is necessary to calculate the time it travels horizontally for the entire 16.0-m distance to the wall. Therefore, we can use $d = v_i \Delta t + \frac{1}{2} a \Delta t^2$ in the x direction, which becomes $d_x = v_{ix} \Delta t + \frac{1}{2} a_x \Delta t^2$. Because $a_x = 0$ for all projectiles, it is just $d_x = v_{ix} \Delta t$. Therefore, 16.0 m = (6.0 m/s)(Δt), or Δt = **2.7 s** (*College Physics* 8th ed. pages 62–68/9th ed. pages 63–71).

(b) Again, similar to question 1 above, it is necessary to calculate the vertical distance d_y of the ball the moment it has traveled horizontally for 16.0 m, or simply for 2.7 s (from the previous question). Therefore, we can still use the same equation, but now in the y direction: $d_y = v_{iy} \Delta t + \frac{1}{2} a_y \Delta t^2$. Notice, though, that because it is a horizontally shot projectile, $v_{iy} = 0$. Thus, $d_y = 0 + \frac{1}{2}(-10 \text{ m/s}^2)(2.7 \text{ s})^2 = -36.5$ m below launch level. The height of the ball above the ground is, then, 50.0 m – 34.8 m = 13.5 m. In terms of the window center, however, it must therefore be 28.0 m –13.5 m, or **14.5 m below the window center** (*College Physics* 8th ed. pages 62–68/9th ed. pages 63–71).

(c) To calculate the final speed of the ball just as it reaches the plane of the wall of apartment building 2, it is necessary to be sure to first find both v_{fy} and v_{fx} because the final speed is the magnitude of a vector sum as shown:

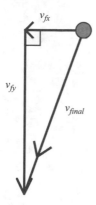

where v_{fx} is 6.0 m/s (constant speed for horizontal motion of a projectile) and v_{fy} can be found from $v_{fy}^2 = v_{iy}^2 + 2ad$ or $v_{fy}^2 = 0 + 2(-10\,\text{m/s}^2)(-36.5\,\text{m})$. Thus, v_{fy} is 27.0 m/s. According to the diagram and the Pythagorean theorem, we can thus write $v_{final}^2 = v_{fy}^2 + v_{fx}^2$ or $v_{final}^2 = (27.0 \text{ m/s})^2 + (6.0 \text{ m/s})^2$, which yields v_f as **27.0 m/s.** Notice that the question did *not* ask for *velocity*, which would have required including a direction with the answer (*College Physics* 8th ed. pages 57–60, 62–68/9th ed. pages 63–71).

(d) The large value for the final speed for the projectile when it has crossed 16.0 m is a result of the component nature of vector addition, and even though the projectile is moving horizontally at 6.0 m/s, it also acquires an increasing downward speed due to the acceleration due to gravity. Thus, when the vector sum (i.e., resultant) of these two velocities is calculated, the dominant speed in the vector equation is the downward one because it is so much larger (*College Physics* 8th ed. pages 57–60, 62–68/9th ed. pages 63–71).

3

NEWTON'S LAWS OF MOTION (STATICS)

(*College Physics* 8th ed. pages 83–86, 94–108/9th ed. pages 86–88, 95–105, 105–112)

The heart of classical physics is undoubtedly dominated by the strength and prevalence of Newton's laws of motion, three strict and time-proven rules that govern everything from blocks sliding on tables to stars orbiting the centers of galaxies. Originally formulated by English physicist Sir Isaac Newton (1642–1727) during the 1680s, these laws, along with Newton's law of gravitation, are generally considered to be the ultimate solution to a problem that had troubled scholars for more than 2000 years: the causes of the motion of objects under the action of outside forces.

NEWTON'S FIRST LAW (THE LAW OF INERTIA) AND EQUILIBRIUM

(*College Physics* 8th ed. pages 85–86, 94–97, 101–104/9th ed. pages 86–88, 95–105, 105–112)

Newton boldly proposed and proved that the motion of objects can be described using only three statements, or laws, the apex of which is the delineation of how motions relate to a force (a push or pull). Recognized by many before him but first formally presented by him is the law of inertia. As translated from Newton's work *The Principia*, the law of inertia reads:

Every body persists in its state of being at rest or of moving uniformly straight forward, except insofar as it is compelled to change its state by force impressed.

In short, the first law states that if something is at rest, it will remain in that state unless an outside force (i.e., net, unbalanced, or resultant force) acts on it, and when such a net force acts, the object has a tendency to experience a change of velocity. Similarly, if the object is moving with constant velocity, it will remain in that state unless, again, a net force acts to alter its motion. In either case, the object is in equilibrium: *static equilibrium* if it is stationary and *dynamic equilibrium* if it is moving at constant velocity. In both cases, equilibrium means *zero net force* and thus *zero acceleration*.

Upon closer examination, the law of inertia is actually a statement of equilibrium, or the condition in which an object is not accelerating and all forces acting on it are equal in size but opposite in direction (i.e., they are balanced). An example is a 3.0-kg book at rest on a table. Making a sketch of all the forces on the book (called a *free-body diagram*) is the first essential aspect of starting any force problem. First, the book is acted upon by the downward pull of gravity, indicated in the free-body diagram by the vector w (for weight, although some textbooks use F_g). Because the book is supported by the table and the book is at rest, the table's support force must be equal to the book's weight, but is directed upward. This force, called the "normal" force, is labeled N (again, some textbooks use F_N) and is represented as shown:

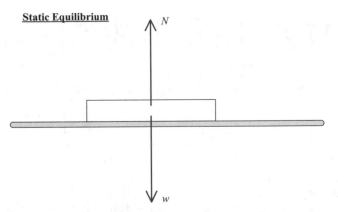

Static Equilibrium

If we take the addition of the forces, this becomes $N + (-w)$ because we must remember that down and to the left are negative vectors. Since the book is at rest, it must mean that both N and w balance and are thus equal. Therefore, their sum must be zero, which is the cornerstone of the law of inertia as well as the subject of statics, where Σ means to add (or "sum") the forces acting on the object:

> $\Sigma F = 0$ is the condition for static equilibrium.

In the metric system (i.e., SI system), the unit of force is the newton, in honor of the noted physicist, and it is the unit of force used exclusively on the AP Exam in Physics. To conceptualize the size of a newton, note it is the equivalent of about a fifth of a pound of force in the English system. Also, a newton is about the weight of an apple, or about the force needed to flick a light switch on or off. A more useful piece of information is that at the surface of Earth, the weight of a 1-kg mass is 9.8 N. The relationship between mass and weight is defined by Newton's second law (discussed below). An object's weight (w) is calculated using

$$w = mg$$

Thus, in the previous diagram, the object's weight is $w = 3.0$ kg $(9.8$ m/s$^2) = 29.4$ N. Therefore, the value of the normal force N acting on the book is found by applying $\Sigma F = 0$, which upon substitution becomes $N + (-w) = 0$, or $N = w$ as expected. Thus, $N = 29.0$ N.

A similar situation occurs if we tie a string to the book and then pull it slowly to the right along the tabletop with a horizontal force of 12.0 N. Because we have introduced a force that is perpendicular to both N and w, we must distinguish these directions and usually do so with x and y axes. In addition to the pull to the right, there is a slowing frictional force to the left ("kinetic" friction because the object is in motion, denoted f_k). Friction is an opposing force that tends to reduce the forward motion of an object. If the pulling force (or tension, T) is small enough such that the book is moving at constant velocity, the acceleration is zero. Then, the condition of equilibrium must be applied to both x and y directions:

$\Sigma F_x = 0$ and $\Sigma F_y = 0$ are the conditions for
dynamic equilibrium.

Dynamic Equilibrium
(constant velocity to the right)

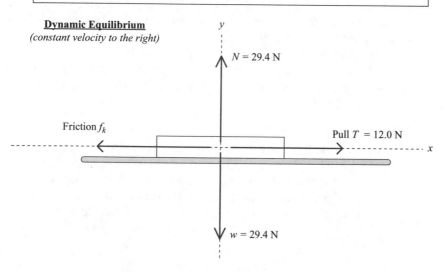

As shown earlier, $\Sigma F_y = 0$ gave $N + (-w) = 0$, or $N = w$ as expected. Thus, $N = 29.4$ N. Now, though, we have a way to solve for the friction force: $\Sigma F_x = 0$ gives $T + (-f_k) = 0$, or $f_k = T$, and the kinetic friction force is 12.0 N.

AP Tip

When preparing to start a statics or dynamics problem, get into the *immediate* habit of sketching a free-body diagram.

AP Tip

Remember that $\Sigma F = 0$ is the "sum" of the forces, which means simply to *add the forces* (keeping + and − for direction) and equate this result to zero. That is the meaning of equilibrium: *balanced forces*.

AP Tip

Be attentive to terms such as *constant velocity* (a problem of *dynamic* equilibrium) and *at rest* (*static* equilibrium). Both indicate that *acceleration is zero*.

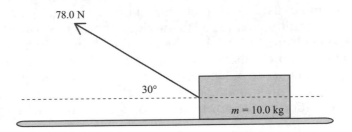

SAMPLE PROBLEM 1

A box of mass 10.0 kg is slid across a floor using a massless rope angled at 30° relative to the horizontal as shown. The box moves at constant velocity, and the tension in the rope is 78.0 N.

(a) Sketch a free-body diagram for the box.

(b) Determine the normal force exerted on the box by the floor.

(c) Determine the force of kinetic friction acting between the box and the floor.

SOLUTION TO PROBLEM 1

(a) When sketching the free-body diagram, realize that N is not the same length as w because part of the tension pulls partly upward (a component, as described in the discussion on vectors and projectiles in Chapter 2). Also notice that the diagram contains only the forces acting, and not their components.

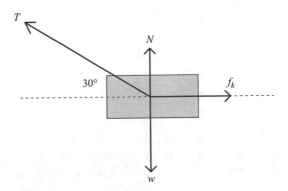

(b) Here, because we have a situation of dynamic equilibrium, we write and apply the conditions of equilibrium: $\Sigma F_y = 0$ becomes $T_y + N - w = 0$ (notice the components of T drawn below), or

$$N = w - T_y \quad (1)$$

Similarly, $\Sigma F_x = 0$ gives $-T_x + (f_k) = 0$, or

$$f_k = T_x \quad (2)$$

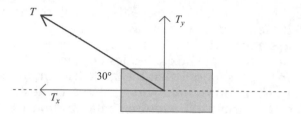

Using the trigonometry of the tension and its components as well as Equation (1) above, we can then find the value of N:
$N = w - T_y$ becomes $N = (10.0 \text{ kg})(9.8 \text{ m/s}^2) - 78.0 \text{ N} (\sin 30°)$, or **$N = 59.0 \text{ N}$**.

(c) From the conditions of equilibrium as done in part (b), this becomes $\Sigma F_x = 0$ gives $-T_x + (f_k) = 0$, or $f_k = T_x$. Note, however, that $T_x = T \cos \theta$. Therefore, $f_k = T \cos \theta = (78.0 \text{ N}) \cos 30° = $ **68.0 N** = **friction force**.

FRICTION: SUBTLE DIFFERENCES

(*College Physics* 8th ed. pages 101–104/9th ed. pages 105–112)

Friction (encompassed in the field of *tribology*) in AP Physics is very basic and comes in two forms: kinetic friction (f_k, as seen already), for situations in which objects slide against a surface, and static friction (f_s), for situations in which static equilibrium occurs but when forces *could* cause motion.

In a world without friction, Newton's laws of motion would be fairly straightforward, but such a world does not exist in our everyday lives. In reality, when objects move against each other, the surfaces constantly rub and grip because, microscopically, there are very minute "hills" and "valleys" onto which objects can grab. In addition, dirt and oils can impede the objects' motion by filling these gaps, acting as adhesives. That is essentially the heart of frictional forces, and, most important, such forces always act to retard, impede, or hinder the forward movement of an object. Such examples exist all around us: walking, moving parts in an engine, a hurricane's impact along a shoreline, a car's tires against the road, and so on.

Two major variables dominate the force of friction. First, close examination of two surfaces in contact reveal great variations in smoothness and texture, and in physics, the variable coefficient of friction (letter μ, which is dimensionless) describes the surface roughness in question. For example, a dirt roadway has a higher coefficient of friction than does an ice-skating rink, and such values typically range from 0.0 to 1.0 (the lower the number, the smoother and more slippery the surfaces in contact). Similarly, friction is also affected by the normal force acting on the object by the surface. For example, in winter when roads are covered with ice and snow, it is typically the smaller, less massive cars that have more trouble achieving traction than large trucks with much higher weights. Therefore, our basic friction equation can be written as

> force of friction = (coefficient of friction)(normal force exerted by the surface)   or $f = \mu N$

Imagine a large, heavy box resting on a floor that you gradually start to pull. If the box doesn't move with a small pull, it is safe to assume an opposing static friction force is acting on the box that prevents you from moving it. What if the box still does not move when you increase your pulling force? It suggests that the static friction force increased as well and will further do so until your pull overcomes the microscopic grip between the surfaces. Therefore, static friction forces increase under the action of an applied force until a maximum value is reached. Kinetic friction, on the other hand, does not behave this way and is constant during the motion of an object against a surface. We can therefore write

$$f_k = \mu_k N$$

$$f_{s\,max} = \mu_s N \quad (\text{otherwise, } f_s \leq \mu_s N)$$

Sample Problem 2

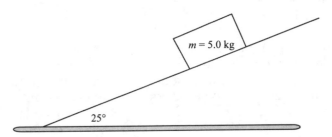

A box of mass 5.0 kg is at rest on an inclined surface angled at 25° relative to the horizontal as shown.
  (a) Sketch a free-body diagram for the box.
  (b) Determine the normal force exerted on the box by the inclined surface.
  (c) Determine the force of static friction acting between the box and the incline necessary to hold the box in place.

Solution to Problem 2
  (a) A free-body sketch is as shown.

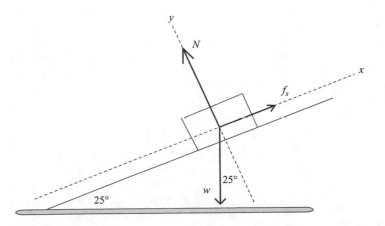

  (b) Here, it is necessary to realize that w has components, with w sin 25° being the x component and w cos 25° opposite N along the negative y axis. $\Sigma F_y = 0$ becomes $N - w_y = 0$, or $N = mg \cos \theta$, which becomes $(5.0 \text{ kg})(9.8 \text{ m/s}^2) \cos 25°$. Therefore, **$N = 44.0$ N.**

(c) In this case, $\Sigma F_x = 0$ gives $-w_x + (f_s) = 0$, or $f_s = w_x$. Therefore, $f_s = w \sin 25° = (5.0 \text{ kg})(9.8 \text{ m/s}^2) \sin 25°$, or **$f_s = 21.0$ N.**

SAMPLE PROBLEM 3

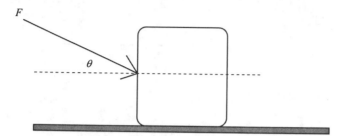

A box of mass M is pushed along a rough, horizontal floor at constant velocity by a force of magnitude F at an angle θ relative to the horizontal as shown. The coefficient of kinetic friction between the box and the floor is μ.

(a) Sketch and label the forces acting on the box.

(b) Determine an expression for the frictional force between the box and the floor in terms of the following variables: g, M, T, μ, θ.

SOLUTION TO PROBLEM 3

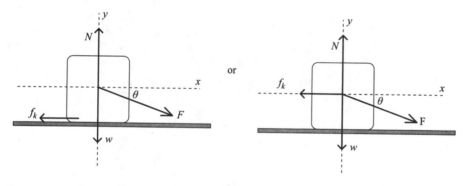

(a) Shown above are two possibilities.

(b) Realize that the applied force F is the only vector with x and y components. We can apply the conditions of equilibrium: $\Sigma F_x = 0$ gives $-f_k + (F_x) = 0$, or $f_k = F_x$, which is

$$f_k = F \cos \theta \qquad (1)$$

Likewise, $\Sigma F_y = 0$ becomes $N - w - F_y = 0$, or $N = w + F_y$, which is

$$N = w + F \sin \theta \qquad (2)$$

Keeping in mind that the question asks for an expression for f_k in terms of the other variables, notice that $f_k = \mu_k N$, which can be used here with Equation (2). So, $f_k = \mu_k N = \mu_k (w + F \sin \theta)$, or **$f_k = \mu_k (mg + F \sin \theta)$**, which contains all the requested variables.

SAMPLE PROBLEM 4

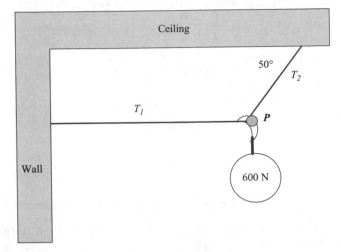

A hooked weight of 600.0 N is hung from two cables with tensions T_1 and T_2 as shown.

(a) Sketch a free-body diagram at point P.
(b) Determine the numerical values of each tension T_1 and T_2.

SOLUTION TO PROBLEM 4

(a) This is the necessary free-body diagram.

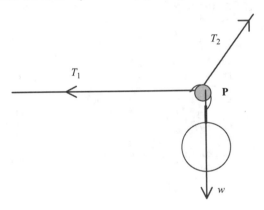

(b) We can apply the conditions of equilibrium: $\Sigma F_x = 0$ gives $-T_1 + (T_{2x}) = 0$, or $T_1 = T_{2x}$, which is

$$T_1 = T_2 \cos 50° \quad (1)$$

Likewise, $\Sigma F_y = 0$ becomes $T_{2y} - 600 = 0$, or $T_{2y} = 600$, which is

$$T_2 \sin 50° = 600 \quad (2)$$

Using Equation (2), solve for T_2: $T_2 = \textbf{783.0 N}$. Then substitute that value back into Equation (1), a common AP problem-solving requirement, solving two systems of equations with two unknown variables. Therefore, $T_1 = T_2 \cos 50° = (783.2 \text{ N}) \cos 50°$, or $T_1 = \textbf{503.0 N}$.

STATICS: STUDENT OBJECTIVES FOR THE AP EXAM

- Know how to analyze situations in which a particle remains at rest, or moves with a constant velocity, under the influence of several forces (i.e., be able to apply two conditions of equilibrium: $\Sigma F_x = 0$ and $\Sigma F_y = 0$).
- Know and write the relationship between the normal and frictional forces on a surface.
- Know how to analyze situations in which a body is pulled or pushed across a rough surface.
- Know how to analyze situations involving friction to calculate the magnitude of the force of friction.
- Know how to solve systems of two equations by substitution.

MULTIPLE-CHOICE QUESTIONS

1. Which of the following are necessary for an object to be in equilibrium: I, net velocity = 0 m/s; II, net acceleration = 0 m/s²; or III, net force = 0 N.
    (A) I only
    (B) III only
    (C) I and III only
    (D) II and III only
    (E) I, II, and III

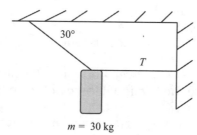

$m = 30$ kg

2. A 30.0-kg box hangs from two different cables as shown above. What is the tension T in the right cable? (*Note:* $\sin 30° = \dfrac{1}{2}$ and $\cos 30° = 0.866$.)
    (A) 175.0 N
    (B) 300.0 N
    (C) 450.0 N
    (D) 520.0 N
    (E) 600.0 N

3. A 40-kg crate is suspended from a beam by two vertical ropes. What is the tension in each rope?
    (A) 10.0 N
    (B) 40.0 N
    (C) 100.0 N
    (D) 200.0 N
    (E) 400.0 N

4.

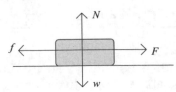

A boy pulls a wooden box along a rough, horizontal floor at a constant speed by means of a force F as shown. Which of the following must be true?
(A) $F > f$ and $N < w$
(B) $F = f$ and $N > w$
(C) $F = f$ and $N = w$
(D) $F > f$ and $N = w$
(E) None of those choices is true.

5.

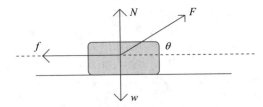

A boy pulls a wooden box along a rough, horizontal floor at a constant speed by means of a force F as shown above. Which of the following must be true?
(A) $F > f$ and $N < w$
(B) $F = f$ and $N > w$
(C) $F = f$ and $N = w$
(D) $F > f$ and $N = w$
(E) None of those choices is true.

6. A brick slides on a level, horizontal surface. Which of the following will increase the frictional force between it and the surface that is in contact with it?
(A) decreasing the surface area in contact
(B) putting a second brick on top of it
(C) increasing the surface area in contact
(D) decreasing the mass of the brick
(E) None of those choices will increase the frictional force.

7.

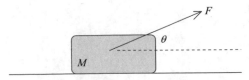

A block of mass M is pulled at a constant speed along a rough, horizontal floor by an applied force F as shown. What is the frictional force acting between the block and surface on which it is sliding equivalent to?
(A) $\mu F (\cos \theta)$
(B) μMg
(C) zero
(D) $F \sin \theta$
(E) $F \cos \theta$

8. A woman stands on a bathroom scale in an elevator that is not moving. The scale reads 500.0 N. The elevator then moves downward at a constant velocity of 5 m/s. What does the scale read while the elevator descends with constant velocity?
    (A) 100.0 N
    (B) 250.0 N
    (C) 450.0 N
    (D) 500.0 N
    (E) 750.0 N

9.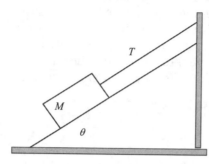

    A block of mass M is held motionless on a frictionless, inclined plane by means of a string attached to a vertical wall as shown. What is the magnitude of the tension T in the string?
    (A) zero
    (B) $Mg (\sin \theta)$
    (C) $Mg (\cos \theta)$
    (D) $Mg (\tan \theta)$
    (E) Mg

10.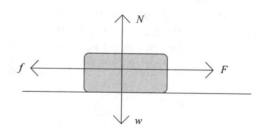

    If the coefficient of kinetic friction μ_k between the block and the surface shown is 0.30 and the magnitude of the frictional force is 80.0 N, which is the approximate weight of the block?
    (A) 1.6 N
    (B) 4.0 N
    (C) 160.0 N
    (D) 270.0 N
    (E) 410.0 N

11. A car travels east with a constant velocity. What is the net force on the car?
    (A) zero
    (B) east
    (C) west
    (D) north
    (E) south

12. What are the units of the coefficient of friction?
    (A) newtons
    (B) newtons²
    (C) kilograms per newton
    (D) The coefficient of friction has no units.
    (E) m/s²N

13. An astronaut orbits Earth in a space capsule whose height above Earth is equal to Earth's radius. How does the inertial mass of the astronaut in the capsule compare to her gravitational mass on Earth?
    (A) It is equal to one-third her mass on Earth.
    (B) It is equal to one-half her mass on Earth.
    (C) It is equal to her mass on Earth.
    (D) It is equal to one-fourth her mass on Earth.
    (E) It is equal to one-sixteenth her mass on Earth.

14.

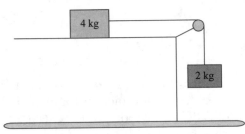

A 4.0-kg block is connected by means of a massless rope to a 2.0-kg block as shown. If the 4.0-kg block is to begin sliding, what must be the coefficient of static friction between that block and the surface?
    (A) less than zero
    (B) greater than 2.0
    (C) greater than 1.0 but less than 2.0
    (D) greater than 0.5 but less than 1.0
    (E) less than 0.5 but greater than zero

15.

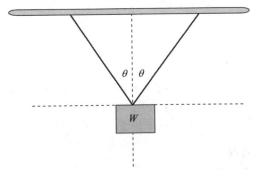

When an object of weight W is suspended from the center of a massless string as shown, what is the tension at any point in the string?
    (A) $2W(\cos \theta)$

    (B) $\dfrac{W \cos \theta}{2}$

    (C) $W(\cos \theta)$

    (D) $\dfrac{W}{2 \cos \theta}$

    (E) $\dfrac{W}{\cos \theta}$

FREE-RESPONSE PROBLEMS

1.

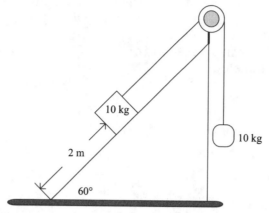

Two 10.0-kg boxes are connected by a massless string that passes over a massless, frictionless pulley as shown. The boxes remain at rest, with the one on the right hanging vertically and the one on the left 2.0 m from the bottom of an inclined plane that makes an angle of 60° relative to the horizontal. The coefficient of static friction between the left-hand box and the incline is 0.30.

(a) On the diagram, draw and label all the forces acting on the box that is on the plane.

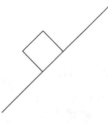

(b) Determine the tension in the string.
(c) Determine the magnitude of the frictional force acting on the box that is at rest on the incline.

2.

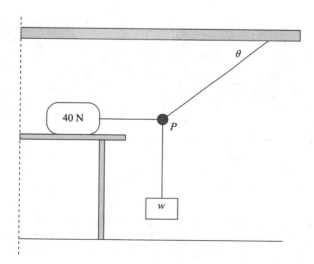

As shown, a 40.0-N block remains at rest on a rough tabletop. It has one massless cord attached to it that is also connected at point P to a similar vertical cord attached to weight w as well as to a third cord angled at $\theta = 30^\circ$ relative to a ceiling. The entire apparatus remains in static equilibrium.

(a) Sketch a free-body diagram for the 40.0-N block on the tabletop.

(b) Sketch a free-body diagram for the hanging weight w.

(c) Sketch a free-body diagram at point P.

(d) Determine the maximum value that w can have if the friction force on the 40.0-N block cannot exceed 12.0 N.

(e) What is the coefficient of friction between the block and the tabletop?

ANSWERS

MULTIPLE-CHOICE QUESTIONS

1. **D** From the definition of equilibrium, an object must be moving at constant velocity or be at rest, which means it cannot be accelerating. An object could have a net velocity of zero and be in equilibrium, but it is not a requirement (an example of which is dynamic equilibrium) (*College Physics* 8th ed. pages 94–97/9th ed. pages 95–105).

2. **D** Sketch a free-body diagram. Resolve the upper tension (T_1) into its components and apply $\Sigma F_x = 0$ and $\Sigma F_y = 0$ to the situation, which gives $\Sigma F_x = 0$, or $T_1 \sin 30 - mg = 0$. Solving for T_1 gives $\boldsymbol{T_1 = 2\ mg}$. Similarly, $\Sigma F_y = 0$, or $-T_1 \cos 30^\circ + T_2 = 0$. Therefore, $\boldsymbol{T = T_1 \cos 30^\circ}$. Substituting $T_1 = 2\ mg$ to eliminate gives $T = (2\ mg) \cos 30^\circ$, or $T = 600(0.866)$, or **520.0 N** (*College Physics* 8th ed. pages 94–97/9th ed. pages 95–105).

3. **D** A quick free-body diagram shows that two vertical cables will equally support the entire weight of the body (which is 400.0 N, *not* 40.0 kg). Therefore, each cable must support only 200.0 N (*College Physics* 8th ed. pages 94–97/9th ed. pages 95–105).

4. **C** Noting that there are no vectors with any components here (i.e., no angles), $\Sigma F_x = 0$ and $\Sigma F_y = 0$ when applied to this diagram clearly show that N must balance w and F must balance f. Therefore, only choice (C) is correct (*College Physics* 8th ed. pages 94–97/9th ed. pages 95–105).

5. **A** This question differs from Question 4 because vector components must be considered in the application of the conditions of static equilibrium. First, $\Sigma F_x = 0$ gives $\Sigma F_x = 0$, or $-f + F_x = 0$, or $f = F_x$. Because F_x is $F \cos \theta$, it must be smaller than F. Therefore, f must be less than F ($f < F$). Similarly, when we apply $\Sigma F_y = 0$, we get $N + F_y = w$, or $N = w - F \cos \theta$ (because $F_y = F \cos \theta$). Thus, N must be smaller than w ($N < w$). Therefore, choice (A) is correct (*College Physics* 8th ed. pages 94–97/9th ed. pages 95–105).

6. **B** Because the frictional force equation is $f = \mu N$, this force depends directly on the normal force, which, for an object on a flat, level surface, equals the weight. Therefore, if the weight is increased, the normal force is increased and thus the frictional force is increased as well (*College Physics* 8th ed. pages 101–104/9th ed. pages 105–112).

7. **E** Apply the conditions of static equilibrium to both the x and y directions. First, $\Sigma F_x = 0$ gives $\Sigma F_x = 0$, or $-f_k + F \cos \theta = 0$, or $\boldsymbol{f_k = F \cos \theta}$. Similarly, when we apply $\Sigma F_y = 0$, we get $N + F \sin \theta - w = 0$, or $\boldsymbol{N = w - F \sin \theta}$. Thus, choice (E) is correct (*College Physics* 8th ed. pages 94–97, 101–104/9th ed. pages 95–105, 105–112).

8. **D** Because it is stated that the elevator is moving with constant velocity (up or down makes no difference), we have a state of dynamic equilibrium and thus no acceleration or net force exists. Therefore, the person's weight is unchanged at 500.0 N (*College Physics* 8th ed. pages 94–97/9th ed. pages 95–105).

9. **B** Apply the conditions of static equilibrium to both the x and y directions (x is along the incline, parallel to the rope, and y is perpendicular to it). First, $\Sigma F_x = 0$ gives $\Sigma F_x = 0$, or $T - w \sin \theta = 0$, or $\boldsymbol{T = Mg \sin \theta}$. Similarly, in the y direction we find $\Sigma F_y = 0$, or $N - w \cos \theta = 0$, or $\boldsymbol{N = Mg \cos \theta}$. Thus, from the x direction information, choice (B) is correct (*College Physics* 8th ed. pages 94–97/9th ed. pages 95–105).

10. **D** Given $\mu_k = 0.3$ and $f_k = 80.0$ N, we can find the weight of the object by realizing that the normal force in this case equals the object's weight. Therefore, $f_k = \mu_k N$, or $80.0 = \dfrac{3}{10} N$. Thus, $N = 800/3$, or $N \sim 266.0$ N. So, the object's **weight is ~ 266.0 N**, closest to choice (D) (*College Physics* 8th ed. pages 94–97, 101–104/9th ed. pages 95–105, 105–112).

11. **A** A situation of dynamic equilibrium implies that no net force exists on the object and thus no acceleration occurs. Therefore, choice (A) is correct (*College Physics* 8th ed. pages 94–97/9th ed. pages 95–105).

12. **D** Given that $f = \mu N$ and $f/N = \mu$, we know that force of friction divided by normal force has units of newtons per newtons, which cancel. Therefore, the coefficient of friction is dimensionless (*College Physics* 8th ed. pages 101–104/9th ed. pages 105–112).

13. **C** Mass is the inherent property of matter that defines the amount of material in a specific volume. Because that amount of material is constant under resting or accelerating conditions, both gravitational and inertial masses are equal (*College Physics* 8th ed. pages 94–97, 101–104/9th ed. pages 95–105, 105–112).

14. **E** Applying the conditions of static equilibrium to both blocks gives $N = 40.0$ and $f_{s\,max} = T$ for the first block on the tabletop. For the hanging block, we have $T = 20.0$ N. The moment the block starts to slip, the condition $f_{s\,max} = \mu_s N$ applies, and from the above we can see that $20.0 = f_{s\,max} = \mu_s(40.0)$. Therefore, $\mu_s = \mathbf{0.5}$. So, if the block is to just begin to slide, the coefficient of static friction must be less than 0.5. If it were larger, the block would remain stationary (*College Physics* 8th ed. pages 94–97, 101–104/9th ed. pages 95–105, 105–112).

15. **D** Applying the conditions of static equilibrium in the y direction gives $\Sigma F_y = 0$, or $T \cos \theta + T \cos \theta - mg = 0$, or $2\,T \cos \theta = mg$.

Therefore, $T = \dfrac{mg}{2 \cos \theta}$, or $T = \dfrac{W}{2 \cos \theta}$ (*College Physics* 8th ed. pages 94–97/9th ed. pages 95–105).

FREE-RESPONSE PROBLEMS

1. (a)

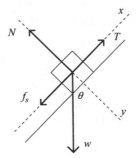

(b) Applying the conditions of static equilibrium to the hanging mass gives $\Sigma F_y = 0$, and we get $T - w = 0$, or $T = mg = 10$ kg (9.8 m/s²), or $\boldsymbol{T = 98.0}$ **N**. Because the pulley simply changes the direction of this force, the tension in the string attached to the mass on the incline is also 98.0 N.

(c) Unfortunately, because this mass is not on the verge of slipping, it is not possible to use the static friction equation ($f_{s\,max} = \mu_s N$), a common error often made in this situation. Instead, apply the conditions of static equilibrium to the left mass shown in the diagram below. First, $\Sigma F_x = 0$ gives $\Sigma F_x = 0$, or $-f_s - w \sin \theta + T = 0$. Therefore, $T = f_s + w \sin \theta$. Solving for the static friction force gives $f_s = T - w \sin \theta$. Substituting gives $f_s = 98.0$ N $- (98.$ N $\sin 60°)$, or $\boldsymbol{f_s}$ = **13.0 N**

(*College Physics* 8th ed. pages 94–97/9th ed. pages 95–105)

2.

(a)

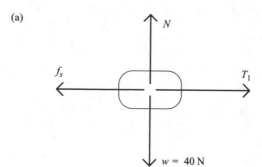

(b)

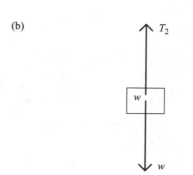

(c)

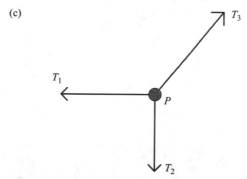

(d) Notice that the maximum value of the static friction force is 12.0 N, and from the three previous free-body diagrams, applying $\Sigma F_x = 0$ and $\Sigma F_y = 0$ gives $N = 40$ N, $f_{s\,max} = T_1$, $w = T_2$, $T_1 = T_3 \cos\theta$, and $T_2 = T_3 \sin\theta$. Because $w = T_2$ and $T_2 = T_3 \sin\theta$, we can write $w = T_3 \sin\theta$, and from the following, we can determine the value of T_3: $T_1 = T_3 \cos\theta = 12.0$, or $T_3 = 12/(\cos 30°) = 13.9$ N. Then, w can be calculated (from the equations above): $w = T_2$ and $T_2 = T_3 \sin\theta$. Therefore, $w = T_3 \sin\theta$, or $w = 13.9 \sin 30°$, or **$w = 7.0$ N.**

(e) From the previous free-body diagrams and because $f_{s\,max}$ is 12.0 N, then T_1 is also 12.0 N, which can be substituted as follows: $T_1 = T_3 \cos\theta = 12.0 = \mu_s N$. Thus, $12.0 = \mu_s(40.0)$, or **$\mu_s = 0.3$.**

(*College Physics* 8th ed. pages 94–97, 101–104/9th ed. pages 95–105, 105–112)

4

Newton's Laws of Motion (Dynamics)

Newton's Second Law of Change and Velocity

(*College Physics* 8th ed. pages 83–92, 94–108/9th ed. pages 86–95, 98–112)

In contrast to Chapter 3, in which the motion of an object was restricted to either rest or constant velocity, the heart of physics lies with Newton's second law, which concentrates on problems dealing with changes of velocity, or *acceleration*. That is what dynamics is all about: objects accelerating under the action of a net force. Taken directly from Newton's impressive work *The Principia* and a 1729 Latin translation, his second law of motion states:

The alteration of motion is ever proportional to the motive force impress'd; and is made in the direction of the right line in which that force is impress'd.

Physicists and scholars have since come to agree that "alteration of motion" refers to a change in velocity of an object (more specifically, "momentum") that is directly proportional to the push or pull (i.e., force) that caused it. This change of velocity (or acceleration) occurs in the direction of the imposed force. As experiments have shown, the rate of acceleration depends inversely on the mass of the object (i.e., the greater the mass, the lower the acceleration for a given force). Today's translation of Newton's second law is

The change of momentum of a body is proportional to the impulse impressed on the body, and happens along the straight line on which that impulse is impressed.

Although many students tend to forget such a long quote, most simply recall the mathematical format of the second law, which is

$$F_{net} = \Sigma F = ma$$

where the force F that causes the object's acceleration a must be a *net* (i.e., *resultant* or *unbalanced*) force acting on the mass m. Unfortunately, students often forget (or are not properly informed) that this force is a *net* force. In problems that encompass two dimensions, it will be necessary to apply $F_{net} = ma$ in each direction of motion in which acceleration occurs. Furthermore, one must be very keen and note that one direction of motion may be equilibrium. In essence, the second law provides a more precise way of defining force, which is any action that causes a body to tend to change the speed or direction with which it is moving. For example, think of a soccer ball sitting on the ground. If you kick that ball with a certain force, the ball will accelerate. If you kick the ball with two times the force, the ball will achieve two times the acceleration. If the ball then bounces off the goalpost and out of bounds, the force of the impact with the goalpost will change the ball's direction or, more precisely, its velocity (and momentum). This type of problem is covered in greater detail in Chapter 6 covering momentum, in which we substitute $\Delta v/\Delta t$ for acceleration in the equation above.

PROBLEM SOLVING AND NEWTON'S SECOND LAW

(*College Physics* 8th ed. pages 83–92, 94–108/9th ed. pages 86–95, 98–112)

Invariably, applying $F_{net} = ma$ to a system to calculate unknown quantities will often require analyzing two directions (x and y directions). Usually, though, only one of those directions will be concerned with the acceleration of the object. The other direction will most likely be in static equilibrium. Thus, it may be likely that several forces could be combining in one direction to provide the acceleration, which requires finding the *net* force. Therefore, to solve dynamics problems, apply these steps:

1. Isolate the body in question and sketch a free-body diagram. Remember that a free-body diagram is a picture with *only* forces, not velocity, vector components, mass, acceleration, or energy.
2. Somewhere next to your free-body diagram, mark the direction of the net force on the object (it is also the direction of the acceleration).
3. In the direction with no acceleration, you can simply apply $\Sigma F = 0$ (i.e., *add* those forces and equate them to zero).
4. In the acceleration direction, find the net force by adding the forces and setting their sum equal to ma (i.e., write $\Sigma F = ma$).
5. Be very careful about directions. Remember that up and to the right are positive y and positive x, respectively, and left and down are negative x and negative y, respectively.

NEWTON'S SECOND LAW AND FRICTION: THE REAL WORLD

(*College Physics* 8th ed. pages 83–92, 94–108/9th ed. pages 86–95, 98–112)

As discussed in Chapter 3, nearly all real-world problems involve some type of friction, an opposing contact force. The simpler cases of static equilibrium involving static friction ($f_{s\,max} = \mu_s N$, otherwise, $f_s \le \mu_s N$) and kinetic friction ($f_k = \mu_k N$) were straightforward:

> *Kinetic friction* (object is accelerating or moving at constant velocity):
> $f_k = \mu_k N$
> *Static friction* (object is stationary): $f_s \le \mu_s N$
> *Static friction* (object is just starting to slip means it is overcoming the maximum f_s): $f_{s\,max} = \mu_s N$

Here are two sample problems involving friction and dynamics.

SAMPLE PROBLEM 1

A hockey puck of mass m slides to the right along a horizontal ice rink and soon comes to rest. The ice–puck interface has a coefficient of kinetic friction of μ_k.

(a) On the diagram below, sketch a free-body diagram of the puck.

(b) Derive an expression for the acceleration of the puck in terms of μ_k and other appropriate constants.

SOLUTION TO PROBLEM 1

(a) Notice that there is a net force of kinetic friction to the left; therefore, the puck's acceleration is also to the left (negative x direction) as shown.

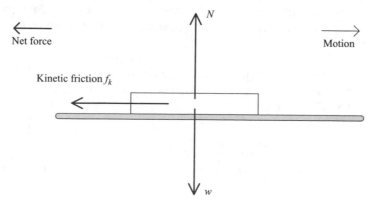

(b) After sketching a free-body diagram, you must determine the direction of the net force (and thus the acceleration), which was shown above. Next, the most important step is applying the dynamics condition, $\Sigma F = ma$, in the negative x-direction, while realizing that $\Sigma F = 0$ in the y direction. Then, $\Sigma F_y = 0$ becomes $N - mg = 0$, or simply

$$N = w \quad (1)$$

and $\Sigma F_x = ma$ becomes

$$-f_k = -ma \quad (2)$$

Next, solve for one variable in terms of another to eliminate it to find the acceleration. Keeping in mind that $f_k = \mu_k N$, we can eliminate f_k from Equation (2), which then becomes $-\mu_k N = -ma$. From Equation (1), however, $N = w$, which is mg. Therefore, we replace N with mg and get $-\mu_k (mg) = -ma$, or $\mu_k g = a$.

SAMPLE PROBLEM 2

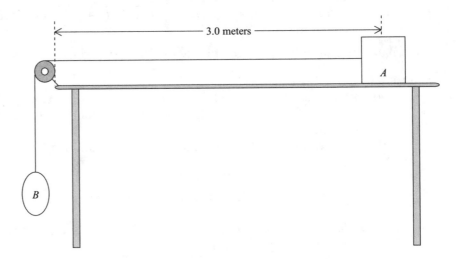

Block A (of mass 12.0 kg) is connected to a massless string that passes over a massless and frictionless pulley that is connected to hanging block B (of mass 5.0 kg) as shown. The center of block A is 3.0 m from the edge of the table where the pulley is attached, and the coefficient of kinetic friction between block A and the horizontal surface is 0.22. The center of block B is 4.0 m above the level ground below.

(a) Block B just begins to move, causing block A to start sliding. Sketch a free-body diagram of blocks A and B in the figure below, while the blocks accelerate. Label all forces in the diagrams.

(b) Determine the acceleration of block B.

(c) If block B falls for 2.0 s, determine how far block B falls. Does block A impact the pulley 2.0 s after it began moving? Explain.

SOLUTION TO PROBLEM 2

(a)

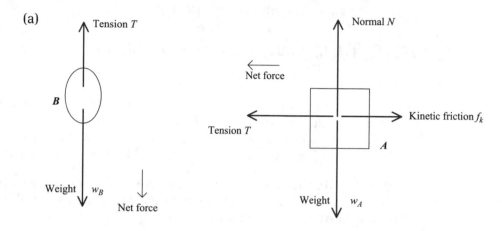

(b) For block B, apply $\Sigma F_x = ma$ (noting the acceleration is in the negative x direction). Thus, $T - m_B g = -m_B a$, or

$$T = -m_B a + m_B g \quad (1)$$

For block A, apply $\Sigma F_x = -ma$. In the vertical direction, apply $\Sigma F_y = 0$. We now have

$$-T + f_k = -m_A a \quad (2)$$

and

$$N = m_A g \quad (3)$$

Now, substitute Equation (1) into Equation (2) to eliminate T and then solve for acceleration: $-(-m_B a + m_B g) + f_k = -m_A a$, or $m_B a + m_A a = m_B g - f_k$. Thus, a becomes

$$a = \frac{m_B g - f_K}{m_B + m_A}$$

Because $f_k = \mu_k m_A g$,

$$a = \frac{m_B g - \mu_K m_A g}{m_B + m_A}$$

Solving gives $a = 1.4$ m/s².

(c) Using $d = v_i \Delta t + \frac{1}{2} a \Delta t^2$ with $v_i = 0$, $a = 1.4$ m/s², and $t = 2$ s, we can find the value of d, the distance fallen: $d = v_i \Delta t + \frac{1}{2} a \Delta t^2 = (0) + \frac{1}{2}(1.4 \text{ m/s}^2)(2 \text{ s})^2$, or $d = 2.8$ m. Therefore, not only will block

B not impact the floor, but block A will not impact the pulley because block A has only moved 2.72 m to the left and the pulley is 3.0 m away. After 2 s, block A will eventually hit the pulley even if block B hits the floor first because the inertia of block A will continue to carry it. If block A hits the pulley before block B hits the floor, the blocks stop completely.

NEWTON'S THIRD LAW: ACTION–REACTION

(*College Physics* 8th ed. pages 83–92, 94–108/9th ed. pages 95–98)

The last of Newton's three laws of motion is typically one that is more familiar to most, perhaps because it possesses a more applicable popular tone. The third law deals with forces and their reciprocals, and it states that all forces occur in pairs. As translated from Latin, Newton's third law states

To every action there is always an equal and opposite reaction: or the forces of two bodies on each other are always equal and are directed in opposite directions.

The third law simply states that for every force acting on *one* object, there is an equally sized (but oppositely directed) force that acts as a response to that first force on a second, *different*, object. For example, if body A exerts a force on body B, simultaneously body B exerts a force of the same magnitude back on body A, with both forces acting along the same line. An sample problem might solidify this concept.

SAMPLE PROBLEM 3

The force of gravity on a person is also known as the person's weight. Thus, "Earth pulling on you" may be considered an action force.

(a) What is the reaction to this force?

(b) Sketch and label both the action and reaction force in the diagram below.

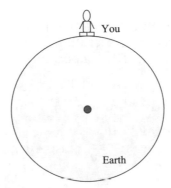

SOLUTION TO PROBLEM 3

(a) To answer a third-law question, simply switch the nouns in the action force:
The action is: **Earth is pulling on you**. The reaction is therefore: **You are pulling on Earth**.

(b) Sketching the action–reaction pair is not complicated, but realize that it is *not* a representation of forces in a free-body diagram. Thus, always answering a question such as that asked in part (a) is imperative before you sketch the action–reaction pair. In a free-body diagram, you are making a sketch of all the forces on one object, whereas in a third-law question, you are sketching a *force pair*, each of which acts on a different object.

OTHER THIRD-LAW EXAMPLES

The action is: *You* kick the *football*.
The reaction is therefore: The *football* kicks *you*.

The action is: The *table* pushes up on the *book* (called the normal force).
The reaction is therefore: The *book* pushes down on the *table*.

The action is: *You* push on the *skater*.
The reaction is therefore: The *skater* pushes back on *you*.

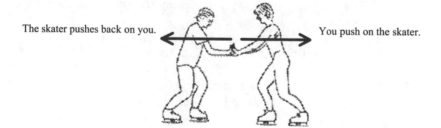

In a manner analogous to that shown in the solution to Sample Problem 3, part (b), the skaters' forces on each other are equal in magnitude but act in opposite directions. Interestingly, although these forces are equal, the accelerations are not: the less-massive skater will have a greater acceleration due to Newton's second law. Again, it is important to note that the action–reaction pair acts on different objects and, contrary to misconception, *do not* cancel each other out. The two forces in Newton's third law are of the same type (i.e., if the road exerts a forward frictional force on an accelerating car's tires, it is also a frictional force that Newton's third law predicts for the tires pushing backward on the road).

DYNAMICS: STUDENT OBJECTIVES FOR THE AP EXAM

- You should understand the relation between force acting on a body and the resulting velocity change.
- You should be able to apply $\Sigma F = ma$ to calculate the acceleration of a body.
- You should be able draw a well-labeled diagram showing all real forces that act on a body (a free-body diagram).
- You should be able to write down the vector equation that results from applying Newton's second law to an accelerating body and take components of this equation along appropriate axes.
- You should understand and be able to identify both action and reaction forces in accordance with Newton's third law of motion.

MULTIPLE-CHOICE QUESTIONS

1. The velocity of a 5.0-N hockey puck sliding across a level ice surface decreases at the rate of 0.5 m/s². What is the coefficient of kinetic friction between the puck and the ice?
    (A) 0.05
    (B) 0.00
    (C) 0.10
    (D) 0.25
    (E) 0.50

2. Complete the following statement: The term *net force* most accurately describes
    (A) the mass of an object.
    (B) the inertia of an object.
    (C) the quantity that has a tendency to change the velocity of an object.
    (D) the quantity that keeps an object moving.
    (E) the quantity that causes displacement.

3. A 15.0-N net force is applied for 6.0 s to a 12.0-kg box initially at rest. What is the speed of the box after 6.0 s?
    (A) 1.8 m/s
    (B) 15. m/s
    (C) 3.0 m/s
    (D) 30. m/s
    (E) 7.5 m/s

4. A book is at rest on a level tabletop. What is the reaction to the pull of gravity on the book?
    (A) the force of Earth pulling on the book
    (B) the force of the table pushing on the book
    (C) the force of the book pushing on the table
    (D) the force of the book pulling on Earth
    (E) the force of friction holding the book still

5. A ball falls straight down through the air under the influence of gravity. There is, however, an air resistance force F given by $F = bv$, where b is a constant and v is the ball's speed. What is the magnitude of the ball's acceleration during its fall?

   (A) $g - b$

   (B) $g - \dfrac{bv}{m}$

   (C) $g + \dfrac{bv}{m}$

   (D) $\dfrac{g}{b}$

   (E) $\dfrac{bv}{m}$

6. A force F gives an object with mass m and acceleration a. If this force is applied to an object of mass $\frac{1}{4}m$, what is the new acceleration?

   (A) $\dfrac{1}{2}a$

   (B) $\dfrac{1}{4}a$

   (C) $2a$

   (D) $4a$

   (E) $8a$

7. A cat of mass 5.0 kg stands on a scale in an elevator that is moving upward at a constant velocity of 10.0 m/s. What approximate value does the scale read?

   (A) 5.0 N

   (B) 50.0 N

   (C) 100.0 N

   (D) 200.0 N

   (E) 1000.0 N

8. A student of mass 100.0 kg is standing on a scale in an elevator car. The elevator is accelerating downward at 5.0 m/s² near the surface of Earth. What approximate value does the scale read?

   (A) 500.0 N

   (B) 150.0 N

   (C) 1000.0 N

   (D) 1500.0 N

   (E) 50.0 N

9. A box of mass m slides along a horizontal floor with constant velocity v. The coefficient of kinetic friction between the box and the floor is μ. What is the net force on the box?

   (A) μmgv

   (B) mgv

   (C) mgv^2

   (D) $\dfrac{\mu mg}{v}$

   (E) 0

10. The pain you experience in your foot when you kick a wall can best be explained by what?
    (A) the force you exert on the wall
    (B) your foot's inertia
    (C) the force the wall exerts on you
    (D) that the wall has more mass than your foot
    (E) our smaller foot bones

11. A horizontal force of 15.0 N is used to push a 2.0-kg block along a tabletop that has a coefficient of friction of 0.15. What is the acceleration of the block?
    (A) 3.0 m/s²
    (B) 6.0 m/s²
    (C) 7.5 m/s²
    (D) 8.5 m/s²
    (E) 10.0 m/s²

12. A 2.0-N rock slides on a frictionless, inclined plane. Which one of the following statements is true concerning the normal force that the plane exerts on the rock?
    (A) The normal force is zero.
    (B) The normal force is 2.0 N.
    (C) The normal force is greater than 2.0 N.
    (D) The normal force is less than 2.0 N but is greater than zero.
    (E) It increases as the angle of inclination, θ, is increased.

13. Blocks of mass M and m are connected by a massless string across a massless, frictionless pulley as shown to the right (called an Atwood's machine). Which of the following represents the acceleration of the block of mass M when released from rest?

    (A) $\dfrac{(M - m)g}{M + m}$

    (B) $\dfrac{(M + m)g}{M - m}$

    (C) $\dfrac{Mg}{M + m}$

    (D) $\dfrac{mg}{M + m}$

    (E) $\dfrac{mg}{m}$

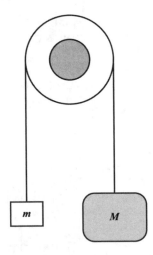

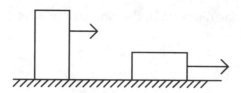

14. Two identical blocks are pulled along a rough surface as suggested in the figure. Which one of the following statements is false?
    (A) The coefficient of kinetic friction is the same in each case.
    (B) A force of the same magnitude is needed to keep each block moving.
    (C) A force of the same magnitude was required to start each block moving.
    (D) The magnitude of the force of kinetic friction is greater for the block on the right.
    (E) The normal force exerted on the blocks by the surface is the same for both blocks.

15. While at rest, a string of negligible mass supports a hanging block that weighs 30.0 N. The breaking strength of the string is 50.0 N. What is the largest acceleration that can be given to the block by pulling up on it with the string without breaking the string?
    (A) 6.0 m/s²
    (B) 6.7 m/s²
    (C) 10 m/s²
    (D) 15 m/s²
    (E) 16.7 m/s²

FREE-RESPONSE PROBLEMS

1. An airplane accelerates uniformly from rest along a level runway as a passenger holds up a thin, massless string to which she has tied a ring of mass m. She notices that as the plane accelerates along the runway, the string makes an angle θ with the vertical as shown.

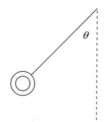

(a) On the diagram of the ring below, sketch the free-body diagram of the ring.

After accelerating uniformly for 40.0 s, the airplane reaches a takeoff speed of 72.0 m/s.

(b) Determine the minimum length of the runway needed for the plane to take off.

(c) Determine the angle θ the string makes with the vertical during the acceleration of the airplane before it takes off.

(d) What additional information would be needed to determine the tension in the string?

2. Two metal guide rails for a 450.0-kg elevator each exert a constant friction force of 110.0 N on the elevator car when it is moving upward with an acceleration of 2.5 m/s² as shown. Attached to the lower right side of the cable hoisting the elevator is a counterweight of mass M. The pulley has negligible mass and friction.

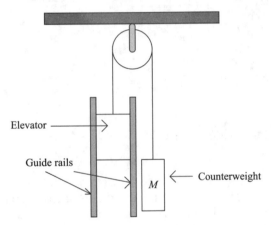

(a) What is the direction of the net force on the elevator car?

(b) On the diagram below, sketch and clearly label all the forces acting on the elevator car during its motion.

(c) Calculate the tension in the cable when the elevator is accelerating as described.

(d) Calculate the mass M the counterweight must have to raise the elevator car with the acceleration as described.

ANSWERS

MULTIPLE-CHOICE QUESTIONS

1. **A** The puck is accelerating as it slides freely on the level surface; thus, apply $\Sigma F = ma$. Sketching the free-body diagram shows $N = w$ (or $N = 5.0$ N), but, more important, $f_k = ma$. Because $f_k = \mu_k N$, we have $\mu_k N = ma$, or $\mu_k mg = ma$, which is just $\mu_k g = a$. Therefore, $a = \mu_k g$ becomes $\frac{1}{2}$ m/s^2 = μ_k (10.0 m/s^2), or μ_k = **0.05** (*College Physics* 8th ed. pages 83–92, 94–108/9th ed. pages 86–95, 98–112).

2. **C** By Newton's second law of motion, the net force is proportional to an object's acceleration. Because acceleration is the rate of change of velocity, the net force imparted to an object is also a quantity that has a tendency to cause an object to change its velocity (*College Physics* 8th ed. pages 83–92/9th ed. pages 86–95).

3. **E** This problem requires finding the acceleration using Newton's second law and then using a kinematics equation to find v_f. So, $F_{net} = ma$, or 15.0 N = (12 kg)a. Therefore, $a = 15/12$ m/s^2. Using $a = \Delta v \, \Delta t$, we can find v_f:

$$\frac{15}{12}\,m/s^2 = \frac{v_f - v_i}{\Delta t} = \frac{v_f - 0}{6s} \qquad \text{or} \qquad v_f = \frac{6(15)}{12} = \frac{15}{2} = \textbf{7.5 m/s}$$

    (*College Physics* 8th ed. pages 83–92, 94–101/9th ed. pages 86–95, 98–105).

4. **D** By Newton's third law, for each action there is an equal but opposite reaction. Because we are told Earth pulls on the book, the reaction to that is the book pulling on the Earth (*College Physics* 8th ed. pages 92–94/9th ed. pages 95–98).

5. **B** In the negative y direction, apply $\Sigma F = ma$ and solve for acceleration (sketch the free-body diagram to show $F = bv$ is upward and mg is downward): $\Sigma F = -ma$, or $bv - mg = -ma$. Thus, $(bv - mg)/m = (bv/m) - g$. Because this equation equals $-a$, solving for acceleration will give $a = g - (bv/m)$ (*College Physics* 8th ed. pages 83–92, 94–101/9th ed. pages 86–95, 98–105).

6. **D** Apply Newton's second law: $F_{net} = ma$, which becomes $F_{net} = (\frac{1}{4} m)a_{new}$. Because each object has the same net force, however, this result can be rewritten as $F_{net} = ma = (\frac{1}{4} m)a_{new}$. Therefore, the new acceleration will be $ma = (\frac{1}{4} m)a_{new}$, or $\textbf{4}a = a_{new}$ (*College Physics* 8th ed. pages 83–92, 94–101/9th ed. pages 86–95, 98–105).

7. **B** Notice that the cat's *mass* (not weight) is given. Thus, the cat's normal weight is $w = mg$, which is approximately 50.0 N. Also notice that the problem states that the elevator is moving

with constant velocity, which therefore means zero acceleration. Thus, it is not a dynamics problem, and the cat's apparent weight remains the same as its normal weight. Therefore, 50.0 N is the answer (*College Physics* 8th ed. pages 85–86, 94–97/9th ed. pages 88–89, 98–105).

8. **A** Applying Newton's second law gives $\Sigma F = ma$, which becomes $F_{net} = -ma$ (downward acceleration given). The free-body diagram shows N upward and w downward, with $-ma$ downward, giving $N - mg = -ma$ (where N is the apparent scale reading), or $N = -ma + mg$. Substituting, we have $N = -(100\ kg)(5\ m/s^2) + (100\ kg)(10.0\ m/s^2) = -500 + 1000$. Therefore, **$N \sim$ 500.0 N** (*College Physics* 8th ed. pages 83–92, 94–101/9th ed. pages 86–95, 98–105).

9. **E** As in Question 7, this situation involves constant velocity and thus there is no acceleration. Because acceleration is zero, by Newton's second law there is no net force (*College Physics* 8th ed. pages 85–86, 94–97/9th ed. pages 88–89, 98–105).

10. **C** Newton's third law states that for all forces, there are equal but opposite forces acting on opposing bodies and that these forces always occur in pairs. Thus, for the force you exert on the wall, there is an equal but opposite force that the wall exerts on your foot, which causes the resistance you feel. That resistance is in turn translated into pain by your brain (*College Physics* 8th ed. pages 92–94/9th ed. pages 95–98).

11. **B** Because the block is sliding horizontally with an applied net force, this question is a dynamics problem in the horizontal direction ($\Sigma F = + ma$), but it is a statics problem in the positive y direction ($\Sigma F = 0$). Thus, a free-body diagram of the object will show $\Sigma F_y = 0$, or $N = mg$. Therefore, $N = 20.0$ N. Substituting into $\Sigma F_x = + ma$ gives $15.0\ N - \mu_k N = ma$, or $15.0\ N - (15/100)(20.0\ N) = (2.0\ kg)(a)$, which then becomes $15.0\ N - (15/5) = (2.0\ kg)(a)$, or $12 = 2a$. Thus, **a = 6.0 m/s²** (*College Physics* 8th ed. pages 83–92, 94–101/9th ed. pages 86–95, 98–105).

12. **D** A sketch of the free-body diagram and $\Sigma F_y = 0$ in the y direction perpendicular to the incline will give $N = 2 \cos \theta$, which states that N is not 2 (the weight) but is slightly less. In addition, N must be larger than zero unless the incline is completely vertical, where θ becomes 90° (*College Physics* 8th ed. pages 83–92, 94–101/9th ed. pages 86–95, 98–105).

13. **A** Isolate each mass (m and M) and sketch a free-body diagram for each, and then apply $\Sigma F = ma$ in the y direction for each. Notice that m accelerates upward and M accelerates downward. Solve by substitution. For mass m, $\Sigma F_y = ma$ gives

$$T - mg = + ma \qquad (1)$$

For mass M, $\Sigma F_y = Ma$ gives

$$T - Mg = -Ma \quad (2)$$

Solving Equation (2) for T and then returning it into Equation (1) will give a solution for the acceleration (keep in mind that both a and T are the same for each mass because the string simply connects them, passing over a single pulley). So, Equation (2) becomes $T = M(g - a)$. Then Equation (1) becomes $M(g - a) - mg = + ma$. Collecting like terms gives $g(M - m) = a(m + M)$, or $\boldsymbol{a = \dfrac{(M - m)g}{(m + M)}}$ (College Physics 8th ed. pages 83–92, 94–101/9th ed. pages 86–95, 98–105).

14. **D** The frictional force depends only on the surface roughness and on the normal force on each object. Because both blocks are on a level surface, their normal forces both equal their weights. Thus, each has the same kinetic (and static) friction force, and statements (B) and (C) are true. Statement (D) contradicts that because the friction equation $f_k = \mu_k N$ does *not* depend on the area A of the objects in contact with the surface. Also, because both objects are the same, statement (A) is also true. Finally, statement (E) is correct because the normal force only depends on the weight of the object on a level surface, and not on the area presented to the surface. Thus, statement (D) is the correct answer (*College Physics* 8th ed. pages 100–101/9th ed. pages 86–95, 98–105).

15. **B** Apply $\Sigma F_y = ma$ in the positive y direction with the constraint that $T_{max} = 50.0$ N. Then, $\Sigma F_y = +ma$ or $T - mg = +ma$. Therefore, 50.0 N – 30.0 N = +(3.0 kg)a. Thus, 20.0 N = (3.0 kg)a, or $\boldsymbol{a = 6.7}$ **m/s²** (*College Physics* 8th ed. pages 101–108/9th ed. pages 105–112).

FREE-RESPONSE PROBLEMS

1. (a) On a free-body diagram, the forces acting are tension (T) and the weight of the ring (w). Notice that there is no forward force to the right (such as velocity or acceleration, a common misconception).

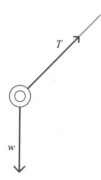

(b) Begin with a variable checklist:

$a_x = ?$ $\quad$ $g = -10$ m/s² $\quad$ $v_i = 0$ m/s $\quad$ $v_f = 72.0$ m/s $\quad$ $\Delta t = 40.0$ s

To calculate the distance d traveled by the jet during the acceleration, use either kinematics equation:

$$v_f^2 = v_i^2 + 2ad \qquad or \qquad d = v_i \Delta t + \frac{1}{2}a\Delta t^2$$

With either equation, we must calculate acceleration using $a = \Delta v / \Delta t = (72 - 0)/40 = 1.8$ m/s². Therefore, the minimum distance traveled by the jet will be $72^2 = 0 + 2(1.8)d$. So, **$d = 1440.0$ m**.

(c) At this point, we must realize that this problem combines statics and dynamics, with the ring accelerating to the right but stationary in the vertical direction. Therefore, $\Sigma F_y = 0$ and $\Sigma F_x = ma$ must be used to set up the equations of motion (noticing where the angle θ is in the diagram). First, $\Sigma F_y = 0$ gives $T \cos \theta - mg = 0$. Thus, **$mg = T \cos \theta$**. Next, $\Sigma F_x = ma$ gives **$T \sin \theta = +ma$**. Because there are two equations with two unknowns, we must solve by substitution. Solve for T and then substitute it in the second equation: $T = mg/\cos \theta$ can be substituted here: $T \sin \theta = +ma$, or, $ma = (mg/\cos \theta) \sin \theta$ which becomes $a = g \tan \theta$. Therefore, 1.8 m/s² $= 10.0$ m/s² $(\tan \theta)$, or $\theta = \mathbf{10.2°}$.

(d) As shown in part (c), to determine the value of the tension in the string, we must know the value of the mass m of the ring.

(*College Physics* 8th ed. page 94/9th ed. pages 98–100)

2. (a) The direction of the net force on the car is the same as the direction of the acceleration of the car, which, as described, is upward (positive y direction).

(b) As shown, the free-body diagram is slightly more complex than what is common from the student's experience. The tension (T) is upward, but because there are two guide rails aside the elevator, there are two normal forces (N) exerted on the elevator by the guide rails. In addition, as described, each guide rail exerts a downward force of kinetic friction (f_k). Finally, the elevator's weight (w) is downward.

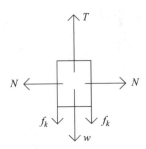

(c) Here, we sketch both free-body diagrams (and F_{net} directions) as shown:

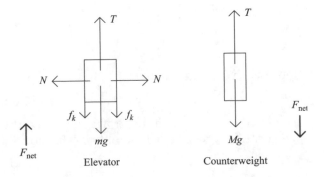

Because the value of M is unknown, we can solve this problem by focusing on the positive y direction of motion of the elevator, applying $\Sigma F_y = +ma$. So, $T - 2f_k - mg = ma$, which can be easily solved for T by substituting all known values. Therefore, $T = ma + 2f_k + mg$, or $T = (450.0 \text{ kg})(2.5 \text{ m/s}^2) + 2(110.0 \text{ N}) + (450.0 \text{ kg})(10.0 \text{ m/s}^2)$. Therefore, $T = \mathbf{5845.0 \text{ N}}$.

(d) Now the focus is on the counterweight's motion in the negative y direction. Applying $\Sigma F_y = -Ma$ gives $T - Mg = -Ma$. Therefore, solving for T gives $T = -Ma + Mg$, or $T = M(-a + g)$ (the objects share a common tension because there is only one pulley redirecting the force). So, $5845.0 \text{ N} = M(-2.5 \text{ m/s}^2 + 10.0 \text{ m/s}^2)$. Therefore, $M = 5845.0 \text{ N}/7.5 \text{ m/s}^2$, or $M = \mathbf{779.3 \text{ kg}}$.

(*College Physics* 8th ed. pages 83–92, 94–101/9th ed. pages 86–95, 98–105)

5

WORK, ENERGY, AND POWER

WHAT IS THE RELATIONSHIP BETWEEN WORK AND ENERGY?

(*College Physics* 8th ed. pages 119–149/9th ed. pages 124–153)

In the everyday sense, we may think we are working hard by studying from a book or typing at a computer for hours, but in the physics sense, the definition of work suggests otherwise. In physics, for work to be performed on an object, a force F must displace an object a distance Δr, with, in general, the force acting in the direction of the displacement. In some instances, the force F and displacement vector Δr may not align and are separated by an angle θ. In those situations, it is necessary to invoke $\cos \theta$ to calculate the work W done by the force, which is

$$W = F \Delta r \cos \theta$$

In cases in which force and displacement are 180° apart, such as when friction acts against the motion of a dragged box, the cosine of 180° gives –1 and thus the work done by the force is *negative*. Similarly, when F and Δr are parallel (i.e., in the same direction), the work done by the force is *positive*. In physics, work is a scalar, not a vector, and its units, derived from the definition, are newton-meters, or N · m. In honor of James Prescott Joule (a 19th-century physicist credited with the discovery of energy conservation), we name the unit of work the joule (abbreviated J). Careful observation of the variables in the equation will show that the joule is a derived unit, equivalent to kilogram m^2/s^2.

Interestingly, a close connection exists between the above definition of work and what we commonly refer to as energy. For very basic problems, Newton's second law ($F_{net} = ma$) is easy to apply, however in situations in which multiple forces exist, it is often more convenient to relate the *net* force (and work) done on an object by using its change of speed. This strategy not only makes problems much easier to solve, but it also allows us to better understand how work and energy are related.

Suppose a horizontal force F is applied to a box on a level floor. As the box accelerates, it is displaced a distance Δr. How does the work done on the box relate to the energy change of the box? Armed with Newton's second law and the kinematics equation $v_f^2 = v_i^2 + 2ad$, we can use the definition of work to discover how work and energy relate. Substituting $F_{net} = ma$ for F in the work equation and taking the force to be in the direction of the displacement ($\cos 0° = 1$) gives

$$W = F\Delta r \cos\theta = (ma)\Delta r \cos\theta = (ma)\Delta r$$

Because Δr represents a displacement, we can solve the above kinematics equation for displacement (which happens to be termed d instead of Δr; nonetheless, they are identical) and substitute to eliminate the variable, which leaves us with work and its relationship to the object's change of velocity, or

$$\frac{v_f^2 - v_i^2}{2a} = d = \Delta r$$

Then, the work equation is

$$W = (ma)\Delta r = (ma)d = (ma)\left[\frac{v_f^2 - v_i^2}{2a}\right] = \left(\frac{m}{2}\right)\left[v_f^2 - v_i^2\right]$$

which can be rearranged to give

$$W = \tfrac{1}{2}mv_f^2 - \tfrac{1}{2}mv_i^2$$

In physics, the quantity $\tfrac{1}{2}mv^2$ is called *kinetic energy* (typically abbreviated KE by textbooks and physicists; AP, however, abbreviates kinetic energy simply K), or energy of motion. In the above equation, there is a difference between quantities (again denoted by Δ), which shows us that the work done on the object by the resultant force causes a *change* in kinetic energy of the object, a valuable and useful rule in problem solving. This relationship is called the *work–energy theorem*. Although this derivation assumed a constant acceleration, the result is true even if the acceleration is not constant. So,

$$\boxed{W = \Delta K = \tfrac{1}{2}mv_f^2 - \tfrac{1}{2}mv_i^2}$$

HOW IS WORK CALCULATED BY A FORCE THAT IS NOT CONSTANT?

(*College Physics* 8th ed. pages 147–149/9th ed. pages 152–154)

What happens if the force acting on a displaced object changes as a function of position x? As shown, the graph on the left represents a basic situation in which the force is constant over the range of the displacement. In the next two graphs, however, the force varies extensively, making the use of the equation $W = F\Delta r$ much less feasible.

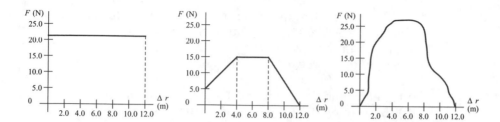

For purposes of AP Physics B, it is necessary to only find the area under simple plots, those that form squares and rectangles (whose areas are $L \times W$) or triangles (whose area is $\frac{1}{2}$ base × height). For example, in the graph on the left, the work done during the 12.0-m displacement would be (~ 21 N)(12.0 m), or about 252.0 J. In the center graph, though, it would be necessary to calculate the area under the line from 0 to 4.0 m (which is a rectangle plus a triangle), add to it the area under the rectangle from 4.0 m to 8.0 m, and finally add to that the triangular area under the line from 8.0 m to 12.0 m. In the graph on the right, we must either resort to using calculus to find the work done or simply approximate the area using this method described.

HOW DOES WORK RELATE TO POWER?

(*College Physics* 8th ed. pages 143–146/9th ed. pages 147–152)

For many practical scientific applications, including the proper functioning of myriad electrical devices in our everyday world, the concept of power is often incorrectly interchanged with energy or work, but it has a very specific definition. In reality, *power* is simply the rate at which energy is being expended or supplied, or, in other words, the rate at which work is being done. For example, what is the rate at which an elevator does work in lifting passengers? What is the rate of energy expended by a runner during a marathon? Power therefore depends inversely on time, just as, for example, acceleration is the rate at which velocity changes; the lower the time, the greater the change of the quantity. Using the definition of work and Newton's second law, power is written as

$$P = \frac{W}{\Delta t} = \frac{F\Delta r\cos\theta}{\Delta t} = Fv_{avg}\cos\theta$$

Therefore, power is

$$\boxed{P = \frac{W}{\Delta t} = Fv_{avg}}$$

The units of power are joules per second, or J/s; the unit is also called a watt, abbreviated W.

SAMPLE PROBLEM 1

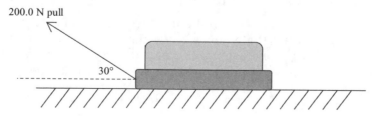

200.0 N pull

30°

A 12.0-kg crate is dragged from rest with an applied force of 200.0 N at an angle of 30° relative to the horizontal as shown. The coefficient of kinetic friction between the floor and crate is 0.4, and the crate is displaced by this force 5.0 m to the left.

(a) Determine the net work done in displacing the crate 5.0 m.
(b) Determine the acceleration of the crate.
(c) Determine the time it takes the crate to travel 5.0 m.
(d) Determine the average power generated by the net force in displacing the crate.

SOLUTION TO PROBLEM 1

(a) A free-body diagram will show that the only forces contributing to the net work are f_k (to the right) and the horizontal component of the 200.0 N force to the left. Therefore, applying the conditions of dynamics, we have $\Sigma F = -ma = F_{net} = -200.0$ N(cos 30°) + $\mu_k N$ = -200.0 N(0.866) + (0.4)N. In the y direction, however, we must apply $\Sigma F = 0$ because we need an expression for the normal force, so 200(sin 30°) + $N - mg$ = 0. Therefore, $N = mg - 200.0$ N(sin 30°) = (12.0 kg)(10.0 m/s²) − 200.0 N(0.5) = 20.0 N. So, $F_{net} = -200.0$ N(0.866) + (0.4)(20.0 N) = −165.0 N. The *net* work is then $W_{net} = F_{net} \Delta r$ = (−165.0 N)(−5.0 m), or W_{net} = **825.0 J**.

Notice that because angle θ between the x component of the 200.0-N force and displacement is zero, cos 0 is 1. As a result, the work due to that component is simply calculated by $W_{net} = -200.0$ N(0.866) Δr. Had this component not been used in the calculation, the product of 200.0 N, 5.0 m, and cos 30°, according to the work equation definition, would still provide the work by this component, to which must be added the work done by friction as calculated above. Either way, the same answer is achieved.

(b) Again, by Newton's second law, we can solve easily for the acceleration: $F_{net} = ma$ = (12.0 kg)(a) = −165.0 N. Therefore, solving for a gives **a = 14.0 m/s²**.

(c) We can calculate the final speed at the end of the 5.0-m interval using the work–energy theorem and then use that value in the kinematics equation $a = \Delta v / \Delta t$ to determine the time. So, $W = \Delta KE = \frac{1}{2} m v_f^2 - \frac{1}{2} m v_i^2$, and substituting gives 825.0 J = $\frac{1}{2}$(12.0 kg) ($v_f^2 - 0$). Thus, v_f = 12.0 m/s. Then, using $a = \Delta v / \Delta t$ we have 14.0 m/s² = (12.0 m/s − 0)/Δt, or **t = 0.86 s**.

(d) The average power will be determined from the net work done by the combination of forces. So, $P = (W_{net}/\Delta t)$ = [(165.0 N)(5.0 m)]/0.86 s, or **P = 959.0 W**.

HOW ARE WORK AND GRAVITY RELATED?

(*College Physics* 8th ed. pages 127–135/9th ed. pages 132–139)

In lifting a backpack from the floor to the top of a table several times, you might notice that your muscles hurt and you feel short of breath. To do this lifting, *you* must work against gravity according to $W = F\Delta r \cos\theta$ where F is now the force you are exerting to lift the object at nearly constant velocity. That force F is simply the weight mg of the object; thus, the work against gravity is $W = F\Delta r = (mg)\Delta r$, or $W = mgh$, where the displacement of the object is simply the height h you raised it. This energy is called *gravitational potential energy* (again, often abbreviated *GPE* by many texts and physicists, but AP refers to it as U_g), which is measured relative to the object's initial position. It is the energy that would be released were the object to fall to its initial position, and Earth does the work. Therefore, whenever the object changes height, a change of gravitational potential energy ΔU_g occurs, written as

$$\Delta U_g = mgh$$

How would this work change if you moved the backpack sideways first instead of directly to the tabletop in a straight, upward path? Would it take more work or less? If you took a different path, would more energy be released when the backpack fell back to the floor? As it turns out, the force in this case, gravity, allows us to recover the potential energy of the raised object, and the work done by us in lifting the backpack is independent of the path taken because gravity acts only vertically downward. Such a force, in which the work done on or by it does not depend on the path taken and is recoverable, is called a *conservative* force. That is, it conserves this energy so that it may be readily used again. Forces such as air drag or kinetic friction cannot easily return the work done against them because they dissipate energy randomly, usually as heat or sound. Therefore, they are called *nonconservative* forces.

WHAT RELATIONSHIP EXISTS BETWEEN SPRINGS AND ENERGY?

(*College Physics* 8th ed. pages 135–140/9th ed. pages 140–145)

Springs are very common and useful devices found in a great variety of everyday tools, from click pens to computer mechanisms to automobiles and even larger equipment. In the late 1670s, British scientist Robert Hooke discovered the important relationship between the force exerted on a spring (the *stress*) and the associated spring elongation or compression (the *strain*). As shown below, a plot of the two quantities (F versus x) reveals a distinct linear relation, with a proportionality constant known as k, the spring constant. This spring constant is a quantity different for every spring, and it explicitly states how much force is needed to elongate or compress the spring by a meter. Hooke's law,

$$F_s = -kx$$

where F_s is the force exerted by the spring and k is in newtons per meter, has a statement within it concerning the spring's restoring capability, denoted by the negative sign. For example, when a spring is elongated, it has a tendency to return to its unstretched position (i.e., equilibrium) as it does when it is compressed (hence the term *restoring force*). The graph shows the relationship between an applied force stretching a spring (or the magnitude of the restoring force) and the elongation of the spring, or $F = kx$. Interestingly, when a spring is cut in half, it becomes stiffer, and experimentation shows that its k value doubles.

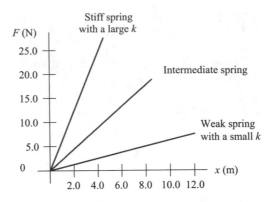

When a spring is compressed (or elongated) a distance x by a force F and then released, it can easily do work simply because upon compression it has stored energy within it. This "spring" potential energy is called elastic potential energy (PE_s) and allows the spring, upon release, to perform a function (such as opening a latch, operating a pop-up toy, or opening a computer CD drive door). Recalling that work may be found from a force–displacement plot by taking the area under the graph, notice that in the graph above, the area under any of the lines is W = area under graph = area of a triangle = $\frac{1}{2}$(base) (height), which becomes $W = \frac{1}{2}(x)(F)$. Substituting $F = kx$ gives $W = \frac{1}{2}(x)$ $(F) = \frac{1}{2}(x)(kx) = \frac{1}{2}kx^2$. Therefore, the work done on or by a spring when it is strained is its *elastic potential energy*, which is sometimes written as *EPE*, although in AP Physics it is abbreviated PE_s. So,

$$PE_s = \frac{1}{2}kx^2$$

When solving energy conservation problems involving springs, be aware that it may be necessary to include the elastic potential energy as part of the object's total mechanical energy as seen in the examples below.

HOW IS TOTAL MECHANICAL ENERGY DESCRIBED?

(*College Physics* 8th ed. pages 127–135/9th ed. pages 132–139)

With some careful observation, an amusement park can serve as an outstanding physics lab! Roller coasters, for example, are perfect for showing the interplay between gravitational potential energy (ΔU_g, stored energy) and kinetic energy (K, energy of motion). When the roller coaster is moving freely, notice at which points its speed is largest and smallest and at which of these locations it is closest to or farthest from the ground. In physics, a great many practical problems can be solved using the principle of conservation, and energy is no exception. With careful measurements, and with the assumption that the work done by nonconservative forces is negligible, it can be shown that at two separate points (such as A and B) in the motion of an object, the sum of K and ΔU_g at those points is a constant, or is conserved. This principle is referred to as the *conservation of mechanical energy* because the energies involved are not concerned with chemical, heat, or atomic processes. Conservation of energy simply means that the sum of all mechanical energies at one location must equal the sum of these energies at another location (and, should the system possess a spring, PE_s must also be included). In equation form,

> ## Law of Conservation of Energy
>
> $$E_{\text{tot } A} = E_{\text{tot } B}$$
>
> or
>
> $$K_A + \Delta U_{gA} + PE_{sA} = K_B + \Delta U_{gB} + PE_{sB}$$

SAMPLE PROBLEM 2

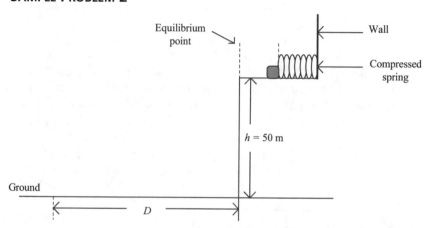

As shown, a 3.0-kg block is held at rest in front of a compressed spring attached to a wall at the top of a 50.0-m-high cliff. The block has compressed the spring 0.80 m from its equilibrium position, and the spring constant is 650.0 N/m. When the block is released, it is propelled off the cliff along a frictionless track.

    (a) Determine the launch speed of the block the moment it reaches the edge of the cliff.

    (b) Determine the total mechanical energy of the block relative to the ground.

    (c) Determine the value of D, the distance from the base of the cliff to the point of impact on the ground.

    (d) Determine the impact speed of the block when it hits the ground.

    (e) Now replace the spring with one having a lower k value and explain how this change will affect (if at all) the time it takes the block to reach the ground and the total mechanical energy of the block.

SOLUTION TO PROBLEM 2

    (a) Here, it is necessary to apply the work–energy theorem (noting that it gives the same result as applying energy conservation) and solve for v_f, where the work done by the spring is equivalent to its PE_s. So, $\frac{1}{2}kx^2 = \Delta K = \frac{1}{2}mv_f^2 - 0$; therefore, $(650.0 \text{ N/m})(0.8 \text{ m})^2 = (3.0 \text{ kg})v_f^2$. Thus, $v_f = \textbf{11.8 m/s}$.

    (b) Here we simply need the kinetic energy K and the gravitational potential energy ΔU_g of the block at the top of the cliff, the moment it has left the spring. Thus, the total mechanical energy becomes

$$K_{\text{top}} + \Delta U_{g \text{ top}} = \tfrac{1}{2}mv_A^2 + mgh = \tfrac{1}{2}(3.0 \text{ kg})(11.8 \text{ m/s})^2 + (3.0 \text{ kg})(10.0 \text{ m/s}^2)(50.0 \text{ m}) = \textbf{1710.0 J} = E_{\text{tot}}.$$

(c) Recalling problems from Chapter 2, we can use the kinematics equation for displacement in the x direction to calculate D. So, $d = v_i \Delta t + \frac{1}{2} a \Delta t^2$, which becomes $D = v_{ix} \Delta t + \frac{1}{2} a_x \Delta t^2$. Because $a_x = 0$, this expression is simply $D = v_{ix} \Delta t$.

The value of the horizontal speed found in part (a) will be used here, but it will also be necessary to find the time of fall. Again, recalling projectile motion, the time can be found using the same displacement equation but in the y direction. So, $d = v_{iy} \Delta t + \frac{1}{2} a_y \Delta t^2$. Recalling that $v_{iy} = 0$ and $a_y = -10.0$ m/s^2, we have -50.0 m $= \frac{1}{2}(-10.0$ m/s$^2) \Delta t^2$. Solving gives $t = 3.2$ s. Next, substituting into the above equation for D gives us $D = v_{ix} \Delta t = (11.8$ m/s$)(3.2$ s$)$, or **$D = 38.0$ m**.

(d) We can determine the impact speed using kinematics or energy conservation (the latter is preferable because vector components are unnecessary). At the moment of impact, the block is at point B and thus has nearly no height (i.e., $h = 0$). Although it still has a total energy of 1710 J, all this energy is now K. Thus, we can write $E_{tot\,B} = K_B + \Delta U_{gB}$, which is $\frac{1}{2} mv_B^2 + 0 = \frac{1}{2}(3.0$ kg$)v_B^2 = 1710.0$ J. Solving for v_B gives an impact speed of **34 m/s**.

(e) The time it takes the block to reach the ground is independent of the spring type as is shown by the kinematics equation used to determine fall time: $d_y = v_{iy} \Delta t + \frac{1}{2} a_y \Delta t^2$. Because $v_{iy} = 0$ and $a_y = g$, the fall time becomes $h = \frac{1}{2} g \Delta t^2$, or $t_{fall} = \sqrt{2h}$. **Therefore, reducing k does not alter the fall time of the block.**

If the spring has a lower k value, it is weaker and thus has less PE_s. Therefore, the lower k value will give the block less initial kinetic energy and **will also reduce the total mechanical energy** of the block.

AP Tip

When solving a problem involving ΔU_g, be sure that you clearly mark your choice of a reference level, where $h = 0$.

AP Tip

When solving a conservation of energy problem, be sure to clearly denote the two (or possibly more) points in the problem at which you need to find E_{total}. It is often convenient to letter them as A, B, C, and so on.

WORK, ENERGY, AND POWER: STUDENT OBJECTIVES FOR THE AP EXAM

- You should understand and use the definition of work to calculate the work done by a specified constant force on a body that undergoes a specified displacement.

■ You should be able to relate the work done by a force to the area under a graph of force versus position and calculate this work in the case in which the force is a linear function of position.

■ You should be able to calculate the change of kinetic energy using the work–energy theorem.

■ You should be able to calculate the work performed by a net force, or each force composing a net force, on a body that undergoes a specific change in speed or kinetic energy.

■ You should be able to calculate the gravitational potential energy of a body in a gravitational field.

■ You should be able to identify situations in which total mechanical energy is or is not conserved.

■ You should be able to apply conservation of energy to bodies that move in a gravitational field and are subject to constraints imposed by strings or surfaces.

■ You should be able to write an expression for the force exerted by an ideal spring and for the associated elastic potential energy in that spring.

■ You should be able to apply conservation of energy to analyze the motion of bodies under the influence of springs.

■ You should be able to calculate the power required to maintain the motion of a body with constant acceleration or constant velocity.

■ You should be able to calculate the work performed by a force that supplies constant power or the average power supplied by a force that performs a specific amount of work.

MULTIPLE-CHOICE QUESTIONS

1. A student weighing 700.0 N climbs at constant speed to the top of an 8.0-m-long vertical rope in 10.0 s. What is the approximate average power expended by the student in overcoming gravity?
(A) 1.1 W
(B) 87.5 W
(C) 560.0 W
(D) 875.0 W
(E) 5600.0 W

2. How much energy is required to stop a car of mass 100.0 kg moving at a speed of 25.0 m/s?
(A) 1150 J
(B) 21,150 J
(C) 31,250 J
(D) 32,250 J
(E) 42,250 J

3. A 5.0-kg block of ice is sliding across a frozen pond at 2.0 m/s. A 7.6-N force is applied in the direction of motion during which time the ice block slides 15.0 m, and then the force is removed. What is the work done by the applied force?
(A) +19.7 J
(B) −114.0 J
(C) +114.0 J
(D) −735.0 J
(E) +735.0 J

4. A 51.0-kg woman runs up a flight of stairs with an average speed of 1.0 m/s. What average power did the woman expend while she was running?
(A) 0.25 kW
(B) 0.51 kW
(C) 0.75 kW
(D) 1.00 kW
(E) 5.00 kW

5. A block of unknown mass falls from rest through a distance of 6.0 m in an evacuated tube near the surface of Earth. What is its speed after it has fallen the 6.0-m distance?
(A) 8.0 m/s
(B) 11.0 m/s
(C) 13.0 m/s
(D) 26.0 m/s
(E) 120.0 m/s

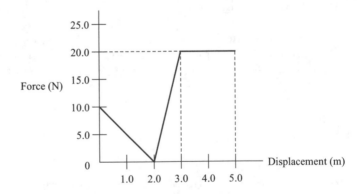

6. The force-versus-displacement graph for an object being pushed along a straight line starting from rest is as shown. After the object has moved a distance of 2.0 m, how much work has been done on it?
(A) 2.5 J
(B) 5.0 J
(C) 10.0 J
(D) 20.0 J
(E) 25.0 J

7. A block of mass m moving with initial velocity v is subjected to a horizontal frictional force on a rough surface. The coefficient of friction between the block and the surface is μ. What distance does the block travel before completely coming to rest?

(A) $\dfrac{v}{2\mu g}$

(B) $\dfrac{v^2}{2\mu m g}$

(C) $\dfrac{v^2}{\mu g}$

(D) $\dfrac{v^2}{2\mu g}$

(E) $\dfrac{v}{2\mu m g}$

8. A spring needs a force of 1.0 N to compress it 0.1 m. Approximately how much work is needed to stretch it 0.4 m?
(A) 0.5 J
(B) 0.8 J
(C) 2.0 J
(D) 4.0 J
(E) 10.0 J

9. A small block at point P is released from rest and slides along the frictionless path toward point Q as shown. At Q, which of the following best describes the speed of the block?

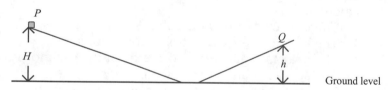

(A) $\dfrac{(H-h)^2}{2g}$

(B) $2g(H-h)$

(C) $\dfrac{H-h}{2g}$

(D) $2g\sqrt{(H-h)}$

(E) $\sqrt{2g(H-h)}$

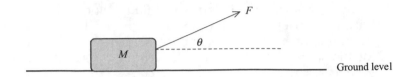

10. A block of mass M is pulled by a constant force F at an angle of θ relative to the level ground, covering a distance L, as shown. Which of the following best represents the work done on the block by force F if θ is 30°?
    (A) $FL \cos 30°$
    (B) $MFL \cos 30°$
    (C) $L \cos 30°$
    (D) $\dfrac{F \cos 30°}{ML}$
    (E) $\dfrac{ML \cos 30°}{F}$

11. Which of the following objects would require the greatest amount of work to stop it?
    (A) an object of mass $3M$ and speed V
    (B) an object of mass $2M$ and speed $3V$
    (C) an object of mass $3M$ and speed $2V$
    (D) an object of mass M and speed $4V$
    (E) an object of mass $4M$ and speed V

12. An elevator car is rising at a constant velocity. Consider the following statements:
    I   The upward force of the cable is constant.
    II The kinetic energy of the elevator is constant.
    III The gravitational potential energy of the elevator is constant.
    IV The acceleration of the elevator is zero.
    V   The kinetic plus potential energies of the elevator is constant.

    Which of the following choices is correct?
    (A) All five statements I through V are true.
    (B) Only statements II and V are true.
    (C) Only statements I, II, and IV are true.
    (D) Only statements IV and V are true.
    (E) Only statements I, II, and III are true.

13. A watt-second is a unit of what?
    (A) force
    (B) velocity
    (C) power
    (D) energy
    (E) displacement

14. A 4.0-kg mass hangs on a spring and stretches it 0.05 m. The spring is then cut exactly in half. The same 4.0-kg mass, when hung on this new spring, will cause the spring to be stretched how far?
    (A) 0.400 m

(B) 0.020 m
(C) 0.100 m
(D) 0.025 m
(E) 0.050 m

15. A block of mass m slides on a frictionless, horizontal table with an initial speed v. It then hits and compresses a spring whose force constant is k and is then brought to rest but does not oscillate. Which of the following describes the maximum compression of the spring?

(A) $\dfrac{v^2}{2g}$

(B) $\dfrac{mgv}{k}$

(C) $\dfrac{mv}{k}$

(D) $v\sqrt{\dfrac{k}{m}}$

(E) $v\sqrt{\dfrac{m}{k}}$

FREE-RESPONSE PROBLEMS

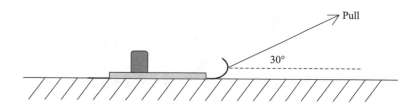

1. A child pulls a 20.0-kg sled (on which a 4.0-kg box sits) from rest along a straight path on a level surface. The child exerts a force of 60.0 N on the sled at an angle of 30° above the horizontal as shown. The coefficient of kinetic friction between the sled and the surface is 0.22.

(a) On the diagram below, draw and label a free-body diagram for the system as it is pulled along the surface.

(b) Calculate the normal force exerted on the sled.
(c) Calculate the acceleration of the sled.
(d) Calculate the net work done on the system as the sled moves a distance of 7.0 m.
(e) Determine the average power developed by the net force acting on the sled during the 7.0-m pull.

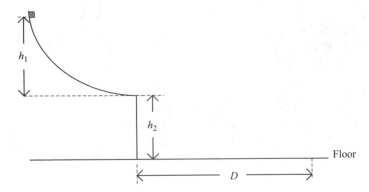

2. As shown, a small, heavy block of mass M rests at the top of a smooth, curved track whose lowest end is a height h_2 above a level, horizontal floor. When released from rest from a height of h_1 above the tabletop, the block accelerates down the track, leaves it horizontally, and strikes the floor at a location that is a distance D from the base of the table. Express your answers in terms of h_1 and h_2 and any necessary constants.

    (a) Derive an expression for the speed of the block the moment it leaves the curved track.
    (b) Derive an expression for the distance D the block travels horizontally before it strikes the floor.
    (c) A student performing this experiment makes the following average measurements: $h_1 = 0.25$ m and $h_2 = 0.90$ m. Although the student actually calculates D as 0.45 m, he measures the average location of impact of the ball with the floor (after five trials) as $D_{avg} = 0.86$ m. Based on your answers to parts (a) and (b), explain any discrepancies in the student's results.

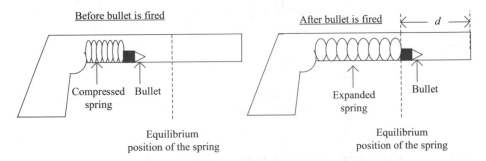

3. A toy gun contains a spring of spring constant $k = 250.0$ N/m. The spring is initially compressed 4.0×10^{-2} m and is then released to propel a bullet of mass 1.0×10^{-2} kg horizontally. The bullet loses contact with the spring the moment the spring passes through its equilibrium position as shown. Thereafter, the bullet travels a distance d through the barrel of the gun.

    (a) Determine the amount of work done by the spring on the bullet in accelerating it to the equilibrium position.
    (b) Determine the ideal speed the bullet should have the moment it is released from the spring at the equilibrium position.
    (c) A student places a photogate assembly at the mouth of the barrel to measure the speed with which the bullet exits the

barrel and determines it to be 4.0 m/s after the bullet has traveled a distance of $d = 2.0$ m. Based on this information, calculate the force of friction between the bullet and the inside of the gun's barrel.

ANSWERS

MULTIPLE-CHOICE QUESTIONS

1. C Because power is the rate at which work is being done, it can be written $P = W/\Delta t = Fv$, which becomes $P = 700.0$ N(8 m/10 s) = **560.0 W** (*College Physics* 8th ed. pages 143–146/9th ed. pages 147–152).

2. C Using the work–energy theorem and solving for W, we have $W = \Delta K = \frac{1}{2}mv_f^2 - \frac{1}{2}mv_i^2 = \frac{1}{2}(100.0$ kg)$[0 - (25.0$ m/s$)^2] = 50(625)$, or $W = $ **31,250 J** (*College Physics* 8th ed. pages 124–126/9th ed. pages 129–132).

3. C From the definition of work, $W = F\Delta r = (7.6$ N)(15.0 m) = **114.0 J**. Notice that it is the work done by the force acting in the direction of motion, *not* in the opposite direction (as friction acts). Therefore, because work and displacement are in the same direction, the work is positive (*College Physics* 8th ed. pages 119–122/9th ed. pages 124–128).

4. B Using $P = Fv$ will provide the solution, where the average force F is the woman's weight mg. Substituting gives $P = Fv = (51.0$ kg$)$ $(10.0$ m/s$^2)(1.0$ m/s), which is 510.0 J/s. It is also 510.0 W, which is the same as 0.51 kW, or $P = $ **0.51 kW** (*College Physics* 8th ed. pages 143–146/9th ed. pages 147–152).

5. B Here, choose the zero gravitational potential energy point at the end of the 6.0-m fall. At the top of the fall, being released from rest, the block has zero kinetic energy. Thus, by energy conservation, we can write $E_{top} = E_{bot}$, or $K_{top} + \Delta U_{g\,top} = K_{bot} + \Delta U_{g\,bot}$, which is $0 + gh_{top} = \frac{1}{2}v_{bot}^2 + 0$. Therefore, $(10.0$ m/s$)(6.0$ m$) = \frac{1}{2}v_{bot}^2$, or $V_{bot} = \sqrt{120.0}$, which is nearly 11.0 m/s. Thus, $v_f = $ **11.0 m/s** (*College Physics* 8th ed. pages 126–134/9th ed. pages 131–140).

6. C The work done by a variable force as a function of distance traveled is the area under the plot on the graph. Therefore, the area from 0 to 2.0 m is that of a triangle: $W = $ area under plot $= \frac{1}{2}bh = \frac{1}{2}(2.m)(10.m) = $ **10.0 J = work done** (*College Physics* 8th ed. pages 147–149/9th ed. pages 152–154).

7. D From the work–energy theorem, we can write $W = \Delta K = \frac{1}{2}mv_f^2 - \frac{1}{2}mv_i^2$ and note that the net force F acting on the block to stop it is kinetic friction $f_k = \mu_k N$, which slows the block through a distance d. Therefore, the work–energy theorem gives $W = \Delta K = \frac{1}{2}mv_f^2 - \frac{1}{2}mv_i^2 = -\mu_k Nd$. Because $v_f = 0$ and the normal force $N = mg$, we have $-\frac{1}{2}mv_i^2 = \frac{1}{2}(mg)d$. Solving for d gives $(mv_i^2)/[2\mu_k(mg)] = d$, or $d = $ **$v^2/2\mu g$**, or choice (D) (*College Physics* 8th ed. pages 124–126/9th ed. pages 129–132).

8. B Here we use Hooke's law $F = -kx$ to calculate the spring constant k and then use the equation for the elastic potential energy (PE_s) or work done by the spring when it is expanded, $W = \dfrac{1}{2}kx^2$. Therefore, $1.0\,\text{N} = K(\frac{1}{10})$, or $k = 10.0\,\text{N/m}$. Substituting values into the next equation gives $W = \frac{1}{2}(10.0\,\text{N/m})(\frac{4}{10})^2$. Solving, we have $W = 5(\frac{16}{100})$, or $\frac{16}{20}$, which is simply **0.8 J** (*College Physics* 8th ed. pages 135–140/9th ed. pages 140–145).

9. **E** Here, we apply energy conservation to points P and Q, noting that at P the block has no kinetic energy as it is released from rest. Thus, we can write $E_P = E_Q$ or $K_P + \Delta U_P = K_Q + \Delta U_Q$, which is $0 + gH$

   $= \frac{1}{2}v_Q^2 + gh$. Therefore, $gH - gh = \frac{1}{2}v_Q^2$, or $v_Q = \sqrt{2g(H-h)}$ (*College Physics* 8th ed. pages 126–134/9th ed. pages 131–140).

10. **A** The work done by a force must be such that the force (or a component of it) is parallel or antiparallel to the direction of the displacement Δr of the object. Because force F fits neither criteria, it is necessary to find the component of F (which is $F\cos\theta$) along the direction of motion. Therefore, the work W performed on the block by the box by F is $W = F\Delta r = (F\cos\theta)L$, which becomes **FL cos 30°** (*College Physics* 8th ed. pages 119–122/9th ed. pages 124–128).

11. **B** Because the work done to stop an object is found from the work–energy theorem (where $K_f = 0$), we can write $W = \Delta K = 0 - \frac{1}{2}mv_i^2$. Therefore, we need to calculate which choice has the greatest initial kinetic energy. Substituting, we find that choice (A) yields $K = \frac{1}{2}(3M)(V)^2 = 1.5\,MV^2$, choice (B) yields $K = \frac{1}{2}(2M)(3V)^2 = 9.0\,MV^2$, choice (C) yields $K = \frac{1}{2}(3M)(2V)^2 = 6.0\,MV^2$, choice (D) yields $K = \frac{1}{2}(M)(4V)^2 = 8.0\,MV^2$, and choice (E) yields $K = \frac{1}{2}(4M)(V)^2 = 2\,MV^2$. Therefore, choice (B), with a value of **9.0 MV²**, requires the greatest work to stop the object (*College Physics* 8th ed. pages 124–126/9th ed. pages 129–132).

12. **C** A discussion of each statement is as follows. Statement I is true because we are told the car is not accelerating, but rather is moving with constant velocity. With statement II, the kinetic energy of the car must be constant because $K = \frac{1}{2}mv^2$ has a dependency on the square of the velocity and must therefore remain the same because v is not changing. Thus, this statement is true. In statement III, the value of U depends on height h, and because the elevator car rises, U must be increasing. Therefore, this statement is false. Statement IV is correct because constant velocity implies no acceleration. With statement V, $K + U_g$ must increase because U_g is increasing even though K remains constant. So, this statement is false. Therefore, statements I, II, and IV are true, making choice (C) the correct answer (*College Physics* 8th ed. pages 126–134/9th ed. pages 131–140).

13. **D** One watt is defined as one joule per second (1 J/s). Therefore, if 1 W is multiplied by 1 s, the second cancels, leaving only the joule. Because the joule is a unit of energy, the correct answer is choice (D) (*College Physics* 8th ed. pages 143–146/9th ed. pages 147–152).

14. **D** This question involves knowing Hooke's law ($F_s = -kx$) and that spring constants k generally *double* when springs are cut in half. Thus, one can substitute values, calculate the original k, and then double it and recalculate with the new value. Instead, we can simply realize that because Hooke's law is a linear relationship, if k is

doubled (for the same force), the displacement x of the mass must be exactly halved. Thus, the spring stretches to half its previous value of 0.05 m and now stretches to **0.025 m** (*College Physics* 8th ed. pages 135–140/9th ed. pages 140–145).

15. **E** By conservation of energy, the kinetic energy of the block is transferred to elastic potential energy upon impacting the spring, which then compresses the spring. Therefore, we can write $E_{before} = E_{after}$, or $K = \frac{1}{2}mv^2 = \frac{1}{2}kx^2$. Thus, $mv^2 = kx^2$. Solving for displacement x gives $(mv^2)/k = x^2$, or $x = v\sqrt{m/k}$ (*College Physics* 8th ed. pages 126–134/9th ed. pages 131–140).

FREE-RESPONSE PROBLEMS

1. (a) A free-body diagram is shown here.

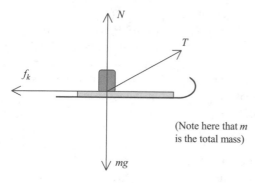

(Note here that m is the total mass)

(b) First, $\Sigma F_y = 0$ gives $N + T \sin\theta - mg = 0$. Thus, $N = mg - T\sin\theta$ so that $N = (24 \text{ kg})(9.8 \text{ m/s}^2) - (60 \text{ N}) \sin 30°$, or **$N = 205.0$ N** (*College Physics* 8th ed. pages 94–97/9th ed. pages 98–102).

(c) First, $\Sigma F_x = ma$ gives $T \cos\theta - f_k = ma$. Thus, $a = (T\cos\theta - f_k)/m$, where $f_k = \mu_k N$. Therefore, the acceleration becomes $a = [(60.0 \text{ N}) \cos 30° - (0.22)(205.0 \text{ N})]/24 \text{ kg}$, or **$a = 0.29$ m/s²** (*College Physics* 8th ed. pages 83–92, 94–101/9th ed. pages 86–95, 98–105).

(d) First, the work done is the result of the horizontal displacement, so we only need to consider the net force in the horizontal direction. Because the displacement is 7.0 m to the right (i.e., x direction), it is necessary to use the net horizontal x force, which is $T\cos\theta - f_k$. Therefore, $W_{net} = F_{net}\Delta r$ gives $W_{net} = (T\cos\theta - f_k)\Delta r$. Substituting gives $W_{net} = (60.0 \text{ N} \cos 30° - 45.1 \text{ N})(7.0 \text{ m})$, or **$W_{net} = 48.0$ J** (*College Physics* 8th ed. pages 119–122/9th ed. pages 124–128).

(e) To determine the power developed, we need either $P = W/\Delta t$ or $P = F_{net}v_{avg}$ where $v_{avg} = (v_i + v_f)/2$. From part (c), we know that the net force on the sled is $T\cos\theta - f_k = ma$, or $(60.0 \text{ N}) \cos 30° - 45.1 \text{ N} = 6.9$ N. Because no value of time is provided, we can use the kinematics equation $v_f^2 = v_i^2 + 2ad$ to determine the average speed v_{avg}. Therefore, $v_f^2 = v_i^2 + 2ad$ becomes $v_f^2 = 0 + 2(0.3 \text{ m/s}^2)(7.0 \text{ m})$ so that $v_f = 2.1$ m/s. The average speed is calculated from $v_{avg} = (v_i + v_f)/2$, which thus gives $v_{avg} = (0 + 2.1 \text{ m/s})/2$, or $v_{avg} = 1.0$ m/s. The power is $F_{net}v_{avg} = (5.9 \text{ N})(1.0 \text{ m/s})$, or **$P = 7.0$ watts** (*College Physics* 8th ed. pages 35–46, 143–146/9th ed. pages 36–47, 147–152).

2. (a) Applying conservation of energy between the highest point (here called A) and the point at which the ball leaves the table (here called B), we can find the horizontal speed of the block as it

leaves the table. So, $E_A = E_B$, which becomes $K_A + \Delta U_{gA} = K_B + \Delta U_{gB}$, or $\frac{1}{2}mv_A^2 + mgh_A = \frac{1}{2}mv_B^2 + mgh_B$. Because $v_A = 0$ and our $h = 0$ point is marked by B, we then have $0 + mgh_A = \frac{1}{2}mv_B^2 + 0$, or $gh_A = \frac{1}{2}v_B^2$. Therefore, $v_B = \sqrt{2gh_1}$, where $h_1 = h_A$ (*College Physics* 8th ed. pages 126–134/9th ed. pages 131–140).

(b) We now have a projectile problem, and to find the horizontal distance D, it is first necessary to find the time of fall using information from the vertical direction. Because d_y is h_2 and $v_{iy} = 0$, we have $h = 0 + \frac{1}{2}g\,\Delta t^2$. Therefore, solving for time gives $t_{fall} = \sqrt{2h_2/g}$. Then, we again apply $d = v_i\,\Delta t + \frac{1}{2}a\,\Delta t^2$, but this time in the horizontal direction to determine D (recalling that $a_x = 0$), which gives $D = v_{ix}\,\Delta t$. From part (a), we have v_{ix} (which is $v_B = \sqrt{2gh_1}$) and can simply substitute both this equation and the one above for t_{fall}. So, $D = \sqrt{2gh_1}\,\sqrt{2h_2/g}$, which is easily simplified to $D = 2\sqrt{h_1 h_2}$ (*College Physics* 8th ed. pages 62–70/9th ed. pages 63–70).

(c) With the measured values of h_1 and h_2 quoted in the problem, the value of $D_{expected}$ is 0.95 m as calculated from the expression found in part (b). Therefore, a value for D of 0.45 m would clearly suggest that the student derived an incorrect expression for D. In addition, the value of $D_{measured}$ must be smaller than $D_{expected}$ (as the student most apparently correctly measured) because the calculated value of D has not incorporated resistance due to friction or air drag. In comparing the student's measured valued of D with the accepted one, we see the former is approximately 10% less than the latter, a fairly realistic estimate for losses due to friction.

3. (a) The work done by the spring in accelerating the bullet is equivalent to the elastic potential energy (PE_s) contained in the spring during its compression. Because k and x are both known, substituting values will give $W = \frac{1}{2}kx^2 = \frac{1}{2}(250.0\ \text{N/m})(4 \times 10^{-2}\ \text{m})^2$, which gives $W = 0.2$ **J** (*College Physics* 8th ed. pages 135–140/9th ed. pages 140–145).

(b) To determine the speed of the released bullet at the equilibrium position, we must realize that it attains all its kinetic energy from the elastic potential energy of the spring. Therefore, we use energy conservation to solve for the bullet's speed, letting the initial compression point in the gun barrel be point A and the equilibrium position at which the bullet is released be point B. Therefore, $E_A = E_B$ which becomes $PE_{sA} = PE_{sB}$. (Notice that the bullet's height relative to a fixed, horizontal reference point has not changed, so we can omit the U_g at points A and B because that value is constant throughout.) Therefore, $kx_A^2 = mv_B^2$, or $0.2\ \text{J} = \frac{1}{2}(1 \times 10^{-2}\ \text{kg})v_B^2$. Solving gives $v_B =$ **6.3 m/s** (*College Physics* 8th ed. pages 126–134/9th ed. pages 131–140).

(c) Here, it is necessary to use the work–energy theorem to determine the work done by friction, using the values of the speeds at point B and at the opening of the gun barrel, where the student measures $v = 4.0$ m/s. Let us call that point C. So, $W = f_k\,\Delta r = \Delta K$, or $f_k\,\Delta r = \frac{1}{2}mv_C^2 - \frac{1}{2}mv_B^2$. Therefore, solving gives $f_k = [\frac{1}{2}m(v_C^2 - v_B^2)]/s$. Substituting given and calculated values yields $f_k = \frac{1}{2}(1 \times 10^{-2}\ \text{kg})[(4.0\ \text{m/s})^2 - (6.3\ \text{m/s})^2]/2.0\ \text{m}$, or $f_k =$ **−0.06 N** (*College Physics* 8th ed. pages 119–122, 124–126/9th ed. pages 124–128, 129–132).

6

IMPULSE AND MOMENTUM

WHAT ARE IMPULSE AND MOMENTUM?

(*College Physics* 8th ed. pages 161–166/9th ed. pages 167–172)

In physics, the quantity *momentum* is something that can be easily seen in our everyday world. When Isaac Newton first set forth the laws of motion, his reference to "state of motion" was understood to be the quantity momentum, a vector whose direction is in the same direction as that of the object's velocity. Thus, as defined, momentum (*p*) is the product of an object's mass *m* and its velocity *v*:

$$p \equiv mv$$

where the SI unit is the kilogram-meter per second, or kg · m/s. In everyday life, for example, a speeding 4000-kg car moving northward has much more momentum than a 10-kg dog walking northward. The dog, however, can have more momentum than the car if, for example, the car is stopped and the dog is still moving. Thus, when the word *motion* is used in physics, it is usually understood that the reference is to *momentum*.

An interesting path to take is to invoke Newton's second law of motion. Recall that the definition of acceleration is $a = \Delta v/\Delta t$ and that we can substitute it into $F = ma$ to acquire $F = ma = m(\Delta v/\Delta t)$, which, upon closer inspection, has momentum secluded within it in the form of $m\Delta v$. For all intents and purposes, problems in AP Physics B will deal with collisions and explosions in which the total mass of a closed system remains constant (unlike, for example, the problem of an accelerating rocket, whose mass changes with time). Therefore, $m\Delta v$ can also be written as $\Delta(mv)$, where m is constant, and is meant as the *change* of momentum (or Δp) of the object in question. Completely written out, it becomes

$$F = ma = m\left(\frac{\Delta v}{\Delta t}\right) = \frac{\Delta(mv)}{\Delta t} = \frac{\Delta p}{\Delta t}$$

Looking carefully, notice that $F = \Delta p/\Delta t$ says that in Newton's second law, the net force on an object is not only the product of mass and acceleration, but is the rate at which the object's momentum *changes*. With a little thought, this concept is completely understandable. For example, if a person kicks a stationary ball, the ball's speed (and thus momentum) changes from zero (i.e., at rest) to some new speed imparted to it by the force of the kick. Thus, that impact (i.e., net force) caused a change of momentum of the ball. Therefore, whenever a force of impact occurs, a tendency to change momentum also occurs.

With a little rearranging, we can solve the above equation for Δp to attain $\Delta p = F\,\Delta t$, where the right-hand expression is defined as *impulse*, a quantity synonymous with *impact* (which can help you remember the meaning of impulse). Denoted by the letter J, impulse is a variable characterized by the average force of impact and the duration over which it acts during a collision or explosion. Notice that impulse, like momentum, is also a vector and is in the direction of the force of impact on the object. Interestingly, its units (newton-seconds, or Ns) are also the same as that of momentum (kilogram-meter per second, or $kg \cdot m/s$) because the unit for newtons is kilogram-meter per second squared, or $kg \cdot m/s^2$. Thus, we have the impulse–momentum theorem:

$$\boxed{\begin{array}{c} \textbf{Impulse} - \textbf{Momentum Theorem} \\ J = F\Delta t = \Delta p \end{array}}$$

SAMPLE PROBLEM 1

A 0.046-kg golf ball initially at rest is struck with a golf club. During the time of the impact (while the force exerted is constant), the ball is compressed by 0.02 m and then leaves the club with a velocity of 44.0 m/s due east.

(a) Determine the impulse imparted to the ball during the collision.
(b) Determine the duration of the collision.
(c) Determine the magnitude of the average force exerted on the ball during the collision.

SOLUTION TO PROBLEM 1

(a) Because both v_i and v_f for the duration of the impact are given, we can use the impulse–momentum theorem to calculate the impulse J. So, $J = \Delta p = m(v_f - v_i)$, which becomes $J = 0.046$ kg(44.0 m/s – 0) = $J =$ **2.0 Ns east**.

(b) From the kinematics relationship $v_f^2 = v_i^2 + 2ad$, we can solve for the acceleration and then use $a = \Delta v/\Delta t$ to determine the collision time. Thus, $v_f^2 = v_i^2 + 2ad$ gives (44.0 m/s)² = 0 + 2a(0.02 m) so $a = 48,400.0$ m/s² (which is huge!). Then, substituting knowns into $a = \Delta v/\Delta t$ gives 48,400.0 m/s² = (44.0 m/s – 0)/Δt, so $\Delta t =$ **9.1 × 10⁻⁴ s**.

(c) Using the impulse–momentum theorem, we can find the average force of impact F; $J = F\,\Delta t$, or 2.0 Ns = F(9.0 × 10⁻⁴ s), which gives $F =$ **2200.0 N**.

WHAT BECOMES OF MOMENTUM DURING A COLLISION OR EXPLOSION?

(*College Physics* 8th ed. pages 166–178/9th ed. pages 172–184)

One of the most fundamental laws of physics, aside from Newton's laws, involves momentum. Think about a large car moving toward a smaller one that is stopped at a red traffic light. If the larger car collides with the smaller one, what happens? The smaller car undoubtedly moves forward, in the direction in which the larger car was moving. Simply put, during a collision (or explosion), momentum is *transferred* from one object to another. Going one step further brings us to the notion of a *closed system* of objects, which, here, is the system of the two cars. In collisions or explosions, there are forces that are internal to the system and forces that are external to the system. Internal forces exist between only the objects in the system, and external forces exist outside of our defined system. With the colliding cars, internal forces are only those of the impact each car exerts on the other. Gravity from Earth, for example, or normal forces or friction would be external to the system. In the absence of external forces, our system is said to be *isolated*. Often, internal forces during an explosion or collision are much greater than external forces and so those external forces (for just a brief time) can be neglected, thus allowing us to approximate an isolated system. Experimentation can easily show (for example, using colliding carts on an air track), that in the absence of external forces, before and after a collision or explosion, the *total momentum* of all objects in a system remains constant. This is the law of conservation of momentum, in which the sum of all the momenta of the objects in the system *prior to* the collision equals the sum of all the momenta of the objects in the system *after* the collision.

Law of Conservation of Momentum

$$p_{isys} = p_{fsys}$$

Keep in mind that collisions are classified based on their ability to conserve kinetic energy, not momentum. *Elastic collisions* are those that conserve both momentum and kinetic energy, when objects collide and do not stick to each other and no energy is transferred to sound or heat (such as air molecules or, in some sense, billiard balls), whereas *inelastic collisions* are those in which momentum is conserved but kinetic energy is not. It can be shown that if the objects stick together, the maximum possible amount of kinetic energy is dissipated, and these collisions are referred to as completely inelastic. In all types of inelastic collisions, mechanical energy is dissipated to other types of energy (such as heat or sound), thereby reducing the total kinetic energy of the objects after the collision.

SAMPLE PROBLEM 2

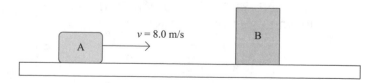

Block A (mass 3.0 kg) moving on a frictionless, horizontal surface collides with stationary block B (mass 5.0 kg) as shown.
Assume the collision is completely *inelastic*.

(a) Determine the final speed of blocks the moment after the collision as they move together.

(b) Determine the change of kinetic energy of the system due to this collision.

Now assume the collision is *elastic*.

(c) Determine the speed of blocks A and B after the collision.

(d) Determine the change of kinetic energy of the system due to this collision.

(e) Determine the average force exerted by block A on block B if the collision time is 0.01 s.

SOLUTION TO PROBLEM 2

(a) By the law of conservation of momentum, we must add the total system momentum before the collision and equate it to that after the collision. Recalling that $p = mv$, we apply $p_{i\,\text{sys}} = p_{f\,\text{sys}}$, which becomes (3.0 kg)(8.0 m/s) + 0 = (3.0 kg + 5.0 kg)v_f, or $v_f = 3.0$ m/s.

(b) Recalling that $K = \frac{1}{2}mv^2$, we find the kinetic energy of the blocks prior to and after the collision: $K_i = \frac{1}{2}m_A v_A^2 + \frac{1}{2}m_B v_B^2 = \frac{1}{2}$ (3.0 kg) (8.0 m/s)^2 + 0 = 96.0 J and $K_f = \frac{1}{2}m_{tot}v_A^2 = \frac{1}{2}$ (8.0 kg)(3.0 m/s)^2 = 36.0 J. Therefore, $\Delta K = 36 - 96 = 60$ J.

(c) By the law of conservation of momentum, the total system momentum before and after the collision must be equal. Thus, $p_{i\,\text{sys}} = p_{f\,\text{sys}}$, which is

$$m_A v_{Ai} + 0 = m_A v_{Af} + m_B v_{Bf} \qquad (1)$$

Because Equation (1) is an elastic collision, we must also write conservation of kinetic energy. So, $K_{i\,\text{sys}} = K_{f\,\text{sys}}$, or

$$\frac{1}{2}m_A v_{Af}^2 + 0 = \frac{1}{2}m_A v_{Af}^2 + \frac{1}{2}m_B v_{Bf}^2 \qquad (2)$$

The solution to this part of the problem involves a great deal of algebra and in the interest of space will only be partially shown here. Rearranging variables in Equation (1) gives $m_A v_{Ai} - m_A v_{Af} = m_A v_{Bf}$, and doing the same in Equation (2) gives $m_A v_{Ai}^2 - m_A v_{Af}^2 = m_B v_{Bf}^2$. To solve, we first divide the two resulting equations, $\dfrac{m_A v_{Ai}^2 - m_A v_{Af}^2}{m_A v_{Ai} - m_A v_{Af}} = \dfrac{m_B v_{Bf}^2}{m_A v_{Bf}}$ and use the following algebraic relationship to reduce further: $x^2 - y^2 = (x + y)(x - y)$. We now substitute back into Equation (1) to solve, which will give the following for each final velocity:

$$V_{Af} = \left(\frac{m_A - m_B}{m_A + m_B}\right) v_{Ai} \quad \text{and} \quad V_{Bf} = \left(\frac{2m_A}{m_A + m_B}\right) v_{Ai}$$

Therefore, $v_{Af} = [(3.0 \text{ kg} - 5.0 \text{ kg})/(3.0 \text{ kg} + 5.0 \text{ kg})](8.0 \text{ m/s})$ and $v_{Bf} = [2(3.0 \text{ kg})/(3.0 \text{ kg} + 5.0 \text{ kg})](8.0 \text{ m/s})$, which gives $v_{Af} = $ **−2.0 m/s** and $v_{Bf} = $ **0.8 m/s**.

(d) Because we are told that it is an elastic collision, the change of kinetic energy is zero because kinetic energy is conserved.

(e) Using the impulse–momentum theorem, we can find the average force of impact F; $J = \Delta mv = F\Delta t$, or $(5.0 \text{ kg})(2.7 \text{ m/s} - 0) = F(0.01 \text{ s})$, which gives $F = $ **1350.0 N**.

AP Tip

When applying the law of conservation of momentum, be sure to *add* the momenta of each object in the system before and after the event (keeping in mind directions for vectors) and then equate their sum. That is the meaning of a conservation law.

IMPULSE AND MOMENTUM: STUDENT OBJECTIVES FOR THE AP EXAM

- You should understand impulse and momentum to relate mass, velocity, and momentum for a moving object and to calculate the total momentum of a system of bodies.
- You should be able to relate impulse to the change in linear momentum and the average force acting on a body.
- You should be able to identify situations in which linear momentum (or its components) is conserved.
- You should be able to apply the conservation of momentum to determine final velocity when two objects move along the same line or at right angles, collide, and stick together, and to calculate the change of kinetic energy of such an event.

MULTIPLE-CHOICE QUESTIONS

1. Which one of the following statements concerning momentum is true?
   (A) Momentum is a force.
   (B) Momentum is a scalar quantity.
   (C) The SI unit of momentum is the kilogram-meter squared per second, or $\text{kg} \cdot \text{m}^2/\text{s}$.
   (D) The momentum of an object is always positive.
   (E) Momentum has the same units as the quantity impulse.

2. A 0.1-kg steel ball is dropped straight down onto a hard, horizontal floor and bounces straight up. Its speed immediately before and immediately after impact with the floor is 10.0 m/s. What is the magnitude of the impulse delivered to the floor by the steel ball?
   (A) 0
   (B) $1 \text{ N} \cdot \text{s}$
   (C) $2 \text{ N} \cdot \text{s}$
   (D) $10 \text{ N} \cdot \text{s}$
   (E) $100 \text{ N} \cdot \text{s}$

3. A beam of n gas molecules is incident upon a barrier at 30° relative to the horizontal as shown. Each molecule has mass m and speed v, and the entire beam is reflected elastically, also at 30°. What is the magnitude of the total change of momentum of the particle beam during this event? (Note: sin 30° = 0.50, cos 30° = 0.87.)
   (A) $2nmv$
   (B) $2nmv(\sin 60°)$
   (C) $nmv(\sin 60°)$
   (D) $nmv(\cos 60°)$
   (E) nmv

4. Which of the following five objects requires the greatest change in its momentum to stop it?

Object	Mass (kg)	Speed (m/s)
(A) Electron	10^{-30}	10^{8}
(B) Oil tanker	10^{8}	10^{-1}
(C) Raindrop	10^{-4}	10
(D) Snail	10^{-2}	10^{-4}
(E) Satellite	10	10^{4}

5. A baseball of mass m (at rest) is struck by a bat so that it acquires a speed v. If t represents the duration of the collision between the bat and the ball, which expression determines the magnitude of the average force exerted on the ball?
   (A) $\frac{1}{2}mv^2$
   (B) $\dfrac{mv}{t}$
   (C) $\frac{1}{2}mv^2 t$
   (D) $\frac{1}{2}\left(\dfrac{mt^2}{v}\right)$
   (E) mvt

6. A sled of mass m is coasting on a frozen river when, while passing under a bridge, a box mass m falls straight down and lands on the sled. The sled and box continue along the original line of motion. How does the kinetic energy of the sled with the box compare to the original kinetic energy of the sled?
   (A) It is one-fourth the original kinetic energy of the sled.
   (B) It is one-half the original kinetic energy of the sled.
   (C) It is three-fourths the original kinetic energy of the sled.
   (D) It is the same as the original kinetic energy of the sled.
   (E) It is two times the original kinetic energy of the sled.

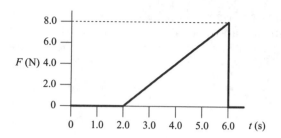

7. A 2.0-kg object is acted upon by a single force in the positive
   x direction as shown. What is the momentum change experienced
   by the object during the first 6 s?
   (A) 16.0 N · s
   (B) 30.0 N · s
   (C) 32.0 N · s
   (D) 40.0 N · s
   (E) 48.0 N · s

8. An in-flight projectile in dynamic equilibrium explodes into several
   fragments. What happens instantaneously to its momentum follow-
   ing this explosion?
   (A) It has been changed into kinetic energy of the fragments.
   (B) It is less than that immediately before the explosion.
   (C) It is the same as that immediately before the explosion, by the
       law of conservation of momentum.
   (D) It is more than that immediately before the explosion.
   (E) It has been changed into radiant energy.

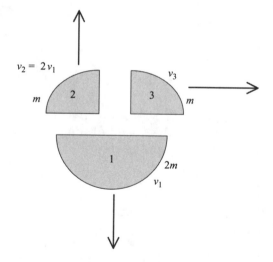

9. A projectile has just exploded into three pieces, with the velocities
   of each piece as shown. What was the speed of the projectile the
   instant before it broke up?
   (A) v_3

   (B) $\dfrac{v_3}{3}$

   (C) $4v_3$

   (D) $\dfrac{v_3}{4}$

   (E) $\dfrac{v_1 + v_2 + v_2}{4}$

10. A rifle of mass M is initially at rest but is free to recoil. It fires a bullet of mass m and velocity $+v$ (relative to the ground). After firing, what is the velocity of the rifle (relative to the ground)?
    (A) $-mv$
    (B) $\dfrac{-Mv}{m}$
    (C) $\dfrac{-mv}{M}$
    (D) $-v$
    (E) $\dfrac{+mv}{M}$

For Questions 11 and 12, refer to the following information.
A space vehicle of mass m has a speed v. At some instant, it explodes into two pieces, each of mass $\frac{1}{2}m$. One of the pieces is at rest just after the separation. This event occurs very far from any celestial body.

11. Which one of the following statements concerning this situation is true?
    (A) The moving piece has speed $2v$.
    (B) The moving piece has speed v.
    (C) The piece at rest possesses kinetic energy.
    (D) The moving piece has speed $\frac{1}{2}v$.
    (E) This process does not conserve momentum.

12. What is the kinetic energy of the moving piece just after the separation?
    (A) 0
    (B) $\frac{1}{4} mv^2$
    (C) $\frac{1}{2} mv^2$
    (D) mv^2
    (E) $2mv^2$

13. A 50.0-kg boy runs at a speed of 10.0 m/s and jumps onto a cart that is initially at rest. If the speed of the cart with the boy on it is 2.50 m/s, what is the mass of the cart?
    (A) 150.0 kg
    (B) 175.0 kg
    (C) 210.0 kg
    (D) 260.0 kg
    (E) 300.0 kg

14. Which one of the following statements concerning an inelastic collision is true?
    (A) Momentum is not conserved, but kinetic energy is conserved.
    (B) Total mass is not conserved, but momentum is conserved.
    (C) Neither kinetic energy nor momentum is conserved.
    (D) Momentum is conserved, but kinetic energy is not conserved.
    (E) The total impulse is equal to the change in kinetic energy.

15. An object of momentum p and mass m is in motion. At the moment it is moving with speed v, what is its kinetic energy?

(A) $\dfrac{2p^2}{m^2}$

(B) $\dfrac{p}{2m}$

(C) $\dfrac{p^2}{2}$

(D) $\dfrac{p^2}{2m}$

(E) $\dfrac{p^2}{2v}$

FREE-RESPONSE PROBLEMS

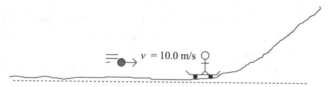

$v = 10.0 \text{ m/s}$

1. A 26.0-kg boy is standing at rest on a 4.0-kg skateboard at the bottom of a frictionless hill as shown. A 5.0-kg ball comes at him with a horizontal velocity of 10.0 m/s to the right, and he catches the ball and remains on the skateboard.

(a) Determine the speed of the boy the moment after he catches the ball.

(b) Determine how high up the hill the boy coasts and momentarily comes to rest.

(c) Sketch the free-body diagram of the boy as he stops on the hill in the diagram below.

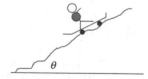

θ

(d) The boy now begins to accelerate down the hill, which is tilted relative to the horizontal by the angle θ. Derive an expression for the boy's acceleration in terms of g and θ.

(e) What percentage of Earth's gravitational acceleration is the boy's acceleration if the angle of the hill is 49°?

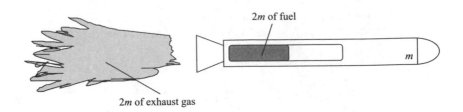

2m of fuel

2m of exhaust gas

2. A rocket of mass *m* initially carries an additional mass of fuel equal to 4*m* as shown. The rocket is in deep space, very far from any stars or planets, and therefore has negligible external forces on it and is initially at rest. The rocket engine fires, causing the rocket to consume (at a constant rate) a mass of 2*m* of fuel expelled out the nozzle as hot gas moving at speed *v* (relative to the original rest frame). Left behind is 2*m* of unburned fuel.
   (a) After the gas is emitted, what is the magnitude of the momentum of the exhaust gas? Express your answer in terms of *m* and *v*.
   (b) After the gas is emitted, what is the speed of the rocket? Express your answer in terms of *m* and *v*.
   (c) If the time during which the gas is expelled is Δ*t*, what was the average force *F* on the rocket during the fuel burn? Express your answer in terms of *m*, *v*, and Δ*t*.
   (d) Explain why the force on the rocket by the gas must have been continuously changing over time Δ*t*.

ANSWERS

MULTIPLE-CHOICE QUESTIONS

1. **E** As defined by Newton's second law, $F_{net} = ma = m(\Delta v/\Delta t) = \Delta p/\Delta t$, momentum is the product of mass (*m*) and velocity (*v*), in the direction of the velocity. Thus, its unit is the kilogram-meter per second, or kg · m/s, which therefore eliminates choices (A), (B), and (C). Similarly, because momentum is a vector quantity, it may have either a positive or negative sign, thus eliminating choice (D). Finally, the impulse–momentum theorem states that, by definition, $J = F\Delta t$, and because $F = ma$, we have $J = F\Delta t = (ma)\Delta t = (m\Delta v/\Delta t)\Delta t = m \Delta v$, which is Δp. Therefore, choice (E) is correct (*College Physics* 8th ed. pages 161–166/9th ed. pages 167–172).

2. **C** When the ball moves downward, its velocity is –10.0 m/s, but the moment after it rebounds, its velocity is +10.0 m/s. Therefore, the impulse delivered to the ball (i.e., the change of momentum Δp) is found by $J = F\Delta t = \Delta p$. Thus, $\Delta p = m\Delta v = m(v_f - v_i) = 0.1$ kg[+10.0 m/s – (–10.0 m/s)] = 0.1 kg(+20.0 m/s) = 2.0 kg · m/s, or $\Delta p = $ **2 N · s** (*College Physics* 8th ed. pages 161–166/9th ed. pages 167–172).

3. **E** The net change of momentum arises from both the change of momentum in the x direction and in the y direction. In the y direction, $\Delta p_y = (mv \sin 30°) - (- mv \sin 30°) = $ **2mv sin 30°**, whereas in the x direction, $\Delta p_x = (mv \cos 30°) - (mv \cos 30°) = $ **0.** Therefore, $\Delta p_{total} = $

$\Delta p_y - \Delta p_x = [mv\left(\frac{1}{2}\right) + mv\left(\frac{1}{2}\right)] - 0 = mv$. So, for n molecules, Δp_{total} is nmv (*College Physics* 8th ed. pages 166–176/9th ed. pages 172–184).

4. **B** The largest change of momentum ($\Delta p = p_f - p_i$) occurs with the object that has the largest initial momentum (p_i) because here in each case $p_f = 0$. Therefore, calculating the initial momentum of each object gives the following and shows that choice (B) is the answer:

Object	Mass (kg)	Speed (m/s)	Initial momentum mv (kg · m/s)
(A) Electron	10^{-30}	10^8	10^{-22}
(B) Oil tanker	$\mathbf{10^8}$	$\mathbf{10^{-1}}$	$\mathbf{10^7}$
(C) Raindrop	10^{-4}	10	10^{-3}
(D) Snail	10^{-2}	10^{-4}	10^{-6}
(E) Satellite	10	10^4	10^5

(*College Physics* 8th ed. pages 161–166/9th ed. pages 167–172)

5. **B** $F = (m\Delta v/\Delta t)$ is the average force exerted on the ball and thus, because $v_i = 0$ and $v_f = v$, this becomes

$$F = \frac{m\Delta v}{\Delta t} = \frac{m(v_f - v_i)}{t} = \frac{m(v_f - 0)}{t}$$

or $F = mv/t$, which is choice (B) (*College Physics* 8th ed. pages 161–166/9th ed. pages 167–172).

6. **B** Applying momentum conservation to the horizontal portion of the motion, $p_i = p_f$, $m_i v_i = m_f v_f$, and solving for v_f gives $v_f = m_i v_i/m_f$. The final mass is $2m$ instead of m, which will cause v_f to decrease by one-half relative to v_i. Therefore, the kinetic energy equation states that $K_f = \frac{1}{2}mv_f^2 = \frac{1}{2}(2m)(\frac{1}{2}v_i)^2 = \frac{1}{4}mv_i^2$, which, upon careful examination, is one-half the original kinetic energy (*College Physics* 8th ed. pages 124–126, 166–176/9th ed. pages 129–132, 172–184).

7. **A** By the impulse–momentum theorem, the change of momentum and force are related by $J = F\Delta t = \Delta p$. Therefore, $\Delta p = F\Delta t$ is used here, where F is the average force occurring in the time interval. From the graph, $F = 0$ during seconds 1 and 2, but from second 2 to second 6 (where $\Delta t = 4$ s), the average force is 4.0 N (because $F_i = 0$ and $F_f = 8.0$ N, their average is 4.0 N). Therefore, $\Delta p = F\Delta t = (4.0$ N$)(4.0$ s$)$, or $\Delta p = \mathbf{16.0\ N \cdot s}$.

Of important note is how this problem can be solved exactly the same way using the area under the Ft graph, which is equal to impulse. For seconds 1 and 2, no area exists, but from second 2 to second 6, the area is that of a triangle, $\frac{1}{2}$ (base × height), which is $\frac{1}{2}$

(4.0 s)(8.0 N), or **16.0 N · s** (*College Physics* 8th ed. pages 161–166/9th ed. pages 167–172).

8. **C** This question is simply a statement of the law of conservation of momentum. In a system in which the net external force is zero, the total momentum of the system of objects is constant during an interaction (i.e., explosion or collision) and thus the momentum before and after the event is constant. Thus, choice (C) is correct (*College Physics* 8th ed. pages 166–176/9th ed. pages 172–184).

9. **D** By the law of conservation of momentum, $p_i = p_f$, and for their respective components, $p_{ix} = p_{fx}$ and $p_{iy} = p_{fy}$. Looking carefully at the diagram, we notice that the final momenta of pieces 1 and 2 are equal ($2mv$) but oppositely directed in the y direction. Thus, they cancel, showing that the initial system's momentum in the y direction must have been zero. Therefore, the momentum of piece 3 must be equal to the entire system momentum before the explosion, or $p_{ix} = p_{fx}$ or $p_{ix} = mv_3$, but because the total mass is $4m$, it becomes $4mv_i = mv_3$, or $v_i = \frac{1}{4}v_3$, which is choice (D) (*College Physics* 8th ed. pages 166–176/9th ed. pages 172–184).

10. **C** By the law of conservation of momentum, the system momentum before and after the firing of the bullet must be constant. Therefore, $p_{isys} = p_{fsys}$, or $0 = +mv + (-Mv_{recoil})$, which gives $mv = Mv_{recoil}$. Therefore, $v_{recoil} = mv/M$. Because we are told that the bullet's velocity is in the positive direction, the rifle's recoil velocity must be in the negative direction; thus, choice (C) is correct (*College Physics* 8th ed. pages 166–176/9th ed. pages 172–184).

11. **A** Applying the law of conservation of momentum before and after the event gives $mv = 0 + \frac{1}{2}mv_f$, and solving gives $v_f = 2v$ (as expected because the first broken piece stopped), which is statement (A). Thus, statements (B) and (D) are eliminated. Statement (D) also is impossible because momentum is conserved in the absence of external forces, and statement (C) is impossible because any object at rest has no kinetic energy (*College Physics* 8th ed. pages 166–176/9th ed. pages 172–184).

12. **D** From Question 11, the speed of the second piece (whose mass is $\frac{1}{2}m$) is $v_f = 2v$. Substituting into the kinetic energy equation gives $K = \frac{1}{2}mv^2 = \frac{1}{2}(\frac{1}{2}m)(2v)^2$, which becomes $\frac{1}{4}m(4v^2)$, or $K = mv^2$ (*College Physics* 8th ed. pages 124–126, 166–176/9th ed. pages 129–132, 172–184).

13. **A** Applying the law of conservation of momentum, $p_i = p_f$ gives $50\ kg(10\ m/s) + 0 = (50\ kg + m)\frac{5}{2}$, which becomes $500\ kg \cdot m/s(\frac{2}{5}) = 50\ kg + m$. Solving gives $m = $ **150.0 kg** (*College Physics* 8th ed. pages 166–176/9th ed. pages 172–184).

14. **D** Collisions are based on whether they are *elastic* (momentum and kinetic energy are conserved) or *inelastic* (momentum is conserved but kinetic energy is not, such as when objects may possibly collide and stick). Thus, statement (D) is correct (*College Physics* 8th ed. pages 166–176/9th ed. pages 172–184).

15. **D**   Recalling that momentum is $p = mv$ and kinetic energy is $K = \frac{1}{2}mv^2$, solving for and replacing v^2 gives $v^2 = (p^2/m^2)$. Thus, $K = \frac{1}{2}m(p^2/m^2)$, or $K = \frac{1}{2}(p^2/m)$, or choice (D) (*College Physics* 8th ed. pages 124–126, 166–176/9th ed. pages 129–132, 172–184).

FREE-RESPONSE PROBLEMS

1. (a) Because we are told that the hill is frictionless, the assumption is that the coefficient of friction is negligible; thus, no external force of friction exists. Therefore, we can apply the law of conservation of momentum, which states that the sum of the momenta of the objects within the system *before the impact* must equal the sum of the momenta of the objects within the system *after the impact*. Therefore, $p_{i\,sys} = p_{f\,sys}$, or (5.0 kg)(10.0 m/s) + 0 = (5.0 kg + 26.0 kg + 4.0 kg)v_f. Solving for v_f gives $v_f =$ **1.4 m/s** (*College Physics* 8th ed. pages 166–176/9th ed. pages 172–184).

    (b) By energy conservation, we can state that the total mechanical energy of the boy–ball–skateboard at the bottom of the hill (just after having caught the ball) is equal to the total mechanical energy at the top of the hill, where they momentarily stop. We need to apply energy conservation because we are searching for the height h above the horizontal to which the boy rises and then stops. Therefore, $E_{total\,bottom} = E_{total\,top}$, which is $K_{bottom} + U_{g\,bottom} = K_{top} + U_{g\,top}$. Because the potential energy at the bottom and the kinetic energy at the top are both zero (no height and no speed, respectively), we then have $\frac{1}{2}$ (35.0 kg)(1.4 m/s)^2 + 0 = 0 + (35.0 kg)(10.0 m/s^2)h. Therefore, $h = $ **0.1 m** (*College Physics* 8th ed. pages 126–134/9th ed. pages 132–140).

    (c) The only forces that act on the object at the top of its path are the normal force N (perpendicular to the hill) and the weight w.

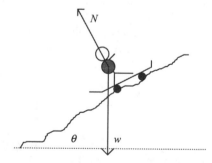

    (d) A hint was given in part (c), the free-body diagram. Now, the object is accelerating, and we thus have a dynamics problem in the negative x direction. We should choose a frame of reference with the x axis parallel to the hill as shown here.

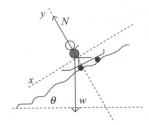

Therefore, $\Sigma F_x = -ma$ gives $mg \sin \theta = -ma$, or the acceleration is $a = g \sin \theta$ (*College Physics* 8th ed. pages 83–92, 94–101/9th ed. pages 86–95, 98–105).

(e) From part (d), $a = g \sin \theta$; thus, all that must be done is to substitute the values given. Therefore, $a = (10.0 \text{ m/s}^2) \sin 49°$, or $a = \mathbf{7.5 \text{ m/s}^2}$. The magnitude of this acceleration relative to Earth's gravitational acceleration is found by taking the ratio of the two: $(7.5 \text{ m/s}^2)/(10.0 \text{ m/s}^2) = 0.75$, or **75% of** g.

2. (a) Because we are told that the gas of mass $2m$ is expelled with speed v, the momentum of the gas as it is expelled is thus $p = mv$, or $p_{gas} = (2m)v$. Thus, $p_{gas} = \mathbf{2mv}$ (*College Physics* 8th ed. pages 161–163/9th ed. pages 167–170).

(b) Here it is necessary to apply the law of conservation of momentum, adding the momenta of the gas and rocket *before the acceleration* and equating it to the sum of the momenta of the gas and rocket *after the acceleration*. Notice that before the expulsion of the gas, the total system mass is $5m$. Therefore, $p_{i \text{ sys}} = p_{f \text{ sys}}$, or $(5m)(0) = -(2m)(v) + (3m)v_{rocket}$. Therefore, $2v = 3v_{rocket}$ because the left side above is zero (no initial momentum). Finally, solving for the rocket's speed gives $v_{rocket} = \frac{2}{3}v$ (*College Physics* 8th ed. pages 166–176/9th ed. pages 172–184).

(c) By the impulse–momentum theorem, the change of momentum of the gas during the time it is expelled is equal to the impulse imparted on it by the force of the rocket, which by Newton's third law is equal but opposite to the force exerted on the rocket by the gas. Therefore, $\Delta p = J = F\Delta t$. Thus, the average force F is the rate of change of momentum of the gas, or

$$F = \frac{\Delta p}{\Delta t} = \frac{p_f - p_i}{\Delta t} = \frac{2mv - 0}{\Delta t} = \frac{2mv}{\Delta t}$$

Thus, the average force is $F = \mathbf{(2mv/\Delta t)}$ (*College Physics* 8th ed. pages 161–166/9th ed. pages 167–172).

(d) The thrust on the rocket by ejected exhaust gases must increase because the exhaust velocity (v_e) of the gases increases while fuel is burned to propel the rocket. The instantaneous thrust is given by $Ma = M(\Delta v/\Delta t) = v_e(\Delta M/\Delta t)$ and continually changes during the time Δt as the burn rate ($\Delta M/\Delta t$) increases, where M is the total mass of the rocket plus the fuel (*College Physics* 8th ed. pages 177–178/9th ed. pages 182–184).

7

CIRCULAR MOTION AND TORQUE

THE PRINCIPLES OF UNIFORM CIRCULAR MOTION

(*College Physics* 8th ed. pages 198–206/9th ed. pages 207–213)

Uniform circular motion represents the motion of an object in a circular path of fixed radius R (or in *part* of such a path, like an arc) under the action of a center-seeking force. Unlike linear motion, where force and velocity are either parallel or antiparallel, the condition for circular motion is that the force and velocity vectors are mutually perpendicular. Therefore, although it is called "uniform" circular motion because the radius of the circle and the speed of the object are constant, the object's tangential *velocity* vector is continuously changing direction and the object therefore accelerates. In this situation, acceleration can occur even though the object's speed is constant (a seeming contradiction).

As shown, taking two separate moments of the object's position in the path will yield two velocity vectors, v_1 and v_2. Taking Δv, or $v_2 + (-v_1)$, shows that their difference is a vector pointing to the circle's center. Recalling from kinematics that $a = \Delta v \, \Delta t$, we now see that the direction of the acceleration is inward (the same direction as Δv) and is called *centripetal acceleration*. By Newton's second law, a net force must be the cause, which is the centrally directed force called *centripetal force*. Equations for these useful relationships are as follows: $a_c = v^2/R$, and because $F_{net} = ma$, we then have $F_C = mv^2/R$.

AP Tip

Differentiate "to the center" and "away from the center" vectors by using positive (+) signs for vectors pointing inward and negative (–) signs for vectors pointing outward.

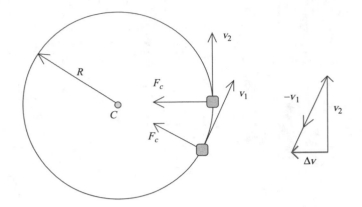

In some instances, several forces may combine to supply the centripetal force (such as tension, gravity, magnetism, or lift), and thus we write $\Sigma F_c = mv^2/R$. Notice that as the object completes one entire revolution, it covers a distance of one circumference (in meters) in a time of one period (T, in seconds), so we can write $v = 2\pi R/T$. To summarize, the three uniform circular motion equations needed for problem solving are as follows:

$$\Sigma F_c = \frac{mv^2}{R} \qquad a_c = \frac{v^2}{R} \qquad v = \frac{2\pi R}{T}$$

SAMPLE PROBLEM 1

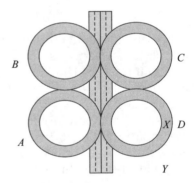

A level, unbanked roadway viewed from overhead possesses four circular, horizontal, level cloverleaf intersections, which are highway entrance/exit ramps (A through D as shown). The coefficient of static friction between the rubber car tires and the roadway asphalt is 0.5, and the diameter of ramp D is 54.0 m. The system of the car and driver, with a total mass of 1300.0 kg, enters ramp D at a constant speed of 8.0 m/s.

(a) Using the following figure to represent the car, sketch and label all the forces acting on the car when it is at point X as viewed from point Y.

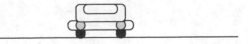

(b) The driver completes one loop along ramp D. Calculate the car's period for this single loop.

(c) Calculate the maximum speed the car can travel along this ramp just before the car begins to slip and starts skidding.
(d) Describe specifically how your answer to part (c) changes if the mass of the car is doubled.

SOLUTION TO PROBLEM 1

(a) A sketch is as shown. Notice that this free-body diagram is the same as if the car were moving away from the observer.

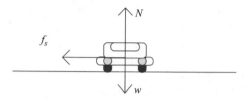

(b) Because both the speed (v = 8.0 m/s) and the circle's diameter (so that its radius R = 27.0 m) are given, the period can be easily calculated using the equation for speed shown above. So,

$$V = \frac{2\pi R}{T}$$

or

$$T = \frac{2\pi R}{v} = \frac{2\pi(27.0 \text{ m})}{8.0 \text{ m/s}}$$

which gives **T = 21.0 s**.
(c) Based on the free-body diagram in part (a), the only force supplying the centripetal force is that of static friction. The moment the car begins to slip, however, the *maximum* static friction force has been overcome, which allows us to write $f_{s\,max}$ = $\mu_s N$ = centripetal force. Therefore, $\mu_s N = mv^2/R$. Because $\Sigma F_y = 0$, we now have $N = mg$. Substituting above gives $\mu_s g = v^2/R$. Solving gives $v = \sqrt{\mu_s Rg} = \sqrt{(0.5)(27.0 \text{ m})(10.0 \text{ m/s}^2)}$, or **$v$ = 12.0 m/s**.
(d) As shown by the equation for the speed v of the car on the curved roadway, the effect of mass is not a factor in the equation. Thus, altering the mass of the car has no effect on the maximum speed the car can attain in rounding this curve.

SAMPLE PROBLEM 2

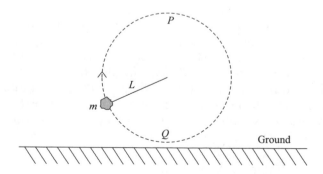

A stone of mass m is attached to a string of length L that is swung clockwise in a vertical circle above the ground as shown. Points P and Q represent the top and bottom, respectively, of the circular path of the stone. While the stone passes through point P, the tension in the string is three times the stone's actual weight, and while passing through point Q, the height of the stone above the ground is negligible. Express all your answers in terms of m, L, and g.

(a) Determine the speed of the stone at point P.
(b) The moment the stone is at point P, the string breaks. Determine the amount of time it takes the stone to reach the ground.
(c) Determine the horizontal distance traveled by the stone the moment it strikes the ground.

SOLUTION TO PROBLEM 2

(a) At the top, point Q, apply $\Sigma F_c = mv^2/R$, noting that we are told that $T = 3mg$. Therefore, we have $T + mg = mv^2/R$, or $3mg + mg = mv^2/R$, which is then $4g = v^2/R$. By noting that R is just L, we then have $2\sqrt{gL} = v$.

(b) The stone now becomes a projectile that falls a vertical distance of one circle diameter, or $2L$. Using the kinematics equation for displacement in the y-direction, we can find the fall time: $d_y = v_{iy}\,\Delta t + \frac{1}{2}a_y\,\Delta t^2$, which becomes $-2L = 0 + \frac{1}{2}(-g)\,\Delta t^2$. Solving for time gives $\Delta t = 2\sqrt{L/g}$.

(c) Here we are looking for d_x. We can use the displacement equation (in the x direction) with the expressions for time found in part (b) and speed found in part (a). Then, $d_x = v_{ix}\,\Delta t + \frac{1}{2}a_x\,\Delta t^2$, or $d_x = v_{ix}\,\Delta t + 0$, which becomes $d_x = \left(2\sqrt{gL}\right)2\sqrt{L/g}$, or $d_x = 4L$.

WHAT SUPPLIES THE CENTRIPETAL FORCE ON A BANKED ROADWAY?

(*College Physics* 8th ed. page 205/9th ed. page 212)

An interesting and useful application of uniform circular motion is the application of this motion to roadways or paths that are tilted (i.e., banked) relative to the horizontal. A perfect example is a raceway track on which sports cars can reach speeds of two to three times those of common vehicles on highways. If a banked roadway is very smooth and nearly frictionless, the question of how the car can stay on the track is the most obvious at the outset. A free-body diagram as shown here can help answer this question. (Notice that this diagram represents a head-on view of the car, not a side view as is often common for objects on an inclined plane.)

In contrast to an object placed on an inclined plane, the x axis is drawn such that it is along the radius of the circular path. Thus, it is the normal force, not the weight, which has x and y components. As a result, the x component of N points radially and thus provides the centripetal force required to hold the car in its circular path. Applying $\Sigma F_c = mv^2/R$ gives $N \sin\theta = mv^2/R$. For example, the maximum speed v that the car can reach without slipping can easily be determined by applying $\Sigma F_y = 0$ as the car is in vertical equilibrium; hence, $\Sigma F_y = N_y - mg = N\cos\theta - mg = 0$.

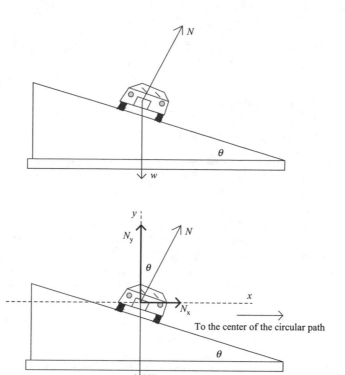

Therefore, $N = mg/\cos\theta$, which can be substituted to find v. So, $N\sin\theta = mv^2/R$ becomes $(g/\cos\theta)\sin\theta = v^2/R$, or $v = \sqrt{gR\tan\theta}$.

THE PRINCIPLES OF TORQUE

(*College Physics* 8th ed. pages 228–232, 236–239/9th ed. pages 235–240, 240–241, 244–247)

Torque is simply the measure of the effectiveness with which a force can cause an extended object to rotate about an axis, centered at a rotation axis called a *pivot*. Examples include seesaws, parts of engines, the use of a wrench or pliers, and opening a door. As shown below in case 1, a force is applied to a bar of length r_1, and in case 2, the same force is applied to a much shorter bar of length r_2 (both bars are attached to pivot point A but are free to turn). In both cases, the bar will have a tendency to rotate (or *torque*) in a clockwise fashion (i.e., in the direction the hands of a clock turn). For case 2, however, the amount of torque will be much less because the distance r_2 (called a *lever* or *moment arm*) is smaller than in case 1. Thus, torque depends directly on this quantity.

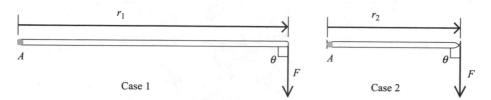

Case 1   Case 2

Not surprisingly, in either case 1 or 2, if the force were increased or decreased, the amount of torque would also be directly affected. As a result, the torque (τ) equation is

$$\tau = rF\sin\theta$$

where θ is the angle between the vectors r and F (which, for all intents and purposes, will nearly always be 90° so that sin 90° = 1; just be aware of the angle between these two vectors).

USING THE RIGHT-HAND RULE FOR TORQUE

(*College Physics* 8th ed. page 231/9th ed. page 238)

The right-hand rule is used in various forms in physics to determine the orientation of vectors in three dimensions. Because τ, r, and F are vectors in the above equation, the equation is called a *cross product*. With a cross product, two vectors that are mutually perpendicular are "crossed" to produce a third vector that is also perpendicular to the original two. For the purposes of AP Physics B, students must be able to determine the "sense" of rotation, which we indicate as clockwise (CW) or counterclockwise (CC), and torque direction. To do so, we use a simple version of the right-hand rule. The predominant convention for rotation sense, which will be used here, is that CC is positive (+) and CW is negative (–). Although there exist many versions of the right-hand rule (see Chapter 13), here it is used in a basic manner to determine the torque direction and rotation sense. The textbook reference mentioned above refers to a version of the right-hand rule that is different from what is shown below, but it also discusses the one shown here.

RIGHT-HAND RULE TO FIND THE SENSE OF ROTATION CAUSED BY THE TORQUE (KEEP YOUR HAND CURLED!)
1. Curl your hand, with your fingers following the direction of rotation of the object (either CW or CC).
2. Your thumb points naturally in the direction of the torque vector (such as *into the page*, using the symbol ⊗, or *out of the page*, using the symbol ⊙).

AP Tip

To help remember the sign difference between clockwise (CW) and counterclockwise (CC) rotations, remember that "CC" (as opposed to "CW") has **two** Cs, with **two** negative signs crossed to make a positive sign. Therefore, CC is (+), and CW (with only one C) has only one negative sign and is thus (–).

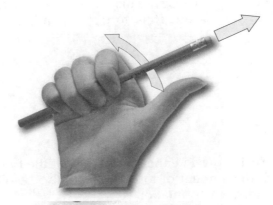

Right Hand Rule (Hand Curled)

TORQUE AND EQUILIBRIUM

Recall that in statics, $\Sigma F = 0$ applies to objects in equilibrium. Similarly, with torque, objects in equilibrium also have a special condition that applies to them. We can write the condition for equilibrium as

$$\Sigma \tau = 0$$

For these situations, simply choose an axis of rotation, add the torques about that axis (bearing in mind the above problem-solving tip), equate to zero, and then solve for unknown quantities. Keep in mind that although you can choose any axis of rotation point, it is wisest to choose a point where one of the torques will be zero because it simplifies calculations.

SAMPLE PROBLEM 3

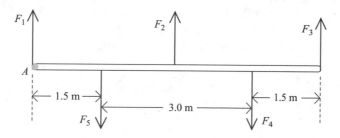

As shown, five forces can act on the 6.0-m bar, causing it to potentially rotate about pivot point A. The forces all act perpendicularly to the bar, the bar is massless, and F_2 acts as the center. Determine the torque (with rotation sense) caused by each force around A.

SOLUTION TO PROBLEM 3

Force F_1: $\tau = 0$ because $r = 0$; the force acts right at the pivot point and thus there is no rotation.
Force F_2: $\tau = +3F_2$ because $r = 3.0$ m; τ is out of the page (◉) and is CC (+).
Force F_3: $\tau = +6F_3$ because $r = 6.0$ m; τ is out of the page (◉) and is CC (+).
Force F_4: $\tau = -4.5F_4$ because $r = 4.5$ m; τ is into the page (⊗) and is CW (−).
Force F_5: $\tau = -1.5F_5$ because $r = 1.5$ m; τ is into the page (⊗) and is CW (−).

SAMPLE PROBLEM 4

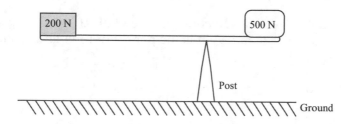

Two weights (500.0 N and 200.0 N) are placed at the ends of a pipe of uniform density weighing 100.0 N as shown. The pipe is to be placed in some manner on a post that serves as a fulcrum (pivot point).
  (a) Determine how much force the post must support.
  (b) Determine where, relative to one end of the pipe, the post must be placed so that the 500.0-N weight balances the 200.0-N weight in the positions shown.

Solution to Problem 4

    (a) The post must support the weight of the two objects as well as the 100.0-N pipe. Therefore, sketching a free-body diagram will show that $\Sigma F_y = 0$, which gives $(-200.0 \text{ N}) + (-100.0 \text{ N}) + (-500.0 \text{ N}) + N = 0$, or $N = \textbf{800.0 N}$.

    (b) Here we must apply $\Sigma\tau = 0$ about the pivot at the top of the post. At this point, where the normal force is 800.0 N, the torque will be zero because the lever arm $r = 0$. We let the length of the pipe be L and the distance of one weight (500.0 N) from the axis be x. The three torques will be

τ from the 200.0-N weight: $+200(L - x)$ (which is CC)
τ from the 100.0-N pipe: $+100(\frac{1}{2}L - x)$ (which is CC)
τ from the normal force N at the post: 0
τ from the 500.0-N weight: $-500x$ (which is CW)

Therefore, $\Sigma\tau = 0$ gives $+200(L - x) + [+100(\frac{1}{2}L - x)] + 0 + (-500x) = 0$, or $200L + 50L + (-200x) + (-100x) + (-500x) = 0$, which gives $x = \textbf{0.31}L$. Thus, the fulcrum at the post must be 0.31L to the left of the 500.0-N weight on the right end.

Circular Motion and Torque: Student Objectives for the AP Exam

■ You should understand uniform circular motion so that you can relate the radius, speed, and rate of revolution to the magnitude of the centripetal acceleration.

■ You should be able to describe the direction of a particle's velocity and acceleration at any time for an object moving in a uniform circle.

■ You should understand the concept of torque to calculate both the magnitude and sense of torque associated with a given force.

■ You should be able to calculate the torque on a rigid body due to gravity.

■ You should be able to state the conditions for translational (dynamic) and rotational equilibrium of a rigid body.

■ You should be able to apply and solve problems using $\Sigma F = 0$ and $\Sigma\tau = 0$ under the combined influence of several coplanar forces applied at different locations.

Multiple-Choice Questions

1. A ball moves with a constant speed of 4.0 m/s along a circular path of radius 0.25 m. What is the period of the ball's motion?
    (A) 0.1 s
    (B) 0.4 s
    (C) 0.7 s
    (D) 1.0 s
    (E) 2.0 s

2. A 0.5-kg rock attached to a string is whirled in a horizontal circle of radius π m such that 20 rotations take 20 s. Which of the following correctly describes the magnitude of the centripetal acceleration (a_c) and the centripetal force (F_c)?
    (A) $a_c = 8\pi^2$, $F_c = 4\pi^3$
    (B) $a_c = 4\pi^3$, $F_c = 2\pi^3$
    (C) $a_c = 4\pi^3$, $F_c = \pi^3$
    (D) $a_c = \pi^2/10$, $F_c = 5\pi^2/100$
    (E) $a_c = \pi^4/5$, $F_c = \pi^4/10$

3. A ball attached to a string is whirled in a horizontal circle of radius R. If the radius of the circle is changed to $4R$ and the same centripetal force is applied by the string, what is the new speed of the ball?
    (A) one-fourth the original speed
    (B) one-half the original speed
    (C) two times the original speed
    (D) the same as the original speed
    (E) four times the original speed

4. A ball is whirled on the end of a string in a horizontal circle of radius R at constant speed v. How can the centripetal acceleration of the ball be increased by a factor of 4?
    (A) by keeping the speed fixed and increasing the radius by a factor of 4
    (B) by keeping the radius fixed and increasing the speed by a factor of 4
    (C) by keeping the radius fixed and increasing the period by a factor of 4
    (D) by keeping the radius fixed and decreasing the period by a factor of 4
    (E) by keeping the speed fixed and decreasing the radius by a factor of 4

5. A particle moves in a circular path of radius π m at a constant speed of 4.0 m/s. What is the time (in seconds) required for one revolution?
    (A) $\pi^2/2$
    (B) $\pi^2/4$
    (C) $\pi/2$
    (D) $2/\pi^2$
    (E) $2/\pi$

6. Which force is responsible for holding a car in a frictionless, banked curve?
    (A) the car's weight
    (B) the horizontal component of the car's weight
    (C) the reaction force to the car's weight
    (D) the vertical component of the normal force
    (E) the horizontal component of the normal force

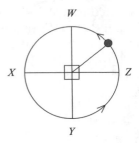

7. As shown, an object on a string moves horizontally in a circle at a constant speed such that one revolution takes 20.0 s. If the arc length from W to X is 25.0 m, what is the magnitude of the centripetal acceleration at X?
   (A) 0.3 m/s²
   (B) 1.0 m/s²
   (C) 1.6 m/s²
   (D) 4.0 m/s²
   (E) 6.0 m/s²

8. A truck moves at a constant speed down one hill and up another along a smoothly curved circular arc from points A to B as shown. Which of the following best represents the directions of the velocity and acceleration of the truck at the instant it is shown?

   (A) ⟵ v ↓ a

   (B) ↖ v ↘ a

   (C) ⟵ v ⟵ a

   (D) ⟵ v ↑ a

   (E) ⟶ v ↑ a

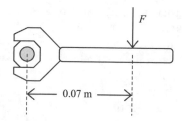

9. A wrench is used to tighten a nut as shown. A 12.0-N force F is applied 0.07 m from the axis of rotation. In units of torque, what is the torque due to the applied force?
   (A) −0.58
   (B) −0.84
   (C) +0.84
   (D) +1.71
   (E) +84.0

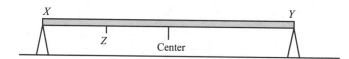

10. A uniform plank of length XY is supported by two equal 120-N forces at X and Y as shown. The support at X is then moved to Z (which is halfway to the plank center). What is the new force at Y after that move is completed?
    (A) 40 N
    (B) 60 N
    (C) 80 N
    (D) 160 N
    (E) 240 N

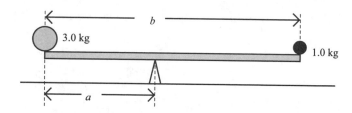

11. A 3.0-kg ball and a 1.0-kg ball are placed at opposite ends of a massless beam so that the system is in equilibrium as shown (not drawn to scale). What is the ratio of length b to length a?
    (A) 2.0
    (B) 2.5
    (C) 3.0
    (D) 4.0
    (E) 5.0

12. When a net torque is applied to a solid object, it has a tendency to produce what?
    (A) static equilibrium
    (B) constant velocity
    (C) rotational stability
    (D) rotation about an axis
    (E) linear acceleration

13. What is an equivalent unit for torque?
    (A) $kg \cdot m^2/s^2$
    (B) $kg^2 \cdot m^3/s$
    (C) $kg^2 \cdot m^2/s^3$
    (D) m^2/s^2
    (E) $kg \cdot m^2/s^3$

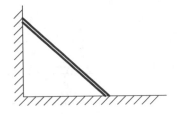

14. A uniform wooden ladder leans against a wall as shown. If the ladder is not to slip, which one of the following statements must be true?
    (A) Only the coefficient of friction between the ladder and the wall must not be zero.
    (B) Only the coefficient of friction between the ladder and the floor must not be zero.
    (C) Both coefficients of friction between the ladder and the wall and the ladder and the floor must not be zero.
    (D) The floor's normal force provides the necessary force to keep the ladder from slipping.
    (E) Both statements (A) and (B) are correct.

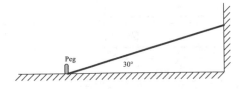

15. A uniform board is 30 m long and weighs 100.0 N. It rests with its upper end against a smooth vertical wall, and its lower end rests on the ground as shown. The board is prevented from slipping by a peg driven in the ground at the lower end of the ladder, and the board makes an angle of 30° with the horizontal. Which one of the following is the approximate force exerted on the board by the wall? (Note: sin 30° = 0.50 and cos 30° = 0.87.)
    (A) 12.0 N
    (B) 18.0 N
    (C) 50.0 N
    (D) 87.0 N
    (E) 150.0 N

FREE-RESPONSE PROBLEMS

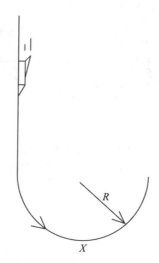

1. A fighter pilot of mass m flies in a vertical dive through a vertical circular arc as shown. She does so at a speed such that the net force on her at point X (the lowest point of the arc) is nine times her actual weight. Her speed at X is v.
   (a) Using the following figure, sketch and label all the forces on the pilot at the moment she passes through point X.

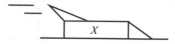

   (b) Derive an expression for the normal force exerted by the seat on the pilot when she is at point X. Leave your answer in terms of m and g.
   (c) Derive an expression for the radius R of the circular arc. Leave your answer in terms of v and g.

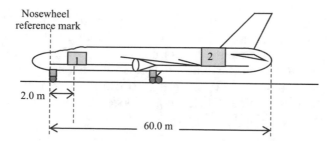

2. As shown in profile, a cargo aircraft of empty weight 1.0×10^6 N is loaded with two packages. Package 1 weighs 5.0×10^4 N, and package 2 weighs 1.0×10^5 N. The package distances are placed relative to a position marker at the nosewheel (as shown by the reference mark), and the distance from the jet's nosewheel to the tail cone is 60.0 m (neglecting the small mass of the jet in front of the wheel). Assume the empty jet's weight acts directly over the main landing gear wheels.

(a) Assume packages 1 and 2 are placed as shown and the jet is on level ground in equilibrium. Sketch the forces that act only on the jet's body that may produce rotation.

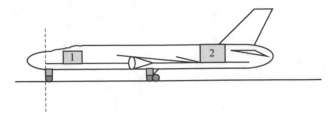

(b) If the jet is being loaded with packages 1 and 2 as shown, calculate the maximum distance package 2 can be from the nosewheel reference mark such that the body of the jet does not rotate backward and fall on its tail.

ANSWERS

MULTIPLE-CHOICE QUESTIONS

1. **B** Because the velocity of the object is $v = 2\pi R/T$, substitute the given values to obtain 4.0 m/s $= 2\pi(\frac{1}{4}$ m$)/T$ or 4.0 m/s $= \pi/2T$ so that $T = \pi/8$, which is about **0.4 s**, or choice (B) (*College Physics* 8th ed. pages 199–206/9th ed. pages 207–213).

2. **B** The given information that 20 rotations occur in 20 s implies that $T = 1$ s. Combining the velocity equation with the centripetal force equation yields $a_c = v^2/R$, or $a_c = (2\pi R/T)^2/R$, which becomes $a_c = (2\pi R)^2/R$ (because $T = 1$). Notice that $R = \pi$, so $\mathbf{a_c = 4\pi^3}$, which eliminates choices (A), (D), and (E). Next, substitute this result for a_c into the centripetal force equation to obtain $F_c = ma_c = m(4\pi^3)$. Because $m = 0.5$ kg, we then have $\mathbf{F_c = 2\pi^3}$, or choice (B) (*College Physics* 8th ed. pages 199–206/9th ed. pages 207–213).

3. **C** Using the equation for centripetal force and subscripts 1 and 2 for the different situations, we can equate the two forces (because we are told they are the same). Because $F_1 = F_2$, we can write $m_1 v^2_1/R_1 = m_2 v^2_2/4R_1$, where R_2 is now $4R_1$. Solving for v_2, the new speed gives $v^2_1 = v^2_2/4$, so $4v^2_1 = v^2_2$, or v_2 is **two times** that of the original speed v_1, which is choice (C) (*College Physics* 8th ed. pages 199–206/9th ed. pages 207–213).

4. **E** Here, we want $a_c = v^2/R$ to increase fourfold, which means the numerator could increase by four times or the denominator could decrease by one-fourth. That implies that the new speed should be two times as large (because squaring it would give $4v^2$, the desired result), or, simply, that the radius should be reduced by one-fourth. This answer is best shown by choice (E) (*College Physics* 8th ed. pages 199–206/9th ed. pages 207–213).

5. **A** Here, use $v = 2\pi R/T$ and solve for T: 4.0 m/s $= 2\pi R/T = 2\pi\pi/T = 2\pi^2/T$, which gives $T = 2\pi^2/4$, or $\mathbf{T = \pi^2/2}$, which is choice (A) (*College Physics* 8th ed. pages 199–206/9th ed. pages 207–213).

6. **E** Taking a slice of the banked roadway with a car on it shows that the inward (i.e., radial) component of N supplies the centripetal force to keep the car on the track. All choices but choice (E) are not radially directed vectors and thus cannot supply F_c. Therefore, choice (E) is correct (*College Physics* 8th ed. page 205/9th ed. page 212).

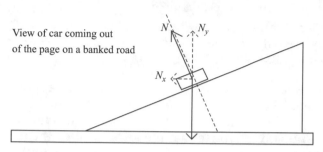

View of car coming out
of the page on a banked road

7. **C** We are told that one-fourth the circumference is 25.0 m so the entire circumference is 100.0 m, thus $100.0 = 2\pi R$, or, $R \sim 16.0$ m. With the given period of 20.0 s, we use $v = 2\pi R/T$, or $v = 2\pi 16.0/20.0 = 16.0\pi/10.0 = 1.6\pi$. Next, substitute into the acceleration equation (carrying out your calculations longhand): $a_c = v^2/R$, or $a_c = (1.6\pi)^2/R$, which is $a_c = (2.56)(10.0)/16.0$ (where $\pi^2 \sim 10.0$). Thus, $a_c = \mathbf{1.6}$ **m/s²**, which is choice (C) (*College Physics* 8th ed. pages 199–206/ 9th ed. pages 207–213).

8. **D** We are told the car moves from A to B, so at the position shown, it is traveling to the left. Therefore, centripetal force (which is radially inward) points directly upward and the velocity (which is tangent to the path) must point left. The only correct answer is choice (D) (*College Physics* 8th ed. pages 199–206/9th ed. pages 207–213).

9. **B** By the torque equation ($\tau = rF \sin \theta$) and the right-hand rule, the torque is into the page ($\otimes$). Therefore, by the right-hand rule for rotation, we have a clockwise torque, which is negative. Thus, choices (C), (D), and (E) can be eliminated. Next, calculate the torque: $\tau = rF \sin \theta$ gives $\tau = -(7.0 \times 10^{-2}$ m$)(12.0$ N$) \sin 90° = -84.0 \times 10^{-2}$ Nm, or $\tau = \mathbf{-0.84}$ **Nm**, which is choice (B) (*College Physics* 8th ed. pages 228–232, 236–239/9th ed. pages 235–240, 240–241, 244–247).

10. **C** Because this system is in equilibrium, apply $\Sigma\tau = 0$ at a location where a force acts to eliminate a torque. Here, point Y is chosen as such, so the torque due to F_Y is zero even though F_Y is the requested unknown variable. The forces that can cause torques are as shown.

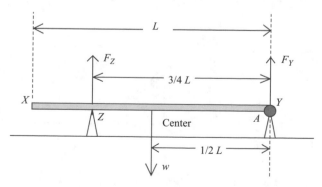

Noting that clockwise torques (CW) are negative and counterclockwise torque (CC) are positive, we have $\Sigma\tau_A = 0$, which becomes $+(L/2)(w) + (-3L/4)(F_z) + 0 = 0$. It is also necessary to resort to applying $\Sigma F = 0$ to determine $F_z + F_y = 240$, which implies that $F_z = 240 - F_y$. We can now substitute into the torque equation above to acquire $+(L/2)(w) + (-3L/4)(240 - F_y) + 0 = 0$, which can be solved for F_y: $(L/2)(w) = (-3L/4)(240 - F_y) + 0 = 0$, or $(4/3L)(L/2)(240) = 240 - F_y$, which becomes $(4/6)(240) = (240 - F_y)$. Thus, **$F_y = 80$ N**, which is choice (C) (*College Physics* 8th ed. pages 228–232, 236–239/9th ed. pages 235–240, 240–241, 244–247).

11. **D** Because this system is in equilibrium, apply $\Sigma\tau = 0$ at the pivot point. The rotation caused by the 3.0-kg mass is counterclockwise (or positive), and the rotation caused by the 1.0-kg mass is clockwise (or negative). Notice that the lever arm for the right mass is $(b - a)$, not b. Thus, using $\tau = rF \sin \theta$ (where $\theta = 90°$), $\Sigma\tau = 0$ becomes $+(a)(3.0 \text{ kg})(10.0 \text{ m/s}^2) + [-(b - a)(1.0 \text{ kg})(10.0 \text{ m/s}^2)] = 0$, which reduces easily to $30.0a = 10.0(b - a)$, or $40.0a = 10.0b$, making **$b/a = 4.0$**, or choice (D), the correct answer (*College Physics* 8th ed. pages 228–232, 236–239/9th ed. pages 235–240, 240–241, 244–247).

12. **D** Torque deals with the effectiveness of a force to produce rotation and thus is not an aspect of equilibrium or any type of linear motion. Therefore, choices (A), (B), (C), and (E) are eliminated, leaving choice (D) as the correct answer (*College Physics* 8th ed. pages 228–232, 236–239/9th ed. pages 235–240, 240–241, 244–247).

13. **A** By the torque equation $\tau = rF \sin \theta$, we can see that the units are simply the product of distance (meters) and force (newtons), or N · m. Recalling Newton's second law as stated by $F = ma$, the unit of force is the product of mass (kilograms) and acceleration (meters per square second). Thus, the fundamental units for torque will be $\tau = rF \sin \theta$, which gives N · m or $[(\text{kg})(\text{m/s}^2)]\text{m}$, which becomes **kg · m²/s²**, or choice (A). (*College Physics* 8th ed. pages 228–232, 236–239/9th ed. pages 235–240, 240–241, 244–247).

14. **B** Upon analysis, the ladder remains in equilibrium because both $\Sigma\tau = 0$ and $\Sigma F = 0$, and as shown, the only force that balances the horizontal normal force N_1 from the wall is the static friction force on the floor acting toward the wall at the bottom of the ladder. In the vertical direction, only w and N_2 balance, and so no other vertical force could balance a vertical friction force at the wall. Therefore, statement (B) is correct (*College Physics* 8th ed. pages 228–232, 236–239/9th ed. pages 235–240, 240–241, 244–247).

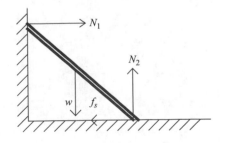

15. **D** The forces that tend to cause torques are shown here, as are the lever arms for N_2 and w. As in Question 10, apply $\Sigma\tau = 0$ at a location where a force acts to eliminate a torque, which here is the point at the peg (A), so that both F and N_1 produce no torques. Thus, N_2 has a lever arm of r_2, 30 sin 30° (as shown), and w has a lever arm of $L/2$, which is (30 cos 30°)/2. Noting that clockwise torques (CW) are negative and counterclockwise torques (CC) are positive, we now have $\Sigma\tau_A = 0$, which becomes $+(r)(N_2) + (-L/2)(w) = 0$, or $+(30 \sin 30°)(N_2) + [(-30 \cos 30°)/2](100) = 0$. Solving for N_2 gives $30(0.5)N_2 = [(30)(0.87)/15](100)$, or $N_2 = \mathbf{87.0\ N}$, which is choice (D) (*College Physics* 8th ed. pages 228–232, 236–239/9th ed. pages 235–240, 240–241, 244–247).

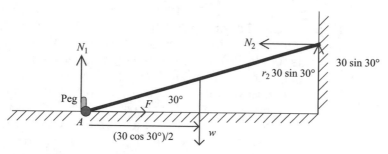

FREE-RESPONSE PROBLEMS

1. (a) A sketch is as shown.

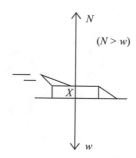

(*College Physics* 8th ed. pages 199–206/9th ed. pages 94–95, 207–213)

(b) We are told that F_{net} at X is 9.0mg; therefore, $\Sigma F_C = mv^2/R = 9.0mg$. Applying $\Sigma F_C = mv^2/R$ at point X gives $N - mg = mv^2/R$, which becomes $N - mg = 9mg$, or $N = \mathbf{10.0mg}$ (*College Physics* 8th ed. pages 199–206/9th ed. pages 207–213).

(c) From part (b), $N - mg = mv^2/R$, which is then $10.0mg - mg = mv^2/R$, or $9g = v^2/R$. Thus, solving for R gives $\mathbf{R = v^2/9g}$ (*College Physics* 8th ed. pages 199–206/9th ed. pages 207–213).

2. (a) A sketch is as shown, where N_1 and N_2 are the normal forces exerted at the landing gear, w_1 and w_2 are the respective weights of the packages, and w_p is the weight of the aircraft (*College Physics* 8th ed. pages 228–232, 236–239/9th ed. pages 235–240, 240–241, 244–247).

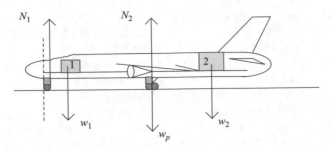

(b) First, simplify the force sketch as shown below and apply $\Sigma F = 0$ to obtain a relation between the given weights and the normal forces, which gives $N_1 + N_2 - w_1 - w_p - w_2 = 0$. Substituting values gives $N_1 + N_2 = 1.15 \times 10^6$ N, which we'll call Equation (1). Then, apply $\Sigma \tau = 0$ about axis A (notice that this change will cause any torque from N_1 to be zero because $r = 0$). We now have (omitting units for clarity) $\Sigma \tau = 0$, or $0 + (-2)(50{,}000) + (-30)(1 \times 10^6) + 30N_2 + (-R)(1 \times 10^5) = 0$. Here, R is the unknown lever arm from package 2 to the nosewheel reference mark. Notice also that signs for CW and CC must be followed above. So, $(-1 \times 10^5) - (3 \times 10^7) + 30N_2 = R(1 \times 10^5)$, which we'll call Equation (2). Realize that as the plane just begins to tip back onto its tail, the nosewheel rises, causing N_1 to go to zero. Thus, substituting Equation (1) into Equation (2) gives $R = 44.0$ m (*College Physics* 8th ed. pages 228–232, 236–239/9th ed. pages 235–240, 240–241, 244–247).

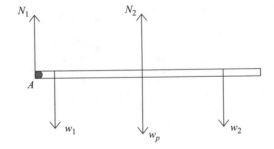

OSCILLATIONS AND GRAVITATION

Unless otherwise stated, the effects of air resistance in these questions are negligible.

WHAT IS SIMPLE HARMONIC MOTION?

(*College Physics* 8th ed. pages 425–428, 445–447/9th ed. pages 437–441, 458–459)

In Chapter 5, we discussed Hooke's law and the nature of a restoring force. In particular, with springs, the force exerted by the spring is always opposite the direction of the strain (displacement x) on the spring; thus, a hanging spring with a mass m attached to it can be displaced, released, and can oscillate up and down due to this restoring force. In the case of springs, this restoring force ($F = -kx$) is always directed back toward the spring's equilibrium point, the point at which the spring "wants" to be at rest, where $x = 0$). When such a restoring force, proportional to displacement, causes this back-and-forth motion, it is said to be a situation of *simple harmonic motion*, which is simply a continuous oscillation around the equilibrium point. (Bear in mind, of course, that friction eventually hinders or damps out such motion, and it is not perpetual.) In nature, many situations exhibit simple harmonic motion, from a small mass swinging on string (called a *bob*) known as a simple pendulum to the oscillations of violin strings and light waves.

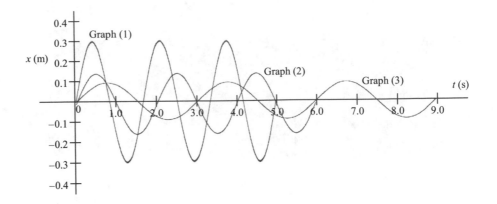

Imagine a mass oscillating vertically on a spring with a pen attached to the end of the spring "writing" against a large paper that is moving horizontally at constant velocity. Careful observation reveals that the pen actually draws a graph that represents the motion of the mass itself, which is a sine curve obeying the position function $x = A \cos(\omega t)$, where $\omega = 2\pi f$, as described below. Thus, we can immediately discover useful features about the simple harmonic motion of the mass by analyzing the sine plot. In doing so, we uncover three very important aspects of simple harmonic motion:

1. *Amplitude (A)* is the magnitude of the maximum displacement $|x|$ from equilibrium, when the mass stops moving. In the graphs above, it is the peak of the crest (or trough): 0.3 m for graph (1), 0.15 m for graph (2), and 0.1 m for graph (3).

2. *Period (T)* is the time for one full cycle of the oscillation. In the graphs above, it is $\frac{5}{3}$ s for graph (1), 2.0 s for graph (2), and 3.0 s for graph (3).

3. *Frequency (f)* (that is, how "often") is the rate at which waves pass a certain point. It is the inverse of period T and is written $f = 1/T$. Its unit is cycles per second, or hertz (Hz).

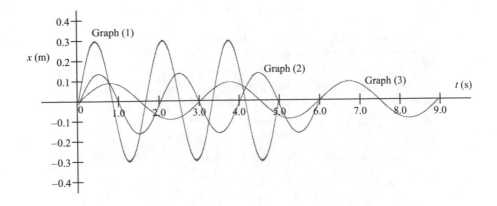

How Do We Describe the Period of an Oscillating Mass?

(*College Physics* 8th ed. pages 432–436/9th ed. pages 445–448)

We can describe the period of an oscillating mass in two ways; by analyzing a simple pendulum and by analyzing a mass on a string.

1. A mass m attached to a string of length L and swinging freely in a vertical plane is a *simple pendulum*. It oscillates in simple harmonic motion about its equilibrium point and has a restoring force due to the gravitation component that is perpendicular to the string. Experimentation and mathematical analysis show that T depends primarily on the pendulum string length L and not on the mass m or amplitude (angle) θ. For angles up to 23°, the period of the pendulum is independent of amplitude to within 1% and obeys the relationship

$$T = 2\pi\sqrt{\frac{L}{g}}$$

2. As can be surmised, a *mass on a spring* (vertical or horizontal) of spring constant k undergoing simple harmonic motion has a period that depends not on L but on k and on the value of the mass m. This relationship is

$$T = 2\pi\sqrt{\frac{m}{k}}$$

Both devices are shown below: the pendulum on the left and the mass–spring system on the right.

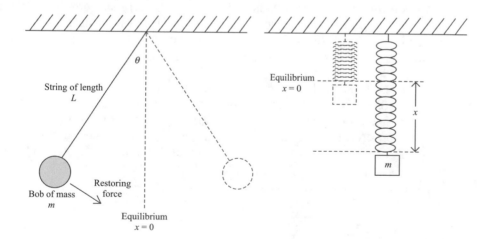

HOW DO VELOCITY AND ACCELERATION RELATE TO THE POSITION X?

(College Physics 8th ed. pages 425–427, 431/9th ed. pages 437–441, 443–444)

For the mass oscillating on a spring, the restoring force is provided by Hooke's law, which is also the net force on the mass. Therefore, we can immediately derive the equation for the acceleration of the mass from Newton's second law of motion, $\Sigma F = F_{net} = ma = -kx$, which gives

$$a = -\frac{kx}{m}$$

Notice that the acceleration is directly proportional to the displacement x and in the opposite direction; also notice that when x is a maximum (at the amplitude A), the acceleration is a maximum, which occurs at the endpoints of the object's travel. This maximum actually occurs when the object is momentarily stopped, in a small way analogous to a ball tossed straight upward: when the ball stops at the top of its path, it still experiences an acceleration.

As for the speed of the oscillating mass, we can apply energy conservation to the situation, using the maximum displacement location (where $x = A$) and comparing it with the total energy at any other location where it is moving to obtain $\frac{1}{2}kA^2 = \frac{1}{2}kx^2 + \frac{1}{2}mv^2$, which can be solved for v to obtain

$$v = \sqrt{\frac{k}{m}(A^2 - x^2)}$$

Careful observation will reveal that when $x = A$ (i.e., at the endpoints of the motion), v goes to zero (as described). In addition, v is a maximum when $x = 0$, which is when the mass is passing through equilibrium (at the center of its motion), as to be expected. The same behavior applies to simple pendulum motion: the speed is a maximum at the center and is zero at the endpoints. The opposite is true for the acceleration: it is zero at the center and is maximum at the endpoints.

SAMPLE PROBLEM 1

A 0.05-kg mass m is attached to a vertical spring as shown, which causes the spring to elongate 0.03 m. The system is then placed on a frictionless, horizontal surface and is set into simple harmonic motion. A graph of the sinusoidal behavior of the mass is shown on the right.

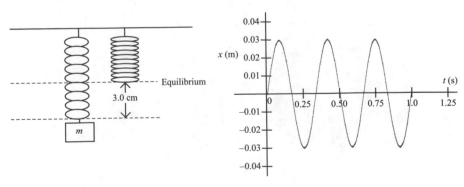

(a) Determine the frequency of oscillation of the mass.
(b) Determine the maximum speed of the mass.
(c) Determine the magnitude of the maximum acceleration of the mass.
(d) A piece of cardboard with negligible mass and large surface area is glued to the bottom of the mass and is again set into simple harmonic motion while hanging vertically. Describe the specific effect this piece of cardboard has on (i) the period of the motion and (ii) the amplitude of the motion.

SOLUTION TO PROBLEM 1

(a) From the graph, the period T is approximately 0.33 s (three complete cycles in 1 s). Therefore, $f = 1/T$ will give approximately **$f = 3.0$ Hz**.

(b) The maximum speed occurs when the mass is passing through equilibrium, when $x = 0$. Therefore, use the v equation quoted earlier (with $A = 0.03$ m from the graph above), but first find the value of k from Hooke's law (when the mass is hung from the vertical spring). So,

$$F = kx = \frac{(0.05 \text{ kg})(10.0 \text{ m/s}^2)}{0.03 \text{ m}} = k$$

which becomes 16.7 N/m. Therefore, the maximum speed is

$$v = \sqrt{\frac{k}{m}(A^2 - x^2)} = \sqrt{\frac{16.7 \text{ N/m}}{0.05 \text{ kg}}[(0.03 \text{ m})^2 - 0]}$$

which gives **$v = 0.5$ m/s**.

More importantly, this solution may be arrived at by considering energy conservation, where the potential energy of the spring at maximum displacement goes into the kinetic energy of the oscillating mass at the equilibrium point. Thus, $\frac{1}{2}mv^2 = \frac{1}{2}kx^2$. Solving for v gives $v = \sqrt{(kx^2/m)}$, the same equation as above, also yielding $v = 0.5$ m/s.

(c) From the acceleration equation quoted earlier, simply substitute values and solve for a:

$$a = \frac{kx}{m} = \frac{(16.7 \text{ N/m})(0.03 \text{ m})}{0.05 \text{ kg}}$$

which gives **$a = 10.0$ m/s²**.

(d) A "fan" attached to the mass should damp out the vibrations quickly by imposing significant air drag on the oscillation. Therefore, the amplitude will die out much more quickly. The period T will remain constant, however; notice that the period equation shows that there is no relationship to air resistance.

HOW DO MASS AND DISTANCE AFFECT MUTUAL GRAVITATIONAL FORCE?

(*College Physics* 8th ed. pages 207–211/9th ed. pages 214–217)

During the late 17th century, Isaac Newton realized that some central force must be responsible for holding the Moon in a closed orbit around Earth. He correctly reasoned that it was also this same force that allowed objects (such as his famed apple) to fall freely in an attractive way to the ground. This central force is what today is referred to simply as *gravity*, and in 1687 Newton published his universal law of gravitation:

$$F = \frac{GMm}{R^2}$$

where M and m are two distinct masses (such as Earth and Moon, an apple and Earth, or a car and a truck) that are separated by distance R (bear in mind that R is not an object radius but rather is the distance between the objects' centers) and G is the universal gravitational constant (6.67×10^{-11} N · m²/kg²), first measured using an ingenious experiment by British scientist Henry Cavendish in 1798. For an object at rest on a planet's surface, this gravitational force of attraction is equivalent to the object's weight, as seen by

$$mg = \frac{GMm}{R^2}$$

which gives an equation for the gravitational acceleration of a planet of mass M and radius R at the surface. Thus,

$$g = \frac{GM}{R^2}$$

Therefore, a planet's gravitational acceleration g is directly proportional to its mass and inversely proportional to the square of its radius. If the object is well above the planet's surface, then R is the distance from the object to the planet's center.

For an object such as a satellite orbiting a planet in a circular path, the gravitational force supplies the centripetal force acting on the orbiting body. Therefore, we can write

$$\Sigma F = F_c = \frac{mv^2}{R} = \frac{GMm}{R^2}$$

which allows us to solve for the speed v of the orbiting body: $v^2 = GM/R$, or $v = \sqrt{GM/m}$. Recalling the previous discussion of uniform circular motion in Chapter 7, this speed can be written as

$$v = \frac{2\pi R}{T}$$

Equating these two expressions allows us to derive the relationship between the orbiting object's period T and its distance R from the central body. Squaring both sides of each v equation gives

$$\frac{GM}{R} = \frac{4\pi^2 R^2}{T^2}$$

which can be rearranged to give

$$T^2 = \frac{4\pi^2 R^3}{GM}$$

This equation is often written as $T^2 = kR^3$ where k is the orbital constant $4\pi^2/GM$ (notice that M is the mass of the central body, not the orbiting mass). So,

$$T^2 = kR^3$$

Notice carefully two implications;

1. The period T of an orbiting body does not depend on its own mass, but only on the mass M of the central body. Therefore, if many objects of varying mass are all placed the same distance R from the central body, they will all orbit with the same period T.

2. The square of the period (T^2) is directly proportional to the cube of the distance (R^3) of the orbiting body, implying that the farther the object is from the central body, the longer it takes the object to complete one orbit. For example, Earth takes 1 year to orbit the Sun, but Saturn, being about ten times more distant from the Sun than Earth is, takes nearly 30 years to complete one orbit.

AP Tip

Remember that when using Newton's law of gravitation, R denotes a *separation between centers of objects* of mass M and m; it is not the radius of a solid object such as a planet or satellite.

WHAT ARE THE IMPORTANT FEATURES OF ORBITS?

(*College Physics* 8th ed. pages 215–218/9th ed. pages 221–224)

For the purposes of AP Physics B, a discussion of the general nature of orbits is sufficient. The nature of orbits is encompassed by the important laws of planetary motion, first formalized by German astronomer Johannes Kepler in the early part of the 17th century, as follows.

Kepler's First Law of Planetary Motion: The orbital paths of planets around the Sun are elliptical in shape, and the Sun remains at one focus of the ellipse of the orbit of each planet, where R represents the average distance of the planet from the Sun.

Kepler's Second Law of Planetary Motion: A line drawn from the planet to the Sun sweeps out equal areas anywhere in the orbital path for equal amounts of time that pass by. When the planet is farthest from the Sun, it is moving slowest, and the path traced approximates a long, narrow triangle. When the planet is closest to the Sun, however, it is moving fastest, and the path traced out appears as a wide, stubby triangle. Calculus shows that the areas of these paths are identical.

Kepler's Third Law of Planetary Motion: The period T of a planet's orbit is related to the orbital distance R, and the farther a planet is from the Sun, the longer its period. This law is a generalized statement based on a circular orbit and was derived earlier as $T^2 = kR^2$, where k is the same for all planets in our solar system (because they all orbit the same body, the Sun).

SAMPLE PROBLEM 2

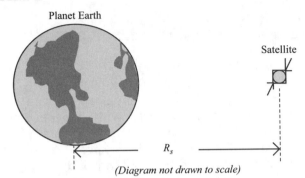

Planet Earth

Satellite

R_s

(Diagram not drawn to scale)

A satellite of mass 1.0×10^4 kg is in a circular orbit around Earth at a distance of R_S from Earth's center, which is three times the radius of Earth R_E, as shown. The mass of Earth is 6.0×10^{24} kg, and the radius of Earth is 6.4×10^6 m.

(a) Determine the orbital period of the satellite in Earth hours.
(b) Determine the net force acting on the satellite as it orbits Earth and state its direction.
(c) Determine the acceleration due to gravity at this location.
(d) This satellite is then moved to an orbit that is three times farther away. Compare mathematically the satellite's new period to its period when it was in the lower orbit.

SOLUTION TO PROBLEM 2

(a) The satellite's period T can easily be found from Kepler's third law, $T^2 = kR^3$, where k is the orbital constant $(4\pi^2)/(GM_E)$. First, calculate the orbital constant for Earth:

$$k = \frac{4\pi^2}{GM_E} = \frac{4(3.14)^2}{(6.7 \times 10^{-11} \text{ N} \cdot \text{m}^2/\text{kg}^2)(6.0 \times 10^{24} \text{ kg})}$$

Thus, $k = 9.8 \times 10^{-14}$ N · m²/kg. Substituting gives $T^2 = 9.8 \times 10^{-14}$ N·m²/kg$[(6.4 \times 10^6$ m$)]^3$ (recalling that the orbit is three times Earth's radius). Taking the square root gives 26,337 s. Noting that 1 h = 3,600 s, we then have **$T = 7.3$ h.**

(b) The net force acting on the satellite is simply the gravitational force

$$F = \frac{GMm}{R^2}$$

Therefore, substituting values gives

$$F = \frac{(6.7 \times 10^{-11} \text{ N} \cdot \text{m}^2/\text{kg}^2)(6.0 \times 10^{24} \text{ kg})(1.0 \times 10^4 \text{ kg})}{(19.2 \times 10^6 \text{ m})^2}$$

So, **$F = 1.1 \times 10^4$ N, toward Earth's center.**

(c) The weight mg is the gravitational force F_g at this location; thus, we can write $g = GM/R^2$. At the location of the satellite (i.e., at $3R_E$, or 19.2×10^6 m), solving for g gives

$$g = \frac{GM_E}{R_S^2} = \frac{(6.7 \times 10^{-11} \text{ N} \cdot \text{m}^2/\text{kg}^2)(6.0 \times 10^{24} \text{ kg})}{(19.2 \times 10^6 \text{ m})^2}$$

or **$g = 1.1$ m/s² at $3R_E$ from the center of Earth**.

(d) As for the original satellite being moved farther away, its orbital radius is now $9R_E$ rather than $3R_E$. Thus, according to $T^2 = kR^3$, when this new distance is substituted, we have $\dfrac{T}{\sqrt{2}}$. Notice that kR_E^3 is simply the original period squared. Therefore, $T_{new}^2 = 27\,T_{old}^2$, or, by taking the square root of both sides, T_{new} becomes 5.2 times T_{old}. Therefore, **the period of the satellite in the higher orbit is 5.2 times its previous value at the lower orbit**.

OSCILLATIONS: STUDENT OBJECTIVES FOR THE AP EXAM

■ You should understand the kinematics of simple harmonic motion.
■ You should be able to sketch or identify a graph of displacement as a function of time and determine from such a graph the amplitude, period, and frequency of the motion.
■ You should be able to write out an appropriate expression for displacement of the form $A \sin \omega t$ or $A \cos \omega t$.
■ You should be able to state qualitatively the relationship between acceleration and displacement for an oscillating object.
■ You should be able to identify points in the motion where the velocity is zero or achieves its maximum positive or negative value.
■ You should be able to identify points in the motion where the acceleration is zero or achieves its maximum positive or negative value.
■ You should be able to state and apply the relation between frequency and period.
■ You should be able to state how the total energy of an oscillating system depends on the amplitude of the motion, sketch or identify a graph of kinetic or potential energy as a function of time, and identify points in the motion where this energy is either all potential or kinetic.
■ You should be able to calculate the kinetic and potential energies of an oscillating system as functions of time, sketch or identify graphs of these functions, and prove that the sum of kinetic and potential energies is constant.
■ You should be able to apply the expression for the period of a mass oscillating on a spring.
■ You should be able to apply the expression for the period of a simple pendulum.

GRAVITATION: STUDENT OBJECTIVES FOR THE AP EXAM

■ You should know Newton's law of gravitation so that you can determine the force that one spherically symmetric mass exerts on another.

■ You should be able to use Newton's law of gravitation to calculate the gravitational field strength at a location outside a spherically symmetric mass.

■ You should understand orbits such that you can recognize that the orbital motion does not depend on the mass of the orbiting body, but only on the mass of the central body.

■ You should be able to describe qualitatively how the velocity, period of revolution, and centripetal acceleration depend on the radius of the orbit, and derive expressions for the velocity and period of revolution for such an orbit.

MULTIPLE-CHOICE QUESTIONS

1. Which one of the following statements is true concerning an object executing simple harmonic motion?
    (A) Its velocity is never zero.
    (B) Its velocity is zero when it is at maximum displacement.
    (C) Its acceleration is never zero.
    (D) Its velocity and acceleration are both zero at minimum displacement.
    (E) Its maximum acceleration is equal to its maximum velocity.

2. A mass M oscillates in simple harmonic motion on a spring whose spring constant is k. If the spring is then cut exactly in half while the mass is doubled, what is the new period of oscillation?

    (A) $2\pi\sqrt{\dfrac{2M}{k}}$

    (B) $4\pi\sqrt{\dfrac{M}{k}}$

    (C) $2\pi\sqrt{\dfrac{M}{k}}$

    (D) $2\pi\sqrt{\dfrac{M}{2k}}$

    (E) $8\pi\sqrt{\dfrac{M}{k}}$

3. When an object oscillating in simple harmonic motion is at its maximum displacement from equilibrium, which of the following is true of its speed and the magnitude of the restoring force?

Speed	Restoring Force
(A) 0	maximum
(B) 0	0
(C) ½ maximum	½ maximum
(D) maximum	½ maximum
(E) maximum	0

4. An object swings on the end of a cord as a simple pendulum with period T. Another object oscillates up and down on the end of a vertical spring, also with period T. If the masses of both objects are doubled, what are the new values for the periods?

   Pendulum   Mass on Spring

   (A) $\dfrac{T}{\sqrt{2}}$ $T\sqrt{2}$

   (B) T $T\sqrt{2}$

   (C) T T

   (D) $T\sqrt{2}$ T

   (E) $T\sqrt{2}$ $\dfrac{T}{\sqrt{2}}$

5. A 2.0-kg mass attached to a spring is oscillating horizontally on a frictionless surface. The total energy of the system is observed to be 10.0 J. If that mass is replaced by a 4.0-kg mass but the amplitude of oscillations and the spring remain the same, what will the approximate total mechanical energy of the system then be?
   (A) 3.3 J
   (B) 5.0 J
   (C) 10.0 J
   (D) 15.5 J
   (E) 20. J

6. A simple harmonic oscillator has a period of 5.0 s and an amplitude of 1.2 m. What is the frequency of the oscillations of this object?
   (A) 0.1 Hz
   (B) 0.2 Hz
   (C) 0.5 Hz
   (D) 1.0 Hz
   (E) 5.0 Hz

7. A person weighing 600 N on Earth travels to a planet with four times the mass and two times the radius of Earth. What is the person's approximate weight on this planet?
   (A) 300 N

   (B) $\dfrac{800}{\sqrt{2}}$ N

   (C) 600 N

   (D) $600\sqrt{2}$ N

   (E) 1,200 N

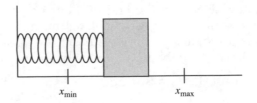

For Questions 8 and 9, refer to the diagram, which shows a block oscillating without friction on the end of a spring. The minimum and maximum lengths of the spring as it oscillates are shown. Graphs (1) through (5) can represent quantities associated with the oscillations as functions of the strain x of the spring.

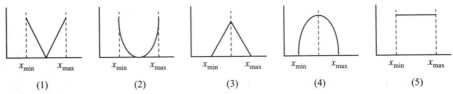

8. Which graph represents the total mechanical energy of the block–spring system as a function of x?
    (A) Graph (1)
    (B) Graph (2)
    (C) Graph (3)
    (D) Graph (4)
    (E) Graph (5)

9. Which graph best represents the kinetic energy of the block as a function of x?
    (A) Graph (1)
    (B) Graph (2)
    (C) Graph (3)
    (D) Graph (4)
    (E) Graph (5)

10. When a 2.0-kg mass is suspended on a particular spring, the spring stretches 40.0 m. What is the period of oscillation of the mass when it is in motion?
    (A) 2π s
    (B) π s
    (C) 4π s
    (D) $\dfrac{\pi}{2}$ s
    (E) $\dfrac{\pi}{4}$ s

11. Gravitational force F exists between uniformly spherical objects A and B separated by a distance R. If the mass of A is doubled and R is tripled, what is the new gravitational force between A and B?

    (A) $\dfrac{2F}{9}$ N

    (B) $\dfrac{2F}{3}$ N

(C) $\dfrac{3F}{2}$ N

(D) $\dfrac{9F}{2}$ N

(E) $6F$ N

12. Two satellites of different masses are in the same circular orbit around Earth. Which one of the following statements is true?
    (A) The magnitude of the gravitational force is zero for both satellites, and the less massive satellite orbits with a shorter period.
    (B) The magnitude of the gravitational force is the same for both satellites but is not zero, and both satellites have the same period.
    (C) The magnitude of the gravitational force is zero for one satellite but not for the other, and the more massive satellite has the greater period.
    (D) The magnitude of the gravitational force depends on the masses of the satellites, and the orbital periods of each satellite are the same.
    (E) The magnitude of the gravitational force varies from point to point in the orbits of the satellites, but the orbital periods of each satellite are the same.

13. Consider a satellite in a circular orbit around Earth. If it were at an altitude equal to two times the radius of Earth, $2R_E$, how would its speed v be related to Earth's radius R_E and the magnitude g of the acceleration due to gravity on Earth's surface?

    (A) $v = \sqrt{\dfrac{gR_E}{9}}$

    (B) $v = \sqrt{\dfrac{gR_E}{2}}$

    (C) $v = \sqrt{\dfrac{gR_E}{3}}$

    (D) $v = \sqrt{\dfrac{gR_E}{4}}$

    (E) $v = \sqrt{2gR_E}$

14. A student measures the gravitational force on a satellite in a circular orbit moving around Earth to be 8,000 N. If the satellite is 4.2×10^7 m from Earth's center and is traveling at a speed of 3,300 m/s, what is the approximate mass of the satellite?
    (A) 3.5×10^4 kg
    (B) 7.0×10^4 kg
    (C) 2.0×10^5 kg
    (D) 9.0×10^6 kg
    (E) 2.5×10^7 kg

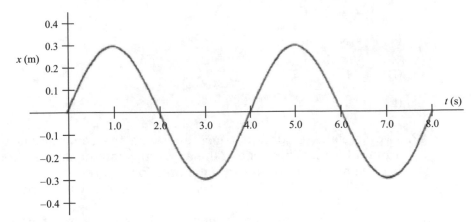

15. The simple harmonic motion of a 2.0-kg mass oscillating vertically on a spring of spring constant k is shown. What is the value of k (in units of N/m²)?

(A) $\dfrac{4}{\pi}$

(B) $\dfrac{\pi^2}{2}$

(C) $2\pi^2$

(D) $\dfrac{8}{\pi^2}$

(E) $\dfrac{\pi^2}{4}$

FREE-RESPONSE PROBLEMS

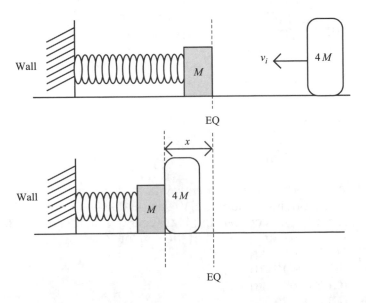

1. A block of mass M is resting on a frictionless, horizontal table as shown and is attached to a relaxed, massless spring of spring constant k at equilibrium (EQ in the figure). A second block of mass

$4M$ and initial speed v_i collides with and sticks to the first block, subsequently compressing the spring by an amount x. Develop expressions for the following in terms of M, k, and v_i:

(a) Determine the speed v of the blocks immediately after the impact.

(b) Determine the maximum compression (strain) x the spring experiences.

(c) Determine the period T of the subsequent simple harmonic motion.

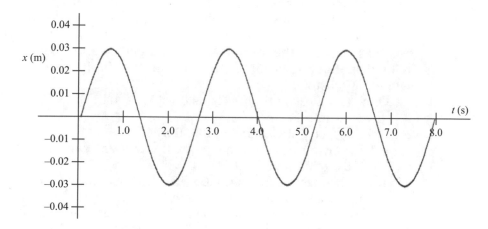

2. The simple harmonic motion of a 0.5-kg mass oscillating on a spring of spring constant k is as shown in the sinusoidal graph.

(a) Determine the amplitude of this oscillatory motion.

(b) Determine the period of this oscillatory motion.

(c) Determine k for this spring.

The mass is now doubled, and the amplitude and the spring itself are unchanged.

(d) Calculate the new period of the oscillating mass.

(e) Sketch the first two cycles of the resulting motion on a displacement versus time graph.

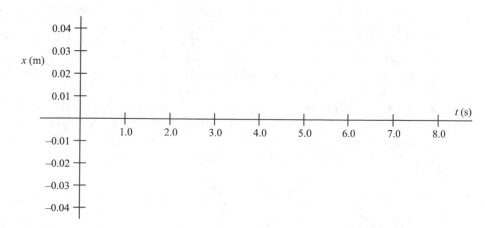

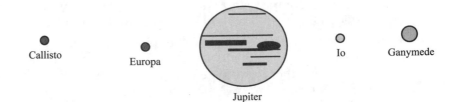

Callisto   Europa   Jupiter   Io   Ganymede

3. To determine the mass of Jupiter, a physics student observes the motions of the moons of that planet (as shown) over the course of several nights. In doing so, she only has the equipment to measure two parameters: the period of the satellites and their orbital velocities. She determines these data for Jupiter's outermost satellite, Callisto:

1. One orbital revolution of Callisto = **17.0 Earth days** (1 Earth day = 86,400 s)
2. Orbital speed of Callisto = **8222.0 m/s**

   (a) From these data, what does the student calculate for the mass of Jupiter?

   (b) If the mass of Earth is 6.0×10^{24} kg, how many times Earth's mass is the student's calculated Jupiter mass?

   (c) According to her astronomical data tables, the student notes that the mass of Jupiter is 318 Earth masses. What percent error in her calculated mass does she calculate?

ANSWERS

MULTIPLE-CHOICE QUESTIONS

1. **B** The acceleration of an object exhibiting simple harmonic motion is $a = -kx/m$, showing that a and x are directly related. Therefore, acceleration is a maximum at maximum displacement, which occurs at the endpoints of the object's motion, when it has stopped. Thus, statement (A) is incorrect. Acceleration is zero when x is zero, so statement (C) is incorrect. Velocity is a maximum at zero displacement, making statements (D) and (E) incorrect. Therefore, statement (B) is the only correct choice (*College Physics* 8th ed. pages 425–428, 431–436/9th ed. pages 437–441, 443–448).

2. **C** According to the period of a mass oscillating on a spring, $T = 2\pi\left(\sqrt{m/k}\right)$. If we replace m with $2M$ and k with $2k$ (because cutting a spring exactly in half gives a new spring with two times the previous k value), we then have

$$T = 2\pi\sqrt{\frac{2M}{2k}} = 2\pi\sqrt{\frac{M}{k}}$$

which is exactly the same as the previous period equation. Thus, choice (C) is correct (*College Physics* 8th ed. pages 425–428, 431–436/9th ed. pages 437–441, 443–448).

3. **A** At its maximum position, the object has stopped, and the restoring force is given by Hooke's law $(F = -kx)$. So, at maximum displacement, x and therefore the acceleration a have their maximum value. Conversely, at the center (equilibrium), when $x = 0$, F is zero and v is largest. Therefore, choice (A) is the only correct choice (*College Physics* 8th ed. pages 425–428, 431–436, 439–441/9th ed. pages 437–441, 443–448, 451–454).

4. **B** The necessary period equations are

    pendulum $T = 2\pi\sqrt{\dfrac{L}{g}}$ mass on a spring $T = 2\pi\sqrt{\dfrac{m}{k}}$

    Notice that the pendulum equation is independent of the bob mass and thus no change in period occurs if m becomes $2m$. Therefore, only choices (B) and (C) can be correct. As for the mass on the spring, notice that its period is proportional to $\sqrt{m}$, which therefore means that the new period will be $\sqrt{2}$ times larger. So, choice (B) is correct (*College Physics* 8th ed. pages 425–428, 431–436, 439–441/9th ed. pages 437–441, 443–448, 451–454).

5. **C** The potential energy of an oscillating mass on a spring is $PE_s = \dfrac{1}{2}kx^2$, which shows no relationship to mass (even though the mass is related to the kinetic energy). Therefore, changing the mass while keeping the displacement x unchanged will not alter the total mechanical energy of the system. Thus, choice (C) is correct (*College Physics* 8th ed. pages 425–436/9th ed. pages 437–448).

6. **B** This question involves only knowing the relationship between period and frequency, which is $T = 1/f$. Thus, the frequency is the inverse of the period, giving $5.0\text{ s} = 1/f$, or $f = 1/5$, or $f = 0.2$ Hz, which is choice (B) (*College Physics* 8th ed. pages 432–435/9th ed. pages 445–448).

7. **C** This problem is a straightforward application of Newton's law of gravitation. Here, the mass M of the planet becomes $4M$ and the radius R becomes $2R$. Therefore, substituting gives

    $$F = \frac{GMm}{R^2} = \frac{G(4M)m}{(2R)^2} = \frac{4GMm}{4R^2} = \frac{GMm}{R^2}$$

    Therefore, the new force (i.e., weight) is the same as the old one, 600 N, which is choice (C) (*College Physics* 8th ed. pages 207–211/9th ed. pages 214–217).

8. **E** At any one point, the total mechanical energy of this oscillating system is comprised of kinetic energy (K) and elastic potential energy (PE_s). Because the height does not vary, gravitational potential energy falls out of both sides of our energy conservation equation, $E_{tot} = K + PE_s$. Notice, however, that at the maximum and minimum values of x shown, the object stops, where its kinetic energy is zero. At these points, PE_s is a maximum, whereas at the center, PE_s is

zero (because $x = 0$), making all the energy kinetic energy. By energy conservation, however, their sum must be constant, assuming no interaction with other external forces. Thus, graph (5) is the only one depicting this situation (*College Physics* 8th ed. pages 130–131, 425–436/9th ed. pages 135–136, 437–448).

9. **D** According to the kinetic energy equation $K = \frac{1}{2}mv^2$, K is proportional to the square of the speed v.

    In addition, as derived earlier, the relation between v and x is

    $$v = \sqrt{\frac{k}{m}(A^2 - x^2)}$$

    Therefore,

    $$K = \frac{1}{2}m\left[\sqrt{\frac{k}{m}(A^2 - x^2)}\right]^2$$

    which simplifies to

    $$K = \frac{1}{2}m\frac{k}{m}(A^2 - x^2) = \frac{k}{2}(A^2 - x^2)$$

    Thus, K is proportional to x^2, and only graph (4), or choice (D), depicts this relationship (*College Physics* 8th ed. pages 124–125, 425–436/9th ed. pages 129–131, 437–448).

10. **C** By Hooke's law, $F = -kx$, we can find the value of the spring constant k, which becomes 2.0 kg(10 m/s²) = $-k$(40.0 m), which gives k = 0.5 N/m. Substituting this result and the value of m into the simple harmonic motion spring period equation gives $T = 2\pi\sqrt{2.0 \text{ kg}/(0.5 \text{ N/m})} = 2\pi\sqrt{4}$, or $T = 4\pi$ s, which is choice (C) (*College Physics* 8th ed. pages 425–428, 431–436/9th ed. pages 437–441, 443–448).

11. **A** This problem is a straightforward application of Newton's law of gravitation. Here, the mass of one becomes $2m$ and the distance R becomes $3R$. Substituting gives

    $$F = \frac{GMm}{R^2} = \frac{GM(2m)}{(3R)^2} = \frac{2GMm}{9R^2} = \frac{2F}{9}$$

    Therefore, the new force is $\frac{2}{9}$ (the old force), or choice (A) (*College Physics* 8th ed. pages 207–211/9th ed. pages 214–217).

12. **D** This problem is an application of both Newton's law of gravitation,

    $$F = \frac{GMm}{R^2}$$

    and Kepler's third law of planetary motion,

    $$T^2 = \frac{4\pi^2}{GM}R^3$$

which relates the period T of the orbit of a mass around a central body to the distance R of the orbiting object from the central body. The value of $4\pi^2/GM$ is the orbital constant that is the same for different objects orbiting the same body, and M refers to the central body mass. Kepler's third law shows that there is no relationship between the period of an orbiting body and its *own* mass. For example, Earth's period of 365 days around the Sun is independent of the mass of Earth. Kepler's third law substantiates choices (B), (D), and (E), but notice that the gravitational force depends directly on *each* object's mass (by Newton's law of gravitation). Therefore, only choice (D) is correct (*College Physics* 8th ed. pages 215–218/9th ed. pages 221–224).

13. **B** In this circular orbit, the centripetal force is supplied by Newtonian gravitation, or

$$\frac{mv^2}{R_s} = \frac{GMm}{R_s^2}$$

where R_s denotes the distance of the satellite from the center of the planet and M is the mass of the Earth. Solving for v gives

$$v^2 = \frac{GMR_s}{R_s^2} \quad \text{which becomes} \quad v = \sqrt{\frac{GM}{R_s}}$$

Earth's self-gravity is described by $g = GM_E/R_E^2$ and we can substitute gR_E^2 for GM_E to obtain

$$v = \sqrt{\frac{GM}{R_s}} = \sqrt{\frac{gR_E^2}{R_s}}$$

Noting that $R_s = 2R_E$ as stated in the problem, we then have

$$v = \sqrt{\frac{gR_E^2}{2R_E}} = \sqrt{\frac{gR_E}{2}}$$

which is choice (B) (*College Physics* 8th ed. pages 215–218/9th ed. pages 221–224).

14. **A** This problem is a straightforward application of Newton's law of gravitation, where $F = 8.0 \times 10^3$ N, $R = 4.2 \times 10^7$ m, $M_E = 6.0 \times 10^{24}$ kg, and $R_E = 6.4 \times 10^6$ m. Omitting units for clarity, we then have

$$F = \frac{GMm}{R^2} = \frac{(6.67 \times 10^{-11})(6.0 \times 10^{24})m}{(4.2 \times 10^7)^2} = 8.0 \times 10^3$$

Because this problem must be performed without a calculator, much approximation can take place. For example, (6.67)(6.0) is nearly midway between 36 and 49, so 40 will do, and 4.2^2 is about 17. Therefore,

$$8.0 \times 10^3 = \frac{(6.67 \times 10^{-11})(6.0 \times 10^{24})m}{(4.2 \times 10^7)^2} \approx \frac{40(10^{-11})(10^{24})m}{17(10^7)^2} \approx \frac{40(10^{13})m}{17(10^{14})}$$

and solving for m gives

$$m \approx \frac{17(8.0 \times 10^3)(10^{14})}{40(10^{13})} \approx \frac{17(8.0 \times 10^{17})}{40(10^{13})} \approx \frac{140 \times 10^4}{40} \approx 3.5 \times 10^4 \text{ kg}$$

Thus, choice (A) is correct (*College Physics* 8th ed. pages 207–211/9th ed. pages 214–217).

15. **B** From the graph, it must be realized that the period of oscillation is 4.0 s (the completion of one full cycle). Thus, $T = 4.0$ s and $m = 2.0$ kg. Using the period equation for the oscillating mass, we have $T = 2\pi\sqrt{m/k}$, or $4.0 \text{ s} = 2\pi\sqrt{2.0 \text{ kg}/k}$. Squaring both sides to eliminate the radical and solving for k gives $16/4\pi^2$, or $k = [2(4\pi^2)]/16$. Therefore, $k = \pi^2/2$ (*College Physics* 8th ed. pages 425–428, 431–436/9th ed. pages 437–441, 443–448).

Free-Response Problems

1. (a) For this collision, we use conservation of momentum to solve for the new speed of the blocks. So, $p_{i \text{ sys}} = p_{f \text{ sys}}$, or $(4M)v_i + 0 = (5M)v_f$. Solving for v_f gives $v_f = \frac{4}{5}v_i$ (*College Physics* 8th ed. pages 166–176/9th ed. pages 172–175).

    (b) The maximum strain comes directly from the impacting kinetic energy of the blocks, which gives the spring PE_s. Therefore, we can use energy conservation to solve this problem, labeling equilibrium as A and x as B. So, $K_A + PE_{sA} + K_B + PE_{sB}$ becomes $\frac{1}{2}mv_A^2 + 0 = 0 + \frac{1}{2}kx_B^2$. Substituting gives $\frac{1}{2}(5M)(\frac{4}{5}v)^2 = \frac{1}{2}kx^2$, where $v_i = v$. Solving for x gives $x = \sqrt{(16Mv^2)/5k}$, or $x = 4v\sqrt{M/5k}$ (*College Physics* 8th ed. pages 135–140/9th ed. pages 140–145).

    (c) The period of a mass oscillating on a spring is given by $T = 2\pi\sqrt{m/k}$. Here, m simply becomes $5M$, so the period T of the simple harmonic motion is $T = 2\pi\sqrt{5M/k}$ (*College Physics* 8th ed. pages 425–428, 431–436/9th ed. pages 437–441, 443–448).

2. (a) The amplitude of this motion is read directly from the y axis on the graph, from the $y = 0$ level (i.e., x axis) up to the peak of the graph, or 0.03 m (*College Physics* 8th ed. pages 445–447/9th ed. pages 458–459).

    (b) Careful observation of the graph shows that three full cycles occur in 8 s. Therefore, one full cycle occurs in $\frac{8}{3}$ s. Thus, the period $T = \frac{8}{3}$ s, or 2.7 s (*College Physics* 8th ed. pages 445–447/9th ed. pages 458–459).

    (c) Here we need to solve the period equation for k, with 0.5 kg substituted for the mass m. So, $T = 2\pi\sqrt{m/k}$ becomes

$\frac{8}{3} = 2\pi\sqrt{0.5 / k}$ or $(8/6\pi)2 = 0.5/k$. Solving for k gives $k = \frac{9}{32}\pi^2 = $ 2.8 N/m (*College Physics* 8th ed. pages 425–428, 431–436/9th ed. pages 437–441, 443–448).

(d) Because the mass was doubled from m to $2m$, careful observation of the period equation will show that the period T is proportional to the square root of mass. Therefore, doubling the mass will increase the period by $\sqrt{2}$. So, $T = 2\pi\sqrt{m / k}$ becomes

$T = 2\pi\sqrt{2m / k} = \sqrt{2}(2\pi)(\sqrt{m / k}) = \sqrt{2}(\frac{8}{3})$ s. Therefore, the period

increases from 2.7 s to 3.8 s (*College Physics* 8th ed. pages 425–428, 431–436/9th ed. pages 437–441, 443–448).

(e) The new plot has a period of 3.8 s; thus, one-half period will be 1.9 s as shown. The crest of the second cycle ends at approximately 5.7 s, and its trough ends at 7.5 s. The amplitude should still remain at 0.03 m as described in the problem (*College Physics* 8th ed. pages 425–428, 431–436/9th ed. pages 437–441, 443–448).

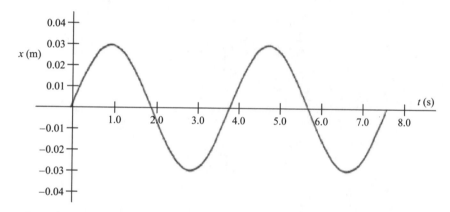

3. (a) This problem can be solved using Kepler's third law for a circular orbit, or simply Newton's law of gravitation (both identical). Because gravity supplies the centripetal force holding Callisto to an orbit, we can cancel terms and write $v^2 = GM/R$, which can be solved for M (Jupiter's mass):

$$\frac{v^2 R}{G} = M$$

Note, though, that it is necessary to find the orbital radius using $v = 2\pi R/T$, which becomes

$$\frac{vT}{2\pi} = R = \frac{(8222.0 \text{ m/s})(17 \times 86{,}400 \text{ s})}{2\pi} = 1.9 \times 10^9 \text{ m}$$

Therefore, using $v^2R/G = M$, we have

$$M = \frac{(8222.0 \text{ m/s})^2(1.9 \times 10^9 \text{ m})}{6.7 \times 10^{-11} \text{ N} \cdot \text{m}^2/\text{kg}^2}$$

So, the mass of Jupiter is 1.9×10^{27} kg.

(b) Take the following ratio to determine the quantity $(1.9 \times 10^{27}$ kg$)/$ $(6.0 \times 10^{24}$ kg$)$, or 323 times greater.

(c) The percent error is calculated as

$$\frac{\text{measured} - \text{accepted}}{\text{accepted}} \times 100\%$$

which is

$$\frac{323.4 - 318}{318} \times 100\% = 1.7\%$$

(*College Physics* 8th ed. pages 207–211, 215–218/9th ed. pages 214–217, 221–224)

9

FLUIDS

WHAT IS A FLUID?

(*College Physics* 8th ed. page 290/9th ed. page 299)

The study of fluids, inasmuch as is required for AP Physics B, outlines two primary branches of this subject at the elementary level: fluids that are stationary (*hydrostatics*) and fluids that are in motion (*hydrodynamics*). In both topics, the relationship between forces causing fluid pressure, how fluid pressure is proportional to fluid velocity, and how fluid pressure varies with depth in a liquid are all of primary importance. In addition, the features of the fluid dictate its behavior under certain conditions. Thus, in terms of understanding the basics of fluid behavior, it is best to consider the fluid as an *ideal* fluid, which satisfies the following constraints:

1. *The fluid is incompressible.* Such a fluid has a constant density throughout.
2. *The fluid is nonviscous.* Such a fluid possesses no internal friction between layers of the fluid that could impede its motion, which allows it to undergo *streamlined* motion.
3. *The fluid moves with no turbulence.* Such a fluid has no irregular motion such that elements of the fluid do not rotate, but simply move forward (i.e., translate).
4. *The fluid motion is steady.* Such a fluid has velocity, density, and pressure at each point in the fluid that do not change with time.

HYDROSTATICS: WHAT RELATIONSHIP EXISTS AMONG PRESSURE, DENSITY, AND DEPTH WITHIN A FLUID?

(*College Physics* 8th ed. pages 276–284/9th ed. pages 279–282, 288–293)

What is heavier, a pound of feathers or a pound of lead? It is important to ask which of these materials takes up more space rather than which is heavier. Of course, lead is the more compact material; thus, an equal amount (or *mass*, *m*, in kilograms) of lead takes up less space (or *volume*, *V*, in cubic meters) than an equal amount of feathers. The combination of mass *m* and volume *V* leads to the a concept of fluids, that of *density*, *ρ*:

$$\rho = \frac{m}{V}$$

The density of a particular material or fluid (measured in units of kilograms per cubic meter, or kg/m³) depends directly on how much matter (or *mass*) is present in a particular volume occupied by the substance. Gold, for example, with a density of 19,300 kg/m³, has nearly nine times the amount of mass per cubic meter than does concrete, with a density of 2200 kg/m³, meaning that an equal mass of gold takes up much less volume than does an equal mass of concrete. (For comparison, the density of water at standard temperature and pressure is 1000 kg/m³.) In fluids, it is also important to realize that the mass of a substance may immediately be calculated using the equation above when only the density and volume are given. Mass, *m*, is also written as $m = \rho V$. For example, the mass of 2 m³ of concrete is $m = (2200 \text{ kg/m}^3)(2 \text{ m}^3) = 4400$ kg.

Although an ideal fluid's mass is uniform for a particular given volume, the force exerted on the bottom of a container holding a fluid depends on both the height *h* of the liquid above the container bottom and the area *A* over which the force is distributed. The combination of the force *F* of the fluid exerted over a certain area *A* (in square meters) gives the fluid's pressure *P* at that location. Thus, the definition of pressure is

$$P = \frac{F}{A}$$

In the above equation, the unit for pressure is newtons per square meter (N/m²), which is called the pascal (Pa). As with the density equation, the pressure equation can be solved for force *F* to give $F = PA$. For common comparison, one pascal (1 N/m²) is equivalent to 1.4×10^{-4} pounds per square inch (lb/in.²), the English unit for pressure. Therefore, the pressure at sea level due to the weight of Earth's atmosphere, which is about 15 lb/in.², is 1.01×10^5 Pa, or 1 atmosphere (1 atm). Similarly, a car tire with 30 lb/in.² has air that is pressurized to 2.02×10^5 Pa, and air on Venus's surface is pressurized to nearly 1.01×10^7 Pa, nearly 100 times that of air pressure at Earth's surface. Notice also that pressure and area are inversely related, implying that as the area of a surface under the same force decreases, the total pressure will increase and vice versa. Hence, it is easier to walk on snow when wearing snowshoes (with a very wide surface contact area) than when wearing normal street shoes (with a small surface contact area).

Consider a "block" of fluid of mass *m* whose top and bottom have area *A*. We can derive the relationship between pressure and depth in a fluid, where F_1 and F_2 are forces on the mass due to the surrounding fluid, as shown.

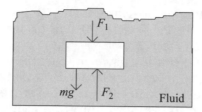

Applying $\Sigma F = 0$, we have $F_2 - F_1 - mg = 0$. Using the pressure and density equations given above, we can rewrite this expression as $P_2 A_2 - P_1 A_1 - \rho V g = 0$. Because $V = Ah$ (where h = the vertical height of the liquid block) and all areas A are equal, we then have $P_2 - P_1 - \rho(h)g = 0$, or $P_2 = P_1 + \rho g h$.

If the block is at the very top of the liquid, then P_1 becomes the downward pressure due to the air above the liquid, which is 1.01×10^5 Pa, written as P_0. Therefore, P_2 is called the *absolute* or *total pressure* on the block. The term $\rho g h$ is called the *gauge pressure* on the block, where h is the depth of the block in the fluid and ρ is the fluid's density. As expected, our fictitious block of liquid can be replaced by a real block of any material beneath the surface of the liquid, which therefore experiences both an absolute and a gauge pressure. To summarize:

$$P = P_0 + \rho g h \quad \text{(absolute or total pressure)} \qquad P_g = \rho g h \quad \text{(gauge pressure)}$$

If you ever swam far below the surface of the water in a swimming pool, you may remember feeling gauge pressure exerted on your body from the weight of the overlying water. Other examples of such submerged objects in water are submarines and all sea life that lives beneath the top of a water layer. Notice that gauge pressure is independent of the shape of the container holding the fluid.

SAMPLE PROBLEM 1

The Super Kamiokande neutrino experiment in Japan is a massive water-filled, cylindrical underground mine that holds about 11,000 sphere-like glass phototubes that detect light emitted when neutrinos pass through the water. The water has a density of 1000 kg/m^3, and the bottom-most phototube is 45 m below the surface of the water.

(a) Determine the gauge pressure on one of the bottom-most phototubes.
(b) Determine the absolute pressure on one of the bottom-most phototubes.
(c) Determine the ratio of the absolute pressure to sea-level pressure on one of the bottom-most phototubes.
(d) If the front of one of the bottom-most phototubes has an area of 0.2 m^2, determine the force exerted on the phototube front.

SOLUTION TO PROBLEM 1

(a) Because the fluid density ρ and the liquid depth h are both given, the gauge pressure can immediately be calculated from $P_g = \rho g h = (1000 \text{ kg/m}^3)(10 \text{ m/s}^2)(45 \text{ m}) = \textbf{4.5} \times \textbf{10}^5 \textbf{ Pa} = \textbf{gauge pressure } P_g$.
(b) The absolute or total pressure on one of the bottom-most phototubes is simply the gauge pressure plus the addition of the

overlying air pressure, 1.01×10^5 Pa. Therefore, $P = P_0 + \rho g h = 1.01 \times 10^5$ Pa $+ 4.5 \times 10^5$ Pa, or **total or absolute pressure** $P = \mathbf{5.51 \times 10^5}$ **Pa.**

(c) The ratio of the answer in part (b) to the pressure at sea level will state how much larger P is relative to 1 atm. Thus, $(5.51 \times 10^5$ Pa$)/(1.01 \times 10^5)$ Pa ≈ 5. **Therefore, the absolute pressure on a bottom-most phototube is five times the sea-level air pressure on Earth.**

(d) According to the pressure equation, the force can be written as $F = PA$. Therefore, the total force on the phototube face is $F = PA = (5.51 \times 10^5$ Pa$)(0.2$ m^2) $\sim \mathbf{1 \times 10^5}$ **N.**

How Do Fluids Act to Provide a Support Force?

(*College Physics* 8th ed. pages 284–290/9th ed. pages 293–299)

What happens to a fluid when an object is placed in it? When an object floats on or near the surface of a liquid, such as in a water bath, two important results occur. First, the object is clearly supported by an upward force exerted by the liquid, called the *buoyant force*, F_B. Second, the fluid is pushed aside, or displaced, and the weight of this displaced fluid is equal to the buoyant force (which is known as Archimedes's principle).

How does the buoyant force compare with the "dry" weight of the object? If the object is hung by a spring scale in air (as shown here in the left-hand diagram) and then in water (right-hand diagram), the reading on the spring scale clearly decreases by an amount equal to the buoyant force.

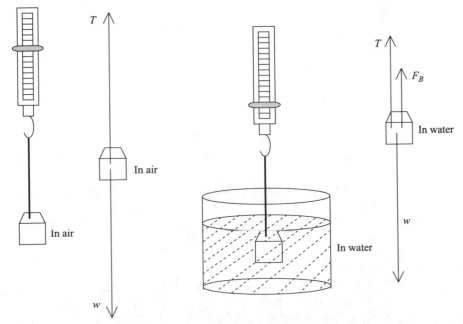

For example, if the scale "in air" in the diagram reads 22 N and then reads 14 N "in water," $\Sigma F = 0$ applied to that situation (see the free-body diagrams) shows that the buoyant force F_B must be 8 N:

$\Sigma F = 0 = T + F_B - w = 0$, or $14 \text{ N} + F_B - 22 \text{ N} = 0$. Therefore, $F_B = 22 \text{ N} - 14 \text{ N} = 8 \text{ N}$.

If, on the other hand, the object is completely submerged (and floats) and if $\Sigma F = 0$, we can write $F - w = 0$, or $F = mg = (\rho V)_{\text{object}} g$.

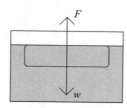

By Archimedes's principle, the weight of the displaced water $[(\rho V)_{\text{water}}]g$ is equivalent to the weight of the submerged object $[(\rho V)_{\text{object}}]g$, which is equal to the buoyant force. Thus, for a fully immersed floating object, the buoyant force F_B is written

$$F_B = \rho g V \quad \text{(buoyant force)}$$

where ρ is the density of the fluid and V is the volume of the displaced liquid (which, again, for a fully submerged object, is equal to the volume of the object). In the case in which the object is partially submerged, however, the weight of the displaced liquid is, of course, less than if the object were fully submerged; therefore, F_B is lower. Thus, the quantity V in the equation above is only the volume of the submerged material, *not* the volume of the entire object. Study Sample Problem 2 to see this further.

AP Tip

When using $F_B = \rho V g$, be sure to differentiate between the volume of the entire object and the volume of that part of the object that is submerged. When the object is fully submerged, V is the total object volume. When it is partially submerged, however, V represents only the volume of the part of the object that is submerged.

SAMPLE PROBLEM 2

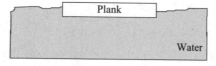

A plank of pine wood (density of 550 kg/m³) of dimensions 4.0 m × 4.0 m × 0.3 m is placed in a water bath whose density is 1000 kg/m³ as shown.

(a) Sketch the forces acting on the floating plank.
(b) Verify by calculation that this plank must float.
(c) Determine the buoyant force on this plank while it is floating.
(d) Determine the percentage of the plank that is not submerged.

SOLUTION TO PROBLEM 2

(a)

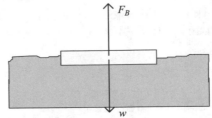

(b) To determine by calculation if the plank floats (other than simply comparing the plank's density with that of water), it is necessary to show that the maximum buoyant force ($F_{B\,max}$) exceeds the weight (mg) of the plank. If $F_{B\,max} > w$, the plank floats. So, $F_{B\,max} = \rho_{liquid}gV_{max}$ = (1000 kg/m³)(10 m/s²)[(4 m)(4 m)(0.3 m)] = 4.8×10^4 N = $F_{B\,max}$. The plank's weight is $w = mg = (\rho V)_{plank}g$ = (550 kg/m³)[(4 m)(4 m) (0.3 m)](10 m/s²) = 2.6×10^4 N = w. **Therefore, the plank must float because $F_{B\,max} > w$.**

(c) The buoyant force on the plank, based on parts (a) and (b) (and because the plank is at rest), is simply the weight of the displaced water, which is balanced by the plank's weight. Thus, **$F_B = 2.6 \times 10^4$ N.**

(d) To determine the percentage of the plank that is above water, it is necessary to calculate the volume of the plank that is submerged so that the ratio $(V_{total} - V_{submerged})/V_{total}$ may be determined. The total volume of the plank that is submerged may be found from the buoyant force: $F_B = \rho_{liquid}gV_{submerged}$. Solving for volume gives

$$V_{submerged} = \frac{F_B}{\rho g} = \frac{2.6 \times 10^4 \text{ N}}{\left(1000 \text{ kg/m}^2\right)\left(10 \text{ m/s}^2\right)} = 2.6 \text{ m}^3$$

Therefore,

$$\frac{V_{total} - V_{submerged}}{V_{total}} = \frac{(4 \text{ m})(4 \text{ m})(0.3 \text{ m}) - 2.6 \text{ m}^3}{\left(4 \text{ m}\right)\left(4 \text{ m}\right)\left(0.3 \text{ m}\right)} = \frac{4.8 \text{ m}^3 - 2.6 \text{ m}^3}{4.8 \text{ m}^3} = 0.46$$

which means that **46% of the plank is above water.**

WHAT HAPPENS TO THE PRESSURE OF A LIQUID IN A CLOSED PIPE?

(*College Physics* 8th ed. pages 281–283/9th ed. pages 288–293)

It has been shown that the pressure within a fluid depends on the depth of the fluid. For a confined fluid, a pressure change must be transmitted evenly throughout the entire fluid, which is true even if the fluid is enclosed in a tube or pipe that has a varying diameter. An example of such a device is a hydraulic lift found at an auto mechanic shop. In this case, a fluid remains enclosed within a pipe of varying diameters, which therefore affects the force on the fluid. This property, first noticed in the early 17th century by French scientist Blaise Pascal, has come to be known as Pascal's principle. It specifically states that any pressure change applied to a fluid in an enclosed pipe is transmitted undiminished through the fluid and to the walls of the container. By employing Pascal's principle, it is possible to input a fairly small force and amplify it, providing a very large output force, as is the case with a hydraulic lift that can raise and lower automobiles.

Because pressure is constant throughout the fluid, we can write $P = F_1/A_1 = F_2/A_2$ at two different locations within the fluid. Thus, Pascal's principle written mathematically becomes $F_1A_2 = F_2A_1$, where A is the cross-sectional area of the pipe enclosing the fluid. For a circular cross section, $A = \pi r^2$. So,

$$F_1A_2 = F_2A_1 \quad \text{(Pascal's principle)}$$

HYDRODYNAMICS: IS THE MASS OF FLUID CONSTANT DURING FLUID FLOW?

(*College Physics* 8th ed. pages 290–293/9th ed. pages 299–302)

How does water behave while passing through the nozzle of a garden hose (where it travels from a wide-diameter tube to a small-diameter opening in the nozzle)? In a section of pipe whose cross-sectional area A_1 is πr_1^2, the fluid moves a distance $d = v_1 \Delta t$ in time Δt. As we have previously seen, the mass m of the fluid may be expressed as ρV; thus, the product of area A_1 and the distance d will be substituted for volume V to give $A_1 v_1 \Delta t$. Therefore, the mass m of fluid passing through this section of the pipe is $\rho V = \rho(A_1 v_1 \Delta t)$. In a separate location of the pipe, however, where the cross-sectional area A_2 is different, the same mass of water must pass through this location because the pipe is closed and the fluid is assumed to be noncompressible to maintain mass conservation. Therefore, in the same time interval Δt, mass m_1 must equal mass m_2, which is $\rho_1(A_1 v_1 \Delta t) = \rho_2(A_2 v_2 \Delta t)$. For the case of an incompressible fluid that is unchanged throughout the pipe (and if the pipe has no leaks), the density ρ cancels from each side to give

$$A_1 v_1 = A_2 v_2 \quad \text{(equation of continuity)}$$

Because the mass flow rate ($\Delta m/\Delta t = \rho A V$) is constant, the product Av is constant, signifying that an inverse relation exists between area A and speed v. When a pipe is narrowly constricted such that A is small, the corresponding effect is to increase v and vice versa. Notice that the mass flow rate has units of kilograms per second, whereas Av has units of cubic meters per second, helping you remember that the former is indeed a rate of *mass* movement and the latter is a rate of *volume* movement.

HOW ARE FLUID SPEED AND PRESSURE RELATED?

(*College Physics* 8th ed. pages 293–299/9th ed. pages 302–305)

In addition to describing the mass flow rate of a fluid through a pipe of varying diameter and the fluid's associated change of speed, there also exists a relationship between fluid pressure and speed in such a pipe, particularly when the pipe changes elevation, causing a change in fluid potential energy. The basis of this relationship, called Bernoulli's equation, lies in the application of energy conservation as applied to an ideal fluid. As a space constraint, its derivation is not shown here (refer to the textbook pages referenced above), but its use is employed in the Sample Problem 3 as well as in Free-Response Question 2.

Bernoulli's equation, written $P + \frac{1}{2}\rho v^2 + \rho gy = $ constant, contains terms that are essentially those of energy conservation. First, notice that fluid pressure P is present, as are $\frac{1}{2}\rho v^2$ and ρgy, which are analogous to kinetic energy (per unit volume) and gravitational potential energy (per unit volume), respectively. Therefore, notice that as the pressure P of the fluid increases, the associated fluid speed v decreases and vice versa.

$$P_1 + \rho gy_1 + \frac{1}{2}\rho v_1^2 = P_2 + \rho gy_2 + \frac{1}{2}\rho v_2^2 \quad \text{(Bernoulli's equation)}$$

An example is the Venturi tube, which is a horizontal tube of varying diameter used to measure the speed of fluid flow (similar tubes, called *pitot tubes*, exist on aircraft to measure airflow). There are countless examples of this principle in our ordinary lives, one of which is evident in Sample Problem 3.

SAMPLE PROBLEM 3

A person suffering from shortness of breath visits a doctor, who discovers that blood flow in an artery (shown here) is severely restricted, noting that the flow at position 2 in the artery is three times faster than at position 1. (For the purposes of this problem, assume human blood is an ideal fluid.)

(a) Based on the information given, comment qualitatively on the diameter of this artery at position 2 relative to that at position 1.

(b) Describe the differences in the blood pressure at position 2 relative to position 1. What can occur as a result of this difference?

(c) Determine the ratio of r_1 to r_2.

(d) If $r_1 = 1.0$ cm, calculate the value of r_2.

(e) If the average density of human blood is 1060 kg/m³ and the blood's speed at position 1 is 0.1 m/s, determine the pressure gradient ΔP between positions 1 and 2 (assume the heights of 1 and 2 are equal).

SOLUTION TO PROBLEM 3

(a) It is stated that blood flow is faster at position 2 than at position 1, which signifies, by the volume flow-rate condition, that **the cross-sectional area (and therefore the diameter) at position 2 must be much narrower than at position 1**. Therefore, the blood vessel has a constriction at position 2 that causes the increase in blood speed.

(b) By Bernoulli's equation, as the speed of the fluid increases, an inverse relation exists with the pressure of the fluid. Thus, because the blood speed has *increased* at position 2, the blood **pressure must be lower at position 2 than at position 1.** This lower pressure may cause a collapse in the artery because there is a greater pressure outside the vessel than inside at position 2.

(c) The ratio can be determined using the volume flow-rate condition $A_1 v_1 = A_2 v_2$, where each cross-sectional area A is πr^2 (note also that it is stated that $v_2 = 3v_1$). We then have $r_1^2 v_1 = r_2^2 v_2$, and solving for the ratio of radii gives $r_1^2/r_2^2 = v_2/v_1$ or $r_1/r_2 = \sqrt{v_2/v_1} = \sqrt{3v_1/v_1} = 1.7$. Therefore, the ratio of r_1 to r_2 is 1.7, or $r_1 = 1.7r_2$.

(d) Based on the calculation in part (c), $r_1 = 1.7r_2$, or $r_2 = 1.0$ cm/1.7. Therefore, $r_2 = 0.59$ cm.

(e) The change of pressure ΔP between positions 1 and 2 can be found by applying Bernoulli's equation to the two locations and calculating the final pressure change $P_1 - P_2$. Because the height of the artery is constant, the terms $\rho g y_1$ and $\rho g y_2$ will drop out, and we can solve for $P_1 - P_2$ as follows: $P_1 + \frac{1}{2}\rho v_1^2 = P_2 + \frac{1}{2}\rho v_2^2$. Rearranging and collecting similar terms on each side gives $P_1 - P_2 = \frac{1}{2}\rho v_2^2 - \frac{1}{2}\rho v_1^2$. Because it is given that $v_2 = 3v_1$, we can substitute to further reduce the equation to $P_1 - P_2 = \frac{1}{2}\rho(3v_1)^2 - \frac{1}{2}\rho v_1^2 = \frac{1}{2}\rho(9v_1^2 - v_1^2) = \frac{1}{2}\rho(8v_1^2) = 4\rho v_1^2$. Substituting for the density and speed will finally give $P_1 - P_2 = 4(1060 \text{ kg/m}^2)(0.1 \text{ m/s})^2 = 42$ Pa. **Therefore, the pressure change ΔP within the artery between points 1 and 2 is 42 Pa.**

FLUIDS: STUDENT OBJECTIVES FOR THE AP EXAM

- You should understand the nature and meaning of mass density ($\rho = m/V$) and how to substitute ρV to solve for mass m.
- You should understand the nature and meaning of pressure P, where $P = F/A$, and how to substitute PA to solve for force F.
- You should understand and be able to calculate gauge pressure ($P = \rho gh$) due to a liquid of depth (or height) h.
- You should understand and be able to calculate absolute pressure P, atmospheric pressure (P_0) plus gauge pressure (ρgh), written as $P = P_0 + \rho gh$.
- You should understand and be able to perform calculations using Pascal's principle ($F_1 A_2 = F_2 A_1$).
- You should understand the nature of floating objects and how they are affected by a buoyant force F_B.
- You should understand, with respect to floating objects, the application of Archimedes's principle and that (1) the volume of liquid that is displaced by a submerged object equals the volume of the material that is submerged and (2) the weight of the displaced material is equal to the (upward) buoyant force exerted by the liquid on the immersed object (i.e., Archimedes's principle).
- You should understand and be able to calculate the maximum buoyant force ($F_{B\,max} = \rho_{liquid}\, g V_{object}$).
- You should understand the nature and characteristics of an ideal fluid.

- You should be able to perform calculations with and should understand the meaning of the equation of continuity ($A_1v_1 = A_2v_2$), which pertains to the speed of an ideal fluid as it passes through constrictions of varying cross-sectional area.
- You should understand and be able to perform calculations using Bernoulli's equation, which states that at any two points (1 and 2) in a flowing ideal fluid, $P + \rho gy + \frac{1}{2}\rho v^2 = $ constant.

MULTIPLE-CHOICE QUESTIONS

1. Water flows with a speed of 5.0 m/s from a 2.0-cm-diameter pipe into a 6.0-cm-diameter pipe. In the 6.0-cm-diameter pipe, what is the approximate speed of the water?
   (A) 0.1 m/s
   (B) 0.6 m/s
   (C) 2.0 m/s
   (D) 3.5 m/s
   (E) 5.0 m/s

2. Water is pumped into one end of a long pipe at the rate of 10.0 m³/s. It emerges at the other end at a rate of 6.0 m³/s. What is the most likely reason for the decrease in the flow rate of this water?
   (A) The water is being pumped uphill.
   (B) The water is being pumped downhill.
   (C) The diameter of the pipe is not the same at the two ends.
   (D) There is a tremendous friction force on the inside walls of the pipe.
   (E) There is a leak in the pipe.

3. In a classroom demonstration, a 73.5-kg physics professor lies on a "bed of nails" that consists of a large number of evenly spaced, relatively sharp nails mounted in a board so that the points extend vertically upward from the board. While the professor is lying down, approximately 1,900 nails make contact with his body. If the area of contact at the point of each nail is 1.26×10^{-6} m², what is the average pressure at each contact point?
   (A) 1.59×10^4 Pa
   (B) 5.71×10^8 Pa
   (C) 1.11×10^{12} Pa
   (D) 1.11×10^6 Pa
   (E) 3.01×10^5 Pa

4. A frog is at rest at the bottom of a lake at a depth y below the surface. If the top surface of the frog has area A, which of the following expressions correctly describes the total downward force F exerted on the frog?
   (A) $(P_0 + \rho gy)A$
   (B) $P_0 A$
   (C) ρgyA
   (D) $(P_0 + \frac{1}{2}\rho v^2)A$
   (E) $P_0 + \rho gy$

5. What are the units of volume flow rate?
   (A) seconds
   (B) kilograms per second
   (C) square meters per second
   (D) cubic meters per second
   (E) cubic meters

6. Liquid water (of density 1000 kg/m³) flows with a speed of 8.0 m/s in a horizontal pipe of diameter 0.2 m. As the pipe narrows to a diameter of 0.04 m, what is the approximate mass flow rate of the water in this constriction (in units of mass flow rate)?
   (A) 0.01
   (B) 0.25
   (C) 0.8
   (D) 240
   (E) 900

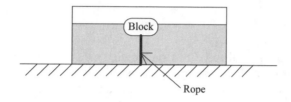

7. A 2-kg wooden block displaces 10-kg of water when it is forcibly held fully immersed (the block is less dense than the water). The block is then tied down such that part of it is submerged as shown, and it displaces only 5 kg of water. What is the approximate tension of the rope?
   (A) 10 N
   (B) 20 N
   (C) 30 N
   (D) 70 N
   (E) 100 N

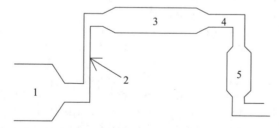

For Questions 8 and 9, refer to the diagram, which depicts a horizontal piping system, viewed from directly overhead, that delivers a constant flow of water through pipes of varying relative diameters labeled 1 through 5.

8. At which of the labeled points is the water in the pipe moving with the lowest speed?
   (A) 1
   (B) 2
   (C) 3
   (D) 4
   (E) 5

9. At which of the labeled points is the water in the pipe under the lowest pressure?
   (A) 1
   (B) 2
   (C) 3
   (D) 4
   (E) 5

10. A hydraulic press has one piston of radius R_1 and another piston of radius R_2. If a 400.0-N force is applied to the piston of radius R_1 and the resulting force exerted on the other piston is 1600.0 N, which of the following is a correct mathematical statement concerning each piston radius?
    (A) $R_2 = R_1$
    (B) $R_1 = 2R_2$
    (C) $R_1 = \sqrt{2}\, R_2$
    (D) $R_2 = 2R_1$
    (E) $R_2 = \sqrt{2}\, R_2$

11. Using the value of atmospheric pressure at sea level, 1.0×10^5 Pa, what is the approximate mass of Earth's atmosphere that is above a flat building that has a rooftop area of 5.0 m²?
    (A) 2.0×10^{-4} kg
    (B) 4.0×10^{-2} kg
    (C) 9.0×10^2 kg
    (D) 5.0×10^4 kg
    (E) 5.0×10^5 kg

12. A person is standing near the edge of a railroad track when a high-speed train passes. By Bernoulli's equation, what happens to the person?
    (A) The person is pushed away from the train.
    (B) The person increases in mass as the train approaches and then decreases in mass as the train recedes.
    (C) The person is pushed upward into the air.
    (D) The person is unaffected by the train.
    (E) The person is pushed toward the train.

13. A fluid is undergoing "incompressible" flow. Which of the following best applies to this statement?
    (A) The pressure at a given point cannot change with time.
    (B) The velocity at a given point cannot change with time.
    (C) The density cannot change with time or location.
    (D) The pressure must be the same everywhere in the fluid.
    (E) The velocity must be the same everywhere in the fluid.

14. A wooden block of density 450 kg/m³ floats on the surface of a pool of stationary liquid water. Which of the following is a correct free-body diagram for this situation, where F = buoyant force, N = normal force, and w = weight?

(A)

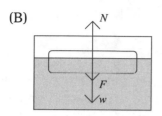

(B)

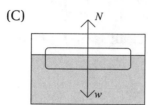

(C)

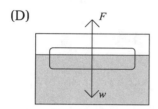

(D)

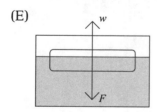

(E)

15. An object with a volume of 2×10^{-2} m³ floats in a tank of water with 70% of its volume exposed above the water. If the density of water is 1000 kg/m³, what is the approximate weight of this object?
    (A) 3 N
    (B) 6 N
    (C) 12 N
    (D) 30 N
    (E) 60 N

FREE-RESPONSE PROBLEMS

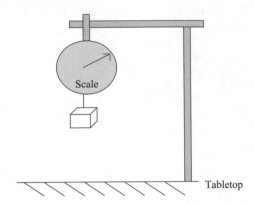

Scale

Tabletop

1. A student hangs an unknown material in the shape of a cube 2.1 cm on a side from a sensitive spring scale that is at rest at sea level on Earth as shown. The scale reads 0.245 N. The student is given the following list of densities of common solids and liquids.

Solids (in kg/m³)		Liquids (in kg/m³)	
Aluminum	2,700	Blood (at 37°C)	1,060
Brass	8,470	Hydraulic oil	800
Concrete	2,200	Mercury	13,600
Diamond	3,520	Water (at 4°C)	1,000
Gold	19,300		
Lead	11,300		
Silver	10,500		
Wood (pine)	550		

(a) According to the table, determine the material the student's cube is most likely made of.
(b) Determine the percent deviation in the student's measurement of the quantity found in part (a).

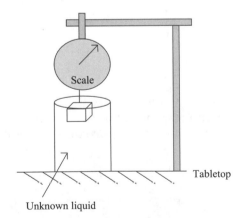

Scale

Tabletop

Unknown liquid

The cube is now fully immersed into a container with an unknown ideal liquid as shown here, and the scale reading is now 0.173 N.

(c) Sketch the free-body diagram of the cube as it remains suspended in the liquid.

(d) What liquid does the student determine is in the container? Support your conclusion with appropriate calculations.

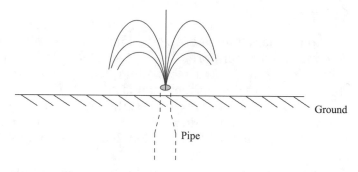

Ground

Pipe

2. A fountain emitting a single stream of water (density 1000 kg/m³) at a playground is fed from a vertical pipe that is below ground but whose opening is at ground level as shown. At the ground-level opening, the pipe's diameter is 0.06 m and the water exits the pipe with a velocity of 9.0 m/s upward.

(a) Determine the maximum height attained by the water after it exits the pipe.

(b) Determine the volume flow rate of the water as it exits the pipe.

(c) Determine the mass flow rate of the water as it exits the pipe.

(d) The fountain's lower end of the underground pipe has a diameter of 0.12 m and is 6.0 m below the ground. Determine the absolute pressure in the underground pipe at a depth of 6.0 m.

(e) The owner of the fountain wishes to launch the water so that it reaches a height of 10.0 m above the ground with the same volume flow rate. She decides to do so by attaching a new nozzle to the pipe at the ground-level opening. Determine what the diameter the new nozzle must be to achieve this height.

ANSWERS

MULTIPLE-CHOICE QUESTIONS

1. **B**   The mass flow rate is $\rho A v$ = constant throughout (i.e., equation of continuity), so $A_1 v_v = A_2 v_2$ can be used to calculate the new speed in the 6.0-cm-diameter pipe (bear in mind that diameter, not radius, is given, but because in the ratio the units of area cancel, the units of centimeter do not need to be changed to meters). We can solve for v_2, substitute $A = \pi r^2$ for each pipe, and solve for v_2:

$$v_2 = \frac{A_1 v_1}{A_2} = \frac{r_1^2 v_1}{r_2^2}$$

Substituting 1 cm for r_1 and 3 cm for r_2 gives

$$v_2 = \frac{(1\,\text{cm})^2 5.0\,\text{m/s}}{(3\,\text{cm})^2}$$

which simplifies to $v_2 = [1(5.0 \text{ m/s})]/9 = \frac{5}{9}$, or $v_2 \approx \mathbf{0.6 \text{ m/s}}$, which is choice (B) (*College Physics* 8th ed. pages 290–293/ 9th ed. pages 299–302).

2. **E** Again, mass flow rate is $\rho Av = $ constant throughout (i.e., equation of continuity). Therefore, $A_1v_1 = A_2v_2$. Because it is stated that the initial flow rate is 10.0 m³/s, this quantity must remain constant throughout the pipe (assuming it is closed). Therefore, because it is stated that the outflow is 6.0 m³/s, the only possible explanation for the discrepancy is that **liquid left the pipe via a leak**, or choice (E) (*College Physics* 8th ed. pages 290–293/9th ed. pages 299–302).

3. **E** This question is a basic application of the definition of pressure, $P = F/A$, where F is the force exerted on one nail (not the entire 1,900 of them). Therefore, the entire weight of the professor (mg) must be distributed over all the nails. Once that value is found, the average pressure per nail can be calculated:

$$P = \frac{F}{A} = \frac{mg/1900}{1.26 \times 10^{-6} \text{ m}^2} = \frac{73.5 \text{ kg}(10.0 \text{ m/s}^2)/1900}{1.26 \times 10^{-6} \text{ m}^2} \approx \frac{735/1900}{1.26 \times 10^{-6}}$$

$$\approx \frac{\left(7.4 \times 10^2\right)/\left(2 \times 10^2\right)}{1.26 \times 10^{-6}} \approx 3.0 \times 10^5 \text{ Pa}$$

or $P \approx \mathbf{3.0 \times 10^5 \text{ Pa}}$, which is the approximate value of choice (E) (*College Physics* 8th ed. pages 276–278/9th ed. pages 279–281).

4. **A** The total force exerted on the frog is derived from the total pressure exerted on the frog due to both the overlying column of water above the frog as well as the overlying column of air above that water, according to $P_{tot}A = F$. Here P_{tot} is the absolute pressure given by $P_{tot} = P_0 + \rho gh$. Therefore, substituting gives $P_{tot}A = F = (P_0 + \rho gh)A$. The depth of the water, however, is y, which replaces h to give $\mathbf{F = (P_0 + \rho gy)A}$, which is choice (A) (*College Physics* 8th ed. pages 276–278, 279–284/9th ed. pages 279–281, 288–293).

5. **D** The equation of continuity gives mass flow rate as Av, or volume per second. Therefore, the units are square meters multiplied by meters per second, or **cubic meters per second**, as shown by choice (D) (*College Physics* 8th ed. pages 290–293/9th ed. pages 299–302).

6. **D** The equation providing mass flow rate is $m/\Delta t$, or simply ρAV. Substituting values gives $(1000 \text{ kg/m}^3)(3.14)(1 \times 10^{-1} \text{ m})^2(8 \text{ m/s}) \sim (3000)(8)(1 \times 10^{-2}) \sim \mathbf{240 \text{ kg/s}}$, which is choice (D) (*College Physics* 8th ed. pages 290–293/9th ed. pages 299–302).

7. **C** It is stated that the block displaces 5 kg of water, which suggests that the weight of the displaced water is $w = mg = 5 \text{ kg}(10 \text{ m/s}^2)$, or 50 N, which, by Archimedes's principle, is also equal to the buoyant force F_B. Next, sketch the free-body diagram and apply the conditions of equilibrium: $\Sigma F = 0$ gives $F_B - T - mg = 0$. So, $F_B - mg = T$, which becomes 50 N $-$ (2 kg)(10 m/s²) = T, or $\mathbf{T = 30 \text{ N}}$, which

is choice (C) (*College Physics* 8th ed. pages 284–290/9th ed. pages 293–299).

8. **A** The mass flow rate is ρAv = constant throughout (i.e., equation of continuity). Therefore, $A_1v_1 = A_2v_2$ shows that the speed v is inversely proportional to the cross-sectional area A of the pipe. So, when A is the largest, the speed is the lowest. The largest pipe diameter shown is 1; therefore, it has the water with the lowest speed (*College Physics* 8th ed. pages 290–293/9th ed. pages 299–302).

9. **B** By Bernoulli's equation, an inverse relationship exists between the square of the speed of the fluid flow and the surrounding pressure according to $P + \rho gy + \frac{1}{2}\rho v^2$ = constant. Because $P \propto 1/v^2$, the pressure P will decrease when the speed of the fluid increases. As seen from the solution to Question 8, the speed of the fluid will be the largest when the area of the pipe is the smallest (i.e., the narrowest). Because the narrowest pipe is pipe 2, it will possess the fastest moving water with the lowest water pressure. Notice also that this pipe is viewed from overhead; thus, all locations are the same height above the ground (*College Physics* 8th ed. pages 290–293, 293–296/9th ed. pages 299–302, 302–305).

10. **D** The pressure is uniform within the press, so, by Pascal's principle, $F_1A_2 = F_2A_1$, which contains each piston's value of R under area A. The area is πr^2, which becomes $F_1(\pi R_2^2) = F_2(\pi R_1^2)$. Solving for the ratio of the radii gives $R_2^2/R_1^2 = F_2/F_1$, which becomes $R_2/R_1 = \sqrt{1600/400}$. Substituting the values of the forces gives $R_2/R_1 = \sqrt{1600/400}$ or $R_2/R_1 = 2$. Therefore, $\mathbf{R_2 = 2R_1}$, which is choice (D) (*College Physics* 8th ed. pages 279–283/9th ed. pages 288–292).

11. **D** Using the relation $P = F/A$, we can calculate the force F on the rooftop and then, realizing that this force is equal to the weight of the overlying air, equate this result to mg by the relation $w = mg$. So, $P = F/A$ becomes $PA = F = mg$, where m is the mass of the air above the rooftop, which simplifies to $PA/g = m$. Substituting gives [(1.0 × 10^5 Pa)(5.0 m²)]/10.0 m/s², so $\mathbf{m = 5.0 \times 10^4 \, kg}$, which is choice (D). (*College Physics* 8th ed. pages 276–278/9th ed. pages 279–281).

12. **E** By Bernoulli's equation, an inverse relationship exists between the speed of the fluid flow and the surrounding pressure according to $P + \rho gy + \frac{1}{2}\rho v^2$ = constant. Because $P \propto 1/v_2$, the pressure P will decrease when the air moving with the speeding train passes by at a higher-than-normal speed. Therefore, this high-speed air will create a region of low pressure on the train side of the person. Thus, the higher air pressure on the platform side of the person creates a pressure gradient, causing the standing person to be moved slightly toward the moving train (*College Physics* 8th ed. pages 293–296/9th ed. pages 302–305).

13. **C** An ideal fluid is nonviscous, possesses a steady motion (i.e., velocity, density, and pressure within the fluid do not change with time), does not experience turbulence, and remains incompressible. An incompressible fluid is one in which the fluid density remains

constant. Therefore, choice (C) is correct (*College Physics* 8th ed. pages 290–291/9th ed. pages 299–302).

14. **D** For an object floating in a liquid, the upward support force of the liquid *is* the buoyant force (F_B), which is equal to the gravitational force ($w = mg$) experienced by the object, but is opposite in direction. Therefore, choice (D) is correct (*College Physics* 8th ed. pages 284–290/9th ed. pages 293–299).

15. **E** To solve this question, it is necessary to use the relation for buoyant force, which relates the submerged volume to the buoyant force, which is equivalent to the weight of the object. We are told that 70% of the object is exposed, and we need to determine how much of the object is submerged according to $F_B = \rho_{liquid}\, g V_{submerged}$. Therefore, $70\%(2 \times 10^{-2}\ m^3) = 1.4 \times 10^{-2}\ m^3$, which signifies that $0.6 \times 10^{-2}\ m^3$ of the object is submerged. The buoyant force (and thus the weight of the object) is $F_B = (1000\ kg/m^3)(10\ m/s^2)(0.6 \times 10^{-2}\ m^3) = 1 \times 10^4(0.6 \times 10^{-2}) = \mathbf{60\ N}$, which is choice (E) (*College Physics* 8th ed. pages 284–290/9th ed. pages 293–299).

FREE-RESPONSE PROBLEMS

1. (a) With the information provided, the student needs to calculate the density of the cube and compare it with those given, finding the volume by the dimensions given and the mass from the weight shown ($w = mg$) on the scale. According to the density equation $\rho = m/V$, we have $\rho = (w/g)/V = w/gV = (0.245\ N)/[10/s^2)(0.021\ m)^3]$, which gives a density of $\rho = 2650\ kg/m^3$. Therefore, the cube is most likely made of **aluminum** (*College Physics* 8th ed. pages 276–278/9th ed. pages 279–281).

   (b) The percent deviation is determined by substituting values:

   $$\% \text{ difference} = \frac{\text{measured} - \text{accepted}}{\text{accepted}} \times 100\%$$

   $$= \frac{2650\ kg/m^3 - 2700\ kg/m^3}{2700\ kg/m^3} \times 100\%$$

   which is approximately **2%**.

   (c) A sketch is as shown.

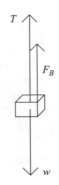

(*College Physics* 8th ed. pages 284–290/9th ed. pages 293–299)

(d) To determine the type of liquid, it is necessary to calculate its density (from the buoyant force equation) and compare it with those given in the chart. Also, because the cube is in equilibrium, we need to apply $\Sigma F = 0$ to find F_B, the buoyant force, in terms of the forces given. So, $\Sigma F = 0$ gives $F_B = mg - T$. Therefore, by $F_B = \rho gV$, we have $mg - T = \rho gV$. As for the volume V, it is stated that the cube is fully immersed; therefore, the volume of displaced liquid is equivalent to the volume of the cube (length × width × height). Solving for density ρ now gives $(mg - T)/gV = \rho$. Substituting values gives the solution for the liquid density: $[(0.245\,N)-(0.173\,N)]/[(10.0\,m/s^2)(0.021\,m)]^3 = \rho$, which gives 777 kg/m³ as the liquid density. According to the table given, this liquid is most likely **hydraulic oil** (*College Physics* 8th ed. pages 284–290/9th ed. pages 293–299).

2. (a) This problem is a kinematics question that simply deals with the maximum height d reached by an object projected straight upward that is in free fall. We can use the kinematics equation $v_f^2 = v_i^2 + 2ad$ for constant acceleration, keeping in mind that at this maximum height, the water velocity is momentarily zero. Solving for d gives $d = v_f^2 - v_i^2/2a = [0 - (9.0\,m/s)^2]/[2(10.0\,m/s^2)$, which gives **$d = 4$ m**. We could also solve this problem by energy conservation, where $K_{bottom} = U_{g\,top}$ (*College Physics* 8th ed. pages 42–46/9th ed. pages 43–47).

(b) The volume flow rate, in cubic meters per second, is given by $A_1v_1 = A_2v_2$ comparing two locations in a pipe. Here we simply need the product of the pipe area A and the speed of the water v_2 at the pipe opening, being careful to realize that pipe diameter D (not radius) was given in the problem. At the pipe opening, we have $A_2v_2 = \pi r_2^2(v_2) = \pi(D/2)^2(v_2) = (3.14)[(0.06\,m)/2]^2(9.0\,m/s) = \mathbf{2.5 \times 10^{-2}}$ **m³/s = volume flow rate**. For ease of calculation in part (d), we have chosen subscript 2 to represent the location at which the water leaves the pipe at ground level (*College Physics* 8th ed. pages 290–293/9th ed. pages 299–302).

(c) The mass flow rate is mass per unit time flow, or $(\rho V)/\Delta t$. It is simply the product of the volume flow rate and the fluid density, here 1000 kg/m³ (water), or ρA_1v_1. Therefore, $\rho A_1v_1 = (1000\,kg/m^3)(2.5 \times 10^{-2}\,m^3/s) = \mathbf{25\,kg/s}$ **= mass flow rate** (*College Physics* 8th ed. pages 290–293/9th ed. pages 299–302).

(d) Because the fluid is in motion, it is necessary to use Bernoulli's equation to determine the pressure at the 6.0-m depth. The location below ground at 6.0 m is labeled position 1 (where $y_1 = 0$ m), and the point at which the water exits the pipe above the ground is labeled position 2 (where $y_2 = 6.0$ m). Here, it is necessary to solve for P_1 at the 6.0-m depth (where P_2 is the atmospheric pressure just at ground level, where the fountain water leaves the pipe). So, $P_1 + \rho gy_1 + \frac{1}{2}\rho v_1^2 = P_2 + \rho gy_2 + \frac{1}{2}\rho v_2^2$. (Notice that v_1 = volume flow rate/pipe area). Leaving units off for clarity and solving, we then have

$$P_1 = P_2 + \rho g y_2 + \frac{1}{2}\rho v_2^2 - \rho g y_1 - \frac{1}{2}\rho \left[\frac{(2.5 \times 10^{-2})}{\pi\left(\dfrac{D}{2}\right)^2} \right]^2$$

Substituting values gives

$$P_1 = \left(1.01 \times 10^5\right) + (1000)(10)(6) + \tfrac{1}{2}(1000)(9)^2 - 0 - \tfrac{1}{2}(1000)\left[\frac{2.5 \times 10^{-2}}{\pi(D/2)^2}\right]^2$$
$$= \left(1.01 \times 10^5\right) + \left(6.00 \times 10^4\right) + \left(4.05 \times 10^4\right) - \left(1.11 \times 10^3\right)$$

or $P_1 = 2.00 \times 10^5$ **Pa.**

(*College Physics* 8th ed. pages 293–296/9th ed. pages 302–305)

(e) Just as in part (a), it is necessary to find the velocity of the water as it leaves the pipe at ground level using kinematics (or energy conservation) relationships. Then, with the same volume flow rate, we solve for the new pipe radius r and finally solve for the pipe diameter (by doubling r). So, $v_f^2 = v_i^2 + 2ad$. Solving for v_i gives $\sqrt{v_f^2 - 2ad} = v$ or $\sqrt{0 - 2(-10 \text{ m/s}^2)(10 \text{ m})} = v_i = 14$ m/s. Because 2.5×10^{-2} kg/s = volume flow rate = Av, we can solve for r and substitute values (omitting units for clarity). So,

$$r = \sqrt{\frac{2.5 \times 10^{-2}}{\pi v}} = \sqrt{\frac{2.5 \times 10^{-2}}{(3.14)(14)}} = 0.024 \text{ m}$$

Thus, the diameter of the new nozzle is 0.048 m, or **4.8 cm** (*College Physics* 8th ed. pages 42–46, 290–293/9th ed. pages 299–302).

10

THERMAL PHYSICS

THE ZEROTH LAW OF THERMODYNAMICS

(*College Physics* 8th ed. pages 322–323/9th ed. pages 332–333)

If objects having different temperatures are placed in an isolated enclosure, eventually all objects will come to the same temperature.

TEMPERATURE SCALES

(*College Physics* 8th ed. pages 324–328/9th ed. pages 333–337)

Temperature is, qualitatively speaking, a property that governs the direction of heat flow. It is a measure of the relative degree of hotness or coldness. Heat will flow from regions of high temperature to regions of low temperature. Heat and temperature are not to be confused; the measurement of heat and the measurement of temperature are entirely different procedures.

The Fahrenheit temperature scale is commonly used in the United States. Under standard conditions, the boiling temperature of water is 212°F and the freezing point is 32°F. The difference between these two temperatures is 180 F°. The rest of the world and the scientific community use the Celsius temperature scale, with the boiling temperature of water at 100°C and the freezing point at 0°C. Between these two temperatures is a difference of 100 C°. The ratios of 100 and 180 reduce to the fractions $\frac{5}{9}$ and $\frac{9}{5}$.

To convert from the Fahrenheit scale to the Celsius scale, we use $T_C = \frac{5}{9}\left(T_F - 32\right)$. To convert from Celsius to Fahrenheit, we use $T_F = \frac{9}{5}T_C + 32$.

AP Tip

When stating a specific temperature, we express the temperature in degrees Fahrenheit (°F) or degrees Celsius (°C). When stating a difference between temperature readings, we express it as Fahrenheit degrees (F°) or Celsius degrees (C°). A temperature of a material and a temperature difference are two distinct things.

Temperature is directly related to the average kinetic energy of the particles of an object. Materials are made of atoms, molecules, ions, or some combination. In general, we will refer to atoms, molecules, and ions as particles.

As the temperature of a material decreases, the kinetic energy of the particles decreases. There is a minimum energy the particles must have, and a decrease below this energy is not possible. This minimum possible energy defines the minimum possible temperature: absolute zero, or –273.15°C. The Kelvin temperature scale is an absolute scale based on this fact.

To convert from the Celsius scale to the Kelvin scale, we use $K = C + 273.15$.

AP Tip

The degree symbol is not used when we express Kelvin temperatures. The temperature is expressed in kelvins, K.

THERMAL EXPANSION OF SOLIDS AND LIQUIDS

(*College Physics* 8th ed. pages 328–334/9th ed. pages 337–342)

In general, when a material—whether solid, liquid, or gas—is heated, it expands as the particles of the material gain kinetic energy. The linear coefficient of thermal expansion α is defined as the change in length per unit length of a material per 1° rise in temperature. Once the coefficient is known, the linear expansion for a material of any length can be calculated for any change in temperature. The change in length of a material is calculated by

$$\Delta L = L_0 \alpha \, \Delta T$$

Area and volume calculations are made by using $\Delta A = A_0 \gamma \, \Delta T$ and $\Delta V = V_0 \beta \, \Delta T$.

SAMPLE PROBLEM 1
A long, thin metal rod has a length of 0.60 m when its temperature is 25.0°C. The rod has a coefficient of linear expansion of $(19.8 \times 10^{-6})(1/°C)$. At what temperature will the rod have a length of 0.60015 m?

SOLUTION TO PROBLEM 1
First, find the change in length:

$$\Delta L = 0.60015 \text{ m} - 0.60 \text{ m} = 1.50 \times 10^{-4} \text{ m}$$

The change in temperature is given by

$$\Delta T = \frac{\Delta L}{L_0 \alpha} = \frac{1.50 \times 10^{-4}\,\text{m}}{(0.60\,\text{m})\left[\left(19.8 \times 10^{-6}\right)\left(1/^\circ\text{C}\right)\right]} = 12.6\,^\circ\text{C}$$

With the change in temperature known, we can determine its final temperature by $\Delta T = T - T_0 = T - 25.0^\circ\text{C} = 12.6^\circ\text{C}$. So, **$T = 37.6^\circ\text{C}$.**

KINETIC THEORY OF GASES

(*College Physics* 8th ed. pages 335–344/9th ed. pages 343–353)

The average kinetic energy, $\bar{K}$, of a gas has been shown to be directly proportional to the absolute or kelvin temperature of the gas. It is known as the kinetic energy interpretation of temperature:

$$\bar{K} = \left(\frac{1}{2}mv^2\right)_{\text{average}} = \frac{3}{2}k_B T$$

where Boltzmann's constant is $k_B = 1.38 \times 10^{-23}$ J/K.

The term $(v^2)_{\text{average}}$ or $(v^2)_{\text{ave}}$ is called the mean square speed of the molecules of a gas. When we take the square root of this term, we obtain the root-mean-square (rms) speed of gas molecules:

$$v_{\text{rms}} = \sqrt{\frac{3k_B T}{m}}$$

SAMPLE PROBLEM 2
Calculate the rms speed of oxygen molecules at 100°C.

SOLUTION TO PROBLEM 2
To calculate the rms speed, we need to find the mass of an oxygen molecule, O_2. So,

$$m = \frac{M}{N_0} = \frac{32 \times 10^{-3}\,\text{kg/mol}}{6.02 \times 10^{23}\,\text{mol}^{-1}} = 5.31 \times 10^{-26}\,\text{kg}$$

$$\frac{1}{2}mv_{\text{rms}}^2 = \frac{3}{2}k_B T$$

and

$$v_{\text{rms}} = \sqrt{\frac{3k_B T}{m}} = \sqrt{\frac{3\left(1.38 \times 10^{-23}\,\text{J/K}\right)\left(100 + 273\right)\,\text{K}}{5.31 \times 10^{-26}\,\text{kg}}} = \textbf{540 m/s}$$

SAMPLE PROBLEM 3
A free electron moves in an isolated environment with an average kinetic energy of 1.60×10^{-20} J. In Celsius degrees, what is the temperature of the environment?

SOLUTION TO PROBLEM 3

The average kinetic energy of the electron is $\bar{K} = \frac{3}{2}k_B T$. Solving for the absolute temperature, we have

$$T = \frac{2\bar{K}}{3k_B} = \frac{2\left(1.60 \times 10^{-20} \text{ J}\right)}{3\left(1.38 \times 10^{-23} \text{ J/K}\right)} = 772.58 \text{ K}$$

The Celsius temperature is $C = T - 273.15 = (772.58 - 273.15)\,^\circ\text{C}$, or $T_C = 500\,^\circ\text{C}$.

AP Tip

Answers should have a reasonable number of significant figures. Do your rounding at the end of the calculations.

THE GAS LAWS

(*College Physics* 8th ed. pages 335–340/9th ed. pages 343–348)

Early experiments on confined gases revealed several basic but important relationships concerning the state variables pressure P, volume V, absolute temperature T, and the number of moles n.

Boyle's law: $\qquad P_1 V_1 = P_2 V_2$

Charles's law: $\qquad \dfrac{V_1}{T_1} = \dfrac{V_2}{T_2}$

General gas law: $\qquad \dfrac{P_1 V_1}{T_1} = \dfrac{P_2 V_2}{T_2}$

Combining these equations gives us

$$PV = nRT \quad \text{(ideal gas law)}$$

In all cases, the volume V of the gas is expressed in cubic meters; pressure P, in pascals, is absolute and not gauge pressure; the absolute temperature T is in kelvins; n is the number of moles of gas; and R is the ideal gas constant 8.31 J/mol K.

SAMPLE PROBLEM 4

A 0.01-m³ sample of oxygen exists under a pressure of 1.52 MPa when its temperature is 25°C. Determine the mass density of the gas. Treat the gas as being ideal.

SOLUTION TO PROBLEM 4

First, write the ideal gas law: $PV = nRT$. We define mass density as $\rho = m/V$. The mass of the oxygen, O_2, present in the sample can be found from $n = m/M$, where m is the mass of O_2 and M is the molecular weight of the O_2. One mol of O_2 is 32×10^{-3} kg.

The ideal gas law can now be written as

$$PV = \frac{m}{M}RT \qquad \text{and} \qquad PM = \frac{m}{V}RT$$

Because $\rho = m / V$, we can write the mass density variation of the ideal gas law: $PM = \rho RT$.

Now we can find the mass density:

$$\rho = \frac{PM}{RT} = \frac{\left(1.52 \times 10^6 \text{ Pa}\right)\left(32 \times 10^{-3} \text{ kg/mol}\right)}{\left(8.31 \text{ J/mol K}\right)\left(25 + 273.15 \text{ K}\right)} = \textbf{19.6 kg} \cdot \textbf{m}^{-3}$$

FIRST LAW OF THERMODYNAMICS AND WORK

(*College Physics* 8th ed. pages 385–398/9th ed. pages 395–410)

Thermodynamics is a branch of both physics and engineering that deals with the conversion of thermal energy into useful work.

The first law of thermodynamics is a statement of the law of conservation of energy. When thermal energy (heat), Q, is transferred to a system, the internal energy, U, of the system increases or the system does work. This law can be expressed as

$$\Delta U = \Delta Q + \Delta W$$

Notice that ΔQ is positive when heat is added to a system and ΔW is positive when work is done on the system. When heat is extracted from a system and work is done by the system, both ΔQ and ΔW must be taken as negative. See the table.

U	Q	W
When ΔU is positive (+), the temperature increases.	When Q is positive (+), heat enters the system.	When W is positive (+), work is done on the system.
When ΔU is negative (–), the temperature decreases.	When Q is negative (–), heat leaves the system.	When W is negative (–), work is done by the system.

SAMPLE PROBLEM 5

Consider the following three systems. What is the change in the internal energy in each system?

(a) System 1 absorbs 2.21 kJ as heat and, at the same instant, does 600 J of work.

(b) System 2 absorbs 1170 J as heat and, at the same time, 500 J of work is done on it.

(c) A total of 6285 J is removed from system 3 as the volume of the system is held constant.

SOLUTION TO PROBLEM 5

(a) Write the first law of thermodynamics:

$$\Delta U = \Delta Q + \Delta W$$

$$\Delta U = 2.21 \times 10^3 \text{ J} + \left(-600 \text{ J}\right) = \textbf{1.61 kJ}$$

(b) Solve for the change in internal energy:

$$\Delta U = \Delta Q + \Delta W$$

$$\Delta U = 1170 \text{ J} + 500 \text{ J} = \mathbf{1.67 \text{ kJ}}$$

(c) The work done at constant volume is $\Delta W = P \, \Delta V = 0$. So, $\Delta U = 6285 \text{ J} - 0 = \mathbf{-6.29 \text{ kJ}}$.

THERMODYNAMIC PROCESSES

(*College Physics* 8th ed. pages 393–398/9th ed. pages 404–410)

During an *isothermal* process, the temperature of the system remains constant, $\Delta T = 0$. There is no change in the internal energy of the gas, and

$$W = -Q$$

The system does an amount of work exactly equal to the quantity of thermal energy transferred to it.

During an *isovolumic*, or *isochoric*, process, $\Delta V = 0$. Because the volume of the system does not change, no work can be done by or on the system, and $W = 0$. All thermal energy entering the system goes into changing the internal energy of that system. So, $\Delta U = Q$.

During an *isobaric* process, the pressure of the system remains constant, and $\Delta P = 0$. When heat is transferred to an isobaric system, the system changes volume to maintain constant pressure. Because this process is not isothermal, the temperature changes, which causes a change in the internal energy of the gas confined.

During an *adiabatic* process, no heat is transferred into or out of the system, and $Q = 0$. The work done on or by such a system changes the internal energy. Therefore, $\Delta U = W$.

SAMPLE PROBLEM 6

A 1.00-kmol sample of helium is taken through the cyclic process as shown. Path *BC* is isothermal. The pressure at point *A* is 1.20×10^5 Pa, the volume at point *A* is 40.0 m³, and the pressure at point *B* is 2.40×10^5 Pa. What are the temperatures at points *A* and *B*, and what is the volume of the gas at point *C*?

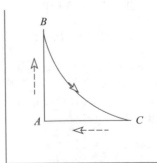

SOLUTION TO PROBLEM 6

Applying the ideal gas law $PV = nRT$ and solving for the temperature T_A, we write

$$T_A = \frac{P_A V_A}{nR}$$

$$T_A = \frac{\left(1.20 \times 10^5 \text{ Pa}\right)\left(40.0 \text{ m}^3\right)}{\left(1.00 \text{ kmol}\right)\left(8.314 \times 10^3 \text{ J/kmol K}\right)} = \textbf{577 K}$$

Because the process AB is isochoric, $T_B = \left(P_B/P_A\right)T_A$. Notice that $P_B = 2P_A$, which makes $T_B = 2T_A$. So, $T_B = \textbf{1150 K}$.

For the volume of the gas at point C, we use $V_C = \left(T_C/T_A\right)V_A$. The process C is isothermal, so $T_C = T_B = 2T_A$. The process CA is isobaric, and $V_C/T_C = V_A/T_A$. So, $V_C = 2V_A$, and then $V_C = \textbf{80.0 m}^3$.

HEAT TRANSFER

(*College Physics* 8th ed. pages 366–377/9th ed. pages 375–386)

Heat transfer involves a transfer of internal energy from one location to another due to temperature difference. Thermal energy can be transferred in three principle ways: conduction, convection, and radiation.

Conduction is heat flow through a material substance by means of molecular collisions transferring kinetic energy from one particle to another. The rate at which heat is conducted from the higher temperature face to the lower temperature face is determined from

$$H = \frac{\Delta Q}{\Delta t} = \frac{kA \, \Delta T}{L}$$

where $H = \Delta Q/\Delta t$ is the time rate of heat flow, k is the thermal conductivity of the substance, A is the cross section, ΔT is the temperature difference in C°, and L is the length of the conductor.

SAMPLE PROBLEM 7
A metal plate 4.0 cm thick has a cross-sectional area of 0.50 m². The inner face of the plate is at a temperature of 100°C, and the outer plate is at 120°C. For the metal, $k = 75.0$ W/m·K. What quantity of heat leaks through the plate each second?

SOLUTION TO PROBLEM 7
The quantity of heat flowing from the outer plate to the inner in a given time period is

$$H = \frac{\Delta Q}{\Delta t} = \frac{kA \, \Delta T}{L}$$

Substituting yields

$$H = \frac{\Delta Q}{\Delta t} = \frac{\left(75.0 \text{ W/mK}\right)\left(0.5 \text{ m}^2\right)\left(120°\text{C} - 100°\text{C}\right)}{0.04 \text{ m}} = \textbf{19 kJ/s}$$

Convection is the heat transfer by the movement of a substance that is either a liquid or a gas. Radiation is heat transfer by electromagnetic radiation. Bodies hotter than their environment radiate infrared radiation that cooler bodies absorb. The surface molecules absorb this energy and gain kinetic energy as a result. In theory, blackbody radiators are ideal radiators. The power, P, a blackbody radiator can emit is a function of the fourth power of the absolute temperature of the radiator. The Stefan–Boltzmann law is

$$P = \varepsilon A\sigma T^4$$

where the constant ε is the emissivity of the radiator, A is the surface area, and the Stefan–Boltzmann constant is $\sigma = 5.67 \times 10^{-8}$ W/m$^2 \cdot$K^4.

SAMPLE PROBLEM 8

A spherical body has a diameter of 0.01 m and is maintained at a temperature of 500°C. Treating the sphere as a blackbody, at what rate is energy being radiated from the sphere?

SOLUTION TO PROBLEM 8

First find the surface area of the sphere:

$$A = 4\pi r^2 = 4\pi\left(0.01 \text{ m}^2\right)$$

$$A = 1.26 \times 10^{-3} \text{ m}^2$$

For a blackbody radiator, we write the Stefan–Boltzmann law: $P = \varepsilon A\sigma T^4$. The Stefan–Boltzmann constant $\sigma = 5.67 \times 10^{-8}$ W/m$^2 \cdot$K^4, and the emissivity of a blackbody is unity, $\varepsilon = 1$. So, $P = \left(1\right)\left(1.26 \times 10^{-3} \text{ m}^2\right)$ $\left(5.67 \times 10^{-8} \text{ W/m}^2 \cdot \text{K}^4\right)\left(500 + 273 \text{ K}\right)^4 = \textbf{25.5 W}$.

HEAT ENGINES

(*College Physics* 8th ed. pages 399–408/9th ed. pages 410–418)

A heat engine is a device of sorts that converts thermal energy into useful work. A heat engine extracts heat, Q_{hot}, from a hot source (a reservoir) at absolute temperature T_{hot} and converts a quantity of this energy into useful work. The remaining heat, Q_{cold}, is dumped into a heat sink (a cold reservoir) at temperature T_{cold}.

The fundamental basis of the functioning of all heat engines is the second law of thermodynamics: the efficiency, e, of heat engines producing mechanical energy is considerably less than 100%. The theoretical efficiency of a heat engine is defined as

$$e = \frac{Q_{hot} - Q_{cold}}{Q_{hot}}$$

In 1824, Sadi Carnot described a cycle for a heat engine that can have the highest possible efficiency. No other heat engine can get more work out of an input of heat than the Carnot engine. Carnot showed that the efficiency of such a cycle is

$$e = \frac{T_{hot} - T_{cold}}{T_{hot}}$$

SAMPLE PROBLEM 9

A heat engine extracts heat from a source at 327°C, does some external work, and dumps the remaining energy into a heat sink at 127°C. If 600 kJ of heat is taken from the heat source, how much work does the engine do? How much heat is dumped into the heat sink?

SOLUTION TO PROBLEM 9

The efficiency of the heat engine is

$$e = \frac{Q_{hot} - Q_{cold}}{Q_{hot}} = \frac{T_{hot} - T_{cold}}{T_{hot}}$$

$$\frac{600 \text{ J} - Q_{cold}}{600 \text{ J}} = \frac{(327 + 273 \text{ } K) - (127 + 273 \text{ } K)}{327 + 273 \text{ } K}$$

$$Q_{cold} = \textbf{400 J}$$

$$W = \Delta Q = 600 \text{ J} - 400 \text{ J} = \textbf{200 J}$$

THERMAL PHYSICS: STUDENT OBJECTIVES FOR THE AP EXAM

- You should understand that the exchange of energy between two objects because of their temperature difference is called heat.
- You should understand that heat added to or removed from a substance causes the material to change in dimensions and should be able to solve problems involving these dimensional changes.
- You should know that heat can be transferred by conduction, convection, and radiation and should be able to solve for the rate at which energy transfer occurs.
- You need to understand that P, V, T, and n amount of gas in a container are related to one another by an equation of state and should be able to solve a problem involving any of these parameters.
- You should know and be able to apply the kinetic theory of gases, in particular the root-mean-square (rms) speed of a molecule.
- You should know the equation for the work done in a thermodynamic process and should be able to apply it to work done on/by a gas.
- You need to understand that work done on a gas is positive and that work done by a gas is negative.
- You should know that work is the area beneath the curve in a PV diagram.
- You should understand and apply the first law of thermodynamics to the various processes.
- You should be able to solve and draw PV diagrams to evaluate work done, heat transferred, and changes in the internal energy.
- You should understand the second law of thermodynamics.
- You should be able to solve multiple-choice questions without a calculator.

MULTIPLE-CHOICE QUESTIONS

1. An ideal gas in a cylinder with a movable piston is made to follow the process graphed by the path $A \to B \to C \to D$. What is the work done on the gas in terms of the initial volume and pressure?

    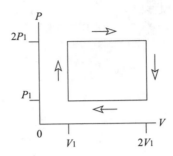

    (A) $P_1 V_1$
    (B) $\sqrt{2} P_1 V_1$
    (C) $2 P_1 V_1$
    (D) $4 P_1 V_1$
    (E) $5 P_1 V_1$

2. What are lines of constant temperature on a PV diagram called?
    (A) isotherms
    (B) isochors
    (C) isobars
    (D) isotopes
    (E) isomers

3. One mole of an ideal gas is held under constant pressure as its volume is increased by a factor of 4. What is the new v_{rms} speed of the molecules compared with the original v_{rms} speed?
    (A) one-half as large
    (B) the same
    (C) $\sqrt{2}$ times as large
    (D) two times greater
    (E) four times greater

4. When a total of 60.0 J of heat is added to a thermodynamic system that does 25.0 J of work, what is the net change in the internal energy of the system?
    (A) +35.0 J
    (B) 0
    (C) −35.0 J
    (D) +85.0 J
    (E) −85.0 J

5. What are lines of constant volume on a PV diagram called?
    (A) isotherms
    (B) isochors
    (C) isobars
    (D) isotopes
    (E) isomers

6. What is the equation of state for an ideal gas?
   (A) $PT = nRV$
   (B) $PV = knRT$
   (C) $PV = \dfrac{M}{R}T$
   (D) $PM = mVRT$
   (E) $PV = nRT$

7. For a thermodynamic system to be in equilibrium, what must be true?
   (A) The pressure must be constant throughout the entire system.
   (B) The values of all the state variables must be constant throughout the system.
   (C) The volume must be constant throughout the entire system.
   (D) The temperature must be constant throughout the entire system.
   (E) All state variables are constant with time at each point in the system.

8. In a closed system, which statement must be true about the work done in the expansion from an initial state to a final state on a *PV* curve?
   (A) The work depends on the endpoints only.
   (B) The work is independent of the path taken.
   (C) The work is the area under the curve.
   (D) The work is the slope of the *PV* curve.
   (E) The work is the product of the pressure and the reciprocal of the volume.

9. What happens to the internal energy of an isolated system?
   (A) It remains constant.
   (B) It is volume dependent.
   (C) It is temperature dependent.
   (D) It is pressure dependent.
   (E) It cannot be determined.

10. To understand the concept of temperature, it is necessary to understand which law?
    (A) zeroth law of thermodynamics
    (B) first law of thermodynamics
    (C) second law of thermodynamics
    (D) third law of thermodynamics
    (E) fourth law of thermodynamics

11. What must happen for two bodies to have the same temperature?
    (A) They must be in thermal contact.
    (B) They must have the same phase.
    (C) They must have the same Celsius difference.
    (D) They must be in thermal equilibrium.
    (E) They must have the same coefficient of temperature.

12. The transfer of heat by the process of convection will occur only where?
    (A) in a vacuum
    (B) in a metal
    (C) in nonmetallic materials
    (D) in the presence of matter
    (E) in a fluid

13. Most of the heat that is lost into space by Earth occurs by what process?
    (A) conduction
    (B) convection
    (C) radiation
    (D) both convection and radiation
    (E) both conduction and convection

14. A gas is taken from an initial state to a final state as shown. How much work is done during this process?

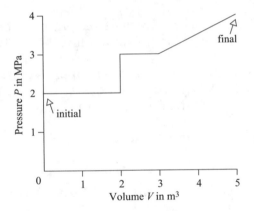

    (A) 3 MJ
    (B) 7 MJ
    (C) 9 MJ
    (D) 11 MJ
    (E) 14 MJ

15. A real gas is slowly changed from state 1 to state 2. During this process, no work is done by or on the gas. What kind of process must it be?
    (A) isothermal
    (B) adiabatic
    (C) isobaric
    (D) isochoric
    (E) isotopic

FREE-RESPONSE PROBLEMS

1. A glass beaker is filled to the brim with 1000.0 mL of an organic liquid when the temperature in the laboratory is 22°C. The liquid has a coefficient of volumetric expansion $\beta_L = 9.4 \times 10^{-4}$ °C^{-1}, and the beaker has a coefficient of linear expansion of $\alpha = 8.3 \times 10^{-6}$ °C^{-1}.

(a) What volume of the liquid overflows from the beaker when the temperature of the system is raised to 90°C?

(b) Calculate the density of the liquid at 90°C if its density at 22°C is 1.22 g/mL.

2. A cylinder contains 4.0 g of He at a gauge pressure of 9.1×10^5 Pa and a temperature of 67°C.

(a) Determine the root–mean–square speed, v_{rms}, for the gas.

(b) Calculate the volume of the cylinder.

(c) Some time later, the cylinder is checked, and the temperature of the gas has dropped to 27°C and the gauge pressure is measured at 5.2×10^5 Pa. How many grams of He have leaked from the container?

(d) Sketch the process on a *PV* diagram.

ANSWERS

MULTIPLE-CHOICE QUESTIONS

1. **A** The area under the graph in a *PV* diagram is equal to the magnitude of the work done on the gas. Thus, **work = P_1V_1**, which is choice (A) (*College Physics* 8th ed. page 387/9th ed. page 397).

2. **A** An isothermal process is one in which the change in internal energy is zero. Because the internal energy depends on the temperature change and if $\Delta U = 0$, then $\Delta T = 0$ and there is no temperature change. The temperature remains the same (*College Physics* 8th ed. page 396/9th ed. page 407).

3. **D** The pressure and the number of moles of the gas are held constant. We know that $V_1/T_1 = V_2/T_2$ and $1/T_1 = 4/T_2$, so we can solve for the new temperature: $T_2 = 4T_1$. Because $v_{rms} \propto \sqrt{T}$, we can determine that the v_{rms} speed is two times greater (*College Physics* 8th ed. pages 337, 342–343/9th ed. pages 345–346, 351–352).

4. **A** Because $\Delta U = Q + W = 60\,J + (-25\,J) = 35\,J$, the work is done by the gas. The net change is +35.0 J (*College Physics* 8th ed. page 388/9th ed. page 399).

5. **B** An isochoric process, also called an isovolumic process, is represented by a vertical line on a *PV* diagram (*College Physics* 8th ed. page 395/9th ed. page 406).

6. **E** The correct statement of the ideal gas law is **PV = nRT** (*College Physics* 8th ed. page 336/9th ed. page 345).

7. **B** The internal energy of any isolated system must remain constant, so $\Delta U = 0$. If the system goes through a cyclic process, the change in the internal energy will be zero and *P, V, T,* and *n* must return to their initial values (*College Physics* 8th ed. page 388/9th ed. page 399).

8. **C** The area under the graph in a *PV* diagram is equal to the magnitude of the work done on the gas (*College Physics* 8th ed. page 387/9th ed. page 397).

9. **A** The internal energy of any isolated system must be constant so that $\Delta U = 0$ (*College Physics* 8th ed. page 388/9th ed. page 399).

10. **A** The zeroth law of thermodynamics is the law of equilibrium. If two objects are in thermal equilibrium, they must be at the same temperature because there is no exchange of energy (*College Physics* 8th ed. page 323/9th ed. page 332).

11. **D** If there is no exchange of energy between the two bodies, they must be in thermal equilibrium and are therefore at the same temperature (*College Physics* 8th ed. page 323/9th ed. page 332).

12. **E** Convection is the transfer of energy due to the movement in fluids (*College Physics* 8th ed. page 371/9th ed. page 380).

13. **C** Radiation is the emission of electromagnetic energy due to the thermal vibrations of molecules of the radiator. In space, there are insufficient numbers of molecules to transfer thermal energy due to conduction or convection (*College Physics* 8th ed. page 372/9th ed. pages 381–382).

14. **E** The area under the graph in a *PV* diagram is equal to the magnitude of the work done on the gas (*College Physics* 8th ed. page 387/9th ed. page 397).

15. **D** Work in a gas is pressure times the change in volume. If there is no change in volume, no work is done. This process is therefore isochoric or isovolumetric (*College Physics* 8th ed. page 395/9th ed. page 406).

FREE-RESPONSE PROBLEMS

1. (a) As the temperature of the system increases, both the volume of the liquid and the capacity of the beaker increase. Because $\Delta V = V_0 \beta \, \Delta T$, the overflow is the difference in the increase in volume, or

$$\Delta V_L - \Delta V_B = \left(\beta_L - \beta_B\right) V_0 \, \Delta T$$

The coefficient of volumetric expansion for the beaker is $\beta_B = 3\alpha_B$. Then

$$\Delta V_L - \Delta V_B = \left(\beta_L - 3\alpha_B\right) V_0 \, \Delta T$$

Substituting yields $\Delta V_L - \Delta V_B = \left[\left(9.4 \times 10^{-4} \ {}^\circ\mathrm{C}^{-1}\right) - 3\left(8.3 \times 10^{-6} \ {}^\circ\mathrm{C}^{-1}\right)\right]$
$$\left(1000 \ \mathrm{mL}\right)\left(90^\circ\mathrm{C} - 22^\circ\mathrm{C}\right)$$

$$\boxed{\Delta V_L - \Delta V_B = 62.2 \ \mathrm{mL}}$$

(b) Mass density is defined as $\rho = m/V$. Because $m = \rho V$, the ratio of the mass densities at different volumes becomes $\rho_0/\rho = V/V_0$. The mass density of the liquid at the elevated temperature is then $\rho = \rho_0\left(V_0/V\right)$. Substituting yields

$$\rho = 1.22 \frac{\text{g}}{\text{mL}} \left(\frac{1000 \text{ mL}}{1000 \text{ mL} + 62.2 \text{ mL}} \right) = \textbf{1.15 g/mL}$$

(*College Physics* 8th ed. pages 328–333/9th ed. pages 337–342)

2. (a) The root-mean-square speed for the gas is found by using

$$v_{\text{rms}} = \sqrt{\frac{3RT}{M}}$$

$$v_{\text{rms}} = \sqrt{\frac{3(8.31 \text{ J/mol K})(67 + 273 \text{ K})}{4 \times 10^{-3} \text{ kg/mol}}} = \textbf{1456 m/s}$$

(b) Next we find the absolute pressure of the gas:

$$PV = nRT$$

$$P_{\text{abs}} = P_{\text{gauge}} + P_{\text{atm}}$$

$$P_{\text{abs}} = 9.1 \times 10^5 \text{ Pa} + 1.01 \times 10^5 \text{ Pa} = 10.11 \times 10^5 \text{ Pa}$$

$$PV = \frac{m}{M} RT$$

We now solve for the volume:

$$V = \frac{mRT}{MP}$$

$$V = \frac{\left(4 \times 10^{-3} \text{ kg}\right)\left(8.31 \text{ J/mol K}\right)\left(340 \text{ K}\right)}{\left(4 \times 10^{-3} \text{ kg/mol}\right)\left(10.11 \times 10^5 \text{ Pa}\right)} = \textbf{2.79} \times \textbf{10}^{-3} \textbf{ m}^3$$

(c) The gauge pressure changes the absolute pressure. So,

$$P_{\text{abs}} = 5.2 \times 10^5 \text{ Pa} + 1.01 \times 10^5 \text{ Pa} = 6.21 \times 10^5 \text{ Pa}$$

$$PV = nRT$$

Solving for the number of moles gives $n = PV/RT$. So,

$$n = \frac{\left(6.21 \times 10^5 \text{ Pa}\right)\left(2.79 \times 10^{-3} \text{ m}^3\right)}{\left(8.31 \text{ J/mol K}\right)\left(300 \text{ K}\right)} = 0.69 \text{ mol}$$

The number of moles of helium lost is $\Delta n = 1.0 \text{ mol} - 0.69 \text{ mol} = 0.31 \text{ mol}$, and the mass is $m = \Delta n \, M = \left(0.31 \text{ mol}\right)\left(4.0 \text{ g/mol}\right) = \textbf{1.24 g}$.

(d) A sketch is as shown.

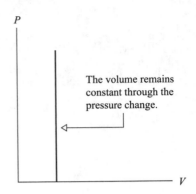

The volume remains
constant through the
pressure change.

(*College Physics* 8th ed. pages 335–345/9th ed. pages 343–354, 406)

ELECTROSTATICS

ELECTRICAL CHARGE

(*College Physics* 8th ed. pages 497–500/9th ed. pages 513–516)

The basic components of all matter are the electron, the proton, and the neutron. An electron carries a negative charge, a proton carries a positive charge, and a neutron is electrically neutral. Charge is quantized, which means that every electron in nature carries the same charge as all other electrons and every proton has the same charge as every other proton.

The SI unit of charge is the coulomb, abbreviated C. The charge of the electron is -1.60×10^{-19} C, and the charge of the proton is $+1.60 \times 10^{-19}$ C.

SAMPLE PROBLEM 1

A metal sphere is given a charge of 1.00 C. How many electrons were removed from the sphere?

SOLUTION TO PROBLEM 1

The elemental charge is $e = 1.60 \times 10^{-19}$ C. So,

$$1.0 \text{ C} \times \frac{1e}{1.60 \times 10^{-19} \text{ C}}$$

The factor for coulombs and electrons is:

$$1 \text{ C} = 6.25 \times 10^{18} \ e$$

We call the magnitude of this charge the elemental charge, *e*. The electron carries the charge –*e*, and the proton carries the charge +*e*. These elemental charges are also denoted as e^- and e^+.

The masses of the elementary particles are

$$m_e = 9.109 \times 10^{-31} \text{ kg}$$

$$m_p = 1.673 \times 10^{-31} \text{ kg}$$

$$m_n = 1.675 \times 10^{-31} \text{ kg}$$

The law of conservation of electrical charge is that the total charge existing in the universe is constant. In a system, the total charge before and after changes remains the same.

In atoms, the proton population of the nucleus equals the electron population that surrounds the nucleus. Atoms that have lost or gained electrons are called ions. An atom that has lost an electron(s), a positive ion, is called a cation:

$$A \rightarrow e^- + A^+$$

An atom that gains an electron(s), a negative ion, is called an anion:

$$A + e^- \rightarrow A^-$$

The usual units of an electrical charge range from several microcoulombs (μC) to several nanocoulombs (nC), with values as follows:

$$1 \ \mu C = 1 \times 10^{-6} \text{ C}$$

$$1 \text{ nC} = 1 \times 10^{-9} \text{ C}$$

Charges larger than several hundred microcoulombs are difficult to produce and maintain. Very large charges are quite dangerous.

Conductors and Insulators

(*College Physics* 8th ed. pages 499–500/9th ed. pages 515–516)

All metal atoms have a common property: they easily lose their valence electrons. Metals may be thought of as positive ions embedded in a sea of free electrons. The electrons belong to the entire metal and are mobile; they are free to move. We call metals conductors of electricity.

Nonmetals have structures that are either atomic or molecular. There are no free electrons. These materials tend to prevent the flow of electricity. We call them insulators.

Electrostatic Attraction, Electrostatic Repulsion, and Electrostatic Force

(*College Physics* 8th ed. pages 500–505/9th ed. pages 517–522)

Electrostatic means electricity at rest, and the words *attraction* and *repulsion* refer to the force that charged bodies exert upon each other at a distance. Like charges repel each other, and unlike charges attract.

Surrounding every positive charge is an electric field. We assign the positive charge to be a source of the electric field. Surrounding a negative charge is an electrical field that we assign to be a field sink, and the field flows into the sink, the charge.

In electrostatic repulsion, like fields interact is such a way as to repel. Two positive charges repel each other, and two negative charges repel each other.

In electrostatic attraction, unlike fields interact to produce electrostatic attraction.

COULOMB'S LAW

(*College Physics* 8th ed. pages 500–505/9th ed. pages 517–522)

The magnitude of the electrostatic force F between charges q_1 and q_2 that are separated by distance R is given by Coulomb's law:

$$F = \frac{1}{4\pi\varepsilon_0}\frac{q_1 q_2}{R^2}$$

where ε_0 is a constant called the permittivity of free space with a value of

$$\varepsilon_0 = 8.85 \times 10^{-12}\frac{C^2}{N\cdot m^2}$$

The constant ε_0 is usually written in terms of a new constant k called the Coulomb constant. We define it as $k = 1/4\pi\varepsilon_0$.

In SI units, we will express the constant as $k = 9 \times 10^9\ N\cdot m^2/C^2$. Coulomb's law now takes the form

$$F = k\frac{q_1 q_2}{R^2}$$

SAMPLE PROBLEM 2
Two fixed point charges, $q_1 = +3\ \mu C$ and $q_2 = -8\ \mu C$, exert an electrostatic force of attraction of 540 N on each other.
   (a) What is their separation?
   (b) How many excess electrons are on point charge q_2?

SOLUTION TO PROBLEM 2
Opposite charges attract, making the force between them electrostatic attraction.
   (a) We can write Coulomb's law and then solve for R:

$$F = k\frac{q_1 q_2}{R^2}$$

$$R = \sqrt{\frac{kq_1q_2}{F}} = \sqrt{\frac{\left(9 \times 10^9 \text{ N} \cdot \text{m}^2/\text{C}^2\right)\left(3 \times 10^{-6} \text{ C}\right)\left(8 \times 10^{-6} \text{ C}\right)}{540 \text{ N}}} = \textbf{0.02 m}$$

(b) Next, we determine the number of excess electrons:

$$8 \times 10^{-6} \text{C} \times \frac{6.24 \times 10^{18} \text{ } e}{1 \text{ C}} = \textbf{5} \times \textbf{10}^{\textbf{13}} \textbf{ } \textit{\textbf{e}}$$

SUPERPOSITION

(*College Physics* 8th ed. pages 503–505/9th ed. pages 519–522)

When a number of charges in a system act on a particular charge, each exerts an electrostatic force. These electrical forces are all calculated separately, one at a time, and are then added as vectors in a process called the superposition principle.

SAMPLE PROBLEM 3
Two fixed point charges, $q_1 = +4$ nC and $q_2 = +6$ nC, are 10 cm apart. What is the force acting on a test charge, $q_0 = +1$ nC, placed midway between q_1 and q_2?

SOLUTION TO PROBLEM 3
Point charge q_1 exerts a force of electrostatic repulsion, F_{10}, to the right on the test charge q_0, and charge q_2 exerts an electrostatic force, F_{20}, to the left of test charge q_0 as shown.

Use Coulomb's law to determine F_{10}:

$$F_{10} = k\frac{q_1q_0}{R^2} = \frac{\left(9 \times 10^9 \text{ N} \cdot \text{m}^2/\text{C}^2\right)\left(4 \times 10^{-9} \text{ C}\right)\left(1 \times 10^{-9} \text{ C}\right)}{\left(0.05 \text{ m}\right)^2} = 1.44 \times 10^{-5} \text{ N at } 0°$$

We do the same for F_{20}:

$$F_{20} = k\frac{q_1q_0}{R^2} = \frac{\left(9 \times 10^9 \text{ N} \cdot \text{m}^2/\text{C}^2\right)\left(6 \times 10^{-9} \text{ C}\right)\left(1 \times 10^{-9} \text{ C}\right)}{\left(0.05 \text{ m}\right)^2} = 2.16 \times 10^{-5} \text{ N at } 180°$$

We can apply the superposition principle to find that these two forces are antiparallel, and their resultant is found by

$$F = F_{10} - F_{20} = 1.44 \times 10^{-5} \text{ N} - 2.16 \times 10^{-5} \text{ N} = -7.2 \times 10^{-6} \text{ N}$$

The negative sign implies that the resultant force acts at 180°. The resultant force acting on q_0 is therefore **7.2 × 10⁻⁶ N at 180°**.

SAMPLE PROBLEM 4

Point charges $q_1 = -2$ nC and $q_2 = -5$ nC are 50.0 cm apart as shown. Where between the charges should a test charge q_0 be placed so that the resultant force acting on it is zero?

SOLUTION TO PROBLEM 4

The force F_{10} acting on point charge q_0 by q_1 is found from Coulomb's law. The test charge will be placed a distance x from q_1, and we write

$$F_{10} = k\frac{q_1 q_0}{x^2}$$

The force F_{20} acting on point charge q_0 by q_2 is also found from Coulomb's law, and q_0 will be placed a distance $0.50 - x$ from q_2. Thus,

$$F_{20} = k\frac{q_2 q_0}{\left(0.5 - x\right)^2}$$

If $F_{10} = F_{20}$, then

$$k\frac{q_1 q_0}{x^2} = k\frac{q_2 q_0}{\left(0.5 - x\right)^2}$$

The terms k and q_0 are common to both sides of the equation and divide out. After cross multiplying, we have

$$q_1\left(0.5 - x\right)^2 = q_2 x^2$$

Dividing both sides by q_1 and expanding gives

$$0.25 - x + x^2 = \frac{q_2}{q_1}x^2$$

$$0.25 - x + x^2 = \frac{5 \times 10^{-9}}{2 \times 10^{-9}}x^2$$

$$0.25 - x + x^2 = 2.5x^2$$

Transposing and simplifying yields $1.5x^2 + x - 0.25 = 0$. Notice that this expression is a quadratic equation of the form $ax^2 + bx + c = 0$ with solutions

$$X = \frac{-b \pm \sqrt{b^2 - 4ac}}{2a} = \frac{-1 \pm \sqrt{1^2 - 4(1.5)(-0.25)}}{2(1.5)}$$

$$x = 0.194 \text{ m} \quad \text{and} \quad x = -0.860 \text{ m}$$

We wanted the position of q_0 between the two point charges. So, q_0 should be placed **0.194 m to the right of q_1**. Notice that we did not need to know the value of q_0 to solve this problem.

ALTERNATE SOLUTION TO PROBLEM 4

An alternate solution uses $F_{10} = F_{20}$ and:

$$k\frac{q_1 q_0}{x^2} = k\frac{q_2 q_0}{(0.5 - x)^2}$$

Here, k and q_0 are common to both sides, so they divide out, leaving

$$\frac{q_1}{x^2} = \frac{q_2}{(0.5 - x)^2}$$

Substituting for the charge on both sides of the equation gives

$$\frac{2 \text{ nC}}{x^2} = \frac{5 \text{ nC}}{(0.5 - x)^2}$$

The nanocoulomb units are common to both sides and divide out. So,

$$\frac{2}{x^2} = \frac{5}{(0.5 - x)^2}$$

Taking the square root of both sides yields $\sqrt{2}/x = \sqrt{5}/(0.5 - x)$. Cross multiplying gives $1.414(0.5 - x) = 2.2311$, or **$x = 0.194$ m**.

THE ELECTRIC FIELD E

(*College Physics* 8th ed. pages 505–510/9th ed. pages 522–526)

Fields are modifications of space. Masses generate a gravitational field, or **g**-field. You cannot see or feel or smell the **g**-field of Earth, but it is there. We can test to see if a **g**-field is present by taking a test body of mass m_0 and dropping it. The **g**-field of the mass interacts with the **g**-field of Earth and falls vertically downward under gravitational force. The gravitational force is the weight of the body, $F = w = mg$.

The electric field, E, is a vector with magnitude and direction. Surrounding all electrical charges are E-fields of intensity E. To test for an E-field, we place a positive test charge q_0 in the field and measure the electrostatic force F acting on it. If q_0 is repelled, the charge creating the field is positive, and if q_0 is attracted, the charge creating the field is negative. We define the E-field as

$$E = \frac{F}{q_0}$$

The magnitude of the E-field can be calculated by using a modification of Coulomb's law:

$$E = k\frac{q}{R^2}$$

The SI unit of the electric field is the newton per coulomb (N/C).

LINES OF FORCE

(*College Physics* 8th ed. pages 510–512/9th ed. pages 526–528)

To aid in visualizing the electric field, the concept of lines of force is frequently used. A line at every point indicates, by its direction, the direction a unit charge would take if placed there, directly away from a positive charge and directly toward a negative charge.

Electric Field Lines

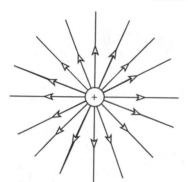 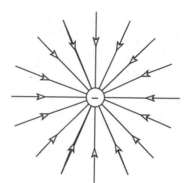

Positive charges behave as a source of an electrical field.

Negative charges behave as a sink for an electrical field.

The direction of a line of force at any point in an electrical field is the same as the direction of the resultant E-field vector at that point. Three rules should be followed when sketching electric field lines:
1. Lines of force never cross one another.
2. Lines of force in a grouping of point charges begin on a positive charge and end on a negative charge.
3. The number of lines leaving a positive charge or ending on a negative charge is proportional to the magnitude of the charges.

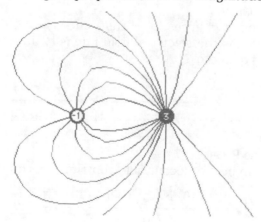

The lines of force associated with point charges $+3q$ and $-q$, illustrating electrostatic attraction.

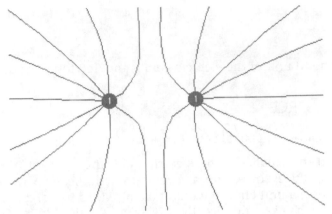

The lines of force associated with point charges $+q$ and $+q$, illustrating electrostatic repulsion.

SAMPLE PROBLEM 5

A charge $q = +2nC$ is placed in a uniform electrical field. In the field, q experiences a force of 4×10^{-4} N. What is the magnitude of the electrical field intensity?

SOLUTION TO PROBLEM 5

Using the definition of the E-field, we write:

$$E = \frac{F}{q} = \frac{4 \times 10^{-4} \text{ N}}{2 \times 10^{-9} \text{ C}} = \textbf{2} \times \textbf{10}^5 \textbf{ N/C}$$

SAMPLE PROBLEM 6

Determine the magnitude of the electrical field 2.0 cm from a point charge $q = +10$ nC.

SOLUTION TO PROBLEM 6

This time, we use the modification of Coulomb's law and substitute:

$$E = k\frac{q}{R^2} = \frac{\left(9 \times 10^9 \text{ N} \cdot \text{m}^2/\text{C}^2\right)\left(10 \times 10^{-9} \text{ C}\right)}{\left(0.02 \text{ m}\right)^2} = \textbf{2.25} \times \textbf{10}^5 \textbf{ N/C}$$

SAMPLE PROBLEM 7

Two fixed point charges, $q_1 = +8\mu C$ and $q_2 = -2\mu C$, are 10 cm apart as shown. What is the electrical field intensity at the midpoint of the line connecting q_1 and q_2?

q_1 E_1 E_2 q_2

|◁---. -- 0.05 m -- .--- -▷◁|◁---. -- 0.05 m -- .--- -▷|

SOLUTION TO PROBLEM 7

First, determine the electric field contributions due to each point charge:

$$E_1 = k\frac{q_1}{R^2} = \frac{\left(9 \times 10^9 \text{ N} \cdot \text{m}^2/\text{C}^2\right)\left(8 \times 10^{-6} \text{ C}\right)}{\left(0.05 \text{ m}\right)^2} = 29 \times 10^6 \text{ N/C to the right}$$

$$E_2 = k\frac{q_2}{R^2} = \frac{\left(9 \times 10^9 \text{ N} \cdot \text{m}^2/\text{C}^2\right)\left(2 \times 10^{-6} \text{ C}\right)}{\left(0.05 \text{ m}\right)^2} = 7.2 \times 10^6 \text{ N/C} \text{ to the right}$$

Applying the superposition principle gives $E = E_1 + E_2 = 29 \times 10^6$ N/C $+ 7.2 \times 10^6$ N/C $= \mathbf{3.6 \times 10^7}$ **N/C to the right**.

Field strengths or field intensities are important for a major reason: they allow us to find force. From $E = F/q$, it is easy to see that

$$F = Eq$$

SAMPLE PROBLEM 8

Two charged, parallel metal plates have a gap of 4.0 mm, and the E-field between the plates is 6000 N/C directed downward. An electron is released from rest from the negative plate.
    (a) What force does the electron experience?
    (b) Calculate the acceleration the electron experiences in the E-field.

SOLUTION TO PROBLEM 8

(a) We use the above equation and substitute:

$F = Eq = Ee = \left(6000 \text{ N/C}\right)\left(1.60 \times 10^{-19} \text{ C}\right) = 9.6 \times 10^{-16}$ N. Because the field is directed downward, the upper plate is positive and the force acting on the electron is upward. The force on the electron is therefore $F = \mathbf{9.6 \times 10^{-16}}$ **N at 90°**.

(b) The acceleration is found from Newton's second law:

$$F = ma \text{ and } a = \frac{F}{m} = \frac{9.6 \times 10^{-16} \text{ N}}{9.11 \times 10^{-31} \text{ kg}} = \mathbf{1.1 \times 10^{15}} \text{ m/s}^2 \text{ upward}$$

ELECTRIC POTENTIAL

(*College Physics* 8th ed. pages 531–541/9th ed. pages 548–558)

Electrical force is a conservative force, and as a result there is an electrical potential energy, U, associated with the electric force, F. The change in electrical potential energy, ΔU, is the work, W, done moving a charged particle in an electric field. In equation form, the work done is $\Delta U = W = Fd = Eq_0 d$.

We define the change in electric potential, ΔV, as

$$\Delta V = \frac{\Delta U}{q_0} = \frac{W}{q_0}$$

The SI unit of electric potential is the volt (V), which is defined as a joule per coulomb (1 V = 1 J/C).

The electric potential can also be calculated by

$$V = k\frac{q}{R}$$

Voltage, or electric potential, is a scalar quantity.

AP Tip

In lifting a mass in a gravitational field a distance h, a force must be applied. The minimum force required is the weight, mg, of the mass. The force does work on Earth–mass system. The work done is $W = mgh$.

SAMPLE PROBLEM 9

How much work is done moving a small body with a charge of +25 μC from point A to point B through a potential difference of 40.0 V?

SOLUTION TO PROBLEM 9

Solving $\Delta V = W/q_0$ for the work done gives $W = \Delta V q_0 = (40.0 \text{ V})$ $(25 \times 10^{-6} \text{ C}) = \mathbf{0.001 \text{ J}}$.

SAMPLE PROBLEM 10

Find the electrical potential 2.0 cm from a point charge $q = -12 \mu$C.

SOLUTION TO PROBLEM 10

The electric potential is:

$$V = k\frac{q}{R} = \frac{(9 \times 10^9 \text{ N} \cdot \text{m}^2 /\text{C}^2)(-12 \times 10^{-6}\text{C})}{0.02 \text{ m}} = \mathbf{-5.4 \times 10^6 \text{ V}}$$

SAMPLE PROBLEM 11

A point charge of $q_1 = +2.0$ μC. is placed at the origin of a frame of reference, and a second point charge of $q_2 = -8.4$ μC. is placed at the position $x = 80.0$ cm as shown. Calculate the potential midway between these point charges.

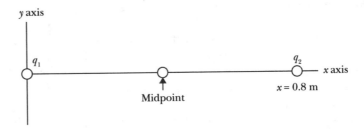

SOLUTION TO PROBLEM 11

The total electric potential of an arrangement of two or more charges by superposition is

$$V = k \, \Sigma \left(\frac{q_i}{r_i}\right) = (9 \times 10^9 \text{ N} \cdot \text{m}^2/\text{C}^2)\left[\left(\frac{2.0 \times 10^{-6}\text{ C}}{0.4 \text{ m}}\right) + \left(\frac{-8.4 \times 10^{-6}\text{ C}}{0.4 \text{ m}}\right)\right]$$

Simplifying the algebra, we have

$$V = \frac{9 \times 10^9 \text{ N} \cdot \text{m}^2/\text{C}^2}{0.4}\left[(2.0)+(-8.4)\right] \times 10^{-6} \text{ C/m} = \mathbf{-1.44 \times 10^5 \text{ V}}$$

Because V is a scalar quantity, the potentials were added algebraically.

SAMPLE PROBLEM 12

In air, a metal sphere of radius $R = 10.0$ cm is given an electrical charge of $q = +100$ nC.

    (a) What is the electrical potential at the surface of the sphere?

    (b) What is the electrical potential at a point 20.0 cm from the surface of the sphere?

    (c) Determine the maximum electrical field intensity for the sphere.

SOLUTION TO PROBLEM 12

    (a) The electrical potential at the surface of the sphere is:

$$V = k\frac{q}{R} = \frac{\left(9 \times 10^9 \ \text{N} \cdot \text{m}^2/\text{C}^2\right)\left(100 \times 10^{-9} \ \text{C}\right)}{0.10 \ \text{m}} = \mathbf{9 \times 10^3 \ V}$$

    (b) The electrical potential at a point 20.0 cm from the surface of the sphere is:

$$V = k\frac{q}{R} = \frac{\left(9 \times 10^9 \ \text{N} \cdot \text{m}^2/\text{C}^2\right)\left(100 \times 10^{-9} \ \text{C}\right)}{0.10 \ \text{m} + 0.20 \ \text{m}} = \mathbf{3 \times 10^3 \ V}$$

    (c) The maximum electrical field intensity exists on the surface of the sphere. So,

$$E = k\frac{q}{R^2} = \frac{\left(9 \times 10^9 \ \text{N} \cdot \text{m}^2/\text{C}^2\right)\left(100 \times 10^{-9} \ \text{C}\right)}{\left(0.10 \ \text{m}\right)^2} = \mathbf{9 \times 10^4 \ N/C}$$

Notice that a relationship exists between E and V:

$$V = \frac{kq}{R} \quad \text{and} \quad E = \frac{kq}{R^2}$$

$$VR = kq = ER^2$$

Therefore,

$$V = ER$$

So, reworking part (c), we then have

$$E = \frac{V}{R} = \frac{9 \times 10^3 \ \text{V}}{0.1 \ \text{m}} = \mathbf{9 \times 10^4 \ V/m}$$

All electrical fields have two properties at every point in space:

1. The electrical field, E, which allows us to calculate the force acting on any charged particle placed at that point
2. Electrical potential, V, which allows us to find the work done transporting a point charge to that position

EQUIPOTENTIAL SURFACES

(*College Physics* 8th ed. pages 543–544/9th ed. pages 559–560)

    A collection of points that all have the same electrical potential constitutes what is called an equipotential surface. The equipotential surfaces of a spherical surface are concentric spheres perpendicular to the electric field lines as shown. **For a region in space where an electric field exists, the equipotential surfaces are always perpendicular to the electrical field lines.**

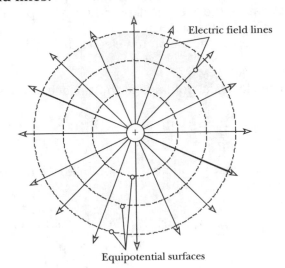

Electric field lines

Equipotential surfaces

The work done to move a charge, q, between two points on an equipotential surface is $W = q \, \Delta V = 0$ because every point on the surface is at the same electric potential.

The surface of a conductor is itself an equipotential surface.

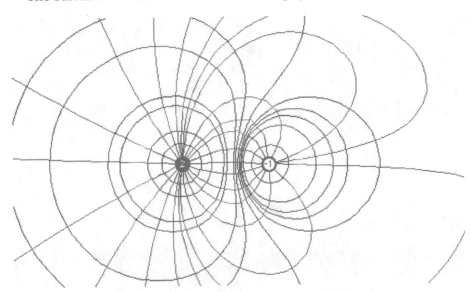

The lines of force and the equipotential lines associated with point charges $+2q$ and $-q$ in electrostatic attraction.

DIELECTRIC STRENGTH

(*College Physics* 8th ed. pages 557–560/9th ed. pages 573–576)

There is a limit to the maximum electrostatic field that air will support. This limit is called the dielectric strength, and for air it is 3×10^6 V/m.

When this value is exceeded, the air molecules in the field ionize, causing the charge creating the field to be reduced. The maximum electrical potential in a medium such as air is related to the maximum electrical field the air will support by

$$V_{max} = E_{max} R$$

SAMPLE PROBLEM 13

Consider Sample Problem 11 again. In air, a metal sphere of radius $R = 10.0$ cm is given an electrical charge of $q = +100$ nC. What is the electrical potential at the surface of the sphere?

SOLUTION TO PROBLEM 13

For a charged metallic sphere, the charge exists on the surface. The maximum electrical potential that can exist on the surface of the sphere is $V_{max} = E_{max} R = (3 \times 10^6 \text{ V/m})(0.10 \text{ m}) = \mathbf{3 \times 10^5}$ **V**. The electrical potential at the surface of Sample Problem 11 is less than this value.

ELECTRICAL POTENTIAL ENERGY

(*College Physics* 8th ed. pages 538–542/9th ed. pages 555–558)

The total energy of a charge in an electrical field is conserved. The electrical potential energy, U, of two point charges separated by distance R is

$$U = k\frac{q_1 q_2}{R}$$

SAMPLE PROBLEM 14

Two point charges, $q_A = +12$ μC and $q_B = -22$ μC, are brought from infinity to a distance of 0.40 m of each other. How much work was done to assemble this system?

SOLUTION TO PROBLEM 14

First, find the electrical potential energy:

$$U = k\frac{q_A q_B}{R} = \frac{(9 \times 10^9 \text{ N·m}^2/\text{C}^2)(+12 \times 10^{-6} \text{ C})(-22 \times 10^{-6} \text{ C})}{0.40 \text{ m}} = \mathbf{-5.9 \text{ J}}$$

Because the particles attract, their fields do –5.9 J of work in assembling the system. To separate the particles to infinity, some outside agent would have to do +5.9 J of work.

SAMPLE PROBLEM 15

Four point charges, $q_1 = 2.5$ μC, $q_2 = -1.5$ μC, $q_3 = 7.5$ μC, and $q_4 = -5.5$ μC, are arranged in a square measuring $x = 0.35$ m on a side.
 (a) How much work was done by outside forces to arrange the charges in the square?
 (b) What is the potential at the center of the square?
 (c) An electron initially at rest starts from a great distance away and moves toward the center of the square. What classical velocity will the electron have when it reaches the center?

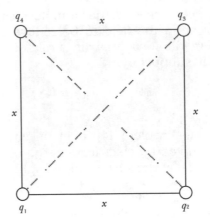

SOLUTION TO PROBLEM 15

(a) The point charges are assembled one charge at a time. To place q_1 requires zero work, $W_1 = 0$, because there are no other charges present. Positioning q_2 requires outside work W_2 that equals the electrical potential energy of q_1 and q_2. So,

$$W_2 = U = k\frac{q_1 q_2}{x} = \frac{k}{x}(q_1 q_2)$$

$$W_2 = \frac{\left(9 \times 10^9 \text{ N} \cdot \text{m}^2/\text{C}^2\right)}{0.35 \text{ m}}\left(2.5 \times 10^{-6}\text{C}\right)\left(-1.5 \times 10^{-6}\text{C}\right)$$
$$= \frac{\left(9 \times 10^9 \text{ N} \cdot \text{m}^2/\text{C}^2\right)}{0.35 \text{ m}}\left[(2.5)(-1.5)\right] \times 10^{-6} \text{ C}$$
$$= -0.096 \text{ J}$$

To place the third point charge, additional work is due to the two point charges already in place. A diagonal of the square forms a right triangle with sides x and hypotenuse $x\sqrt{2}$. Each diagonal has a length $x\sqrt{2}$. So,

$$W_3 = kq_3\left(\frac{q_1}{x_{13}} + \frac{q_2}{x_{23}}\right)$$
$$= kq_3\left(\frac{q_1}{x\sqrt{2}} + \frac{q_2}{x}\right)$$

$$W_3 = \left(9 \times 10^9 \text{ N} \cdot \text{m}^2/\text{C}^2\right)\left(7.5 \times 10^{-6} \text{ C}\right)\left[\left(\frac{2.5 \times 10^{-6} \text{ C}}{\sqrt{2}(0.35 \text{ m})}\right) + \left(\frac{-1.5 \times 10^{-6} \text{ C}}{0.35 \text{ m}}\right)\right]$$

Simplifying gives

$$W_3 = \left(9 \times 10^9 \text{ N} \cdot \text{m}^2/\text{C}^2\right)\left(7.5 \times 10^{-6} \text{ C}\right)\left[\left(\frac{2.5}{0.49}\right) + \left(\frac{-1.5}{0.35}\right)\right] \times 10^{-6} \text{ C/m} = 0.055 \text{ J}$$

Positioning point charge q_4 requires work of W_4:

$$W_4 = kq_4 \left(\frac{q_1}{x_{14}} + \frac{q_2}{x_{24}} + \frac{q_3}{x_{34}} \right)$$

$$= kq_4 \left(\frac{q_1}{x} + \frac{q_2}{x\sqrt{2}} + \frac{q_3}{x} \right)$$

$$W_4 = \left(9 \times 10^9 \text{ N} \cdot \text{m}^2/\text{C}^2\right)\left(-5.5 \times 10^{-6} \text{ C}\right)\left\{ \left(\frac{2.5 \times 10^{-6} \text{ C}}{0.35 \text{ m}} \right) + \left[\frac{-1.5 \times 10^{-6} \text{ C}}{\left(\sqrt{2}\right)\left(0.35 \text{ m}\right)} \right] \right.$$

$$\left. + \frac{\left(7.5 \times 10^{-6} \text{ C}\right)}{0.35 \text{ m}} \right\}$$

Simplifying yields

$$W_4 = \left(9 \times 10^9 \text{ N} \cdot \text{m}^2/\text{C}^2\right)\left(-5.5 \times 10^{-6} \text{ C}\right)\left[\left(\frac{2.5}{0.35} \right) + \left(\frac{-1.5}{0.49} \right) + \frac{\left(7.5\right)}{0.35} \right]$$

$$\times 10^{-6} \text{ C/m} = -1.26 \text{ J}$$

Therefore, the total work is

$$\Sigma W = W_1 + W_2 + W_3 + W_4$$

$$\Sigma W = 0 + (-0.096 \text{ J}) + 0.055 \text{ J} + (-1.26 \text{ J}) = \mathbf{-1.30 \text{ J}}$$

(b) With all the point charges in place, the potential at the center is

$$V = V_1 + V_2 + V_3 + V_4 = k \left[\frac{q_1 + q_2 + q_3 + q_4}{\left(0.5x\right)\left(\sqrt{2}\right)} \right]$$

$$V = \left(9 \times 10^9 \text{ N} \cdot \text{m}^2/\text{C}^2\right)\left[\frac{2.5 - 1.5 + 7.5 - 5.5}{\left(0.175\right)\left(\sqrt{2}\right)} \right] \times 10^{-6} \text{ C/m} = \mathbf{1.09 \times 10^5 \text{ V}}$$

(c) The electron must lose electrical potential energy because $\Delta U = Ve$. So, $\Delta U = \left(1.09 \times 10^5 \text{ V}\right)\left(-1.60 \times 10^{-19} \text{ C}\right) = -1.75 \times 10^{-14} \text{ J}$. This electrical potential energy becomes kinetic energy at the center of the square, and $K = 1.75 \times 10^{-14} \text{ J}$. Therefore, $K = \frac{1}{2}mv^2$ m and

$$v = \sqrt{\frac{2K}{m}} = \sqrt{\frac{2\left(1.74 \times 10^{-14} \text{ V}\right)}{9.11 \times 10^{-31} \text{ kg}}} = \mathbf{1.96 \times 10^8 \text{ m/s}}$$

THE PARALLEL-PLATE CAPACITOR

(*College Physics* 8th ed. pages 546–548/9th ed. pages 563–565)

One of the most useful electrical devices in many aspects of electricity is the parallel-plate capacitor. The plates are metal and are separated by a plate gap, d. Connecting the capacitor to a battery charges the plates. Think of a battery as an electron pump. It removes electrons from what becomes the positive plate and places an equal number of electrons on what becomes the negative plate (charging a capacitor is done by electrostatic repulsion). It takes a brief period of time to charge the capacitor, and then the battery can be removed. The magnitude of the charges on the plates are equal: $\left|q_{plate\,1}\right| = \left|q_{plate\,2}\right|$. The amount of charge on each plate is proportional to the potential difference, V, across the plates:

$$C = \frac{q}{V}$$

We call the constant of proportionality, C, the capacitance of the capacitor.

The SI unit of capacitance is the farad, F, which is defined as 1 F = 1 C/V. The farad is a very large unit. The usual capacitance of a capacitor is on the order of several microfarads, μF, to several picofarads, pF. In short:

$$1 \ \mu F = 1 \times 10^{-6} \ F$$

$$1 \ nF = 1 \times 10^{-9} \ F$$

$$1 \ pF = 1 \times 10^{-12} \ F$$

The upper plate in the diagram shown here has been charged positive. The field always points from positive charge to negative. Ignoring the edges of the plates, the electrical field between the plates is uniform.

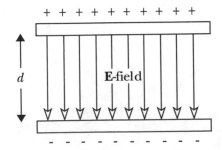

For a parallel-plate capacitor, the relationship between the electrical field, E, between the plates, the potential difference across the plates, and the plate gap is

$$V = Ed$$

SAMPLE PROBLEM 16

A parallel-plate capacitor has a potential difference of 100 V across its plates and a plate gap of 2.0 mm. What electric field, E, exists between the plates?

SOLUTION TO PROBLEM 16

The electrical field is found by:

$$E = \frac{V}{d} = \frac{100 \text{ V}}{2 \times 10^{-3} \text{ m}} = 5 \times 10^4 \text{ V/m}$$

The student should prove that 1 N/C = 1 V/m.

The equipotential surfaces between the plates of a parallel capacitor are planes that are perpendicular to the field lines as shown.

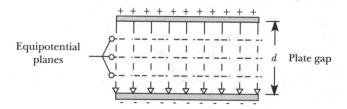

The capacitance of a parallel-plate capacitor can be calculated by using

$$C = \varepsilon_0 \frac{A}{d}$$

where ε_0 is the permittivity constant of free space and A is the area of one of the plates. This equation gives us information about how well an E-field is set up in space. In SI units, $\varepsilon_0 = 8.85 \times 10^{-12} \text{ C}^2 / \text{N} \cdot \text{m}^2$.

SAMPLE PROBLEM 17

A set of capacitor plates each measure 10.0 cm by 12.0 cm, and they have a plate gap of 3.0 mm. Calculate the capacitance.

SOLUTION TO PROBLEM 17

The area of one of the plates is

$$120 \text{ cm}^2 \times \frac{1 \text{ m}^2}{1 \times 10^4 \text{cm}^2} = 120 \times 10^{-4} \text{m}^2$$

Therefore,

$$C = \varepsilon_0 \frac{A}{d} = \frac{\left(8.85 \times 10^{-12} \text{ C}^2/\text{N} \cdot \text{m}^2\right)\left(120 \times 10^{-4} \text{m}^2\right)}{3 \times 10^{-3} \text{ m}} = 35 \text{ pF}$$

DIELECTRICS

(*College Physics* 8th ed. pages 557–560/9th ed. pages 573–578)

When an insulating material called a dielectric is inserted between the plates of a capacitor, the capacitance increases. The dielectric is represented by a dimensionless quantity called the dielectric constant, κ. With a dielectric inserted between the plates, the capacitance becomes

$$C = \kappa \varepsilon_0 \frac{A}{d}$$

SAMPLE PROBLEM 18

A parallel-plate capacitor of plate gap $d = 2.0$ mm has a capacitance $C_0 = 3.0$ μF. A battery is used to charge the plates with a potential difference $V_0 = 600$ V. After the charging process, the battery is removed.

(a) What is the potential difference across the capacitor when a 2.0-mm-thick slab of a dielectric of $\kappa = 7.5$ is sandwiched between the plates?

(b) What is the new capacitance?

(c) What is the permittivity of the dielectric?

SOLUTION TO PROBLEM 18

Proportionally, the dielectric constant is $\kappa = V_0/V$, and

(a) $V = V_0/\kappa = 600$ V$/7.5 =$ **80 V**

(b) $C = \kappa C_0 = 7.5\left(3.0 \times 10^{-6} \text{ F}\right) =$ **2.25 μF**

(c) $\varepsilon = \kappa \varepsilon_0 = 7.5\left(8.85 \times 10^{-12} \text{ C}^2/\text{N} \cdot \text{m}^2\right) =$ **6.64 $\times$ 10^{-11} C^2/N $\cdot$ m^2**

ELECTRICAL ENERGY STORED IN A CAPACITOR

(*College Physics* 8th ed. pages 555–557/9th ed. pages 571–573)

Parallel-plate capacitors not only produce uniform electrical fields between their plates and store charge on the plates; they also store electrical energy. The energy stored in the field between the plates may be calculated by

$$U = \tfrac{1}{2}CV^2$$

or

$$U = \tfrac{1}{2}qV$$

or

$$U = \tfrac{1}{2}\left(\frac{q^2}{C}\right)$$

SAMPLE PROBLEM 19

A parallel-plate capacitor with a plate gap of 0.6 mm has a capacitance of 6.0 μF. A battery charges the plates with a potential difference of 500 V and is then disconnected.

(a) Calculate the energy stored in the capacitor.

(b) What charge exists on the plates?

SOLUTION TO PROBLEM 19

(a) Because the capacitance and potential difference are given, we will use $U = \tfrac{1}{2}CV^2$ to find the energy stored. Therefore, $U = \tfrac{1}{2}CV^2 = \tfrac{1}{2}\left(6.0 \times 10^{-6}\text{F}\right)\left(500 \text{ V}\right)^2 =$ **0.75 J**.

(b) The charge is then:

$$q = CV = \left(6.0 \times 10^{-6} \text{ F}\right)\left(500 \text{ V}\right) = 3 \times 10^{-3} \text{ C, or } \textbf{3 mC}$$

COMBINATIONS OF CAPACITORS

(*College Physics* 8th ed. pages 549–555/9th ed. pages 565–571)

Electrical circuits frequently contain two or more capacitors grouped together to serve a particular function. In considering the effect of such groupings, it is convenient to use a circuit diagram. In such diagrams, electrical components are represented by symbols. The symbol for a battery is a set of unequal parallel lines. The high-potential terminal (+ terminal) of a battery is represented by the longer line. The capacitor is diagrammed as a set of equal-length parallel lines. Wires are shown as lines that connect components. Electrical circuit diagrams are also called electrical schematics.

When capacitors are arranged in parallel, their equivalent capacitance is the arithmetic sum of the individual capacitors:

$$C_{eq} = C_1 + C_2 + C_3 + \ldots$$

SAMPLE PROBLEM 20
Three capacitors, $C_1 = 0.5 \ \mu F$, $C_2 = 0.3 \ \mu F$, and $C_3 = 0.2 \ \mu F$, are arranged in parallel. Calculate the equivalent capacitance, C_{eq}.

SOLUTION TO PROBLEM 20
We start with a circuit diagram and then substitute values:

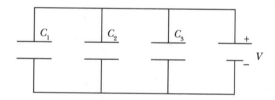

$$C_{eq} = C_1 + C_2 + C_3 = \left(0.5 + 0.3 + 0.2\right) \mu F = \mathbf{1.0 \ \mu F}$$

When capacitors are arranged in series, the reciprocal of the combined capacitance is the sum of the reciprocals of the capacitors:

$$\frac{1}{C_{eq}} = \frac{1}{C_1} + \frac{1}{C_2} + \frac{1}{C_3} + \cdots$$

SAMPLE PROBLEM 21
Three capacitors, $C_1 = 0.5 \ \mu F$, $C_2 = 0.3 \ \mu F$, and $C_3 = 0.2 \ \mu F$, are arranged in series. Calculate the equivalent capacitance, C_{eq}.

SOLUTION TO PROBLEM 21
Again, we start with a diagram and substitute:

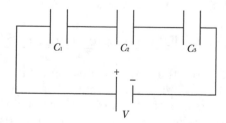

$$\frac{1}{C_{eq}} = \frac{1}{C_1} + \frac{1}{C_2} + \frac{1}{C_3} = \frac{1}{0.5 \ \mu F} + \frac{1}{0.3 \ \mu F} + \frac{1}{0.2 \ \mu F}$$

$$C_{eq} = 0.097 \ \mu F$$

SAMPLE PROBLEM 22

(a) Calculate the total capacitance of the circuit shown here.

(b) Find the charge on each capacitor in the circuit.

(c) Calculate the voltage drop across capacitor C_2.

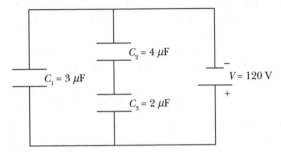

SOLUTION TO PROBLEM 22

(a) Capacitors C_2 and C_3 are in series with each other, and their equivalent capacitance is

$$\frac{1}{C_{eq}} = \frac{1}{C_1} + \frac{1}{C_2} = \frac{1}{4 \mu F} + \frac{1}{2 \mu F}$$

$$C_{eq} = 1.33 \ \mu F$$

The circuit is now reduced as shown here.

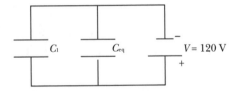

The two remaining capacitances are arranged in parallel, and $C = C_1 + C_{eq} = 3 \ \mu F + 1.33 \ \mu F = \textbf{4.33 } \mu \textbf{F}$.

(b) The total charge in the capacitors is $q = CV = (4.33 \ \mu F)(120 \ V) = 520 \ \mu C$. The charge q_1 on C_1 is $q_1 = C_1 V = (3 \ \mu F)(120 \ V) = \textbf{360 } \mu \textbf{C}$, and the remaining charge is $q - q_1 = 520 \ \mu C - 360 \ \mu C = 160 \ \mu C$. The 160 μC must be deposited on capacitors C_2 and C_3. So, $q_2 = q_3 = \textbf{160 } \mu \textbf{C}$.

(c) The voltage drop is $V = q_2/C_2 = \textbf{40 V}$.

ELECTROSTATICS: STUDENT OBJECTIVES FOR THE AP EXAM

■ You should know that there are two fundamental charges.

■ You should understand Coulomb's law for the fundamental electrostatic force between point charges and that the electrical fields produced by these charges are vector quantities with magnitude and direction.

- You should know how to use the equations, identify the charges, and sketch the directions for the forces and field in solving problems that involve these quantities.
- You should know that potential difference and electrical potential, closely related concepts, are scalar quantities.
- You should know how to use the equations, identify the charges, and solve problems involving potential difference and electrical potential.
- You should know that the equations of potential difference and electrical potential can be used to solve conservation of energy and work–energy theorem problems.
- You should know the relationship between electric field lines and equipotential lines and be able to sketch them.
- You should know that the electron volt, eV, is a unit of work and energy.
- You should be able to work with a capacitor, a device that stores energy.
- You should be able to solve multiple-choice questions without a calculator.

MULTIPLE-CHOICE QUESTIONS

1. A body that has been charged by conduction has what charge?
   (A) half the charge as the charged object brought near it
   (B) the same charge as the charged object brought near it
   (C) the same charge as the charged object that touched it
   (D) the opposite charge as the charged object brought near it
   (E) the opposite charge as the charged object that touched it

2. When the distance between two point charges is increased, what happens to the force between the point charges?
   (A) It increases directly with the distance.
   (B) It decreases directly with the distance.
   (C) It increases inversely with the distance.
   (D) It increases directly with the square of the distance.
   (E) It decreases inversely with the square of the distance.

3. Which one of the following statements is true about the electric field at the surface of a conductor?
   (A) It is always zero.
   (B) It is never zero.
   (C) It is parallel to the surface.
   (D) It is perpendicular to the surface.
   (E) It is identical to the field within the conductor.

4. A positive charge, in vacuum, is released from rest in a nonuniform electrical field. What happens to the positive charge?
   (A) It moves perpendicular to the field with constant velocity.
   (B) It moves parallel to the field with constant velocity.
   (C) It accelerates in the direction of the field.
   (D) It accelerates perpendicularly to the field.
   (E) It moves only along equipotential lines.

5. Two point charges are spaced by a distance x and exert mutual attractive forces of F on each other. If the charges are separated by a distance of $x/3$, what is the new mutual force?
    (A) F
    (B) $F/3$
    (C) $F/9$
    (D) $3F$
    (E) $9F$

6. Which one of the following statements is true about an electron moving in a direction opposite to the electrical field?
    (A) Both its potential energy and electrical potential remain constant.
    (B) Its potential energy increases, and its electrical potential decreases.
    (C) Its potential energy decreases, and its electrical potential increases.
    (D) Its potential energy increases, and its electrical potential increases.
    (E) Its potential energy decreases, and its electrical potential decreases.

7. The concept of difference in electrical potential is closely associated with which one of the following?
    (A) mechanical force on an electron
    (B) work per unit quantity of electrical charge
    (C) resistance of a section of copper wire
    (D) charge of a electron
    (E) charge of a proton

8. A point charge of 3 mC is placed in a uniform electrical field. The point charge experiences an electrical force of 6 nN. What is the magnitude of the field?
    (A) 2 μN/C
    (B) 0.2 μN/C
    (C) 20 μN/C
    (D) 18 μN/C
    (E) 0.5 μN/C

9. Electrical potential energy can be expressed in terms of what unit?
    (A) N/C
    (B) F
    (C) V
    (D) eV
    (E) C/V

10. To move a 2-C charge from point A to point B, 10 J of energy is required. What is the potential difference between the two points?
    (A) 0.2 V
    (B) 0.5 V
    (C) 5 V
    (D) 10 V
    (E) 20 V

11. Which one of the following statements is true concerning the work done by an external force in moving an electron at constant speed between two points in an electrical field?
    (A) The work done depends only on the displacement of the electron.
    (B) The work done is always positive.
    (C) The work done is always 0 J.
    (D) The work done is always negative.
    (E) The work done depends on the total distance covered.

12. Which one of the following statements applies to an equipotential surface in an electrical field?
    (A) It must be parallel to the electric field at any point.
    (B) It must be perpendicular to the electric field at any point.
    (C) It must never cross a field line.
    (D) It must be equal to the electric field at every point.
    (E) It must be randomly oriented to the electric field at every point.

13. A negative charge in a vacuum, if it is free to move, tries to move in what way?
    (A) in the direction of the electrical field
    (B) away from infinity
    (C) toward infinity
    (D) from low potential to high potential
    (E) from high potential to low potential

14. If the voltage across a capacitor is doubled, what happens to the energy in the capacitor?
    (A) It doubles.
    (B) It triples.
    (C) It quadruples.
    (D) It halves.
    (E) It stays the same.

15. A dielectric having a dielectric constant 4 is inserted between the plates of a parallel-plate capacitor. What happens to the capacitance?
    (A) It increases by a factor of 4.
    (B) It decreases by a factor of 4.
    (C) It increases by a factor of 16.
    (D) It decreases by a factor of 16.
    (E) It stays the same.

FREE-RESPONSE PROBLEMS

1. A tiny sphere of mass 8×10^{-13} kg and charge $q = -4.8 \times 10^{-18}$ C is placed between the plates of a parallel-plate capacitor with plate gap $d = 20.0$ mm. The sphere remains suspended in the electric field of the capacitor as shown.

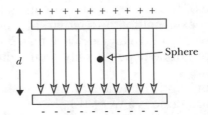

(a) On the diagram, show the forces acting on the sphere.
(b) How many electrons are in excess on the sphere?
(c) What is the strength of the field?
(d) Determine the potential difference across the plates.
(e) The charge is removed from the field. Both upper and lower plates are symmetrical, and each measures 25.0 cm by 25.0 cm. Find the capacitance of the capacitor.
(f) What charge exists on the lower plate of the capacitor?

2. Four identical charges of +6.0 μC are arranged in a square that measures $R = 0.04$ m on a side as shown.

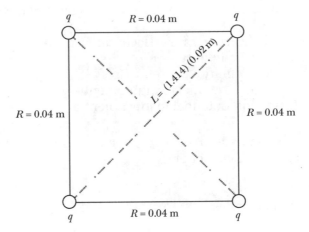

(a) Find the electrical field at the center of the square.
(b) Determine the electrical potential at the center of the square.

Answers

Multiple-Choice Questions

1. **C** The only charge that can move in a conductor is the negative charge. If you bring a rod with a negative charge near an isolated neutral body, the negative charge will move away, causing polarization. On contact, some of the negative charge will transfer into the positive region, neutralizing some of the positive charge. When the rod is removed, there is a net negative charge (*College Physics* 8th ed. pages 499–500/9th ed. pages 513–517).

2. **E** Coulomb's law establishes that the electrical force is an inverse square law (*College Physics* 8th ed. pages 500–501/9th ed. pages 517–518).

3. **D** The electrical field is radially outward for a positive charge (radially inward for a negative charge) and is therefore perpendicular to the surface of the conductor (*College Physics* 8th ed. pages 506–507/9th ed. pages 522–523).

4. **C** The electrical field has the same direction as the force acting on a positive charge. Because the field is defined as directed outward from a positive charge, a positive particle will accelerate in the direction of the field (repelled by a positive charge) (*College Physics* 8th ed. page 506/9th ed. page 522).

5. **E** Coulomb's law is an inverse square law (*College Physics* 8th ed. page 501/9th ed. page 517).

6. **C** An electron will move toward the positive end of the field, increasing its kinetic energy (a decrease in electrical potential energy). Electrons accelerate from regions of low potential to regions of high potential (*College Physics* 8th ed. pages 533–536/9th ed. pages 549–552).

7. **B** Electrical potential difference V_{AB} is defined as the change in electrical potential energy per unit charge, which is the work per unit charge done by a force in moving the charge from point A to point B in the field (*College Physics* 8th ed. page 536/9th ed. page 552).

8. **A** Substituting values gives $E = F/q = (6 \times 10^{-9} \text{ N})/(3 \times 10^{-3} \text{ C}) = 2 \text{ μF/C}$ (*College Physics* 8th ed. page 506/9th ed. page 522).

9. **D** Because $W = qV$, an electron dropped through a potential difference of 1 V gains 1 eV in kinetic energy (*College Physics* 8th ed. page 543/9th ed. page 559).

10. **C** Substituting values gives $W = q \, \Delta V$ and $\Delta V = W/q = 10 \text{ J}/2 \text{ C} = 5 \text{ V}$ (*College Physics* 8th ed. page 542/9th ed. page 558).

11. **A** Because work is done by a conservative force, it only depends on the endpoints and not on the path taken between those points (*College Physics* 8th ed. page 532/9th ed. page 549).

12. **B** Equipotentials are perpendicular to the electric field at any point (*College Physics* 8th ed. pages 543–544/9th ed. pages 550–560).

13. **D** A negative charge will accelerate from the low potential to the high potential of the field (*College Physics* 8th ed. page 532/9th ed. page 549).

14. **C** Energy stored in the field between the plates is given by $U = \frac{1}{2}CV^2$. If V becomes two times as large, then U becomes four times as large (*College Physics* 8th ed. page 555/9th ed. pages 571–572).

15. **A** Capacitance is multiplied by a factor κ when a dielectric fills the plate gap. Because $C = \kappa C_0$ and $\kappa = 4$, the capacitance is increased by a factor of 4 (*College Physics* 8th ed. page 558/9th ed. page 574).

FREE-RESPONSE PROBLEMS

1. (a)

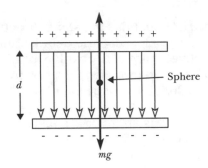

(b) Substituting values gives $4.8 \times 10^{-18} \text{C} \times \left(1 \text{ e}/1.60 \times 10^{-19} \text{ C}\right) = $ **30 e**.

(c) In static equilibrium, the upward electrostatic force acting on the negative sphere equals the weight of the sphere. So, $qE = mg$, and

$$E = \frac{mg}{q} = \frac{\left(8 \times 10^{-13} \text{ kg}\right)\left(9.8 \text{ m/s}\right)}{4.8 \times 10^{-18} \text{ C}} = \textbf{1.63} \times \textbf{10}^{\textbf{6}} \textbf{ V/m}$$

(d) The potential difference can be found by $V = Ed = \left(1.63 \times 10^{6} \text{ V/m}\right)$ $\left(20 \times 10^{-3} \text{ m}\right) = $ **33 kV**.

(e) The capacitance is

$$C = \varepsilon_0 \frac{A}{d} = \frac{\left(8.85 \times 10^{-12} \text{ F/m}\right)\left(0.025 \text{ m}\right)^2}{20 \times 10^{-3} \text{ m}} = \textbf{0.28 pF}$$

(f) The charge on the lower plate is $q = CV = \left(0.28 \times 10^{-12} \text{ F}\right)$ $\left(1.63 \times 10^{6} \text{ V}\right) = $ **9.24 nC**.

(*College Physics* 8th ed. pages 506, 538, 546–547/9th ed. pages 523, 553, 562–563)

2. (a) The distance, L, from the center of the square to each point charge is half the length of the diagonal of the square. So,

$$L = \sqrt{2}\frac{R}{2} = \left(1.414\right)\left(\frac{0.04 \text{ m}}{2}\right) = 0.028 \text{ m}$$

The charges q are identical and so are the distances L. Logically, the magnitude of the electrical field vectors, E, for each charge will all be equal. The directions will differ and will be directed along the diagonals. Therefore, **by symmetry, the E-field pattern will be zero**.

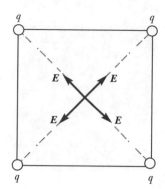

To calculate the resultant electrical field at the center of the square, first determine the x component of the resultant **E**-vector:

$$E_x = E\left(\cos 45°\right) + E\left(\cos 135°\right) + E\left(\cos 225°\right) + E\left(\cos 315°\right)$$

$$E_x = \left(0.707\right)E + \left(-0.707\right)E + \left(-0.707\right)E + \left(0.707\right)E = 0$$

Next, find the y component of **E**:

$$E_y = E\left(\sin 45°\right) + E\left(\sin 135°\right) + E\left(\sin 225°\right) + E\left(\sin 315°\right)$$

$$E_y = \left(0.707\right)E + \left(0.707\right)E + \left(-0.707\right)E + \left(-0.707\right)E = 0$$

Both the x component and the y component of the resultant **E** are zero, which means that the resultant electrical field intensity at the center of the square is itself zero and **E = 0**.

(b) Even though the field intensity at the center of the square is zero when identical charges are at each vertex, it does not necessarily mean that the electrical potential is likewise zero. The electrical potential due to i number of charges at a given point is found by $V = k \Sigma \left(q_i/r_i\right)$. Here, $i = 4$ charges, and the electric potential is calculated by

$$V = \frac{k}{L}\left(q_1 + q_2 + q_3 + q_4\right)$$

$$V = \left(\frac{9 \times 10^9 \text{ N} \cdot \text{m}^2/\text{C}^2}{0.028 \text{ m}}\right)\left(6.0 + 6.0 + 6.0 + 6.0\right) \times 10^{-6} \text{ C} = \mathbf{7.71 \times 10^6 \text{ V}}$$

There is electrical potential at the center of the square.

(*College Physics* 8th ed. pages 505–510, 535–538/9th ed. pages 522–526, 552–555)

12

DC Circuits

Electric Current, *I*

(*College Physics* 8th ed. pages 570–575/9th ed. pages 590–596)

Certain materials, metals in particular, are better conductors of electricity than others. When a conductive path is provided between two points originally at different potentials, charge will move. Current is defined as the flow of charge q, and the intensity of the current, I, is defined as the time rate of flow of charge, or

$$I = \frac{q}{t}$$

The SI unit of current is the ampere, A. We define the ampere as $1\,A = 1\,C/s$.

The direction of current is a matter of convention. Because the concept of positive charge is basic to electrical terminology, the direction of conventional current is from positive (+) to negative (−). On the other hand, current in metallic conductors is a matter of electron flow, which is from negative (−) to positive (+).

AP Tip

The direction of conventional current is always the same as the direction that positive charges would move, even if the actual current consists of a flow of electrons.

When current through a conductor is always in the same direction, it is called direct current, or DC.

AP Tip

Current means running or flowing, and it is not proper to say that a "current flows." *Current* used in conjunction with the word *flows* is a redundancy.

SAMPLE PROBLEM 1

A charge of 22.0 C flows through a cross section of wire every minute.

  (a) What is the current?

  (b) How many electrons go through the cross section each minute?

SOLUTION TO PROBLEM 1

(a) $I = \dfrac{q}{t} = \dfrac{22 \text{ C}}{60 \text{ s}} = 0.37 \text{ A}$

(b) $22.0 \text{ C} \times \dfrac{1 \text{ e}}{1.60 \times 10^{-19} \text{ C}} = 1.37 \times 10^{20} \text{ e}$

EMF

(*College Physics* 8th ed. pages 594–595/9th ed. pages 616–617)

Although emf, ε, and potential difference, ΔV, are both measured in volts, there is a real distinction between them. The emf is defined as the work per unit charge done by a battery or a generator on the charges in moving them around the circuit. Potential difference between two points is defined as the work per unit charge done by the electrical forces in moving the charge from one point to the other. It is convenient to think of a source of emf as a kind of pump that acts on a charge to bring it to a higher potential energy.

The SI unit of emf is the volt, defined as 1 V = 1 J/C. A seat of emf will perform 1 J of work on each 1-C charge that passes through it.

The most familiar source or seat of emf is the battery. A battery should be thought of as a *charge pump* that sends conventional current into a closed circuit. The seat of emf gives the current electrical energy, and the resistors in the circuit use up that energy.

RESISTANCE

(*College Physics* 8th ed. pages 575–576/9th ed. pages 596–597)

Resistance, R, is a physical characteristic of matter. Every material offers some resistance to electrical current. Good conductors such as the metals copper, silver, and aluminum offer very little resistance to current. Nonconductive materials such as rubber, plastic, and glass offer very high resistance to current.

The SI unit of resistance is the ohm (Ω), defined as 1Ω = 1 volt/ampere = 1 V/A.

OHM'S LAW

(*College Physics* 8th ed. pages 575–576/9th ed. pages 596–597)

Ohm's law is the fundamental law in electricity that makes it possible to determine the potential difference, V, across the ends of a resistor when the current, I, through it and its resistance, R, are known. Ohm's law for a resistor is

$$V = IR$$

AP Tip

Circuit diagrams will greatly help in understanding a problem. Draw diagrams when working and solving problems.

SAMPLE PROBLEM 2

A battery is directly connected to a small lightbulb. The battery maintains a potential difference of 6.0 V across the lightbulb. If the current in the circuit is 0.5 A, what is the resistance of the lightbulb?

SOLUTION TO PROBLEM 2

First, make a circuit diagram. The lightbulb is a resistor, and we show it in the circuit diagram as such.

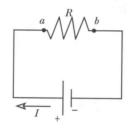

The voltage drop across R is V_{ab} = 6.0 V. So, $R = R/I$ = 6.0 V/0.5 A = **12 Ω**.

Although the resistance calculated in Sample Problem 2 is assumed to be the resistance of the lightbulb, it actually includes the resistance of the connecting wires and the resistance of the battery. In practice, we use wires of very low resistance, so this factor can be neglected in most calculations. Internal resistance in many sources of emf can be quite low and as a result can be neglected in some of our problem work.

We call the drop in voltage across the resistor an IR drop.

POWER

(*College Physics* 8th ed. pages 580–583/9th ed. pages 601–604)

Electrical power is the rate at which energy is produced or used. Sources of emf do work on charge and give it energy. The power output of an emf source is

$$P_0 = I\mathcal{E}$$

Resistors use electric energy, and the rate at which heat is dissipated in a circuit is called the power loss. The power loss in a resistor is given by

$$P = IV = I^2R = \frac{V^2}{R}$$

The power output of the seat of emf equals the power loss in the external circuit.

SAMPLE PROBLEM 3

A resistor uses 12.5 A when connected across 120 V.

    (a) What is the resistance of this electrical component?
    (b) Determine the power loss through the resistor.

Solution to Problem 3

(a) $R = V/I = 120 \text{ V}/12.5 \text{ A} = \textbf{9.6 }\boldsymbol{\Omega}$

(b) $P = IV = (12.5 \text{ A})(120 \text{ V}) = \textbf{1.5 kW}$

Sample Problem 4

A 420-W resistor with a resistance of 60 Ω is used in a circuit.

(a) Determine the potential difference across the ends of the resistor.

(b) What current passes through the resistor?

Solution to Problem 4

Notice that the rules for the use of significant figures are not followed when using resistance in calculations because resistors are not calibrated to have significant figure values. Instead, they may have a tolerance of as much as ±20%, so the value of a 60-Ω resistor could range from 48 Ω to 72 Ω. Be reasonable with your answers and do not exceed two decimal places in your problem work. Do any rounding at the end of your calculations.

(a) $P = V^2/R$ and $V = \sqrt{PR} = \sqrt{(420 \text{ W})(60 \text{ }\Omega)} = 159 \text{ V}$

(b) $I = V/R = 159 \text{ V}/60 \text{ }\Omega = \textbf{2.65 A}$

Sample Problem 5

A battery has an emf, $\mathcal{E} = 24.0 \text{ V}$. When connected in a circuit, it delivers a current of 3.4 A. The battery has an internal resistance of 1.5Ω.

(a) What is the terminal voltage?

(b) There is an external resistor in the circuit. What is the potential difference across this resistance?

(c) What is the power loss in this external resistor?

Solution to Problem 5

(a) $V_T = \mathcal{E} - Ir = 24.0 \text{ V} - (3.4 \text{ A})(1.5 \text{ }\Omega) = \textbf{18.9 V}$

(b) The external resistor must use whatever voltage the battery puts into the external circuit. The external resistance has a potential difference of **18.9 V**.

(c) $P = IV = (3.4 \text{ A})(18.9 \text{ V}) = \textbf{64.3 W}$

Resistivity, ρ

(*College Physics* 8th ed. pages 577–579/9th ed. pages 598–599)

Several factors determine the resistance of any section of wire: (1) the length L; (2) the cross-sectional area A; and (3) the resistivity ρ, a property of the material of which the wire is composed. The resistivity indirectly gives a measure of how well a current will be conducted through a piece of wire. Resistivity is related to resistance by the relationship

$$R = \rho \frac{L}{A}$$

Sample Problem 6

A 120-m-long sector of circular wire has a diameter of 1.2 mm. The wire has a resistivity $\rho = 3.6 \times 10^{-8} \text{ }\Omega \cdot \text{m}$.

(a) What is the resistance of this length of wire?
(b) What is the potential difference across the ends of the wire when a current of 2.4 A is sent through it?

SOLUTION TO PROBLEM 6

The radius of the wire is $r = 0.6 \times 10^{-3}$m.
   (a) Then,

$$R = \rho \frac{L}{A} = \frac{\left(3.6 \times 10^{-8}\ \Omega \cdot m\right)\left(120\ m\right)}{\pi \left(0.6 \times 10^{-3}\ m\right)^2} = \mathbf{3.8\ \Omega}$$

   (b) $V = IR = \left(2.4\ A\right)\left(3.8\ \Omega\right) = \mathbf{9.2\ V}$

RESISTORS IN SERIES

(*College Physics* 8th ed. pages 595–597/9th ed. pages 617–620)

When two or more resistors are connected in series in an electrical circuit as shown, the current through all parts of the series combination is the same.

The sum of the voltage drops across the resistors in series is the sum of the voltage drop across each resistor. The equivalent resistance, R_{eq}, of the resistors in series is the sum of their resistances:

$$R_s = R_1 + R_2 + R_3 + \ldots$$

AP Tip

The current through resistors in series is the same in each resistor, and the potential difference across them is additive.

SAMPLE PROBLEM 7

The three resistors, $R_1 = 12\ \Omega$, $R_2 = 6\ \Omega$, and $R_3 = 8\ \Omega$, are arranged in series.
   (a) Find the equivalent resistance of the combination.
   (b) The resistors are connected to a seat of emf. The current through the resistors is 2.4 A. What is the *IR* drop across junctions *a* and *b*?

SOLUTION TO PROBLEM 7

   (a) First, make a diagram.

For a set of resistors combined in series, the equivalent resistance is the sum of the resistors as shown, and $R_s = R_{ab} = R_1 + R_2 + R_3 = 12\ \Omega + 6\ \Omega + 8\ \Omega = 26\ \Omega$. The three resistors behave like a single 26-Ω resistor.

$$R_{ab} = 26\ \Omega$$

$$a \longrightarrow \wedge\!\wedge\!\wedge \longrightarrow b$$

(b) The *IR* drop between junctions *a* and *b* is $V_{ab} = IR_s = (2.4\ \text{A})(26\ \Omega) = \textbf{6.2 V}.$

RESISTORS IN PARALLEL

(*College Physics* 8th ed. pages 598–600/9th ed. pages 620–623)

When resistors are arranged in a parallel combination, the current splits as shown. The sum of the currents in each branch is equal to the current that enters the combination. The voltage drop across the combination is equal to the voltage drop across each resistor in parallel.

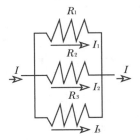

The reciprocal of the equivalent resistance, R_{eq}, of the resistors in parallel is the sum of the reciprocals of the individual resistances:

$$\frac{1}{R_{eq}} = \frac{1}{R_1} + \frac{1}{R_2} + \frac{1}{R_3} + \ldots$$

SAMPLE PROBLEM 8

The three resistors, $R_1 = 12\ \Omega$, $R_2 = 6\ \Omega$, and $R_3 = 8\ \Omega$, are arranged in parallel.
  (a) Calculate their equivalent resistance.
  (b) Junctions *a* and *b* are connected across an emf. If a current of 2.4 A enters junction *a*, what is the *IR* drop across junctions *a* and *b*?
  (c) What is the current through each resistor in the parallel bank?

SOLUTION TO PROBLEM 8
  (a) First, make a diagram of the resistor arrangement.

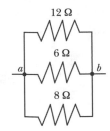

For a set of resistors combined in parallel, the equivalent is the sum of the resistors.

$$\frac{1}{R_{eq}} = \frac{1}{R_{ab}} = \frac{1}{R_1} + \frac{1}{R_2} + \frac{1}{R_3} = \frac{1}{12\ \Omega} + \frac{1}{6\ \Omega} + \frac{1}{8\ \Omega} = 0.375\ \frac{1}{\Omega}$$

$$R_{eq} = R_{ab} = \frac{1}{0.375}\ \Omega = \mathbf{2.67\ \Omega}$$

The three resistors in parallel function as a single 2.67-Ω resistor as shown.

$$R_{ab} = 2.67\ \Omega$$

$$a \longrightarrow\!\!\bigwedge\!\!\bigvee\!\!\longrightarrow b$$

(b) Current $I = 2.4$ A enters the resistor at point a. The IR drop is

$$V_{ab} = IR_s = (2.4\ A)(2.67\ \Omega) = \mathbf{6.4\ V}$$

(c) Each resistor in parallel undergoes the same voltage or IR drop, and that is 6.4 V. So, the current in R_1 is

$$I_1 = \frac{V_{ab}}{R_1} = \frac{6.4\ V}{12\ \Omega} = \mathbf{0.53\ A}$$

The current in R_2 is

$$I_2 = \frac{V_{ab}}{R_2} = \frac{6.4\ V}{6\ \Omega} = \mathbf{1.07\ A}$$

The current in R_3 is

$$I_3 = \frac{V_{ab}}{R_3} = \frac{6.4\ V}{8\ \Omega} = \mathbf{0.80\ A}$$

The sum of the currents going through the resistors in a parallel bank must equal the current entering the bank. As a check, add the currents of the resistors in parallel:

$$I = I_1 + I_2 + I_3 = 0.53\ A + 1.07\ A + 0.80\ A = 2.4\ A$$

They do check.

AP Tip

The largest resistance in parallel carries the smallest current, and the smallest resistor in parallel carries the largest current. Current tends to take the path of least resistance.

COMBINATION CIRCUITS

(*College Physics* 8th ed. pages 600–603/9th ed. pages 623–625)

In most electrical circuits, resistors are wired partly in series and partly in parallel. In such circuits, the rules for determining the equivalent resistance are applied to each part of the circuit for circuit analysis.

SAMPLE PROBLEM 9

The electrical circuit diagram shown here contains a seat of emf with zero internal resistance, three resistors, an ammeter, and voltmeter. Ammeters are electrical instruments designed to measure electric current. An ammeter has low resistance and is connected in series so that all the current passes through it. Voltmeters are designed to measure the potential difference across a resistor. Voltmeters have a high resistance and are connected in parallel across a resistor.

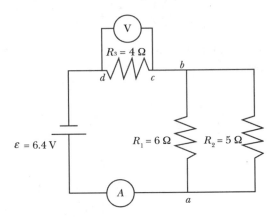

Perform the following analysis on the circuit.
  (a) Find the total resistance of the circuit.
  (b) What current will the ammeter A read?
  (c) Determine the current in each resistor.
  (d) What will the voltmeter V across resistor R_3 read?
  (e) Calculate the power output of the battery.
  (f) Find the power drop in each resistor.

SOLUTION TO PROBLEM 9

Current I is issued from the positive terminal of the battery. The full current passes through the ammeter. At junction a, the current splits and current I_1 goes through R_1 and current I_2 passes through R_2. Currents I_1 and I_2 merge at junction b. See the figure below.

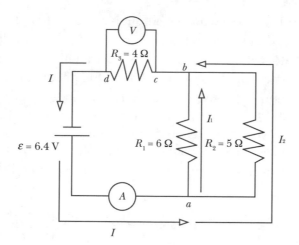

(a) Resistors R_1 and R_2 are in parallel, and their equivalent resistance is

$$\frac{1}{R_{12}} = \frac{1}{R_1} + \frac{1}{R_2}$$

Using another approach, we can find that the equivalent resistance is also the reciprocal of the sum of the reciprocals, or

$$R_{12} = \frac{1}{1/R_1 + 1/R_2} = \frac{1}{1/6\ \Omega + 1/5\ \Omega} = \frac{1}{11/30\ \Omega} = \frac{30\ \Omega}{11} = 2.73\ \Omega$$

Resistor R_3 is in series with the 2.73-Ω resistance, and the equivalent resistance, R_{eq} of the circuit is $R_{eq} = R_3 + 2.73\ \Omega = 4\ \Omega + 2.73\ \Omega =$ **6.73 Ω**.

(b) The current issued by the battery, which is the current read by the ammeter, is found by using Ohm's law:

$$I = \frac{\mathcal{E}}{R_{eq}} = \frac{6.4\ \text{V}}{6.73\ \Omega} = \textbf{0.95 A}$$

(c) At junction a, the current splits and current I_1 goes through R_1 and current I_2 passes through R_2. All resistors suffer the same IR drop in parallel. The equivalent resistance, R_{12}, of R_1 and R_2 was found in part (a) to be $R_{12} = 2.73\ \Omega$. By Ohm's law,

$$V_{12} = IR_{12} = (0.95\ \text{A})(2.73\ \Omega) = 2.59\ \text{V}$$

$$I_1 = \frac{V_{12}}{R_1} = \frac{2.59\ \text{V}}{6\ \Omega} = \textbf{0.43 A}$$

$$I_2 = \frac{V_{12}}{R_2} = \frac{2.59\ \text{V}}{5\ \Omega} = \textbf{0.52 A}$$

(d) What will the voltmeter V across resistor R_3 read? The voltmeter will read the IR drop across R_3. The full current passes through R_3, and by Ohm's law, $V_3 = IR_3 = (0.95\ \text{A})(4\ \Omega) = \textbf{3.80 V}$.

(e) The battery power output is the product of the current issued to the circuit and the emf: $P_{output} = I\mathcal{E} = (0.95\ \text{A})(6.4\ \text{V}) = \textbf{6.08 W}$.

(f) Resistors R_1 and R_2 are in parallel, and the power dissipated in each can be found by taking the product of the current squared and the resistance. So, for resistor 1, $P_1 = I_1^2 R_1 = (0.43\ \text{A})^2 (6\ \Omega) = \textbf{1.11 W}$, and for resistor 2, $P_2 = I_2^2 R_2 = (0.52\ \text{A})^2 (5\ \Omega) = \textbf{1.35 W}$. Resistor R_3 is in series, and then the power drop can be calculated by taking the product of the IR drop and the current through the resistor. So, $P_3 = IV_3 = (0.95\ \text{A})(3.80\ \text{V}) = \textbf{3.61 W}$.

ELECTRIC CIRCUITS: STUDENT OBJECTIVES FOR THE AP EXAM

- You should know the definition for electrical current in a conductor and be able to apply it.
- You should know that the direction of the current in a conductor is, by convention, the direction in which positive charge carriers flow.
- You should know and be able to apply Ohm's law and the power equations to both conductors and the entire DC circuit.
- You should know how to calculate the resistance of a conductor from its physical parameters.
- You should know how to draw and read schematic diagrams of the components in a direct-current circuit.
- You should know how to solve for equivalent resistance in series circuits, parallel circuits, and combination circuits.
- You should know how to solve for current, voltage, and power for an entire circuit and for each component of the circuit.
- You should know how to solve for terminal voltage in a DC circuit.
- You should be able to solve multiple-choice questions without a calculator.

MULTIPLE-CHOICE QUESTIONS

1. A set of resistors that are connected in parallel will have what feature?
   (A) the same charge across their ends
   (B) the same current passing through them
   (C) different potential differences
   (D) the same power dissipation
   (E) the same potential difference

2. Which one of the following equations expresses the resistance of a length L of circular wire in terms of its resistivity, ρ, and cross section, A?
   (A) $R = \rho LA$
   (B) $R = \rho A/L$
   (C) $R = \rho L/A$
   (D) $R = AL/\rho$
   (E) $R = A/\rho L$

3. Electrical current through a conductor is a measure of what?
   (A) the work done moving charge carriers
   (B) the drop in potential that charge carriers experience per unit time
   (C) the quantity of charge moving through a given cross section per unit time
   (D) the drift velocity of the charge carriers
   (E) the kinetic energy gained by the charge carriers

4. The same potential difference is applied to two wires. Wire 1 carries two times the current as wire 2. If the resistance of wire 2 is R, what is the resistance of wire 1?
   (A) $R/4$
   (B) $R/2$
   (C) R
   (D) $2R$
   (E) $4R$

5. The circuit shown contains three resistors. What is the equivalent resistance of the resistors?

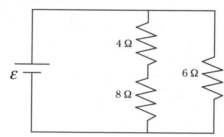

   (A) 1.85 Ω
   (B) 4 Ω
   (C) 8.67 Ω
   (D) 10.4 Ω
   (E) 18 Ω

6. Which one of the following equations expresses the power P dissipated in an ohmic material in terms of its resistance R and the potential difference ΔV across the resistance?
   (A) $P = R\,\Delta V$
   (B) $P = \Delta V/R$
   (C) $P = \Delta V^2/R$
   (D) $P = R^2/\Delta V$
   (E) $P = R(\Delta V)^2$

7. To maintain a current through an electrical conductor, which one of the following statements must be true?
   (A) The conductor must be a metal.
   (B) There must be a drop in resistance across the conductor.
   (C) The conductor must have net free charge.
   (D) There must be a potential difference between the ends of the conductor.
   (E) The conductor must have electrical resistance.

8. Which one of the following statements about the terminal potential of a battery is true?
   (A) It is equal to the emf of the battery by definition.
   (B) It is equal to the emf of the battery minus the terminal resistance of the battery.
   (C) It is equal to the emf of the battery divided by the terminal resistance of the battery.
   (D) It is equal to the emf of the battery only when no current is drawn from the battery.
   (E) It is equal to the emf of the battery only when a large current is drawn from the battery.

9. Two resistors, A and B, are connected in series across a potential difference V_{AB}. The current carried by resistor A is I. What is the current carried by resistor B?
   (A) $4I$
   (B) $2I$
   (C) I
   (D) $0.5I$
   (E) $0.25I$

10. The current through and the voltage across a resistor are to be measured in an electrical circuit. How should an ammeter and voltmeter be connected to the resistor?
    (A) It does not matter how the meters are connected.
    (B) The ammeter is connected in series and the voltmeter in parallel with the resistor.
    (C) The ammeter is connected in parallel and the voltmeter in series with the resistor.
    (D) Both meters are arranged in parallel with the resistor.
    (E) Both meters are arranged in series with the resistor.

11. Of the graphs shown, which one illustrates the relationship between the resistance R and the length L of a piece of copper wire that is maintained at a constant temperature?

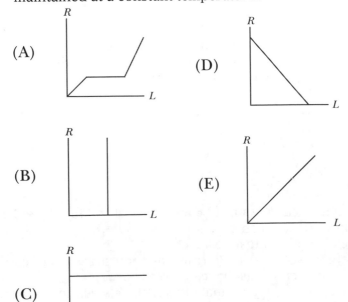

12. Which one of the following best defines the emf?
    (A) the maximum force that accelerates electrons through a wire when connected to a battery
    (B) the maximum capacitance between the terminals of a battery
    (C) the maximum potential difference between the terminals of a battery
    (D) the maximum force that accelerates protons through a wire when connected to a battery
    (E) the maximum electrical potential energy stored in a battery

13. One ohm is equal to which one of the following?
    (A) 1 V/C
    (B) 1 J·s/C²
    (C) 1 J/s
    (D) 1 W/A
    (E) 1 A/J

14. Two 10-Ω resistors and four 20-Ω resistors are connected in series to a 24.0-V battery that has no internal resistance. What current passes through each resistor?
    (A) 0.24 A
    (B) 2.40 A
    (C) 4.17 A
    (D) 417 A
    (E) 2400 A

15. An old battery in a flashlight has a 6.0-V emf and an internal resistance of 0.5 Ω. What is the terminal voltage of the battery when the current is 1.0 A?
    (A) 0.5 V
    (B) 5.5 V
    (C) 6.5 V
    (D) 7.0 V
    (E) 7.5 V

FREE-RESPONSE PROBLEMS

1. Consider the electrical circuit diagram shown here. The battery has an emf, $\mathcal{E}$, of 12.0 V. The resistors are $R_1 = 12.0\ \Omega$, $R_2 = 4.0\ \Omega$, $R_3 = 8.0\ \Omega$, and $R_4 = 22.0\ \Omega$. The battery has an internal resistance $r = 0.50\ \Omega$.

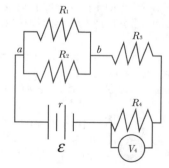

    (a) Determine the current, I, issued by the battery.
    (b) Calculate the terminal voltage of the battery.

(c) Find the current through R_1 and R_2.
(d) What is the total power output of the battery?
(e) What will meter V_4 read?

2. The circuit diagram shown here has a battery with an emf, ε. The ammeter in the circuit diagram reads 2.4 A. Resistors $R_1 = R_2 = R_3 = 18 \, \Omega$, $R_4 = 8.0 \, \Omega$, and $R_5 = 4.0 \, \Omega$. The internal resistance of the battery is negligible.
(a) Calculate the emf of the battery.
(b) What is the voltage drop, the IR drop, between junctions a and d?
(c) Determine the power loss between junctions c and d.

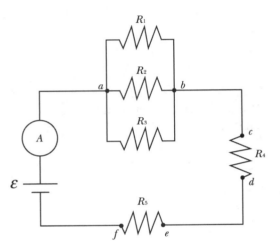

ANSWERS

MULTIPLE-CHOICE QUESTIONS

1. **E** A set of resistors connected in parallel will all have the same potential difference because each is connected to the same two points in the electrical circuit (*College Physics* 8th ed. page 578/9th ed. page 620).

2. **C** Resistance of an ohmic wire is dependent on its physical characteristics. Resistance is directly proportional to resistivity and the length of wire and inversely proportional to the cross-sectional area of the wire (*College Physics* 8th ed. page 577/9th ed. page 597).

3. **C** Current is the rate at which charge moves through and perpendicular to a cross section in a given time period (*College Physics* 8th ed. page 570/9th ed. pages 590–591).

4. **B** Ohm's law, $V = IR$, applies in this situation. Because V is the same, then $(2A)R_1 = (1A)R$ and $\mathbf{R_1} = \mathbf{R/2}$. (*College Physics* 8th ed. page 576/9th ed. pages 596–597).

5. **B** The 4-Ω and 8-Ω resistors are in series, and they function as a 12-Ω resistor. The 12-Ω resistor is in parallel with the 6-Ω resistor,

and their sum is 12 Ω/3 Ω = **4 Ω** (*College Physics* 8th ed. pages 600–601/9th ed. pages 624–625).

6. **C** Power is the rate at which energy is delivered to a resistor. By definition, $P = W/t$, and the work done is $W = q\,\Delta V$. We can write $P = q\,\Delta V/t$, and because Ohm's law is $\Delta V = IR$, power can then be expressed as $P = I\,\Delta V = I^2 R$, or $\mathbf{P = \Delta V^2/R}$ (*College Physics* 8th ed. page 581/9th ed. page 601).

7. **D** Charge moves in an electrical conductor as long as there is a potential difference between the ends of the conductor (*College Physics* 8th ed. page 574/9th ed. page 595).

8. **D** A device that maintains a potential difference between two points is a source of emf. A battery converts chemical energy into electrical energy. The terminal voltage across the battery is equal to the emf when (1) no current is drawn from the battery or (2) the internal resistance is negligible when it is delivering current (*College Physics* 8th ed. pages 594–595/9th ed. pages 616–617).

9. **C** The resistors are in series, and the current is the same everywhere (*College Physics* 8th ed. page 595/9th ed. page 617).

10. **B** An ammeter is a device that measures the electrical current without appreciably altering it. It reads the current entering or leaving a resistor; therefore, it must be in series with the resistor. A voltmeter has a large resistance and will not greatly alter the current in the resistance if it is placed in parallel with the resistor (*College Physics* 8th ed. pages 574–575/9th ed. pages 595–596).

11. **E** Resistance is directly proportional to the length, and $R = f(L)$ is linear with a positive slope and zero intercept (*College Physics* 8th ed. pages 577–578/9th ed. pages 597–599).

12. **C** The terminal voltage of a source of emf is given by $\Delta V = \mathcal{E} - Ir$. The voltage ΔV is maximum when $Ir = 0$. Therefore, either no current is drawn from the battery or the internal resistance is negligible when it is delivering current (*College Physics* 8th ed. pages 594–595/9th ed. pages 616–617).

13. **B** Ohm's law is $V = IR$. Using SI units, $1\text{ V} = 1\,\Omega \times 1\text{ A}$, $1\text{ V} = 1\text{ J/C}$, and $1\text{ A} = 1\text{ C/s}$, making the ohm unit (J/C)/(C/s), which yields $\mathbf{1\ \Omega} = \mathbf{J \cdot s/C^2}$ (*College Physics* 8th ed. pages 536, 570, 576/9th ed. pages 552, 591, 596).

14. **A** Resistance in series is additive. Thus, $2(10\ \Omega) + 4(20\ \Omega) = 100\ \Omega$. Then $V = IR$, so $\mathbf{I = 0.24\ A}$ (*College Physics* 8th ed. pages 594–595/9th ed. pages 617–620).

15. **B** Terminal voltage is defined as $V_t = \mathcal{E} - Ir$. Upon substitution, $V_t = 6.0V - (1.0\text{ A})(0.5\ \Omega)$, or $\mathbf{V_t = 5.5\ V}$ (*College Physics* 8th ed. pages 594–595/9th ed. pages 616–617).

FREE-RESPONSE PROBLEMS

1. (a) Ohm's law for a circuit is written as $\varepsilon = I \Sigma R$. Before we find the current issued by the battery, we need the total resistance of the entire circuit. Resistors R_1 and R_2 are in parallel with respect to each other, and their combined resistance, R_{ab}, is

$$R_{ab} = \frac{1}{1/R_1 + 1/R_2} = \frac{1}{1/12\ \Omega + 1/4\ \Omega} = \frac{1}{1/12\ \Omega + 3/12\ \Omega} = \frac{1}{4/12\ \Omega} = \frac{12}{4}\ \Omega = 3\ \Omega$$

where R_{ab}, R_3, R_4, and the internal resistance r of the battery are all in series and the total or equivalent resistance, ΣR, of the entire circuit is then $\Sigma R = R_{ab} + R_3 + R_4 + r = 3\ \Omega + 8\ \Omega + 22\ \Omega + 0.50\ \Omega = 33.5\ \Omega$. From Ohm's law:

$$I = \frac{\varepsilon}{\Sigma R} = \frac{12.0\ V}{33.5\ \Omega} = \textbf{0.36 A}$$

(b) By definition, the terminal voltage is $V_t = \varepsilon - Ir = 12.0\ V - (0.36\ A)(0.5\ \Omega) = \textbf{11.82 V}$.

(c) Resistors R_1 and R_2 are in parallel, and their equivalent resistance, R_{ab}, is known from part (a). Each resistor in parallel suffers the same voltage drop V_{ab}, and that is given from Ohm's law: $V_{ab} = IR_{ab} = (0.36\ A)(3\ \Omega) = 1.08\ V$. The same current enters the parallel branch at junction a then splits into currents I_1 and I_2. The current I_1 through resistor R_1 is

$$I_1 = \frac{V_{ab}}{R_1} = \frac{1.08\ V}{12\ \Omega} = \textbf{0.09 A}$$

The current I_2 through resistor R_2 is

$$I_2 = \frac{V_{ab}}{R_2} = \frac{1.08\ V}{4\ \Omega} = \textbf{0.27 A}$$

(d) The power output of a battery with internal resistance can be found by $P_{out} = IV_t = (0.36\ A)(11.82\ V) = \textbf{4.26 W}$.

ALTERNATE SOLUTION TO PART (D)

The power output of a seat of emf is $P_{out} = I\varepsilon = (0.36\ A)(12.0\ V) = 4.32\ W$. An internal resistance r dissipates some of the energy produced by the battery into heat, however. The internal resistance uses up some of the power output, and that amount is $P = IV = I(Ir) = I^2r = (0.36\ A)^2(0.50\ \Omega) = 0.065\ W$. The actual power output of the battery is then $P_{out} = 4.32\ W - 0.065\ W = \textbf{4.26 W}$.

(e) Voltmeters are placed in parallel with resistance, so V_4 will read the drop in voltage across resistor R_4. By Ohm's law, $V_4 = IR_4 = (0.36\ A)(22.0\ \Omega) = \textbf{7.92 V}$.

(*College Physics* 8th ed. pages 595–603/9th ed. pages 617–625)

2. (a) First, determine the equivalent resistance, R_{eq}, of the entire circuit. Starting with the parallel bank,

$$R_{ab} = \frac{1}{1/R_1 + 1/R_2 + 1/R_3} = \frac{1}{1/18\ \Omega + 1/18\ \Omega + 1/18\ \Omega} = \frac{1}{3/18\ \Omega} = \frac{18\ \Omega}{3} = 6\ \Omega$$

The remainder of the circuit is in series, and $R_{eq} = R_{ab} + R_4 + R_5 = 6\ \Omega + 8\ \Omega + 4\ \Omega = 18\ \Omega$. So, from Ohm's law, $\mathcal{E} = IR_{eq} = (2.4\ \text{A})(18\Omega) = \textbf{43.2 V}$.

(b) The IR drop across ab is found by $V_{ab} = IR_{ab} = (2.4\ \text{A})(6\ \Omega) = 14.4\ \text{V}$, and across cd, it is found by $V_{cd} = IR_4 = (2.4\ \text{A})(8\ \Omega) = 19.2\ \text{V}$. Therefore, between junctions a and d, it is $V_{ad} = V_{ab} + V_{cd} = 14.4\ \text{V} + 19.2\ \text{V} = \textbf{33.6 V}$.

(c) The power loss across $R_4 = R_{cd}$ is $P_{cd} = I^2 R_{cd} = (2.4\ \text{A})^2 (8\ \Omega) = \textbf{46.1 W}$.

(*College Physics* 8th ed. pages 595–603/9th ed. pages 617–625)

13

THE MAGNETIC FIELD

MAGNETS AND MAGNETISM

(*College Physics* 8th ed. pages 626–630/9th ed. pages 648–652)

The forces magnets exert on one another are rather complicated. Sometimes they attract one another, and sometimes they repel. Most magnets have two ends, which are called the north-seeking pole, N-pole, and the south-seeking pole, S-pole, because the north end always points toward the north magnetic pole of the Earth when magnets are suspended and allowed to rotate freely. These poles behave somewhat like electric charges; that is, like poles repel, and unlike poles attract.

But there is no other resemblance. Magnets cannot be broken into a single N-pole and into a single S-pole. No one has ever observed a magnetic monopole. Unlike electric charge, which is strictly conserved, magnets can be created and destroyed. If a permanent magnet is heated above a certain critical temperature, the Curie temperature, it loses all of its magnetic properties and behaves like an ordinary piece of iron. Placing a piece of iron into contact with a strong permanent magnet gives the piece of iron weak magnetic properties. Magnetism is a property that can be acquired or lost without regard to conservation laws.

Magnetism is an interaction between moving electric charges. Electric charges create electric fields, but only moving electric charges create magnetic fields. The magnetic field is in addition to the electric field. The charge has an electric field whether the charge is moving or not.

Magnets affect the space around them. Space is modified into a magnetic field that we can call a **B**-field. Magnetic fields have vector properties, they have an intensity **B** and a direction in space. Just as electric field lines are useful in describing electric fields, magnetic flux lines are useful for visualizing the magnetic field. Magnetic flux is defined as leaving the N-pole of a magnet and entering the S-pole. Unlike electric field lines, magnetic flux lines do not have origins and end points—they form continuous loops.

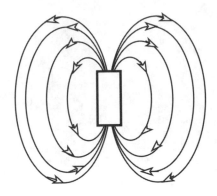

FORCE ON A MOVING CHARGE

(*College Physics* 8th ed. pages 630–633/9th ed. pages 652–655)

All moving charged particles generate a magnetic field. Electrons in atoms move in some fashion in atomic orbitals. Even the electron itself spins, giving it magnetic properties.

Consider a charged particle, q, moving through a magnetic field in a region in space where there is no electric field. The charge will experience a magnetic force, F_B. This force is dependent on several variables, including the charge q of the particle and its speed and its direction.

At any point in space in a magnetic field there is one particular direction in which the charge can move so that the force acting on it is zero, regardless of the speed. The relationship between the magnitude of charge q, its velocity v, the strength of the **B**-field and the magnetic force F_B acting on the charge is

$$F_B = qvB\sin\theta$$

Charge q is a scalar quantity, velocity **v** is a vector, the magnetic field **B** is a vector and the force F_B is also a vector. The angle θ is the angle between **v** and **B**. When $\theta = 0°$ or $180°$, $\sin 0° = 0$ making **v** and **B** parallel, the magnetic force on the charge is zero.

The SI unit of magnetic field, **B**, is the tesla, T, and it is defined as

$$1\,T = 1\,N/(C \cdot m/s) = 1\,N/A \cdot m$$

Note: The tesla is not a fundamental unit. It is related to the newton, the ampere, and the meter. The newton and the ampere are in turn related to the fundamental units of length, mass, time, and charge.

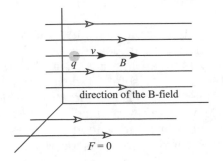

Motion in any other direction will always produce a force. When $\theta = 90°$, sin 90° = 1, making **v** and **B** perpendicular, and the magnetic force is a maximum at

$$F_B = qvB$$

The direction of magnetic force on a positive charge that is moving perpendicular to the plane of the velocity vector **v** and the magnetic field vector **B** is found by the *right-hand charge rule: the right hand is open and the thumb points in the direction of the magnetic force. The fingers point in the direction of the velocity and the palm of the hand points in the direction of the magnetic field.* For a negative charge the direction of the force vector is reversed.

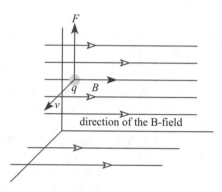

direction of the B-field

AP Tip

Since the magnetic force F_B is perpendicular to the velocity vector **v**, it is a purely deflecting force. It changes the direction of **v** and not the speed. Because there cannot be a component of magnetic force along the motion, there is no tangential acceleration. *No work can be done on the moving charge q by the B-field and no change in energy can take place.*

SAMPLE PROBLEM 1
A proton of charge $q = +e$, mass 1.67×10^{-27} kg and speed $v = 2.9 \times 10^6$ m/s orbits in a magnetic field of $B = 1.5$ T directed into the page.
   (a) What is the radius of the orbit?
   (b) Find the force the magnetic field exerts on the particle.

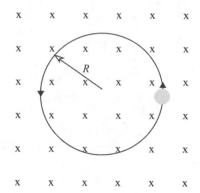

SOLUTION TO PROBLEM 1

(a) The magnetic force provides the centripetal force to the orbiting particle.

$$F_B = \frac{mv^2}{R} = qvB$$

Solving for R:

$$R = \frac{mv}{qB} = \frac{\left(1.67 \times 10^{-27}\,kg\right)\left(2.9 \times 10^6\,m/s\right)}{\left(1.5\,T\right)\left(1.60 \times 10^{-19}\,C\right)} = 0.02\,m$$

(b) The magnetic force is

$$F_B = qvB = (1.60 \times 10^{-19}\,C)(2.9 \times 10^6\,m/s)(1.5\,T) = 7.0 \times 10^{-13}\,N$$

SAMPLE PROBLEM 2

A *velocity selector* is a device that is operated in vacuum and utilizes crossed **E**- and **B**-fields between a set of parallel-plate capacitors to select positively charged ions +q of only one velocity. The ions are projected into the perpendicular fields at varying speeds. Particles with velocities sufficient to make the magnetic force equal and opposite to the electric force pass through the slit undeflected. Slower moving ions will be deflected out of the plane of the page, while those with greater speed will be deflected into the page.

(a) Show that the speed of these particles is found from $v = \frac{E}{B}$.

(b) It is desired to have a beam of protons with a speed of 7.0×10^3 m/s. If $B = 0.25$ T, what is the strength of the electric field?

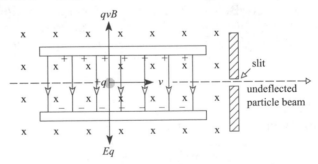

SOLUTION TO PROBLEM 2

(a) The upward force on +q is qvB by the right-hand charge rule. The downward force is qE. Equating the upward and downward forces:

$$qvB = qE \text{ and } v = \frac{E}{B}$$

(b) $E = vB = (7.0 \times 10^3$ m/s$)(0.25$ T$) = 1.8 \times 10^3$ N/C

In vacuum, the path of a charged particle moving in a magnetic field depends on the mass, charge, and velocity of the particle and on the magnetic field intensity. If a beam of positively charged ions all having the same velocity and charge is projected into a uniform magnetic field and is perpendicular to the field, the ions will be bent into a circular path dependent upon their mass. Those ions with smaller mass will move in a path with a smaller radius than more massive ions with the same charge. This is the principle of the *mass spectrograph,* a device used to separate ions of a given element into groups according to the mass of the ions. The diagram represents the two major parts of a mass spectrograph.

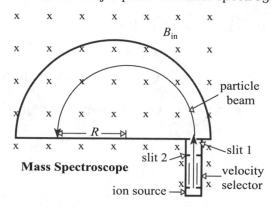

The first part is the ion source and velocity selector. The velocity selector is also referred to as a velocity filter. The ion source produces a beam of ions of varying velocities. The beam is directed into the velocity selector with crossed **E**- and **B**-fields. The **B**-field across the velocity selector is a secondary **B**-field to the primary field of the spectrograph. With the proper **E** and secondary **B,** across the velocity selector, only ions with a velocity $v = \dfrac{E}{B_s}$ will enter slit 2 and then through slit 1 into the mass spectrograph.

The second part of the mass spectrograph is the portion that separates ions of equal velocity and charge according to differences in mass. The beam of ions enters a D-shaped chamber between the poles of an electromagnet that produces the primary **B**-field of intensity B. Within the chamber, the ions move in a semicircular path of radius R under the influence of the **B**-field.

The magnetic field exerts centripetal force on each ion of mass m.

$$F_C = \frac{mv^2}{R} = qvB$$

and the mass of the ion is

$$m = \frac{BqR}{v}$$

SAMPLE PROBLEM 3

Ions of charge $q = +e$ are produced in the ion source of a mass spectrograph operated with a primary **B**-field of 0.40 T. The ion beam is directed into the velocity selector of Sample Problem 2 and then emerges with a velocity of 7.0×10^3 m/s. The ions enter the mass spectrograph where they travel a semicircular path of radius 7.2×10^{-3} m. Calculate the mass of one of these ions.

Solution to Problem 3

The charge of an ion is $q = +e = +1.60 \times 10^{-19}$ C and the mass is found by

$$m = \frac{BqR}{v} = \frac{(0.40 \text{ T})(1.60 \times 10^{-19} \text{ C})(7.2 \times 10^{-3} \text{ m})}{7.0 \times 10^3 \text{ m}/\text{s}} = 6.6 \times 10^{-26} \text{ kg}$$

Force in a Current-Carrying Wire

(*College Physics* 8th ed. pages 633–636/9th ed. pages 655–658)

The charge carriers in a wire under a potential difference are constrained to travel inside the conductor. When the charges are so constrained, the transverse force on them due to an external magnetic field is transmitted to the conductor.

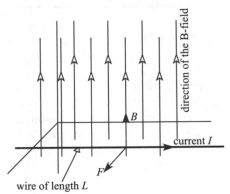

The magnetic force the wire experiences in the **B**-field is related to the current I, the length L of the segment of wire exposed to the field, and the intensity B of the field as

$$F_B = ILB$$

In the event that L makes an angle θ with the field, the relationship becomes

$$F_B = ILB \sin \theta$$

Sample Problem 4

A wire connected across a potential difference carries a current $I = 2.4$ A. The wire is inserted into a magnetic field at a right angle to the field of **B** = 0.5 T, which is directed into the page. If a length, $L = 0.5$ m is exposed to the field as illustrated, what force acts on the wire?

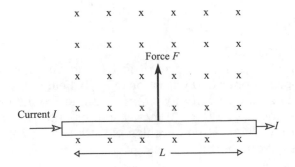

SOLUTION TO PROBLEM 4

By the right-hand charge rule, the **B**-field exerts an upward force on the wire segment. The magnitude of the force is

$$F_B = ILB = (2.4 \text{ A})(0.5 \text{ m})(0.5 \text{ T}) = \textbf{0.6 N upward}$$

MAGNETIC FIELD OF A LONG STRAIGHT CURRENT-CARRYING WIRE

(*College Physics* 8th ed. pages 642–646/9th ed. pages 664–667)

The magnetic lines of force near a current-carrying wire are in the form of concentric circles. The relationship between the direction of the magnetic field and the direction of the current in the wire is given by the _right-hand current rule_: *when a wire is grasped by the right hand in such a way that the thumb points in the direction of the current, the fingers encircle the wire in the same sense as the magnetic field.*

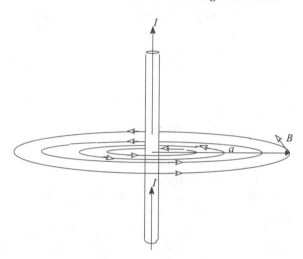

The magnitude of the **B**-field at a point near a long current-carrying wire is proportional to the current I, carried in the wire and is inversely proportional to the perpendicular distance, a, from the point to the center of the wire. The expression is written as

$$B = k_B \frac{I}{a}$$

Here k_B is a constant of proportionality. In the SI, the unit of the magnetic field strength, B, is the tesla, T. The tesla can be defined by taking the constant k_B to be exactly 2×10^{-7} T · m/A. This constant is usually written as $k_B = \frac{\mu_o}{2\pi}$, and μ_0 is called the magnetic permeability of free space. Its value is $\mu_o = 4\pi \times 10^{-7}$ T·m/A. $B = k_B \frac{I}{a}$ now becomes

$$B = \frac{\mu_o I}{2\pi a}$$

The gauss, G, is a common unit of the magnetic field strength. It is related to the tesla by 1 T = 10^4 G *or* 1 G = 10^{-4} T.

SAMPLE PROBLEM 5

A 2.00 m long, 1.20 mm diameter wire having a resistivity of $1.50 \times 10^{-6} \Omega \cdot m$ is connected to a 12.0 V battery. What is the magnitude of the **B**-field at a perpendicular distance of 1.0 cm from the center of the wire?

SOLUTION TO PROBLEM 5

First, we have to find the resistance of the wire and the current in the wire. Resistance is related to resistivity by

$$R = \rho \frac{L}{A} = \frac{\rho L}{\pi r^2} = \frac{\left(1.50 \times 10^{-6} \Omega \cdot m\right)\left(2.00 \text{ m}\right)}{\pi \left(0.060 \times 10^{-3} \text{m}\right)^2} = 2.65 \ \Omega$$

The current is found by using Ohm's law:

$$I = \frac{V}{R} = \frac{12.0 \text{ V}}{2.65 \Omega} = 4.52 \text{ A}$$

Now, the magnetic field strength 1.0 cm from the wire is

$$B = \frac{\mu_o I}{2\pi a} = \frac{\left(4\pi \times 10^{-7} \text{ T m}/\text{A}\right)\left(4.52 \text{ A}\right)}{2\pi \left(0.01 \text{ m}\right)} = \mathbf{9.0 \times 10^{-5} \text{ T}}$$

SAMPLE PROBLEM 6

Two parallel wires of length 1.0 m are 8.0 cm apart and carry respective currents of $I_1 = 8.0$ A and $I_2 = 6.0$ A.
  (a) Determine the magnetic force on wire 2 due to wire 1 when the currents are parallel.
  (b) Calculate the magnetic force on wire 2 due to wire 1 when the currents are antiparallel.

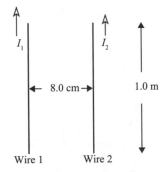

SOLUTION TO PROBLEM 6

  (a) First find the **B**-field at the position of wire 2 due to wire 1. The right-hand current rule indicates B at the position of wire 2 is directed into the page. The magnitude of B is then

$$B = \frac{\mu_o I}{2\pi r} = \frac{\left(4\pi \times 10^{-7} \text{T} \cdot \text{m/A}\right)\left(8.0 \text{ A}\right)}{2\pi \left(0.08 \text{ m}\right)} = \mathbf{2.0 \times 10^{-5} \text{ T}}$$

The force on the 1.0 m length of wire 2 is then
$F_M = ILB \sin \theta = (6.0 \text{ A})(1.0 \text{ m})(2.0 \times 10^{-5} \text{ T})(\sin 90°) = \mathbf{1.2 \times 10^{-4} \text{ N}}$
to the left

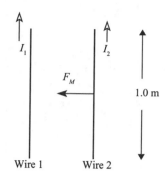

(b) The current in wire 2 is reversed, but the force will have the same magnitude and the opposite direction.

$F_M = 1.2 \times 10^{-4}$ N to the right

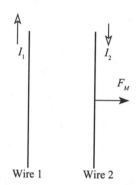

MAGNETIC FIELD AT THE CENTER OF A COIL

(*College Physics* 8th ed. pages 646–650/9th ed. pages 669–673)

The magnetic field produced by a current-carrying wire is greatly increased if the wire is wound into a circular coil with many turns. The magnetic field created by a flat coil carrying current I is complex as shown here.

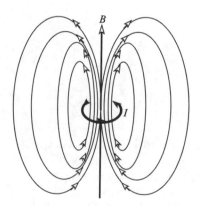

For a flat circular coil of n turns and radius a, we can calculate the **B**-field at the very center of the coil, and it is

$$B = \frac{\mu_o nI}{2a}$$

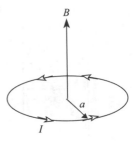

SAMPLE PROBLEM 7

A flat circular coil of 10 turns of wire has a radius of 4.0 cm. Determine the **B**-field at the center of the coil when a current of 4.0 A is circulated through the coil.

SOLUTION TO PROBLEM 7

$$B = \frac{\mu_o nI}{2a} = \frac{\left(4\pi \times 10^{-7}\,\text{T·m/A}\right)(10)(4.0\,\text{A})}{2(0.04\,\text{m})} = 6.3 \times 10^{-4}\,\text{T}$$

MAGNETIC FIELD OF A SOLENOID

(*College Physics* 8th ed. pages 646–649/9th ed. pages 670–672)

The solenoid is a helix, a long tube of many turns of wire *N*. The word *solenoid* itself stems from the Greek and means "tube."

The ideal parallel-plate capacitor has many uses, but two of its major uses are that a uniform electric field can be established between the plates and that electrical energy is stored in the field. The ideal solenoid will maintain a uniform magnetic field between its ends and will store magnetic energy in the field.

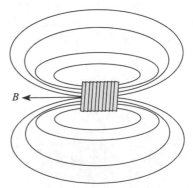

Solenoids are found in doorbells, speaker systems, TVs, computers, and relays that control furnaces and air conditioners. The MRI used in medical centers is a giant solenoid.

The magnetic field *B* established in a solenoid that is circulating current *I* through the *N* turns of wire is found by the equation

$$B = \frac{\mu_o NI}{L}$$

We can define the number of turns per unit length as $n = \frac{N}{L}$.

Then we can write $B = \mu_o nI$.

SAMPLE PROBLEM 8

A 0.4 m long solenoid has 1600 turns. The magnetic field at the center of the solenoid is $B = 0.05$ T. What current circulates through the wrappings of the solenoid?

SOLUTION TO PROBLEM 8

From the solenoid equation, $B = \dfrac{\mu_o NI}{L}$, we write the current as being

$$I = \frac{BL}{\mu_o N} = \frac{(0.05\text{ T})(0.4\text{ m})}{(4\pi \times 10^{-7}\text{ T}\cdot\text{m/A})(1600)} = \textbf{10 A}$$

FARADAY'S LAW OF INDUCTION

(*College Physics* 8th ed. pages 663–676/9th ed. pages 688–701)

Michael Faraday discovered magnetic induction, the creation of an electric field by a magnetic field. Magnetic induction ranks with electromagnetism as one of the fundamental principles on which our modern technology is based. Electromagnetism provides the means by which electric energy can be converted into mechanical work; magnetic induction provides the means by which mechanical work can be converted into electric energy. All of our electric power comes from generators that operate on the principle of magnetic induction.

The magnetic flux ϕ_M through a loop of wire is defined as the product of the magnetic field that penetrates the loop and the area penetrated, or

$$\phi_M = BA$$

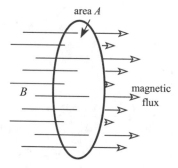

Faraday's law of magnetic induction states that when magnetic flux through a loop changes by an amount $\Delta\phi_M$ in a time period Δt, the emf induced in the loop during time period Δt is

$$\mathcal{E} = -\frac{\Delta\phi_M}{\Delta t}$$

When a conductor moves through a magnetic field and experiences a change in magnetic flux, the induced emf is called *motional emf*. For **N** loops, we write Faraday's law as

$$\mathcal{E} = -N\frac{\Delta\phi_M}{\Delta t}$$

The SI unit of magnetic flux ϕ_M is the weber, Wb, and it is defined as 1 Wb = 1 T·m².

SAMPLE PROBLEM 9

Imagine a moving conductor of length $L = 0.2$ m sliding along a stationary conducting loop with a velocity $v = 2.0$ m/s. The loop, as shown, contains a resistor $R = 4.0$ Ω. The **B**-field has an intensity **B** = 0.5 T and is directed into the page. As the conductor slides to the right, the magnetic flux penetrating the loop increases as the area of the loop increases. An emf is induced in the loop as a result of this motion, and a current is also induced in the circuit.

(a) Calculate the magnitude of the motional emf.

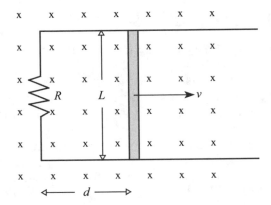

(b) What current is induced in the loop?

(c) What is the direction of this current?

SOLUTION TO PROBLEM 9

(a) The magnitude of the induced motional emf is

$$|\mathcal{E}| = \frac{\Delta\phi_M}{\Delta t} = \frac{\Delta(BA)}{\Delta t}$$

B is constant and

$$|\mathcal{E}| = \frac{\Delta(BA)}{\Delta t} = \frac{B\Delta A}{\Delta t} = \frac{B\Delta(Ld)}{\Delta t}$$

The length of the conductor L is constant and

$$|\mathcal{E}| = BL\frac{\Delta d}{\Delta t} = BLv = (0.5 \text{ T})(0.2 \text{ m})(2.0 \text{ m/s}) = \textbf{0.2 V}$$

(b) The current is found by using Ohm's law:

$$I = \frac{\mathcal{E}}{R} = \frac{0.2 \text{ V}}{4.0 \text{ Ω}} = \textbf{5} \times \textbf{10}^{-2} \textbf{ A}$$

(c) The direction of the induced emf and the direction of any resulting induced current is determined by Lenz's law:
The direction of the induced emf is such as to oppose the change in magnetic flux that causes the induced emf.

The induced current is counterclockwise.
The words *change* and *flux* are very important. Consider the word *change*. Lenz's law says that when the flux is increasing, the induced emf tries to make it decrease; when flux is decreasing, the induced emf tries to make it increase. Note that Lenz's law does not say the induced emf opposes the magnetic *field*, but rather it says induced emf opposes the *change* in magnetic *flux*.

AP Tip

If the magnitude of the flux through a circuit is *increasing*, the induced **B**-field is in the *opposite* direction of the primary field. If the magnitude of the flux through a circuit is *decreasing*, the induced field is in the *same* direction as the primary field.

Lenz's law is required by the law of conservation of energy.

THE MAGNETIC FIELD: STUDENT OBJECTIVES FOR THE AP EXAM

- You should know and be able to apply the expression used for the magnitude of the magnetic field.
- You should know that force, velocity, and magnetic field intensity are all vector quantities that are mutually perpendicular to one another.
- You should be able to apply the right-hand rule for a positive charge to determine the direction of the unknown parameter when the other two are known.
- You should be able to state and apply the equation for the magnetic force on a moving conductor.
- You should be able to relate the magnetic force on a moving charge in a magnetic field that causes the particle to alter its direction of travel to the centripetal force and to evaluate the equations to solve for any unknown parameter either mathematically or by diagram.
- You should know and be able to apply the second right-hand rule to the direction of the magnetic field produced by a long straight wire carrying a current.
- You should be able to calculate the magnitude and direction of the **B**-field produced in a closed loop.
- You should know and be able to apply Faraday's and Lenz's laws for the magnitude and direction of the induced emf or current in closed loops.
- You should be able to draw or explain graphs involving changes in magnetic flux or induced emf as a function of time.
- You must be able to solve multiple-choice questions without a calculator.

MULTIPLE-CHOICE QUESTIONS

1. Magnetic field lines produced by a long straight wire carrying a current are
    (A) in the same direction as the current.
    (B) opposite to the direction of the current.
    (C) concentric circles around the wire.
    (D) radially outward from the wire.
    (E) radially inward toward the wire.

2. A horizontal straight wire carrying a large current from east to west is placed over a magnetic compass. The end of the needle marked **N** will
    (A) point north.
    (B) point south.
    (C) point east.
    (D) point west.
    (E) keep rotating in a circle.

3. If a constant current is sent through a helical coil of length L, the coil will
    (A) become shorter.
    (B) become longer.
    (C) oscillate along its central axis.
    (D) rotate about a central axis.
    (E) produce zero magnetic field at its center.

4. At a given instant, an electron is moving in the positive x direction in a uniform magnetic field directed in the positive z direction. When viewed from a point on the positive z axis, the subsequent motion of the electron is
    (A) along the x axis.
    (B) counterclockwise around a circle in the xy plane.
    (C) clockwise around a circle in the xy plane.
    (D) in the positive z direction.
    (E) in the negative z direction.

5. Why doesn't a constant uniform magnetic field do work on a moving charged particle?
    (A) Magnetic fields are conservative fields.
    (B) Magnetic force is velocity dependent.
    (C) Magnetic fields are vector fields, and work is a scalar quantity.
    (D) Magnetic fields are scalar fields, and work is a vector quantity.
    (E) Magnetic force is always perpendicular to the velocity of the particle.

6. Increasing the number of turns of wire in a coil placed in a region of changing magnetic field, while making no other changes,
    (A) establishes an equilibrium.
    (B) maintains a steady-state system.
    (C) does not change the emf in the system.
    (D) causes an increase in the induced emf.
    (E) causes a decrease in the induced emf.

7. A negatively charged particle enters a uniform magnetic field that is perpendicular to the particle's velocity. Which of the following is true of the particle's kinetic energy and direction?

Kinetic Energy	Direction of Particle
(A) Increases	Changes
(B) Decreases	Changes
(C) Stays the same	Changes
(D) Stays the same	Stays the same
(E) Increases	Stays the same

8. A bar magnet is pushed through a flat coil of wire. The induced emf is greatest when the
(A) north pole is pushed through first.
(B) magnet is pushed through rapidly.
(C) magnet is pushed through slowly.
(D) south pole is pushed through first.
(E) magnet is at equilibrium with the coil.

9. The fundamental SI unit for the magnetic field is the
(A) gauss.
(B) newton/ampere.
(C) ampere meter.
(D) tesla.
(E) ohm meter.

10. The law providing the statement that an induced current is in such a direction as to oppose the change producing it is attributed to
(A) Gauss.
(B) Coulomb.
(C) Ampère.
(D) Maxwell.
(E) Lenz.

11. An electrical current can be induced in a closed circuit without the use of a battery or other electrical power supply by moving the circuit through
(A) an electrical field.
(B) a magnetic field.
(C) a gravitational field.
(D) a coulombic field.
(E) a Gaussian field.

12. The region in space surrounding a moving electron contains
(A) a gravitational field only.
(B) a magnetic field only.
(C) an electric field only.
(D) both an electric and a magnetic field.
(E) neither an electric nor a magnetic field.

13. The phenomenon of magnetism is best understood in terms of
(A) the existence of magnetic poles.
(B) magnetic fields associated with the movement of charged particles.
(C) force fields between electrons and nuclei.
(D) electric fields.
(E) flux lines.

14. Each of the positive ions that pass through crossed electric and magnetic fields without being deflected have the same
    (A) speed.
    (B) mass.
    (C) momentum.
    (D) energy.
    (E) potential.

15. The magnetic flux through a 100-turn coil changes uniformly from a constant 0.01 Wb to 0.05 Wb in 2.0 s. The magnitude of the induced emf during this time is
    (A) 0.5 V.
    (B) 1.0 V.
    (C) 2.0 V.
    (D) 2.5 V.
    (E) 5.0 V.

FREE-RESPONSE PROBLEMS

1. Each electron in a beam of electrons travels with the same velocity of 1.50×10^7 cm/s. The beam is bent 90° through an arc length $s = 4.25$ mm by a uniform magnetic field perpendicular to the beam path.

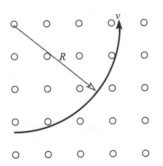

   (a) What is the magnetic field strength?
   (b) How much time is required for an electron to travel through the 90° arc?
   (c) What centripetal force does an electron experience in the magnetic field?
   (d) Through what potential difference were the electrons accelerated to acquire their velocity?

2. A square loop of wire 20.0 cm on a side enters a region in space where a magnetic field of 1.6 T is directed into the page and confined in a square of dimensions 70.0 cm by 70.0 cm. The loop of wire has a constant velocity $v = 10.0$ cm/s perpendicular to the **B** field as shown.

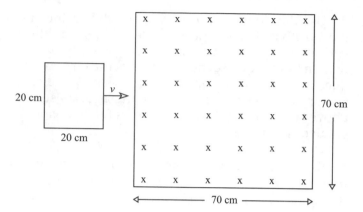

(a) i.   What is the direction of the current in the loop as it enters the field?
   ii.   What is the direction of the current in the loop as it leaves the field?
   iii. Justify your answers.
(b) i.   How long does it take the loop to enter the magnetic field once the right-hand side contacts the field?
   ii.   How long does the loop, once the right-hand side first contacts the field, spend in crossing the field?
   iii. How long does it take the loop to exit the field once the right-hand side reaches the edge of the field?
(c) What is the magnitude of the induced emf as it enters and leaves the **B**-field?
(d) Graph the emf as a function of time as the loop completely enters and completely emerges from the magnetic field.
(e) If the loop of wire has a resistance of 40.0 Ω, what is the magnitude of the induced current in the loop?
(f) Calculate the magnetic flux in the loop when it is completely immersed in the field.

ANSWERS

MULTIPLE-CHOICE QUESTIONS

1. **C**   Use the right-hand rule for the direction of the magnetic lines of force. The thumb is pointed in the direction of the current and the curl of the fingers show the field lines are concentric circles with the wire (*College Physics* 8th ed. pages 642–644/9th ed. pages 665–666).

2. **B**   Using the right-hand rule with your thumb pointed east to west, your circled fingers will point south (*College Physics* 8th ed. page 642/9th ed. page 665).

3. **A**   A constant current sent through a helical coil of some length *L* produces a strong and a fairly uniform magnetic field in its center (the field is weaker at the ends). One end of the coil behaves as the north end of a bar magnet and the other end behaves as the south end. The magnetic force between the ends will cause the coil to become shorter (*College Physics* 8th ed. pages 631, 640–641/9th ed. pages 653, 669–670).

4. **B** Use the right-hand rule with the thumb indicating the force on the positive charge, the extended fingers as the direction of the velocity vector, and the **B**-field indicated by the palm of the hand. Remember to reverse the direction of the force because the charge in question is negative. Since the force is perpendicular to the velocity vector, the electron will move counterclockwise when viewed from above (+z direction) (*College Physics* 8th ed. pages 631, 640–641/9th ed. pages 653, 662–664).

5. **E** Since the force is perpendicular to the velocity, it is perpendicular to the charge in linear displacement of the particle, $W = R\Delta(\cos \theta) = 0$ (*College Physics* 8th ed. page 631/9th ed. page 653).

6. **D** Faraday's law of magnetic induction indicates the emf induced is proportional to the number of turns (*College Physics* 8th ed. pages 666–667/9th ed. pages 691–692).

7. **C** Since the magnetic force on a charged particle is perpendicular to the velocity, no work is done by the force and thus there is no change in the kinetic energy. There is, however, a change in the direction of the charged particle. (*College Physics* 8th ed. pages 639–642/9th ed. pages 661–664).

8. **B** The induced emf given by Faraday's law relates the strength of the induced emf to the rate change in flux per unit time (*College Physics* 8th ed. pages 666–668/9th ed. pages 691–692).

9. **D** The tesla is the SI unit for the magnetic field. $1 \text{ T} = \dfrac{\text{N}}{\text{C} \cdot \dfrac{\text{m}}{\text{s}}}$, which can be written as $\dfrac{\text{N}}{\text{A} \cdot \text{m}}$. (An alternative form is to relate the tesla to a $\dfrac{\text{Wb}}{\text{m}^2}$ since **B** was initially defined as the magnetic flux/unit area.) (*College Physics* 8th ed. page 630/9th ed. page 653).

10. **E** Lenz's law explains the negative sign in Faraday's law. It is used to determine the direction the induced current will flow in a closed loop (*College Physics* 8th ed. pages 667, 674–676/9th ed. pages 692–695).

11. **B** Faraday's law of electromagnetic induction relates how an induced emf and a current are set up in a closed loop as long as there is relative motion between the magnet and the loop (*College Physics* 8th ed. pages 663–668/9th ed. pages 688–695).

12. **D** An electric field exists in a region of space surrounding a charged body. If the charge is moving, it also sets up a magnetic field (*College Physics* 8th ed. pages 505, 627, 642–643/9th ed. pages 522, 649, 664–665).

13. **B** We define the properties of a magnetic field at a point in space in terms of the magnetic force F_B exerted on a charge moving with some velocity v and the sine of the angle between the velocity and the magnetic field (*College Physics* 8th ed. pages 630–631/9th ed. pages 652–655).

14. **A** A velocity selector is a region in which the charged particles of a specific velocity pass undeflected. The electric field and the magnetic field are perpendicular to each other. $F_B = F_E$. Since $qvB = qE$, the velocity is found from $v = \dfrac{E}{B}$ (*College Physics* 8th ed. page 658/9th ed. page 682).

15. **C** The induced emf given by Faraday's law relates the strength of the induced emf to the rate change in flux per unit time (*College Physics* 8th ed. pages 666–668/9th ed. pages 691–694).

FREE-RESPONSE PROBLEMS

1.

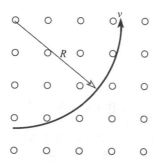

(a) To determine the strength of the magnetic field, we first need the radius of curvature, R, of the electron beam. Arc length s is related to radius by

$$s = \theta R \text{ and } \theta = 90° = \frac{\pi}{2}$$

then

$$R = \frac{s}{\theta} = \frac{4.25 \times 10^{-3}\,\text{m}}{\pi/2\ \text{rad}} = 2.71 \times 10^{-3}\,\text{m}$$

$$B = \frac{mv}{eR} = \frac{\left(9.11 \times 10^{-31}\,\text{kg}\right)\left(1.50 \times 10^{7}\,\text{m/s}\right)}{\left(1.60 \times 10^{-19}\,\text{C}\right)\left(2.71 \times 10^{-3}\,\text{m}\right)} = \mathbf{3.15 \times 10^{-2}\ T}$$

(b) The time period is

$$t = \frac{s}{v} = \frac{4.25 \times 10^{-3}\,\text{m}}{1.50 \times 10^{7}\,\text{m/s}} = \mathbf{2.83 \times 10^{-10}\ s}$$

(c) The magnetic field provides the centripetal force:

$$F_C = F_M = qvB = evB = \left(1.60 \times 10^{-19}\,\text{C}\right)\left(1.50 \times 10^{7}\,\text{m/s}\right)\left(3.15 \times 10^{-2}\,\text{T}\right) = \mathbf{7.56 \times 10^{-14}\ N}$$

(d) The potential difference is related to the kinetic energy by $Ve = \dfrac{1}{2}mv^2$.

Solving for V: $V = \dfrac{mv^2}{2e} = \dfrac{\left(9.11 \times 10^{-31}\,\text{kg}\right)\left(1.50 \times 10^7\,\text{m/s}\right)^2}{2\left(1.60 \times 10^{-19}\,\text{C}\right)} = \mathbf{640\ V}$

(*College Physics* 8th ed. pages 639–642/9th ed. pages 661–664)

2.

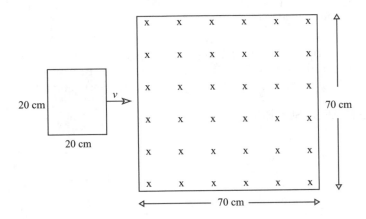

(a) i. Counterclockwise

ii. Clockwise

iii. Before the square loop enters the field, the flux through the loop is zero. As the loop enters the field, the flux increases until the left edge of the loop is just inside the field. The flux decreases to zero as the loop leaves the field.

Before the loop enters the field, no motional emf is induced in it because no field is present. As the right side of the square loop enters the magnetic field, the magnetic flux directed into the page increases. According to Lenz's law, the induced current is counterclockwise because it must produce a magnetic field directed out of the page. The motional emf, BLv, arises from the magnetic force experienced by the charge carriers in the right side of the loop.

Once the loop is entirely in the field, the change in the magnetic flux is zero. This happens because, once the left side of the loop enters the field, the motional emf induced in it cancels the motional emf present in the right-hand side of the loop.

As the right-hand side of the loop leaves the field, the flux inward begins to decrease, a clockwise current is induced, and the induced emf is $-BLv$. As soon as the left-hand side leaves the field, the emf decreases to zero.

(b) i. $v = \dfrac{x}{t}$ and $t = \dfrac{x}{v} = \dfrac{0.2\ \text{m}}{0.10\ \text{m/s}} = \mathbf{2.0\ s}$

ii. $t_{\text{total}} = \dfrac{L}{v} = \dfrac{0.70\ \text{m}}{0.10\ \text{m/s}} = \mathbf{7.0\ s}$

iii. $t = \dfrac{x}{v} = \dfrac{0.2 \text{ m}}{0.10 \text{ m/s}} = \textbf{2.0 s}$

(c) $\mathcal{E} = BLv = (1.6 \text{ T})(0.2 \text{ m})(0.1 \text{ m/s}) = \textbf{3.2} \times \textbf{10}^{-2} \textbf{ V}$

(d) Two seconds are required for the loop to completely enter the magnetic field. During that time period, an emf of 0.032 V is induced. From 2.0 to 5.0 s, there is no change in flux and no motional emf. Another two seconds is required for the loop to exit the field. During this interval, an emf of –0.032 V is induced. The graph should look the one shown here.

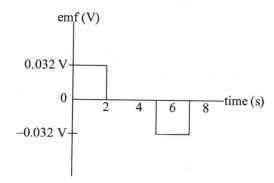

(e) Current is found by using Ohm's law:

$$I = \dfrac{\mathcal{E}}{R} = \dfrac{3.2 \times 10^{-2} \text{ V}}{40.0 \ \Omega} = \textbf{8.0} \times \textbf{10}^{-4} \textbf{ A}$$

(f) The magnetic flux in the loop when it is completely immersed in the field is

$$\phi_M = BA = (1.6 \text{ T})(4 \times 10^{-2} \text{ m}^2) = \textbf{6.4} \times \textbf{10}^{-2} \textbf{ Wb}$$

(*College Physics* 8th ed. pages 670–675/9th ed. pages 697–701)

14

WAVE MOTION

WHAT ARE THE PROPERTIES OF WAVES AND WHAT TYPES OF WAVES EXIST?

(*College Physics* 8th ed. pages 443–447/9th ed. pages 455–459)

Several of the most basic wave properties such as amplitude, frequency, and period were discussed in Chapter 8 (Oscillations & Gravitation); this chapter proceeds with further information about waves and also describes the effects of wave interference.

What is a wave? First, it is better to understand a *pulse*, which is a single disturbance in a medium (such as water, dirt, air, or a toy Slinky) that causes the particles in that medium to vibrate in a manner similar to simple harmonic motion. Once such a vibration occurs, energy is transferred and spread among the interconnecting particles of the medium, which allows the pulse to move (*propagate*). Eventually, the pulse dies out as it transfers all of its remaining energy to the medium. It is vital to understand that the *energy* of the pulse is being propagated, *not* the particles in the medium. The particles in the medium simply oscillate around an equilibrium position as the pulse passes. A water wave, for example, only causes the water molecules to move up and down as the pulse passes, and it is the energy (proportional to the pulse's amplitude) which is transported, not the water itself. A series of pulses sent at a constant rate constitutes a *periodic wave*.

Many waves are present in nature, but two basic wave types are categorized on both their appearance and the manner in which the particles of the medium oscillate to propagate the wave. The first is a *transverse* wave in which the particle oscillations are perpendicular (i.e., transverse) to the direction of motion of the wave. Take, for example, a common Slinky, a very soft coiled spring whose behavior can be used to represent a wave through nearly any medium. To see how the Slinky particles move, attach a small flag to a coil to represent a Slinky particle, as shown. Hold the Slinky firmly outstretched at both ends on a level floor and apply a quick impulse by the hand perpendicularly to the side of the Slinky to see that as the wave propagates, the flag moves side to side, or transverse to the motion of the pulse. To some extent, ocean waves and earthquake shear waves can serve as approximate examples of transverse waves.

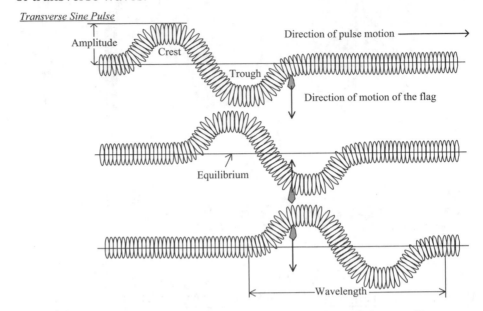

Transverse Sine Pulse

In contrast to a transverse wave, the particles of the medium may instead oscillate *along* the direction of motion of the wave itself, and this type of wave is termed a *longitudinal* wave. In the Slinky example, when the pulse is created along the Slinky by bunching up and releasing coils, the flag first moves in the direction of the pulse, but then as the pulse passes, the flag is forced back toward its equilibrium position by a restoring force (here, Hooke's law). As a result, the flag (or particle of the medium), oscillates around equilibrium. Sound is the most common type of longitudinal wave, as air particles act analogously to the coils of the spring, oscillating as the wave transfers energy, which is proportional to the amplitude (or loudness) of a sound wave. Regions where particles are bunched closely together are *compression* regions, while opposite locations where particles are spread out are regions of *rarefaction*.

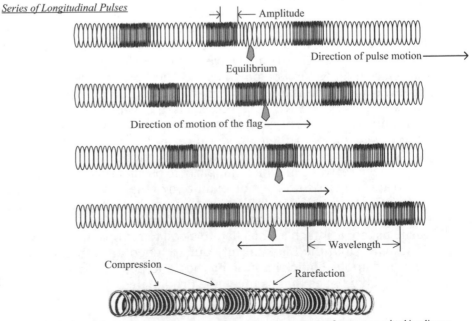

Series of Longitudinal Pulses

WHAT IS THE WAVE EQUATION?

(*College Physics* 8th ed. pages 443-447, 737–738/9th ed. pages 455–459, 767–768)

As outlined in the early portion of Chapter 8, primary features of waves include amplitude A, frequency f, period T, wavelength λ, and speed v. At this point, it is left to show the relation among f, T, v, and λ. Recall that $v = \dfrac{\Delta d}{\Delta t}$, where the distance Δd traveled by a single wave is its wavelength, λ, and the time Δt it takes for the wave to pass a certain point is equal to one wave period, T. Therefore, the wave speed v is $v = \dfrac{\Delta d}{\Delta t} = \dfrac{\lambda}{T} = \dfrac{\lambda}{\frac{1}{f}} = f\lambda$ or $v = f\lambda$. This relation holds for all types of waves: sound, light, transverse, longitudinal, and so on. Note that the *product* of frequency and wavelength remain constant for a fixed wave speed, which therefore implies that a reciprocal relationship exists between f and λ, such that a decrease in one causes a corresponding increase in the other so that their product (v) is constant. This is particularly important when studying the electromagnetic spectrum (i.e., light), as there exists a wide range of types of light whose characteristics are related to their frequency and wavelength.

$$v = f\lambda$$

As shall be discussed shortly, the speeds of waves in various materials depend on many characteristics of the material (e.g., temperature, elasticity, tension); however, the preceding wave equation will always hold true for a wave in a particular medium.

HOW DO WAVES INTERACT AT BOUNDARIES?

(*College Physics* 8th ed. pages 443–447/9th ed. pages 455–459, 462–463)

Predominantly, a wave traveling in a particular uniform medium can encounter either a *firm* or *fixed* boundary (such as an immovable hard barrier) or a *soft* or *free* boundary (such as a weakly composed material like a string). As anticipated, the most obvious behavior a wave experiences as it meets a new medium is reflection, in which part or all of the wave is returned toward its source (a more in-depth discussion of this as it applies to light is given in Chapter 16). Examples of this include sound or Slinky waves meeting a wall, light waves meeting a denser material, or a Slinky wave meeting a string connected to the Slinky.

How are the wave's characteristics affected by reflection? Imagine an overhead view of a long weak Slinky that is on a level floor and fixed to a clamp that is attached to an immobile wall (as shown). When a single transverse pulse is sent along the Slinky, some of the energy of the pulse is transmitted to the second material, as evidenced by seeing slight movement of the clamp (the same is easily shown when a student's firmly placed hand is substituted for the clamp). Since the pulse reflects, it too takes some of the initial energy back toward its source. With waves, the amount of energy transported by the wave is directly proportional to the square of the amplitude of the wave. Thus, since energy was transferred, the reflected wave's energy (and amplitude) have decreased. More importantly, a reflection from a fixed boundary produces an inverted pulse, shifted by 180° (often referred to as a *phase shift*). While the explanation for this is rather involved, it is primarily due to Newton's third law (action-reaction) in action between the Slinky particles and the firm boundary.

As for the speed of the reflected pulse, it remains unchanged because it is traveling the same medium, which depends solely on the properties of the medium. Additionally, since all the particles of the medium vibrate at the same rate (i.e., with the same frequency), the incident pulse has the same frequency as the reflected pulse. By the wave equation shown earlier, since the speed and frequency of the reflections are unchanged, their wavelengths are unchanged also.

Single Transverse Pulse Reflection at a Firm Boundary

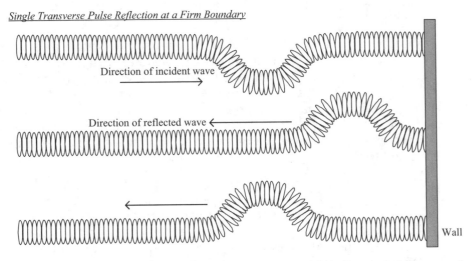

The single pulse reflecting from a firm barrier is straightforward, but the reflection of a sine or other periodic wave is somewhat more elaborate. As shown, when the trough meets the boundary first, it inverts and becomes a crest, and reflects first, while the wave's original crest inverts to a trough, and then follows the first reflection. Therefore, even though the phase of the reflected sine wave appears unchanged, it too has experienced a 180° phase shift relative to the incident wave.

Transverse Sine Wave Reflection at a Firm Boundary

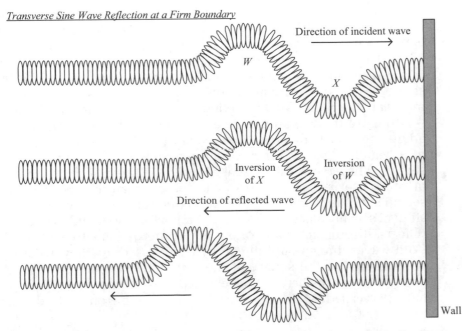

In contrast to reflections off firm barriers, a pulse reflecting from a soft or free boundary does not invert (i.e., there is no shift in phase of the wave). Imagine the Slinky now tied to a long string that is free to move easily. The fact that the string is not firmly fixed causes the pulse to reflect without a phase shift, but note the reflection's amplitude decreases, as shown. Additionally, notice that part of the original pulse is transmitted to the string with a greater amplitude, due in part to the lower density of the string.

Single Transverse Pulse Reflection at a Free Boundary

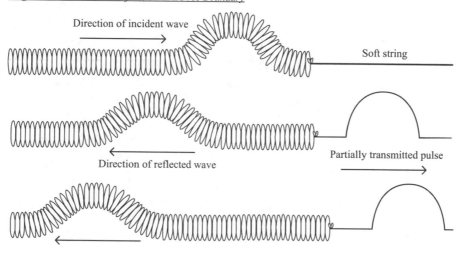

WHAT HAPPENS WHEN WAVES INTERFERE?

(*College Physics* 8th ed. pages 448–449/9th ed. pages 461–462)

The interference of waves is of huge importance in physics as all sorts of waves surround us in the physical world. When two or more waves meet in the same medium, the waves are said to *interfere*, a specific situation in which a new wave is temporarily formed; the new wave takes on the characteristics that are the net effect of the two individual waves. When parts of these waves combine to enhance each other, the interference is said to be *constructive*, but when parts cancel or destroy each other, the interference is *destructive*, as detailed later.

CONSTRUCTIVE INTERFERENCE

Consider two sine pulses of the same amplitude (+2 units, for example, as shown) that are moving in opposing directions in the same medium. As each pulse encounters the other, the two momentarily overlap such that a new pulse whose amplitude is the sum of the amplitudes of the individual pulses (namely, +4 units) is briefly formed. A moment later, the pulses will continue in their original directions. Similarly, this may occur if the pulses have different amplitudes; however, both must have either a trough or a crest to experience *constructive interference* ("CI" for short). The sum of the individual displacements of the waves combining to form a larger pulse is termed the *principle of superposition*.

The Principle of Superposition: When two waves interfere, the resulting displacement of the medium at any location is the algebraic sum of the displacements of the individual waves at that same location.

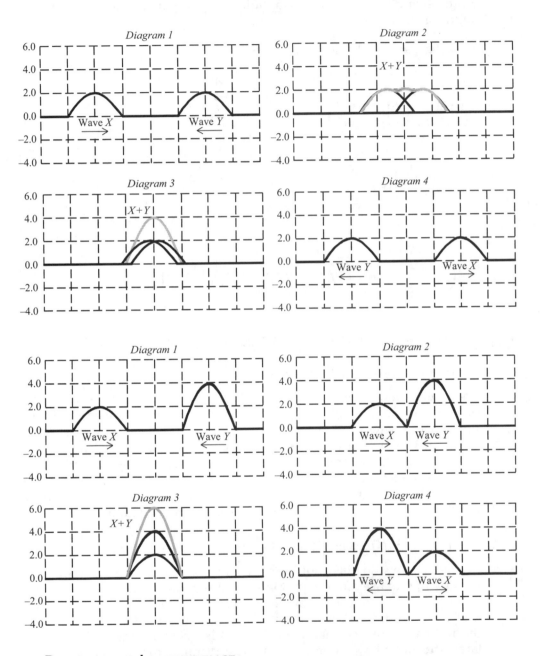

DESTRUCTIVE INTERFERENCE

In contrast to constructive interference, pulses with opposing displacements (such as one with a crest and one with a trough) that meet from opposing directions in the same medium will also superimpose, but they may cancel in places (again, by the principle of superposition). For example, as shown, wave X and wave Y approach each other from opposite directions, and each has the same amplitude (but that of X of –2 units). In Diagram 2, note that X and Y are just about over each other, meaning that, by the principle of superposition, their resultant amplitude is + 2 units + (–2 units), or zero. This means that the moment the pulses are vertically aligned, they completely cancel. During their superposition here (or, as shown by the second set of four diagrams, the *partial* cancellation of the pulses), the waves are said to be experiencing *destructive interference* (DI) simply because they are "destructive" to each other.

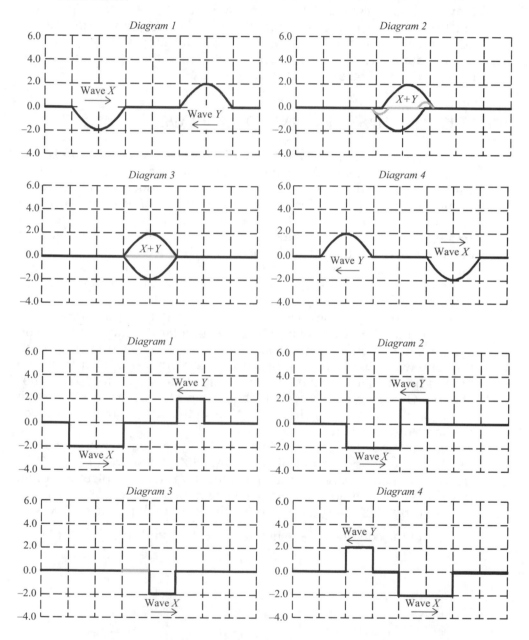

SAMPLE PROBLEM 1

Two traveling waves of equal frequency superimpose in the same medium. One wave has an amplitude of 10 cm and the other has an amplitude of 15 cm. Which of the following gives the best description of the amplitude A of the resultant wave?

(A) $5 \leq A \leq 25$
(B) $10 \leq A \leq 15$
(C) $A = 5$ cm
(D) $A = 15$ cm
(E) $A = 25$ cm

SOLUTION TO PROBLEM 1

In this problem, note there is no statement as to whether or not the amplitude values constitute troughs or crests in the wave. Therefore, if they are both crests, the maximum amplitude A of the resultant wave must be 10 cm + 15 cm or 25 cm. Similarly, if one is a trough and the other a crest, the magnitude of the maximum amplitude A would be 5 cm (from either −10 cm + 15 cm, or −15 cm + 10 cm). Therefore, the best answer is choice (A).

WHAT IS THE PHASE OF POINTS ON A WAVE?

An important matter to bear in mind when working with problems dealing with wave interference is the relative location of parts of one particular wave. For example, compare the first four diagrams shown in the Constructive Interference section with those in the Destructive Interference section and notice that those in the first set depict two crests about to interfere. Both crests are said to be *in phase* as they depict points with the same *displacement*. However, under destructive interference, where a crest meets a trough, the two pulses are said to be *out of phase* by half a wave, or 180°. The pulses have opposing displacements and therefore cancel.

Waves, or points on a wave, that are said to be *in phase* have locations that are experiencing the same angular displacement and the same relative motion. Such points from two waves can overlap such that one wave that is superimposed over the other begins at the same time as the other, or is coherent, and their relative relationship does not change. On a single wave, points that are *in phase* are exactly one full wave (or 360°) apart, implying that points in the medium will experience the same displacement.

Similarly, points may be *out of phase* by any value, but for purposes of identification, points out of phase by 180° (half a wave) and 90° (a quarter of a wave) are easiest to locate. Note that complete (or total) destructive interference occurs when waves or wave points are out of phase by 180°, 540°, or any other integral multiple of half waves, satisfying the condition $\dfrac{n\lambda}{2}$, where $n = 1, 3, 5, 7$, and so on.

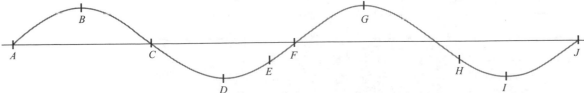

Points that are in phase (separated by one λ or 360°): Points AF, BG, DI, FJ.

Points that are out of phase by 180° (or λ/2 apart): Points AC, BD, CF, DG, EH, GI.

Points that are out of phase by 90° (or λ/4 apart): Points AB, BC, CD, DF, FG, IJ.

WHAT IS THE NATURE OF SOUND WAVE INTERFERENCE?

(*College Physics* 8th ed. pages 473–475/9th ed. pages 488–489)

Just as with the elementary examples of transverse waves experiencing interference discussed earlier, sound (longitudinal) waves interfere and experience both CI and DI. Suppose a listener at point P stands directly between two sound speakers A and B, each emitting the same waves in phase with each other.

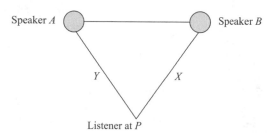

Speaker A Speaker B

Y X

Listener at P

These sound waves, will always meet at the overlapping point P such that rarefactions from A's wave will meet rarefactions from B's wave. Similarly, compressions of each wave will also meet, thereby creating a situation heard by the listener at P as a location of increased volume, simply because constructive interference has occurred at point P. This occurs because the distances Y and X between the listener at P and each speaker are the same, or, more importantly, the *path difference* ($\Delta L = Y - X$) between these lengths is zero. Let's say that each wavelength is $\lambda = 1$ meter. Note that, if either Y or X were increased by 1 meter, 2 meters, 3 meters, and so on (i.e., an integral number of full wavelengths), the listener would also hear a louder than usual sound. These distances may also be referred to as multiples of half waves (i.e., 1 meter = two half waves, 2 meters = four half waves, etc.), so that we can write the condition for constructive interference of sound waves arriving at a location that is situated near two sound sources as follows:

$$\Delta L = \frac{n\lambda}{2} \text{ where } n = 0, 2, 4, 6, \ldots$$

Condition for sound wave *constructive interference*, where ΔL is the path difference between the listener and the sources.

where n is an integer that represents the number of half waves that exist in the difference between the lengths of the listener from each sound source.

Similarly, again referring to the diagram shown, if either Y or X is increased by 0.5 meter (i.e., half a wavelength), then the waves arriving at P will now be half a wave out of phase, meaning that rarefactions will meet compressions, a situation that now creates destructive interference. Further changing the *difference* of the distances by 0.5 meter (or by multiples of half a wavelength) will create additional regions of destructive interference as detected by the listener. In contrast to CI points, these locations will exhibit reduced sound intensity. The condition for destructive interference of sound waves is therefore written as follows:

$$\Delta L = \frac{n\lambda}{2} \text{ where } n = 0, 1, 3, 5, \ldots$$

Condition for sound wave *destructive interference*, where ΔL is the path difference between the listener and the sources.

SAMPLE PROBLEM 2

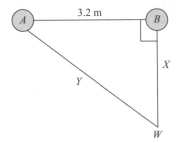

As shown, two sound speakers, A and B, are separated by 3.2 meters, and a stationary listener stands at point W. The listener is a distance Y from speaker A and a distance X from speaker B. The two speakers emit identical, in-phase sound waves such that it is observed that the largest wavelength that produces a minimum in sound intensity (volume) at W is 1.6 meters.

(a) Determine the values of X and Y that satisfy the described condition.

(b) Describe the resultant sound intensity (volume) the person would hear if positioned such that $Y = X$.

SOLUTION TO PROBLEM 2

(a) As the problem states that a minimum in sound is heard associated with the largest wavelength of 1.6 meters, this signifies a situation of destructive interference (DI) in which $n = 1$. Therefore, by the condition of DI, this becomes $\Delta L = \frac{n\lambda}{2} = \frac{(1)\lambda}{2} = \frac{\lambda}{2}$, implying that the difference in path lengths ($\Delta L = Y - X$) between the listener and the speakers must be half a wavelength, or ½(1.6 m) = 0.8 m. Thus, $\Delta L = Y - X = 0.8$. This implies that $Y = 0.8 - X$ so it is necessary to find two unknowns.

From the diagram, the Pythagorean theorem gives $(3.2\,\text{m})^2 = Y^2 + X^2$ or $(3.2\,\text{m})^2 - X^2 = Y^2$. From the previous part, we can square Y and equate these two relationships: $Y^2 = (0.8 - X)^2 = (3.2\,\text{m})^2 - X^2$. This becomes $0.64 + 1.6X + X^2 = X^2 + 10.2$ so that solving gives $X = 6.0$ meters. Therefore, since $Y - X = 0.8$, this gives $Y = 6.8$ meters.

(b) If $Y = X$, that would imply that the path difference ($\Delta L = Y - X$) between the listener and the speakers is zero, which therefore results in a maximum sound intensity (volume) at this location.

WHAT FACTORS AFFECT THE SPEED OF WAVES IN A STRING AND SOUND WAVES IN AIR?

(*College Physics* 8th ed. pages 447–448 (strings), 459–463 (sound)/9th ed. pages 459–461 (strings), 473–478 (sound))

As there are many applications of wave motion to musical instruments, it is common to first study the basic movement of waves along stretched, taut strings that have firmly fixed endpoints. A basic derivation using Newton's second law is valuable to understanding such waves. First, as shown, we magnify the very peak of the wave pulse on the string, which can be assumed to be a small circular arc. As the rope segment is pulled by the equal tensions T, note that the y components of those forces provide the centripetal force, F_c.

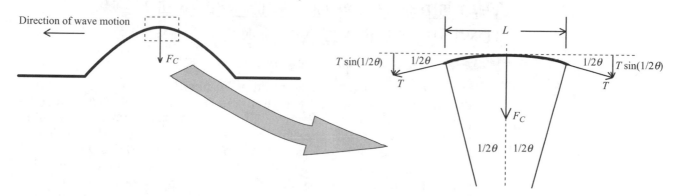

Therefore, $\Sigma F = F_c = \dfrac{mv^2}{R}$ or $2\left[T\sin\left(\dfrac{1}{2}\theta\right)\right] = \dfrac{mv^2}{R}$. Using the small angle approximation $\sin\left(\dfrac{1}{2}\theta\right) \approx \dfrac{1}{2}\theta$, this then becomes $T\theta = \dfrac{mv^2}{R}$. Next, looking carefully at the vertical triangular shape created by this arc of length L, for a small angle θ the length L is simply $L = R\theta$, or $\theta = \dfrac{L}{R}$. Substituting this into the previous equation for centripetal force yields $T\theta = T\left(\dfrac{L}{R}\right) = \dfrac{mv^2}{R}$. Solving for v gives $v^2 = \dfrac{TR}{m}\left(\dfrac{L}{R}\right)$ or $v = \sqrt{\dfrac{TL}{m}} = \sqrt{\dfrac{T}{m/L}}$, where m/L is referred to as the string's linear mass density (often referred to as μ; however, to avoid confusion with coefficient of friction, it will simply be left as m/L). The speed of the wave along the string is therefore dependent on the string tension and inversely dependent on the square root of the string's linear mass density. We are careful here to avoid using T for the tension, as it may be confused with T for period; thus, F is often used for the variable tension.

$$v = \sqrt{\frac{Tension}{m/L}}$$

Transverse wave speed on a string under tension

Similarly, the speed of sound depends on the medium in which the wave travels, whether it is through a solid, liquid, or gas. In each case, the speed of sound is very different due in part to the density of the material, with its fastest value in solids (almost 6000 m/s in steel) and its slowest value in gases (about 343 m/s in room temperature air). Therefore, the denser the material, the faster the speed of sound. Additionally, the speed of sound in a medium is also a function of the temperature of the material. More precisely, the speed of sound in the air depends on the square of the Kelvin temperature, so that if the air temperature, for example, is doubled, the speed of sound increases by $\sqrt{2}$, while quadrupling the temperature increases the speed of sound by $\sqrt{4}$, or 2.

WHAT IS THE NATURE OF STANDING WAVES ALONG STRINGS, ROPES, AND SLINKYS?

(*College Physics* 8th ed. pages 473–479/9th ed. pages 488–494)

When the string (or rope or Slinky) is fixed firmly at one end while the other is connected to a tuning fork, mechanical oscillator, or a person's hand, the string may be vibrated in such a manner as to reflect transverse waves with the same frequency, amplitude, and wavelength in accordance with the principle of superposition. When viewed with a strobe light in a darkened room, these waves actually do appear to stand still, or appear to "snake" along, hence the name *standing waves*. Interestingly, it was a dramatic example of a standing wave induced by wind that collapsed the famous Tacoma Narrows bridge in 1940.

Closer examination of the standing wave will reveal that each wave is separated into two different regions; those that oscillate, or displace the medium, and those that do not. The regions where the medium is experiencing maximum displacement are called *antinodes* (AN), while locations that show no motion are called *nodes* (N). It is easy to remember the latter because a *no*de has *no* motion. The resonant frequency with the fewest antinodes is called the *fundamental*, or first harmonic (as shown), and only one half wave fills the region spanned by the string length L such that the following condition results: $L = \frac{1}{2}\lambda$ or $\lambda = 2L$. By the wave equation, $v = f\lambda$, substituting this gives the condition for all the harmonics that exist on the string: $v = f\lambda$ or $v = f(2L)$, which gives $f_n = \frac{nv}{2L}$, where n = number of antinodes (or number of half waves), $v =$ the wave speed, and L = the length of the string. Oscillating the string at greater and greater frequencies can drive the string to exhibit higher harmonics, such as $n = 2, 3,$ and 4, as shown later. Stringed instruments of all varieties exhibit standing wave behaviors, particularly when played in the "open," or fundamental, position.

$$f_n = \frac{nv}{2L}$$

Fundamental frequencies of standing waves on a string where n = number of **antinodes** or _**half** wavelengths_ along the string (1, 2, 3, …), $v =$ the wave speed, and L = the length of the string that is resonating.

FUNDAMENTAL FREQUENCIES FOR STANDING WAVE HARMONICS ALONG A STRING

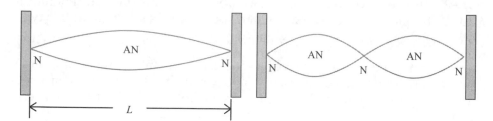

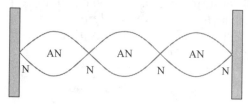

$n = 1$ (i.e., 1 antinode or 1 half wave exists along the string) (*fundamental* or *first harmonic*)

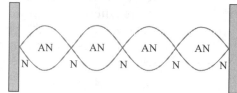

$n = 2$ (i.e., 2 half waves exist along the string) (second harmonic)

$n = 3$ (i.e., 3 antinodes or 3 half waves exist along the string) (*third harmonic*)

$n = 4$ (i.e., 4 antinodes or 4 half waves exist along the string) (*fourth harmonic*)

WHAT IS THE NATURE OF STANDING WAVES IN TUBES AND PIPES?

(*College Physics* 8th ed. pages 480–484/9th ed. pages 495–499)

Just as there are many applications of standing waves on strings in the world of music, so too are there applications of standing waves in open and partially closed pipes (or tubes), such as with a pipe organ or other wind instrument. In such pipes, standing longitudinal waves can exist as the result of constructive interference of sound waves that reflect within the pipe. The key to understanding what is happening depends on whether the reflected wave exists in a tube that is open at both ends or one that is open only at one end. In the case with one closed end, standing waves are set up such that a node exists at the closed end since the movement of the air is restricted. This means that an antinode must exist at the tube opening. Therefore, both cases are different, as outlined next.

FUNDAMENTAL FREQUENCIES FOR STANDING WAVE HARMONICS IN A TUBE OPEN AT BOTH ENDS

In a tube that is open at both ends, sound can emanate from either open end, which therefore suggests that an antinode (AN) must exist there, since sound's volume is proportional to the amplitude of the wave, where the antinode is. If the tube's length is L, then an integral number of half waves will fit into the tube. For example, when the air in the tube is resonating at its lowest frequency, the fewest number of antinodes exist in the tube, with one node (N) at the center. Thus, $n = 1$, and one half wave resonates in the tube. That relation simply implies $L = \frac{1}{2}\lambda$ or $\lambda = 2L$. By the wave equation, $v = f\lambda$; substituting this gives the condition for all the harmonics that exist when sound waves resonate in this type of tube; $v = f\lambda$ or $v = f(2L)$, which gives $f_n = \frac{nv}{2L}$ where n is simply the number of nodes (or half waves) that exist in the tube. Since transverse waves are much easier to sketch and visualize, they have been used to represent additional harmonics in the following diagrams, where harmonics for $n = 2, 3,$ and 4 are also shown.

$$f_n = \frac{nv}{2L}$$

Fundamental frequencies of standing waves in a tube open at *both* ends where n = number of **nodes** or **_half wavelengths_** in the tube (1, 2, 3, …), v = the wave speed, and L = the length of the resonating air column in the tube.

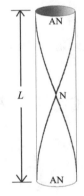 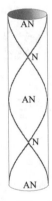 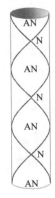 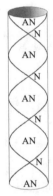

| $n = 1$ (i.e., 1 node or 1 half wave fits in the tube) (*fundamental* or *first harmonic*) | $n = 2$ (i.e., 2 nodes or 2 half waves fit in the tube) (*second harmonic*) | $n = 3$ (i.e., 3 nodes or 3 half waves fit in the tube) (*third harmonic*) | $n = 4$ (i.e., 4 nodes or 4 half waves fit in the tube) (*fourth harmonic*) |

FUNDAMENTAL FREQUENCIES FOR STANDING WAVE HARMONICS IN A TUBE OPEN ONLY AT THE TOP END

In a tube that is open at only at one end, sound can only emanate from the open end, which therefore still suggests that an antinode (AN) must exist there; however, a node (N) must exist at the closed end. If the tube's length is L, then an integral number of quarter waves will instead now fit into the tube (note the difference between this and the tube open at both ends). For example, when the air in the tube is resonating at its lowest frequency, only one antinode and node exist in the tube, which means only one quarter wave is resonating. Thus, $n = 1$. Note, however, that it is impossible to achieve the next resonant harmonic with $n = 2$, but instead, the next (and all subsequent) harmonics occur when n is an odd value of quarter waves. Looking at $n = 1$ gives $L = \frac{1}{4}\lambda$ or $\lambda = 4L$. By the

WAVE MOTION ❖ 329

wave equation, $v = f\lambda$; substituting this gives the condition for the all the harmonics that exist when sound waves resonate in this type of tube; $v = f\lambda$ or $v = f(4L)$ which gives $f_n = \dfrac{nv}{4L}$ where n is simply the number of quarter waves that exist in the tube. Again, transverse waves for the additional harmonics $n = 3, 5,$ and 7 are shown in the following diagrams.

$$f_n = \frac{nv}{4L}$$

Fundamental frequencies of standing waves in a tube open at *one* end where n = number of **quarter wavelengths** in the tube $(1, 3, 5, \ldots)$, v = the wave speed, and L = the length of the resonating air column in the tube.

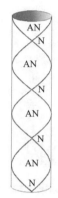

| $n = 1$ (i.e., ¼ wave fits in the tube) (*fundamental* or *first harmonic*) | $n = 3$ (i.e., ¾ wave fits in the tube) (*second harmonic*) | $n = 5$ (i.e., ⁵⁄₄ wave fits in the tube) (*third harmonic*) | $n = 7$ (i.e., ⁷⁄₄ wave fits in the tube) (*fourth harmonic*) |

HOW DOES THE DETECTION OF SOUND WAVES CHANGE WHEN THERE IS RELATIVE MOTION?

(*College Physics* 8th ed. pages 468–473/9th ed. pages 482–488)

How does our perception of longitudinal sound waves change if the source or the listener is moving? A perfect example of this occurs when a train or ambulance blowing a whistle of fixed frequency passes you as you stand nearby and listen. In both of these circumstances, careful observation reveals that the observer detects a higher pitch (or frequency) of sound waves as the vehicle (i.e., source) approaches, and a lower pitch of waves as the vehicle recedes, all relative to the original pitch emitted by the source. First discovered in 1842 by Austrian physicist Christian Doppler and later verified by Dutch chemist Buys Ballot, this apparent change of frequency is known as the Doppler effect and is measurable not only with sound waves but with light waves as well.

Why does the Doppler effect occur? As shown, the most prominent cause is the changing distance between the wave source and the observer. When the source (emitting a wave of constant frequency f_0) is approaching the observer, arriving sound waves cover less and less distance to the observer, such that these waves bunch up, compress, and arrive more frequently. Thus, the observer perceives sound waves arriving at a more frequent rate (i.e., with a higher frequency, f'). Similarly, as the source of waves recedes from the observer, the distance between the two now increases, and the waves arrive less frequently. Therefore, the detected pitch (or frequency) decreases. In the most basic manner, this is a brief but effective description of the Doppler effect. It is important to note that this apparent change of frequency is simply due to the relative motion of the source in comparison with the observer. A similar effect would occur if the source were stationary and the observer moved; however, at all times, the actual emitted frequency f_0 is constant.

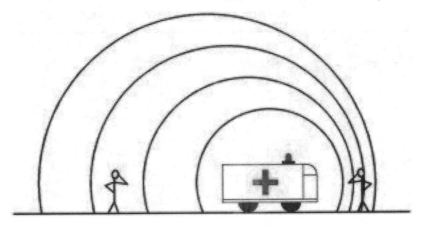

The mathematical derivation of the Doppler effect formulas is very lengthy and is omitted here for the sake of brevity (consult the Serway textbook if need be). For the sake of AP Physics B, the student must know the qualitative aspects of both the reduced frequency of recession and the increased frequency of approach according to the formulas shown. In these equations, note that f_0 is simply the emitted frequency of the wave, f' is the detected frequency of the wave, and v_s represents the source or observer speed. The speed of the waves in the medium (which for nearly all problems will be air) is v and is typically the speed of sound at STP, 343.0 m/s, unless otherwise noted. Recall that since the approach frequency must be the largest detected, it is easy therefore to remember that it is that equation that contains the negative sign in the denominator, signifying that the fraction will be larger than if there were a plus sign. Note what occurs for an approaching source when its speed v_s equals the speed of the wave v in the medium.

$$f' = \frac{f_0}{1 - \dfrac{v_s}{v}}$$

Source/Observer Approaching
(f' increases)

$$f' = \frac{f_0}{1 + \dfrac{v_s}{v}}$$

Source/Observer Receding
(f' decreases)

SAMPLE PROBLEM 3

You are standing on the passenger loading platform at a train station when a train approaches you with an initial constant speed of 8 m/s. The train is blowing its whistle with a frequency of 350 Hz; however, it then begins to slow down uniformly until it passes you moving at a speed of 2 m/s. The speed of sound in the air around you and the train is 340 m/s.

    (a) Determine the change in frequency that you detect during the deceleration of the train to the time it passes by you.

    (b) Determine the change of wavelength between the two waves you detect.

SOLUTION TO PROBLEM 3

    (a) Here the train is approaching a stationary observer, and thus the detected frequency of the approaching sound waves can be determined by $f' = \dfrac{f_0}{1 - \dfrac{v_s}{v}}$, where $f_0 = 350$ Hz and $v = 340$ m/s.

Since it is stated that the train changes speed, it will be necessary to calculate f' twice in order to determine the frequency change Δf. This therefore becomes (omitting units for clarity) $f' = \dfrac{f_0}{1 - \dfrac{v_s}{v}} = \dfrac{350}{1 - \dfrac{3}{340}} = 358$ Hz for the first speed. The next

frequency is; $f' = \dfrac{f_0}{1 - \dfrac{v_s}{v}} = \dfrac{350}{1 - \dfrac{2}{340}} = 352$ Hz for the second speed.

The frequency shift Δf is therefore $358 - 352 = 6$ Hz.

    (b) According to the wave equation $v = f\lambda$, the wavelength shift is $\dfrac{v}{\Delta f} = \Delta\lambda$, which is $\dfrac{343\ m/s}{6\ Hz} = \Delta\lambda = 57.2$ m.

WHAT IS THE NATURE OF BEATS?

(College Physics 8th ed. pages 484–486/9th ed. pages 499–500)

What happens if two sound waves of differing frequencies interfere? Standing waves exist because of reflections that involve waves of the same shape, frequency, and wavelength, although the resulting interference pattern of two waves of slightly different frequencies alternates between constructive and destructive. Taking images of two such waves and overlapping them will easily reveal that points alternately reinforce and cancel with a definite and new frequency. This new frequency, because it is clearly demarcated by these two distinct points, is called the *beat frequency*, or f_{beat}.

As shown, both superimposed waves on the top are of slightly different frequencies; however, when they combine, both constructive and destructive interference occur, providing the beat frequency as shown by the enhanced amplitudes in the bottommost image. By the principle of superposition, regions of the first two waves, which coincide in phase, add to provide the final beat wave amplitude; however, regions that are at and near 180° out of phase experience destructive interference, as shown in the resulting beat wave in the bottom image.

You may consult the Serway text for the full derivation of how to calculate the beat frequency, but it is essentially equal to the *difference* in frequency of the two frequencies that interfere to produce the beats.

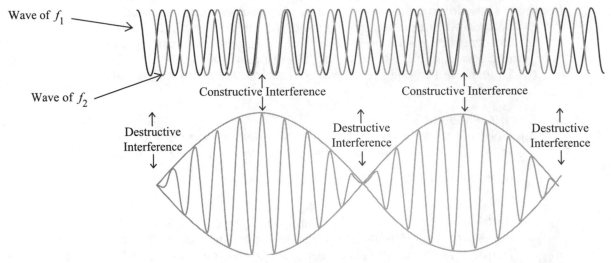

Wave of f_1

Wave of f_2

Constructive Interference

Constructive Interference

Destructive Interference

Destructive Interference

Destructive Interference

Thus, if two sound waves with frequencies of 436 and 488 Hz are played simultaneously, a beat frequency of (488 – 436) or 52 Hz will be detected. It is interesting to note that, for the most part, the human ear cannot detect beats with frequencies of 7 Hz and below, and it is the ability of very talented string musicians to detect slight changes in the beat frequency as a means to tuning their instruments.

$$f_{beat} = |f_2 - f_1|$$

Beat frequency

SAMPLE PROBLEM 4
Two tuning forks are struck and vibrate with the frequencies of 526 and 530 Hz, respectively.
   (a) Determine the beat frequency.
   (b) Determine how many beats will be heard after 20 seconds pass.

SOLUTION TO PROBLEM 4
   (a) The beat frequency is the difference in the two frequencies;
       $f_{beat} = |530 Hz - 526 Hz|$ or, $f_{beat} = 4$ Hz.
   (b) From (a), the beat frequency is 4 beats per second, or 4 cycles per second. Therefore, in a time of 20 seconds, the following number of beats will be heard:

$$20 \; \cancel{seconds} \; \left(4 \frac{beats}{\cancel{second}} \right) = 80 \text{ cycles or } 80 \text{ beats}$$

WAVE MOTION: STUDENT OBJECTIVES FOR THE AP EXAM

■ You should know and understand the primary properties of periodic waves, and the nature of transverse and longitudinal waves.
■ You should be able to sketch and identify graphs that represent traveling waves and determine amplitude, wavelength, and frequency of a wave from such a graph.
■ You should be able to state and apply the relation among wavelength,

frequency, and velocity for a wave.

■ You should be able to sketch or identify graphs that describe reflection of a wave from the fixed or free end of a string.

■ You should qualitatively know what factors determine the speed of waves on a string and the speed of sound in air.

■ You should be able to apply the principle of superposition to traveling waves moving in opposite directions and describe how a standing wave may be formed by superposition.

■ You should understand the physics of standing waves so that you can sketch possible standing wave modes for a stretched string that is fixed at both ends, and determine the amplitude, wavelength, and frequency of such standing waves.

■ You should be able to understand and describe standing sound waves in a pipe that has either open or closed end, and determine the wavelength and frequency of such standing waves.

■ You should understand the Doppler effect for sound so that you can explain the mechanism that gives rise to a frequency shift in the case of both the moving source and the moving observer.

■ You should be able to understand the nature of wave interference in order to understand phase relationships, the nature of interference of sound waves, and the phenomenon of beats.

MULTIPLE-CHOICE QUESTIONS

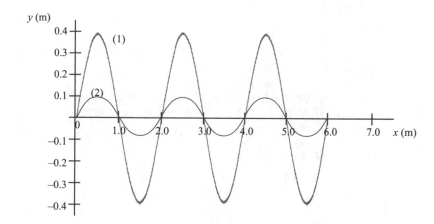

1.   Shown are two transverse waves, (1) and (2), each which have the same speed v. Which of the following is a correct statement?
   (A) Both waves (1) and (2) have equal amplitudes; however, the wavelength of wave (1) is four times larger than the wavelength of wave (2).
   (B) The amplitude of both waves (1) and (2) is 1.0 meter; however, the wavelength of wave (1) is 0.4 meter and the wavelength of wave (2) is 0.1 meter.
   (C) The wavelengths of both waves (1) and (2) are equal; however, the frequency of wave (1) is four times greater than that of wave (2).
   (D) Both waves (1) and (2) have equal wavelengths; however, the amplitude of wave (2) is one-fourth that of wave (1).
   (E) The frequency of wave (1) is four times that of wave (2); however, both waves have the same wavelength.

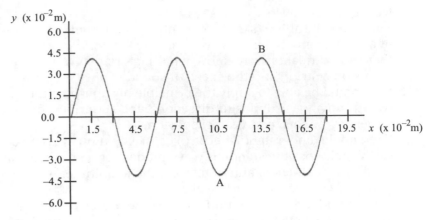

For Questions 2 and 3, refer to the diagram, depicting the displacement of a vibrating string versus position along the string. The periodic waves in the string have a speed of 0.10 m/s, and A and B are two points on the string.

2. What is the wavelength of the wave?
   (A) 3×10^{-2} m
   (B) 6×10^{-2} m
   (C) 9×10^{-2} m
   (D) 12×10^{-2} m
   (E) 15×10^{-2} m

3. What is the frequency of the wave?
   (A) 0.60 Hz
   (B) 0.90 Hz
   (C) 1.11 Hz
   (D) 1.67 Hz
   (E) 2.88 Hz

4. A periodic wave of speed v and wavelength λ passes a point with a frequency f. Which of the following pairs of equations is correct for this wave?
   (A) $\dfrac{v}{f} = \lambda$ and $Tf = 1$
   (B) $f = v\lambda$ and $T = \dfrac{1}{f}$
   (C) $\dfrac{T}{T} = \lambda$ and $v = f\lambda$
   (D) $f = \dfrac{1}{T}$ and $f = v\lambda$
   (E) $v = f\lambda$ and $Tf = \lambda$

5. Which of the following best represents the frequency of a standing wave moving with a speed v on a string of length L fixed at both ends, which contains one antinode?
   (A) $\dfrac{5v}{2L}$
   (B) $\dfrac{2v}{L}$
   (C) $\dfrac{v}{2L}$
   (D) $\dfrac{v}{L}$
   (E) $\dfrac{3v}{2L}$

6. A rope of length 2.0 m is stretched between two fixed points and supports transverse standing waves with a fundamental frequency of 30 Hz. What is the ratio of the frequency of the fourth harmonic to the frequency of the second harmonic?
   (A) 3:1
   (B) 1:2
   (C) 1:3
   (D) 1:1
   (E) 2:1

7. A 10-m-long rope is fixed at both ends and supports a standing wave with a total of 5 nodes. If a transverse wave travels at 15 m/s along this rope, what is the frequency of the standing wave that exists?
   (A) 0.3 Hz
   (B) 0.5 Hz
   (C) 2.5 Hz
   (D) 3 Hz
   (E) 5 Hz

8. A guitar string is plucked and set into vibration. The vibrating string disturbs the surrounding air, resulting in a sound wave. Which table entry is correct?

	Wave in the String	Sound Wave in Air
(A) The wave is transverse.	yes	yes
(B) The wave speed increases if the medium temperature rises.	no	yes
(C) The wave is longitudinal.	yes	yes
(D) The wave is transmitted by particle vibrations.	no	yes
(E) The wave transports energy.	yes	no

9. A rope of length 5 m is stretched to a tension of 40 N. If the mass of the rope is 0.5 kg, at what speed would a transverse wave with a wavelength of 4 m travel?
   (A) 0.5 m/s
   (B) 2 m/s
   (C) 5 m/s
   (D) 20 m/s
   (E) 200 m/s

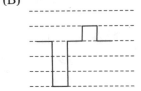

10. As shown, two rectangular waves A and B approach each other. Which of the following diagrams best represents the interference of A and B?

(A)

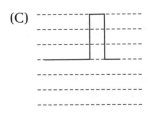

(B)

(C)

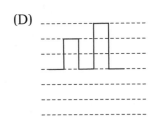

(D)

(E)

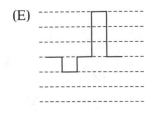

11. A small vibrating object *S* moves across the surface of a level, water-filled wave tank, producing the waves shown, which move with speed *v*. The object is traveling in what direction and with what speed relative to the speed of the waves produced?

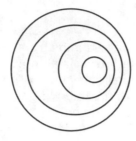

Direction	Speed
(A) right	< *v*
(B) left	< *v*
(C) right	> *v*
(D) right	= *v*
(E) left	= *v*

12. A car moving to the west at a speed of 35 m/s emits a continuous 220 Hz sound from its horn as it approaches a stationary pedestrian observer. If the speed of sound is 343 m/s, what is the frequency heard by the observer?
    (A) 9.7 Hz
    (B) 176 Hz
    (C) 200 Hz
    (D) 218 Hz
    (E) 245 Hz

13. A snugly held rope is tied tightly to a hook attached to a wall. Which of the following is a correct statement regarding a transverse wave traveling along the rope as it reflects from the hook?
    (A) The reflected wave's amplitude is inverted, and none of the wave's energy is transferred to the barrier.
    (B) The reflected wave's amplitude is inverted, and some of the wave's energy is transferred to the barrier.
    (C) The reflected wave's amplitude is not inverted, and none of the wave's energy is transferred to the barrier.
    (D) The reflected wave's amplitude is not inverted, and some of the wave's energy is transferred to the barrier.
    (E) The incident wave's energy is always completely absorbed by the barrier, and no reflection occurs.

14. A pipe that is open at both ends is 1.7 m long. If the speed of sound is 340 m/s in the pipe, what is the fundamental frequency of this pipe?
    (A) 17 Hz
    (B) 34 Hz
    (C) 100 Hz
    (D) 170 Hz
    (E) 340 Hz

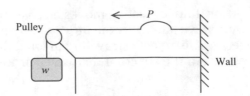

15. As shown, a weight *w* hangs from a string over the end of a pulley, and a wave pulse *P* travels along the string. The time required for the pulse *P* to travel one length of the string will not be affected by changing which of the following?
    (A) the amplitude of the pulse
    (B) the length of the string from the wall to the pulley
    (C) the ratio of mass to length of the string
    (D) the weight of the hanging mass
    (E) the density of the string

FREE-RESPONSE PROBLEMS

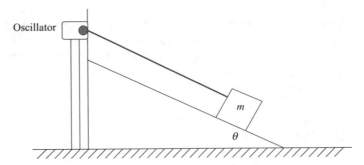

1. As shown, a 15-kg block *m* is attached to a 0.6-m-long string of linear density $\mu = 1.2 \times 10^{-2}$ kg/m as it rests on a frictionless inclined plane at angle θ relative to the horizontal. The upper end of the string is attached to an oscillator that drives the string at a constant frequency of 180 Hz, and the angle of inclination θ is adjustable from 20° to 80°.
   (a) Sketch a free-body diagram of the block in the diagram.

   (b) Determine the two angles that will produce standing wave harmonics on this string.
   (c) Sketch the standing waves on the string associated with the angles in your answer to (b) in these diagrams.

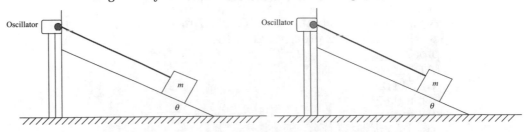

   (d) Determine the speed of each of the standing waves.
   (e) Explain what effect, if any, doubling the mass of the block would have on the angles that produce standing waves on this string.

2. Sound waves are sent into an air-filled tube that is 0.9 m long and closed at one end. The air in the tube is observed to resonate at several frequencies, the lowest of which is 95 Hz.

(a) In the tube cross sections shown, sketch transverse waves to represent the vibrational modes of the waves for the three lowest resonant frequencies.

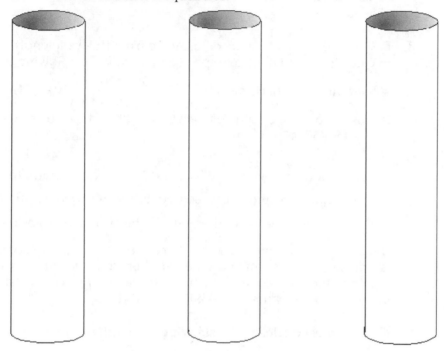

(b) Determine the n and frequency values for the next two harmonics that exist in the tube above 95 Hz.

(c) Determine the wavelengths of each of the three harmonic waves that exist in the tube.

(d) Determine the speed of each of the three harmonic waves that exist in the tube.

(e) The region of air within the tube is doubled in length. Describe the effects this may have on the fundamental resonance frequency within the tube. Justify your answer with appropriate calculations.

ANSWERS

MULTIPLE-CHOICE QUESTIONS

1. **D** The amplitude of wave (1) is the vertical displacement at the peak of the crest or trough, which is approximately 0.4 m (read directly from the vertical axis), while the amplitude of wave (2) is approximately 0.1 m. The wavelength of each is the horizontal distance for one full wave to complete its cycle, which for wave (1) is 2.0 m (read directly from the horizontal axis) and is also the same for wave (2). As for frequency, since it is stated that each wave has the same speed and both waves have the same wavelength, each wave will therefore have the same frequency. Therefore, both waves have the same wavelength, however, wave (1) has an amplitude that

is four times that of wave (2), which is best represented by choice (D) (*College Physics* 8th ed. pages 443–447/9th ed. pages 455–459).

2. **B** The wavelength of the wave shown is the horizontal distance for one complete cycle, which, according to the graph, is 6.0×10^{-2} m, or choice (B) (*College Physics* 8th ed. pages 443–447/9th ed. pages 455–459).

3. **D** The frequency f can be determined from the wavelength λ found in Question 2 and the wave speed equation, $v = f\lambda$. Solving for f and substituting, this becomes $f = \dfrac{v}{\lambda} = \dfrac{1 \times 10^{-1} \text{ m/s}}{6 \times 10^{-2} \text{ m}} = \dfrac{1}{6} \times 10 \sim 1.7 \text{Hz}$, which is closest to choice (D) (*College Physics* 8th ed. pages 443–447/9th ed. pages 455–459).

4. **A** Here, both the relations $v = f\lambda$ and $T = \dfrac{1}{f}$ are necessary to answer this question. Solving the speed equation for wavelength λ gives $\dfrac{v}{f} = \lambda$ and using the second equation, the product of period T and frequency f must be 1: $Tf = 1$. Therefore, the only correct answer is choice (A). None of the other answer choices portrays correct algebra, and thus each is incorrect (*College Physics* 8th ed. pages 443–447/9th ed. pages 455–459).

5. **C** This question deals with standing waves on a string, the harmonic frequencies for which are given by $f_n = \dfrac{nv}{2L}$, where n represents the number of antinodes on the string, v is the wave's speed, and L is the length of the string. In this case, the question states that the string has one antinode, and thus this standing wave is the fundamental (or first harmonic), in which $n = 1$. Therefore, the frequency for this wave simply becomes $f_n = \dfrac{nv}{2L} = \dfrac{(1)v}{2L} = \dfrac{v}{2L}$, which is choice (C) (*College Physics* 8th ed. pages 473–479/9th ed. pages 488–494).

6. **E** This question also deals with standing waves on a string, the harmonic frequencies for which are given by $f_n = \dfrac{nv}{2L}$, where n represents the number of antinodes on the string, v is the wave's speed and L is the length of the string. Since the question requests the ratio of the frequency of the fourth harmonic (i.e., f_4 where $n = 4$) to the second harmonic (i.e., f_2 where $n = 2$), using $f_n = \dfrac{nv}{2L}$, this becomes $\dfrac{f_4}{f_2} = \dfrac{\frac{4v}{2L}}{\frac{2v}{2L}}$, which simplifies to $\dfrac{f_4}{f_2} = \dfrac{4v}{2L}\left(\dfrac{2L}{2v}\right) = \dfrac{4}{2} = 2$. Therefore, the correct answer is a 2:1 ratio, or choice (E) (*College Physics* 8th ed. pages 473–479/9th ed. pages 488–494).

7. **D** This question also deals with standing waves on a string, the harmonic frequencies for which are given by $f_n = \dfrac{nv}{2L}$, where n represents the number of antinodes on the string, v is the wave's speed, and L is the length of the string. Here, it is stated that five nodes exist, which implies that only four antinodes exist, meaning that just two full wavelengths exist in the 10 meter length of the string. Since it is also stated that the wave speed is 15 m/s, and because four antinodes exist, this is a fourth harmonic f_4 such that

   $$f_4 = \frac{4v}{2L} = \frac{4(15\frac{m}{s})}{2(10\,m)} = \frac{30}{10}\,Hz = 3\,Hz.$$ This is best shown by answer choice

   (D) (*College Physics* 8th ed. pages 473–479/9th ed. pages 488–494).

8. **B** This question asks the student to distinguish the factors affecting both the speed of transverse string waves and longitudinal sound waves in air. The former, whose value is $v = \sqrt{\dfrac{Tension}{m/L}}$, depends directly on the square root of the string tension (i.e., force) and inversely on the square root of the mass of the string m divided by its length L. Similarly, the speed of a longitudinal sound wave in air depends directly on the square root of the air temperature T. Thus, of the choices given, (A) is incorrect as sound waves are not transverse, (B) correctly states that a sound wave's speed will increase if the temperature increases and that a string's transverse wave will not, (C) incorrectly states that the string wave is longitudinal, (D) incorrectly states that only sound waves arise from particle vibrations, and (E) incorrectly states that sound waves do not transport energy. Thus, the correct answer is choice (B) (*College Physics* 8th ed. pages 447–448 (strings), 459–463 (sound)/9th ed. pages 459–461 (strings), 473–478 (sound)).

9. **D** This question deals with the speed of transverse waves on strings, according to the equation $v = \sqrt{\dfrac{Tension}{m/L}}$. Here, carefully note that the length of the string L (5 m) rather than the wavelength λ (4 m) is used in the above equation. Therefore, substituting and solving for the speed v gives $v = \sqrt{\dfrac{40\,N}{(0.5\,kg)/(5\,m)}} = \sqrt{\dfrac{5(40)}{1/2}} = \sqrt{400} = 20$ m/s, which is choice (D) (*College Physics* 8th ed. pages 447–448 (strings), 459–463 (sound)/9th ed. pages 459–461 (strings), 473–478 (sound)).

10. **E** This question requires knowledge of the wave superposition, which involves basic interference. As waves pass through each other, superposition simply involves realizing that the amplitudes of interfering waves add, bearing in mind that amplitudes can be negative. Therefore, parts of the waves A and B shown will cancel and others will reinforce. Wave B has been redrawn here with thick lines and superimposed over wave A. Therefore, it can be seen that the left portions of A and B will partly cancel while all of the right portions of the two waves will completely reinforce. The final amplitude of the left part of the new wave must be (+1 + –2 units =

−1 unit) tall and the right portion will be (+2 + 1 units = + 3 units) in amplitude. Thus, the new wave must appear as shown, which is choice (E) (*College Physics* 8th ed. pages 448–449/9th ed. pages 461–462).

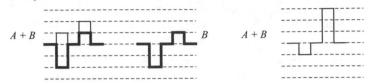

11. **A** This question deals with the aspects of the Doppler effect in which a moving source of waves portrays the unique wave pattern shown in the diagram. When the object moves as it emits waves, the wave fronts pile up on the side from which they were emitted, as the source emitting them continually moves over waves it just emitted. Therefore, in this question, the wave fronts are piled up to the right of the diagram, implying the source is moving to the right (answer choices (A), (C), and (D)). As for the wave speeds, they must all be less than that of the source, otherwise a bow shock would form at the location of the wave emission, which takes on a triangular wave front appearance as the waves move faster than the source itself. Therefore, the correct answer is choice (A) (*College Physics* 8th ed. pages 468–473/9th ed. pages 482–488).

12. **E** This question also deals with the aspects of the Doppler effect in a very elementary manner. Since the Doppler effect involves an apparent shift in frequency detected by relative motion between an observer and a wave source (here it's the car's horn), it first must be realized that, in this case, the wave source is approaching the observer. As a result, emitted waves bunch up at a greater rate in the direction in which they were emitted than in the opposite direction. Therefore, the stationary observer will simply detect waves arriving *more frequently* (i.e., with a greater frequency), and so the only answer that is a frequency greater than the 220 Hz of the source waves is choice (E) (*College Physics* 8th ed. pages 468–473/9th ed. pages 482–488).

13. **B** When incident upon a boundary, a wave (or pulse) can either reflect completely inverted or not inverted. In either case, energy is always partly transferred to the medium of the barrier (whether it is a firm barrier or a weak one), thus eliminating choice (E). Additionally, by Newton's third law, when a pulse impacts a firm barrier, an equal but opposite force is exerted on the rope carrying the pulse, causing the pulse invert as it reflects. This is not the case if the rope is connected loosely to another rope, or string, when the pulse returns uninverted. The best answer, therefore, is choice (B) (*College Physics* 8th ed. pages 449–450/9th ed. pages 462–463).

14. **C** Here it is necessary to recall the resonant properties of pipes, in this case a pipe that is open at both ends. Recall that in such a pipe an antinode (maximum volume for a sound wave) exists at the open ends and that the resonant frequencies are given by $f_n = \dfrac{nv}{2L}$, where n represents the number of *nodes* in the

pipe (not antinodes, as with standing waves on a string). Here, since $n = 1$ and $v = 340$ m/s, the fundamental frequency becomes $f_1 = \dfrac{nv}{2L} = \dfrac{(1)(340 \text{ m/s})}{2(1.7 \text{ m})} = \dfrac{340 \text{ m/s}}{3.4 \text{ m}} = 100$ Hz, which is choice (C) (*College Physics* 8th ed. pages 480–484/9th ed. pages 495–499).

15. **A** This question deals with the application of the wave speed equation $v = \sqrt{\dfrac{Tension}{m/L}}$, which depends on the string mass, length, and tension as shown, as applied to a taut string. The time t for the pulse P to travel along the string of length L will simply be, from kinematics, $t = \dfrac{L}{v}$, where v is the wave pulse speed. Combining these two equations gives $t = \dfrac{L}{v} = \dfrac{L}{\sqrt{\dfrac{Tension}{m/L}}} = \dfrac{L}{\dfrac{\sqrt{Tension}}{\sqrt{m/L}}} = \dfrac{L\sqrt{m/L}}{\sqrt{Tension}}$, which

shows that the wave travel time depends on the string mass (and therefore its weight and density), its length and the string tension (choice (D), the hanging weight). Therefore, only amplitude, choice (A), is not a factor in determining the wave speed along the string (*College Physics* 8th ed. pages 447–448 (strings), 459–463 (sound)/ 9th ed. pages 459–461 (strings), 473–478 (sound)).

FREE-RESPONSE PROBLEMS

1. (a) The forces acting on the block are tension T, the normal force N, and the block's weight w (*College Physics* 8th ed. page 94/9th ed. page 98).

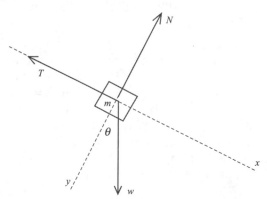

(b) It is necessary to combine both the wave speed equation $v = \sqrt{\dfrac{Tension}{\mu}}$ (where μ is the mass per unit length, or linear density, of the string) and the equation for the standing wave fundamental frequencies on a string, $f_n = \dfrac{nv}{2L}$, to solve for the angle θ. The key is to understand that applying $\sum F_x = 0$ shows that the x component of the weight vector balances the tension T in the string or, $T - mg \sin\theta = 0$, which becomes $T = mg \sin\theta$. Therefore, the standing wave frequencies f_n become $f_n = \dfrac{nv}{2L} = \dfrac{n}{2L}\sqrt{\dfrac{Tension}{\mu}} = \dfrac{n}{2L}\sqrt{\dfrac{mg \sin\theta}{\mu}}$. Rearranging and solving this for $\sin\theta$ gives $\dfrac{2Lf_n}{n} = \sqrt{\dfrac{mg\,\sin\theta}{\mu}}$, which becomes $\dfrac{2Lf_n}{n}\sqrt{\dfrac{\mu}{mg}} =$

$\sqrt{\sin\theta}$. Therefore, $\left(\dfrac{2Lf_n}{n}\sqrt{\dfrac{\mu}{mg}}\right)^2 = \sin\theta$. Since everything on the

left side of the equation but n is a constant, this may be further

reduced: $\left(\dfrac{2Lf_n}{n}\sqrt{\dfrac{\mu}{mg}}\right)^2 = \left(\dfrac{4L^2f_n^2}{n^2}\left(\dfrac{\mu}{mg}\right)\right) = \dfrac{1}{n^2}\left(\dfrac{4L^2f_n^2\mu}{mg}\right) = \sin\theta$. We

can finally solve for θ to give $\sin^{-1}\left[\dfrac{1}{n^2}\left(\dfrac{4L^2f_n^2\mu}{mg}\right)\right] = \theta_n$, which

is separated in this way so that everything inside the inner
parentheses is a constant for this problem. Furthermore, with
values for this problem, it simplifies to

$\sin^{-1}\left[\dfrac{1}{n^2}\left(\dfrac{4(0.6\text{ m})^2(180\text{ Hz})^2(1.2\times10^{-2}\text{ kg/m})}{(15\text{ kg})(9.8\text{ m/s}^2)}\right)\right] = \theta_n$ or $\sin^{-1}\left[\dfrac{1}{n^2}(3.8086531)\right] = \theta_n$.

Therefore, when $n = 1$ (one antinode), this becomes
$\sin^{-1}[3.8086531] = \theta_1$, which is undefined (as $\sin\theta \le 1$ always).
If $n = 2$ (two antinodes), this becomes $\sin^{-1}[0.952163] = \theta_2$, or
$\theta_2 = 72.2°$. When $n = 3$ (three antinodes), this becomes
$\sin^{-1}[0.4321837] = \theta_3$, or $\theta_3 = 25.0°$. Lastly, when $n = 4$ (four antinodes), this becomes $\sin^{-1}[0.2380408] = \theta_4$, or $\theta_4 = 13.8°$. As the
problem gave a constraint for the angle θ (from 20° to 80°), the
only standing waves produced on this string are the second and
third harmonics ($n = 2$ and $n = 3$) at angles of 72.2° and 25.0°,
respectively (*College Physics* 8th ed. pages 473–479/9th ed. pages
488–494).

(c) Even though the angles are different, for the sake of simplicity
the same incline will be used for both standing waves (the incline
at 25.0° is shown on the left whereas that of the 72.2° is on the
right). The first standing wave, at $\theta = 25.0°$, has two antinodes
and three nodes. This means that one full wave is shown along
the string and one full wave is reflected. For the angle $\theta = 72.2°$,
the wave has three antinodes and four nodes, implying that three
half waves occupy the 0.6-m length of the string (*College Physics*
8th ed. pages 473–479/9th ed. pages 488–494).

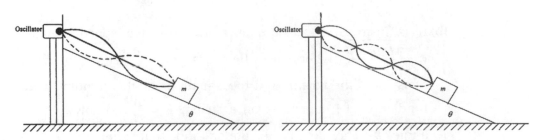

(d) To determine the wave speed, all that is necessary is the relation
$v = f\lambda$ for both angles. In the first case, $n = 2$, and thus a full wave
fills the 0.6 m length of the string. Therefore, $\lambda_1 = 0.6$ m and $f = 180$ Hz
(given), the first speed v_1 is $v_1 = f\lambda_1 = (180\text{ Hz})(0.6\text{ m}) = 108\text{ m/s} = v_1$.

For the second standing wave, note that three half waves fill the 0.6 meter string length, or $\frac{3}{2}\lambda_2 = 0.6$ m or $\lambda_2 = 0.4$ m. Therefore, v_2 becomes $v_2 = f\lambda_2 = (180 \text{ Hz})(0.4 \text{ m}) = 72 \text{ m/s} = v_2$ (*College Physics* 8th ed. pages 443–447, 737–742/9th ed. pages 455–459, 767–770).

(e) According to the equation relating the angle to the number of antinodes derived in (b) (which is $\sin^{-1}\left[\frac{1}{n^2}\left(\frac{4L^2 f_n^2 \mu}{mg}\right)\right] = \theta_n$),

any change in mass would result in a decrease in the angle causing resonant standing waves on the string because the angle is inversely related to the mass. For example, if m becomes $2m$, then θ_1 becomes 1.9°, θ_2 becomes 28.0°, and θ_3 becomes 12.2°.

2. (a) The first three vibrational modes are shown, with $n = 1$ having a quarter wave in the tube, $n = 3$ having three quarter waves, and $n = 5$ having five quarter waves (*College Physics* 8th ed. pages 480–484/9th ed. pages 495–499).

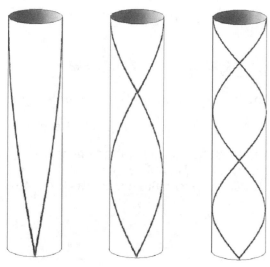

(b) Since each of the harmonics of resonating air in a tube open at only one end must occur in units of odd numbers of quarter wavelengths in the tube with an antinode at each tube opening, the n values for all three harmonics in this question must be $n = 1$, 3, and 5 (as evidenced in the sketches for part (a); one, three, and five quarter waves exist in each tube). Similarly, the frequencies associated with both $n = 3$ and $n = 5$ harmonics are simply those multiples of the fundamental. Therefore, since f_1 is 95 Hz, the second harmonic f_3 then becomes (3)(95), or 285 Hz. Lastly, f_5 is (5)(95) or 475 Hz. This solution, as well as the sketches for part (a), are in accordance with the equation for the fundamental frequencies in the tube, $f_n = \frac{nv}{4L}$, where n is the number of quarter waves in the tube (*College Physics* 8th ed. pages 480–484/9th ed. pages 495–499).

(c) The wavelengths of these waves may each be determined by the combination of $f_n = \frac{nv}{4L}$ and $v = f\lambda$. Substituting the latter into the former gives $f_n = \dfrac{n(f\lambda)}{4L}$, which becomes $4L = n\lambda$, or $\dfrac{4L}{n} = \lambda$.

Therefore, the corresponding wavelengths are as follows (*College Physics* 8th ed. pages 480–484/9th ed. pages 495–499):

$$\lambda_1 = \frac{4L}{1} = 4(0.9 \text{ m}) = 3.6 \text{ m} = \lambda_1 \qquad \lambda_3 = \frac{4L}{3} = \frac{4(0.9 \text{ m})}{3} = 1.2 \text{ m} = \lambda$$

$$\lambda_5 = \frac{4L}{5} = \frac{4(0.9 \text{ m})}{5} = 0.72 \text{ m} = \lambda_5$$

(d) For each situation shown, the wave speed v may be calculated using $v = f\lambda$ and the corresponding values of f and λ from parts (b) and (c). Note that the following products produce the same result, since the wave speed here depends only on properties of the air (*College Physics* 8th ed. pages 443–447, 459–463 (sound), 480–484/9th ed. pages 459–461 (strings), 473–478 (sound), 495–499):

$$v_1 = f_1\lambda_1 = (95 \text{ Hz})(3.6 \text{ m}) = 342 \text{ m/s} \quad v_3 = f_3\lambda_3 = (285 \text{ Hz})(1.2 \text{ m}) = 342 \text{ m/s}$$

$$v_5 = f_5\lambda_5 = (475 \text{ Hz})(0.72 \text{ m}) = 342 \text{ m/s}$$

(e) If the length of the tube is doubled, becoming $2L$, the new fundamental frequency at $n = 1$ becomes $f_1 = \dfrac{(1)v}{4(2L)} = \dfrac{v}{8L}$ which is one-half the original fundamental frequency when the tube length was L. Therefore, the fundamental frequency is now 47.5 Hz (*College Physics* 8th ed. pages 480–484/9th ed. pages 495–499).

15

WAVE OPTICS

DISPERSION

(*College Physics* 8th ed. pages 742–746/9th ed. pages 771–775)

Measurements on the refraction of light as it passes from air into glass show that the degree of refraction is dependent upon wavelength. Light of all wavelengths is reduced in speed in glass, but violet light, which is refracted the greatest amount, travels slower than red light, which is refracted least. This effect is called *dispersion*. The diagram shows the result of directing a narrow beam of white light at one face of a glass prism.

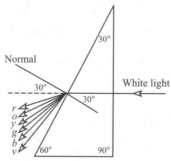

Dispersion of white light

The initial beam is separated into beams of various colors, from which we conclude that white light is actually a mixture of light of various colors. The band of colors that emerges from the glass prism is known as a *spectrum*. When the ray of white light is broken into its components, each component color is deviated by a different angle, for example, δ_r for red light and δ_v for violet light. The *angular dispersion* Ψ between the violet and red regions is the difference between the deviations: $\Psi = \delta_v - \delta_r$.

SAMPLE PROBLEM 1

Consider the 30°-60°-90° glass prism in the preceding diagram. The glass has an index of refraction of $n_r = 1.62$ for a particular wavelength of red light and $n_v = 1.72$ for a particular wavelength of violet light. To three significant figures:
(a) What is the deviation angle, δ_r for red light and the deviation angle for this violet light δ_v?
(b) What is the angular dispersion, Ψ ?

SOLUTION TO PROBLEM 1

(a) The angle of incidence and the angle of refraction of the white light on the vertical side of the prism is 0°, but on the slanted side of the prism the ray of white light has an angle of incidence of 30.0°. The angles of refraction are different for each color.

Using Snell's law to find the angle of refraction of the red light: $n_1 \sin \theta_1 = n_2 \sin \theta_2$.

Solving for θ_2:

$$\theta_2 = \sin^{-1}\left(\frac{n_1}{n_2}\sin\theta_1\right) = \sin^{-1}\left[\left(\frac{1.62}{1.00}\right)\sin 30.0°\right] = 54.1°$$

The deviation angle for red light = $\delta_r - 30.0° = 54.1° - 30.0° = \mathbf{24.1°}$
Using Snell's law to find the angle of refraction of the violet light: $n_1 \sin \theta_1 = n_2 \sin \theta_2$.

Solving for θ_2:

$$\theta_2 = \sin^{-1}\left(\frac{n_1}{n_2}\sin\theta_1\right) = \sin^{-1}\left[\left(\frac{1.72}{1.00}\right)\sin 30.0°\right] = 59.3°$$

The deviation angle for violet light = $\delta_r - 30.0° = 59.3° - 30.0° = \mathbf{29.3°}$
(b) The angular dispersion: $\Psi = \delta_v - \delta_r = 29.3° - 24.1° = \mathbf{5.2°}$.

Dispersion in water droplets is responsible for rainbows, which are seen when the sun is behind the observer who is facing the rain. Dispersion is especially conspicuous in diamonds. The sparkle of a cut diamond is due in part to its high index of refraction and in part to the way it is cut.

ELECTROMAGNETIC WAVES

(*College Physics* 8th ed. pages 791–795/9th ed. pages 746–749)

When a stone is thrown into water, a disturbance is created by the energy added to the water by the stone. Water is a medium that reacts to the disturbance by creating water waves that carry the outside energy away from the point of the disturbance. We say that water waves radiate away from the point of the disturbance at some wave speed. Slam a book on a desktop, a disturbance is created in the surrounding air and the air, the medium, reacts by creating a sound wave that carries the energy away from the point of disturbance. Here we say that sound waves radiate away from the point of the disturbance at the speed of sound.

The electrons in the outer portions of atoms have both electrical and magnetic properties. Disturb the atom with heat or electrical energy and these outer electrons are displaced to higher electron positions in what is now an excited atom. The electrons create electromagnetic waves as they accelerate back to their ground states. The electromagnetic waves carry the added energy away from the atom at the speed of light. These electromagnetic waves are classified as *light*.

Note that water waves are carried in the medium water. Sound waves travel in the medium air. Electromagnetic waves do not need a medium. Light travels in vacuum as well as in air, water, or glass.

Visible light is not the only type of electromagnetic wave. All electromagnetic waves share the basic properties of frequency f and wavelength λ, and they all travel at the same speed in vacuum, the speed of light c. The speed of light is related to these properties by $c = f\lambda$.

Because of the small wavelengths of light radiation, it is convenient to define a smaller unit of measure. The SI unit is the *nanometer* (*nm*). One nanometer (1 nm) is defined as one-billionth of a meter, or 1 nm = 10^{-9} m.

The student should be aware that some textbook authors express the wavelength of light in terms of an older unit, the millimicron (mμ). The student should verify that 1 nm = 1 mμ. An even older unit of wavelength measure is still in use. It is the angstrom (Å). The angstrom was originally defined as 1 Å = 1×10^{-10} m making 1 nm = 10 Å.

The names given to various portions of the electromagnetic spectrum are simply for the convenience in describing the region of the spectrum where they are found. In many instances, there is considerable overlap between classifications. There is no sharp dividing point between one type of electromagnetic radiation and the next. Every form of electromagnetic waves is produced by the same thing—accelerating electrical charges.

Electromagnetic Radiation	Sources	Wavelength Range
Radio waves	Radio waves are the result of accelerating electrons through a transmitting antenna by an oscillator. Radio waves are the basis of television and radio communications systems.	From more than 10^4 m to about 0.1 m.
Microwaves	Electronic devices produce microwaves. Radar systems generate microwaves, and microwave ovens, which produce a wavelength of $\lambda = 12.2$ cm, are a common household device.	From approximately 0.3 m to 10^{-4} m.
Infrared waves (IR)	Molecules and room temperature objects produce infrared waves. Some IR is produced by outer electron transitions in excited atoms.	From 10^{-3} m to 700 nm.
Visible light	Visible light is the part of the electromagnetic spectrum the human eye detects. Light is produced by electron transitions in the outer electron shell of excited atoms and molecules. The sensitivity of the human eye is at a maximum of 550 nm at yellow green.	From 700 nm for red light to 400 nm for violet light.
Ultraviolet waves (UV)	Ultraviolet waves are produced by electron transitions in the outer shells of excited atoms. The surface of the sun produces great quantities of UV.	From about 400 nm to 0.6 nm.

(Continued)

Electromagnetic Radiation	Sources	Wavelength Range
X-rays	The most common source of X-rays is the deceleration of high-energy electrons bombarding a heavy metal target in a vacuum tube. X-rays are also produced by the electron transitions that follow the removal of electrons from the inner electron shells of heavy metal atoms.	From approximately 10^{-8} m to 10^{-12} m.
Gamma rays	Gamma rays are the result of the rearrangement of neutrons and electrically charged protons in the nucleus after alpha or beta radioactive decay. Gamma rays are a component of high-energy cosmic radiation that enters the Earth's atmosphere from deep space. Matter-antimatter interactions also produce gamma rays.	From about 10^{-10} m to less than 10^{-14} m.

SAMPLE PROBLEM 2
(a) Calculate the frequency of yellow light, $\lambda = 600$ nm.
(b) Find the wavelength of radio waves whose frequency is $f = 1.00$ MHz.

SOLUTION TO PROBLEM 2
(a) The frequency is found using $f = \dfrac{c}{\lambda} = \dfrac{3.00 \times 10^8 \text{ m/s}}{600 \times 10^{-9} \text{ m}} = \mathbf{5.00 \times 10^{14} \text{ Hz.}}$

(b) Solving for wavelength: $\lambda = \dfrac{c}{f} = \dfrac{3.00 \times 10^8 \text{ m/s}}{1.00 \times 10^6 \text{ s}^{-1}} = \mathbf{300 \text{ m.}}$

CONDITIONS FOR INTERFERENCE

(*College Physics* 8th ed. pages 790–791/9th ed. pages 824–825)

In our study of mechanical waves, we saw that two waves could, by superposition, add together constructively or destructively. In constructive interference, the amplitude of the resultant wave is the sum of the amplitudes of the interacting waves. In destructive interference, the resultant amplitude is less than the sum of the interacting waves or even zero. Light waves also interact constructively or destructively. The interference between light waves is an interaction of the electromagnetic fields of the individual waves.

Light waves having a constant phase relationship with one another are said to be *coherent*. Laser beams have this property. On the other hand, light streaming from the sun or a lightbulb consists of a great number of short segments of sinc waves and the phase of one segment is not related to any other, and such light is said to be *incoherent*. Two coherent waves of the same wavelength (*monochromatic light*) may interfere. This means they can undergo constructive interference, or they may cancel one another out as in destructive interference.

There are two conditions that must be met in order to produce interference:

1. The light source must be coherent meaning it emits light of the same phase.

2. The light must be monochromatic meaning the wavelengths are identical.

YOUNG'S DOUBLE-SLIT EXPERIMENT

(*College Physics* 8th ed. pages 791–795/9th ed. pages 825–830)

In 1801 Thomas Young conducted a brilliant experiment that established the wave theory of light. He directed monochromatic light on a screen with a single narrow slit that behaved like a point source S. The light passes through the single slit and encounters a second screen with two narrow slits A and B. Each slit acts as a secondary source emitting coherent light.

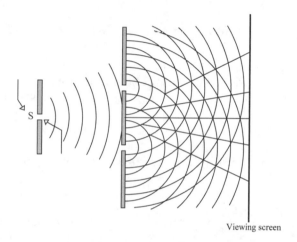

Viewing screen

Two wave fronts emanate from these slits. Where crests coincide, the light is reinforced, and where a crest encounters a trough, the light cancels. The two sets of waves are directed on a screen where one sees a pattern of bright and dark bands.

Consider point P on the viewing screen as shown on the diagram. Note that the diagram is not to scale. The screen is positioned a perpendicular distance L from the screen containing slits A and B that are separated by a distance d.

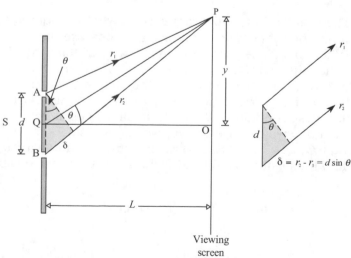

$$\delta = r_2 - r_1 = d \sin \theta$$

Viewing screen

Both r_1 and r_2 are the distances rays travel from the slits to the screen. The rays emanating from A and B have the same frequency and the same amplitude and start out in phase. The intensity of the light at point P is the result of light from both slits. Light from slit B travels further than a wave from slit A by an amount $d \sin\theta$. This distance is called the path difference δ, where

$$\delta = r_2 - r_1 = d \sin\theta$$

This equation assumes that r_1 and r_2 travel in parallel lines because $L \gg d$.

The value of the path difference determines whether the two waves are in phase at *point P*. If the path difference is either zero or some integral multiple of the wavelength λ, the waves will be in phase and constructive interference will take place.

The condition for constructive interference and bright fringes at point P is

$$d \sin\theta_{bright} = m\lambda \qquad \text{where } m = 0, \pm 1, \pm 2, \ldots$$

The number m is the *order number*. The central bright fringe at $\theta_{bright} = 0$ is the zeroth-order maximum. The maximum on each side of the zeroth-order maximum, where $m = \pm 1$, is called the first-order maximum, and so forth.

When the path difference is an odd multiple of $\lambda/2$, then the two waves arriving at point P are 180° out of phase and cause destructive interference. The condition for destructive interference and dark fringes at point P is

$$d \sin\theta_{dark} = \left(m + \frac{1}{2}\right)\lambda \qquad \text{where } m = 0, \pm 1, \pm 2, \ldots$$

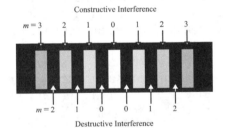

The spacing in the diagram is somewhat exaggerated. The spacing between the fringes is not uniform and increases as θ increases.

When $m = 0$, the path difference is $\lambda/2$, which is the first dark fringe on either side of the central maximum. When $m = 1$, the path difference is $3\lambda/2$, which is the condition for the second dark fringe, and so forth.

In addition to the assumption of $L \gg d$, we also assume that $d \gg \lambda$. Under these conditions, θ is quite small; usually less than 4°. For such a small angle, we can use the approximation $\sin\theta = \tan\theta$. Then from the triangle OPQ: $y = L \tan\theta \approx L \sin\theta$. From this equation and $d \sin\theta_{bright} = m\lambda$, we find the positions of bright fringes measured from O by

$$y_{bright} = \frac{\lambda L}{d} m \qquad \text{where } m = 0, \pm 1, \pm 2, \ldots$$

And for dark fringe positions:

$$y_{\text{dark}} = \frac{\lambda L}{d}\left(m + \frac{1}{2}\right) \qquad \text{where } m = 0, \pm 1, \pm 2, \ldots$$

Will there be an infinite number of fringes on a screen where constructive and destructive fringes occur? The $\sin\theta$ cannot exceed one. Thus, there is an upper limit to the values of m. The maximum value of m is the integer closest to the value but smaller than d/λ. There are a finite number of constructive and destructive interference fringes regardless the size of the screen.

AP Tip

Constructive interference occurs when the waves arrive in phase with one another.

AP Tip

Destructive interference occurs when the phase difference is a half-integral number of wavelengths.

SAMPLE PROBLEM 3

In a Young's double-slit experiment, two slits are 0.02 mm apart. The screen is located 1.80 m from the source, and the third-order bright fringe is located 12.50 cm from the central fringe.
  (a) Determine the wavelength of the source.
  (b) Where will the first dark fringe appear?
  (c) What is the distance between the first dark fringe and the third-order bright fringe?

SOLUTION TO PROBLEM 3

  (a) Since θ is small, we can use $\sin\theta = \tan\theta$ and can substitute y/L for θ. For a third-order bright fringe, $m = 3$. The wavelength is then found by using

$$\lambda = \frac{y_{\text{bright}}d}{mL} = \frac{(0.125 \text{ m})(2.00 \times 10^{-5}\text{m})}{3(1.80 \text{ m})} = \textbf{4.63} \times \textbf{10}^{-7} \textbf{ m} = \textbf{463 nm}$$

  (b) For the first dark fringe, $m = 0$. The position of the first dark fringe is found from

$$y_{\text{dark}} = \frac{\lambda L}{d}\left(m + \frac{1}{2}\right) = \frac{(4.63 \times 10^{-7}\text{m})(1.80 \text{ m})}{2(2.00 \times 10^{-5}\text{m})} = \textbf{2.08 cm}$$

  (c) The difference is simply $\Delta y = 12.6 \text{ cm} - 2.1 \text{ cm} = \textbf{10.5 cm}$.

THIN FILMS

(*College Physics* 8th ed. pages 796–800/9th ed. pages 830–836)

Interference effects are commonly observed in thin films such as thin layers of oil on water and the thin surface of a soap bubble. The varied colors observed when incoherent white light is incident on such films result from the interference of light waves reflected from the two surfaces of the film.

Consider a thin film of thickness t as illustrated here. The light incident on the film is incident in a direction that is perpendicular to the surface of the film. The principle involved here would be the same for a different angle to the surface, but the calculations become more complicated, and so we will deal with light being perpendicular to the surface of the film. The incident ray is partially reflected at the top of the film, surface A, as it travels from a material of index of refraction n_1 to the film that has an index of refraction of n_2. For clarity, the reflected ray, ray 1, is displaced slightly to the left.

The remainder of the incident ray is transmitted through the film and reaches its bottom, surface B, where it encounters another medium with an index of refraction n_3 and is partially reflected and partially transmitted into the new material of index of refraction n_3.

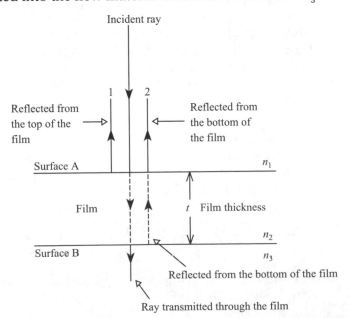

The reflected ray, ray 2, then travels back to the top surface of the film where it is now transmitted into the material of original incidence n_1. We have two rays that travel together away from the upper surface of the film: ray 1, which is reflected from the top of the film, and ray 2, which is reflected from the bottom of the film. These two rays can, in general, interfere with one another.

To determine whether the reflected rays interfere constructively or destructively we note the following rules.

1. A light wave traveling from a medium of index of refraction n_1 toward a medium of index of refraction n_2 undergoes a 180° (π radian) phase change on reflection when $n_2 > n_1$. There is no phase change in the reflected light wave if $n_2 < n_1$.

2. The wavelength of light λ_n in a medium with index of refraction n is given by $\lambda_n = \lambda/n$ where λ is the wavelength of light in vacuum.

According to the first rule, ray 1, which is reflected from surface A, undergoes a phase change of 180° with respect to the incident ray. Ray 2, which is reflected from lower surface B, undergoes no phase change with respect to the incident ray. Ray 1 is 180° out of phase with ray 2, which is equivalent to a path difference of $\lambda_n/2$. We must also consider the fact that ray 2 travels an extra distance of $2t$ before the two rays can recombine above surface A.

If $2t = \lambda_n/2$, then rays 1 and 2 recombine in phase and constructive interference takes place. The condition for constructive interference in thin films is

$$2t = \left(m + \frac{1}{2} \right) \lambda_n \qquad \text{where } m = 0, 1, 2, \dots$$

The preceding conditions take two factors into account:

1. The difference in path length for the two rays, the term $m\lambda_n$.
2. The 180° phase change upon reflection, the term $\lambda_n/2$.

Since $\lambda_n = \lambda/n$, we can write the *condition for constructive interference* in thin films as

$$2nt = \left(m + \frac{1}{2} \right) \lambda \qquad \text{where } m = 0, 1, 2, \dots$$

If the extra distance $2t$ traveled by ray 2 is a multiple of λ_n, the two waves combine out of phase, and destructive interference results. The *condition for destructive interference* in thin films is

$$2nt = m\lambda \qquad \text{where } m = 0, 1, 2, \dots$$

The equations for constructive and destructive interference are valid when and only when there is one phase reversal! This occurs when the media above and below the thin film both have indices of refraction greater than the index of refraction of the film or when both have indices of refraction less than the film ($n_1 > n_2 < n_3$ or $n_1 < n_2 > n_3$).

When the film is placed between two different media, one having a lower index of refraction than the film and one of higher index of refraction, the preceding equations are reversed ($n_1 < n_2 < n_3$ or $n_1 > n_2 > n_3$).

AP Tip

For thin film interference, an extra half-wavelength phase shift occurs when light reflects off an optically denser medium, going from a material of lesser index of refraction to one with a greater index of refraction.

SAMPLE PROBLEM 4

A student observes the interference of light with a soap bubble ($n = 1.33$) surrounded by air ($n = 1.00$).

(a) What is the minimum thickness for yellow light, $\lambda = 580$ nm, to be strongly reflected when the soap bubble is illuminated by white light and observed from directly above?

(b) What is the minimum thickness needed to remove the yellow light, $\lambda = 580$ nm from the reflection of white light from the soap bubble.

(c) In a third thin-film interference observation, an organic material ($n = 1.36$) is placed on a layer of glass ($n = 1.50$). What wavelength of white light is strongly reinforced in the reflected light if the film has a thickness of 184.0 nm?

SOLUTION TO PROBLEM 4

(a) The light coming from air to the soap bubble encounters a medium of higher index of refraction and undergoes a 180° phase shift in the reflection from the upper surface. Reflection from the lower surface is in phase.

Minimum thickness means that $m = 0$. Since $n_{air} > n_{bubble} < n_{air}$, we write

$$2n_{film}t = \left(m + \frac{1}{2}\right)\lambda$$

Solving for the thickness of the film, t:

$$t = \left(m + \frac{1}{2}\right)\frac{\lambda}{2n_{film}} = \left(0 + \frac{1}{2}\right)\frac{\lambda}{2n_{film}} = \frac{\lambda}{4n_{film}} = \frac{580 \text{ nm}}{4(1.33)} = \mathbf{109 \text{ nm}}$$

(b) The minimum thickness for destructive interference to occur requires a path length in the film of $\lambda/2$. The ray reflected from the lower surface of the film has traveled a total length of λ. The minimum thickness requires $m = 1$, and then $2n_{film}t = m\lambda$.

Solving for t:

$$t = \frac{m\lambda}{2n_{film}} = \frac{1(580 \text{ nm})}{2(1.33)} = \mathbf{218 \text{ nm}}$$

(c) The ray reflected from the upper surface undergoes a phase shift of 180°. The ray reflected from the lower surface also undergoes a phase shift of 180° Since $n_1 < n_2 < n_3$ and for constructive interference $m = 1$: $2n_{film}t = m\lambda$.

Solving for λ:

$$\lambda = \frac{2n_{film}t}{m} = \frac{2(1.36)(184 \text{ nm})}{1} = \mathbf{500 \text{ nm}}$$

OPTICAL COATINGS

(*College Physics* 8th ed. page 799/9th ed. pages 652–655)

Interference in a thin film is desirable to reduce unwanted reflections from the glass of a camera lens or the lenses of a pair of binoculars. Lenses are often coated with thin films of transparent, durable materials such as magnesium fluoride, MgF_2. Destructive interference in an optical coating minimizes unwanted reflections from glass.

SAMPLE PROBLEM 5

To produce a minimum reflection of wavelengths near the middle of the visible spectrum, 550 nm, how thick of a coating of MgF_2 ($n = 1.38$) should be vacuum-coated on a camera lens ($n = 1.55$)?

SOLUTION TO PROBLEM 5

Consider incident light to be normal to the surface of the film.

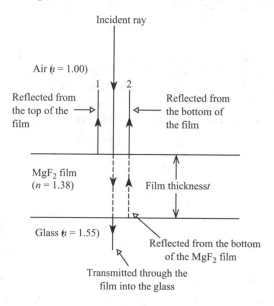

We wish to cause destructive interference between ray 1 and ray 2 so that maximum energy passes into the glass. A phase change occurs with each ray for both the upper and the lower surfaces of the MgF_2 film. Since $n_1 < n_2 < n_3$ and for destructive interference and setting $m = 0$, we can write $2n_{film}t = \left(m + \dfrac{1}{2}\right)\lambda$.

Solving for the film thickness:

$$t = \left(m + \frac{1}{2}\right)\frac{\lambda}{2n_{film}} = \frac{\lambda}{4n_{film}} = \frac{550\text{ nm}}{4(1.38)} = \textbf{99.6 nm}$$

DIFFRACTION

(*College Physics* 8th ed. page 802/9th ed. pages 836–837)

Light travels in straight lines in a uniform medium but commonly changes directions where there is a change of medium or a change in the properties of a single medium. This, of course, is the cause of reflection and refraction. Careful observation shows that there is also a slight bending around opaque objects placed in a beam of light. The spreading of light into the region behind an obstacle is called *diffraction*. Diffraction occurs in accordance with Huygen's principle and is an interference phenomenon.

Any obstacle placed into a light beam coming from a point source will cause diffraction effects under proper conditions. A slit, a thin wire, and a razor edge are examples of such objects. A razor's edge illuminated by a beam of monochromatic light from a point source casts a shadow that is not geometrically sharp. A small amount of light bends around the edge into the geometric shadow, and a series of alternating light and dark bands are found to border the shadow.

If a hole on a screen is illuminated by monochromatic light, the image formed on a screen is not a single well-defined spot of light but rather a series of light and dark rings.

SINGLE-SLIT DIFFRACTION

(*College Physics* 8th ed. pages 803–805/9th ed. pages 837–839)

Consider a beam of monochromatic light illuminating a narrow slit of width *a*. In the following illustrations, sets of arrows were drawn to suggest that the wave front can be imagined to consist of many coherent secondary sources. Rays going straight ahead are all in phase and when they fall on a screen they will appear as a bright band.

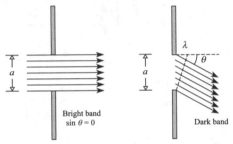

Bright band
$\sin \theta = 0$

Dark band

In the diagram on the right, consider the two rays 1 and 4. Note in the diagram that these two light sources are distance *a*/2 apart. They give an interference pattern much like that from double slits; that is, when $(a/2)\sin \theta = \lambda/2$, these two waves cancel. Consider another pair of rays just below 1 and 4. These, too, also cancel. Moving down the slit in this manner, we can see that each ray can be paired off with another ray that will cancel it.

Repeat the process dividing the slit into four parts rather than two and using similar reasoning. The effective slit spacing is *a*/4, so $(a/4) = \sin\theta = \lambda/2$, or $a\sin\lambda = 2\lambda$. We can divide the slit into six zones and then eight zones and so on. The general result is

$$\sin\theta_{dark} = \frac{m\lambda}{a} \qquad \text{where } m = 1, 2, 3 \dots \text{ single-slit minima}$$

Do not confuse this with the condition for maxima in the double-slit experiment, even though the equations appear similar.

SAMPLE PROBLEM 6

In a laboratory experiment, a student observes a diffraction pattern in which a single slit, of width *a*, is illuminated by monochromatic light of wavelength $\lambda = 540$ nm.

    (a) If the first dark band is 5.2° from the central axis, what is the width of the slit?

    (b) At what angle will the student locate the third dark band?

SOLUTION TO PROBLEM 6

(a) Solving for the width a:

$$a = \frac{m\lambda}{\sin\theta_{dark}} = \frac{(1)(5.4 \times 10^{-7}\,m)}{\sin 5.2°} = \mathbf{6 \times 10^{-6}\ m}$$

(b) To find the angle, we use

$$\sin\theta_{dark} = \frac{m\lambda}{a} \quad \text{and} \quad \theta_{dark} = \sin^{-1}\left(\frac{m\lambda}{a}\right) = \sin^{-1}\left[\frac{3(5.4 \times 10^{-7}\,m)}{6 \times 10^{-6}\,m}\right] = \mathbf{15.7°}$$

THE DIFFRACTION GRATING

(*College Physics* 8th ed. pages 805–807/9th ed. pages 839–842)

The principles of interference and diffraction find importance in measuring wavelengths of light with the optical diffraction grating. A grating for use with transmitted light, the diffraction grating is a glass plate ruled with a large number of equally spaced opaque lines, usually several thousand lines per centimeter. A grating is specified in terms of its number of lines per centimeter. The spacing, d, between the rulings is the inverse of the line population per centimeter. If a grating is specified as having 2,500 lines/cm or 2,500 cm^{-1}, the spacing is $d = 1/N = 1/2,500$ cm^{-1} $= 4.0 \times 10^{-4}$ cm $= 4.0 \times 10^{-6}$ m. A diffraction grating is basically a system with a large number of optical slits.

The interference pattern produced by a diffraction grating is a series of sharp, widely spaced bright fringes that are called *principal maxima*. Dark regions with a number of weak secondary maxima separate the principal maxima fringes. The angle at which a principal maximum appears is dependent on the wavelength of light that passes through the grating. The grating acts like a prism by sending various components of white light off in different directions. Unlike the prism, the diffraction grating spreads light over a wider range.

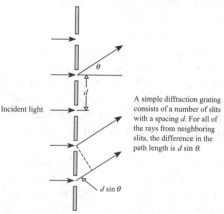

A simple diffraction grating consists of a number of slits with a spacing d. For all of the rays from neighboring slits, the difference in the path length is $d \sin \theta$.

To find the angles at which principal maxima are formed, consider a diffraction grating of large number of slits where each one is separated by a distance d, as illustrated in the diagram. A beam of light of wavelength λ illuminates the left side of the grating and is diffracted to the right on to a screen on to a distant screen. At angle θ to the incident direction, the path difference between adjacent slits is $d \sin \theta$ as shown.

Constructive interference and a principal maximum produced by a diffraction grating occurs when the path difference is an integral number of wavelengths, λ:

$$d \sin\theta = m\lambda \qquad \text{where } m = 0, \ \pm1, \ \pm2, \ ...$$

When a grating has more lines per centimeter, d is smaller and the angle θ becomes greater spreading the incoming light over a wider range of angles.

SAMPLE PROBLEM 7

A diffraction grating, ruled with 200 lines per millimeter, is used to determine the wavelength of a monochromatic light source. If the third-order spectrum occurs at an angle of 19.0°, what is the wavelength of the source?

SOLUTION TO PROBLEM 7

First, we need to determine the width of the lines:

$$d = \frac{1}{200 \text{ mm}^{-1}} = 5 \times 10^{-3} \text{mm} = 5 \times 10^{-6} \text{m}$$

To find the wavelength, we use $d \sin \theta = m\lambda$, and

$$\lambda = \frac{d \sin\theta}{m} = \frac{(5 \times 10^{-6} \text{m}) \times (\sin 19°)}{3} = \textbf{543 nm}$$

WAVE OPTICS: STUDENT OBJECTIVES FOR THE AP EXAM

- You should know that all electromagnetic waves travel with the same speed, c, in a vacuum and be able to state and relate the relationship between speed, wavelength, and frequency of these waves.
- You should know the difference between the parts of the electromagnetic spectrum and their sources.
- You should be able to explain why dispersion occurs for the visible part of the electromagnetic spectrum.
- You should know and be able to state what is necessary for two or more light waves to produce interference phenomena.
- You must be able to state and mathematically apply the equations for constructive and destructive interference in the *Young's double-slit experiment.*
- You must be able to relate a 180° phase change due to reflection at the boundary between two media when $n_2 > n_1$, and recognize that there is no phase change at the boundary between the two media when $n_2 < n_1$.
- You must also recognize that the interference between the waves reflected from the upper and lower surface of a thin film also depends on the path length $2t$ in the film before the waves combine at the upper surface.

■ You must be able to solve for thin-film interference, both constructive and destructive, when one and two phase changes occur at the boundaries between the media.

■ You must be able to apply the equations for constructive and destructive interference in a diffraction pattern.

■ You must be able to solve multiple-choice questions without a calculator.

MULTIPLE-CHOICE QUESTIONS

1. Two sources are said to be coherent. This means they
   (A) are polarized.
   (B) have the same amplitude.
   (C) have different wavelengths.
   (D) maintain a constant phase with respect to each other.
   (E) have different frequencies.

2. In a double-slit interference pattern, decreasing the distance, d, between the slits by ½ results in a change in the distance between the fringes by a factor of
   (A) ¼.
   (B) ½.
   (C) 1.
   (D) 2.
   (E) 4.

3. In a double-slit interference pattern, decreasing the distance, d, between the slits causes the width of the fringes to
   (A) increase.
   (B) decrease.
   (C) remain the same.
   (D) increase then decrease.
   (E) decrease then increase.

4. In a double-slit interference pattern, destructive interference occurs when the path difference between two waves is
   (A) even multiples of $\lambda/2$.
   (B) odd multiples of $\lambda/2$.
   (C) the same.
   (D) even multiples of λ.
   (E) odd multiples of λ.

5. In a double-slit interference pattern, using different wavelengths of light to produce the fringes, the fringes are closer together when the slit is illuminated with
   (A) blue light.
   (B) green light.
   (C) yellow light.
   (D) orange light.
   (E) red light.

6. In thin-film interference, there is a 180° phase change at the boundary between two media for a ray traveling from medium with index of refraction n_1 to second medium with index of refraction n_2, when
    (A) $n_1 = n_2$.
    (B) $n_1 > n_2$.
    (C) $n_1 < n_2$.
    (D) $n_1 = 1/2\ n_2$.
    (E) $n_1 = 2n_2$.

7. A soap bubble ($n = 1.33$) is floating in air ($n = 1.00$). For a ray of light incident on the soap bubble from air, the minimum thickness of the soap bubble for constructive interference to occur is given by
    (A) $t = \lambda n/2$.
    (B) $t = 2\lambda/n$.
    (C) $t = \lambda$.
    (D) $t = \lambda/4n$.
    (E) $t = 4\lambda/n$.

8. If the soap bubble in multiple-choice Question 7 is illuminated by 450 nm light, the minimum thickness of the film is most nearly
    (A) 85 nm.
    (B) 112 nm.
    (C) 169 nm.
    (D) 338 nm.
    (E) 677 nm.

9. The spreading of light from its original line of travel is called
    (A) reflection.
    (B) refraction.
    (C) diffraction.
    (D) dispersion.
    (E) polarization.

10. Increasing the number of lines per centimeter (the ruling) on a diffraction grating
    (A) allows one to use longer wavelengths of light.
    (B) allows one to use shorter wavelengths of light.
    (C) increases the spread of the spacing between principal maxima.
    (D) decreases the spread of the spacing between principal maxima.
    (E) produces no change in the spacing between principal maxima.

11. In a single-slit experiment, increasing the width of the slit results in
    (A) widening the diffraction pattern.
    (B) narrowing the diffraction pattern.
    (C) no change in the diffraction pattern.
    (D) reversing the diffraction pattern.
    (E) production of no diffraction pattern.

12. A diffracting grating is used to determine the wavelength of light. In using the same grating, illuminated by red light compared to blue light, the angle for the first-order maxima
    (A) is equal for both red and blue light.
    (B) is greater for red light than blue light.
    (C) is smaller for red light than blue light.
    (D) is independent of the wavelength of light.
    (E) is independent of the frequency of light.

13. Light of wavelength $\lambda = 600$ nm falls on a soap bubble ($n = 1.33$) from air ($n = 1.00$). What is the change in phase for light reflected from the upper surface?
    (A) $0°$
    (B) $\pi/2$
    (C) π
    (D) $\lambda/2$
    (E) $\lambda/1.33$

14. Light of wavelength $\lambda = 600$ nm falls on a soap bubble ($n = 1.33$) from air ($n = 1.00$). The wavelength of light in the soap bubble is most nearly
    (A) 800 nm.
    (B) 600 nm.
    (C) 450 nm.
    (D) 340 nm.
    (E) 300 nm.

15. Light of wavelength $\lambda = 500$ nm falls on a diffraction grating whose ruling produces a spacing between the slits of 1.00×10^{-5} m. How many principal maxima can be observed?
    (A) 5
    (B) 10
    (C) 15
    (D) 20
    (E) 25

FREE-RESPONSE PROBLEMS

1. A student conducts an interference experiment using a laser source of monochromatic light of wavelength $\lambda = 635$ nm.
   (a) The light is incident on a double slit having a separation of $d = 0.04$ mm. At what angle will the second-order
       i. maximum occur?
       ii. minimum occur?
   (b) The light is incident on a single slit of separation $a = 0.04$ mm. At what angle will the second-order
       i. maximum occur?
       ii. minimum occur?
   (c) If the screen is 1.50 m from the double slits, what is the linear separation between the first-order maximum and the fourth-order maximum?
   (d) The student places the double-slit film in water ($n = 1.33$) and illuminates it with monochromatic light of $\lambda_{air} = 635$ nm. What is the angle of the second order maximum?

2. Monochromatic light of wavelength $\lambda = 630$ nm is directed on a diffraction grating ruled with 300 lines per mm. Determine the
   (a) angle for the first-order maxima.
   (b) angle for the third-order maxima.
   (c) angle between the first- and third-order maxima.
   (d) maximum number of orders that can be observed.

ANSWERS

MULTIPLE-CHOICE QUESTIONS

1. **D** Coherent sources must (1) maintain a constant phase with respect to each other and (2) have the same wavelength (*College Physics* 8th ed. pages 790–791/9th ed. pages 824–825).

2. **D** In a double-slit interference pattern, decreasing the distance, d, between the slits results in an increase between the fringe and the central axis, $y_{bright} = \dfrac{\lambda L m}{d}$. If d decreases by a factor of $\dfrac{1}{2}$, the distance between the fringe and the central maxima increase by a factor of 2 (*College Physics* 8th ed. pages 791–795/9th ed. pages 825–830).

3. **A** In a double-slit interference pattern, when the separation, d, between the slits is decreased, the width of the fringes increases $\Delta y = \dfrac{\lambda L}{d}$ (*College Physics* 8th ed. pages 791–795/9th ed. pages 825–830).

4. **B** For destructive interference between two waves in the Young's double-slit experiment, the path length must be an odd multiple of $\lambda/2$ (*College Physics* 8th ed. pages 792–793/9th ed. pages 826–828).

5. **A** A smaller wavelength, blue light, results in the fringe pattern being closer together, $y_{bright} = \dfrac{\lambda L m}{d}$ (*College Physics* 8th ed. pages 791–795/9th ed. pages 825–830).

6. **C** A wave of light traveling from a medium of lower index of refraction to one of higher index of refraction undergoes a 180° phase change when $n_2 > n_1$ (*College Physics* 8th ed. pages 795–797/9th ed. pages 829–833).

7. **D** Constructive interference in a soap bubble where n_2 is greater than n_1 occurs when $2t = \left(m + \dfrac{1}{2}\right)\lambda_n$. A 180° shift occurs at the upper surface, and a 180° shift occurs because the wave must travel down to the lower surface and back up to the upper surface. Since $\lambda_n = \lambda/n$, the equation can be rewritten as $2t = \left(m + \dfrac{1}{2}\right)\dfrac{\lambda}{n}$. The minimum thickness is $m = 0$. This yields $t = \lambda/4n$ (*College Physics* 8th ed. pages 796–797/9th ed. pages 831–833).

8. **A** Minimum thickness occurs for $t = \lambda/4n$. Illumination by 450-nm light requires that $t = \dfrac{450 \text{ nm}}{4(1.33)}$. Therefore, $t = 85$ nm (*College Physics* 8th ed. pages 796–797/9th ed. pages 831–833).

9. **C** Diffraction is the spreading out of light from its initial line of travel (*College Physics* 8th ed. page 802/9th ed. page 836).

10. **C** Increasing the number of lines per centimeter, N, on a diffraction grating will increase the spacing between principal maxima. Since $d = 1/N$ and $m\lambda = d \sin\theta$, as d increases, the angle increases—

therefore, the spacing increases (*College Physics* 8th ed. pages 805–808/9th ed. pages 839–842).

11. **B** As the width of the slit in a single-slit diffraction pattern is increased, the pattern narrows. The central band becomes narrower, and secondary bands move closer to the central band (*College Physics* 8th ed. page 802–805/9th ed. pages 836–839).

12. **B** In the equation, $m\lambda = d\sin\theta$, both m and d are the same, thus as λ varies so does $\sin\theta$. Red light has a wavelength λ of about 700 nm, and blue light has a wavelength λ of about 450 nm (*College Physics* 8th ed. pages 720–722, 800–802/9th ed. pages 746–749, 839–842).

13. **C** A wave of light traveling from a medium of lower optical density to one of higher optical density undergoes a phase change of 180° at the interface between the two media (*College Physics* 8th ed. pages 795–797/9th ed. pages 830–831).

14. **C** The wavelength of light in the soap bubble is given by $\lambda_n = \lambda/n$ (*College Physics* 8th ed. pages 795–797, 802/9th ed. pages 829–833).

15. **D** In the equation, $m\lambda = d\sin\theta$, the maximum number of orders occurs when $\sin\theta = 90°$. Therefore, $m = d/\lambda$, and substituting $m = \dfrac{1\times10^{-5}\,m}{5\times10^{-7}\,m}$ yields $m = 20$ (*College Physics* 8th ed. pages 805–808/9th ed. pages 839–842).

FREE-RESPONSE PROBLEMS

1. (a) i. The angle for the second-order maximum is given by

$$d\sin\theta_{bright} = (m\lambda) \qquad \text{where } m = 0,\ \pm1,\ \pm2,\ \dots$$

Solving for θ:

$$\theta_{bright} = \sin^{-1}\left(\frac{m\lambda}{d}\right) = \sin^{-1}\left[\frac{2\left(6.35\times10^{-7}m\right)}{4.0\times10^{-5}m}\right] = \mathbf{1.82°}$$

ii. The angle for the second-order minimum is given by

$$d\sin\theta_{dark} = \left(m+\frac{1}{2}\right)\lambda \qquad \text{where } m = 0,\ \pm1,\ \pm2,\ \dots$$

The second order minimum occurs at

$$\theta_{dark} = \sin^{-1}\left(\frac{1.5\lambda}{d}\right) = \sin^{-1}\left[\frac{1.5\left(6.35\times10^{-7}m\right)}{4.0\times10^{-5}m}\right] = \mathbf{1.36°}$$

(b) The equation for part (a) i. $\sin\theta_{bright} = \dfrac{m\lambda}{d}$ and part (b) i. $\sin\theta_{dark} = \dfrac{m\lambda}{a}$ have the same form, *but* they do not mean the same thing. In part (a) the equation describes the *bright* regions in a two-slit interference pattern where d is the separation of the slits A and B.

In part (b), the equation describes the *dark* regions in a single-slit interference pattern where a is the single-slit width.

i. $a\,\sin\theta_{bright} = \left(m + \dfrac{1}{2}\right)\lambda$ where $m = 0,\ \pm 1,\ \pm 2,\ \ldots$

Solving for θ:

$$\theta_{bright} = \sin^{-1}\left(\frac{1.5\lambda}{a}\right) = \sin^{-1}\left[\frac{1.5\left(6.35 \times 10^{-7}\,\text{m}\right)}{4.0 \times 10^{-5}\,\text{m}}\right] = \textbf{1.36°}$$

ii. $\theta_{dark} = \sin^{-1}\left(\dfrac{m\lambda}{a}\right) = \sin^{-1}\left[\dfrac{2\left(6.35 \times 10^{-7}\,\text{m}\right)}{4.0 \times 10^{-5}\,\text{m}}\right] = \textbf{1.82°}$

(c) The linear separation is given by

$$y_{bright} = \frac{\lambda L m}{d}\ \ \text{and}$$

$$\Delta y = \left(y_4 - y_1\right) = \frac{6.35 \times 10^{-7}\,\text{m} \times 1.5\,\text{m} \times \left(4 - 1\right)}{4.0 \times 10^{-5}\,\text{m}} = \textbf{0.071 m}$$

(d) The angle for the second-order maximum is

$$\lambda_n = \frac{\lambda}{n} = \frac{635\ \text{nm}}{1.33} = 477.4\ \text{nm}$$

$$\theta = \sin^{-1}\left(\frac{m\lambda}{d}\right) = \sin^{-1}\left[\frac{2\left(4.77 \times 10^{-7}\,\text{m}\right)}{4.0 \times 10^{-5}\,\text{m}}\right] = \textbf{1.37°}$$

(*College Physics* 8th ed. pages 791–794, 802–804/9th ed. pages 825–829)

2. (a) First, we need to find d:

$$d = \frac{1}{300\ \text{mm}^{-1}} = 3.33 \times 10^{-6}\,\text{m}$$

The angle for the first-order maxima is

$$\theta_1 = \sin^{-1}\left(\frac{m\lambda}{d}\right) = \sin^{-1}\left[\frac{1\left(6.30 \times 10^{-7}\,\text{m}\right)}{3.33 \times 10^{-6}\,\text{m}}\right] = \textbf{10.9°}$$

(b) The angle for the third-order maxima is

$$\theta_3 = \sin^{-1}\left(\frac{m\lambda}{d}\right) = \sin^{-1}\left[\frac{3\left(6.30 \times 10^{-7}\,\text{m}\right)}{3.33 \times 10^{-6}\,\text{m}}\right] = \textbf{34.6°}$$

(c) The angle between the first- and third-order maxima is
$$\Delta\theta = 34.6° - 10.9° = \textbf{23.7°}$$

(d) The maximum number of orders that can be observed:
The maximum number of orders occurs when $\theta = 90°$ since $\sin 90° = 1$
$$m = \frac{d}{\lambda} = \frac{3.33 \times 10^{-6}\,\text{m}}{6.30 \times 10^{-7}\,\text{m}} = \textbf{5.28}$$

You *cannot* have a partial order. The maximum number of orders that can be observed under the given conditions is **5**.

(*College Physics* 8th ed. pages 805–808/9th ed. pages 839–842)

16

GEOMETRICAL OPTICS

WHAT IS THE NATURE OF THE REFLECTION OF LIGHT?

(*College Physics* 8th ed. pages 733–736/9th ed. pages 762–766)

When a light ray is incident upon a reflective material, it is a simple demonstration to show that the angle of the incoming ray (called the *angle of incidence*, θ_1 or θ_i) equals the angle of the outgoing ray (the *angle of reflection*, θ_2 or θ_R). Known as the law of reflection, this occurs because, even though light travels in a straight path until it encounters a boundary, light exhibits particle-like properties, approximately analogous to the path of a linearly projected object. The convention for measuring the angles is to use a line that is perpendicular to the surface boundary, which is called a normal, N. When reflection occurs, the incident and reflected rays remain in the same medium, in contrast to refraction, to be discussed shortly.

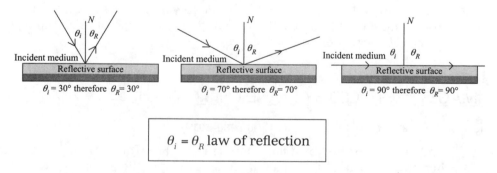

$\theta_i = 30°$ therefore $\theta_R = 30°$ $\theta_i = 70°$ therefore $\theta_R = 70°$ $\theta_i = 90°$ therefore $\theta_R = 90°$

$$\theta_i = \theta_R \text{ law of reflection}$$

As shown in the diagrams, this type of reflection, called *regular* or *specular reflection*, occurs only when the surface is smooth (such as with a mirror, a window, a level lake, or a polished automobile) simply because all the surface normals are parallel. A rough surface (such as newspaper), in contrast, causes *diffuse reflection* in which reflected rays do not leave the surface parallel to each other because the surface normals are not parallel. Provided surface variations are very small relative to the incident light's wavelength, reflection will be regular.

AP Tip

Keep in mind that angles are measured relative to the normal N, not the surface boundary. Thus, when $\theta_i = 90°$ (ray incident *along the boundary*), the angle of reflection is 90°, not 0°. Similarly, when $\theta_i = 0°$ (ray incident *along the normal*), the angle of reflection is 0°, not 90°.

SAMPLE PROBLEM 1

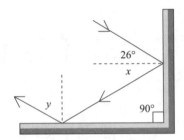

As shown, an incident ray of light is reflected twice from two flat perpendicular mirrors. What are the correct values of angles x and y?

	Value of x	Value of y
(A)	26°	26°
(B)	26°	64°
(C)	38°	52°
(D)	52°	26°
(E)	64°	26°

SOLUTION TO PROBLEM 1

According to the law of reflection, angle x must equal 26°, which immediately gives its complement, 90° − 26° or 64°. Since the sum of the angles in the triangle formed by the first reflection and the two mirrors must be 180°, the angle in the lower left of that triangle is 26°. The complement to that is 64° which gives the angle of reflection y, 64°. Thus, the correct choice is (B).

IMAGES PRODUCED BY PLANE MIRRORS

(*College Physics* 8th ed. pages 759–762/9th ed. pages 790–793)

The images formed by a flat (plane) mirror are well-known as everyone has stood in front of such a mirror, as shown in the figure. Incident rays of light (such as rays 1, 2, and 3) from an object a distance s_o from the mirror reflect according to the law of reflection, and those reflections (rays 1a, 2a, and 3a) diverge from the mirror's surface. The observer sees these rays diverging as if they emanated from a point behind the mirror, called the *image point*, which is a distance s_i behind the mirror. The image, however, really isn't there. Since the light rays only appear to come from this point, the image is called a *virtual image*; had its reflections instead converged at a point, it would be termed a *real image*. Tracing the reflections behind the mirror (rays 1b, 2b, and 3b) reveals the formation of the image.

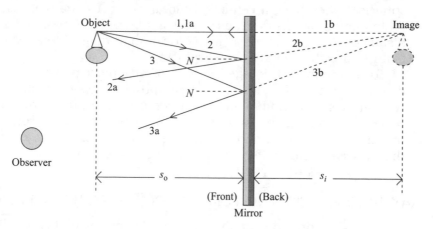

SUMMARY OF IMAGE PROPERTIES FOR PLANE MIRRORS

1. Image height (h_i) is the same size as the object height (h_o).
2. Image distance is the same as the object distance (i.e., $s_i = s_o$).
3. Images produced by plane mirrors are upright and virtual.
4. Images produced by plane mirrors are laterally reversed (reversed left-right).

SAMPLE PROBLEM 2

An object is placed 1 m in front of a plane mirror. An observer stands 3 m behind the object. For what distance must the observer focus his eyes in order to see the image of the object?

(A) 1 m
(B) 2 m
(C) 3 m
(D) 4 m
(E) 5 m

SOLUTION TO PROBLEM 2

The image distance of the object in the plane mirror is the same as the object distance, meaning the image distance is 1 meter behind the mirror, and thus 2 meters from the actual object in front of the mirror. Additionally, since the observer is an additional 3 meters in front of the mirror, the total distance of the observer from the image is 3 m + 2 m or 5 meters, choice (E).

IMAGES PRODUCED BY CONVEX MIRRORS

(*College Physics* 8th ed. pages 764–769/9th ed. pages 795–800)

Bending a plane mirror outward creates a convex mirror, reflections from which appear distorted relative to those of a plane mirror since surface normals diverge (hence, a convex mirror is a *diverging* mirror). Typically spherical, a convex mirror is commonly used for security purposes and for side-view vehicle mirrors because its outward curvature provides a larger field of view than does a plane mirror although it always produces smaller images (i.e., $h_i < h_o$). Since convex mirrors are spherical, they have a center of curvature C, a negative focal point f (both behind or "inside" the mirror), and a radius R which is twice the distance from the mirror as is the focal point f (i.e., $R = 2f$). Note these features are shown in Sample Problem 3.

To determine the image location of an object placed in front of a convex mirror, it is necessary to compose a ray diagram, a series of several rays of light (a minimum of two is needed) from the object that reflect according to the law of reflection. As with plane mirrors, to locate the image, trace reflected rays behind the mirror to the point where they intersect. Sample Problem 3 illustrates these steps.

RAY-TRACING GUIDELINES FOR CONVEX (DIVERGING) MIRRORS

1. A ray drawn from the object to the mirror that is parallel to the optical axis reflects as if it had emanated from the focal point f behind the mirror.
2. A ray drawn from the object that comes from (or may *appear to be* coming from) the center of curvature C reflects back on itself, through C.
3. A ray drawn from the object that comes from (or may *appear to be* coming from) the focal point f reflects parallel to the optical axis.
4. Back-tracing these *diverging* reflections shows they intersect *behind* the mirror, the image location.

While an accurate ray diagram is useful for locating the image produced by the convex mirror, one may also calculate the exact size and position of this image by using the following relationships (derivations of which are omitted here for brevity), both of which may serve as a check for the other. First, the equation

$$\frac{1}{f} = \frac{1}{s_i} + \frac{1}{s_o}$$

is known as the thin lens equation, as it also applies to images produced by lenses (to be seen later in this chapter). In the equation, as described earlier, s_o represents the object distance, s_i represents the image distance, and f is the mirror's focal length. Straightforward use of the lens maker's equation is common in AP Physics calculations. However, there are occasions in which it must be used in tandem with the magnification (M) equation (a dimensionless quantity), which may be written as either the ratio of the image height (h_i) to the object height (h_o), or that of the image distance (s_i) to the object distance (s_o).

$$M = \frac{h_i}{h_o} = -\frac{s_i}{s_o}$$

SAMPLE PROBLEM 3

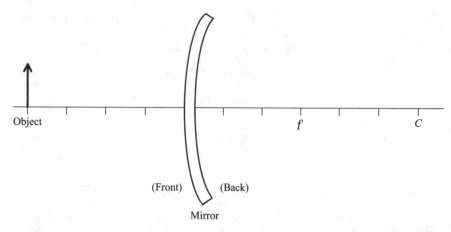

An object (represented by the arrow) that is 7 cm tall is placed 20 cm in front of the reflective side of a convex mirror whose focal length is 15 cm, as shown.

(a) Construct a ray diagram to locate the image formed by this convex mirror.

(b) Determine the image distance.

(c) Determine the magnification of the image.

(d) Determine the image height.

(e) Is the image real or virtual? Explain.

SOLUTION TO PROBLEM 3

(a) The diagram is as shown (drawn in accordance with the ray-tracing guidelines described earlier) with reflections labeled 1a, 2a, and 3a and back-traced reflections labeled as 1b, 2b, and 3b. Note that the image appears where 1b, 2b, and 3b intersect, as described, and that the image is behind the mirror, is upright, and, since it is formed from divergent rays, is a virtual image.

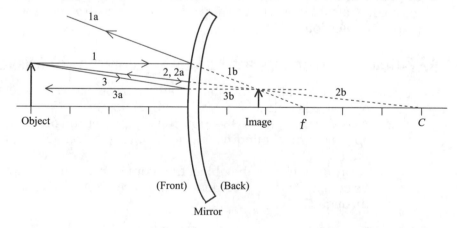

(b) Here it is necessary to use the thin lens equation, with the following in our variable checklist: $f = -15$ cm, $R = 30$ cm, $s_o = 20$ cm, $h_o = 7$ cm, $s_i = ?$ Therefore, substituting and solving:

$$\frac{1}{f} = \frac{1}{s_i} + \frac{1}{s_o} \text{ becomes } \frac{1}{f} - \frac{1}{s_o} = \frac{1}{s_i} \text{ or } \frac{1}{-15} - \frac{1}{20} = \frac{1}{s_i}, \text{ which}$$

gives $s_i = -8.6$ cm. The negative solution indicates that the image is behind the mirror and is virtual.

(c) Using the magnification equation and substituting gives $M = \dfrac{h_i}{h_o} = -\dfrac{s_i}{s_o}$ or $M = -\dfrac{-8.6 \text{ cm}}{20 \text{ cm}}$, which gives **M = 0.43**.

(d) Image height is h_i, which can be determined from both the answer to (c) and the magnification equation: $M = \dfrac{h_i}{h_o} = -\dfrac{s_i}{s_o}$ or $Mh_o = h_i$. Substituting gives $(0.43)(7 \text{ cm}) = h_1$ or **h_i = +3.0 cm** (upright).

(e) As the image is formed from the intersection of divergent rays 1a, 2a, and 3a, it is virtual.

SUMMARY OF IMAGE PROPERTIES FOR CONVEX MIRRORS

1. Image height is always smaller than the object height (i.e., $h_i < h_o$).
2. Image distance is less than the object distance (i.e., $s_i < s_o$).
3. Images produced by convex mirrors are upright and virtual.
4. Images produced by convex mirrors are laterally reversed (reversed left-right).

IMAGES PRODUCED BY CONCAVE MIRRORS

(*College Physics* 8th ed. pages 762–764/9th ed. pages 793–795)

Imagine now bending a plane mirror inward to form a bowl-shaped (concave) reflective surface. Images produced by convex mirrors are fairly straightforward for nearly all values of s_o, but those produced by concave mirrors are quite varied, depending greatly upon object distance s_o. The most instructive way to learn and reinforce images formed by concave mirrors is to sketch ray diagrams for five main object positions, which will yield very different image results, as shown. Additionally, concave mirrors have the greatest versatility in terms of practical use, ranging from telescope mirrors to cosmetic makeup mirrors. Calculations concerning such mirrors are left for a free-response question.

RAY-TRACING GUIDELINES FOR CONCAVE (CONVERGING) MIRRORS

1. A ray drawn from the object to the mirror that is parallel to the optical axis reflects through the focal point f.
2. A ray drawn from the object that passes through (or may *appear to be* coming from) the focal point f reflects parallel to the optical axis.
3. A ray drawn from the object that comes from (or may *appear to be* coming from) the center of curvature C reflects back on itself, through C.

CASE 1: OBJECT IS PLACED WELL BEYOND **R**

Rays 1, 2, and 3 from Sample Problem 3 have been drawn (as have their respective reflections), and the image is located where these reflections intersect. Therefore, when the object is very far from the mirror, its image is inverted, smaller, and real (not virtual, since it is formed from reflections *converging* at a point). This is the basis for the reflecting telescope.

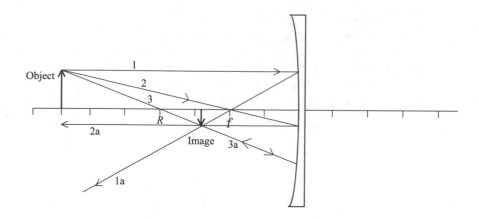

CASE 2: OBJECT IS PLACED AT R

In this situation, only rays 1 and 2 from Sample Problem 3 have been drawn (as have their respective reflections), as the object is already at C (the same as R), and the image is located where these reflections intersect. Therefore, when the object is at the center of curvature C, its image is inverted, the same size (i.e., $s_i = s_o$ and $h_i = h_o$), and real (since it is formed from reflections *converging* at a point).

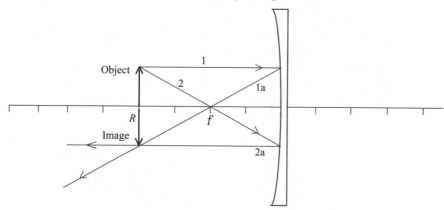

CASE 3: OBJECT IS PLACED BETWEEN R AND f

Again, due to diagram size constraints, only rays 1 and 2 from Sample Problem 3 have been drawn (as have their respective reflections), and the image is located where these reflections intersect, which is much farther beyond s_o. Therefore, when the object is between R and f, its image is inverted, larger (i.e., $s_i > s_o$ and $h_i > h_o$), and real (since it is formed from reflections *converging* at a point).

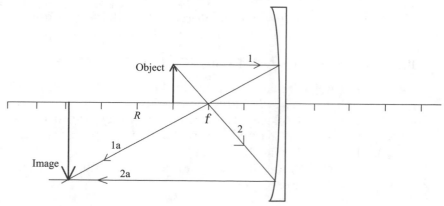

CASE 4: OBJECT IS PLACED AT *f*

Here is the most curious aspect of placing an object in front of a concave mirror. When placed directly at the focal point *f*, notice that the two reflections 1a and 2a neither diverge nor converge, meaning the rays are always parallel. Therefore, even though moving the object closer and closer to the mirror produces a larger and larger image, this is only true up to the focal point *f*; when the object is at *f*, no image is produced.

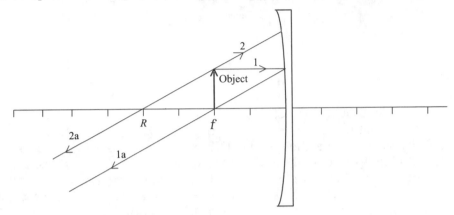

CASE 5: OBJECT IS PLACED INSIDE *f*

Once again, for clarity, only rays 1 and 2 from Sample Problem 3 and their reflections have been drawn, and note the image is now clearly virtual because the reflections diverge. Therefore, when the object is *inside* the focal point *f*, its image is upright, larger (i.e., $h_i > h_o$), and virtual. This situation represents a cosmetic mirror, in which a person's face is inside *f* so as to enlarge it.

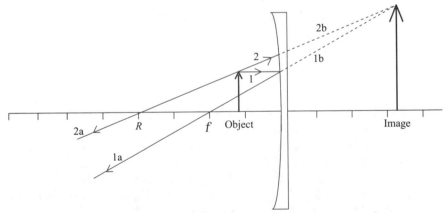

For the sake of review and reinforcement, a table of signs for mirror variables follows the image summary list shown below.

SUMMARY OF IMAGE PROPERTIES FOR CONCAVE MIRRORS

1. For objects placed well beyond *R*, the image is smaller than the object (i.e., $h_i < h_o$), inverted, and real.
2. For objects placed at *R*, the image is the same size as the object (i.e., $h_i = h_o$), inverted, and real and is also placed at *R* (i.e., $s_i = s_o$).
3. For objects placed between *R* and *f*, the image is larger than the object (i.e., $h_i > h_o$), inverted, and real, and is farther from the lens than the object (i.e., $s_i > s_o$).

4. For objects placed inside f, the image is larger than the object (i.e., $h_i > h_o$), is upright, virtual, and behind the mirror.

Sign Conventions for Curved Mirrors					
Quantity	Symbol	In Front of Mirror	In Back of Mirror	Upright Image	Inverted Image
Object distance	s_o	+	−		
Image distance	s_i	+	−		
Focal length	f	+	−		
Image height	h_i			+	−
Magnification	M			+	−

WHAT IS THE NATURE OF THE REFRACTION OF LIGHT?

(*College Physics* 8th ed. pages 736–742/9th ed. pages 765–771)

In contrast to reflection, the refraction of light concerns light rays that are transmitted from one medium into a second medium, rather than simply returning to the same medium as with reflection. Refraction of light involves two major properties: (a) light decreases its speed, and (b) it changes direction (colloquially referred to as "bent," which is technically incorrect as light travels along a straight, not bent, path). The degree to which light decreases its speed depends on the optical density of the medium into which is passes, known as the index of refraction, n. This is a dimensionless quantity that is the ratio of the speed of light in vacuum c to that of the speed v in that particular medium. Tables of n values are often given in textbooks, however, insofar as the AP Physics examination is concerned, particular values for a problem are given as needed. This relationship is

$$n = \frac{c}{v}$$

Despite changing its speed, a light wave passing across the boundary between the two media does not change its *rate* of passage (i.e., frequency f), as waves neither accumulate at the boundary nor are they created or destroyed there. According to the wave relationship $v = f\lambda$, since v decreases and f remains constant, there is a corresponding decrease in wavelength λ (i.e., λ's behavior is proportional to that of v).

This fact, in accordance with the equation $n = \frac{c}{v}$ will give the relationship between n and λ; $n_1\lambda_2 = n_2\lambda_1$.

Furthermore, with the application of geometry to the passage of a light ray from one medium of index of refraction n_1 into a second medium of index of refraction n_2, we can derive Snell's law, which relates the angle of incidence (θ_1) to the angle of refraction (θ_2). Analogous to the law of reflection, Snell's law allows one to determine the angle of refraction of the light within the second medium. In some instances, Snell's law must be used twice when the first refracted ray enters a second transparent medium and refracts a second time.

$$n_1 \sin \theta_1 = n_2 \sin \theta_2 \text{ (Snell's law)}$$

Careful note must be taken when making ray diagrams of refractions because, when light passes from a less optically dense medium to a denser one, the ray turns *toward* the normal in the second medium. In contrast, when a light ray leaves a denser medium and enters a less dense one, it turns *away* from the normal. This is summarized briefly in the diagram below and is very important to bear in mind.

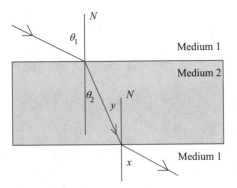

Angle x is equal to angle θ_1, angle y is equal to angle θ_2, and the two light rays in medium 1 are parallel.

WHAT IS TOTAL INTERNAL REFLECTION?

(*College Physics* 8th ed. pages 748–751/9th ed. pages 777–780)

In the unique situation in which light originates from an optically denser material (such as water) and refracts into a less dense material (such as air), the light may remain within the first material if its angle of incidence in the denser medium exceeds a certain angle, called the *critical angle*, θ_c. If the light is incident at the critical angle, the refracted ray remains at the boundary, neither leaving the first medium nor entering the second. That angle (the angle of refraction) is therefore 90° (as shown). Using Snell's law for such a situation gives

$$n_1 \sin \theta_c = n_2 \sin (90°) \text{ or } n_1 \sin \theta_c = n_2(1) \text{ which is } \sin \theta_c = \frac{n_2}{n_1}$$

When the light's angle of incidence exceeds θ_c, the ray is trapped in the first (denser) medium, creating a situation known as total internal reflection in which the light reflects off the boundary and remains in the first medium. Reducing the angle of incidence to below θ_c allows the ray of light to exit the medium and enter the second, less dense material. A common example of such behavior occurs in the use of fiber optic systems that transmit information via light signals in a virtually undiminished fashion over great distances. It is of great importance to realize that total internal reflection can occur only when light passes from an optically denser material to a less dense material, never the other way around. As shown by the critical angle equation, if this were to occur, $\sin \theta_c$ would be > 1, which is impossible.

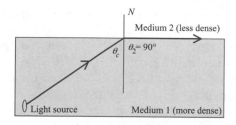
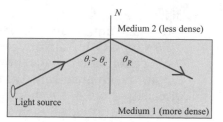

SAMPLE PROBLEM 4

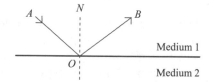

The diagram shows total internal reflection. Which of the following statements is incorrect?

(A) Angle *AON* is the angle of incidence.

(B) Angle *AON* = angle *BON*.

(C) The speed of light in medium 2 is greater than that in medium 1.

(D) Angle *AON* must be the critical angle.

(E) If angle *AON* were increased, total internal reflection would still occur.

SOLUTION TO PROBLEM 4

At first inspection, choices (A) and (B) are correct statements, and thus are not correct answer choices. Also, as the problem states that total internal reflection is occurring, the optically denser medium must be the top one, medium 1, since the ray is reflecting back into it. This signifies that light travels faster in medium 2 than in medium 1, which is choice (C), and thus that choice is not correct for the question. Additionally, if angle *AON* were the critical angle, then angle *BON* would be 90°, which it clearly isn't. Therefore, angle *AON* must be greater than the critical angle, since it is reflecting back into the medium, which also means choice (E) is correct and does not answer the question. Therefore, choice (D) is an incorrect statement, which is the correct choice.

IMAGES PRODUCED BY CONCAVE LENSES

(*College Physics* 8th ed. pages 773–782/9th ed. pages 805–816)

In contrast to light incident upon curved mirrors, our discussion now focuses on light that passes through transparent materials of varying thicknesses, or lenses. The simplest type to analyze is the double concave lens, which has two identically curved surfaces with equal radii of curvature, 2f and 2f, with focal points f and –f on each side. Diagrams of concave lens rays are similar in nature to those drawn for convex mirrors as they mimic the same type of image (i.e., smaller than the object for all values of s_o except when $s_o = 0$). These lenses always produce upright, virtual, but smaller images and are the type used in eyeglasses for those who are nearsighted (i.e., see nearby objects clearly but see distant objects blurred). Note also that when performing calculations, the focal length is also denoted by a minus sign, –f.

Again, as with mirrors, many rays of light may be drawn to determine the location of an image; however, aside from the following sample ray diagram, hereafter only two rays (rays 1 and 2) will be used for the sake of clarity. Note again that images are formed by tracing any diverging rays back through the lens, as shown here by rays 1b and 3b. Those diverging rays (along with ray 2) all intersect on the left side of the lens to produce a virtual image. Hence, this lens is also called a diverging lens.

Ray-Tracing Guidelines for Concave (Diverging) Lenses

1. A ray drawn from the object to the lens that is parallel to the optical axis refracts through the lens as if it emanated from the focal point f on the same side of the lens as the object.
2. A ray drawn from the object to the center of the lens passes through unrefracted, continuing straight.
3. A ray drawn from the object that comes from (or may *appear to be* coming from) the focal point f on the other side of the lens refracts through the lens parallel to the optical axis.

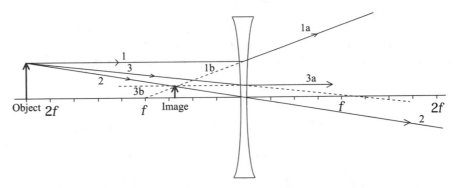

Summary of Image Properties for Concave (Diverging) Lenses

1. Image height is always smaller than the object height (i.e., $h_i < h_o$).
2. Image distance is less than the object distance (i.e., $s_i < s_o$).
3. Images produced by concave lenses are upright and virtual.

Images Produced by Convex Lenses

(*College Physics* 8th ed. pages 773–782/9th ed. pages 805–816)

Double convex lenses are by far the most versatile as they produce a wide range of images for varying object distances s_o. Analogous to concave mirrors, convex lenses can both diverge and converge light, as shown hereby the basic ray diagrams, which address the five main cases of object position in front of this lens type. Since this is the case, convex lenses can produce both real and virtual images, both large and small, and are commonly used as magnifying glasses and eyeglass lenses for individuals who are farsighted (i.e., see distant objects clearly, but see near objects blurred). Here, as with concave lenses, both surfaces have identical radii of curvature, 2f and 2f, with focal points f and –f on each side.

Again, as with mirrors, many rays of light may be drawn to determine the location of an image, however, for the sake of clarity, only two rays, rays 1 and 2, will be used in the diagrams. As with previous ray diagrams, note that the image is formed by either the intersection of refracted rays (in the case of converging rays), or by the intersection of back-traced refracted rays (in the case of diverging rays). Also note that, as shown in the chapter's free-response questions, the thin lens equation may easily be used to verify all image positions and image heights for each of the ray diagram cases shown here. Note that in the "Sign Conventions for Lenses" table, "in front" refers to the same side as the object, whereas "in back" or "behind" refers to the side of the lens without the object.

RAY-TRACING GUIDELINES FOR CONVEX (CONVERGING) LENSES

1. A ray drawn from the object to the lens that is parallel to the optical axis refracts through the focal point f on the other side of the lens.
2. A ray drawn from the object to the center of the lens passes through the lens unrefracted, continuing straight.
3. A ray drawn from the object that comes from (or may *appear to be* coming from) the focal point f refracts through the lens parallel to the optical axis.
4. The three rays above *converge* on the opposite side of the lens, and the point at which they intersect forms the image.

CASE 1: OBJECT IS PLACED WELL BEYOND 2f

In this most basic case, the object is placed very far from $2f$, and the resulting image formed on the opposite side of the lens is inverted and real, formed directly by the intersection of the two refracted rays shown. Note that $s_i < s_o$ and that $h_i < h_o$. This arrangement is the basis of the refracting telescope and of elements in single-lens reflex camera lens assemblies.

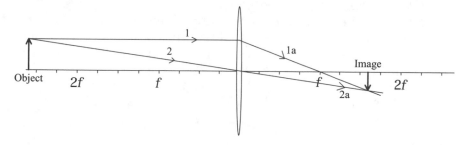

CASE 2: OBJECT IS PLACED AT 2f

Here, due greatly to symmetry, the object placed at $2f$ gives an identical image at $2f$ on the opposite side of the lens; however, it is inverted and real. Note also that $s_i = s_o$ and that $h_i = h_o$.

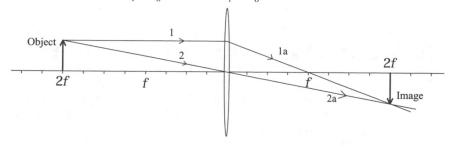

CASE 3: OBJECT IS PLACED BETWEEN 2f AND f

When the object is placed within 2f, the resulting image formed on the opposite side of the lens progressively increases in size as s_o decreases. Additionally, this image is still inverted and real, formed directly by the intersection of the two refracted rays shown. Now, however, note that $s_i > s_o$ and that $h_i > h_o$.

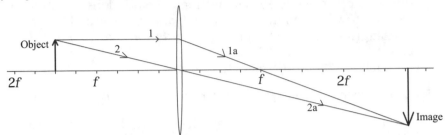

CASE 4: OBJECT IS PLACED AT f

Just as with the concave mirror, when the object is placed at f of the convex lens, the ensuing refracted light rays neither converge nor diverge, but leave the lens parallel to each other. As a result, the rays never intersect and thus no image is ever formed.

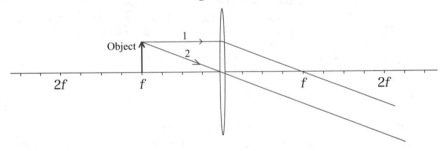

CASE 5: OBJECT IS PLACED INSIDE f

Probably the most interesting case of this lens is when the object is placed inside f, causing a virtual and upright image to be formed on the side of the lens shared by the object. Even more useful is the fact that the image is enlarged (i.e., M > 1), which serves to allow the lens in this situation to be used as a magnifying glass.

Note that $s_i > s_o$ and that $h_i > h_o$.

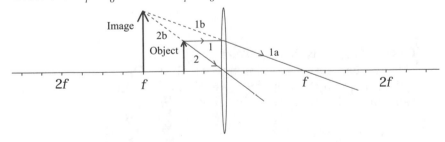

SUMMARY OF IMAGE PROPERTIES FOR CONVEX (CONVERGING) LENSES

1. For objects placed outside of 2f, the image is always smaller than the object (i.e., $h_i < h_o$), is inverted, is real, and appears on the opposite side of the lens.

2. For objects placed at 2f, the image is the same size as the object (i.e., $h_i = h_o$), is inverted, is real, and appears at 2f on the opposite side of the lens (i.e., $s_i = s_o$).

3. For objects placed between 2f and f, the image is larger than the object (i.e., $h_i > h_o$), is inverted, is real, and appears on the opposite side of the lens.

4. For objects placed at f, no image is produced.

5. For objects placed inside f, the image is larger than the object (i.e., $h_i > h_o$), is upright, is virtual, and appears on the same side of the lens as the object.

Sign Conventions for Lenses					
Quantity	Symbol	In Front of Lens	In Back of Lens	Converging Lens	Diverging Lens
Object distance	s_o	+	–		
Image distance	s_i	–	+		
Focal length	f			+	–

IMAGES PRODUCED BY TWO LENSES

(*College Physics* 8th ed. pages 773–782/9th ed. pages 805–816)

There exists a myriad of applications of multiple lens arrangements in the everyday world, but solving a double lens problem is the most elaborate of this type that is currently required for the AP Physics exam. Essentially, it is simply two lens problems, with the object used to create an image through the first lens, then that subsequent image is used as the object for the second lens. Once the second image is traced, the problem is in essence complete. Therefore, simply remember that the image formed by the first lens serves as the object for the second lens. Even though such problems are fairly rare occurrences on the AP Physics exam, it is wise to know how to complete them.

ALTERING THE AMOUNT OF REFRACTION

For the most part, nearly all AP Physics lens problems will involve actual common glass lenses that exist where one would typically expect them to be—in a room surrounded by air. What, however, occurs should either the lens material change or the entire lens assembly be immersed in a transparent material (such as water) that has an index of refraction that is greater than that of air, but less than that of the glass?

In the first instance, if the lens material were changed to a greater index of refraction, a greater degree of refraction would occur. Therefore, the lens' focal points would move closer to the lens, changing the values of s_i as per the thin lens equation. Similarly, if the opposite occurred, and the lens were made of a less optically dense material with a lower index of refraction, less refraction would occur, moving the focal points further from the lens surface. In short, the greater the change of indices of refraction between the two media, the greater the degree of refraction, and the less the change of indices of refraction between the two media, the less the degree of refraction.

In the second instance, a similar result occurs. In the same manner as just previously described, the *difference* between indices of refraction alters the degree of refraction of the light passing through the media. If, for example, the lens is immersed in water (whose $n = 1.33$, which is greater than that of air at $n = 1.00$) rather than in air, less refraction would occur through the lens when rays of light passed from the water to the lens, as the difference between the respective indices of refraction is less than in the previous case. Again, while not a common question on the AP Physics exam, it is important to understand how altering the two media affects the resulting refraction of light.

GEOMETRICAL OPTICS: STUDENT OBJECTIVES FOR THE AP EXAM

- You should be able to determine how the speed and wavelength of light change when light passes from one medium into another.
- You should be able to show on a diagram the directions of reflected and refracted rays.
- You should be able to use Snell's law to relate the directions of the incident ray and the refracted ray, and the indices of refraction of the media.
- You should be able to identify conditions under which total internal reflection will occur.
- You should understand image formation by plane or spherical mirrors.
- You should be able to relate the focal point of a spherical mirror to its center of curvature ($R = 2f$).
- You should be able, given a diagram of a curved mirror with the focal point shown, to locate by ray tracing the image of a real object and determine whether the image is real or virtual, upright or inverted, enlarged or reduced in size.
- You should understand image formation by concave or convex lenses.
- You should be able to determine whether the focal length of a lens is increased or decreased as a result of a change in curvature of its surface or in the index of refraction of the material of which the lens is made or the medium in which it is immersed.
- You should be able to determine by ray tracing the location of the image of a real object located inside or outside the focal point of the lens, and state whether the resulting image is upright or inverted, real or virtual.
- You should be able to use the thin lens equation to relate the object distance, image distance, and focal length for a lens and to determine the image size in terms of the object size (i.e., magnification).
- You should be able to analyze simple situations in which the image formed by one lens serves as the object for another lens.

MULTIPLE-CHOICE QUESTIONS

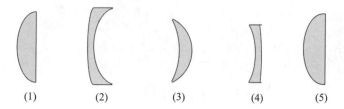

1. Which three glass lenses shown, when placed in air, will cause incident parallel light rays to converge?
   (A) 1, 2, and 3
   (B) 2, 3, and 4
   (C) 1, 4, and 5
   (D) 1, 3, and 5
   (E) 2, 4, and 5

2. Which one of the following statements is not a characteristic of an image formed by an object in front of a plane mirror?
   (A) The image is real.
   (B) The magnification is +1.
   (C) The image is always upright.
   (D) The image is laterally reversed.
   (E) The image and object distances are equal in magnitude.

3. The radius of curvature of a spherical convex mirror is 50 cm. What is its focal length?
   (A) +25 cm
   (B) −25 cm
   (C) +50 cm
   (D) −50 cm
   (E) +100 cm

4. A beam of light passes from air into water. Which is necessarily true?
   (A) The frequency is unchanged, and the wavelength increases.
   (B) The frequency is unchanged, and the wavelength decreases.
   (C) The wavelength is unchanged, and the frequency decreases.
   (D) Both the wavelength and the frequency increase.
   (E) Both the wavelength and the frequency decrease.

5. Which one of the following expressions determines the critical angle for quartz ($n = 1.50$) immersed in oil ($n = 1.10$)?

(A) $\theta_c = \dfrac{1.50}{1.10}$

(B) $\theta_c = \dfrac{1.10}{1.50}$

(C) $\theta_c = \sin^{-1}\left(\dfrac{1.10}{1.50}\right)$

(D) $\theta_c = \sin\left(\dfrac{1.10}{1.50}\right)$

(E) $\theta_c = \tan^{-1}\left(\dfrac{1.10}{1.50}\right)$

6. An object is placed 30 cm in front of a concave spherical mirror that has a radius of curvature equal to 40 cm. Which one of the following phrases best describes the image?
(A) virtual and located at infinity
(B) real and located 60 cm from the mirror
(C) real and located 120 cm from the mirror
(D) virtual and located 60 cm from the mirror
(E) virtual and located 120 cm from the mirror

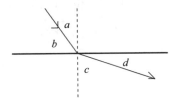

7. The horizontal line in the image shown above represents the boundary between two different media, one of which is diamond (whose index of refraction is 2.42) and the other is air. Two arrowed light rays are passing through each medium. Which of the following is correct for the diagram shown?

(A) $\dfrac{\sin a}{\sin b} = 2.42$

(B) $\dfrac{\sin b}{\sin a} = 2.42$

(C) $\dfrac{\cos a}{\cos c} = 2.42$

(D) $\dfrac{\sin a}{\sin c} = \dfrac{1}{2.42}$

(E) $\dfrac{a}{c} = 2.42$

8. A concave mirror has a radius of curvature of 4.0 m. A dog sits in front of the mirror so that the dog appears 2.5 times taller than its actual height. If the image of the dog is upright, how far is it sitting from the mirror?
   (A) 1.2 m
   (B) 2.2 m
   (C) 4.2 m
   (D) 5.0 m
   (E) 7.0 m

9. Which of the following diagrams best represents the relationship between the image distance and object distance for an object placed in front of a plane mirror?

   (A)

   (B)

   (C)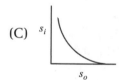

   (D)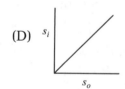

   (E)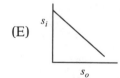

10. A converging lens with focal length of 12 cm produces a 3-cm-high virtual image of a 1-cm-tall object. Which entry in the table is correct?

	Image Distance	Image Location
(A)	8 cm	same side of lens as object
(B)	8 cm	opposite side of lens from object
(C)	12 cm	opposite side of lens from object
(D)	24 cm	opposite side of lens from object
(E)	24 cm	same side of lens as object

11. If n_{water} = 1.33 and n_{glass} = 1.50, then total internal reflection at an interface between this glass and water
    (A) occurs whenever the light goes from glass to water.
    (B) occurs whenever the light goes from water to glass.
    (C) may occur when the light goes from glass to water.
    (D) may occur when the light goes from water to glass.
    (E) can never occur at this interface.

12. A 3-cm-tall object is placed 25 cm from a diverging lens whose focal length is –10 cm. Which most accurately describes the image?
    (A) The image is virtual and upright with a magnification of +0.29.
    (B) The image is virtual and upright with a magnification of −0.29.
    (C) The image is real and inverted with a magnification of +0.72.
    (D) The image is virtual and inverted with a magnification of −0.72.
    (E) The image is virtual and upright with a magnification of +0.84.

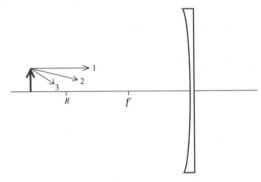

For questions 13 through 15, refer to this diagram, which depicts an erect arrow placed on the optical axis in front of a concave spherical mirror. The three light rays 1, 2, and 3, leave the top of the arrow. Ray 1 is parallel to the optical axis, ray 2 passes through f, and ray 3 passes through R.

13. Which ray(s) will pass through f after reflection?
    (A) 1 only
    (B) 2 only
    (C) 3 only
    (D) both 1 and 2
    (E) 1, 2, and 3

14. Which ray(s) will reflect back on itself (themselves)?
    (A) 1 only
    (B) 2 only
    (C) 3 only
    (D) both 1 and 2
    (E) 1, 2, and 3

15. Which of the following groups of terms best describes the image of the arrow formed by this mirror?
    (A) real, erect, enlarged
    (B) virtual, inverted, reduced
    (C) virtual, erect, enlarged
    (D) real, inverted, enlarged
    (E) real, inverted, reduced

FREE-RESPONSE PROBLEMS

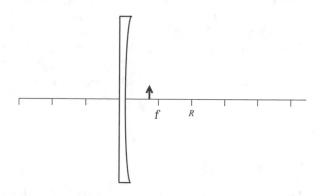

1. As shown in the diagram, a 3-cm-tall arrow is placed 15 cm in front of the reflective side of a concave spherical mirror whose radius of curvature is 40 cm.
   (a) Using at least two light rays, locate the image on the diagram.
   (b) Is this image real or virtual? Justify your answer.
   (c) Determine the image distance.
   (d) Determine the image height.
   (e) Beyond the scope of the physics classroom, what might be a useful application of such a mirror in the everyday world? Explain.

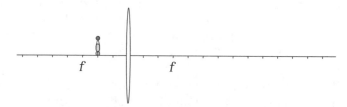

2. As shown in the diagram, a small toy whose height is 6 cm is placed 10 cm to the left of a large, thin, converging lens whose focal length is 15 cm and whose index of refraction is 1.50.
   (a) Calculate the image distance of the toy as seen in the converging lens.
   (b) Calculate the image height of the toy as seen in the converging lens.

   A diverging lens of focal length −20 cm and index of refraction 1.50 is now placed 50 cm to the right of the first lens.

   (c) On the diagram, draw an appropriate ray diagram to locate the final image of the toy that will now be formed by the lens combination.

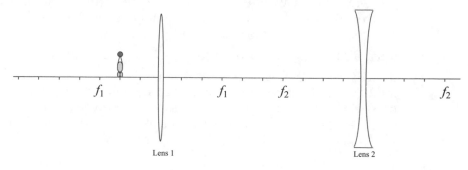

(d) Calculate the image distance of the toy as seen by the combination of lenses.

(e) Calculate the height of the final image.

(f) Is the final image real or virtual? Justify your answer.

(g) The toy and entire lens combination are immersed in a still water bath ($n = 1.33$). Explain how this affects the final image location compared with your answers to (c) and (d).

Answers

Multiple-Choice Questions

1. **D** Lenses that cause light to converge are thicker at the center and thinner at the edges, which is shown only by lenses 1, 3, and 5. Diverging lenses are the opposite in shape; thinner at their centers, and thicker at the edges, as shown by lenses 2 and 4. Therefore, choice (D) is correct (*College Physics* 8th ed. pages 773–779/9th ed. pages 805–814).

2. **A** All images produced by plane (flat) mirrors are erect (upright) and therefore virtual, with a magnification equal to +1 (i.e., the image size equals the object size, or $h_i = h_o$). Also, plane mirror images are laterally reversed (i.e., left-right reversed). Therefore, the choice that does not depict a plane mirror characteristic is choice (A), as a real image is an inverted one, which is never produced from an object in front of a plane mirror (*College Physics* 8th ed. pages 759–762/9th ed. pages 790–793).

3. **B** Since the mirror is spherical in shape, the radius of curvature R is a radius of the sphere, which according to the relationship $f = \dfrac{R}{2}$ is twice the focal length f. Therefore, if $R = 50$ cm, $f = 25$ cm. Additionally, since the mirror is a convex mirror, whose focal point lies behind the mirror's surface, this value is negative. Thus, choice (B) is correct (*College Physics* 8th ed. pages 764–769/9th ed. pages 795–800).

4. **B** When light passes from one transparent medium to another, it is refracted (i.e., changes direction) because the speed of light changes between the two media according to the relation $n = \dfrac{c}{v}$. Passing into the new medium, the wave fronts must pass at the same rate (i.e., same frequency) as they had in the first medium; otherwise, the wave fronts would either accumulate at the boundary or be destroyed/created at the boundary, which is impossible. Therefore, as a consequence of the change of frequency, the light's wavelength must also change according to $v = f\lambda$ or $\lambda = \dfrac{v}{f}$. Since v and λ are directly related, should v decrease, λ will decrease. Therefore, when light passes from air into water, its frequency f remains constant, however, because its speed v decreases, its wavelength λ must also decrease, as stated by choice (B) (*College Physics* 8th ed. pages 737–739/9th ed. pages 767–771).

5. **C** The critical angle θ_c is the angle of incidence of light passing from a denser transparent medium into a less dense medium such that the angle of refraction is 90°, with the refracted beam traveling along the boundary between the two media. Therefore, according to Snell's law, this is $n_1 \sin \theta_c = n_2 \sin(90°)$, which becomes $n_1 \sin \theta_c = n_2$.

Solving for the critical angle then gives $\sin \theta_c = \dfrac{n_2}{n_1}$ or $\theta_c = \sin^{-1}\left(\dfrac{n_2}{n_1}\right)$.

Substituting gives the final answer; $\theta_c = \sin^{-1}\left(\dfrac{1.10}{1.50}\right)$, which is choice (C) (*College Physics* 8th ed. pages 748–751/9th ed. pages 777–780).

6. **B** Since both the radius of curvature R and the object distance s_o are given, the thin lens equation may be used to determine the image distance s_i. Thereafter, the magnification equation can be used to determine both the size and orientation of the image (which may also be determined by making a ray diagram). Thus, $\dfrac{1}{f} = \dfrac{1}{s_i} + \dfrac{1}{s_o}$ can be solved for s_i as follows (noting that $R = 2f$ and omitting units for clarity); $\dfrac{1}{20} = \dfrac{1}{s_i} + \dfrac{1}{30}$ or $\dfrac{1}{20} - \dfrac{1}{30} = \dfrac{1}{s_i}$. Therefore, $s_i = 60$ cm. By the magnification equation, $M = -\dfrac{s_i}{s_o}$ we have $M = -\dfrac{60}{30} = -2$ suggesting that the image is inverted, real, and enlarged, appearing 60 cm in front of the mirror, which is choice (B) (*College Physics* 8th ed. pages 762–769/9th ed. pages 793–801).

7. **D** Careful observation of the diagram reveals that the top medium must be the optically denser material, which is diamond, and air is the lower medium (since $c > a$). Then, according to Snell's law, the relation between the incident angle (a) and the refracted angle (c) can be determined, where medium 1 is diamond and medium 2 is air. Thus, $n_1 \sin \theta_1 = n_2 \sin \theta_2$, which becomes $2.42 \sin a = 1.00 \sin c$.

Therefore, the final answer becomes $\dfrac{\sin a}{\sin c} = \dfrac{1.00}{2.42}$, which is choice (D) (*College Physics* 8th ed. pages 748–751/9th ed. pages 777–780).

8. **A** Multiple steps are required to solve this problem, which is asking for the object distance, s_o. Begin by realizing that $f = 2.0$ m since it was given that $R = 4.0$ m (by the relation $R = 2f$). Additionally, the magnification of the image is given as 2.5 (or 5/2, making hand calculations easier), which gives the important relation: $M = -\dfrac{s_i}{s_o} = 2.5$ or $s_i = -2.5\,s_o$. Next, substituting this into the thin lens equation and solving for s_o will give the answer (omitting units for clarity): $\dfrac{1}{f} = \dfrac{1}{s_i} + \dfrac{1}{s_o}$ gives $\dfrac{1}{2} = \dfrac{1}{-2.5 s_o} + \dfrac{1}{s_o}$ or $\dfrac{1}{2} = \dfrac{1}{s_o}\left(\dfrac{1}{-5/2} + \dfrac{1}{1}\right) = \dfrac{1}{s_o}\left(-\dfrac{2}{5} + \dfrac{5}{5}\right) = \dfrac{1}{s_o}\left(\dfrac{3}{5}\right)$ $s_o = 2\left(\dfrac{3}{5}\right) = \dfrac{6}{5}$. Therefore, $s_o = 1.2$ m, choice (A) (*College Physics* 8th ed. pages 762–769/9th ed. pages 793–801).

9. **D** An image in a plane mirror is the same distance from the mirror as is the object itself (i.e., $s_i = s_o$) and has the same height as the object (i.e., $h_i = h_o$). Therefore, a linear relation exists between s_i and s_o, which signifies that a plot of one as a function of the other will produce a straight diagonal line, shown only by choice (D) (*College Physics* 8th ed. pages 759–762/9th ed. pages 790–793).

10. **E** The question requires the student to determine the image distance (s_i) from $f = 12$ cm, $h_i = 3$ cm, and $h_o = 1$ cm. Therefore, it will be necessary to use both the magnification equation $M = \dfrac{h_i}{h_o} = -\dfrac{s_i}{s_o}$ and the thin lens equation $\dfrac{1}{f} = \dfrac{1}{s_i} + \dfrac{1}{s_o}$ (omitting units for clarity) in a manner that was similar to that of question 8. First, the magnification of the image is $M = \dfrac{h_i}{h_o} = \dfrac{3}{1} = 3$ and from this, we see that $3 = -\dfrac{s_i}{s_o}$ or $s_i = -3s_o$. Next, the thin lens equation gives $\dfrac{1}{12} = \dfrac{1}{-3s_o} + \dfrac{1}{s_o}$ or

$$\frac{1}{12} = \frac{1}{s_o}\left(-\frac{1}{3} + \frac{3}{3}\right) \text{ or } \frac{1}{12} = \frac{1}{s_o}\left(\frac{2}{3}\right)$$ Therefore, $s_o = 8$ cm. From the fact that $s_i = -3s_o$, this gives $s_i = -24$ cm, signifying that the image is on the same side as the object and is upright (which can be shown by a ray diagram). Therefore, the correct answer is (E) (*College Physics* 8th ed. pages 773–781/9th ed. pages 805–816).

11. **C** Total internal reflection (TIR) can only occur when a ray of light passes from a more optically dense medium to a less optically dense medium. In the case of this question, TIR can only occur when light passes from the glass (higher density) into the water (lower density), which is best stated by answer choice (C). Note that it is not required for the ray to be incident upon the glass-water boundary at the critical angle θ_c, as simple refraction would occur if the angle of incidence were less than θ_c. Hence, TIR *may* occur, but it does not exclusively occur (*College Physics* 8th ed. pages 748–751/9th ed. pages 777–780).

12. **A** All images produced by objects in front of diverging lenses are always upright (i.e., erect) and smaller than the original object (i.e., $M < 1$), which allows choices (C) and (D) to be eliminated. Using the thin lens equation $\dfrac{1}{f} = \dfrac{1}{s_i} + \dfrac{1}{s_o}$ and the magnification equation $M = \dfrac{h_i}{h_o} = -\dfrac{s_i}{s_o}$ the correct answer may be determined. Therefore (finding a common denominator and omitting units for clarity), $-\dfrac{1}{10} = \dfrac{1}{s_i} + \dfrac{1}{25}$ becomes $-\dfrac{1}{10} - \dfrac{1}{25} = \dfrac{1}{s_i} = -\dfrac{5}{50} - \dfrac{2}{50}$ so that $s_i = -7$cm, indicating a virtual, upright image that is on the same side of the lens as is the object. The object's magnification is therefore $M = -\dfrac{s_i}{s_o} = +\dfrac{7}{25} \approx +\dfrac{1}{3}$. Therefore, the best answer is choice (A) (*College Physics* 8th ed. pages 773–781/9th ed. pages 805–816).

13. **A** Of the three rays of light shown in the diagram, the only ray that will reflect through f is ray 1, which is parallel to the optical axis, choice (A). Ray 2 cannot reflect through f since it is incident through f and will instead reflect parallel to the optical axis, the reverse of ray 1. Since ray 3 is incident through the radius of curvature R, it will return along this path as, by the law of reflection, the angle of incidence of this ray relative to the normal is 0°. Ray 3 is incident along a radius of the sphere, which is the same as a normal to the reflective surface and thus it returns through R (*College Physics* 8th ed. pages 762–769/9th ed. pages 793–801).

14. **C** As per the explanation given for the answer to Question 13, ray 3 is the only ray that will reflect back onto itself as it is incident along a normal to the circular surface of the mirror. Thus choice (C) is the correct answer (*College Physics* 8th ed. pages 762–769/9th ed. pages 793–801).

15. **E** The qualitative aspects of the image of the arrow formed by the mirror may be easily shown using a ray diagram, recalling that the image is formed where the three primary reflections intersect. As per the explanation given to Question 13, ray 1 reflects through f, ray 2 reflects parallel to the optical axis, and ray 3 reflects back on itself, as shown by the dotted lines in this diagram.

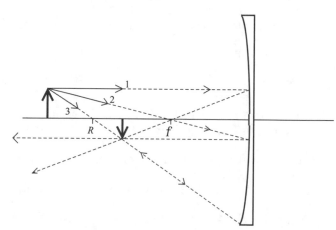

Since the incident rays originated from the head of the arrow, the reflected rays intersect at the head of the image of the arrow, which, as shown, is smaller, inverted, and therefore real, which is choice (E) (*College Physics* 8th ed. pages 762–769/9th ed. pages 793–801).

FREE-RESPONSE PROBLEMS

1. (a) As shown, ray 1, incident parallel to the optical axis, reflects through f (ray 1a), while ray 2, incident along a line apparently emanating from f, reflects parallel to the optical axis (ray 2a). To locate the image top, retrace the reflections (rays 1a and 2a) back behind the mirror until they intersect, giving the enlarged, upright image shown (*College Physics* 8th ed. pages 762–769/9th ed. pages 793–801).

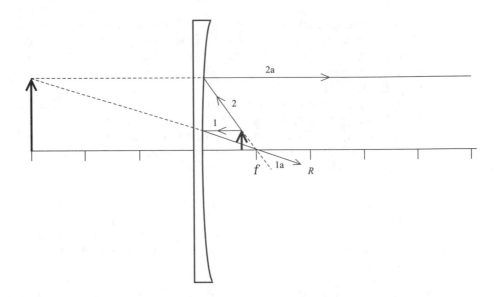

(b) This image is virtual as it is upright and the light rays forming it only appear to emanate (diverge) from it, and do not actually intersect to form it (*College Physics* 8th ed. pages 759–760, 762–769/9th ed. pages 790–801).

(c) Here it is necessary to use the thin lens equation to calculate the image distance, s_i, with $f = 20$ cm (since the radius of curvature R is given as 40 cm, and the relation between R and f is $R = 2f$) and $s_o = 15$ cm. Therefore, $\dfrac{1}{f} = \dfrac{1}{s_i} + \dfrac{1}{s_o}$ gives $\dfrac{1}{20} = \dfrac{1}{15} + \dfrac{1}{s_i}$ or $\dfrac{1}{20} - \dfrac{1}{15} = \dfrac{1}{s_i}$; thus $s_i = \mathbf{-60}$ **cm** (*College Physics* 8th ed. pages 762–769/9th ed. pages 793–801).

(d) To determine the image height h_i, it is necessary to use the value of the image distance from part (c), and then use the magnification equation (omitting units for clarity): $M = \dfrac{h_i}{h_o} = -\dfrac{s_i}{s_o}$. This becomes $M = -\dfrac{-60}{15} = 4$. Therefore, the image height h_i, can easily be calculated: $4 = \dfrac{h_i}{h_o} = \dfrac{h_i}{3}$ or $h_i = \mathbf{12}$ **cm** (*College Physics* 8th ed. pages 762–769/9th ed. pages 793–801).

(e) A concave mirror, which magnifies an object placed inside the focal point f, serves many purposes, one of which is as a cosmetic makeup mirror in which a person's head is placed inside f in order to magnify the face (*College Physics* 8th ed. pages 767–769/9th ed. pages 799–801).

2. (a) To calculate s_i, it is necessary to use the thin lens equation $\dfrac{1}{f} = \dfrac{1}{s_i} + \dfrac{1}{s_o}$ where $f = 15$ cm and $s_o = 10$ cm. Therefore (omitting units for clarity) $\dfrac{1}{f} = \dfrac{1}{s_i} + \dfrac{1}{s_o}$ gives $\dfrac{1}{15} = \dfrac{1}{s_i} + \dfrac{1}{10}$ or $\dfrac{1}{15} - \dfrac{1}{10} = \dfrac{1}{s_i}$ thus $s_i = \mathbf{-30}$ **cm** (*College Physics* 8th ed. pages 773–779/9th ed. pages 767–771).

(b) To determine the image height h_i, it is necessary to use the image distance from part (a) and then use the magnification equation (omitting units for clarity): $M = \dfrac{h_i}{h_o} = -\dfrac{s_i}{s_o}$. This becomes $M = -\dfrac{-30}{10} = 3$. Therefore, the image height h_i, can easily be calculated; $3 = \dfrac{h_i}{h_o} = \dfrac{h_i}{6}$ or h_i = **18 cm** (*College Physics* 8th ed. pages 773–779/9th ed. pages 767–771).

(c) The first image, determined by the back-traced intersection of refracted rays 1b and 1d, is at 30 cm to the left of lens 1, and as expected, it is larger than the object since the object is inside the focal point. This image is now used as the object for lens 2, as shown in the second ray diagram (which ignores the presence of the first lens). The final image, labeled s_{i2}, lies just inside f_2 and is upright, virtual, and smaller than the original object (*College Physics* 8th ed. pages 773–779/9th ed. pages 767–771).

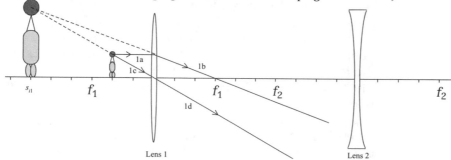

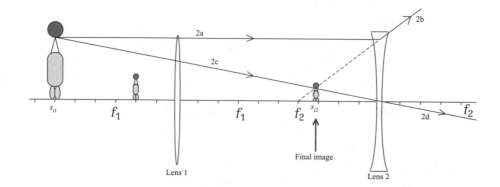

(d) Because the image created by the converging lens is now serving as the object for the diverging lens on the far right, the new object distance becomes the distance that s_{i1} is from the diverging lens, which is 30 cm + 50 cm (distance between the lenses) = 80 cm. The thin lens equation can now be used to calculate the new s_i (labeled s_{i1} in the second ray diagram). Therefore (omitting units for clarity), $\dfrac{1}{f} = \dfrac{1}{s_i} + \dfrac{1}{s_o}$ gives $-\dfrac{1}{20} = \dfrac{1}{80} + \dfrac{1}{s_i}$ or $-\dfrac{1}{20} - \dfrac{1}{80} = \dfrac{1}{s_i}$; thus, $s_i = $ **– 16 cm** (*College Physics* 8th ed. pages 773–779/9th ed. pages 767–771).

(e) As done in part (b), it is necessary to use the result from part (d) as well as the magnification equation $M = \dfrac{h_i}{h_o} = -\dfrac{s_i}{s_o}$ in order to determine h_i. Omitting units for clarity, this becomes $M = -\dfrac{-16}{80} = 0.2 = M$. Therefore, the new image height $h_{i'}$ can easily be calculated (noting that value for h_o must be 18 cm, the height of the first image, which is used as the object for the second lens): $0.2 = \dfrac{h_i}{h_o} = \dfrac{h_i}{18}$ or $h_i = (0.2)18 \text{ cm} = \textbf{3.6 cm} = \textbf{h}_i$ (*College Physics* 8th ed. pages 773–779/9th ed. pages 767–771).

(f) Based on both the ray diagrams and the preceding calculations, the final image produced by both lenses is virtual as it is upright and on the same side of the lens as the object. Also, the light rays forming it only appear to emanate (diverge) from it, and do not actually intersect to form it (*College Physics* 8th ed. pages 759–760, 762–769/9th ed. pages 790–792, 793–801).

(g) Placing the entire lens arrangement in a water bath with an index of refraction that is higher than the air ($n = 1.00$) in which the lenses were originally placed will reduce the degree of refraction by Snell's law. For example, ray 1b in the diagram to the solution to (c) would not refract through f_1 but would refract further to the right of the lens. As a result, when this ray is traced behind the lens to meet ray 1d, the two will intersect closer to the lens, thus yielding an image distance s_i that is smaller than the original value. Additionally, the image will be smaller than that calculated in (b).

Second, when this first image is used as the object for the diverging lens, ray 2b will refract not as if it had come from f_2, but from further to the left of f_2, which will therefore intersect with ray 2d further to the left, making the final image taller and to the left of f_2 (*College Physics* 8th ed. pages 736–742/9th ed. pages 765–771).

17

MODERN PHYSICS

PLANCK'S QUANTUM THEORY

(*College Physics* 8th ed. pages 870–872/9th ed. pages 911–913)

In 1903, Max Planck theoretically showed that light streams from light sources as tiny lumps of energy that he called quanta and each quantum of light has an energy related to the frequency of the light. That relationship is

$$E = hf$$

where h is called Planck's constant and has a value $h = 6.63 \times 10^{-34}\,\text{J} \cdot \text{s}$ and f is the frequency of the light.

MASS-ENERGY EQUIVALENCE

(*College Physics* 8th ed. pages 859–860/9th ed. pages 899–900)

One of the major ideas developed in the special theory of relativity was the equivalence of mass and energy. Einstein showed that mass and energy were the same thing but in two different forms related by the equation

$$E = mc^2$$

Here c is the speed of light, $3 \times 10^8\,\dfrac{\text{m}}{\text{s}}$. A very tiny mass can yield a very large quantity of energy.

The usual SI unit of energy is the joule, J. There is another way of expressing energy that is convenient in modern physics, and that is in terms of the electron volt, eV. When an electron falls through a potential difference, work is done on the electron and that quantity of work is $1.60 \times 10^{-19}\,\text{J}$. We define the electron volt as

$$1\ \text{eV} = 1.60 \times 10^{-19}\,\text{J}$$

SAMPLE PROBLEM 1

Calculate the rest-mass energy of an electron in both joules and MeV.

SOLUTION TO PROBLEM 1

Write the Einstein mass-energy relationship. Note this is the only relationship from relativity that is needed for AP Physics B.

$$E = mc^2$$

$$E = \left(9.11 \times 10^{-31} \text{ kg}\right)\left(3.00 \times 10^8 \ \frac{m}{s}\right)^2 = 8.20 \times 10^{-14} \text{ J}$$

Converting to MeV:

$$8.20 \times 10^{-14} \text{ J} \times \frac{1 \text{ eV}}{1.60 \times 10^{-19} \text{ J}} \times \frac{1 \text{ MeV}}{1 \times 10^6 \text{ eV}} = 0.51 \text{ MeV}$$

Is the reverse true? Can energy be converted into matter? Under certain conditions the answer is yes.

SAMPLE PROBLEM 2

A gamma ray photon passes very close to a $^{238}_{92}$U where the photon is converted into an electron pair, an electron, and a positron. What maximum wavelength can the gamma ray have and what is its frequency?

SOLUTION TO PROBLEM 2

Two electrons, the electron and its antiparticle, are created in the process.

$$\gamma \rightarrow e^- + e^+$$

Maximum wavelength implies minimal energy and that means there is just enough energy for the pair creation.

Rest-mass energy of the pair: $E = 2m_e c^2$

Energy of the photon: $E = \dfrac{hc}{\lambda}$

$$2m_e c^2 = \frac{hc}{\lambda}$$

$$2\lambda m_e c = h$$

$$\lambda = \frac{h}{2m_e c}$$

$$\lambda = \frac{6.63 \times 10^{-34} \text{J} \cdot \text{s}}{2\left(9.11 \times 10^{-31}\text{kg}\right)\left(3.00 \times 10^8 \ \frac{m}{s}\right)} = 1.21 \times 10^{-12} \text{ m}$$

Frequency is related to wavelength by

$$c = \lambda f$$

$$f = \frac{c}{\lambda}$$

$$f = \frac{3.00 \times 10^8 \; \text{m}/\text{s}}{1.21 \times 10^{-12} \; \text{m}} = 2.48 \times 10^{20} \; \text{Hz}$$

SAMPLE PROBLEM 3

The reverse process to particle-antiparticle pair creation is pair annihilation. Determine the minimum energy, in joules, released when a proton annihilates an antiproton to form two identical gamma ray photons.

SOLUTION TO PROBLEM 3

$$p^+ + \overline{p}^- \; \rightarrow \; \gamma + \gamma$$

The energy release is

$$E = mc^2 = 2m_p c^2$$

$$E = 2\left(1.67 \times 10^{-27} \text{kg}\right)\left(3 \times 10^8 \; \text{m}/\text{s}\right)^2 = 3.01 \times 10^{-10} \text{J}$$

THE PHOTOELECTRIC EFFECT

(*College Physics* 8th ed. pages 872–875/9th ed. pages 913–916)

In his series of papers published in 1905, Albert Einstein stated that light is emitted in the form of particles (Planck's quanta) he called photons and each photon carries energy $E - hf$. Einstein suggested a solution to a problem that had baffled scientists for a number of decades. When certain types of light irradiated metallic surfaces, the surfaces acquired positive electrical charge. Einstein stated that the photons struck surface electrons and were absorbed by them. Surface electrons are bound by an energy we call the work function, ϕ. If the incoming photons had enough energy, not only would surface electrons leave the surface of the metal, but they would leave with a kinetic energy:

$$K = hf - \phi$$

SAMPLE PROBLEM 4

A potassium wafer is irradiated with monochromatic ultraviolet light of $\lambda = 250$ nm and intensity of 2.00 W/m². Photoelectrons are emitted from the surface of the metal. If potassium has a work function of $\phi = 2.21$ eV, (a) what is the maximum kinetic energy of the photoelectrons? (b) What is the rate of photoelectron emission from the surface of the potassium if the surface is 40% efficient as an emitter?

SOLUTION TO PROBLEM 4

(a) First, write the Einstein photoelectric equation:

$$K = hf - \phi$$

$$K = \frac{hc}{\lambda} - \phi$$

$$K = \frac{\left(6.63 \times 10^{-34} \text{ J} \cdot \text{s}\right) 3.00 \times 10^{8} \frac{\text{m}}{\text{s}}}{\left(250 \times 10^{-9} \text{m}\right)} - 2.21 \text{ eV} \times \frac{1.60 \times 10^{-19} \text{J}}{1 \text{ eV}}$$

$$K = 4.42 \times 10^{-19} \text{J}$$

ALTERNATE SOLUTION:

(a) Express h in terms of eV s:

$$h = 6.63 \times 10^{-34} \text{J} \cdot \text{s} \times \frac{1.00 \text{ eV}}{1.60 \times 10^{-19} \text{J}} = 4.14 \times 10^{-15} \text{ eV}$$

$$K = hf - \phi$$

$$K = \frac{hc}{\lambda} - \phi$$

$$K = \frac{\left(4.14 \times 10^{-15} \text{eV} \cdot \text{s}\right)\left(3 \times 10^{8} \frac{\text{m}}{\text{s}}\right)}{\left(250 \times 10^{-9} \text{m}\right)} - 2.21 \text{ eV}$$

$$K = 2.76 \text{ eV}$$

As a check:

$$4.42 \times 10^{-19} \text{J} \times \frac{1.00 \text{ eV}}{1.60 \times 10^{-19} \text{J}} = 2.76 \text{ eV}$$

(b) Since the light is monochromatic, each photon carries the same energy.

$$E = \frac{hc}{\lambda}$$

$$E = \frac{\left(6.63 \times 10^{-34} \text{J} \cdot \text{s}\right)\left(3.00 \times 10^{8} \frac{\text{m}}{\text{s}}\right)}{250 \times 10^{-9} \text{m}}$$

$$E = 7.95 \times 10^{-19} \frac{\text{J}}{\text{photon}}$$

Only 40% of the radiation falling on the surface of the potassium is effective for photoelectrons.

$$2.00 \frac{\text{W}}{\text{m}^{2}} \times 0.40 = 0.80 \frac{\text{J}}{\text{m}^{2} \cdot \text{s}}$$

For each effective photon, there is one photoelectron.

$$0.80 \frac{\text{J}}{\text{m}^{2} \cdot \text{s}} \times \frac{1 \text{ photon}}{7.95 \times 10^{-19} \text{J}} = 1.01 \times 10^{18} \frac{\text{photoelectrons}}{\text{m}^{2} \cdot \text{s}}$$

X-RAYS

(*College Physics* 8th ed. pages 875–878/9th ed. pages 916–920)

Although X-rays secured their name from "X = unknown," it is now well established that they are high-energy electromagnetic waves of very short wavelength. Bombarding a heavy metal target with high-energy electrons in an X-ray tube generates continuous X-rays. The high-energy electrons are abruptly stopped, and a major portion of the kinetic loss is converted into electromagnetic radiation, X-rays.

SAMPLE PROBLEM 5

A 50.0 kV X-ray tube is used to generate continuous X-rays.
(a) Calculate the kinetic energy of one of the electrons accelerated across the 50.0 kV potential difference immediately before it impacts the anode.
(b) What is the wavelength of the maximum energy X-ray produced in the tube?

SOLUTION TO PROBLEM 5

(a) The kinetic energy of the electron is:

$$K = \frac{1}{2}mv^2 = Ve$$

$$K = \left(5.00 \times 10^4 V\right)e$$

$$K = 5.00 \times 10^4 eV$$

(b) Maximum X-ray energy implies that 100% of the kinetic energy of the electron is converted to electromagnetic radiation.

$$h = 6.63 \times 10^{-34} J \cdot s = 4.14 \times 10^{-15} eV \cdot s$$

$$K = E = \frac{hc}{\lambda}$$

$$\lambda = \frac{hc}{E}$$

$$\lambda = \frac{\left(4.14 \times 10^{-15} eV \cdot s\right)\left(3.00 \times 10^8 \frac{m}{s}\right)}{\left(5.00 \times 10^4 eV\right)}$$

$$\lambda = 2.48 \times 10^{-11} m$$

THE COMPTON EFFECT

(*College Physics* 8th ed. pages 879–880/9th ed. pages 920–922)

While making a spectroscopic study of scattered X-rays in 1923, Arthur H. Compton discovered a new phenomenon now known as the Compton effect. Compton proved conclusively an X-ray may collide with an electron and bounce off with reduced energy in another direction. This is analogous to the collision between two billiard balls. His experiment demonstrated that photons had momentum. Light behaves as both a wave and a stream of particles.

DE BROGLIE WAVES

(*College Physics* 8th ed. pages 880–882/9th ed. pages 922–924)

In 1924, Louis de Broglie made the suggestion that this dual particle-wave character of light should apply as well to moving objects. His suggestion was based on the general observation that nature often reveals a physical or a mathematical symmetry. His reasoning that the wavelength, λ, and the momentum, p, of a particle must be related by the equation

$$\lambda = \frac{h}{p} = \frac{h}{mv}$$

The de Broglie equation states that as the momentum of a particle increases, the de Broglie wavelength decreases. The equation is simplicity itself, yet it has become one of the most important in modern-day physics. De Broglie's hypothesis was experimentally proven correct in 1927.

SAMPLE PROBLEM 6
Determine the de Broglie wavelength of a 27°C thermal neutron. The mass of the neutron is $1.67 \times 10^{-27}\,\text{kg}$.

SOLUTION TO PROBLEM 6
The de Broglie wavelength is given by $\lambda = \frac{h}{mv}$. Before we find the wavelength, we need to find v. The kinetic energy of the neutron is related to temperature by

$$K = \frac{1}{2}mv^2 = \frac{3}{2}k_B T$$

$$mv^2 = 3k_B T$$

$$v^2 = \frac{3k_B T}{m}$$

$$v = \sqrt{\frac{3k_B T}{m}}$$

$$v = \sqrt{\frac{3\left(1.38 \times 10^{-23}\,\frac{\text{J}}{\text{K}}\right)(273 + 27)\text{K}}{1.67 \times 10^{-27}\,\text{kg}}}$$

$$v = 2.73 \times 10^3\,\frac{\text{m}}{\text{s}}$$

$$\lambda = \frac{h}{mv}$$

$$\lambda = \frac{6.63 \times 10^{-34} \text{J} \cdot \text{s}}{\left(1.67 \times 10^{-27} \text{kg}\right)\left(2.73 \times 10^{3} \frac{\text{m}}{\text{s}}\right)} = 1.45 \times 10^{-10} \text{m}$$

THE ATOMIC MASS UNIT

(*College Physics* 8th ed. page 914/9th ed. page 958)

In the study of nuclear physics, the masses of nuclei and nucleons are expressed in terms of the *unified atomic mass unit*, u, where a neutral C-12 atom is defined to be precisely 12.000 000 u. The unified atomic mass unit is $\frac{1}{12}$ of the mass of the C-12 atom. It is advantageous to express the unified atomic mass unit in terms of its rest-mass energy.

AP Tip

Calculations involving nuclear reactions involve working with masses expressed to six decimal places. Set your calculators to deal with six decimal place calculations. The usual rules for significant figures are not followed here.

SAMPLE PROBLEM 7
What is the rest-mass energy, in MeV, of the unified mass unit, u?

SOLUTION TO PROBLEM 7
In terms of SI mass, the unified atomic mass unit, u, is defined as

$$1.000\ 000\ \text{u} = 1.660540 \times 10^{-27} \text{kg}$$

Write the Einstein mass-energy relationship:

$$E = mc^2$$

$$E = \left(1.660540 \times 10^{-27} \text{kg}\right)\left(2.997924 \times 10^{8} \frac{\text{m}}{\text{s}}\right)^2$$

$$E = 1.492419 \times 10^{-10} \text{J} \times \frac{1.00\ \text{MeV}}{1.602218 \times 10^{-13} \text{J}}$$

$$E = 931.494\ \text{MeV}$$

or:

$$1.00\ \text{u} = 931.494\ \text{MeV}$$

AP Tip

Use this conversion factor, $931.494\ \frac{\text{MeV}}{\text{u}}$, to all three decimal places when determining the energy in nuclear reactions.

NUCLEI AND NUCLEONS

(*College Physics* 8th ed. pages 913–915/9th ed. pages 957–960)

Atomic nuclei are composed of nucleons. Only nucleons are found in the nucleus, and these are protons and neutrons. Electrons are extranuclear in their nature and are never present in the nucleus. The proton population of a nucleus is the atomic number, Z. The total nucleon population is called the mass number, A, and the neutron population, N, is then $N = A - Z$.

Nuclear species are symbolically expressed as $_Z^A X$. The O-16 nuclear symbol is then $_8^{16}O$. The O-16 nucleus contains 16 nucleons, 8 of which are protons and 8 are neutrons.

Nuclei of the same element that have different neutron populations are called isotopes. C-12, $_6^{12}C$, and C-13, $_6^{13}C$ are isotopes.

NUCLEAR BINDING ENERGY

(*College Physics* 8th ed. pages 916–917/9th ed. pages 960–961)

The rest mass of a nucleus is less than all of the rest masses of its constituent nucleons. The decrease in mass is due to the fact that negative energy is required to hold nucleons together in the nucleus. The binding energy, B, is found by taking the differences between the rest-mass energies of the constituent nucleons and the rest-mass energy of the final nucleus, M_A.

> ### AP Tip
>
> Tabulations of masses of isotopes are atomic masses and not nuclear masses. The electrons are included, but this is not a problem. In determining energies, initial values are subtracted from final values eliminating the electron masses.

SAMPLE PROBLEM 8
Calculate both the binding energy and the binding energy per nucleon of the $_8^{16}O$ nucleus.

SOLUTION TO PROBLEM 8
The mass of a hydrogen atom is 1.007 825 u, the neutron is 1.008 665 u, and O-16 is 15.994 915 u.

The mass of the hydrogen atom, H, not the mass of the proton, is used. In the subtraction in this problem, all electron masses are eliminated from the final answer.

The binding energy of a nucleus of Z protons and N neutrons is defined as

$$B = (Zm_H + Nm_n - M_A)\ 931.494\frac{\text{MeV}}{\text{u}}$$

$$B = \left[\left(8 \times 1.007\ 825\ \text{u}\right) + \left(8 \times 1.008\ 665\ \text{u}\right) - \left(15.994\ 915\ \text{u}\right)\right]\left(931.494\ \frac{\text{MeV}}{\text{u}}\right)$$

$$B = 127.62 \text{ MeV}$$

The binding energy per is the binding energy divided by the nucleon population.

$$\frac{B}{A} = \frac{127.619 \text{ MeV}}{16 \text{ nucleons}} = 7.98 \frac{\text{MeV}}{\text{nucleon}}$$

SAMPLE PROBLEM 9

A gamma ray photon is used to photodisintegrate a deuteron into a proton and a neutron as: ${}_1^2\text{H} + \gamma \rightarrow {}_1^1\text{H} + {}_0^1\text{n}$. Calculate the minimum energy of the photon and the frequency of the associated electromagnetic wave.

SOLUTION TO PROBLEM 9

Minimum energy implies the proton and neutron are at rest after the disintegration.

$$E = \left(m_H + m_n - M_D \right) \times 931.494 \frac{\text{MeV}}{\text{u}}$$

$$E = \left(1.007\ 825 \text{ u} + 1.008\ 665 \text{ u} - 2.014\ 102 \text{ u} \right) \times 931.494 \frac{\text{MeV}}{\text{u}}$$

$$E = 2.22 \text{ MeV}$$

$$E = hf$$

$$f = \frac{E}{h}$$

$$f = \frac{\left(2.22 \text{ Mev} \right) \left(\dfrac{1.60 \times 10^{-13} \text{ J}}{1.00 \text{ MeV}} \right)}{6.63 \times 10^{-34} \text{ J} \cdot \text{s}}$$

$$f = 5.37 \times 10^{20} \text{Hz}$$

Note that when a neutron and a proton come under the strong nuclear force, they merge to become a deuteron: ${}_0^1\text{n} + {}_1^1\text{H} \rightarrow {}_1^2\text{H} + 2.224 \text{ MeV}$. The energy will be released as a 2.22 MeV gamma ray having a frequency of 5.37×10^{20} Hz.

RADIOACTIVITY

(*College Physics* 8th ed. pages 918–926/9th ed. pages 962–971)

Discovery has its own chain reaction. The discovery of X-rays by Becquerel in 1895 set the stage for Becquerel's discovery of radioactivity a year later. Over the next decade, a number of scientists investigated radioactivity and eventually unraveled its mysteries. Of all of the known nuclei, fewer than 300 are stable, while nearly five times that number are unstable—radioactive. In the lightest nuclei, the number of protons and neutrons are about equal ($Z \approx N$). As the number of protons and neutrons increase in higher Z, the number of neutrons becomes greater than the proton population ($N > Z$). Increased neutron population in a heavier nucleus serves to buffer the repulsive Coulomb force between protons. A point is reached where there are too many neutrons in a nucleus and the nucleus becomes unstable—radioactive. Radioactive nuclei stabilize themselves by undergoing radioactive decay, and there are several modes of radioactive decay.

Alpha decay is a spontaneous nuclear reaction that takes place in heavy, neutron-rich (too many neutrons) radioactive nuclei ($Z > 61$). A parent nucleus X emits an alpha particle ^4_2He or $^4_2\alpha$ and forms a daughter nucleus Y. The nuclear reaction for this decay is

$$^A_Z\text{X} \rightarrow {}^4_2\text{He} + {}^{A-4}_{Z-2}\text{Y}$$

SAMPLE PROBLEM 10

Write the balanced alpha decay reactions for $^{239}_{94}\text{Pu}$, $^{238}_{92}\text{U}$, $^{230}_{90}\text{Th}$, $^{222}_{86}\text{Rn}$, and $^{214}_{84}\text{Po}$.

SOLUTION TO PROBLEM 10

$$^{239}_{94}\text{Pu} \rightarrow {}^4_2\text{He} + {}^{235}_{92}\text{U}$$

$$^{235}_{92}\text{U} \rightarrow {}^4_2\text{He} + {}^{231}_{90}\text{Th}$$

$$^{230}_{90}\text{Th} \rightarrow {}^4_2\alpha + {}^{226}_{88}\text{Ra}$$

$$^{222}_{86}\text{Rn} \rightarrow {}^4_2\text{He} + {}^{218}_{84}\text{Po}$$

$$^{218}_{84}\text{Po} \rightarrow {}^4_2\alpha + {}^{214}_{82}\text{Pb}$$

Note that each alpha decay results in a new nucleus two atomic numbers lower on the periodic table.

AP Tip

The alpha particle is a helium nucleus, and its nuclear notation is commonly expressed either as ^4_2He or $^4_2\alpha$. The student should be familiar with both notations.

Energy, called the Q-value, is released in the alpha decay process, $^A_Z\text{X} \rightarrow {}^4_2\text{He} + {}^{A-4}_{Z-2}\text{Y} + Q$. Alpha decay can only take place if $Q > 0$ and

$$Q > (M_X - M_Y - M_\alpha) \times 931.494 \frac{\text{MeV}}{\text{u}}$$

The Q-value is calculated by

$$Q = (M_X - M_Y - M_\alpha) \times 931.494 \frac{\text{MeV}}{\text{u}}$$

SAMPLE PROBLEM 11

Calculate the Q-value for the alpha decay of Ra-226.

SOLUTION TO PROBLEM 11

First, write the balanced nuclear reaction for Ra-226.

$$^{226}_{88}Ra \rightarrow \ ^{222}_{86}Rn + \ ^{4}_{2}\alpha + Q$$

From an atomic mass table:

$$M_{Ra} = 226.025\ 406\ u$$
$$M_{Rn} = 222.017\ 574\ u$$
$$M_{\alpha} = 4.002\ 603\ u$$

Now calculate the Q-value:

$$Q = (M_X - M_Y - M_{\alpha}) \times 931.494\frac{MeV}{u}$$

$$Q = (226.025\ 406\ u - 222.017\ 574\ u - 4.002\ 603\ u) \times 931.494\frac{MeV}{u}$$

$$Q = 4.87\ MeV$$

The alpha particle carries away nearly 4.8 MeV of the Q-value as kinetic energy where the recoiling Rn-222 nucleus carries away approximately 0.1 MeV.

Negative beta decay takes place in neutron-rich (too many neutrons), radioactive nuclei. The process is complex and involves the creation of a beta particle and antineutrino by the weaker interaction and intermediate W⁻ and Z° bosons. Very basically, a neutron is converted into a proton with the emission of the beta particle and antineutrino. A parent nucleus X decays by emitting the beta particle $^{0}_{-1}e$ or $^{0}_{-1}\beta$ and an antineutrino $^{0}_{0}\overline{V}$ and forms a daughter nucleus Y. The nuclear reaction for this decay process is:

$$^{A}_{Z}X \rightarrow \ ^{0}_{-1}e + \ ^{0}_{0}\overline{V} + \ ^{A}_{Z+1}Y$$

The beta particle is an electron. Note that electrons (beta particles) do not exist in the nucleus; the beta particle and antineutrino are created in the decay process. Both leave the surface of the nucleus at near the speed of light.

SAMPLE PROBLEM 12

Write balanced reactions for the beta decay of: $^{239}_{92}U$, $^{239}_{93}Np$, $^{90}_{38}Sr$, $^{14}_{6}C$, and $^{3}_{1}H$.

SOLUTION TO PROBLEM 12

$$^{239}_{92}U \rightarrow \ ^{0}_{-1}e + \ ^{0}_{0}\overline{V} + \ ^{239}_{93}Np$$

$$^{239}_{93}Np \rightarrow \ ^{0}_{-1}e + \ ^{0}_{0}\overline{V} + \ ^{239}_{94}Pu$$

$$^{90}_{38}Sr \rightarrow \ ^{0}_{-1}\beta + \ ^{0}_{0}\overline{V} + \ ^{90}_{39}Y$$

$$^{14}_{6}C \rightarrow \ ^{0}_{-1}e + \ ^{0}_{0}\overline{V} + \ ^{14}_{7}N$$

Note that each beta decay results in a new nucleus one atomic number higher on the periodic table.

Positron decay takes place in neutron-poor (too few neutrons) radioactive nuclei. These nuclei are not found in nature—they are artificially made in nuclear laboratories. The positron process is complex and involves the creation of a positron (electron antiparticle) and neutrino by the weaker interaction and intermediate W^+ and Z^o bosons. Basically, a proton is converted into a neutron with the emission of the positron and neutrino. A parent nucleus X decays by emitting the beta particle $_{+1}^{0}e$ or $_{+1}^{0}\beta$ and a neutrino $_{0}^{0}v$ and forms a daughter nucleus Y. The nuclear reaction for this decay is

$$_{Z}^{A}X \rightarrow {_{+1}^{0}}e + {_{0}^{0}}v + {_{Z-1}^{A}}Y$$

The positron is an antielectron. Note that positrons do not exist in the nucleus; the positron and neutrino are created in the decay process. Both leave the surface of the nucleus at near the speed of light.

SAMPLE PROBLEM 13
Write the positron decay reactions for $_{26}^{53}Fe$, $_{17}^{33}Cl$, $_{15}^{28}P$, $_{8}^{14}O$, and $_{6}^{11}C$.

SOLUTION TO PROBLEM 13

$$_{26}^{53}Fe \rightarrow {_{+1}^{0}}e + {_{0}^{0}}v + {_{25}^{53}}Mn$$
$$_{17}^{33}Cl \rightarrow {_{+1}^{0}}e + {_{0}^{0}}v + {_{16}^{33}}S$$
$$_{15}^{28}P \rightarrow {_{+1}^{0}}\beta + {_{0}^{0}}v + {_{14}^{28}}Si$$
$$_{8}^{14}O \rightarrow {_{+1}^{0}}e + {_{0}^{0}}v + {_{7}^{14}}N$$
$$_{6}^{11}C \rightarrow {_{+1}^{0}}\beta + {_{0}^{0}}v + {_{5}^{11}}B$$

Note that each positron decay results in a new nucleus one atomic number lower on the periodic table.

The nucleons of a nucleus that has undergone alpha or some form of beta decay are left in an excited state. To stabilize itself, the excited nucleus discards the excitation energy as a gamma ray photon γ. The excited state is short-lived and emits a gamma ray about 10^{-8} s. A star (*) indicates an excited state, and both the daughter and the parent nucleus have the same nucleon and proton populations. The nuclear reaction for this decay process is

$$_{Z}^{A}X^{*} \rightarrow {_{Z}^{A}}Y + \gamma$$

SAMPLE PROBLEM 14

Write the nuclear reactions for the gamma emission of: $^{53}_{25}\text{Mn}^*$, $^{33}_{16}\text{S}^*$, $^{28}_{14}\text{Si}^*$, $^{14}_{7}\text{N}^*$, and $^{11}_{5}\text{B}^*$.

SOLUTION TO PROBLEM 14

$$^{53}_{25}\text{Mn}^* \rightarrow \, ^{53}_{25}\text{Mn} + \gamma$$

$$^{33}_{16}\text{S}^* \rightarrow \, ^{33}_{16}\text{S} + \gamma$$

$$^{28}_{14}\text{Si}^* \rightarrow \, ^{28}_{14}\text{Si} + \gamma$$

$$^{14}_{7}\text{N}^* \rightarrow \, ^{14}_{7}\text{N} + \gamma$$

$$^{11}_{5}\text{B}^* \rightarrow \, ^{11}_{5}\text{B} + \gamma$$

NUCLEAR REACTIONS

(*College Physics* 8th ed. pages 927–929/9th ed. pages 971–972)

An excellent source of neutrons is a mixture of radium and beryllium. To understand the mechanism involved, we need to consider the following nuclear reactions:

$$^{226}_{88}\text{Ra} \rightarrow \, ^{222}_{86}\text{Rn} + ^{4}_{2}\text{He}$$

$$^{9}_{4}\text{Be} + ^{4}_{2}\text{He} \rightarrow \, ^{12}_{6}\text{C} + ^{1}_{0}\text{n}$$

Alpha particles from the radium strike beryllium nuclei producing neutrons. The neutrons produced are not monoenergetic. Most nuclear reactions are carried out in nuclear physics laboratories using high-energy particle accelerators.

SAMPLE PROBLEM 15

Tritium, H-3 nuclei, are bombarded with deuterons, H-2, producing helium nuclei, He-4, and neutrons. This type of nuclear reaction is usually represented as

$$X + x \rightarrow Y + y$$

The symbol X represents the target nucleus, x is the projectile, Y is the resulting nucleus, and y represents the fragment. The Q-value of the reaction is calculated using

$$Q = \left[(M_X + m_x) - (M_Y + m_y) \right] \times 931.494 \frac{\text{MeV}}{\text{u}}$$

Calculate the reaction Q-value for $^{3}_{1}\text{H} + ^{2}_{1}\text{H} \rightarrow \, ^{4}_{2}\text{He} + ^{1}_{0}\text{n} + Q$. Note that the projectile and fragment particles are given in the nuclear reaction.

SOLUTION TO PROBLEM 15

The reaction could also be written as $X(x,y)Y$ or $^{3}_{1}\text{H}(d, n)^{4}_{2}\text{He}$.

Find the reaction Q-value:

$$M_{H-3} = 3.016 \ 049 \text{ u} \qquad M_{He-4} = 4.002 \ 603 \text{ u}$$

$$m_d = 2.014 \ 102 \text{ u} \qquad m_n = 1.008 \ 665 \text{ u}$$

$$M_{H-3} + m_d = 5.030 \ 151 \text{ u} \qquad M_{He-4} + m_n = 5.011 \ 268 \text{ u}$$

$$Q = \left[(M_X + m_x) - (M_Y + m_y)\right] \times 931.494 \frac{\text{MeV}}{\text{u}}$$

$$Q = \left[(5.030\ 151\ \text{u}) - (5.011\ 268\ \text{u})\right] \times 931.494 \frac{\text{MeV}}{\text{u}}$$

$$Q = 17.59\ \text{MeV}$$

The reaction Q-value is positive indicating that energy is in excess by 17.59 MeV.

SAMPLE PROBLEM 16

Consider the alpha-neutron nuclear reaction $^{27}_{13}\text{Al}(\alpha, \text{n})^{30}_{15}\text{P}$. Calculate the reaction Q-value.

SOLUTION TO PROBLEM 16

First, write the alpha-neutron nuclear reaction:

$$^{27}_{13}\text{Al} + {}^{4}_{2}\text{He} \rightarrow {}^{30}_{15}\text{P} + {}^{1}_{0}\text{n} + Q$$

Calculate the Q-value:

$$M_{Al} = 26.981\ 535\ \text{u} \qquad\qquad M_P = 29.978\ 320\ \text{u}$$
$$m_{\alpha} = 4.002\ 603\ \text{u} \qquad\qquad m_n = 1.008\ 665\ \text{u}$$
$$M_{Al} + m_{\alpha} = 30.984\ 138\ \text{u} \qquad\qquad M_P + m_n = 30.986\ 985\ \text{u}$$

$$Q = \left[(M_X + m_x) - (M_Y + m_y)\right] \times 931.494 \frac{\text{MeV}}{\text{u}}$$

$$Q = \left[(30.084\ 138\ \text{u}) - (30.986\ 985\ \text{u})\right] \times 931.494 \frac{\text{MeV}}{\text{u}}$$

$$Q = -2.65\ \text{MeV}$$

$Q < 0$, making the reaction endoergic. Such nuclear reactions cannot take place spontaneously. Energy in excess of 2.65 MeV must be added to the system to induce nuclear reaction.

NUCLEAR FISSION

(*College Physics* 8th ed. pages 937–940/9th ed. pages 982–986)

Hahn and Strassman discovered nuclear fission in 1938. When a slow or thermal neutron enters a nucleus of fissionable material, like $^{235}_{92}\text{U}$ or $^{239}_{94}\text{Pu}$, the neutron is captured and the nucleus splits—fissions with a large release of energy. Uranium U-235 and plutonium Pu-239 are fissionable materials. Chemical reactions liberate energies on the order of several electron volts, eV, where nuclear fission releases energies on the order of 180 MeV. When nuclear fission occurs, two fission fragments A and B are formed along with several neutrons and a large Q-value. We can write the fission reaction as

$$^{235}_{92}\text{U} + {}^{1}_{0}\text{n} \rightarrow A + B + x{}^{1}_{0}\text{n} + Q$$

or as

$$^{239}_{94}\text{Pu} + {}^1_0\text{n} \rightarrow \text{A} + \text{B} + x{}^1_0\text{n} + Q$$

The fission fragments are asymmetric.

SAMPLE PROBLEM 17

A thermal neutron is used to initiate nuclear fission in a stationary U-235 nucleus. Calculate the Q-value for $^{235}_{92}\text{U} + {}^1_0\text{n} \rightarrow {}^{144}_{56}\text{Ba} + {}^{89}_{36}\text{Kr} + 3{}^1_0\text{n} + Q$.

SOLUTION TO PROBLEM 17

The thermal neutron has an energy less than 0.1 eV. Since the energy released in a single fission far exceeds 100 MeV, the energy of the incoming thermal neutron is ignored in the calculations.

In this problem, the masses of the fission fragments are only given to four decimal places, and we will calculate with the given masses.

$$M_U = 235.0439 \text{ u} \qquad\qquad M_{Ba} = 143.9605 \text{ u}$$
$$m_n = 1.0087 \text{ u} \qquad\qquad M_{Kr} = 88.8640 \text{ u}$$
$$3m_n = 3.0261 \text{ u}$$
$$M_U + m_n = 236.0526 \text{ u} \qquad M_{Ba} + M_{Kr} + 3m_n = 235.8506 \text{ u}$$

$$Q = \left[\left(M_U + m_n\right) - \left(M_{Ba} + M_{Kr} + 3m_n\right)\right] \times 931.494 \frac{\text{MeV}}{\text{u}}$$

$$Q = \left[\left(236.0526 \text{ u}\right) - \left(235.8506 \text{ u}\right)\right] \times 931.494 \frac{\text{MeV}}{\text{u}}$$

$$Q = 188.16 \text{ MeV}$$

The fission fragments and fission neutrons share the 188.16 MeV as kinetic energy. Fissionable materials have a high density, and the fission fragments are quickly stopped from transforming their energy into thermal energy. Nuclear fission releases gigantic quantities of heat.

The isotope Pu-239 does not exist in nature but is made in a type of nuclear reactor called a breeder reactor. The uranium isotope U-238 does not participate in slow neutron-induced nuclear fission. In the breeder reactor, U-238 absorbs a neutron and forms the short-lived U-239 isotope. U-239 is a beta emitter and forms element 93 that is also is a short-lived beta emitter. The end product is Pu-239.

SAMPLE PROBLEM 18

Ignoring the Q-values, write the nuclear reactions for the formation of Pu-239 from U-238 in the breeder reactor.

SOLUTION TO PROBLEM 18

Write the reaction for the absorption of the neutron by U-238:

$$^{238}_{92}\text{U} + {}^1_0\text{n} \rightarrow {}^{239}_{92}\text{U}$$

The beta decay is

$$^{239}_{92}\text{U} \rightarrow {}^0_{-1}\text{e} + {}^0_0\bar{\nu} + {}^{239}_{93}\text{Np}$$

and the next beta decay:

$$^{239}_{92}\text{Np} \rightarrow {}^0_{-1}\text{e} + {}^0_0\bar{\nu} + {}^{239}_{94}\text{Pu}$$

THERMONUCLEAR FUSION

(*College Physics* 8th ed. pages 941–943/9th ed. pages 986–988)

Nuclear fission is a nuclear reaction where massive, fissionable nuclei absorb a neutron, causing them to split into two fission fragments with the release of several neutrons and energy on the order of 180 MeV per fission. Nuclear fusion is a nuclear process in which light nuclei fuse or join in a more massive nucleus with an energy release on the order of 10 to 20 MeV per fusion.

Light nuclei have to collide before they fuse. Surrounding each nucleus is an electrostatic coulomb barrier that repels other nuclei. Colliding nuclei require high kinetic energy and great pressure to overcome the electrostatic barriers. Light nuclei heated to millions of degrees have such kinetic energies to bring nuclei into direct contact allowing fusion reactions. These nuclear reactions are called thermonuclear fusion reactions.

Thermonuclear fusion reactions are the reactions that drive stars and fuel the fireball of a thermonuclear device—a hydrogen bomb. Lithium-6 deuteride is a fuel used in thermonuclear devices.

SAMPLE PROBLEM 19

Under extreme temperature and pressure, Li-6 and deuterium, H-2, will undergo thermonuclear fusion as $^6_3\text{Li} + ^2_1\text{H} \rightarrow ^4_2\text{He} + ^4_2\text{He} + Q$. Calculate the reaction Q-value.

SOLUTION TO PROBLEM 19

Write the nuclear reaction:

$$^6_3\text{Li} + ^2_1\text{H} \rightarrow ^4_2\text{He} + ^4_2\text{He} + Q$$

Calculate the reaction Q-value:

$$M_{Li} = 6.015\ 122\ \text{u} \qquad\qquad M_{He} = 4.002\ 603\ \text{u}$$
$$m_d = 2.014\ 102\ \text{u} \qquad\qquad m_{He} = 4.002\ 603\ \text{u}$$
$$M_{Li} + m_d = 8.029\ 224\ \text{u} \qquad\qquad M_{He} + m_{He} = 8.005\ 206\ \text{u}$$

$$Q = \left[(M_X + m_x) - (M_Y + m_y)\right] \times 931.494\ \frac{\text{MeV}}{\text{u}}$$

$$Q = \left[(8.029\ 224\ \text{u}) - (8.005\ 206\ \text{u})\right] \times 931.494\ \frac{\text{MeV}}{\text{u}}$$

$$Q = 22.37\ \text{MeV}$$

MODERN PHYSICS: STUDENT OBJECTIVES FOR THE AP EXAM

- Know and use the mass-energy relationship.
- Know and use Planck's quantum equation.
- Know and use the photoelectric effect equation and be able to apply it to graphical solutions.
- Know the Compton scattering concept.

■ Know and use the de Broglie particle-wave dualism concept.
■ Have an understanding of the Bohr hydrogen atom.
■ Know and understand the symbols for atomic number *Z*, neutron number *N*, and mass number *A* and be able to use them correctly in radioactive decay and binding energy problems.
■ Know the decay processes for (a) alpha, (b) beta, and (c) gamma and be able to balance nuclear reactions.
■ Know the difference between nuclear fission and fusion and be able to balance their nuclear reactions.
■ Be able to calculate *Q*-values in nuclear reactions.
■ Be able to calculate the binding energy of nuclei.
■ You must be able to solve multiple-choice questions without a calculator.

MULTIPLE-CHOICE QUESTIONS

1. Compton scattering gives the evidence for the
   (A) particle nature of light.
   (B) wave nature of light.
   (C) particle nature of matter.
   (D) wave nature of matter.
   (E) photoelectric effect.

2. The photoelectric effect describes the
   (A) relationship between a photon and the charge on the electron.
   (B) production of light when electrical current exists in a thin filament.
   (C) electric current produced when electromagnetic radiation strikes a metallic surface.
   (D) production of light in an incandescent bulb.
   (E) production of light when an electron is captured by an ion.

3. If a physics experiment shows that blue light will not produce photoelectrons from the surface of a particular metal, photoelectrons may possibly be produced by using light that is
   (A) red.
   (B) ultraviolet.
   (C) green.
   (D) infrared.
   (E) microwave.

4. Isotopes of an element have the same
   (A) *A* and *Z* numbers.
   (B) *A* but a different *Z* number.
   (C) *Z* but a different *A* number.
   (D) neutron number.
   (E) *A* but a different *N* number.

5. To fission nuclei of Pu-239, which of the following is used to initiate the fission reaction?
   (A) proton
   (B) neutron
   (C) neutrino
   (D) gamma ray
   (E) positron

6. When a gamma ray is emitted from a radioactive nucleus, the mass number of the nucleus
   (A) increases by 1.
   (B) decreases by 1.
   (C) does not change.
   (D) increases by 2.
   (E) decreases by 2.

7. The material that serves as both fuel and product in a breeder reactor is
   (A) $_{1}^{1}\text{H}$
   (B) $_{94}^{239}\text{Pu}$
   (C) $_{92}^{235}\text{U}$
   (D) $_{92}^{238}\text{U}$
   (E) $_{0}^{1}\text{n}$

8. When the velocity of a electron is increased by a factor of 2, its de Broglie wavelength changes by a factor of
   (A) $\frac{1}{4}$.
   (B) $\frac{1}{2}$.
   (C) 1.
   (D) 2.
   (E) 4.

9. The energy of a photon is
   (A) inversely proportional to the square of the frequency of the photon.
   (B) inversely proportional to the frequency of the photon.
   (C) proportional to the square of the frequency of the photon.
   (D) directly proportional to the frequency of the photon.
   (E) independent of the frequency of the photon.

10. Rutherford's alpha particle scattering experiments with gold foil showed
    (A) the wave nature of matter.
    (B) the particle nature of light.
    (C) that electrons can be diffracted.
    (D) that the atom has a small positive core.
    (E) that photons behave like particles.

11. In 1917, Rutherford conducted the first transmutation of N-14 into O-17 through the following nuclear reaction: $^{14}_{7}N + ^{4}_{2}He \rightarrow ^{17}_{8}O + ?$. The identity of the missing particle is
(A) an electron.
(B) a positron.
(C) a neutron.
(D) a proton.
(E) an alpha particle.

12. Determine the atomic number Z and the nucleon number A for the following nuclear reaction: $^{23}_{Z}Na\left(^{3}_{2}He, ^{2}_{1}H\right)^{A}_{12}Mg$.

	Z	A
(A)	11	22
(B)	11	23
(C)	11	24
(D)	12	23
(E)	12	24

13. What is the importance of using thermal neutrons in nuclear reactions?
(A) Thermal neutrons capture results in nuclear fission.
(B) Thermal neutrons are released in alpha decay.
(C) Thermal neutrons accompany gamma ray photons.
(D) Thermal neutrons initiate thermonuclear fusion.
(E) Thermal neutrons are important in forming helium nuclei.

14. The momentum p of a photon is given in terms of the frequency f, the wavelength λ, and Planck's constant h by
(A) $p = hf$
(B) $p = h\lambda$
(C) $p = \dfrac{hf}{\lambda}$
(D) $p = \dfrac{hc}{\lambda}$
(E) $p = \dfrac{h}{\lambda}$

15. When a negative beta particle is emitted from a radioactive nucleus, the mass number of the nucleus
(A) increases by 1.
(B) decreases by 1.
(C) does not change.
(D) increases by 2.
(E) decreases by 2.

FREE-RESPONSE PROBLEMS

1. Given the spontaneous decay reaction: $^{232}_{92}U \rightarrow ^{228}_{90}Th + ^{4}_{2}He + Q$.
(a) Calculate the Q-value for the reaction.
(b) Is this decay possible? Justify your answer.
(c) Determine the binding energy of the U-232 nucleus.

(d) Find the binding energy per nucleon given that the mass of the U-232 = 232.037 156 u , Th-228 = 228.028 741 u , He-4 = 4.002 603 u , H = 1.007 825 u, and the neutron = 1.008 665 u.

2. An electron, in vacuum, is directed against a tungsten metal target. In doing so, the electron falls through a difference in electrical potential of $9 \times 10^3 \, \text{V}$.
   (a) What is the kinetic energy of a single electron as it impacts the target?
   (b) Determine the classical velocity of the electron as it strikes the surface.
   (c) What is the de Broglie wavelength prior to impact?
   (d) All of the kinetic energy of the electron, as it impacts the surface, is converted into pure electromagnetic energy. What is the frequency of this electromagnetic radiation?
   (e) Calculate the wavelength of the radiation.

ANSWERS

MULTIPLE-CHOICE QUESTIONS

1. **A** The scattering of X-rays from various targets strongly supports the photon concept. The Compton shift equation experimentally supports this shift in wavelength (*College Physics* 8th ed. page 879/9th ed. pages 920–921).

2. **C** Light striking a metallic surface will give rise to photoelectrons and hence a photoelectric current when the energy of the photon is greater than the energy binding an electron to the surface of the metal (*College Physics* 8th ed. page 872/9th ed. pages 913–916).

3. **B** The speed of light is given by $c = \lambda f$. The higher the frequency, the shorter the wavelength. Ultraviolet light has a higher frequency than blue light (*College Physics* 8th ed. page 721/9th ed. page 741).

4. **C** The isotopes of an element have the same Z number but different A numbers (*College Physics* 8th ed. page 913/9th ed. page 957).

5. **B** Fission of Pu-239 is initiated by neutrons. Since there is no coulombic barrier to their absorption, the compound nucleus that is formed is in a highly energetic state and will split into two fission fragments almost instantaneously with two or three free neutrons also appearing with the fragments (*College Physics* 8th ed. page 937/9th ed. pages 982–983).

6. **C** The gamma decay of an excited nucleus to a lower energy state is similar to the emission of light from an excited atom. There is no change in either mass number or charge (*College Physics* 8th ed. page 924/9th ed. pages 968–969).

7. **B** A breeder reactor will produce more fissionable fuel than it uses. The reaction begins with neutron absorption by a U-238 nucleus and

subsequent beta decay to Np-239 that is followed by an additional beta decay into Pu-239 which is fissionable (*College Physics* 8th ed. page 939/9th ed. page 984).

8. **B** The de Broglie wavelength is $\lambda = \dfrac{h}{mv}$ and if $v = 2v$, then $\lambda_{new} = \dfrac{1}{2}\lambda$ (*College Physics* 8th ed. pages 880–881/9th ed. pages 922–924).

9. **D** The energy of a photon is given by $E = hf$. (*College Physics* 8th ed. page 873/9th ed. page 915).

10. **D** The Rutherford alpha-scattering experiment used techniques in moving the gold foil target and showed that the Thomson model of the atom was incorrect. Only a positive core (nucleus) could account for the electrostatic repulsion of alpha particles through the large angles observed (*College Physics* 8th ed. page 891/9th ed. pages 934–935).

11. **D** In nuclear reactions, the Z numbers and the A numbers must be conserved. To conserve, the answer is a proton, ^1_1H (*College Physics* 8th ed. page 927/9th ed. pages 971–972).

12. **C** In a nuclear decay, charge and mass number must be conserved (*College Physics* 8th ed. page 927/9th ed. pages 971–972).

13. **A** Slow neutrons are more likely to cause a fission of a U-235 nucleus than a fast neutron (*College Physics* 8th ed. page 940/9th ed. page 985).

14. **E** The energy of a photon can be expressed as $E = \dfrac{hc}{\lambda}$ and its momentum as $p = \dfrac{E}{c}$, which yield $p = \dfrac{h}{\lambda}$ (*College Physics* 8th ed. page 881/9th ed. pages 922–923).

15. **C** Charge and mass number must be conserved in nuclear reactions. In the negative beta decay process, $^A_ZX \rightarrow {}^0_{-1}\beta + {}^0_0\nu + {}^A_{Z+1}Y$, the mass number does not change, and the Z number increases by 1 (*College Physics* 8th ed. page 922/9th ed. page 967).

FREE-RESPONSE PROBLEMS

1. (a) Write the nuclear reaction for the spontaneous alpha decay of U-232:

$$^{232}_{92}U \rightarrow {}^{228}_{90}Th + {}^4_2He + Q$$

The required masses are

$$M_{U\text{-}232} = 232.037\ 156\ u$$
$$M_{Th\text{-}228} = 228.028\ 741\ u$$
$$M_\alpha = 4.002\ 603\ u$$
$$M_H = 1.007\ 825\ u$$
$$M_n = 1.008\ 665\ u$$

Calculating the Q-value:

$$Q = (M_{\text{U-232}} - M_{\text{Th-228}} - M_{\alpha}) \times 931.494 \frac{\text{MeV}}{\text{u}}$$

$$Q = (232.037\ 156\ \text{u} - 228.028\ 741\ \text{u} - 4.002\ 603\ \text{u}) \times 931.494 \frac{\text{MeV}}{\text{u}}$$

$$Q = 5.41\ \text{MeV}$$

(b) The Q-value is positive, $Q > 0$, making the alpha decay of U-232 possible.

(c) The U-232 nucleus has $Z = 92$ protons and $N = 140$ neutrons. The binding energy is

$$B = \left(Zm_H + Nm_n - M_A\right) \times 931.494 \frac{\text{MeV}}{\text{u}}$$

$$B = \left[\left(92 \times 1.007\ 825\ \text{u}\right) + \left(140 \times 1.008\ 665\ \text{u}\right) - \left(232.037\ 156\ \text{u}\right)\right]\left(931.494\ \frac{\text{MeV}}{\text{u}}\right)$$

$$B = 1766.0\ \text{MeV}$$

(d) The binding energy per nucleon is the binding energy divided by the nucleon population.

$$\frac{B}{A} = \frac{1766.0\ \text{MeV}}{232\ \text{nucleons}}$$

$$\frac{B}{A} = 7.61\ \frac{\text{MeV}}{\text{nucleon}}$$

(*College Physics* 8th ed. pages 916–917, 921–924/9th ed. pages 960–961, 965–969).

2. (a) Since the electron falls through a potential difference of $9 \times 10^3\,\text{V}$, its kinetic energy is

$$K = Vq = \left(9 \times 10^3\,\text{V}\right)e$$

$$K = 9 \times 10^3\,\text{eV} \times \frac{1.60 \times 10^{-19}\,\text{J}}{1\ \text{eV}} = 1.44 \times 10^{-15}\,\text{J}$$

(b) To find the velocity of the electron, we write

$$K = \frac{1}{2}mv^2$$

and

$$v = \sqrt{\frac{2K}{m}} = \sqrt{\frac{2(1.44 \times 10^{-15}\,\text{J})}{9.11 \times 10^{-31}\,\text{kg}}} = 5.62 \times 10^7 \frac{\text{m}}{\text{s}}$$

(c) The de Broglie wavelength is

$$\lambda = \frac{h}{mv}$$

$$\lambda = \frac{6.63 \times 10^{-34}\,\text{J} \cdot \text{s}}{\left(9.11 \times 10^{-31}\,\text{kg}\right)\left(5.62 \times 10^7 \, \text{m}\middle/\text{s}\right)} = 1.29 \times 10^{-11}\,\text{m}$$

(d) $E = hf$

$$f = \frac{E}{h} = \frac{1.44 \times 10^{-15}\,\text{J}}{6.63 \times 10^{-34}\,\text{J} \cdot \text{s}} = 2.17 \times 10^{18}\,\text{Hz}$$

(e) The wavelength of the electromagnetic radiation is

$$c = \lambda f$$

$$\lambda = \frac{c}{f} = \frac{3 \times 10^8 \, \text{m}\middle/\text{s}}{2.17 \times 10^{18} \, 1\middle/\text{s}} = 1.38 \times 10^{-10}\,\text{m}$$

(*College Physics* 8th ed. pages 872–874, 880–882/9th ed. pages 914–916, 922–924)

Part III

Practice Tests

PRACTICE TEST 1

AP Physics B
Section I: Multiple-Choice Questions
Time: 90 minutes
70 Questions

Directions: Each of the following questions or incomplete statements is accompanied by five suggested answers or completions. Select the correct response to each question.

Hand calculators are not allowed on this part of the test.

The Table of Information is allowed, but not the AP B Equations.

1. The velocity versus time graph of a particle moving in a linear manner is a straight line with a positive slope. This graph shows that the particle
   (A) has zero velocity.
   (B) has a constant negative velocity.
   (C) has a constant positive velocity.
   (D) has a constant negative acceleration.
   (E) has a constant positive acceleration.

2. If the velocity and acceleration of a particle in motion have opposite signs,
   (A) the position of the particle is constant.
   (B) the particle is at rest.
   (C) the particle is slowing down.
   (D) the velocity of the particle is in the positive direction.
   (E) the velocity of the particle is in the negative direction.

3. A projectile is fired from ground level into two-dimensional space with initial speed v_0 at launch angle θ_0. When the projectile reaches its maximum altitude,
   (A) its acceleration and velocity are nonzero.
   (B) its acceleration becomes zero but its velocity is nonzero.

   (C) its acceleration is nonzero but its velocity becomes zero.
   (D) its acceleration and velocity both become zero.
   (E) its acceleration and velocity are both positive.

4. Ignoring air resistance, at what angle should a projectile be projected into two-dimensional space to reach its theoretical maximum range?
   (A) 0°
   (B) 45°
   (C) 54°
   (D) 60°
   (E) any set of complementary angles

5. A particle of mass m moving in a straight line on a smooth, frictionless surface experiences an increase in velocity. This increase in velocity indicates
   (A) the presence of a force in the same direction as the direction of the velocity vector.
   (B) the presence of a force acting perpendicular to the direction of the velocity vector.
   (C) the absence of a force.
   (D) the presence of a force acting antiparallel to the velocity vector.
   (E) the absence of a resultant or net force.

6. The component of the contact force perpendicular to a surface is called the
   (A) frictional force.
   (B) gravitational force.
   (C) inertial force.
   (D) normal force.
   (E) weight.

7. The inertia of a body tends to cause it to
   (A) accelerate.
   (B) decelerate.
   (C) be attracted to the center of Earth.
   (D) experience a frictional force.
   (E) continue moving at present velocity.

8. A 1.0-kg mass is at rest on the surface of a laboratory table. The net force acting on the mass is
   (A) 0 N
   (B) 1.0 kg
   (C) 1.0 N
   (D) 9.8 kg
   (E) –9.8 N

9. The acceleration due to gravity on the surface of the Moon is approximately one-sixth of that of the surface of Earth. What force is required to accelerate a mass of 25.0 kg on the surface of the Moon?
   (A) one-sixth of the force required on the surface of Earth
   (B) the same as the force required on the surface of Earth
   (C) six times greater than the force required on the surface of Earth
   (D) five-sixths of the force required on the surface of Earth
   (E) five times greater than the force required on the surface of Earth

10. A 500-kg elevator car accelerates upward at 2.0 m/s². What is the magnitude of the force exerted by the support cable?
    (A) 500 N
    (B) 980 N
    (C) 1500 N
    (D) 4900 N
    (E) 5900 N

11. For most surface-to-surface contacts,
    (A) the coefficient of static friction is greater than the coefficient of kinetic friction.
    (B) the coefficient of kinetic friction is greater than the coefficient of static friction.
    (C) the coefficient of static friction will equal the coefficient of kinetic friction.
    (D) the static frictional force will exceed the normal force.
    (E) the kinetic frictional force will exceed the normal force.

12. A block is placed at the top of an inclined plane that is tilted at 45°. The coefficient of static friction for the surfaces is 0.32, and the coefficient of kinetic friction for the surfaces is 0.30. When the block is released,
    (A) it remains at rest on the inclined plane.
    (B) it slides down the plane with constant velocity.
    (C) it accelerates down the plane.
    (D) it remains in a state of impending motion.
    (E) it slides a short distance and stops.

13. A wooden crate sits on an inclined plane without slipping. As the angle of inclination is decreased, the normal force
    (A) increases.
    (B) decreases.
    (C) does not change.
    (D) is directed downward.
    (E) is directed upward.

14. A body travels uniformly in a horizontal, circular orbit. The orbiting body
    (A) is in translational equilibrium and has no net force or acceleration.
    (B) moves with constant velocity.
    (C) is accelerating toward the center of the circle.
    (D) experiences tangential acceleration.
    (E) accelerates away from the center of the circle.

15. When compressing a spring, the work done by the spring force is
    (A) negative because work is always a negative quantity.
    (B) negative because the spring pushes back in the direction opposite to its displacement.
    (C) zero because work is only done by a force external to the spring.
    (D) positive because the end of the spring is moved through a finite displacement.
    (E) positive because work is always a positive quantity.

16. Consider a mass m moving in a horizontal circle with uniform motion. The work done on the mass by the centripetal force is zero because the centripetal force
    (A) is parallel to the displacement.
    (B) is perpendicular to the displacement.
    (C) is a fictitious force.
    (D) returns the mass to its starting place at the end of each period of motion.
    (E) is tangent to the velocity.

17. On a force versus displacement graph, the work done is
    (A) the vertical intercept.
    (B) the slope of the curve.
    (C) the area beneath the curve.
    (D) the intercept on the displacement axis.
    (E) the maximum of the curve.

18. A particle experiences a decrease in its kinetic energy. According to the work–kinetic energy theorem,
    (A) there is work done by the particle.
    (B) the force acting on the particle was not constant.
    (C) there is no work done on or by the particle.
    (D) the velocity of the particle remains a constant.
    (E) the distance the particle travels is a constant.

19. If the height of a particle of mass m at rest above the ground is doubled, its gravitational potential energy is multiplied by a factor of
    (A) 0.25.
    (B) 0.5.
    (C) 1.
    (D) 2.
    (E) 4.

20. Two unequal masses hang from the ends of a massless cord that passes over a frictionless pulley. The masses are released from rest. Which of the following statements is true about the kinetic energy K and the potential energy U of the system?
    (A) $\Delta U = 0$ and $\Delta K = 0$
    (B) $\Delta U = 0$ and $\Delta K > 0$
    (C) $\Delta U < 0$ and $\Delta K > 0$
    (D) $\Delta U > 0$ and $\Delta K < 0$
    (E) $\Delta U < 0$ and $\Delta K = 0$

21. In a one-dimensional system, a force is conservative if it is a
    (A) function of time and position.
    (B) function of time.
    (C) function of position.
    (D) linear function of time.
    (E) quadratic function of position.

22. The net impulse on a particle is equal to
    (A) the total applied force.
    (B) the particle's total momentum.
    (C) the change in the particle's momentum.
    (D) the change in the particle's displacement.
    (E) the work done on the particle.

23. Ignoring air resistance, as a body falls to the surface of Earth, its momentum
    (A) remains constant because it is in free fall.
    (B) increases because of the external force of gravity.
    (C) remains a constant but its kinetic energy increases.
    (D) increases but its kinetic energy remains constant.
    (E) increases but its kinetic energy decreases.

24. A uniform meterstick has a weight of 1.00 N and is supported at the 20.0-cm mark by a frictionless pivot. A 4.00-N weight will place the meterstick into a state of rotational equilibrium if it is located at which of the following positions on the meterstick?
(A) 7.50 cm
(B) 12.5 cm
(C) 27.5 cm
(D) 42.5 cm
(E) 57.5 cm

25. Astronauts experience *weightlessness* because
(A) they are beyond the range of Earth's gravitational attraction.
(B) they have no weight beyond two Earth radii.
(C) the gravitational pull of the sun in one direction equals that of Earth in the opposite direction.
(D) the motion of the spacecraft produces a centrifugal force balancing the gravitational force of Earth.
(E) they are always in a state of free fall toward Earth.

26. A communications satellite is in a circular orbit well above Earth's atmosphere. Which of the following is true?
(A) There is only one force acting on the satellite.
(B) There are two forces acting on the satellite, and their resultant is zero.
(C) There are two forces acting on the satellite, and their resultant is not zero.
(D) There are three forces acting on the satellite.
(E) Neither (A), (B), (C), or (D) is true.

27. Two blocks of mass $M_A = m$ and $M_B = 2m$ are pushed across a frictionless table by a constant horizontal force F. The blocks remain in contact. Block M_B experiences a net force of

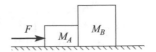

(A) $\frac{2}{3}F$
(B) F
(C) $\frac{3}{2}F$
(D) $2F$
(E) $3F$

28. In a system that is undergoing simple harmonic motion, the potential energy is a maximum when
(A) the displacement is a maximum.
(B) the displacement is zero.
(C) the acceleration is zero.
(D) the force is zero.
(E) the kinetic energy is a maximum.

29. The velocity of sound in air depends on
(A) the wavelength of the sound wave.
(B) the temperature of air.
(C) the frequency of the sound wave.
(D) the amplitude of the wave.
(E) the velocity of the source producing the wave.

30. A fluid pressure of 1 pascal is equal to
(A) 1 atmosphere.
(B) 1 kg/m3.
(C) 1 bar.
(D) 1 N/m2.
(E) 1 mm of Hg.

31. The buoyant force of a fluid is
(A) the product of the volume of the displaced fluid and the mass density of the object.
(B) a function of the mass of the submerged object.
(C) always greater than the weight of the submerged object.
(D) less than the weight of the displaced fluid if the object sinks.
(E) equal to the weight of the displaced fluid.

32. The process of heat transfer involving the direct transfer of kinetic energy from more energetic to less energetic particles is called
(A) sublimation.
(B) evaporation.
(C) conduction.
(D) convention.
(E) radiation.

33. If the absolute temperature of a lamp filament were doubled, the energy radiated each second by the bulb would
(A) remain constant.
(B) double.
(C) quadruple.
(D) increase by a factor of 8.
(E) increase by a factor of 16.

34. A block of plastic floats in water. The buoyant force acting on it is equal to
(A) the weight of the plastic block.
(B) the mass of the plastic block.
(C) the difference of the plastic block and the weight of the displaced water.
(D) the product of the surface area of the block and mass of water displaced.
(E) the product of the surface area of the block and weight of water displaced.

35. If the mass and pressure of an ideal gas are held constant while the volume is allowed to double, the temperature changes by a factor of
(A) 0.2.
(B) 0.5.
(C) 1.
(D) 2.
(E) 4.

36. Which of the graphs illustrates the relationship between frequency and period?

(A)

frequency f

(B)
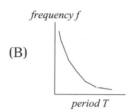
period T

frequency f
(C)
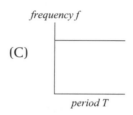
period T

(D)
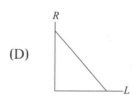

frequency f
(E)
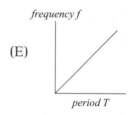
period T

37. The work done by a system during any thermodynamic process
(A) depends only on the starting and ending points.
(B) depends on the path taken during the process.
(C) is equal to the quantity of heat added to the system.
(D) is equal to the final value of the internal energy of the system.
(E) is equal to the change in the internal energy of the system.

38. Which graph illustrates the relationship between the resistance and the length of a piece of copper wire maintained at constant temperature?

(A)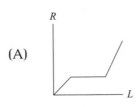

(B)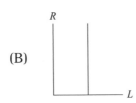

(C)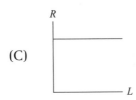

(D)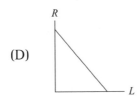

(E)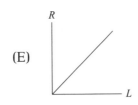

39. Doubling the separation of two identical negative charges causes the force of electrostatic repulsion to change by a factor of
(A) 4.
(B) 2.
(C) 1.414.
(D) 0.5.
(E) 0.25.

40. A small particle is considered to be negative when it has
(A) dipole properties.
(B) an excess of protons.
(C) a deficiency of neutrons.
(D) a deficiency of electrons.
(E) an excess of electrons.

41. The electric potential inside a hollow conductor that carries a surface charge is
(A) zero.
(B) infinite.
(C) greater at points near the surface than near the center.
(D) greater at points near the center than at the surface.
(E) equal to the electric potential at the surface.

42. When work is done by an external force in moving an electron at a constant speed between two points in an electric field, the work done is
(A) always positive.
(B) always zero.
(C) always negative.
(D) dependent only on the total distance traversed.
(E) dependent only on the displacement.

43. The capacitance of a capacitor
(A) depends on the geometry of the two conductors that make up the capacitor.
(B) decreases if the charge on the plates is increased.
(C) increases if the charge on the plates is increased.
(D) decreases if the voltage across the plates is increased.
(E) increases if the voltage across the plates is increased.

44. The process of accumulating charge on the plates of a capacitor
    (A) involves work being done by the electric field of the capacitor.
    (B) requires a maximum energy density between the plates.
    (C) requires work to be done by an external agent.
    (D) involves no energy transfer because the plates contain charges of opposite sign.
    (E) involves work being done on one plate and work being done by the charge on the other plate for a net work of zero.

45. The difference between the terminal voltage of a battery and its emf is due to
    (A) internal resistance.
    (B) the circuit load.
    (C) external resistance.
    (D) current delivered.
    (E) potential of the circuit.

46. Resistors connected in series all have
    (A) the same charge.
    (B) the same current.
    (C) varying potential differences.
    (D) the same power dissipation.
    (E) the same potential difference.

47. The magnitude of the force exerted on a current-carrying wire placed in an external magnetic field is directly proportional to
    (A) the magnitude of the current.
    (B) the direction of the current.
    (C) the strength of the magnetic field.
    (D) factors (A) and (C) only.
    (E) all the factors (A), (B), and (C).

48. A proton with velocity v to the right enters a uniform magnetic field that is directed out of the page. After the proton enters the field, it will be
    (A) deflected out of the plane of the page.
    (B) deflected into the page.
    (C) deflected upward.
    (D) deflected downward.
    (E) unaffected.

49. A proton moves in a circular orbit of radius R in a uniform magnetic field. Doubling the velocity of the particle causes the radius to change by a factor of
    (A) $0.25R$.
    (B) $0.5R$.
    (C) R.
    (D) $2R$.
    (E) $4R$.

50. A current in a solenoid produces a uniform magnetic field inside the solenoid. The strength of the field is directly proportional to
    (A) the magnitude of the current.
    (B) the direction of the current.
    (C) the area of the solenoid.
    (D) all the factors (A), (B), and (C).
    (E) factors (A) and (C) only.

51. In an elastic collision between two bodies,
    (A) both momentum and kinetic energy are conserved.
    (B) both momentum and potential energy are conserved.
    (C) neither momentum or kinetic energy are conserved.
    (D) neither momentum or potential energy are conserved.
    (E) only momentum is conserved.

52. When the south pole of a bar magnet approaches a loop, an emf is induced so that the magnetic field of the loop
    (A) increases as the magnet gets closer.
    (B) decreases as the magnet gets closer.
    (C) points away from the south pole of the approaching magnet.
    (D) points toward the south pole of the approaching magnet.
    (E) none of the above statements are correct.

53. Nuclear decay leads to a type of electromagnetic radiation called
    (A) infrared.
    (B) visible light.
    (C) ultraviolet.
    (D) X-rays.
    (E) gamma rays.

For Questions 54 to 56:
    I = real
    II = virtual
    III = upright
    IV = inverted
    V = smaller than
    VI = same size as the object
    VII = larger than the object

54. The image formed by a concave mirror of an object that is located at the center of curvature of the mirror is
    (A) I, III, and V.
    (B) I, III, and VI.
    (C) I, III, and VII.
    (D) II, IV, and V.
    (E) I, IV, and VI.

55. For an object located at a distance beyond twice the focal length of a diverging lens, the image is
    (A) I, III, and V.
    (B) I, IV, and V.
    (C) II, III, and V.
    (D) II, III, and VII.
    (E) I, IV, and VII.

56. For an object located at a distance between one and two focal lengths from a converging lens, the image is
    (A) I, III, and V.
    (B) II, IV, and V.
    (C) I, III, and VI.
    (D) II, III, and VII.
    (E) I, IV, and VII.

57. A real image is one that is characterized as an image that is
    (A) formed by a mirror and not by a lens.
    (B) formed by a lens and not by a mirror.
    (C) inverted with respect to the object.

(D) not inverted with respect to the object.
(E) formed by light rays that actually pass through the image point.

58. For an object positioned a distance L in front of a plane mirror, the distance between the object and the image formed by the mirror is
    (A) 0.25L.
    (B) 0.5L.
    (C) 2L.
    (D) 3L.
    (E) 4L.

59. An electron enters the magnetic field as shown. Which way will the electron be deflected?

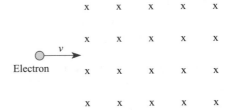

(A) It will be deflected toward the top of the page.
(B) It will be deflected toward the bottom of the page.
(C) It will go undeflected.
(D) It will be deflected into the page.
(E) It will be deflected out of the page.

60. The advantage of using a diffraction grating over Young's apparatus is
    (A) a wider pattern.
    (B) a narrower pattern.
    (C) wider dark fringes.
    (D) the absence of bright fringes.
    (E) sharper bright lines.

61. In Young's double-slit experiment, the two beams of light must
    (A) travel at different speeds.
    (B) be nonmonochromatic.
    (C) originate at the same source.
    (D) originate at two different sources.
    (E) travel the same distance to the screen.

62. Four charges of equal magnitude and charge $+q$ are arranged at the corners of a square of sides d as shown. Which arrow illustrates the net electrostatic force acting on the charge at the lower-right-hand corner of the square?

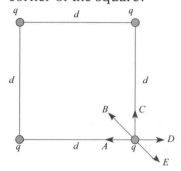

(A) A
(B) B
(C) C
(D) D
(E) E

63. According to the de Broglie equation, if the momentum of the particle is tripled, the corresponding change in the wavelength of the matter wave will change by a factor of
(A) 1/9.
(B) 1/3.
(C) 3.
(D) 9.
(E) zero.

64. Compton scattering refers to the scattering of
(A) electrons by photons.
(B) photons by electrons.
(C) photons by photons.
(D) protons by photons.
(E) photons by protons.

65. When a positron is emitted from a radioactive nucleus, the atomic number of that nucleus
(A) is increased by 1.
(B) is decreased by 1.
(C) does not change.
(D) is increased by 2.
(E) is decreased by 2.

66. In a chain reaction involving U-235, the nuclide that is both a reactant and a product, is
(A) $_{1}^{1}\text{H}$.
(B) $_{94}^{239}\text{Pu}$.
(C) $_{92}^{235}\text{U}$.
(D) $_{92}^{238}\text{U}$.
(E) $_{0}^{1}\text{n}$.

67. When a radioactive nucleus decays, it emits an alpha particle, causing the atomic number of the daughter nucleus to
(A) increase by 4.
(B) increase by 2.
(C) remain unchanged.
(D) decrease by 2.
(E) decrease by 4.

68. A β^- radioactive decay happens in an unstable nucleus when
(A) a proton is converted into an electron by the strong force.
(B) a proton is converted into a neutron by the strong force.
(C) a neutron is converted into a proton by the weak force.
(D) a neutron is converted into an alpha particle by the weak force.
(E) a neutron is converted into a beta particle by the weak force.

69. $_{84}^{216}\text{Po}$ decays into $_{82}^{212}\text{Pb}$ by emitting what nuclear radiation?
(A) alpha
(B) beta negative
(C) beta plus
(D) gamma
(E) X-ray

70. The mass number of a nucleus is equal to the number of
(A) protons.
(B) neutrons.
(C) nucleons.
(D) neutrinos.
(E) positrons.

STOP
END OF SECTION I

IF YOU FINISH BEFORE TIME IS CALLED, YOU MAY CHECK YOUR WORK ON THIS SECTION. DO NOT GO ON TO SECTION II UNTIL YOU ARE TOLD TO DO SO.

AP Physics B
Section II: Free-Response Problems
Time: 90 minutes

Directions: Solve each of the following problems. Unless the directions indicate otherwise, respond to all parts of each question.

Hand calculators are permitted on this part of the test.

The Table of Information and the Advanced Placement Physics B Equations are allowed.

1. Consider the diagram shown here, which is not drawn to scale. A 2.0-kg block is initially held at rest at position A. The curved portion of the curve, path AB, is frictionless. The entire horizontal section from point B to the wall has a kinetic coefficient of friction $\mu_k = 0.10$.

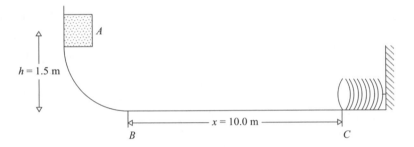

(a) The block is released from rest, and it slides along the curve to point B. What is the speed of the block when it reaches point B?

(b) The block continues sliding and reaches point C. What is the velocity of the block just before it makes contact with the horizontal spring?

(c) If the spring has a constant $k = 30.00$ N/m, by what distance does the block compress the spring before momentarily coming to rest? Consider the spring to be massless.

(d) Where will the block ultimately come to rest?

2. A parallel-plate capacitor, in vacuum, has a plate gap of 2.0 mm and is charged with a 100.0 V battery as shown.

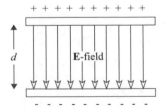

(a) Calculate the intensity of the electrical field existing between the plates.

(b) If the plates measure 10.0 cm by 20.0 cm, what is the capacitance of the arrangement?

(c) How many electrons are in excess on the negative plate?

(d) An electron is released from rest from the surface of the negative plate. What acceleration does the electron experience?

(e) Calculate the velocity of the electron on impact with the positive plate.

(f) How much work does the electrical field do to the electron in accelerating it across the plate gap to the positive plate?

3. Consider an ideal gas that is taken along the path $A \to B \to C \to D \to A$ as shown. The initial internal energy of the system at point A is $U_A = 20$ kJ.

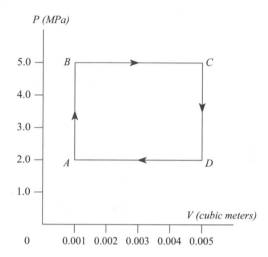

P (MPa)

V (cubic meters)

(a) For parts i through iv, determine the work done on each path.
   i. $A \to B$
   ii. $B \to C$
   iii. $C \to D$
   iv. $D \to A$
   v. What is the net work done in the cycle?

(b) If 10 kJ of heat enters the system along path $A \to B$, what is the internal energy of the system at B?

(c) The internal energy of the gas at point C is 70 kJ. How much thermal energy entered or left the system along path $B \to C$? Justify your answer.

(d) What is the net change in the thermal energy entering or leaving the system as it returns to point A? Justify your answer.

4. A double slit is illuminated by monochromatic light of wavelength $\lambda = 620$ nm. The slits are spaced by 3.20 μ.

(a) If the light starts out at the two slits in phase with each other, at what angle will the first minimum occur?

(b) If the light starts at the two slits with a phase difference of 180°, at what nonzero angle does the first minimum occur?

(c) When two rays start at the slits with no phase difference, the first minimum takes place at an angle of θ. How much of a time delay must there be with one wave so that there will be a maximum at angle θ?

5. A pair of copper rails are separated by 12.0 cm and are connected at one end across a resistor $R = 8.00\ \Omega$ as shown. The rails are arranged perpendicular to a magnetic field, $B = 0.75$ T, that is directed out of the page. A copper bar of length $L = 12.0$ cm is pulled to the right at 3.60 m/s.

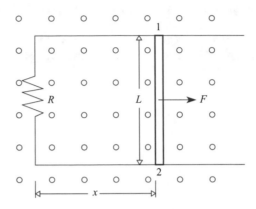

(a) Calculate the induced emf.
(b) What power is supplied to the resistor?
(c) Determine the induced current.
(d) Calculate the magnetic flux through the loop when $x = 12.0$ cm.
(e) What is the direction of the induced current. Justify your answer.
(f) Which end of the copper bar is positive (+)? Justify your answer.

6. A beam of deuterons, $^2_1$H, is used to bombard a sample of lithium-6, $^6_3$Li, in a particle accelerator. The beam is directed against the sample for 10.0 minutes and the current across the particle accelerator is 12.5 mA.

(a) What total charge is delivered to the lithium-6 sample in the 10.0 min of operation?
(b) Calculate the number of deuterons that collide with the lithium-6 sample in the 10.0 min of operation.
(c) Consider a single deuteron as it collides with a single lithium-6 nucleus causing the nuclear reaction $^6_3$Li + $^2_1$H → $^4_2$He + $^4_2$He + Q, where Q, the Q value, is the energy released in the reaction. The masses of the particles, in mass units u, are

$$M_{Li\text{-}6} = 6.015\ 122\ u \qquad M_{He\text{-}4} = 4.002\ 603\ u$$
$$m_{H\text{-}2} = 2.014\ 102\ u \qquad m_{He\text{-}4} = 4.002\ 603\ u$$

Calculate the Q value, in megaelectronvolts (MeV) of the nuclear reaction.

(d) Each alpha particle, $^4_2$He nucleus, has an equal share of the Q value as kinetic energy.
   i. What is the velocity of each alpha particle?
   ii. What is the de Broglie wavelength of each alpha particle?

END OF EXAMINATION

ANSWERS

ANSWER KEY FOR MULTIPLE-CHOICE QUESTIONS

1. E	11. A	21. C	31. E	41. E	51. A	61. C
2. C	12. C	22. C	32. C	42. E	52. C	62. E
3. A	13. A	23. B	33. E	43. A	53. E	63. B
4. B	14. C	24. B	34. A	44. C	54. E	64. B
5. A	15. B	25. E	35. D	45. A	55. C	65. B
6. D	16. B	26. A	36. B	46. B	56. E	66. E
7. E	17. C	27. A	37. B	47. D	57. E	67. D
8. A	18. A	28. A	38. E	48. D	58. C	68. C
9. B	19. D	29. B	39. E	49. D	59. B	69. A
10. E	20. C	30. D	40. E	50. A	60. E	70. C

EXPLANATIONS FOR THE MULTIPLE-CHOICE ANSWERS

1. **E** The acceleration is the slope of a velocity versus time graph. Because the slope is positive, the acceleration is positive (*College Physics* 8th ed. pages 31–33/9th ed. pages 33–35).

2. **C** The velocity and the acceleration vectors are in opposite directions; therefore, the speed is decreasing, or slowing down (*College Physics* 8th ed. pages 31–33/9th ed. pages 33–35).

3. **A** A projectile, a particle, that moves in two-dimensional space is always under the acceleration due to a gravitational force: the free-fall acceleration acting downward. At the peak of the trajectory, the v_y component of the velocity is zero, but the v_x component is constant (assuming air resistance is negligible) (*College Physics* 8th ed. pages 62–70/9th ed. pages 63–71).

4. **B** The range equation, $R = (v_0^2 \sin 2\theta)/g$, gives the horizontal distance from the origin of the projectile to the point where y is again zero. The maximum distance occurs when $\sin 2\theta = 1$, which implies an angle of $\theta = 45°$. (You should try to derive this equation yourself; it is always a good idea to practice deriving the equations for the AP B Test!) (*College Physics* 8th ed. page 63/9th ed. page 69).

5. **A** Newton's second law, $\Sigma F = ma$ applies. If the velocity increased, the acceleration and, therefore, the force are in the same direction as the velocity (*College Physics* 8th ed. pages 86–87/9th ed. pages 89–90).

6. **D** The normal force is the force the surface exerts upward on a body (*College Physics* 8th ed. page 93/9th ed. pages 96–97).

7. **E** Inertia is the tendency of a body to remain in its original state of motion (*College Physics* 8th ed. page 85/9th ed. page 89).

8. **A** The net force is the vector sum of all external forces exerted on the body. Because it is at rest on the table, F_g is 9.8 N downward, the normal n is 9.8 N upward, and $\Sigma F = 0$ (*College Physics* 8th ed. pages 89–91/9th ed. pages 92–93).

9. **B** The mass of the body has not changed, only its weight. It is one-sixth its weight on Earth. The condition $\Sigma F = ma$ still applies (*College Physics* 8th ed. page 90/9th ed. page 93).

10. **E** Newton's second law applies, $\Sigma F = ma$, and $T - W = ma$. Substituting into the equation gives $T - 4900\ \text{N} = 500\ \text{kg}\left(2.0\ \text{m/s}^2\right) = 5900\ \text{N}$ (*College Physics* 8th ed. pages 97–101/9th ed. pages 101–105).

11. **A** The coefficients of static friction are generally larger than the coefficients of kinetic friction (*College Physics* 8th ed. pages 97–104/9th ed. pages 105–108).

12. **C** The frictional force on the block is given by $f_s = \mu_s N$ if the block is about to slip and $f_k = \mu_k N$ if it is moving. Because the expression for the gravitational component of the force along the plane is $mg \sin \theta$ then $\Sigma F_x = mg \sin \theta - \mu_s mg \cos \theta$. If the block is stationary, then $\mu_s = \tan \theta$. If the block is accelerating, then $\mu_k = \tan \theta$. Because the tangent of $45° = 0.707$, which is greater than μ, the body is accelerating down the incline (*College Physics* 8th ed. pages 97–104/9th ed. pages 105–108).

13. **A** The normal force on the body sitting on the incline is given from $\Sigma F_y = 0$ and $N = W \cos \theta$. As the angle decreases, the cosine increases and the normal increases (*College Physics* 8th ed. pages 97–104/9th ed. pages 101–103).

14. **C** Acceleration is change in velocity with respect to time. The speed (magnitude of the velocity) is not changing but its direction is, so a force directed perpendicular to the velocity is required. Both the force and the acceleration are directed along the radius toward the center of the circle (*College Physics* 8th ed. pages 199–207/9th ed. pages 207–214).

15. **B** The spring force points in a direction opposite the motion because it is a force that returns the body to its original position (*College Physics* ed. pages 136–140, 425–427/9th ed. pages 140–145, 437–438).

16. **B** Here, $W = (F \cos \theta)\,\Delta x$. The angle between the force and the displacement is 90°, and no work is done on the body by the centripetal force because it is perpendicular to the tangential velocity (*College Physics* 8th ed. pages 119–121, 202–203/9th ed. pages 124–127, 209–210).

17. **C** Work on a force versus displacement graph is the area under the curve (*College Physics* 8th ed. pages 148–150/9th ed. pages 152–154).

18. **A** The object can do work decreasing its kinetic energy, which is the work–energy theorem (*College Physics* 8th ed. pages 124–127/9th ed. pages 129–132).

19. **D** Gravitational potential energy is given by $U = mgy$, and if the height doubles, the potential energy doubles (*College Physics* 8th ed. pages 127–130/9th ed. pages 132–136).

20. **C** As the smaller mass descends, the kinetic energy of the system will increase because both bodies will increase in speed. The potential energy must decrease for that to happen (*College Physics* 8th ed. pages 130–133/9th ed. pages 135–138).

21. **C** A conservative force depends only on the endpoints of its path, not on the route between those endpoints (*College Physics* 8th ed. pages 126–127/9th ed. pages 131–132).

22. **C** The change in the impulse equals the change in the momentum (*College Physics* 8th ed. pages 126–127/9th ed. pages 168–169).

23. **B** The speed and therefore the kinetic energy increases because gravity exerts a force on the body during the time that it falls (*College Physics* 8th ed. pages 161–163/9th ed. pages 168–169).

24. **B** When the meterstick is placed into rotational equilibrium, the net torque on the meterstick is zero. The meterstick is a uniform body, and its center of mass is at the 50.0-cm mark. Placing the meterstick on a pivot at the 20.0-cm mark gives a moment arm of 30.0 cm for the meterstick. Because $-R_1F_1 + R_2F_2 = 0$, substituting yields $-(30.0 \text{ cm})(1.00 \text{ N}) + R_2(4.00 \text{ N}) = 0$ and $R_2 = 7.50$ cm. The moment arm is the distance from the point of application of the force to the pivot point; therefore, the 4.00-N weight must be placed at 12.5 cm (*College Physics* 8th ed. pages 228–239/9th ed. pages 235–247).

25. **E** Astronauts in orbit around Earth feel "weightless" because their acceleration is the same as the spacecraft. Newton's second law, $n + mg = -ma_y$, applies, and because the normal $n = 0$, the equation yields $g = -a_y$ (*College Physics* 8th ed. pages 99–100, 203/9th ed. pages 103–104, 210).

26. **A** The only force on the satellite is the centripetal force provided by Newton's law of universal gravitation. The satellite is in a circular orbit and well above the frictional effects of the atmosphere (*College Physics* 8th ed. pages 202–203, 207–208, 216/9th ed. pages 209–210, 214–215, 222).

27. **A** By Newton's second law, $F = (3m)a$ and $a = F/3m$. The entire system has the same acceleration. Block M_B experiences a force exerted by M_A, and that force is $F' = (2m)a = (2m)(F/3m) = 2/3F$ (*College Physics* 8th ed. pages 97–101/9th ed. pages 101–105).

28. **A** The potential energy is maximum when $x = A$. It is zero when $x = 0$ (*College Physics* 8th ed. pages 428–429/9th ed. pages 441–442).

29. **B** The velocity of sound is temperature dependent, and $v = \left(331 + 0.6T_C\right)$ m/s (*College Physics* 8th ed. page 462/9th ed. page 477).

30. **D** Pressure is defined as force per unit area. The SI unit for pressure—the pascal, Pa—is 1 N/m² (*College Physics* 8th ed. page 277/9th ed. page 280).

31. **E** Archimedes's principle states that a body completely or partially submerged in a fluid is buoyed up by a force equal in magnitude to the weight of the displaced fluid (*College Physics* 8th ed. page 284/9th ed. pages 293–294).

32. **C** On an atomic scale, kinetic energy is transferred by more energetic atoms, molecules, or electrons to less energetic particles during collisions (*College Physics* 8th ed. pages 228–239/9th ed. pages 235–247).

33. **E** The rate of energy transfer by radiation $P = \sigma A \varepsilon T^4$ is proportional to T^4. As the temperature doubles, the power increases by a factor of 16 (*College Physics* 8th ed. page 372/9th ed. page 382).

34. **A** The object floats because for the two forces acting on it, F_B upward is equal to F_g downward (*College Physics* 8th ed. page 286/9th ed. page 295).

35. **D** Charles's law, $V_1/T_1 = V_2/T_2$, applies in this situation. If V doubles, then T doubles (*College Physics* 8th ed. page 336/9th ed. page 345).

36. **B** Period and frequency are reciprocals of each other, and $f = 1/T$ is hyperbolic (*College Physics* 8th ed. page 434/9th ed. page 447).

37. **B** The work done in a thermodynamic process depends on the path between the initial and the final states (*College Physics* 8th ed. page 387/9th ed. page 397).

38. **E** Resistance of a wire is $R = \rho(L / A)$, making R directly proportional to L (*College Physics* 8th ed. page 577/9th ed. page 597).

39. **E** Coulomb's law is an inverse square law where

$$F = \frac{1}{4\pi\varepsilon_o} \frac{q_1 q_2}{R^2}$$

When the radius is doubled, the force is one-fourth as large (*College Physics* 8th ed. pages 500–501/9th ed. page 517).

40. **E** Because the only charge on a body that can move is the electron, something that is negatively charged has an excess of electrons. If it has a deficit of electrons, it is positively charged (Commit this principle to memory!) (*College Physics* 8th ed. pages 497–500/9th ed. pages 513–516).

41. **E** The electrical potential at all points on a charged conductor is the same, both inside the conductor and on its surface (*College Physics* 8th ed. pages 497–500/9th ed. pages 529–530).

42. **E** For a negative charge moved between two points in an electrical field, we find the work done by the work–energy theorem, $W = \Delta K + |q|Ed$. When speed is constant, $W = \Delta K + |q|Ed$ (*College Physics* 8th ed. pages 532–533/9th ed. pages 548–550).

43. **A** The capacitance of a device depends on the physical geometry of the conductors, the plate size, the plate spacing, and the substance filling the gap between the plates (*College Physics* 8th ed. pages 546–548/9th ed. pages 562–567).

44. **C** As charge is added to a plate of the capacitor (equal magnitude of charge due to electrostatic repulsion on the other plate, but opposite sign), ΔV will increase linearly. It requires work to transfer more charge against the change in the potential (*College Physics* 8th ed. pages 555–557/9th ed. pages 571–573).

45. **A** The terminal voltage of a battery is $V_t = \varepsilon - Ir$. The internal resistance lowers the voltage output of the battery (*College Physics* 8th ed. page 595/9th ed. page 617).

46. **B** Resistors in series must have the same current because there is only one path between them (*College Physics* 8th ed. pages 595–596/9th ed. pages 617–618).

47. **D** The magnetic force is given by $F = BIl \sin \theta$. The magnitude of the force is proportional to the magnetic field strength and the magnitude of the current, not its direction (*College Physics* 8th ed. pages 633–636/9th ed. pages 655–658).

48. **D** The right-hand rule shows that the proton is deflected downward (*College Physics* 8th ed. pages 630–633/9th ed. pages 652–655).

49. **D** Because the centripetal force F_C acting on the charge is equal to the magnetic force F_B acting on the charge, we can write $mv^2/r = Bqv$. Solving for the radius gives $r = mv/Bq$. Doubling the velocity increases the radius by a factor of 2 (*College Physics* 8th ed. pages 639–642/9th ed. pages 661–664).

50. **A** The magnetic field inside the center of a solenoid is given by $B = \mu_0 nI$, where n is the number of turns per unit length and B is directly proportional to I (*College Physics* 8th ed. pages 648–650/9th ed. pages 670–673).

51. **A** An elastic collision is defined as one in which both momentum and kinetic energy are conserved (*College Physics* 8th ed. page 169/9th ed. page 176).

52. **C** This wording is Lenz's law. The direction of the induced current (magnetic field) is such that it opposes what induced it (*College Physics* 8th ed. pages 667–688/9th ed. pages 692–693).

53. **E** Gamma decay is the emission of photons that have higher energy than visible light (*College Physics* 8th ed. page 924/9th ed. page 968–969).

54. **E** If the object is located at the center of curvature, the mirror is concave. Because $C/2 = f$ and $1/f = 1/p + 1/q$, we have that $2/C = 1/C + 1/q$ and $q = C$. The image is real and inverted. The magnification M is given by $h_1/h_0 = -q/p$, which gives an image the same size as the object (*College Physics* 8th ed. pages 762–769/9th ed. pages 793–799).

55. **C** For an object located at any distance for a diverging lens, the image is virtual, upright, and smaller (*College Physics* 8th ed. pages 773–779/9th ed. pages 805–809).

56. **E** For an object located between f and $2f$ for a converging lens, the image is real, inverted, and larger (*College Physics* 8th ed. pages 773–779/9th ed. pages 805–809).

57. **E** By definition, whenever reflected light actually passes through a point, the image is real. This definition applies to images formed by refracted light as well (*College Physics* 8th ed. page 762/9th ed. page 793).

58. **C** The image formed by a flat mirror appears as far behind the mirror as the object is in front of it (*College Physics* 8th ed. pages 759–760/9th ed. pages 790–791).

59. **B** The right-hand rule applies in this case. The force is exerted downward because the particle entering the field is an electron (*College Physics* 8th ed. pages 630–633/9th ed. pages 653–655).

60. **E** Intensity distribution for a diffraction grating produces a sharper principal maximum and a broad range of dark areas. Young's double-slit experiment produces broad, bright fringes (*College Physics* 8th ed. pages 791–794, 805–807/9th ed. pages 825–829, 839–841).

61. **C** The light source must be coherent; therefore, it must be the same source because two sources would emit light independent of the other. They would not be in phase (*College Physics* 8th ed. pages 790–791/9th ed. page 825).

62. **E** The charges are positive; therefore, the net force on the charge located in the lower right-hand corner must point away from the charge. The net force in the x direction is the repulsive force between the two on the lower edge pointing to the right plus the F_x component of the force between the two along the diagonal pointing downward toward the right. The net force in the y direction is the repulsive force between the two on the right vertical edge pointing downward plus the F_y component of the force between the two along the diagonal pointing downward to the right. Because the charges are the same and the angle along the diagonal is 45°, the Pythagorean theorem will yield a force pointing at 315° (*College Physics* 8th ed. pages 500–505/9th ed. pages 517–522).

63. **B** The de Broglie wavelength is given by $\lambda = h/p$. If the momentum triples, the wavelength changes by a factor of 1/3 (*College Physics* 8th ed. pages 880–882/9th ed. pages 922–924).

64. **B** Compton scatter is the change in the wavelength of a scattered photon colliding with an electron (*College Physics* 8th ed. pages 879–880/9th ed. pages 920–922).

65. **B** The decay form for positron emission is $^A_Z X \rightarrow ^A_{Z-1}Y + ^0_{+1}\beta + ^0_0\nu$. Charge and mass numbers must balance (*College Physics* 8th ed. pages 922–923/9th ed. pages 967–968).

66. **E** U-235 is fissionable by thermal neutrons. When the compound excited nucleus fissions into two asymmetrical fission fragments, several neutrons are also emitted (*College Physics* 8th ed. pages 937–940/9th ed. pages 982–985).

67. **D** The decay form for alpha emission is $^A_Z X \rightarrow ^4_2He + ^{A-4}_{Z-2}Y$ (*College Physics* 8th ed. pages 921–922/9th ed. pages 965–966).

68. **C** A neutron is converted into a proton by the weak force. The proton remains in the nucleus, and because charge and mass numbers must balance, the negative beta particle is emitted from the nucleus (*College Physics* 8th ed. pages 922–923/9th ed. pages 967–968).

69. **A** Because the Z number has changed by 2 and the mass number has changed by 4, the particle emitted must be an alpha particle (*College Physics* 8th ed. pages 921–922/9th ed. pages 965–966).

70. **C** The mass number of the nucleus is equal to the sum of the number of protons and the number of neutrons present in the nucleus, the nucleon population of the nucleus (*College Physics* 8th ed. page 913/9th ed. page 957).

ANSWERS TO FREE-RESPONSE PROBLEMS

Question 1 [15 points]

(a) 4 points

The path AB is a conservative path, and we write the law of conservation of mechanical energy as $\Delta K + \Delta U = 0 = (K - K_0) + (U - U_0)$.

[2 points for a statement of the law of conservation of energy]

The initial kinetic energy is zero, and the final gravitational potential energy of the block is zero: $\frac{1}{2}mv_B^2 - mgh = 0$

[1 point for knowing initial kinetic energy and final potential energy are both zero]

and

$$v_B = \sqrt{2gh} = \sqrt{2(9.8 \text{ m/s}^2)(1.50 \text{ m})}. \text{ So, } v_B = \textbf{5.42 m/s.}$$

[1 point for correct answer with correct units]

(b) 3 points

The nonconservative force of friction acts along the horizontal. The law of conservation of mechanical energy for a nonconservative force is written as $\Delta K + \Delta U = -W_f$. Only the kinetic energy changes.

[1 point for knowing only the kinetic energy changes]

So, $\frac{1}{2}mv_C^2 - \frac{1}{2}mv_B^2 = -fx = -\mu_k mgx$.   Solving   for v_c gives

$v_C = \sqrt{v_B^2 - 2\mu_k gx} = \sqrt{(5.42 \text{ m/s})^2 - 2(0.10)(9.8 \text{ m/s}^2)(10.0 \text{ m})}$, so,

$v_C = \textbf{3.13 m/s}$.

[1 point for correct working equation]
[1 point for correct answer with correct units]

(c) 4 points

Friction is a factor in finding s. Here, $\Delta K + \Delta U = -W_f$.

[1 point for statement of work and energy]

Again there is no change in the gravitational potential energy, but there is a change in the spring potential energy when it is fully compressed.

[1 point for knowing it is spring potential energy]

So, $0 - \frac{1}{2}mv_C^2 + \frac{1}{2}ks^2 = -\mu_k mgs$ and $ks^2 + 2\mu_k mgs - mv_C^2 = 0$. Then,
$(30.0 \text{ N/m})s^2 + 2(0.10)(2.00 \text{ kg})(9.8 \text{ m/s}^2)s - (2.00 \text{ kg})(3.13 \text{ m/s})^2 = 0$,
which is a quadratic equation. Putting it in the form $ax^2 + bx + c = 0$
gives $30s^2 + 3.92s - 19.59 = 0$.

[1 point for setting up the quadratic equation]
Only the positive root is meaningful: $s = \textbf{|0.746 m|}$

[1 point for correct answer with correct units]

(d) 4 points

Let x' be the distance the block slides from point C to where it comes to rest.

[1 point for recognizing distance to rest]

So, $\Delta K + \Delta U = -W_f$. The block is at rest at s and again at x'. Both kinetic energies are zero. So, $0 - \frac{1}{2}ks^2 = -\mu_k mg(x'+s) = \frac{1}{2}(30.0 \text{ N/m})(0.745 \text{ m})^2 = (0.10)(2.00 \text{ kg})(9.8 \text{ m/s}^2)(x'+s) = x'+s = x' + 0.746 \text{ m} = 4.26 \text{ m}$. Therefore, $\textbf{x}' = \textbf{3.51 m to the left of C}$.

[1 point for correct working equation]
[1 point for correct substitution]
[1 point for correct answer with correct units]

(*College Physics* 8th ed. pages 122–131, 135–140/9th ed. pages 128–136, 140–145)

Question 2 [15 points]
(a) 2 points

The electrical field is, by definition, $E = V/d$. So,

[1 point for correct equation]

$$E = \frac{100 \text{ V}}{2 \times 10^{-3} \text{ m}} = \textbf{5.0} \times \textbf{10}^4 \textbf{ V/m} = \textbf{5.0 x 10}^4 \textbf{ N/C}$$

[1 point for correct answer with correct units]

(b) 2 points

The area of the top plate is $200 \text{ cm}^2 = 200 \times 10^{-4} \text{m}^2$, and $C = \varepsilon_0(A/d)$.
So,

$$C = \left(8.85 \times 10^{-12} \text{ C}^2/\text{Nm}^2\right)\frac{200 \times 10^{-4} \text{ m}^2}{2 \times 10^{-3} \text{ m}} = \mathbf{88.5 \times 10^{12}} \ \boldsymbol{F = 88.5 \text{ pF}}$$

[1 point for correct substitution]
[1 point for correct answer with correct units]

(c) 2 points

Start with $q = CV$. Then, $q = \left(88.5 \times 10^{-12} \text{F}\right)\left(100 \text{ V}\right) = 88.5 \times 10^{-10} \text{C}$

$$88.5 \times 10^{-10} \text{ C} \times \frac{1e^-}{1.6 \times 10^{-19} \text{ C}} = \mathbf{5.53 \times 10^{10}} \ \boldsymbol{e^-}$$

[1 point for correct e⁻/C conversion]
[1 point for correct answer with correct units]

(d) 3 points

Start with $F = ma = Eq = Ee$. Then,

$$a = \frac{Ee}{m_e} = \frac{\left(5 \times 10^4 \text{ N/C}\right)\left(1.60 \times 10^{-19} \text{ C}\right)}{9.1 \times 10^{-31} \text{ kg}} = \mathbf{8.78 \times 10^{15} \text{ m/s}^2}$$

[1 point for correct working equation]
[1 point for correct substitution]
[1 point for correct answer with correct units]

(e) 3 points

Start with $Ve = \frac{1}{2}mv^2$. Then,

$$v = \sqrt{\frac{2Ve}{m_e}} = \sqrt{\frac{2\left(100 \text{ V}\right)\left(1.60 \times 10^{-19} \text{ C}\right)}{\left(9.11 \times 10^{-31} \text{ kg}\right)}} = \mathbf{5.93 \times 10^6 \text{ m/s}}$$

[2 points for correct working equation]
[1 point for correct answer with correct units]

Alternate solution to (e) 3 points

$$v^2 = v_0^2 + 2ad$$

$$v = \sqrt{2ad} = \sqrt{2\left(9.5 \times 10^{15} \text{ m/s}^2\right)\left(2 \times 10^{-3} \text{ m}\right)} = \mathbf{5.93 \times 106 \text{ m/s}}$$

[2 points for correct working equation]
[1 point for correct answer with correct units]

(f) 3 points

Here, we use $W = Ve$. So, $W = (100 \text{ V})e = 100 \text{ eV}$, and $\boldsymbol{W = 1.60 \times 10^{-17} \text{ J}}$.

[2 points for correct working equation]
[1 point for correct answer with correct units]

Alternate solution to (f) 3 points $W = \Delta K = K = \frac{1}{2} m_e v^2$

$$W = \tfrac{1}{2}\left(9.11 \times 10^{-31} \text{ kg}\right)\left(5.93 \times 10^6 \text{ m/s}\right)^2 = \mathbf{1.60 \text{ ë } 10^{-17}} = \mathbf{100 \text{ eV}}$$

[2 points for correct working equation]
[1 point for correct answer with correct units]

(College Physics 8th ed. pages 506–508, 532–536, 546–548/9th ed. pages 522– 524, 532–533, 561–565)

Question 3 [15 points]

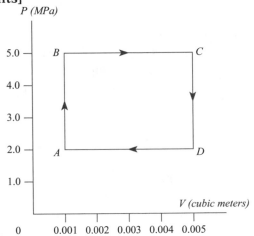

(a) **6 points**

i. 1 point

The path $A \rightarrow B$ is an isovolumetric process. The work done is $W_{A \rightarrow B} = P \, \Delta V = P(0) = 0.$

[1 point for correct answer with correct units]

ii. 1 point

The path $B \rightarrow C$ has a volume change, and $W_{B \rightarrow C} = -P \Delta V = -\left(5.0 \times 10^6 \text{ Pa}\right)(0.005 - 0.001) \text{ m}^3 = \mathbf{-2.0 \times 10^4 \text{ J}}$. Work is negative because the system expands.

[1 point for correct answer with correct units]

iii. 1 point

The path $C \rightarrow D$ is isovolumetric. The work done is $W_{C \rightarrow D} = P \, \Delta V = P(0) = 0.$

[1 point for correct answer with correct units]

iv. 1 point

The path $D \to A$ has a volume change, and $W_{B \to C} = -P \, \Delta V = -\left(2.0 \times 10^6 \text{ Pa}\right)\left(0.001 - 0.005\right) \text{ m}^3 = \mathbf{8.0 \times 10^3 \, J}$. Work is positive because the system is compressed. Work is done on the system.

[*1 point for correct answer with correct units*]

v. 2 points

(The net work is the sum of the work along the individual paths or the area under the curve:

$$W_{A \to B} + W_{B \to C} + W_{C \to D} + W_{D \to A}$$

$$0 + \left(-2.0 \times 10^4 \text{ J}\right) + 0 + \left(8.0 \times 10^3 \text{ J}\right) = \mathbf{-1.2 \times 10^4 \, J}$$

[*2 points for correct answer with correct units*]

(b) 3 points

The internal energy at point B is found by using the first law of thermodynamics:

$$U_B - U_A = Q_{A \to B} - W_{A \to B}$$

[*1 point for first law of thermodynamics*]

$$U_B - \left(20 \times 10^3 \text{ J}\right) = \left(10 \times 10^3 \text{ J}\right) - 0$$

$$\mathbf{U_B = 30 \times 10^3 \, J}$$

[*2 points for correct answer with correct units*]

(c) 3 points

The internal energy of the gas at point C is 70 kJ. So,

[*1 point for knowing the internal energy at point C*]

$$U_C - U_B = Q_{B \to C} - W_{B \to C}$$

$$70 \times 10^3 \text{ J} - 30 \times 10^3 \text{ J} = Q_{B \to C} - \left(-20 \times 10^3 \text{ J}\right)$$

$$\mathbf{Q_{B \to C} = 20 \times 10^3 \, J}$$

[*2 points for correct answer with correct units*]

A quantity of 20×10^3 J of heat enters the system as the internal energy increases, and negative work was done by the system in expanding.

(d) 3 points

By the first law of thermodynamics, $\Delta U = \Delta Q - \Delta W$. The internal energy of the ideal gas returns to its original state in the cyclic process, making $\Delta U = 0$.

[*1 point for knowing the change in internal energy is zero*]

The net work done in the process is $W = -12 \times 10^3$ J. So, $0 = \Delta Q - \left(-12 \times 10^3 \text{ J}\right) = \Delta Q = -12 \times 10^3$ **J**. Therefore, 12×10^3 J of thermal energy is left in the system, and ΔQ must be negative.

[2 points for correct answer with correct units]

(*College Physics* ed. pages 385–392/9th ed. pages 395–404)

Question 4 [15 points]

    (a) 5 points

The first minimum will occur at

$$\sin\theta = \frac{\lambda}{2d} = \frac{620 \times 10^{-9} \text{ m}}{2\left(3.20 \times 10^{-6} \text{ m}\right)} = 0.097$$

[2 points for correct working equation]
[1 point for correct substitution]

$$\theta = \sin^{-1}\left(0.097\right) = \mathbf{5.6°}$$

[2 points for correct answer with correct unit]

    (b) 5 points

The waves start out 180° out of phase, and the two waves will be able to interfere destructively. The first minimum will occur at $\theta = 0$, where the central maximum would have been located. Additional minima occur when there is a difference in path length that is a half integral number of wavelengths. The first nonzero angle where we obtain a minimum is when the difference in path length is λ, which will occur when

$$\sin\theta = \frac{\lambda}{d} = \frac{620 \times 10^{-9} \text{ m}}{3.20 \times 10^{-6} \text{ m}} = 0.194$$

[2 points for correct working equation]
[1 point for correct substitution]

and

$$\theta = \sin^{-1}\left(0.194\right) = \mathbf{11.2°}$$

[2 points for correct answer with correct unit]

    (c) 5 points

A minimum can be converted to a maximum by adding a phase difference of 180°, or having a time delay by a factor of a half. So, $c = \lambda f = \lambda/T$ and $T = \lambda/c$. Because the time delay is $T/2$,

[2 points for correct working equation]

$$\frac{T}{2} = \frac{\lambda}{2c} = \frac{620 \times 10^{-9} \text{ m}}{2\left(3 \times 10^8 \text{ m/s}\right)} = \mathbf{1.03 \times 10^{-15} \text{ s}}$$

[*1 point for correct substitution*]
[*2 points for correct answer with correct unit*]

(*College Physics* 8th ed. pages 790–795/9th ed. pages 824–829)

Question 5 [15 points]

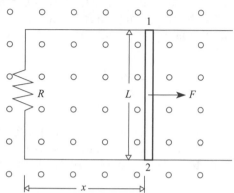

(a) 3 points

The induced emf is found by using:

$$|\varepsilon| = BLv = (0.750T)(0.12\ m)(3.60\ m/s) = \mathbf{0.324\ V}$$

[*1 point for correct substitution*]
[*2 points for correct answer with correct unit*]

(b) 3 points

The power drop in the resistor is

$$P = \frac{\varepsilon^2}{R} = \frac{(0.324\ V)^2}{8.00\ \Omega} = \mathbf{1.31 \times 10^{-2}\ W}$$

[*1 point for correct substitution*]
[*2 points for correct answer with correct unit*]

(c) 2 points

From Ohm's law,

$$I = \frac{\varepsilon}{R} = \frac{0.324\ V}{8.00\ \Omega} = \mathbf{4.05 \times 10^{-2}\ A}$$

[*2 points for correct answer with correct unit*]

(d) 2 points

The area of the loop at the moment $x = 12.0\ cm$ is $(0.12\ m)^2 = 1.44 \times 10^{-2}\ m^2$.

[*1 point for correct area*]

The magnetic flux through the loop is $\phi_B = BA = (0.750T)(1.44 \times 10^{-2}\ m^2) = \mathbf{1.08 \times 10^{-2}\ Wb}$.

[*1 point for correct answer and units*]

(e) 3 points

The direction of the induced current is **clockwise**. According to Lenz's law, whenever an emf is induced, the induced current must be in a direction such as to oppose the change by which the current is induced. Moving the bar to the right increases the flux through the loop. By the right-hand rule, a current is established clockwise to oppose the increase in flux.

[1 point for direction]
[2 points for correct reason]

(f) 2 points

The bottom of the bar, end 2, is **positive (+)**. The force moving the bar to the right causes the positive charge carriers to be accelerated downward to the bottom of the bar.

[1 point for direction]
[1 point for correct reason]

(*College Physics* 8th ed. pages 670–675/9th ed. pages 697–701)

Question 6 [15 points]

(a) 3 points

To find current, use $I = q/t$, or $q = It$. So, $q = \left(12.5 \times 10^{-3}\,\text{A}\right)\left(600\text{ s}\right)$ = **7.5 C.**

[1 point for correct equation]
[1 point for correct substitution]
[1 point for correct answer with correct unit]

(b) 2 points

The number n of deuterons is found by taking the total charge and the charge on a single deuteron. So,

$$n = \left(7.5\text{ C}\right)\left(\frac{1\ e}{1.6 \times 10^{-19}\text{ C}}\right) = \textbf{4.7} \times \textbf{10}^{\textbf{19}}\textbf{ deuterons}$$

[1 point for correct e^-/C conversion]
[1 point for correct answer with correct units]

(c) 4 points

The Q value is

$$Q = \left[(M_X + m_x) - (M_Y + m_y)\right] \times 931.494\,\text{MeV/u}$$
$$Q = \left[(8.029\ 224\text{u}) - (8.005\ 206\text{u})\right] \times 931.494\ \text{MeV/u}$$

[1 point for correct working equation]
[2 points for correct substitutions]

Q = 22.37 MeV

[1 point for correct answer with correct units]

(d) i. 4 points

Each alpha particle has a kinetic energy of 22.37 MeV/2 = 11.19 MeV.

[1 point for recognizing the energy is divided by two particles]

Expressing the kinetic energy in joules gives

$$K = 11.19 \text{ MeV} \left(\frac{1.6 \times 10^{-13} \text{ J}}{1 \text{ MeV}} \right) = 1.79 \times 10^{-12} \text{ J}$$

Find the mass in kilograms:

$$m = (4.002\ 603 \text{ u}) \left(\frac{1.66 \times 10^{-27} \text{ kg}}{1 \text{ u}} \right) = 6.65 \times 10^{-27} \text{ kg}$$

[1 point for correct mass]

Calculate the velocity:

$$K = \tfrac{1}{2} mv^2$$

$$v = \sqrt{\frac{2K}{m}}$$

[1 point for correct working equation]

$$v = \sqrt{\frac{2\left(1.79 \times 10^{-12} \text{ J}\right)}{6.65 \times 10^{-27} \text{ kg}}} = \textbf{2.32} \times \textbf{10}^{7} \textbf{ m/s}$$

[1 point for correct answer with correct units]

ii. 2 points

The de Broglie wavelength is found by using $\lambda = h/mv$:

$$\lambda = \frac{6.63 \times 10^{-34} \text{ J} \cdot \text{s}}{\left(6.65 \times 10^{-27} \text{ kg}\right)\left(2.32 \times 10^{7} \text{ m/s}\right)} = \textbf{4.30} \times \textbf{10}^{-15} \textbf{ m}$$

[1 point for correct substitution]
[1 point for correct answer with correct unit]
(*College Physics* 8th ed. pages 880–882, 927–929/9th ed. pages 922–924, 971–973)

Calculating Your Score

Section I: Multiple-Choice

_____ × 1.2857 = _____

Number Correct   Weighted Section I Score
(out of 70)   (If less than zero, enter
                    zero; do not round)

Section II: Free Response

Question 1 _____ × 1.0000 = _____
           (out of 15)   (Do not round)

Question 2 _____ × 1.0000 = _____
           (out of 15)   (Do not round)

Question 3 _____ × 1.0000 = _____
           (out of 15)   (Do not round)

Question 4 _____ × 1.0000 = _____
           (out of 15)   (Do not round)

Question 5 _____ × 1.0000 = _____
           (out of 15)   (Do not round)

Question 6 _____ × 1.0000 = _____
           (out of 15)   (Do not round)

Sum = _____

Weighted Section II Score
(Do not round)

Composite Score

_____ + _____ = _____
Weighted   Weighted   Composite Score
Section I Score   Section II Score   (Round to nearest
                                    whole number)

AP Grade Conversion Chart

Composite Score Range	AP Grade
112–180	5
85–111	4
57–84	3
40–56	2
0–39	1

PRACTICE TEST 2

AP Physics B
Section I: Multiple-Choice Questions
Time: 90 minutes
70 Questions

Directions: Each of the following questions or incomplete statements is accompanied by five suggested answers or completions. Select the correct response to each question.

Hand calculators are not allowed on this part of the test.

The Table of Information is allowed, but not the AP B Equations.

1. The position versus time graph of a particle moving in a linear manner is a straight line with a negative slope as shown.

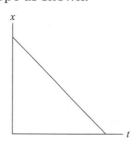

This graph shows that the particle has
(A) a negative position intercept.
(B) a constant negative velocity.
(C) a constant positive velocity.
(D) a constant negative acceleration.
(E) a velocity that decreases at a constant rate.

2. For a compact body thrown vertically downward, the acceleration of the body is
(A) always zero.
(B) changing from 9.8 m/s² upward to 9.8 m/s² downward.
(C) changing from 9.8 m/s² downward to 9.8 m/s² upward.
(D) always 9.8 m/s² upward.
(E) always 9.8 m/s² downward.

3. If body M_1 has twice the mass of body M_2, the force necessary to produce the same acceleration for both bodies is
(A) the same.
(B) two times greater for body M_1 as for body M_2.
(C) two times greater for body M_2 as for body M_1.
(D) four times greater for body M_1 as for body M_2.
(E) four times greater for body M_2 as for body M_1.

For Questions 4 and 5: A 200.0-N box is pulled to the right at constant speed by a 100.0-N force acting at an angle of 30.0° with respect to the horizontal as shown.

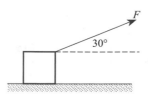

4. The normal force exerted on the block is most nearly equal to
(A) 113 N.
(B) 150 N.
(C) 200 N.
(D) 250 N.
(E) 287 N.

5. The coefficient of kinetic friction between the box and the floor is most nearly equal to
   (A) 0.58.
   (B) 0.50.
   (C) 0.43.
   (D) 0.25.
   (E) zero.

6. If the distance a spring is stretched from its equilibrium position is doubled, the elastic potential energy of the spring is multiplied by a factor of
   (A) 0.25.
   (B) 0.5.
   (C) 1.
   (D) 2.
   (E) 4.

7. The work–energy theorem states that
   (A) the work done equals the change in the net force.
   (B) the work done equals the change in kinetic energy.
   (C) the work done equals the net force divided by the net kinetic energy.
   (D) the work done equals the product of the net force and the net kinetic energy.
   (E) the work done equals the product of the mass and the velocity.

8. At a given instant, the acceleration of a particle is zero. That means that the velocity of the particle is
   (A) constant.
   (B) increasing.
   (C) decreasing.
   (D) changing direction.
   (E) zero.

9. An object is released from rest from a height of 4.0 km. The object reaches a constant speed called terminal velocity. At terminal velocity,
   (A) the acceleration is equal to g.
   (B) the force of air resistance is zero.
   (C) the effect of gravity has become negligible.
   (D) the force of air resistance is equal to the weight of the object.

(E) the effect of gravity increases as the object gets closer to the ground.

10. The total mechanical energy in a system is conserved only if
    (A) the potential energy in the system is zero.
    (B) the kinetic energy is a constant.
    (C) the forces are conservative forces.
    (D) the forces are nonconservative forces.
    (E) the system is at rest.

11. Sound waves travel in a medium of uniform density. Which sound waves have the greater speed?
    (A) The sounds with the longer wavelengths have the greater speed.
    (B) The sounds with the shorter wavelengths have the greater speed.
    (C) The sounds with the higher frequencies have the greater speed.
    (D) The sounds with the lower frequencies have the greater speed.
    (E) All wavelengths have the same speed.

12. The graph of the x-directed force acting on a body is shown.

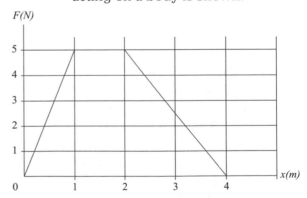

The work done by the force over the interval $0'' x'' 4\,\text{m}$ is
(A) 10 J.
(B) 12.5 J.
(C) 15 J.
(D) 17.5 J.
(E) 20 J.

13. The basic principle of conservation of energy states that if no work is done on a closed system by a nonconservative force,
    (A) the kinetic energy is always a constant.
    (B) the gravitational potential energy is always a constant.
    (C) the elastic potential energy is always a constant.
    (D) the total energy is a constant.
    (E) the total energy is nonconstant.

14. Conservative forces behave in such a way as to guarantee that when a particle returns to a particular position, it will have
    (A) no change in kinetic energy.
    (B) an increase in kinetic energy.
    (C) a decrease in kinetic energy.
    (D) an undeterminable kinetic energy.
    (E) no relationship to kinetic energy.

15. When the kinetic energy of a given particle is increased by a factor of 4, its momentum changes by a factor of
    (A) 0.25.
    (B) 0.5.
    (C) 1.
    (D) 2.
    (E) 4.

16. A perfectly elastic collision is one in which
    (A) momentum is not conserved.
    (B) kinetic energy is conserved.
    (C) no forces exist during the collision process.
    (D) the particles couple.
    (E) the colliding particles must have the same mass.

17. The momentum of a car rounding a curve at constant speed is
    (A) constant because the speed of the car is a constant.
    (B) not constant because the kinetic energy of the car is a constant.
    (C) constant because the kinetic energy of the car is a constant.
    (D) constant because the specific impulse is constant.
    (E) not constant because there is an external force acting on the car.

18. To calculate torque, one must know
    (A) the magnitude of the applied force.
    (B) the length of the moment arm.
    (C) the direction of the applied force.
    (D) the magnitude of the applied force and the length of the moment arm.
    (E) the magnitude of the applied force, the length of the moment arm, and the direction of the applied force.

19. The acceleration due to gravity at a point in space $2R_E$ above the surface of Earth, where R_E as the radius of Earth is most nearly
    (A) 1.1 m/s^2.
    (B) 2.4 m/s^2.
    (C) 4.9 m/s^2.
    (D) 9.8 m/s^2.
    (E) 19.6 m/s^2.

20. A communications satellite is in an elliptical orbit well above Earth's atmosphere as shown. At what point in the orbit does the satellite have its lowest speed?

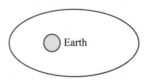

    (A) It has its lowest speed when it is nearest Earth.
    (B) It has its lowest speed when it is farthest from Earth.
    (C) It has its lowest speed when it is moving toward Earth.
    (D) It has its lowest speed when it is moving away from Earth.
    (E) It has the same speed at all points in its orbit.

21. A body in simple harmonic motion has
    (A) constant speed.
    (B) constant acceleration.
    (C) constant restoring force.
    (D) changing acceleration.
    (E) changing total energy.

22. Two waves of the same frequency traveling in opposite directions along a string. When they meet, these waves will not
    (A) follow the principle of superposition.
    (B) reflect off each other.
    (C) remain transverse.
    (D) continue to carry energy.
    (E) pass through each other.

23. The speed of a sound wave is determined by
    (A) the amplitude of the wave.
    (B) the intensity of the sound wave.
    (C) the speed of the source producing the wave.
    (D) the speed of the observer hearing the wave.
    (E) the medium in which the wave travels.

24. A stretched wire is attached to a wall at points 1 and 5 as shown. When the wire is vibrating in its first harmonic frequency, the nodes are at what points?

    (A) 1 and 5 only
    (B) 1, 3, and 5
    (C) 2, 3, and 4
    (D) 1, 2, 3, 4, and 5
    (E) 2 and 4 only

25. Two sounds of equal amplitude but slightly different frequencies are emitted from a sound source, which gives rise to
    (A) standing wave forms.
    (B) beats.
    (C) amplification.
    (D) constructive interference.
    (E) destructive interference.

26. An incompressible, ideal fluid flows through a horizontal pipe and encounters a region where the diameter is doubled. The ratio of the fluid velocity in the larger-diameter pipe to that in the smaller-diameter pipe is
    (A) 1 to 2.
    (B) 1 to 1.414.
    (C) 1 to 4.
    (D) 2 to 1.
    (E) 4 to 1.

27. A wood block floats with 65% of its entire volume submersed in water. What is the mass density of the wood?
    (A) 3.5 kg/m^3
    (B) 6.5 kg/m^3
    (C) 350 kg/m^3
    (D) 650 kg/m^3
    (E) 980 kg/m^3

28. Substance A has a mass density of 3000 kg/m^3, and substance B has a mass density of 4000 kg/m^3. To obtain equal masses of each of these two substances, the ratio of the volume of substance A to the volume of substance B will be equal to
    (A) 3:1
    (B) 4:3
    (C) 3:4
    (D) 4:1
    (E) 1:4

29. The relationship that exists between the pressure and the volume of a gas expressed by Boyle's law holds true
    (A) if the density remains constant.
    (B) if the temperature is constant.
    (C) for real gases under any conditions.
    (D) if the gas can expand with increasing pressure.
    (E) for all ideal gases under any conditions.

30. A closed system absorbs heat Q and has an equal amount of positive work W done on it. What is the change in the internal energy of the system?
    (A) Q
    (B) $2Q$
    (C) $-2Q$
    (D) $Q/2$
    (E) zero

31. The work done by a gas on a piston in a cylinder can be obtained from the graph as shown, provided the horizontal axis represents what?

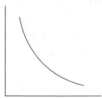

(A) volume
(B) temperature
(C) number of moles
(D) density
(E) internal energy

32. When the thickness of a wall is doubled, the rate of heat conduction through the wall
(A) doubles.
(B) increases by a factor of 4.
(C) decreases by a factor of 4.
(D) is reduced by one-half.
(E) remains constant.

33. A circular hole is cut in the center of a sheet of metal. When the sheet is heated, the area of the hole
(A) does not change.
(B) always increases.
(C) always decreases.
(D) is dependent only on the coefficient of expansion for the metal.
(E) is dependent only on the temperature change.

34. Each second, Earth receives approximately 1.5×10^{17} J of energy from the Sun through a process called
(A) conduction.
(B) convection.
(C) radiation.
(D) evaporation.
(E) sublimation.

35. In the Compton effect, the wavelength shift λ depends on
(A) the initial wavelength.
(B) the initial frequency.
(C) the scattering material.
(D) the binding energy of the material.
(E) the photon scatter angle.

36. The difference between the pressure inside and outside a tire is called
(A) absolute pressure.
(B) atmospheric pressure.
(C) gauge pressure.
(D) fluid pressure.
(E) air pressure.

37. At what temperature will the internal motion of the particles of a substance be a minimum?
(A) −273°C
(B) −40°C
(C) 3.98°C
(D) 0°C
(E) 100°C

38. According to the kinetic theory, molecules of a gas in a confined container at a given temperature all have the same
(A) kinetic energy.
(B) momentum.
(C) direction of motion.
(D) speed.
(E) V_{rms} speed.

39. Lines of constant pressure on a PV diagram are called
(A) isotherms.
(B) isochors.
(C) isobars.
(D) isotopes.
(E) isomers.

40. A gas bubble escapes the bottom of a pond and expands by a factor of 4 by the time it reaches the surface. The temperature of the water at the bottom of the pond is the same as on the surface. If atmospheric pressure is 100 kPa, what is the absolute pressure at the bottom of this pond?
(A) 103 kPa
(B) 120 kPa
(C) 206 kPa
(D) 300 kPa
(E) 400 kPa

41. An adiabatic process is a process in which
   (A) no heat enters or leaves the system.
   (B) the temperature of the system is constant.
   (C) the pressure of the system is constant.
   (D) the volume of the system is constant.
   (E) the mass of the system is constant.

42. The work done by an ideal gas can be determined from a *PV* diagram as
   (A) the intercept on the pressure axis.
   (B) the intercept on the volume axis.
   (C) the area beneath the curve.
   (D) the slope of the curve.
   (E) the change in the direction of isotherm.

43. One electronic charge is
   (A) 1.00 C.
   (B) 1.60×10^{-19} C.
   (C) 1.60×10^{19} C.
   (D) 6.25×10^{-18} C.
   (E) 6.25×10^{18} C.

44. The direction of the electric field vector in space is
   (A) away from the position of a positive test charge.
   (B) toward the location of a positive test charge.
   (C) antiparallel to the direction of the electrostatic force on a positive test charge at that point in space.
   (D) parallel to the direction of the electrostatic force on a positive test charge at that point in space.
   (E) perpendicular to the direction of the electrostatic force on a positive test charge at that point in space.

45. The electrical potential at a position 3.0 m away from a point charge of –5.0 nC is
   (A) +15 V.
   (B) +5.0 V.
   (C) zero.
   (D) –5.0 V.
   (E) –15 V.

46. The electrical field intensity at a position 3.0 m away from a point charge of –5.0 nC is
   (A) 15.0 N/C radially outward.
   (B) 5.0 N/C radially outward.
   (C) zero.
   (D) 5.0 N/C radially inward.
   (E) 15.0 N/C radially inward.

47. How much work must be done by the electrical field in bringing a 1.0-nC charge from infinity to a position 3.0 m away from a –5.0-nC charge?
   (A) +5.0 nJ
   (B) +15.0 nJ
   (C) zero
   (D) –5.0 nJ
   (E) –15.0 nJ

48. If a charged particle is placed into a magnetic field, it experiences zero magnetic force
   (A) if it has a negative charge.
   (B) if it has a positive charge.
   (C) when it moves at constant speed perpendicular to the magnetic field lines.
   (D) if there is an electrical field present.
   (E) if it is at rest.

49. A circular loop of copper wire of resistance *R* lies in the plane of the page. A magnetic field is directed through the loop out of the page. If the magnetic field suddenly is removed,
   (A) a momentary clockwise current is induced in the loop.
   (B) a momentary counterclockwise current is induced in the loop.
   (C) no current is induced because the area remains constant.
   (D) no current is induced because the loop does not rotate.
   (E) no current is induced because a resistance is present.

50. The emf across a coil of N turns is given by which of the following terms?

    (A) $-N\dfrac{\Delta\phi}{\Delta t}$

    (B) $N\dfrac{\Delta\phi}{\Delta t}$

    (C) $-N\dfrac{\Delta t}{\Delta\phi}$

    (D) $N\dfrac{\Delta A}{\Delta t}$

    (E) $-N\dfrac{\Delta A}{\Delta t}$

51. A proton, traveling north, enters a magnetic field of strength B. Because of the magnetic field, the proton curves downward. What is the direction of the field?
    (A) downward
    (B) upward
    (C) east
    (D) west
    (E) north

52. A resistor operates at 120.0 V and has a power rating of 60.0 W. The current through the resistor is
    (A) 0.25 A.
    (B) 0.5 A.
    (C) 1.0 A.
    (D) 1.5 A.
    (E) 2.0 A.

53. The work done in moving a small positive charge against an electric field does not depend on the path taken through the field. What kind of force field is the electrostatic field?
    (A) quantized
    (B) potential
    (C) scalar
    (D) conservative
    (E) nonconservative

54. A wire carries a current I vertically downward. What is the direction of the force caused by the magnetic field of Earth acting on the wire?
    (A) vertically north
    (B) vertically south
    (C) horizontally east
    (D) horizontally west
    (E) circular clockwise

55. A circular coil is held flat on a horizontal surface. A bar magnet is held at rest above the coil with its N-pole pointing downward. When the magnet is released from rest, what is the direction of the induced current in the coil?
    (A) It alternates.
    (B) There is no current.
    (C) The direction is clockwise.
    (D) The direction is counterclockwise.
    (E) Not enough information is provided to determine the direction.

56. The rapid deceleration of high-speed electrons when they strike a metal in a cathode-ray tube gives rise to a type of electromagnetic radiation called
    (A) infrared.
    (B) visible light.
    (C) ultraviolet.
    (D) X-rays.
    (E) gamma rays.

For Questions 57 and 58:
    I. real
    II. virtual
    III. upright
    IV. inverted
    V. smaller than the object
    VI. same size as the object
    VII. larger than the object

57. The image formed by a plane mirror is
    (A) II, III, and VI.
    (B) I, III, and VI.
    (C) II, III, and V.
    (D) I, III, and V.
    (E) II, III, and VII.

58. The image formed by a concave mirror of an object that is located between the focus and the surface of the mirror is
    (A) I, III, and VII.
    (B) I, IV, and V.
    (C) II, III, and VII.
    (D) II, IV, and V.
    (E) I, IV, and VII.

59. In Young's double-slit experiment, doubling the slit spacing for monochromatic light results in
    (A) doubling the fringe spacing.
    (B) reduces the fringe spacing by one-half.
    (C) increases the brightness of the maximum.
    (D) reduces the brightness of the maximum.
    (E) changes the central maximum to a minimum.

60. For a thin film bounded on both sides by media each of lower index of refraction, maximum constructive interference occurs if the optical path difference is
    (A) 2λ.
    (B) $3\lambda/2$.
    (C) λ.
    (D) $\lambda/2$.
    (E) $\lambda/4$.

61. The Bohr model of the atom is also known as the
    (A) plum pudding model.
    (B) planetary model.
    (C) raisin muffin model.
    (D) de Broglie wave model.
    (E) blackbody model.

62. A temperature on the order of 10^8 K is required to drive a fusion reactor. Why is such a high temperature required?
    (A) to initiate nuclear fission
    (B) to separate electrons from nuclei
    (C) to form a plasma
    (D) to overcome the Coulomb forces of repulsion between the protons
    (E) to initiate thermonuclear fission

63. In nuclei of different isotopes of the same element, there are the same number of
    (A) protons.
    (B) neutrons.
    (C) nucleons.
    (D) neutrinos.
    (E) electrons.

64. The MeV is a unit of
    (A) charge.
    (B) voltage.
    (C) energy.
    (D) potential.
    (E) radioactivity.

65. The emf of a battery is
    (A) the maximum electric potential energy stored in the battery.
    (B) the maximum potential difference between the terminals of the battery.
    (C) the maximum capacitance between the terminals of the battery.
    (D) the force that accelerates electrons through a wire when the battery is connected to it.
    (E) the force that accelerates protons through a wire when the battery is connected to it.

66. The kilowatt-hour is a unit of
    (A) current.
    (B) power.
    (C) potential drop.
    (D) energy.
    (E) resistance.

67. Which of the following nuclei is produced when $^{214}_{83}\text{Bi}$ undergoes alpha decay?
    (A) $^{210}_{81}\text{Tl}$
    (B) $^{210}_{83}\text{Bi}$
    (C) $^{210}_{79}\text{Au}$
    (D) $^{212}_{81}\text{Tl}$
    (E) $^{212}_{79}\text{Au}$

68. Light bends as it moves from one medium into another with differing indices of refraction is due to a change in what property of light?
    (A) amplitude
    (B) frequency
    (C) speed
    (D) period
    (E) color

69. Which of the following statements concerning an object totally submerged in water is true?
(A) The buoyant force depends on the mass of the object.
(B) The buoyant force depends on the weight of the object.
(C) The buoyant force depends on the volume of water displaced.
(D) The buoyant force is independent of the mass density of water.
(E) The buoyant force increases with depth in the water.

70. Bernoulli's principle is a statement of
(A) hydrostatic equilibrium.
(B) thermal equilibrium.
(C) hydrodynamics.
(D) charge conservation.
(E) energy conservation.

STOP
END OF SECTION I

IF YOU FINISH BEFORE TIME IS CALLED, YOU MAY CHECK YOUR WORK ON THIS SECTION. DO NOT GO ON TO SECTION II UNTIL YOU ARE TOLD TO DO SO.

AP Physics B
Section II: Free-Response Problems
Time: 90 minutes

Directions: Solve each of the following problems. Unless the directions indicate otherwise, respond to all parts of each question.

Hand calculators are permitted on this part of the test.

The Table of Information and the Advanced Placement Physics B Equations are allowed.

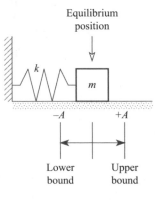

Equilibrium position

1. Consider a block of mass $m = 0.50$ kg attached to a spring of elastic constant $k = 10.0$ N/m that is fastened to a rigid wall as shown. The mass is pulled to the right a distance of $x = 3.0$ cm and is then released from rest, and the mass oscillates on the frictionless, horizontal surface.
    (a) What force was used to pull the block 3.0 cm to the right of the equilibrium position?
    (b) What initial acceleration does the block experience when released from rest at $+A$?
    (c) What is the frequency of oscillation of the mass?
    (d) How much work does the spring do on the block returning it from amplitude position $+A$ to the equilibrium position?
    (e) What is the maximum kinetic energy of the block?
    (f) Where will it have maximum kinetic energy?
    (g) Sketch the graphs of the kinetic energy K as a function of x and the total energy E as a function of x.

2. A laboratory beaker contains water and is at rest on a scale that reads 50.0 N. A brass cylinder having a volume $V = 900$ cm^3 is suspended from a string, lowered into the water, and suspended there as shown. Brass has a mass density of 8.60×10^3 kg/m^3.
    (a) What is the weight of the cylinder?
    (b) What buoyant force acts on the cylinder?
    (c) Determine the tension in the string.
    (d) What is the reading on the scale with the brass suspended in the water?

3. Consider the electric circuit shown. Four identical lightbulbs A, B, C and D are arranged in the circuit with a battery having an emf of 10.0 V.

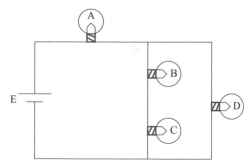

(a) If lightbulb A is removed from the circuit, what happens to the other lightbulbs? Are they brighter or dimmer?
(b) If lightbulb B is removed from the circuit, what happens to the other lightbulbs? Are they brighter or dimmer?
(c) If lightbulb D is removed from the circuit, what happens to the other lightbulbs? Are they brighter or dimmer?

Resistors as shown in the diagram now replace the lightbulbs of the above circuit.

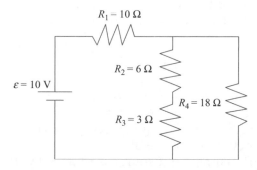

(d) Calculate the current issued by the battery.
(e) Find the voltage drop across the 18-Ω resistor.
(f) Determine the power loss in the 18-Ω resistor.

4. A ray of monochromatic light having a wavelength λ = 600 nm in air enters a second medium where it has an angle of incidence of 35°. The refracted angle in the medium is 21°.
(a) What is the frequency of light in air?
(b) Sketch all rays and angles at the air–medium interface, labeling each. Determine the index of refraction in the medium.
(c) What is the speed of light in the medium? What is the wavelength λ in the medium?
(d) If the ray originates in the denser medium, what is the critical angle for the medium-to-air surface?
(e) The medium has a depth of 2.0 m. The ray entering from the air strikes the upper surface of the medium, is refracted at 21°, and then is reflected from the bottom of the medium. Find the horizontal distance between the incident ray and the emerging ray.

5. An ion of mass 2.4×10^{-26} kg orbits clockwise in an extensive uniform magnetic field of 1.3 T that is projected out of the page as shown. The magnitude of the charge on the ion is $|q| = |2e|$, and the radius of the orbit is 2.0 cm.

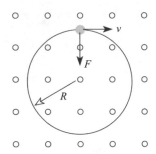

   (a) Calculate the centripetal acceleration experienced by the orbiting ion.
   (b) Does the ion have a positive (+) or negative (–) charge? Justify your answer.
   (c) What is the magnetic force acting on the orbiting ion?
   (d) How much work does the magnetic force do on the ion during each orbit?
   (e) What is the period of each orbit?
   (f) What current does the orbiting ion generate?

6. A 10-W monochromatic light source produces light having a wavelength of 480 nm.
   (a) How many photons of this light are produced per second?
   (b) What is the frequency of these photons?
   (c) The light irradiates a metallic surface and causes photoelectrons to just leave the surface. Calculate the work function of this metal.
   (d) The 480-nm light source is replaced with a different 10-W monochromatic light source of wavelength 420 nm. What is the speed of the photoelectrons as they leave the surface of the metal?

END OF EXAMINATION

ANSWERS

ANSWER KEY FOR MULTIPLE-CHOICE QUESTIONS

1. B	11. E	21. D	31. A	41. A	51. C	61. B
2. E	12. B	22. B	32. D	42. C	52. B	62. D
3. B	13. D	23. E	33. B	43. B	53. D	63. A
4. B	14. A	24. A	34. C	44. D	54. C	64. C
5. A	15. D	25. B	35. E	45. E	55. D	65. B
6. E	16. B	26. C	36. C	46. D	56. D	66. D
7. B	17. E	27. D	37. A	47. E	57. A	67. A
8. A	18. E	28. B	38. E	48. E	58. C	68. C
9. D	19. A	29. B	39. C	49. B	59. B	69. C
10. C	20. B	30. B	40. E	50. A	60. D	70. E

EXPLANATIONS FOR THE MULTIPLE-CHOICE ANSWERS

1. **B** The average velocity is the slope of the line between two points. Because the graph is linear with negative slope, the velocity is constant and negative (*College Physics* 8th ed. pages 28–31/9th ed. pages 29–32).

2. **E** The compact body falls freely under the influence of gravity alone. Compact implies little surface area and negligible friction. In this case, $a = -g = -9.8$ m/s² (*College Physics* 8th ed. pages 42–46/9th ed. pages 43–47).

3. **B** Newton's second law applies, and $F_1 = m_1 a$ and $F_2 = m_2 a$. Because $a = a$, $F_1/F_2 = m_1/m_2$ (*College Physics* 8th ed. pages 86–89/9th ed. pages 89–92).

4. **B** The normal force is determined by writing the $\Sigma F_y = 0$ equation. The normal is $n + F_y - W = 0$ and is therefore $200 \text{ N} - (100 \text{ N}) \sin 30° = 150$ N (*College Physics* 8th ed. pages 92–98/9th ed. pages 95–103).

5. **A** The coefficient of kinetic friction is determined from $\Sigma F_x = 0$ because the box is moving at constant speed. So, $\Sigma F_x = F \cos\theta = \mu_k n$. Substituting into the equation gives $100.0 \text{ N} \cos 30° = \mu_k \times 150$ N. The coefficient of kinetic friction is $\mu_k = 86.6 \text{ N}/150 \text{ N} = \mu_k = 0.58$ (*College Physics* 8th ed. pages 101–104/9th ed. pages 105–108).

6. **E** Elastic potential energy is $U_s = \frac{1}{2}kx^2$. If x doubles, the potential energy increases by a factor of 4 (*College Physics* 8th ed. pages 135–140/9th ed. pages 140–145).

7. **B** By the work–kinetic energy theorem, the net work done is equal to the change in the kinetic energy, $W_{net} = \Delta K = (K - K_0)$ (*College Physics* 8th ed. pages 124–126/9th ed. pages 129–131).

8. **A** Because the acceleration is zero, Newton's first law applies in this case. The speed of the body and direction are both constant (*College Physics* 8th ed. pages 85–86/9th ed. pages 88–89).

9. **D** For the speed to be constant (terminal velocity), the net force acting on the body must be zero. The two forces on the body are F_R upward and F_g downward. They must be equal to each other (*College Physics* 8th ed. pages 85–86/9th ed. pages 88–89).

10. **C** Conservation means that the total initial energy of a system must equal the final energy. The conservative forces acting depend only on the endpoints and not the path taken between the endpoints (*College Physics* 8th ed. pages 445–447/9th ed. pages 131–132).

11. **E** The speed is the product of the wavelength and frequency in a uniform medium (*College Physics* 8th ed. pages 290–291/9th ed. pages 457–459).

12. **B** The work done is the area beneath a force versus displacement graph (*College Physics* 8th ed. pages 147–150/9th ed. pages 152–154).

13. **D** If only conservative forces are applied, the initial energy of the system is equal to the final energy of the system (*College Physics* 8th ed. pages 126–133/9th ed. pages 131–138).

14. **A** Because $W_{net} = \Delta K$, and if only conservative forces act, the net work on the object in moving it along a closed loop must be zero, which means that $K = K_0$ (*College Physics* 8th ed. pages 126–127/9th ed. pages 131–132).

15. **D** Given $K = \frac{1}{2}mv^2$ and $p = mv$, if the mass remains constant and the kinetic energy increases by a factor of 4, the velocity has increased by a factor of 2. Thus, the momentum will increase by a factor of 2 (*College Physics* 8th ed. pages 124–161/9th ed. pages 130, 167–168).

16. **B** For a collision to be perfectly elastic, both momentum and kinetic energy must be conserved (*College Physics* 8th ed. page 169/9th ed. page 176).

17. **E** Here, $F \Delta t = m \Delta v$. To round a curve at constant speed, a centripetal force must be applied. This force produces the centripetal acceleration needed to change the direction of motion of the car (*College Physics* 8th ed. pages 162–163,199–203/9th ed. pages 168–169, 207–211).

18. **E** Torque is defined as $\tau = rF \sin \theta$ (*College Physics* 8th ed. pages 229–231/9th ed. pages 236–238).

19. **A** The acceleration due to gravity, g, can be calculated by equating the weight of the body to the force existing between the two bodies through Newton's law of universal gravitation: $mg = Gmm_E/R^2$. Thus, at any point in Earth's gravitational field, g will depend on the mass of Earth, and the distance of the body is from the center of Earth. So, $(9.8 \text{ m/s}^2)(R_E)^2 = g_{\text{location}}(R_E + 2R_E)^2$, which yields $9.8 \text{ m/s}^2/9 = 1.1 \text{ m/s}^2$ (*College Physics* 8th ed. pages 219–221/9th ed. pages 217–219).

20. **B** The total energy of the Earth–satellite system is a constant, the law of conservation of mechanical energy applies in this case. At its greatest distance from Earth, the satellite has its greatest gravitational potential energy and least kinetic energy. The speed of the satellite will be least when it is farthest from Earth (at apogee) (*College Physics* 8th ed. pages 215–216/9th ed. pages 221–222).

21. **D** A body in simple harmonic motion moves in one dimension under the action of an elastic restoring force. Because $F = ma$ and $F = -kx$, then $ma = -kx$ and the acceleration is $a = -kx/m$. The acceleration varies according to $-x$ (*College Physics* 8th ed. pages 425–427/9th ed. pages 437–440).

22. **B** Two traveling waves of the same frequency can meet and pass through each other without being altered or destroyed. The superposition principle applies (*College Physics* 8th ed. pages 448–450/9th ed. pages 461–463).

23. **E** The speed of sound depends on an elastic property that is characteristic of the medium and an inertial property, the mass density ρ, of the medium (*College Physics* 8th ed. pages 461–463/9th ed. pages 476–478).

24. **A** The first harmonic is the fundamental; thus, the only nodes are at positions 1 and 5, the two fixed ends of the string, and $L = \lambda/2$ (*College Physics* 8th ed. page 475/9th ed. page 490).

25. **B** It is an interference that alternates from constructive to destructive because of the slight difference in frequency. The result is an alteration of sound intensity called beats. The beat frequency is $f_b = |f_2 - f_1|$ (*College Physics* 8th ed. pages 484–486/9th ed. pages 499–500).

26. **C** The equation of continuity, $A_1v_1 = A_2v_2$, applies in this situation. The flow rate through the pipe is constant. Reducing area causes an increase in the velocity of the fluid (*College Physics* 8th ed. pages 290–291/9th ed. pages 299–300).

27. **D** An object that floats or is partially submerged experiences a buoyant force provided by the displaced fluid that is equal to the weight of the object: $\rho_{\text{obj}}/\rho_{\text{fluid}} = V_{\text{fluid}}/V_{\text{obj}} = 0.65$. Substituting in the density of water gives $\rho_{\text{obj}}/1000 \text{ kg/m}^3 = 0.65$, and the density of the object is $\rho_{\text{obj}} = 650 \text{ kg/m}^3$ (*College Physics* 8th ed. page 286/9th ed. page 295).

28. **B** Density is mass per unit volume, and because the masses are equal we can write $\rho_A V_A = \rho_B V_B$. The ratio is $V_A/V_B = \left(4000 \text{ kg/m}^3\right)/\left(3000 \text{ kg/m}^3\right) = \frac{4}{3}$ (*College Physics* 8th ed. page 276/9th ed. page 279).

29. **B** Boyle's law for a confined amount of a gas shows that $P_1 V_1 = P_2 V_2$ as long as the number of moles of the gas and the temperature are constant (*College Physics* 8th ed. page 336/9th ed. page 345).

30. **B** The first law of thermodynamics applies in this case. Heat is absorbed by the system, and Q is positive. Work is positive because it is done on the system. The values are equal, and the change in U is equal to $2Q$ (*College Physics* 8th ed. pages 388–389/9th ed. pages 398–400).

31. **A** Work is the area beneath a force versus displacement curve. Using $W = F\Delta x$ and multiplying both the numerator and the dominator by area gives $W = (F/A)(A\Delta x)$. Work is now expressed as $W = |P\Delta V|$. The horizontal axis must be volume (*College Physics* 8th ed. page 387/9th ed. page 397).

32. **D** Thermal conductivity is given by $H = Q/t = (kA\,\Delta t)/L$. When L is doubled, the conductivity H is reduced by half (*College Physics* 8th ed. pages 366–367/9th ed. pages 375–376).

33. **B** The area of the hole acts as if were made of the same material as the metal plate that surrounds it. As the sheet of metal expands, so does the hole (*College Physics* 8th ed. pages 327–332/9th ed. pages 337–341).

34. **C** Energy transfer is done by conduction, convection, and radiation. Space is a vacuum (too few molecules that are too far apart). There is no way to transfer energy by contact between molecules or movement of fluids (*College Physics* 8th ed. pages 366–374/9th ed. pages 375–384).

35. **E** The Compton effect describes the shift in wavelength when a photon strikes an electron that is initially at rest: $\Delta\lambda = \lambda - \lambda_0 = (h/m_e c)(1 - \cos\theta)$. The shift is dependent on the photon scatter angle (*College Physics* 8th ed. pages 879–880/9th ed. pages 920–922).

36. **C** The absolute pressure: $P_{abs} = P_{atm} + P_{gauge}$ and $P_{gauge} = P_{abs} - P_{atm}$ (*College Physics* 8th ed. pages 276–283/9th ed. pages 279–282).

37. **A** On a plot of pressure versus the Celsius temperature, extrapolating the pressure to zero gives a temperature of –273°C. The force ($F = PA$) the molecules exert on the other molecules and the walls of the container would be zero. Kinetic energy of the gas would go to zero, and there would be no translation motion of the individual molecules (There will be internal motion, however.) (*College Physics* 8th ed. pages 324–326/9th ed. pages 333–335).

38. **E** The kinetic theory relates the Kelvin temperature to the V_{rms} speed, and $V_{rms} = \sqrt{(3k_B T/m)} = \sqrt{(3RT/M)}$ (*College Physics* 8th ed. pages 342–343/9th ed. pages 351–352).

39. **C** The process in which the pressure remains constant is an isobaric process. The lines representing constant pressure are isobars (*College Physics* 8th ed. page 386/9th ed. page 397).

40. **E** Boyle's law, $P_1 V_1 = P_2 V_2$, will apply because the temperature remains constant. The ratio of the volume is $P_1/P_2 = V_1/V_2 = \frac{4}{1}$. The absolute pressure at the surface P_1 is 100 kPa, and the absolute pressure P_2 at the bottom where the bubble is released is 400 kPa (*College Physics* 8th ed. pages 279–284/9th ed. pages 288–292).

41. **A** An adiabatic process is defined as one in which no thermal energy crosses a boundary. No heat enters or leaves the system (*College Physics* 8th ed. pages 393–395/9th ed. pages 404–406).

42. **C** Work is the area under a force versus x graph. The work done on or by an ideal gas is $W = -P\,\Delta V = (F/A)(A\,\Delta x)$ (*College Physics* 8th ed. pages 385–386/9th ed. pages 395–398).

43. **B** The charge on one electron or one proton is $e = 1.60 \times 10^{-19}$ C (*College Physics* 8th ed. page 501/9th ed. page 518).

44. **D** By definition, it is parallel to the direction of the electrostatic force on a positive test charge at that point in space (*College Physics* 8th ed. pages 505–507/9th ed. pages 522–524).

45. **E** The electrical potential at a point in space due to a negative charge is negative and is determined by $V = Kq/R$ (*College Physics* 8th ed. pages 538–539/9th ed. pages 555–557).

46. **D** The electrical field intensity at a point in space due to a negative charge is radially inward and is given by $E = Kq/R^2$ (*College Physics* 8th ed. pages 505–507/9th ed. pages 522–523).

47. **E** The work done in assembling two charges is given by $U = Kq_1 q_2/R$. Because the charges are –5.0 nC and +1.0 nC, the work represents a decrease in potential energy (*College Physics* 8th ed. pages 539–541/9th ed. pages 556–558).

48. **E** For a charged particle of either sign to experience a force, it must have some velocity because the magnetic force is $F_B = Bqv \sin\theta$ (*College Physics* 8th ed. pages 630–631/9th ed. pages 652–653).

49. **B** An emf is induced in the wire in response to the change in the flux permeating the coil. Faraday's law is $\mathcal{E} = -N(\Delta\phi/\Delta t)$, and Lenz's law gives the direction of the current as $I = \mathcal{E}/R$. Because the current is in such a direction to cause a B-field to set up that opposes the drop in the original field (B_0 out of the page),

the loop current is counterclockwise and the induced B-field is out of the page. The right-hand rule applies (*College Physics* 8th ed. pages 666–667/9th ed. pages 691–692).

50. **A** Use $\mathcal{E} = -N(\Delta\phi/\Delta t)$, Faraday's law, and Lenz's law (*College Physics* 8th ed. pages 666–667/9th ed. pages 691–692).

51. **C** The magnitude of the force is given by $F_B = Bqv \sin\theta$. The right-hand rule gives the direction of the force. The velocity of the proton is north, and the force on it is downward. The B-field points east (*College Physics* 8th ed. pages 666–667/9th ed. pages 652–653).

52. **B** Power is given by $P = IV$, and substitution gives $I = 0.5\,\text{A}$ (*College Physics* 8th ed. pages 580–584/9th ed. pages 601–604).

53. **D** A conservative field depends only on the endpoints and not the path between those endpoints. The electrical force is conservative, as is the electrical field (*College Physics* 8th ed. page 532/9th ed. page 549).

54. **C** The right-hand rule applies in this case. The force is given by $F_B = B\ell v \sin\theta$, which is east because the current is downward, and the B-field of Earth points south to north (*College Physics* 8th ed. pages 633–636/9th ed. pages 652–655).

55. **D** Faraday's law and Lenz's law apply. The magnetic field is increasing in the coil. The induced current opposes the increase in the magnetic flux (*College Physics* 8th ed. pages 666–667/9th ed. pages 691–692).

56. **D** X-rays are produced when high-speed electrons abruptly slow down as they strike a metal plate (*College Physics* 8th ed. pages 875–876/9th ed. pages 916–917).

57. **A** The image formed by a plane mirror is virtual, upright, the same size, and as far behind the mirror as the object is in front of it (*College Physics* 8th ed. pages 759–762/9th ed. pages 790–793).

58. **C** The image formed by an object placed between the focus and the mirror is always virtual, upright, and enlarged (*College Physics* 8th ed. pages 762–768/9th ed. pages 793–798).

59. **B** In Young's double-slit experiment, $d \sin\theta = m\lambda$. If the distance to the screen is large—that is, if $L \gg d$—we can substitute $\tan\theta$ for $\sin\theta$, which will yield $y_{\text{bright}} = \lambda Lm/d$. If d doubles, y_{bright} is reduced by a factor of 2 (*College Physics* 8th ed. pages 791–795/9th ed. pages 825–829).

60. **D** A ray coming from n_1 goes through a 180° phase inversion when $n_2 > n_1$. There is no change in the reflected ray from the lower surface because $n_2 > n_1$. Thus, the optical difference in the film must be $\lambda/2$

for constructive interference to occur on the upper surface (*College Physics* 8th ed. pages 796–797/9th ed. pages 830–833).

61. **B** The Bohr atom consists of a lone proton with an electron orbiting it. It is the planetary model because it resembles a planet orbiting a star (*College Physics* 8th ed. pages 894–897/9th ed. pages 937–940).

62. **D** Fusion combines lighter nuclei into heavier ones. The temperature must be extremely high (about 10^7 K for $^1_1$H) for the kinetic energy of the protons to overcome the repulsive Coulomb force acting between the protons (*College Physics* 8th ed. pages 941–942/9th ed. pages 986–988).

63. **A** Isotopes have the same Z number (proton number) but different A numbers (protons plus neutrons) (*College Physics* 8th ed. page 913/9th ed. page 957).

64. **C** The MeV is a unit of energy equal to 1.60×10^{-13} J (*College Physics* 8th ed. page 543/9th ed. page 559).

65. **B** The emf of a battery is equal to the terminal voltage when (a) the current is zero or (b) the internal resistance is negligible when it is delivering current. If either (a) or (b) applies, the emf is the maximum potential difference (*College Physics* 8th ed. page 595/9th ed. page 617).

66. **D** Power is work per unit time. A kilowatt-hour is a unit of energy (*College Physics* 8th ed. page 581/9th ed. page 602).

67. **A** Alpha decay is the emission of a helium nuclei $^4_2$He, a radioactive decay process. The reaction is $^{214}_{83}$Bi $\rightarrow$ $^4_2$He $+$ $^{210}_{81}$Tl (*College Physics* 8th ed. pages 921–922/9th ed. pages 965–966).

68. **C** The index of refraction of a medium is given by $n = c / v$. Light obliquely entering a medium of higher density will bend toward the normal because of an abrupt speed change at the interface between the two media (*College Physics* 8th ed. page 737/9th ed. page 767).

69. **C** Archimedes's principle applies in this case. A body completely submerged in a fluid is buoyed up by a force equal in magnitude to the weight of the fluid displaced by the body (*College Physics* 8th ed. pages 284–286/9th ed. pages 293–295).

70. **E** Bernoulli's equation is a statement of conservation of energy applied to an ideal fluid (*College Physics* 8th ed. page 543/9th ed. page 559).

Answers to Free-Response Problems

Question 1 [15 points]

(a) 2 points

Hooke's law allows us to calculate the force: $F = kx = (10.0 \text{ N/m})(0.03 \text{ m})$, and $F = \textbf{0.3 N}$.

[1 point for correct substitution]
[1 point for correct answer with correct units]

(b) 2 points

To find the initial acceleration, which is also the maximum acceleration, we relate Hooke's law and Newton's second law of motion. The block will be accelerated to the left. So, $F = ma = kx = a = -F/m = -0.3 \text{ N}/0.5 \text{ kg}$, or $a = \textbf{0.6 m/s}^2$.

[1 point for correct substitution]
[1 point for correct answer with correct units]

(c) 2 points

Frequency f is related to the spring constant k and the mass m of the oscillating body by

$$f = \frac{1}{2\pi}\sqrt{\frac{k}{m}}$$

$$f = \frac{1}{2\pi}\sqrt{\frac{10 \text{ N/m}}{0.50 \text{ kg}}}$$

$$f = \textbf{0.71 Hz}$$

[1 point for correct substitution]
[1 point for correct answer with correct units]

(d) 3 points

At the amplitude position, the kinetic energy of the body is zero.

[1 point for knowing the kinetic energy is zero]

All the energy of the body at $\pm A$ is elastic potential energy. The work done on the system is the gain in elastic potential. So, $W = U_s = \frac{1}{2}kA^2 = \frac{1}{2}(10.0 \text{ N/m})(0.030 \text{ m})^2$, or $W = \textbf{4.5} \times \textbf{10}^{-3}$ **J** = **4.5 mJ**.

[1 point for correct substitution]
[1 point for correct answer with correct units]

(e) 2 points

The law of conservation of mechanical energy for the system is $E = U_s + K$.

[1 point for knowing the conservation of mechanical energy]

When the oscillating body has maximum kinetic energy, the elastic potential energy is zero. The total energy is the maximum kinetic energy, or $K_{max} = 4.5 \times 10^{-3}$ J = 4.5 mJ.

[1 point for correct answer with correct units]

(f) 2 points

The body has zero kinetic energy at the amplitude positions, $\pm A$.

[*1 point for knowing zero kinetic energy at amplitude positions*]

Therefore, **the maximum kinetic energy occurs at the equilibrium position.**

[*1 point for knowing this to be true*]

(g) 2 points

The graph of kinetic energy versus x is parabolic as shown. The endpoints are $\pm A$. The maximum kinetic energy occurs at K_{max}.

[*1 point for each correctly sketched graph*]

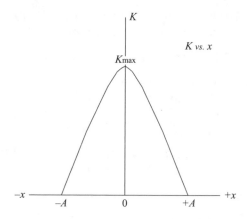

The total energy E in a system is a constant with endpoints $\pm A$ as shown.

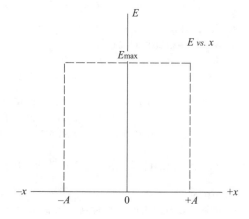

(*College Physics* 8th ed. pages 425–432/9th ed. pages 437–445)

Question 2 [15 points]

(a) 4 points

The weight w of the cylinder is $w = mg = \rho V g = (8.60 \times 10^3 \text{ kg/m}^3)(900 \times 10^{-6} \text{ m}^3)(9.8 \text{ m/s}^2)$, or **$w = 75.9$ N.**

[*1 point for correct working equation*]
[*1 point for correct substitution*]
[*2 points for correct answer with correct units*]

(b) 3 points

The buoyant force is the weight of the displaced water in the beaker.

[1 point for knowing buoyant force is the weight of the displaced water]

So, $B =$ weight of displaced water $= m_w g = \rho_w V_w g = \left(1000 \text{ kg/m}^3\right) \left(900 \times 10^{-6} \text{ m}^3\right)\left(9.8 \text{ m/s}^2\right)$, or $B = 8.82$ N.

[1 point for correct substitution]
[1 point for correct answer with correct units]

(c) 4 points

The brass cylinder is in a state of equilibrium, and all the up forces equal all the down forces.

[1 point for knowing the system is in equilibrium]

Acting upward on the cylinder is the string with tension T and the buoyant force B of the water. Acting downward is the weight of the cylinder, w_{brass}. So, $T + B = w_{brass} = T = w_{brass} - B = 75.9$ N $- 8.82$ N, or $T = 67.1$ N.

[1 point for knowing the buoyant force is upward]
[2 points for correct answer with correct units]

(d) 4 points

By Newton's third law, the brass cylinder exerts a downward force of magnitude B on the liquid.

[1 point for expressing Newton's third law]

The scale must balance the weight of the beaker and water, which was measured at 50.0 N, plus the downward reaction force of the buoyant force B. The new scale reading is $F_n = F + B = 50.0$ N $+ 8.82$ N, or $F_n = 58.2$ N.

[1 point for knowing the reaction force to the buoyant force is downward]
[2 points for correct answer with correct units]

(*College Physics* 8th ed. pages 284–290/9th ed. pages 293–299)

Question 3 [15 points]

When the lightbulbs in the circuit are on, the intensity in lightbulb A is the brightest because it receives the entire current. The current divides in the parallel arrangement, and the branch containing lightbulb D has a smaller resistance than the other branch. Therefore, lightbulb D is dimmer than A but brighter than B and C, which are equal.

(a) 1 point

When lightbulb A is removed from the circuit, all the lightbulbs go out because the circuit is broken.

[1 point for correct answer]

(b) 2 points

When lightbulb B is removed, this part of the circuit is broken. Lightbulbs A and D are equally bright, but A is dimmer than in the original circuit and D is brighter.

[2 points for correct explanation]

(c) 2 points

When lightbulb D is removed, A, B, and C are equally bright. Lightbulb A is dimmer than before, and B and C are brighter than before.

[2 points for correct explanation]

(d) 5 points

First, simplify the circuit and find the total resistance. Resistors R_2 and R_3 are in series with each other and add to find their equivalent resistance R_{23}. So, $R_{23} = R_2 + R_3 = 3\Omega + 6\Omega = 9\Omega$ as shown.

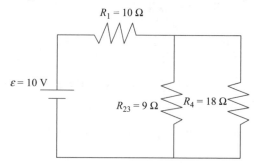

$R_1 = 10\ \Omega$

$\varepsilon = 10\ V$

$R_{23} = 9\ \Omega$ $R_4 = 18\ \Omega$

Resistors R_{23} and R_4 are in parallel, and their equivalent resistance, R_{234}, is found from

$$\frac{1}{R_{234}} = \frac{1}{R_{23}} + \frac{1}{R_4} = \frac{1}{9\ \Omega} + \frac{1}{18\ \Omega} = \frac{3}{18\ \Omega}$$

$$R_{234} = 6$$

[2 points for correct answer with correct units]
The circuit is now reduced as shown.

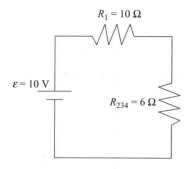

$R_1 = 10\ \Omega$

$\varepsilon = 10\ V$

$R_{234} = 6\ \Omega$

[1 point for reducing the circuit]

The remaining resistors are now arranged in series, and their equivalent resistance is $R_{eq} = R_1 + R_{234} = 10\Omega + 6\Omega = \textbf{16}\ \Omega$. The current issued by the battery is found by using Ohm's law: $\varepsilon = IR_{eq}$. So, $I = \varepsilon/R_{eq} = 10\ V/16\ \Omega$, or $I = \textbf{0.625 A}$.

[2 points for correct answer with correct units]

(e) 3 points

The 18 Ω resistor is in the parallel bank, and the equivalent resistance there is 6 Ω. All resistors in parallel suffer the same drop in voltage.

[1 point for knowing the voltage drop is the same]

So, $V_{234} = IR_{234} = (0.625\ \text{A})(6\Omega)$, or $V_{234} = \textbf{3.75 V}$.

[2 points for correct answer with correct units]

(f) 2 points

The power drop across the 18 Ω resistor is found from $P = V^2/R_4 = (3.75\ V)^2/18\Omega$, or $P = \textbf{0.78 W}$.

[2 points for correct answer with correct units]

(*College Physics* 8th ed. pages 595–603/9th ed. pages 617–625)

Question 4 [15 points]

(a) 2 points

The speed of light in air is $c = \lambda f$, and $f = c/\lambda = (3\times10^8\ \text{m/s})/(600\times10^{-9}\ \text{m})$, or $f = \textbf{5}\times\textbf{10}^{\textbf{14}}$ **Hz**.

[2 points for correct answer with correct units]

(b) 6 points

A sketch of the ray trace is as shown.

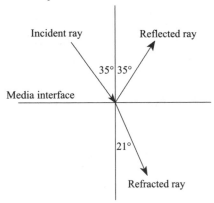

[4 points for correct sketch and angles]

The index of refraction for the medium is found by $n_1 \sin\theta_1 = n_2 \sin\theta_2$:

$$n_2 = \frac{n_1 \sin\theta_1}{\sin\theta_2} = \frac{(1.0)(\sin 35°)}{\sin 21°}$$

$$n_2 = \textbf{1.6}$$

[1 point for correct substitution]
[1 point for correct answer]

(c) 2 points

The speed of light v in a medium other than air is

$$v = \frac{c}{n} = \frac{(3\times10^8\ \text{m/s})}{1.6}$$

$$v = 1.9 \times 10^8 \text{ m/s}$$

[1 point for correct answer with correct units]

The wavelength in the medium is related to the wavelength in air by $\lambda_{medium} = \lambda_{air}/n = 600$ nm/1.6, or $\lambda_{medium} = $ **375 nm**.

[1 point for correct answer with correct units]

(d) 1 point

The sine of the critical angle in a medium is $\sin\theta_{critical} = 1/n_{medium}$ $= 1/1.6$, so $\theta_{critical} = $ **38.7°**.

[1 point for correct answer with correct units]

(e) 4 points

The depth of the medium is 2.0 m, and the horizontal distance from the point enters the medium to where it strikes the bottom is *x* as shown.

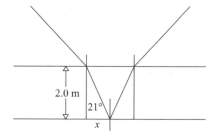

The depth and the distance *x* along with the ray form a right triangle. The adjacent and opposite sides of the triangle are used to find *x*. So, $\tan 21° = x/2.0$ m and $x = (2.0 \text{ m})(\tan 21°) = 0.768$ m.

[2 points for correct answer with correct units]

The ray is reflected from the bottom, and horizontally it travels 2*x*, or 1.54 m.

[1 point for doubling the distance]

The distance between the incident and emerging rays is **1.54 m**.

[1 point for correct answer with correct units]

(*College Physics* 8th ed. pages 733–741/9th ed. pages 762–770)

Question 5 [15 points]
(a) 3 points

To find the centripetal acceleration, we need to find the speed of the ion. The centripetal force is

$$\frac{mv^2}{R} = qvB$$

$$v = \frac{qBR}{m} = \frac{2(1.60 \times 10^{-19} \text{ C})(1.3T)(0.02 \text{ m})}{2.4 \times 10^{-26} \text{ kg}} = 3.47 \times 10^5 \text{ m/s}$$

[1 point for correct working equation]
[1 point for correct substitution]

$$a_c = \frac{v^2}{R} = \frac{\left(3.47 \times 10^5 \text{ m/n}\right)^2}{0.02 \text{ m}} = \textbf{6.0} \times \textbf{10}^{\textbf{12}} \textbf{ m/s}^2$$

[1 point for correct answer with correct units]

(b) 2 points

The ion has a **negative (–) charge**. The right-hand rule fails here, indicating that a negative particle orbits in the **B**-field.

[1 point for correct answer]
[1 point for reason for answer]

(c) 2 points

Because the mass of the ion and its acceleration are known, we can calculate the force by using Newton's second law of motion. So, $F = ma = (2.4 \times 10^{-26} \text{ kg})(6.0 \times 10^{12} \text{ m/s}^2)$, or **1.4 × 10⁻¹³ N**.

[1 point for correct substitution]
[1 point for correct answer with correct units]

(d) 2 points

Because there is no change in kinetic energy, the speed is a constant, so the work done is zero. Therefore, $W = \Delta K = 0$.

[1 point for correct answer]
[1 point for reason for answer]

(e) 3 points

To find the period, the circumference of the circular orbit must be found:

$$v = \frac{C}{T} = \frac{2\pi R}{T}$$

$$T = \frac{2\pi R}{v} = \frac{2\pi \left(0.02 \text{ m}\right)}{3.47 \times 10^5 \text{ m/s}}$$

[1 point for correct working equation]
[1 point for correct substitution]

T = 3.6 × 10⁻⁷ s

[1 point for correct answer with correct units]

(f) 3 points

The current is given by

$$I = \frac{q}{T} = \frac{2e}{T} = \frac{2\left(1.60 \times 10^{-19} \text{ C}\right)}{3.6 \times 10^{-7} \text{ s}}$$

[1 point for correct working equation]
[1 point for correct substitution]

I = 8.9 × 10⁻¹³ A

[1 point for correct answer with correct units]

(*College Physics* 8th ed. pages 639–642/9th ed. pages 661–664)

Question 6 [15 points]

(a) 4 points

Each photon carries an energy

$$E = hf = \frac{hc}{\lambda} = \frac{\left(6.63 \times 10^{-34}\,\text{J·s}\right)\left(3 \times 10^{8}\,\text{m/s}\right)}{480 \times 10^{-9}\,\text{m}} = 4.14 \times 10^{-19}\,\text{J/photon}$$

[1 point for correct working equation]
[1 point for correct energy per photon]

The light source is 10.0 W, or 10 W = 10 J/s. Then 10 J/s = 1 photon/(4.14 × 10^{-19} J), or **2.4 × 10^{19} photons/s**.

[2 points for correct answer with correct units]

(b) 4 points

Each photon has a frequency

$$f = \frac{c}{\lambda} = \frac{3 \times 10^{8}\,\text{m/s}}{480 \times 10^{-9}\,\text{m}}$$

[1 point for correct working equation]
[1 point for correct substitution]

***f* = 6.25× 10^{14} Hz**

[2 points for correct answer with correct units]

(c) 3 points

To calculate the work function of this metal, we need the Einstein photoelectric equation, $K = hf - \phi$.

[1 point for photoelectric equation]

In this case, the energy of each incoming photon is 4.14 × **10^{-19}** J. Because the photoelectrons just leave the surface, $K = 0$, and the work function is $\phi = hf =$ **4.14** × **10^{-19}** J.

[1 point for knowing K = 0 at the surface]
[1 point for correct answer with correct units]

(d) 4 points

To find the speed, we need the kinetic energy of the photoelectrons under these new conditions. So,

$$K = \frac{hc}{\lambda} - \phi = \frac{\left(6.63 \times 10^{-34}\,\text{J·s}\right)\left(3 \times 10^{8}\,\text{m/s}\right)}{420 \times 10^{-9}\,\text{m}} - 4.14 \times 10^{-19}\,\text{J} = 6.0 \times 10^{-20}\,\text{J}$$

[1 point for correct substitution]
[1 point for correct answer with correct units]

Kinetic energy and speed are related by

$$v = \sqrt{\frac{2K}{m}} = \sqrt{\frac{2\left(6 \times 10^{-20}\,\text{J}\right)}{9.11 \times 10^{-31}\,\text{kg}}}$$

***v* = 3.6 × 10^{5} m/s**

[1 point for correct working equation]
[1 point for correct answer with correct units]

(*College Physics* 8th ed. pages 872–875/9th ed. pages 913–916)

CALCULATING YOUR SCORE

SECTION I: MULTIPLE-CHOICE

$$\underline{\hspace{3cm}} \times 1.2857 = \underline{\hspace{3cm}}$$

Number Correct   Weighted Section I Score
(out of 70)   (If less than zero, enter
zero; do not round)

SECTION II: FREE RESPONSE

Question 1 $\underline{\hspace{2cm}}$ $\times 1.0000 =$ $\underline{\hspace{3cm}}$
         (out of 15)   (Do not round)

Question 2 $\underline{\hspace{2cm}}$ $\times 1.0000 =$ $\underline{\hspace{3cm}}$
         (out of 15)   (Do not round)

Question 3 $\underline{\hspace{2cm}}$ $\times 1.0000 =$ $\underline{\hspace{3cm}}$
         (out of 15)   (Do not round)

Question 4 $\underline{\hspace{2cm}}$ $\times 1.0000 =$ $\underline{\hspace{3cm}}$
         (out of 15)   (Do not round)

Question 5 $\underline{\hspace{2cm}}$ $\times 1.0000 =$ $\underline{\hspace{3cm}}$
         (out of 15)   (Do not round)

Question 6 $\underline{\hspace{2cm}}$ $\times 1.0000 =$ $\underline{\hspace{3cm}}$
         (out of 15)   (Do not round)

                              Sum = $\underline{\hspace{3cm}}$

                              Weighted Section II Score
                                 (Do not round)

COMPOSITE SCORE

$$\underline{\hspace{3cm}} + \underline{\hspace{3cm}} = \underline{\hspace{3cm}}$$

Weighted   Weighted   Composite Score
Section I Score   Section II Score   (Round to nearest
                                      whole number)

AP GRADE CONVERSION CHART

Composite Score Range	AP Grade
112–180	5
85–111	4
57–84	3
40–56	2
0–39	1

AP TABLES OF INFORMATION

CONSTANTS AND CONVERSION FACTORS

Proton mass, $m_p = 1.67 \times 10^{-27}$ kg	Electron charge magnitude, $e = 1.60 \times 10^{-19}$ C
Neutron mass, $m_n = 1.67 \times 10^{-27}$ kg	1 electron volt, $1\ eV = 1.60 \times 10^{-19}$ J
Electron mass, $m_e = 9.11 \times 10^{-31}$ kg	Speed of light, $c = 3.00 \times 10^8$ m/s
Avogadro's number, $N_0 = 6.02 \times 10^{23}$ mol^{-1}	Universal gravitational constant, $G = 6.67 \times 10^{-11}$ m^3/kg·s^2
Universal gas constant, $R = 8.31$ J/(mol·K)	Acceleration due to gravity
Boltzmann's constant, $k_B = 1.38 \times 10^{-23}$ J/K	at Earth's surface, $g = 9.8$ m/s^2

1 unified atomic mass unit,	$1u = 1.66 \times 10^{-27}$ kg $= 931$ MeV/c^2
Planck's constant,	$h = 6.63 \times 10^{-34}$ J·s $= 4.14 \times 10^{-15}$ eV·s
	$hc = 1.99 \times 10^{-25}$ J·m $= 1.24 \times 10^3$ eV·nm
Vacuum permittivity,	$\varepsilon_0 = 8.85 \times 10^{-12}$ C^2/N·m^2
Coulomb's law constant,	$k = 1/4\pi\varepsilon_0 = 9.0 \times 10^9$ N·m^2/C^2
Vacuum permeability,	$\mu_0 = 4\pi \times 10^{-7}$ (T·m)/A
Magnetic constant,	$k' = \mu_0/4\pi = 1 \times 10^{-7}$ (T·m)/A
1 atmosphere pressure,	1 atm $= 1.0 \times 10^5$ N/m$^2 = 1.0 \times 10^5$ Pa

UNIT SYMBOLS							
	meter,	m	mole,	mol	watt,	W	farad,	F
	kilogram,	kg	hertz,	hz	coulomb,	C	Tesla,	T
	second,	s	newton,	N	volt,	V	degree Celsius,	°C
	ampere,	A	pascal,	Pa	ohm,	Ω	electron-volt,	eV
	kelvin,	K	joule,	J	henry,	H		

PREFIXES

Factor	Prefix	Symbol
10^9	giga	G
10^6	mega	M
10^3	kilo	k
10^{-2}	centi	c
10^{-3}	milli	m
10^{-6}	micro	μ
10^{-9}	nano	n
10^{-12}	pico	p

VALUES OF TRIGONOMETRIC FUNCTIONS FOR COMMON ANGLES

θ	0°	30°	37°	45°	53°	60°	90°
$\sin \theta$	0	1/2	3/5	$\sqrt{2}/2$	4/5	$\sqrt{3}/2$	1
$\cos \theta$	1	$\sqrt{3}/2$	4/5	$\sqrt{2}/2$	3/5	1/2	0
$\tan \theta$	0	$\sqrt{3}/3$	3/4	1	4/3	$\sqrt{3}$	∞

The following conventions are used in this exam

    I. Unless otherwise stated, the frame of reference of any problem is assumed to be inertial.

    II. The direction of any electric current is the direction of flow of positive charge (conventional current).

    III. For any isolated electric charge, the electric potential is defined as zero at an infinite distance from the charge.

    IV. For mechanics and thermodynamics equations, W represents the work done on a system.

ADVANCED PLACEMENT PHYSICS B EQUATIONS

NEWTONIAN MECHANICS		ELECTRICITY AND MAGNETISM	
$v = v_0 + at$	a = acceleration	$F = -\dfrac{1}{4\pi\varepsilon_0}\dfrac{q_1 q_2}{r^2}$	A = area
$x = x_0 + v_0 t + \dfrac{1}{2}at^2$	F = force	$E = \dfrac{F}{q}$	B = magnetic field
$v^2 = v_0^2 + 2a(x - x_0)$	f = frequency	$U_E = qV = \dfrac{1}{4\pi\varepsilon_0}\dfrac{q_1 q_2}{r}$	C = capacitance
$\Sigma \mathbf{F} = \mathbf{F}_{net} = m\mathbf{a}$	h = height	$E_{avg} = -\dfrac{V}{d}$	d = distance
$F_{fric} \le \mu N$	J = impulse	$V = \dfrac{1}{4\pi\varepsilon_0}\Sigma_i \dfrac{q_i}{r_i}$	E = electric field
$a_c = \dfrac{v^2}{r}$	K = kinetic energy	$C = \dfrac{Q}{V}$	ε = emf
$\tau = rF \sin\theta$	k = spring constant	$C = \dfrac{\varepsilon_0 A}{d}$	F = force
$\mathbf{p} = m\mathbf{v}$	ℓ = length	$U = \dfrac{1}{2}QV = \dfrac{1}{2}CV^2$	I = current
$\mathbf{J} = \mathbf{F}\Delta t = \Delta \mathbf{p}$	m = mass	$I_{avg} = \dfrac{\Delta Q}{\Delta t}$	ℓ = length
$K = \dfrac{1}{2}mv^2$	N = normal force	$R = \dfrac{\rho L}{A}$	P = power
$\Delta U_g = mgh$	P = power	$V = IR$	Q = charge
$W = F\Delta r \cos\theta$	p = momentum	$P = IV$	q = point charge
$P_{avg} = \dfrac{W}{\Delta t}$	r = radius or distance	$C_p = \Sigma_i C_i$	R = resistance
$P = Fv \cos\theta$	T = period	$\dfrac{1}{C_s} = \Sigma_i \dfrac{1}{C_i}$	r = distance
$\mathbf{F}_s = -k\mathbf{x}$	t = time	$R_s = \Sigma_i R_i$	t = time
$U_s = \dfrac{1}{2}kx^2$	U = potential energy	$\dfrac{1}{R_p} = \Sigma_i \dfrac{1}{R_i}$	U = potential (stored) energy
$T_s = 2\pi\sqrt{\dfrac{m}{k}}$	v = velocity or speed	$F_B = qvB \sin\theta$	V = electric potential or potential difference
$T_p = 2\pi\sqrt{\dfrac{\ell}{g}}$	W = work done on system	$F_B = BI\ell \sin\theta$	v = velocity or speed
$T = \dfrac{1}{f}$	x = position	$B = \dfrac{\mu_0}{2\pi}\dfrac{I}{r}$	ρ = resistivity
$F_G = -\dfrac{Gm_1 m_2}{r^2}$	μ = coefficient of friction	$\phi_m = BA \cos\theta$	θ = angle
$U_G = -\dfrac{Gm_1 m_2}{r}$	θ = angle	$\varepsilon_{avg} = \dfrac{\Delta\phi m}{\Delta t}$	ϕ_m = magnetic flux
	τ = torque	$\varepsilon = B\ell v$	